Amerasia

Amerasia

Elizabeth Horodowich

Alexander Nagel

ZONE BOOKS · NEW YORK

2023

ZONE BOOKS
633 Vanderbilt Street
Brooklyn, NY 11218

Printed in the United States of America.

Distributed by Princeton University Press,
Princeton, New Jersey, and Woodstock, United Kingdom

Library of Congress Cataloging-in-Publication Data
Names: Horodowich, Elizabeth, 1970– , author. | Nagel, Alexander, 1964– , author.
Title: Amerasia / Elizabeth Horodowich and Alexander Nagel.
Description: New York : Zone Books, 2023. | Includes bibliographical references and index. | Summary: "This book explores the many ways in which European artists, writers, and cartographers described and represented an Amerasian continuum in the first two centuries after Columbus" — Provided by publisher.
Identifiers: LCCN 2022049956 (print) | LCCN 2022049957 (ebook) | ISBN 9781942130833 (hardback) | ISBN 9781942130840 (eBook)
Subjects: LCSH: Geographical myths. | Amerasia.
Classification: LCC GR940.H67 2023 (print) | LCC GR940 (ebook) | DDC 398.23/4—dc23/eng/20230109
LC record available at https://lccn.loc.gov/2022049956
LC ebook record available at https://lccn.loc.gov/2022049957

Contents

If we were to see as much of the world as we do not see, we would perceive, one might believe, a perpetual multiplication and vicissitude of forms.

Si nous voyions autant du monde comme nous n'en voyons pas, nous apercevrions, comme il est à croire, une perpétuelle multiplication et vicissitude de formes.

—MICHEL DE MONTAIGNE, "DES COCHES," 1588

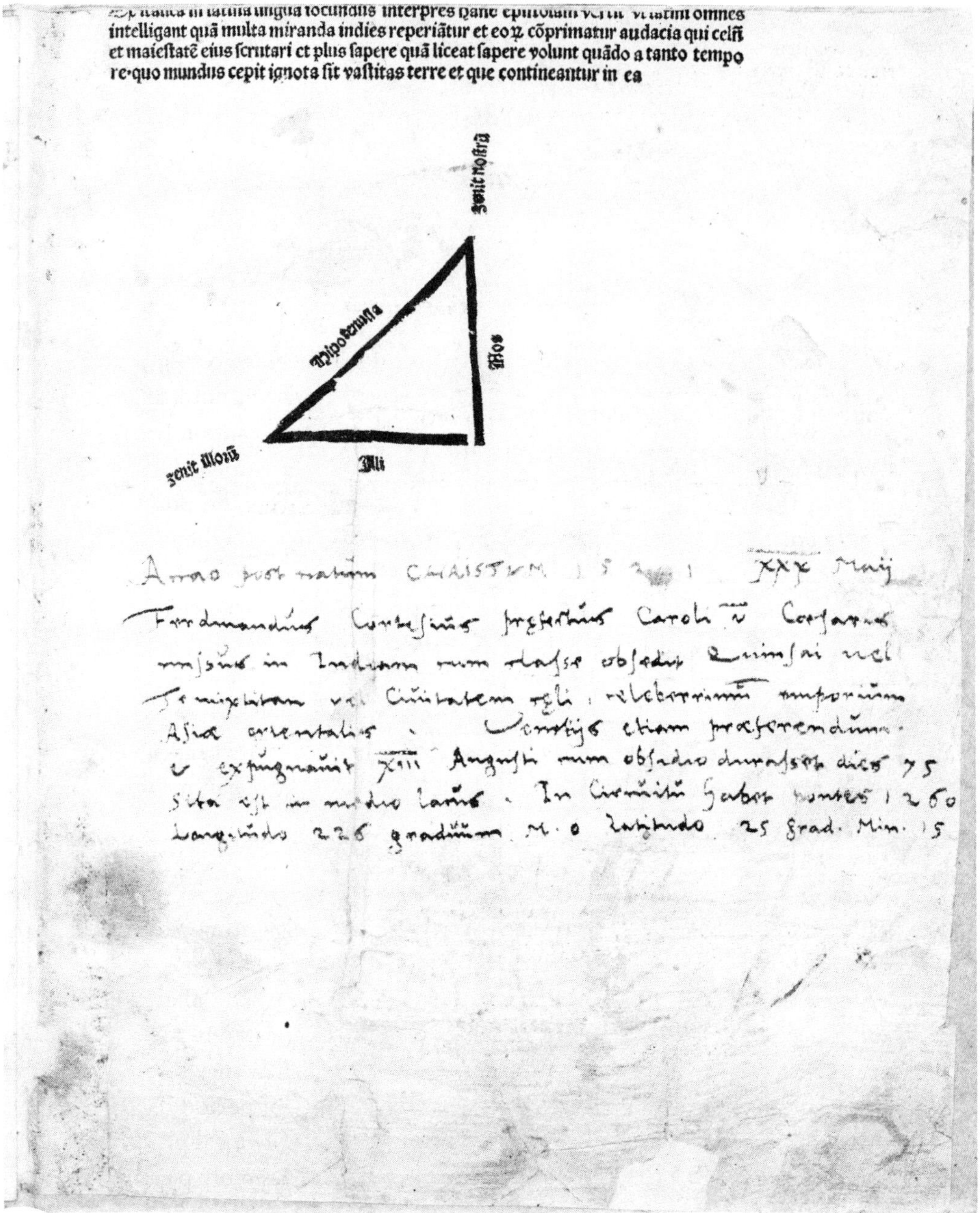
intelligant quā multa miranda indies reperiātur et eoꝝ cōprimatur audacia qui celū
et maiestatē eius scrutari et plus sapere quā liceat sapere volunt quādo a tanto tempo
re quo mundus cepit ignota sit vastitas terre et que contineantur in ea

I.1 Hernán Cortés, conqueror of China. Handwritten annotation of the early 1520s on Amerigo Vespucci, *De novo mundo* (1505). Rostock, University Library.

INTRODUCTION

The Unsettlement of the World

In the early 1520s, a reader of a 1505 Latin edition of Amerigo Vespucci's famous letter "On the New World" added a handwritten note, also in Latin, with a spectacular new world update: the Spanish captain Hernán Cortés has lately conquered the capital of the Chinese empire. On May 30, 1521, the note reports, Cortés laid siege to Quinsay (the Southern Song capital Hangzhou, which had been effusively described by Marco Polo), "also known as Temixtitam or the City of Heaven, most famous trading capital of eastern Asia, also much esteemed by the Venetians, and finally subdued on the 13th of August after the siege had gone on 75 days."[1] Temixtitam was a common European spelling for the Mexica capital Tenochtitlan. Although Cortés himself never claimed it, the idea that Tenochtitlan was a Chinese capital and Moctezuma a Chinese emperor persisted for decades in authoritative European maps and publications (fig. I.1).

Amerasia as a Meeting Place

This book studies the long record of a new world spanning Asia and America, in geographical conceptions, military campaigns, ethnographic inquiries, travel accounts, collecting practices, pictures and allegories, and the whole European imaginary produced and propagated by all these practices. We call this imaginary Amerasia, a neologism that serves as a meeting place for the consideration of a wide array of period sources that might otherwise remain disparate oddities or simply local phenomena. We also use it as an embankment against the extremely powerful view that from the time of Columbus's "discovery of America" Europe revealed the new world and thus led the whole world into the modern future. We present instead a protracted and unsettled process of European self-orientation that unfolded over two centuries after the explorations of Columbus and Vespucci. Europe in this account is emphatically not the center of the world and not yet in a commanding position in the world, but emerges as an unrelenting generator of a world imaginary, in maps, travel accounts, epic poems, collecting practices, and images of all kinds. We propose that Amerasia was a major axis around which this world imaginary was configured, an unsettled zone where east meets west, modernity folds into antiquity, and otherness, whether conceived in strictly antipodal terms or not, is always self-implicating. Amerasia was above all a geographic construction in continual redefinition, and so served as a reflection of Europe's own unsettling as it went through its own process of identity formation, provoked in good part by the intensive awareness that its own position in the world and in history was being radically redefined. The meeting place of Amerasia gives some structure to this less familiar story, one that it is now possible to hear.

A round feather mosaic now in Vienna was brought from Mexico to Europe probably as early as 1520 (fig. I.2). Now recognized as a Mexica shield made around 1500, its imagery is still in debate, the fierce animal in bright blue feathers identified by some scholars as an *ahuitztotl*, a legendary, spiny, dog-like beast that lures people to their death in the water, while other scholars point out that the furriness of this figure is at odds with the *ahuitztotl*'s traditional smoothness. Many believe it represents a fox, a symbol of war and an animal revered by Mexica warriors as well as by the *amantecas* or featherworkers who made these objects. In the earliest European inventories, however, from the late sixteenth and early seventeenth centuries, the animal is described as a dragon. No inventory ventured to say where the work originated until 1788, when it was said to be a parasol from China, an origin story perhaps informed by the long-held view that it depicted a dragon. It is likely that the feather roundel was believed to be Chinese long before 1788. Over the nineteenth century, the origin of the piece was changed to "Indian" and then "Ancient Mexican."[2]

There are many other such examples. A Mexica obsidian mirror, also in Vienna, was described as Chinese as late as the nineteenth century.[3] A Mixtec manuscript now in Vienna was given to Pope Clement VII sometime in the 1520s and was described not long after as being from "south India," *India Meridionalis*, which referred not to the southern tip of what today is called the subcontinent of India but rather to an imagined peninsula to the east even of the Malay peninsula—a new world so far to the east that it is shown in period maps to be not many degrees of longitude from America. In the 1679 catalogue of the Imperial Library of Vienna the Vienna Codex crowns the collection as the last item, concluding a list of the library's *Orientalia*.[4] Another Mixtec manuscript now in Bologna was called a "book from India" in the 1530s, then by the middle of the seventeenth century became a "book from China," and then in 1677 was described as a book with "hieroglyphs from Mexico." Provenances could

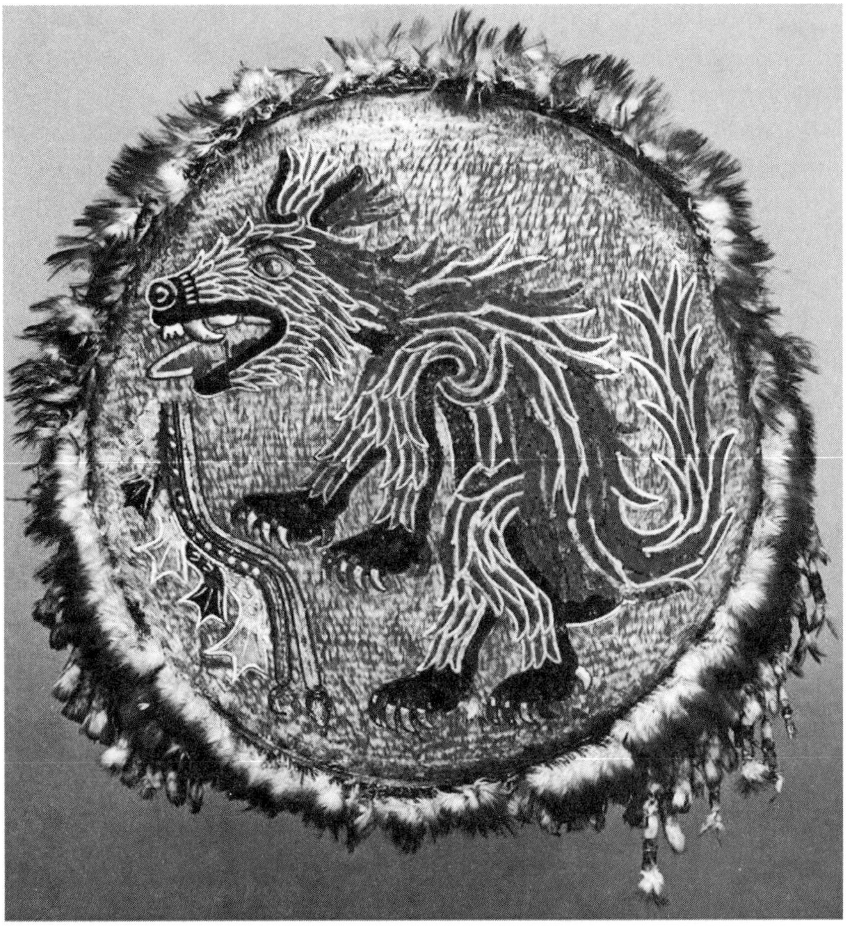

I.2 Chinese, Indian, or Mexican? Chimalli (shield), 70 cm in diameter, feathers, gold leaf, cotton fibers, leather, and reed (ca. 1500). Vienna, Weltmuseum.

shift in the other direction, when what we identify as Asian objects were classed as American, as when a piece of Japanese armor was described as a "shield of Moctezuma," or a Javanese *kris*, a figured sword handle, was taken as a Taíno household god or *zemi*.[5]

The Amerasian imaginary studied in this book yields a plethora of such cases of what appears to be geographical and cultural-historical confusion, over more than two centuries: Columbus identifying and naming cannibals on the basis of old tales of Asian human-eating races (chapter 1), the inclusion of east Asia in the cartography of the "new world" (chapter 2), Amerasian Magi (chapter 3), the island of Columbus's first colony (Hispaniola, called Haiti by the locals) identified with Japan (chapter 4), representations of Asian populations arrayed in Brazilian Tupi feather gear (chapters 5 and 12), Cuban crocodiles taken to be Asian snakes described by Polo (chapter 6), Mangi (Polo's name for southern China) identified with Mexico (chapter 7), islands of California rich in "Oriental pearls" (chapter 8), serious discussion about whether the female warrior tribes of Brazil were the same as the Scythian Amazons described in antiquity (chapter 9), and about whether the eastern biblical emporium Ophir was Peru (chapter 10), theories of the ancient discovery of America by the Chinese (chapter 11), the reuse of the very same images to represent cannibals of Java and cannibals of the Caribbean; or to represent Indians in colonial Jamestown and Indians of the Mughal empire (chapter 12); the presentation of evidence that American Indian tribes originated in the lost tribes of Israel, and that early Christians had found their way to the Americas (chapter 13), the discovery of an ancient Egyptian root system connecting Chinese, Japanese, and Mexican cultures (chapter 14), the investing of the allegorical figure of America with Asian attributes (chapters 15 and 16), and finally the very real transformation of Mexico and the material culture of New Spain by imports and immigration from Asia (chapter 17).

This collaborative project began a number of years ago as an informal and then ongoing exchange of examples of Amerasian thinking that cropped up here and there in the secondary literature and in primary sources. As the examples piled up, what at first seemed like glitches in knowledge or curious episodes began to look more like possible applications of shared premises. As patterns started to emerge in the evidence, we found ourselves letting go of the old idea, still routinely found in the literature, that Columbus's erroneous belief that he had reached the Indies was soon dispelled — that the confusion was cleared up by Vespucci's "new world" letter of 1502, or by Martin Waldseemüller's naming of America in 1507, or by the humanist Peter Martyr's collection of writings "on the new world" (*De orbe novo*), or by the circumnavigation of the globe by Ferdinand Magellan's crew in 1520–22, or by the regular crossing of the Pacific by the Manila merchant galleons after 1565, or by the depiction of America as a fourth (or fifth) part of the world from the later sixteenth century on. Digging into these episodes and their consequences, we found that each supposed turning point in fact generated more Amerasian speculation — theories about migration, biblical interpretation, geographical extrapolations, as well as the kind of speculation that funded expeditions in search of Asian riches. As the evidence grew, it became necessary to coordinate the information from different arenas — accounts of exploration, map-making, collecting practices, natural-historical treatises, historical accounts, poetic works, and visual representations in various media — so as to develop a sense of how the world came into view at specific times and places, and eventually to trace basic arcs of development over decades and centuries, even while respecting the differences among locales.

The result is the present study, organized as a series of short chapters in roughly chronological sequence, each focused on a particular object or set of objects — maps, artifacts, images, books — that crystallize Amerasian thinking at particular junctures of European culture. The objects or cluster of objects bring into view the Amerasian imaginary as it took shape in specific settings ranging from Brazil and Portugal, Peru, Mexican New Spain, and Spain, various centers in Italy, German-speaking and Netherlandish publishing hubs, and the French and English realms. Given the range of materials and centers of production, this book cannot be much more than a preliminary cabinet display of the phenomenon, sketching the trajectory of a worldview while at the same time offering some sense of the texture of specific ventures in image-crafting, cartography, exploration, history-writing, collecting, and, generally, "worldmaking." The chapters proceed from the initial reception of Columbus's first journey through to the eighteenth century, with an Epilogue that considers the revival (or persistence?) of Amerasian ideas into the present time. An Afterword by Timothy Brook offers a brief analysis of corresponding views of the world from the Chinese side.

Beyond Exoticism

When dealing with a phenomenon as expansive and unwieldy as Amerasia, the skeptical questions continually arise: Was this not mostly negligence? Were they not just mixing up various things that seemed above all remote? Is this confusion not due, first, to empirical error (faulty geographical and cultural knowledge), and, second, to exoticist indifference about far-away places? This basic skepticism has become fairly standard in the field, gaining new strength in recent years as scholars aim to expose Eurocentrism and provincialize Europe. One is reminded of Saul Steinberg's 1976 map-illustration "View of the World from Ninth Avenue," where beyond Tenth Avenue is the Hudson river and a strip of New Jersey, beyond which is an undifferentiated expanse marked by places like Kansas, Nebraska, and Las Vegas in rough relation to each other, with Mexico and Canada to either side, beyond them the Pacific Ocean, and on the horizon in the distance low undifferentiated mounds labeled Japan, China, and Russia. If this is how early modern Europeans looked at the world from their parlors and studies and taverns and churches, then why should the Amerasian axis be singled out as particularly coherent or consequential?

Our answer is that Europe in the sixteenth century was in fact not much like Saul Steinberg's 1970s New York. The inhabitants of Europe were not yet certain of their centrality in the world, and at the same time they were deeply informed about the shape of the Asian old world, and deeply invested in stories about how the movements out of Asia had produced their own culture. Legends of different kinds insistently told them that their origins as humans lay in the earthly paradise at the eastern limit of the world, or in the Noachic repopulation of the world after the Flood. History was then reshaped by the birth and death of Jesus in the Levant and the sending of the Apostles over the surface of the world from there, bringing the Christian religion to the Latin West, where churches, images, and spiritual tracts in turn continually oriented Latin Christians back towards the Holy Land in the east. All understood that the Egyptian and Greek worlds grounded Roman civilization, which in turn embraced the eastern Christian religion. In an eastward return, the Roman capital was moved to a city named Constantinople after the first Christian emperor, and now the seat of a highly authoritative Christian Church with its own liturgies and hierarchy, an eastern Church that virtually every Latin Christian had to concede was closer to the original sources and forms of Christian life. On a more practical level, many of the things that gave flavor, color, and meaning to the lives of people living in the western peninsula known as Europe came from the east—spices, silks, jewels, some of the finest pigments, most technical and scientific knowledge, as well as many of the inherited stories. The medieval Latin West was on the margins of the known world and knew itself to be on the margins, looking across time and space towards various eastern centers. It came naturally to Latins (later known as Europeans) to see culture, religion, and history as the result of flows of people, materials, artifacts, and ideas.

Europeans brought to their encounters with what they called new worlds a robust ability to see human reality as a dynamic and ongoing layering of spatial and temporal relations. The encounter with territories and peoples that the ancient authorities knew only imperfectly or not at all brought the shape of the world and thus the meaning of history newly and urgently into question, an unsettling of knowledge that provoked significant efforts of reordering. Europeans did not give up on their tendency to organize global reality in meaningful terms, even if their efforts remained provisional and open-ended for decades and centuries. A number of basic cosmological paradigms—primary among them the zonal/climatic organization of the world by latitude and the robust and extensible idea of India beyond the Ganges (both explained in chapter 1)—came into effective use, with the result that Amerasia emerged as a salient cultural-geographical configuration, in fact a primary laboratory for studying how far cultures can travel and how similarity can be articulated over a range of difference. This basic configuration was consistently sustained by the widespread cultural habit of applying the term "new world" to both east Asian and American territories (as explained in chapter 2).

The debate rages among historians over how important a role Europe played globally in the early modern period, but none doubt that Europeans played an extraordinarily active and influential part in the technology of *depicting* the world. In the sixteenth and seventeenth centuries, a veritable industry of map-making and global imagery arose in Europe, a world-picturing activity whose impact was soon felt around the world. Just as images of outer space — of the solar system and galaxies — have coalesced into a common if variable iconography over the last fifty years, Europe in the sixteenth century generated a constellation of images of "the world" in maps, in poems and narratives, and in works of visual art, making "worldmaking" a ubiquitous cultural practice in the early modern period.[6]

If viewed with modern maps and modern cultural-geographical categories in mind, Amerasian connections and mergings look like meaningless jumbles. It seems as if features or artifacts from one locale have been decontextualized and fairly arbitrarily thrown into association with things from other far away places. It looks like exoticism. According to Peter Mason, the free and highly variable use of features originally drawn from American life, such as feather garments, in European images of Asians and Africans reveals an exoticist taste for foreignness that was largely indifferent to provenance.[7] We propose that there was no strict sense of American origin because the place America was not in focus in the modern sense; it was strongly and persistently associated with Asia, sometimes through Africa. According to Amerasian logic, there was every reason to imagine that feathers might be worn by a hunter in Brazil as well as by a fisherman in the Indian Ocean. Moreover, the category of the "exotic" itself has a history; it was not a ready-made cultural predisposition, available at all times. Almost unknown in the sixteenth century, the word "exotic" came into more frequent use in the seventeenth century as a technical term to designate nonnative botanical species. Only at the very end of the seventeenth century and more commonly in the eighteenth century was it employed in the modern, cultural sense to mean "coming from far away and looking strange."[8]

Rather than dating a European taste for exoticism from the period of Columbus and Bartolomeu Dias, or even from later decades, we propose a now largely forgotten "pre-exoticist" model that dominated European representational practices during the sixteenth and most of the seventeenth centuries. In this phase, provenance was configured according to consistent early modern geographic and cosmological principles that organized multiple levels of cultural practice — from maps and globes (studied throughout this book), to representations of new world flora and fauna (chapters 5, 8, and 14), to biblical criticism (chapters 3, 7, and 13), to the narrative structure of travel accounts (chapter 6), to the figuring of the parts of the world (chapter 16), to the organization and inventorying of European collections (chapters 12 and 17). These principles and the institutions they underwrote sustained the Amerasian view. If one begins with preconceived ideas about place based on modern geographical models — where America is America and Asia is Asia — then it will certainly seem as if early modern people assigned objects to the wrong places, implying a culture of exoticism and an indifference to where things came from. Perhaps future research will demonstrate that Europeans gradually layered new routines of exoticism on top of Amerasian thinking, in the end burying the Amerasian idea altogether. When the exoticizing process happened, it did so unevenly; our final chapters explore how strains of Amerasian thought continued to shape ideas about global geography well into the eighteenth century. This is not to say that terms were never used loosely or that basic errors were not made (about geography, or about where a given object or cultural form or material originated), but rather than see them as the default setting we propose that errors or indifference were the exception, and that efforts to use terms and assign provenances in meaningful and reasoned ways were the norm.

Let us take a few examples of how the evidence can be read in period terms. On most sixteenth-century maps, the water on the far side of Mexico was designated not as the Pacific but as the traditional Southern Sea, Mar de Sur, which was known to border on China, a body of water sometimes represented as a gulf in a world that did not know the Bering Strait. In some important sixteenth-century maps and treatises, Mexico is in fact a province of China, meaning that it was not a laughable error to identify a Mixtec manuscript or a piece of Mexica featherwork as Chinese. If, alternatively, China is understood as "Upper India" (*India superior*) and America is understood as an eastern extension of the Indian sphere (whether as *India meridionalis*, *India orientalis*, *India nova*, or *India extra Gangem*), as we routinely find in geographical treatises and maps of the period, then it is not wild flailing to change the provenance of such an item from Chinese to Indian, but, rather, a prudent reassignment of the object from the subregion of China to larger India, the macro-geographical category. Later, in the seventeenth century, after a well-established transpacific trade had produced intensive cultural exchanges between Asia and America and new interactivity within the subregions of Asia and America, and as objects from all these regions came back to Europe in merged streams, there were very good reasons for provenances to mingle in new ways in European collections and accounts.

The Tools We Hold

The set of relations we are bringing together under the term Amerasia are in fact highly various and unsystematic. We might think of them as a spectrum or range, though even that is too neat a model. In some cases, as when maps identify Haiti as Japan, we have a relation of *identity*: this place is in fact the Asian island described by Polo. In other cases, as when Columbus or Vespucci imagine themselves not far from the earthly paradise or when Bartolomé de Las Casas considers the Spanish Indies "the last part of what in antiquity was called India," we are dealing with an idea of *extension*: this place, hitherto unknown, is an extension of lands described in the Bible or in other ancient sources. In other cases, as when Lorenzo Pignoria interprets both Japanese and Mexica culture as part of an ancient Egyptian diaspora, or José de Acosta understands the American Indians to be descendants of Asians, we have a relation of *derivation*: this place was settled long ago by Asian immigrants, who brought with them their wisdom traditions and language forms. In yet other cases, as when a Mexican painter imagines feathers on the inhabitants of India, or the inhabitants of the east and west Indies are typified above all by their nudity, we have a relation of *association*: these people inhabit climatically similar latitudes, with many shared flora and fauna, and thus are bound to exhibit strong similarities. At the farthest extreme of Amerasian thinking, as when Michel de Montaigne compares the "cannibals" of Brazil to the Scythian warriors of antiquity, we have relations of *analogy*: we know these are distant places and peoples, yet they are comparable in their habits, culture, and morals. In some cases, for example when Asian and American objects are presented side by side at the imperially sponsored convent of the Descalzas Reales in Madrid, all of them labeled "Indian," it is in fact difficult to know whether the relation was understood to be one of identity, or extension, or derivation, or mere association.

The point is not to try to refine or firm up this admittedly loose typology, as if it could be made to correspond, finally, with the ways people actually thought in the past. Even in the same location and at the same date, one person might see identity where another sees only association, and even a single individual could be inconsistent, sliding up or down the scale of possibilities without ever resolving the question in a given case. Insofar as they thought of it at all, the new-world phenomenon was for Europeans most often an experience of this range of possibilities, with no resolution. To imagine such a range is above all a heuristic tool, for the benefit of present-day scholars and readers, helping us to see relations among period expressions that might otherwise fall apart into odd anecdotes.

Heuristic tools, like the neologism Amerasia or the typology of associations just outlined, are helpful because they are not so easily confused with period tools. However, in many areas of the study of early modern world-making confusion between our tools and theirs is rife. As we have already seen, the terms Mexico or America or India or new world, although exactly the same as the ones modern scholars use, were used in different contexts and with different meanings in the early modern period. The same goes for the term continent, so often used by modern historians of cartography. The early modern use of the word continent, a descriptive term referring to the geological fact of a landmass that is not an island, most certainly does not map onto the modern use of that term.[9] Then there are all the terms that are no longer common, such as "torrid zone" or "part of the world" (*pars mundi*), and are essential to this story. As used in the period, all of these terms—both the ones we do and don't use today—are foreign to modern geographical thinking yet fundamental to Amerasian views of the world. Metageographical concepts are highly effective, then and now; the main thing is to be clear about which are ours and which theirs.

Likewise, to plot Columbus's or other explorers' voyages on modern maps, so that we see travel lines that land in the Caribbean or Brazil, with Asia nowhere to be seen, is to reinforce an unhelpful historical telescoping according to which Columbus brought into being the world we now inhabit. The 1507 map by the Dutch cosmographer Johannes Ruysch (see fig. 4.12) offers a better guide to inhabiting the world we are trying to understand, as does the 1507 map by Waldseemüller (see fig. 2.7), the one that names America for the first time, if it is considered carefully as a whole. So long as the period accounts are set into the coordinates of modern geography, they will seem full of mistakes, conflations, and confusions. To bring Amerasia into view, therefore, is to encounter resistance built into the modern methods and tools used to study it, a resistance that goes deeper than the question of toponymic description. The modern organization of historical study by field areas, themselves derived from modern metageographical models, is structurally predisposed to misrecognize Amerasian associations as confusions, often quaint or humorous, or just embarrassing glitches soon to be dispelled. Confusion implies that one thing has been mistaken for another; but what if we are dealing with a world before the separation that would make such confusions possible?

We propose that the confusion was not theirs, but between one set of models and tools and another.

Amerasia is hardly the only unwieldy geocultural formation created by the European imagination. Various large geocultural formations organize and shape perceptions of the world today, both in the popular imagination and in academic studies. Unlike ones still in use, such as Africa, Amerasia is simply a formation that has fallen out of use, remaining only in traces here and there. Despite its many subregions and widely varying linguistic and material cultures, Africa remains a powerfully unifying construct, a testament to the power of an ancient Greco-Roman metageographical concept enshrined by modern European colonial, administrative, and educational institutions. In the late medieval and early modern worlds, the regions along the arc of the Niger River, the heavily forested lands of the Congo Basin, and the Islamic commercial sultanates of the Swahili coast did not conceive of themselves as parts of a singular geographic entity; the modern conception of Africa arises from the era of European colonial partition of these territories in the second half of the nineteenth century. Metageographical thinking did not begin with the nineteenth-century categories. It was alive and well in the sixteenth century, but the categories were different. The emergent macro-category in that period was the "new world," which stretched from the newly encountered territories in Asia to those across the Atlantic, a new world that was presented in many period publications as fully half of the world—180 degrees of the globe's 360. The thirst for travel accounts and images of the newly encountered peoples, the new collections of artifacts from the Indies, the industry of cosmographies and world maps—all these new cultural expressions constituted the emergent sixteenth-century field of "new world studies."

With the Amerasian macro-category in place as an organizing tool, apparent anomalies can be recast as applications of forms of knowledge. Rather than say that the Venetian mapmaker Giovanni Francesco Camocio "placed the American toponym of *Tuchiano* in Asia," implying that Camocio needed to move it to do so, we say, "Camocio shows us that *Tuchiano* is in Asia." Rather than describe the Pacific Ocean in the Amerasian world as "dramatically shrunken," or even call it the Pacific, or even call it an ocean, to stay close to the historical sources is to allow, as the case suggests, that it was not an ocean but a sea, or perhaps the waters of an archipelago. Rather than fixing a body of water with the modern term such as the Caribbean, which places it on a modern map far from Asia, we allow it to be the South China Sea, or the Sea of the Indies, as the sources suggest. In these ways, rediscovering Amerasia demands a persistent recalibration of our perceptions, senses, and language.

If Amerasia suspends and exposes the modern myth of continents, therefore, it is not because it simply stitches together the continents of America and Asia as constituted by modern geography. Rather, it resolves the world into a thoroughly non-modern configuration, one that, for example, occasionally drew Africa into the Amerasian formation. As Europeans sought out new routes to Goa and Calicut in the wake of the voyage of Vasco da Gama, all European seaborne traffic to India moved along the African coast, pulling Africa into the relationship between Europe and India. The administrative affairs of Portuguese trade with Africa were managed by the Casa da Guiné, which was renamed Casa da India e da Guiné (and then often shortened to Casa da India) after the circumnavigation of Africa by Vasco da Gama in 1497 established a sea route to India. Ships returning to Lisbon were filled with items from a variety of ports in Portuguese nodes in Indian Ocean trade networks, yet the goods unloaded there, including goods from both India and Africa, that were sent on for sale throughout Europe were registered as having arrived generically from the Estado da Índia, an identifier that very likely colored their provenance from then onward.[10]

Apart from the administrative paper trail, there were cartographic and cosmographic reasons for occasionally associating Africa both with India and South America. On medieval *mappaemundi*, the Indian Ocean is minimized and Ethiopia and India are pressed together. Europeans alternatively located Prester John in both Ethiopia and India, and when in August of 1441 missions of the Patriarch of Alexandria came to Florence from the Ethiopian Convent of Jerusalem, these people were considered "Indians from Greater India sent by Prester John."[11] Africa, metonymically represented by Ethiopia, was a hinge that could be associated with both Asia and America, an Ethiopian lability that goes back as far as Homer, who in the opening words of the Odyssey spoke of the Ethiopians who inhabited both the westernmost and the easternmost parts of the world.[12] Though we do not explore this phenomenon in depth here, we bring out African elements in Amerasian thinking wherever the sources make it evident, even as we acknowledge that the relations need to be understood better.

Amerasia is not the only instance of a geographic-cultural formation that is foreign to modern thinking. Pierre Schneider has explored the pervasive conflation of Ethiopia and India in ancient Greco-Roman thought.[13] Similarly, the art historian Byron Hamann encourages us to see both sides of the early modern Atlantic as a "Mediterratlantic" space.[14] Ricardo Padrón has explored an early modern "transpacific" space, the idea that the Spanish conceived of the coasts of Asia and America and the sea in between them as one continuous world. Padrón's interests are close to ours, with the difference that his study is focused on Spanish imperial ideology; we propose that Amerasian thinking developed broadly throughout Europe, in diverse ways and for a variety of reasons.

Interactivity and Unsettling

Amerasia is not merely a Western idea imposed on other realities. It is an emergent matrix for understanding the world that unfolded out of exchanges — verbal, material, artifactual — with the communities and lands encountered by Europeans during the period that began with the Portuguese voyages to Africa and Columbus's voyages across the ocean. As the very first images of Columbus's 1492–93 voyage make clear (see chapter 1), the islanders he encountered revealed, so it appeared to him, a world held together by water-based transportation and trade, in strong contrast to the primarily landmass-based trade of the traditional *oikoumene* and the Silk Road. The Portuguese encountered similarly connected maritime worlds in the Indian ocean and the Indonesian archipelago beyond Malacca. A new, water-based reality, made evident by the way Native inhabitants used and made sense of their environments, soon came to dominate Western conceptions of global expansion (in stark comparison to Ming China, as Brook's Afterword explores in this volume), and this vision then transformed European understandings of antiquity. In the wake of the new world explorations European commentators reimagined an ancient world connected by water and thus extending into the new world. Even after crossing the body of water to the west of Mexico, and in part because they crossed it, Europeans could now imagine contacts spanning Asia and America that had occurred in the ancient past and that had already shaped the cultures they were encountering (see chapters 3, 5, and 14). Early modern navigation not only made certain discoveries possible; it introduced a conceptual shift away from the traditional Ptolemaic land-mass model of human habitation and migration.[15]

Amerasia could not have arisen without the constant interaction with Indigenous communities and voices. Although these communities were decimated and their voices were suppressed if not silenced, they had a significant role to play in shaping European ideas about specific territories and about the world altogether during this period.[16] Their voices — literally the sounds they made — informed Amerasian thinking from the moment they responded to the inevitable questions the strange visitors asked on first encounter: What is the name of this place? What is the name of your ruler? Are there more powerful kingdoms farther on? Where does the metal you are wearing come from? What is the name of this fruit? The new arrivals would listen intently to what came out of the mouths of the natives of the place, hoping and expecting to hear echoes of names contained in biblical, mythological, or ancient lore. As we will see in chapter 1, when the inhabitants of Haiti, renamed Hispaniola by Columbus, spoke of a place called Cibao that had gold, the navigator heard the word Cipangu, or Japan, an island off the coast of Asia that Polo had said was rich in gold.

For these reasons, this book adopts Indigenous place names (insofar as they are known) when describing episodes of first contact, in an effort to gain some access to the "acoustemology" of first encounters.[17] For further stages of interaction and colonization, we adopt the toponyms, sometimes more than one for the same place, used by period actors and mapmakers as territories entered a wider discourse, a discourse that registered Indigenous place names and terminology even as colonization progressed and European renamings piled up. As a result, readers of this book will occasionally be thrown off their modern global positioning systems, coming closer to the disorientation and unclarity felt by soldiers, missionaries, and settlers, as well as by the writers and compilers of accounts and by the readers they found both in Europe and in European colonies in different parts of the world.

To emphasize dialogue is not to claim that these early modern encounters produced understanding and harmonious exchange. The interactions that informed the Amerasian matrix began under conditions of invasion and then continued to unfold as Native communities faced persecution and institutionalized oppression. Pressed for information about the surrounding geography and resources, and about their beliefs and traditions, their responses jolted European frameworks of understanding, or evaded them, or in flashes of apparent understanding seemed to illuminate them.[18] Nonetheless, these were multidirectional exchanges.[19] The utterances, habitus, and lifeworld of Indigenous populations confronted Europeans in the sounds of their worldscape, in the astonishing products of their artisans, in their knowledge and use of their environment, in the pathways of their trade networks, in their aquatic imaginary, cosmovisions, and origin legends, in their radically different social structures, and in the survival strategies they elaborated in response to invasion. The invaders and settlers found themselves, in the words of Eduardo Viveiros de Castro, confronted by the fact of possible other worlds, ones whose consequences were being drawn out in their own experience of them and the effect of these encounters on their own thinking.[20]

This dialogue did not subside quickly, and Amerasia did not disappear within years or decades as telescoping modern narratives would have it. It was a major organizing paradigm of the world for two centuries, accompanying and possibly enabling the rise of Europe as an idea. The eighteenth century did see a definitive shift to a modern understanding of global geography, in part as a result of the voyages of Vitus Bering and James Cook, in part due to advances in the European understanding of longitude, though the sense of a special relationship between America and Asia persisted well into the nineteenth century (see the Epilogue). Amerasia subsided as colonialism came into its modern form, as disciplines for the study of "Oriental" cultures and literatures and, later, of Native American cultures were established; as the European myth of continents came into resolution and as modern geography as taught by Europeans reshaped understandings of the earth; and as western museums organized the productions of world cultures according to European categories. J. Jorge Klor de Alva has warned against projecting these later colonialist models of geography and history onto the early modern period.[21] Against the view that would present this period as an early stage of the colonialist era of the eighteenth and nineteenth centuries, Hamann has proposed to see the earlier encounters, incursions, and colonizations in their alterity—"an alien, violent, connected world."[22]

Amerasia is an array of signs pointing to an unsettling, a field of unsettling. The various and wide-ranging applications of the idea of "new world" in the Amerasian centuries are repeated admissions that all of this—this land, these resources, these objects, these people—are part of something else: Asia is larger and even more various than we thought; or rather, this may be part of Asia, but only if we adapt our idea of Asia; or, it is just something else that needs to be understood in relation to what we thought we knew. The cohesive yet malleable Amerasian view allowed this shifting and unsettlement to unfold. It held space for the thinking of margins and extremes: India beyond the Ganges, the new world, the torrid zone that turns out to be inhabited, the antipodes, the vicinity of paradise, utopia. The imaginary of Amerasia was populated but migratory; it was in play. It reflected Europe's own unsettling, caused by having come to recognize that there are other worlds. Ultimately, Amerasia brought home the truth that the new world was not this or that newly encountered territory but in fact the whole world, now coming into a new configuration and a new interconnectedness, with unknown consequences for the understanding of both the past and the future. Amerasia was an index of the unsettlement of the world.

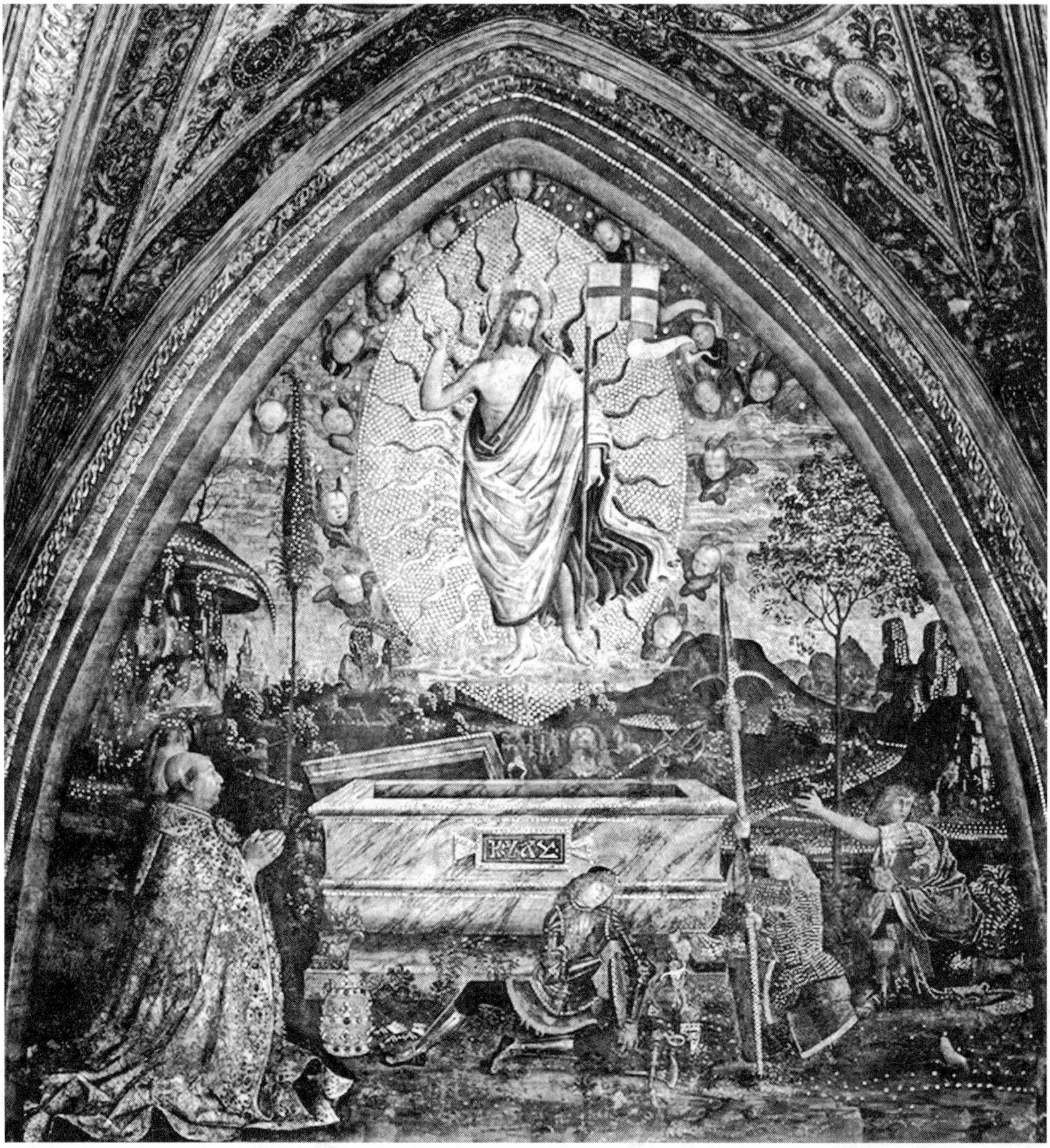

1.1 In the distance, under the golden blaze of the resurrected Christ, one of the first European representations of the people encountered by Christopher Columbus. Pinturicchio, *Resurrection of Christ*, fresco (1494–95). Vatican City, Borgia Apartments.

ONE

Emergent Amerasia: India Beyond the Ganges

In the *Resurrection of Christ* painted by Pinturicchio in 1494–95, we see Christ hovering above the tomb in a mandorla (fig. 1.1). The fresco belongs to a cycle of scenes of the Life of Christ in the so-called Sala dei Misteri in the Vatican palace, one room of the apartments of Pope Alexander VI, Rodrigo Borgia. Among all the scenes in these rooms, this one, figuring Christ's triumph over death, contains a portrait of the pope, who kneels below and to the left. His even, prayerful attitude is in stark contrast to those of the soldiers who have been guarding the tomb, and who respond in different ways to Christ's reemergence. One soldier is asleep, his shield carrying a reflection of the artist himself; one stands in awe looking up at the risen Christ; another looks out at us, while a fourth points out the miracle to others outside the scene. The tomb carries a prominent and legible inscription in characters no viewer of this painting could read, though they would have understood them to have been written in a Near Eastern language, reminding them that this event occurred in Jerusalem.

Naked Indians

Directly above the tomb and below Christ's mandorla, next to the upturned head of the soldier on the other side of the tomb, is a group of figures that came into new visibility and under new scrutiny after a 2006 conservation campaign on the fresco (fig. 1.2). One figure seems to be leaning on a long staff. The group of naked men is not still but animated, even alert, aware they have been seen. A horse raises an excited leg, his mouth open, whinnying. The extensions we see emerging from one figure's head are probably not locks of hair but feathers. Who are these people?

Various scholars have affirmed that this is one of the first visual documents to register the existence of the people encountered by Columbus, who brought back some of these island people from his first voyage.[1] When he went back across the ocean on his better-funded second

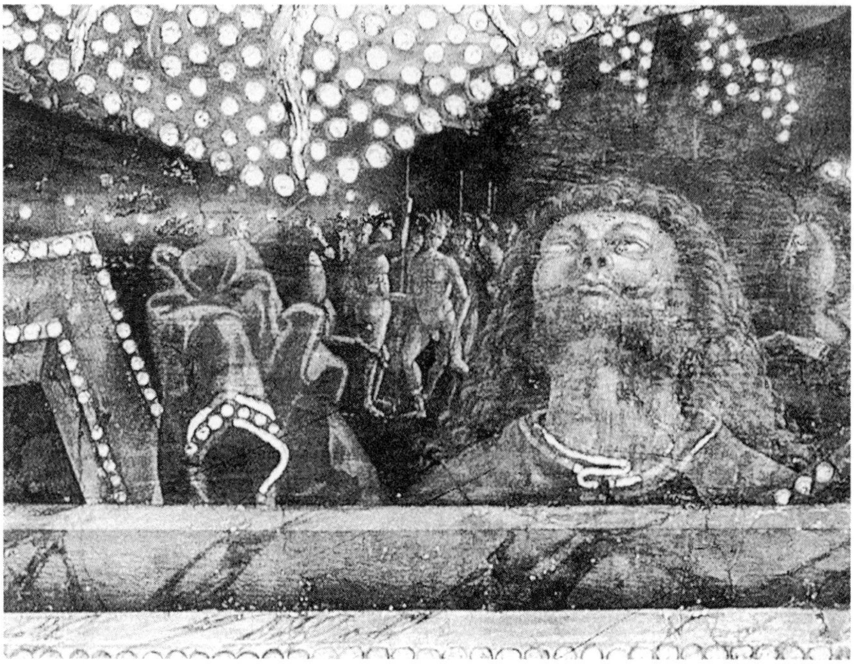

1.2 Pinturicchio, *Resurrection*, detail of figure 1.1.

expedition of 1493, he took along horses. Alexander VI, a Spanish pope, was acutely aware of these developments. The best evidence for connecting Pinturicchio's fresco to Columbus's expeditions comes from a letter written by Columbus on February 15, 1493, during his return from his first voyage, to Luis de Santángel, the finance minister who had personally funded Columbus's expedition after the Spanish monarchs had rejected Columbus's plan to reach the Indies by traveling west. The letter was a digest of information from his log and reported his impressions of the islands he had explored across what he and his contemporaries called the Ocean Sea. Soon after his landfall in Lisbon on March 4, the admiral had two copies of this letter dispatched by courier to the Spanish court, unleashing the first document announcing news of his voyage to lands possibly never before visited by a European. Printed editions began to appear right away in Barcelona (March/April 1493), Rome (May 1493), and soon after in Basel, Paris, and Antwerp, as well as in a variety of other European cities within months of his return, spreading the news with an efficiency and speed barely imaginable in the manuscript age. The Spanish crown circulated it purposefully in order to claim rights to these new lands and ward off potential competitors. Europe was blanketed with copies and translations; by one estimate, its presses published three thousand copies of Columbus's letter, making it a best-seller in its day.[2]

A woodcut accompanying the 1494 Basel edition of the letter shows some nude Native peoples fleeing the new Spanish arrivals on the island called Haiti by the Taíno inhabitants, renamed Hispaniola by Columbus (fig. 1.3). As in Pinturicchio's fresco, the naked figures in the woodcut, many of them bald, huddle in a group. The two figures shown arriving

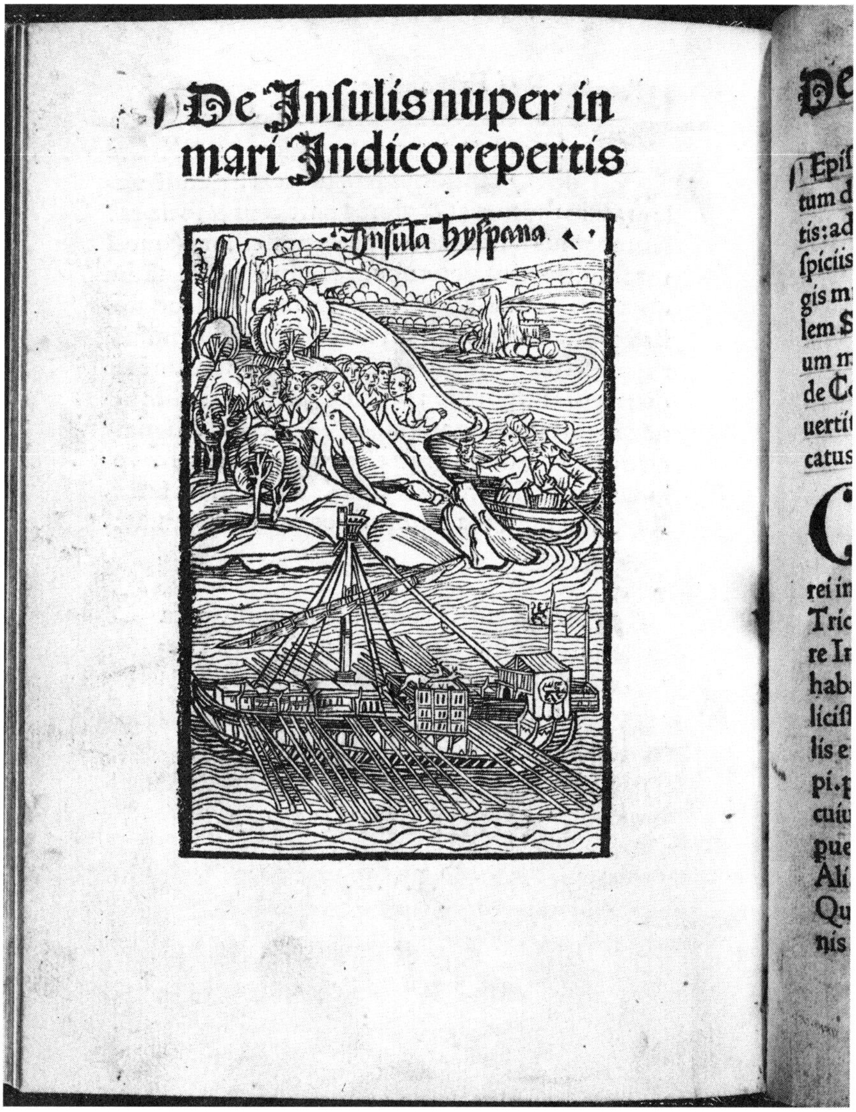

1.3 Amerasian trade in the islands recently discovered by Columbus. *The Island of Hispaniola.* Woodcut on paper. *Epistola de insulis nuper inventis* (Basel: Johannes Bergmann de Olpe, 1494).

along the coast in a boat are not the natives of the place, for they are fully dressed. Yet they are not Europeans; one is shown wearing a turban and the other a Phrygian cap, marking them as eastern traders. This publication announcing a spectacular new European discovery also broadcasts the idea that this new world was not in fact new to everyone in the world. Here, as in Pinturicchio's fresco, the newly discovered lands to the west are connected to the known Orient. This detail corresponds with Columbus's description of a trade network connecting various islands with what he imagined to be an Asian mainland, not far away. Intriguingly, the ship at the bottom of the woodcut is not a representation of Columbus's ship; instead, it presumably belongs to the traders visiting the coast in the dinghy. As for the locals, Columbus observes in his letter that although their canoes do not have sails, they are impressive vessels, equipped with many oars, big enough to hold seventy to eighty men and able to travel over far distances. Although it is a highly abbreviated image, the woodcut clarifies that before Columbus's arrival, as narrated in the accompanying letter, these people were part of a far-flung network connecting them to Asian seafarers using ships comparable to those of Columbus's crew and equipped with proper rigging.[3]

Echoing the frontispiece woodcut, visions of Asia play a fundamental role in the text of Columbus's letter.[4] The admiral claims that he had landed on the edge of the Indian Ocean, in the province of Cathay (*la provincia de Catayo)* or in the Indies (*las Indias*). With consequences lasting until the present day, he describes its inhabitants as Indians (*Indios*), uses the word *Indias* or *Indios* ten times in his short letter. The term *India* derived from the Proto-Indo-European word for the Indus River, which was applied by Greek and Roman cosmographers to a vaster encompassing region stretching from Africa in the West to the farthest reaches of Asia, as yet imperfectly understood, in the East. Columbus describes islands lush and fertile beyond belief, rich in gold and spices, and abounding in rhubarb, cinnamon, and other plants native to China and Southeast Asia. He notes that La Navidad, the fort he ordered to be erected on Hispaniola, is located near gold mines that were well situated for the trade that would soon begin with the Great Khan on the Chinese mainland (*commo de aquella de alla del grand can, adonde aura grand trato et grand ganança*). Local Indians, he writes, report the existence of people who eat human flesh (*comen carne humana*), whom he calls "monsters" (*monstruos*). As in the Basel print, he notes how they travel in their many canoes "through all the islands of India" (*corren todas las yslas de India*) and describes another local legend about a tribe of female warriors who inhabit an island east of Hispaniola called Matinino (today Martinique). He speculates that men visit this island only intermittently for mating, a report that drew on Marco Polo's description of an "island of women" located in the Indian Ocean.[5] He also understands from the Indigenous people he encountered that a large island exists nearby that "abounds in countless gold" (*en esta ay oro sin cuenta*), reaffirming Polo's and other Europeans' descriptions of eastern lands.

According to the historian Edmundo O'Gorman, Columbus was unwavering in his belief that "he had reached Asia, he was in Asia, and it was from Asia that he returned. No one, nothing, to the day of his death, ever made him relinquish this cherished conviction."[6] His personal log recounting his first voyage, transcribed and transmitted by Bartolomé de Las Casas (also known as his *Diario*, which was not published until 1825), confirms that Columbus believed he had arrived in the part of Asia known as the Indies.[7] In Michele de Cuneo's letter to Hieronymo Annari, written in October 1495 and describing Columbus's second voyage in which Cuneo took part, he reports that Columbus associated either Guadeloupe or Jamaica with the Kingdom of Sheba, rich in gold and frankincense, and believed the nearby mainland was Cathay.[8] Columbus's conviction about the nearness of China (or his desperation to prove it) was so pressing that he made his crew swear an oath, on pain of corporal punishment, that on Cuba they had reached the Asian mainland.[9] As we will see in chapter 2, the Asian orientation of Columbus's first voyages gained traction only later, in his third voyage, when he landed on a large landmass that he believed was connected to the terrestrial paradise. On his fourth voyage, he continued to make a series of eastern identifications in the area around Panama (see chapter 6).[10]

Despite the evidence of nude populations, an absence of great cities, and no contact with the Great Khan or his representatives, Columbus remained committed to his vision, due in large part to the authoritative texts that the navigator drew on to make sense of the nature of the world. These included a 1480 edition of Pierre d'Ailly's *Imago Mundi*, which depicts a seemingly boundless Asia characterized by lush vegetation, immense rivers, and countless Indian islands abounding in wealth, and the 1489 edition of Pliny the Elder's *Historia Naturalis*, which similarly offers a lengthy description of Asian lands. Aeneas Sylvius Piccolomini's *Historia rerum ubique gestarum locorumque descriptio*, also owned by Columbus, described an Asia inhabited by both civilized peoples as well as cannibals and Amazons. Perhaps most informative for Columbus was the 1485 abridged Latin Antwerp edition of Polo's *Le livre des merveilles*, which Columbus had learned about from the Florentine cosmographer Paolo dal Pozzo Toscanelli. Columbus's copies of these four texts have been preserved, and all contain his copious annotations. He was also reported to own *The Book of John*

Mandeville (conditioning his vision of human flesh-eaters and Amazons) and *The Letter of Prester John.*[11] Accounts of far eastern journeys fired and shaped Columbus's conviction that he had reached the Indies.

Farthest Reaches of India Beyond the Ganges

The numerous Latin versions of the navigator's letter published in the late fifteenth century were almost all entitled Letter of Columbus . . . Concerning the Recent Discovery of the Islands of India Beyond the Ganges (Epistola Christofori Colom . . . de Insulis Indi[a]e supra Gangem nuper inuentis). To understand what "India beyond the Ganges" meant to Columbus and his contemporaries, it is necessary to review the historical geography of India, which had long been a plural and unstable discursive category for European commentators. As the literary scholar Marianne O'Doherty puts it, "the Indies are a plural entity throughout the later medieval period because travellers, geographers, cartographers, and audiences engage in an endless process of reinventing them in accordance with their own or their culture's changing knowledge, needs, fears, and desires."[12] India (or in the plural, the Indies) was both a real place reached by travelers past and present and an imagined encounter with extremes, climatic, botanical, and animal.[13] The works of a great variety of classical and late antique writers such as Herodotus, Pliny, Solinus, Strabo, and Diodorus first established India's character for European audiences, developed in the thirteenth and fourteenth centuries, when a variety of merchants and missionaries, including Odoric of Pordenone, Polo, Niccolò de' Conti, and (perhaps) John Mandeville, built upon these ancient accounts to provide a rich portrait of this part of the world.[14] In these depictions, layered over the centuries, Europeans described India as a vast, populous, urbanized and civilized region filled with seemingly endless marvels, luxury goods, and extraordinary and monstrous peoples. India was famously visited by Thomas the Apostle, who evangelized a portion of India shortly after the resurrection of Christ, and later became home to the legendary priest-king Prester John and his Christian kingdom. A long tradition placed it in the vicinity of the earthly paradise. As a conceptual and spatial unit, India became an orienting point of reference in the medieval imagination: an insular, littoral, tropical, and maritime region at the most distant eastern reaches of the world.[15] India's alterity and otherworldliness were features of its geographical extremity and liminality; it was, for Europeans, a land that embodied both edge and origin.

Two elements of the traditional image of India, its multipartite geography and its tropical climate producing exuberant fertility, figured frequently in Amerasian conceptions of the new world. For Hellenistic and

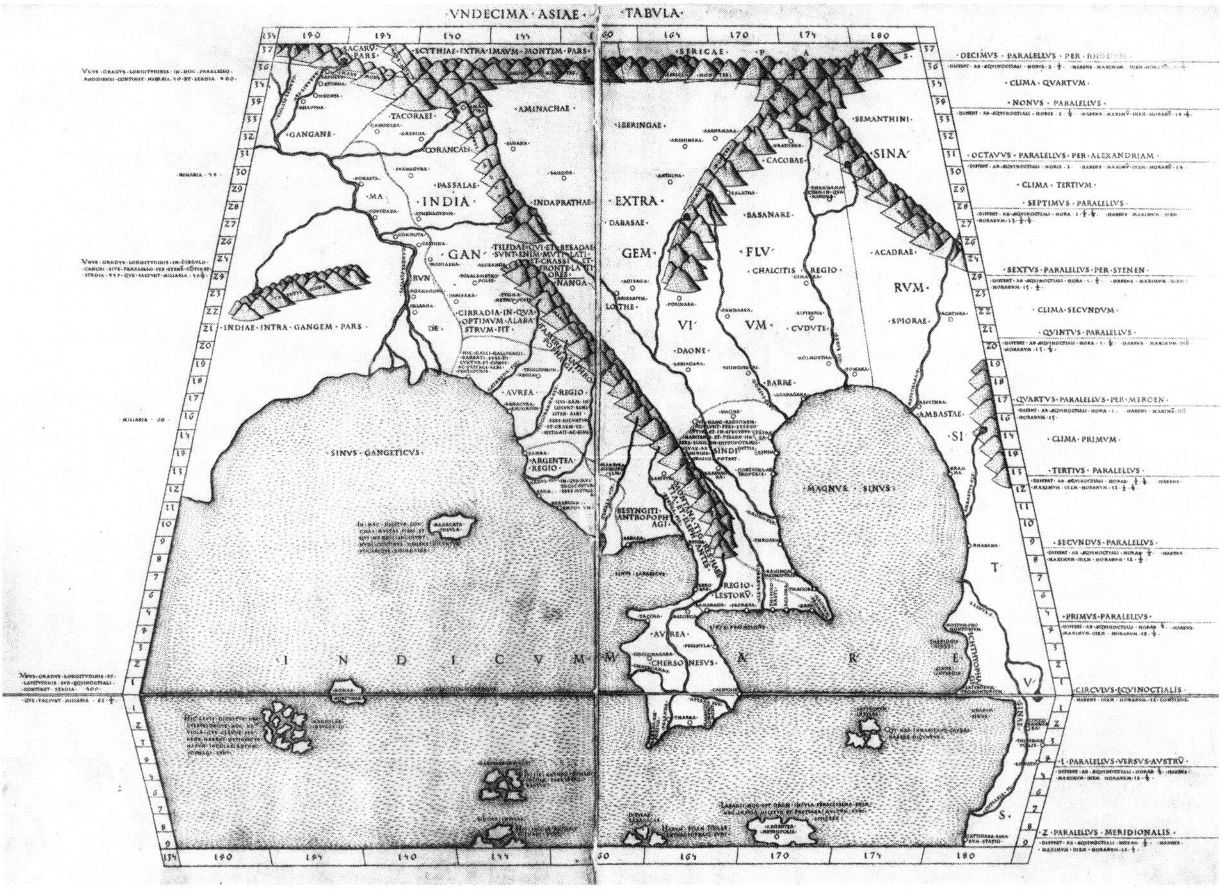

1.4 Ptolemy's eleventh map of easternmost Asia grounded the mental universe of European observers of the Age of Encounters for over a century after the Columbian voyages. Copper engraving on paper, 34.2 × 25.4 cm. *Descriptio undecimae tabulae Asiae*, from *Claudii Pthlolomei Alexandrini cosmographia* (Rome, 1478). Stanford University, Ruderman Map Collection.

Roman geographers — most notably Claudius Ptolemy — India was divided by the Ganges into two regions: *India intra Gangem*, comprising the lands between the Indus and the Ganges Rivers, and *India extra Gangem*, or India beyond the Ganges to the east, which included mainland and maritime Southeast Asia, the lands between India and China (*Sinarum Situs*), and islands beyond the mainland, as we see in Ptolemy's map of Asia (fig. 1.4).[16] The land beyond the Ganges was the remotest, its eastern and southern extent not known even to Ptolemy, and thus it was also the most fabled of the parts of India.

By the later Middle Ages, European cosmographers sometimes began to depict India in a tripartite configuration.[17] The fifteenth-century

Venetian traveler de' Conti, who visited India, Southeast Asia, and possibly part of China, affirmed that "all India is divided into three parts: one, extending from Persia to the Indus; the second, comprising the district from the Indus to the Ganges; and the third, all that is beyond."[18]

In addition to India's multipartite geography, the second component of European understandings of India that informed and sustained the development of the idea of Amerasia was India's climate and latitude. As the historian Nicolás Wey Gómez has demonstrated, thinking about latitude rather than longitude directly motivated Columbus's ventures. Columbus had set out to explore the "torrid zone" between the Tropics of Cancer and Capricorn, thought by several ancient authorities to be uninhabitable, or inhabited only by marvelous creatures, and to prove, among other things, that they were temperate and habitable. The discovery that the tropics were in fact highly fertile and inhabited made possible descriptions of the Caribbean and its people that corresponded in many ways to descriptions of India, thought to occupy the same latitude.[19] The association of the new world and Asian tropics may help explain why the vault mosaic of the chapel of Saint Helena in the church of Santa Croce in Gerusalemme in Rome, commissioned probably before 1503 by the Cardinal Bernardin de Carvajal, a Spanish prelate well informed about the Iberian discoveries and a correspondent of the new world chronicler Peter Martyr d'Anghiera, shows an American macaw and new world maize in the vicinity of a representation of the four rivers of the earthly paradise, traditionally placed in the easternmost part of the earth (see chapter 5). The fact that many of the newly discovered lands from India to New Spain occupied the same climatic zone determined by latitude reinforced the association connecting them, as can be seen well after Columbus in the writings of the Spanish naturalist Gonzalo Fernández de Oviedo. Commonality by latitude produced an association robust enough to persist even as the mileage between the two Indies, including a growing knowledge of the Pacific, expanded greatly over the following decades.[20] This latitudinal or Macrobian system of organizing the world, as we shall see, continued to make sense in the early modern period and refused to simply go away even as four-part models of the world began to take shape (see chapters 8 and 13).

For classical and medieval geographers, India was characterized by its remoteness and extravagance, as well as its expansive but vague extent. India beyond the Ganges teemed with lions, tigers, elephants, parrots, men with tails, *Anthropophagi* or human flesh-eaters, "the best cinnamon," and "very much gold."[21] The lands of the Golden Peninsula (the Golden Chersonesus, the name used by classical geographers for the Malay

Peninsula) were also populated with human flesh–eaters who inhabited seemingly infinite islands in this region, including the Maniolae Islands, "occupied by cannibals called *Manioli*."[22] Beginning with Columbus, a great variety of early modern travelers would look for, and often locate, many of these elements in their explorations of the lands in the western Atlantic, and the island-dotted Indian expanse in particular would dominate the imagination of countless European explorers, writers, and cartographers (see chapters 6 and 8).

Above all, India beyond the Ganges was the ever-farther shore where Western geographical knowledge faltered into silence. According to Ptolemy, the region of the Sinae, the ancient term for the lands of China and the easternmost part of India beyond the Ganges, "is terminated . . . on the east by the meridian [the 180th degree of longitude] marking the unknown land," beyond which existed a people who appeared to isolate themselves as much as possible from the rest of the world.[23] The characteristics of this region—that it was remote, little-known, and unclear in its boundaries—allowed the extremes of *India extra Gangem* to become, in the later Middle Ages, an invitation to imaginings of extravagant foreignness. For example, de' Conti speculates in the mid–fifteenth century that India beyond the Ganges "excels the others in riches, politeness, and magnificence" and was home to sumptuous buildings, rich merchants, and inhabitants leading "a refined life, removed from all barbarity and coarseness."[24] Even more important, because their limits were not fully understood, it was possible for these lands to be both new *and* part of a configuration known to exist since antiquity. Even decades later, Columbus's son Ferdinand Columbus explained that his father had called these islands the Indies not because they were the same as the Indian lands visited by previous European travelers, but because "they were the eastern part of India beyond the Ganges, to which no cosmographer set limits [i.e., to the east], nor boundaries with another land or province to the east, save with the ocean. And because these lands were the unknown eastern part of India, and had no name of their own, he named them after the nearest adjoining land, calling them the west Indies."[25] An extensive and malleable geographical imaginary, this part of the world informed Europeans' understanding of the new world for the next century and more.

The publication of Columbus's letter neatly coincided with another formative publication about India: Cristoforo da Bollate's first printed edition of de' Conti's account of his voyage to India, *Indies Rediscovered* (*India recognita*) (Milan, 1492), which had been composed approximately fifty years earlier and included in the fourth book of Poggio Bracciolini's widely read *On the Vicissitudes of Fortune (De varietate fortunae)*. In addition to defining the geography of the three parts of India, de' Conti's text offered a digest of information on the Indies, describing the geography, flora, fauna, clothing, architecture, and general riches of India. When news of the Columbian voyages reached Europe the year after Bollate's publication, these printed accounts worked together to generate a wave of European interest in and enthusiasm for the new "Indians" encountered during the recent voyages to both East and West.

News of the Indian New World Reaches Italy

With so many printed versions of Columbus's letter in circulation, the news traveled fast, reaching not only envoys and ambassadors but also a wider public.[26] The Florentine priest Giuliano Dati turned Columbus's story into a street song, published in a cheaply printed leaflet that today survives in a few original copies. His "Letter on the Islands Newly Discovered by the King of Spain" (*La lettera dell'isole che ha trovato nuovamente il Re di Spagna*, 1493), in which he refashions Columbus's letter in the poetic form of ottava rima, meant to be performed live, conveying to the listening public a sense of immediacy and awe associated with the Columbian voyages. Taking apart and reassembling Columbus's letter into a ballad partly in the singer's voice and partly in that of Columbus, the *Lettera dell'isole* brought to the streets of Florence a vivid account of the deeds of the Italian admiral and about foreign lands laden with untold wealth and inhabited by strange people.

Dati's first song was so popular that he quickly composed two sequels, "The Great Magnificence of Prester John, Lord of Greater India and of Ethiopia" (*La gran magnificentia del Prete Ianni Signore dell'India Maggiore & dell'Etiopia*, 1493–94), and "The Second Song of India" (*Il secondo cantare dell'India*, 1494–95), which describe the resplendent court of the mythic Christian Indian monarch Prester John and the marvels of India. Both were illustrated with woodcuts of traditional Plinian monsters, including pygmies, hermaphrodites, and headless men.[27] Responding to the excitement over the recent discoveries, the three poems contributed to the association of the lands explored by Columbus with the fabled lands of India.[28]

According to Dati, gold, silver, gems, and spices are found in all of these lands; he specifically mentions cinnamon and rhubarb in Columbus's Indies.[29] In *La lettera*, Dati notes that "the land was abundant in many different fruits," leaving Columbus and his men "amazed at the luxuriance that we found; there are green trees which I believe never shed their leaves." In *La gran magnificentia*, Columbus describes how in Prester

John's India, "their land is fertile and healthy, and abounds in fruit."[30] Beyond the abundance celebrated in all three songs, they all present the Indians as a particularly agreeable race. In *La lettera*, Dati has Columbus exclaim, "Gentle lord, I could not relate the affability of this race," and in *La gran magnificentia* Dati claims that "rarely do they feel violence or any animosity; they aren't a traitorous or thieving people, nor are they adulterers, liars, or thieves."[31] Marvel and awe are equally evoked in the three songs. In *La lettera*, for instance, he notes that those who haven't seen the riches of these lands "do not know the world's marvels," and in *Il secondo cantare* he exclaims, "about these great things that I sing to you, some will not believe."[32] Above all, in all three *cantari*, these are tropical places, sharing a common Indian climate.[33] By following his original poem *La lettera*—based on Columbus's letter to Santángel—with two subsequent poems about India, all of which describe identical landscapes and people, Dati presented Columbus's islands not as a dramatic new discovery but as an extension of Indian geography.[34] The Indies of Asia and the Indies of Columbus were either commensurate or proximate.[35]

Visions of India and Asia, first developed in ancient and medieval accounts and then, blossoming in Columbus's letter, went on to inform a great variety of early chronicles that described the lands Europeans encountered across the Atlantic. Among the first entries of Martyr d'Anghiera's widely read new world reports, published in 1510 as *De Orbe Novo* or *Decades of the New World* but circulated and read aloud in European educated circles from 1493 on, is one from 1493 in direct response to Columbus's voyage. Martyr writes, "the parrots brought from there and many other things show that these islands taste of the soil of India, either because of their proximity or because of their natural properties." This summary observation, which was to be developed in countless ways during the following decades, shows that Amerasian thinking could be grounded in an imagined propinquity ("because of their proximity") or a climatic association ("because of their natural properties") or both.[36] In the same report, the chronicler notes that when Columbus landed on Hispaniola, he saw the Native peoples gathering fleeces from trees "just as among the Chinese."[37] In another entry from April 23, 1501, Martyr relays Columbus's claim that Hispaniola was the Far Eastern capital "Ophir, about which one reads in the third book of Kings."[38] Sailing west and passing the islands of Cuba and Jamaica, Martyr reports, Columbus believed "he had reached close to the Golden Chersonese, the beginning of our east beyond Persia."[39] Ideas and turns of phrase like these, first recorded in Columbus's letter, established what would become a long-standing pattern of Europeans finding Asia across the ocean to the west.

Alpha Omega, or Where East Meets West

Perhaps the most dramatic moment of geographical clarity in Martyr's accounts comes in his description of Columbus's landing in Cuba:

> He [Columbus] called the beginning [of the island] Alpha Omega, because he thinks that there lies the boundary of our orient, since the sun sets there, and of our occident, since it rises there. For he insists that the beginning of "India beyond the Ganges" is to the West [of here], and in fact comes to its ultimate limit [here]. Nor indeed is this utterly absurd, since the cosmographers have left the boundaries of the Gangean India undefined, and many are of the opinion that the shores of India are not far from the coasts of Spain.[40]

For a variety of ancient and medieval cosmographers, all this made sense; Asia was so expansive that its eastern shores approached Europe.[41] Martyr gave these vague ideas traction by offering his readers reports of real voyages to real places: Cuba (or here, more specifically, Cape Maisi, at the eastern extremity of Cuba) was the place where "East" and "West" met. To put it another way, sailing west eventually brought Columbus to a point where "East" and "West" came into definition by meeting in the same place. The associations also extended to areas further south. As Martyr reports, when in 1500 Vicente Yáñez Pinzón and his nephew Arias Pinzón sailed along the coast of Paria, in what is today northeastern Venezuela, they believed they were "beyond the city of Cathay and the Indian shore beyond the Ganges."[42] The placement of the Alpha Omega line, a widening contact zone that contemporaries called the new world, shifted in the coming decades, but the basic idea persisted for centuries. From the moment Columbus returned from his first voyage, Europeans understood and perpetuated the idea that the lands he had explored were an extension of Asia.

Martyr's reports also dramatize the fact that knowledge of the new contact zone necessarily involved dialogue across difference, a continually informative acoustic phenomenology. On April 23, 1501, Martyr reports that Columbus sent thirty men "to explore the region of Cipangu, otherwise Cibao," revealing that upon hearing the name of the Haitian province of Cibao, where Native peoples indicated there would be a great quantity of gold as well as woods full of spices, Columbus found acoustic confirmation that this land was Japan.[43] As this example illustrates, from the very beginning, Columbus and his men asked the people they encountered what they called themselves, who their ruler was, and what name they gave their lands and vicinities. Columbus and a great variety of future explorers received Indigenous information by word of mouth, asking further leading questions, and in the process giving form to Amerasian ideas. Amerasia as a concept was not simply imposed on a passive Native population but was formed through encounters with Indigenous knowledge traditions and a sonic landscape of Indigenous naming, which is not to say the process wasn't continually marked by ellipses, misunderstandings, and (frequently enough) misdirections.

Limits of Visibility

Some of Martyr's early letters may have had a role to play in the formation of the restless group of naked figures on the far side of the tomb in Pinturicchio's Vatican fresco for Pope Alexander VI (see figs 1.1–2). In a letter of September 13, 1493, to Cardinal Ascanio Sforza (who, having crucially supported Borgia in his election as Pope Alexander VI in 1492, was duly rewarded by the new pope with the powerful position of vice chancellor), Martyr writes that the island discovered by Columbus is populated by Native peoples who go naked and yet have a political structure ("the island has many chieftains") and a developed culture of military contest among tribes ("they wear each other out in constant wars . . . using bows and spears pointed and ablaze"), a description that generally accords with what Pinturicchio shows in his grouping of naked and apparently battle-ready Native peoples.[44] In the fresco, the figure with arm raised seems to be leaning on a long staff, perhaps corresponding to the spears made of cane stalks described by Columbus in his letter. Next to the Europeans' stepping horses, these naked Indians seem to be engaged in a sort of dance, some with mouths open, as if in a war chant. In a letter of December 29, 1494, to the Roman humanist Pomponio Leto, a prominent intellectual figure also favored by Pope Alexander VI, Martyr offers a resonant vignette that perhaps best accords with what Pinturicchio shows: "The natives are amazed at the sound of trumpets and kettle-drums; they are astounded by the thunder of war machines, by the stepping and running of the horses and their trappings; they whisper, they stand still and in astonishment, mouth open, intrigued by every aspect of our possessions."[45] The artist in the Vatican and the Roman humanist patronized by the Pope inhabited a shared vision of an Amerasian new world.

The *Resurrection* presents a view toward the tomb of Christ, toward Jerusalem, and in the distance somewhere beyond the tomb, farther east, we see these figures, hazy yet distinctly foreign. The naked Native peoples painted by Pinturicchio may or may not accept the news of Christ's resurrection, which is happening far from them but also directly above them. Or they may only ever receive that news through the filter of their own beliefs and traditions. Whereas the rest of the fresco is painted in full color, these figures are in ghostly grisaille. They are not yet dressed, which is to say they are not yet figures, in the sense of characters in a known story. It is not yet clear how they will figure in history or what their relationship is to that raining gold. For now, they are people far to the east of Jerusalem, hovering at the limits of visibility and understanding.

• • •

Coda: Amerasian Cannibals

The fashioning of the word *cannibalism*, a Columbian neologism, merged Asian soundscapes with those encountered across the Atlantic. The earliest reference to eaters of human flesh in the lands of the western Atlantic appear in Columbus's journal from his first voyage or *Diario* on November 4, 1492, as summarized and transcribed by the Dominican friar Las Casas. On the island of Cuba, looking for evidence of Asia, Columbus presented the local Taíno with samples of cinnamon and pepper, Indian products that he had brought with him from Spain. They responded with gestures to indicate that nearby, to the southwest, he could find these things. He similarly showed them gold and pearls, and "some old men answered that in a place that they called Bohío there was an infinite quantity of gold . . . and that there were pearls as well." Then, primed as he was to believe that Asia was close at hand, Columbus learned from his informants that to the southeast, "far from there, there were one-eyed people and others with dogs' muzzles who ate human beings; upon seizing a person, they cut his throat and drank his blood and cut off his genitals."[46]

Having just arrived on these islands, Columbus probably could not have extracted such detail through gestures alone, but his knowledge of Asia supplemented lapses in understanding, since he had read about islands populated with dog-headed men and human flesh–eaters in a variety of medieval travel accounts to Asian lands. Columbus then brought some locals with him as he continued to explore other nearby islands, reaching Bohío on November 23. These Native informants "said it [Bohío] was very large and that there were people upon it who had one eye in the middle of their foreheads and others whom they called cannibals, of whom they showed themselves to have a great fear."[47] In this fateful passage, the word *cannibals* makes its first entry into European history and culture.[48] On November 26, Las Casas reports that "all the people whom he has found up to today, [Columbus] says, have the greatest fear of the people of Caniba, or Canima, and they say that the latter live on this island of Bohío." Columbus's Indigenous informants "could not speak, fearing that the people here were going to eat them, and he could not rid them of the fear. They said that the people here had only one eye each and dogs' faces, but the admiral believed that they were lying. The admiral felt that

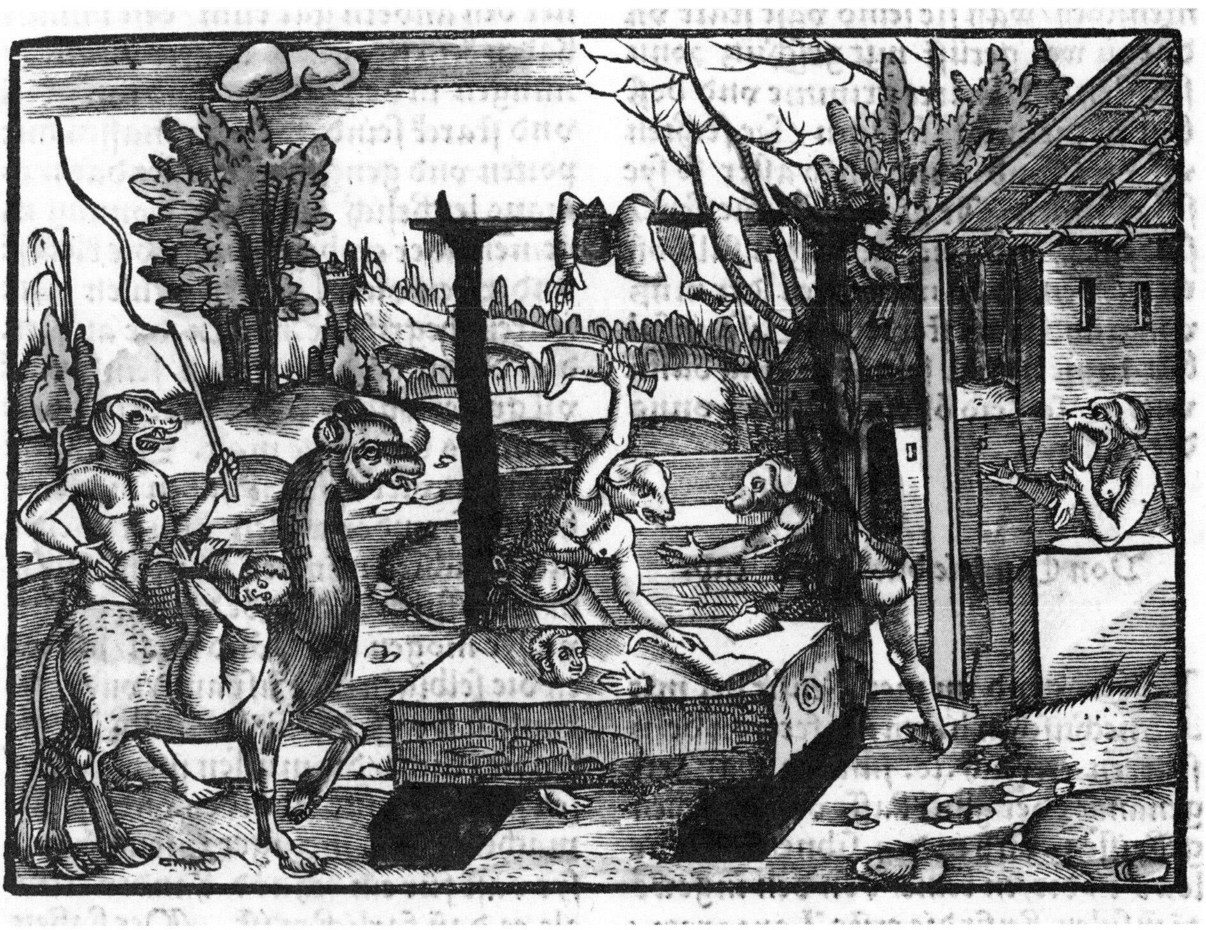

1.5 Dog-headed Asian cannibals among the Caribs. Hand-colored woodcut, 10.5 × 14.4 cm. Lorenz Fries, *Uslegung der Mercarthen oder Carta marina* (Strasbourg, 1525).

the people who used to capture them must belong to the Grand Khan's dominion." Although Columbus wasn't entirely sure about the accuracy of the information he was receiving, the rhyming morphemes can (i.e., dog)/Khan had begun to echo in his mind.[49] On December 11, they fully coincide, when Columbus remarks that "that Caniba is nothing other than the people of the Grand Khan, who must be very close to here."[50]

By associating what he heard from the Taíno about the man-eating Caribs, Columbus effectively attached selected sounds from Indigenous speech—from Taíno defamations of their traditional enemy—to what he already knew about Asia. He heard the Arawak world "Cariba" and rendered it "Caniba," perhaps under the influence of the word for dog (*cane/canis*) in association with the man-eaters in Asia described by Polo as "similar to dogs" (*canibus similes*); Columbus then went one step further and identified the Caribs/Canibs as subjects of the Great Khan himself. A brilliant, early Amerasian constellation thus came into being: the three words *canis*, *caniba*, and *khan* (spelled Can in the log transcriptions that have come down to us) became associated into a phonetic family connecting Pliny's Cynocephalus, the insulting Arawak name for their neighbors, and the historical Mongols of China, a sonic convergence that Columbus took as decisive further empirical proof that he was in or near Asia.[51]

Columbus's Amerasian cannibals proliferated from this point forward. The widely publicized editions of Vespucci's voyages generated a nearly endless series of images of cannibal feasts (see fig. 2.3). As the historian Surekha Davies has pointed out, Martin Waldseemüller's 1516 *Carta marina* (see fig. 2.10) placed cannibals in Asia, plotted not far from the newly discovered lands, making an Amerasian expanse of man-eaters from Asia to the western Atlantic perfectly imaginable.[52] Based on this linguistic conflation, in another of the earliest representations of the peoples in the western Atlantic, the Strasbourg cartographer Lorenz Fries depicted dog-headed cannibals carving up human remains, associating the human flesh–eating inhabitants of the western Atlantic with the dog-headed peoples of Asia (fig. 1.5).

As the literary scholar Margarita Zamora explains, European knowledge of new worlds "is not created by an individual genius working alone; it is the product of intellectual give and take, of the movement of ideas back and forth, of conversations comprising many voices."[53] Amerasia was a European formation, but one that emerged and was consistently shaped in seemingly endless misunderstanding-ridden verbal interactions with local communities.[54] Not only the concept, but the very word cannibal is an Amerasian creation formed by such interchanges, with powerful consequences for centuries to come.

TWO

What Did the Term *New World* Mean?

In February 1502, just before Columbus set out on his fourth voyage in May of that year, Valentim Fernandes, a Moravian printer working in Lisbon, produced a compendium of three translations in service to the Portuguese King Manuel I: an excerpt from Marco Polo's *Description of the World* (*Divisament dou monde*), book four of Poggio Bracciolini's *On the Vicissitudes of Fortune* (*De Varietate Fortunae*), which included Niccolò de' Conti's account of his travels in India, and a 1499 letter by the Genoese merchant Girolamo da Santo Stefano describing his travels from the Levant to India and as far as Pegu and Sumatra—all of them treatises on the Indies.[1] Addressing the Portuguese king, Fernandes introduces the book by praising Portuguese expansion in both Africa and Asia. Beginning with Bartolomeu Dias's circumnavigation of the Cape of Good Hope, Fernandes boasts: "Dias . . . had been chosen like Joshua to enter into that new world, which we can indeed call the Promised Land."[2]

For Fernandes as for many others in the period, the parts of Asia recently reached by European navigators were a new world, filled with "new and marvelous things from new lands."[3] As Fernandes's collection of texts suggests, there was a natural link between Polo's travels, Portuguese expansion, and the concept of new worlds. By relating Polo to "the new" and "the new" to Polo, Fernandes brought Polo's text into contemporary relevance as an invaluable source of information about Asia that could guide the Portuguese king and his explorers in their most recent spectacular expeditions. In his colophon, Fernandes states directly that he undertook his translation "as a service to God and as an instruction for all those who now go to the Indias."[4] The epoch-making discovery of Fernandes's day, as he points out in the preface to his translation of Polo, was that the Portuguese had found the beginnings of the East at the limits of the West, now made accessible to Europeans as a result of Gaspar Corte-Real's landing in what is today called Newfoundland: "Beginning

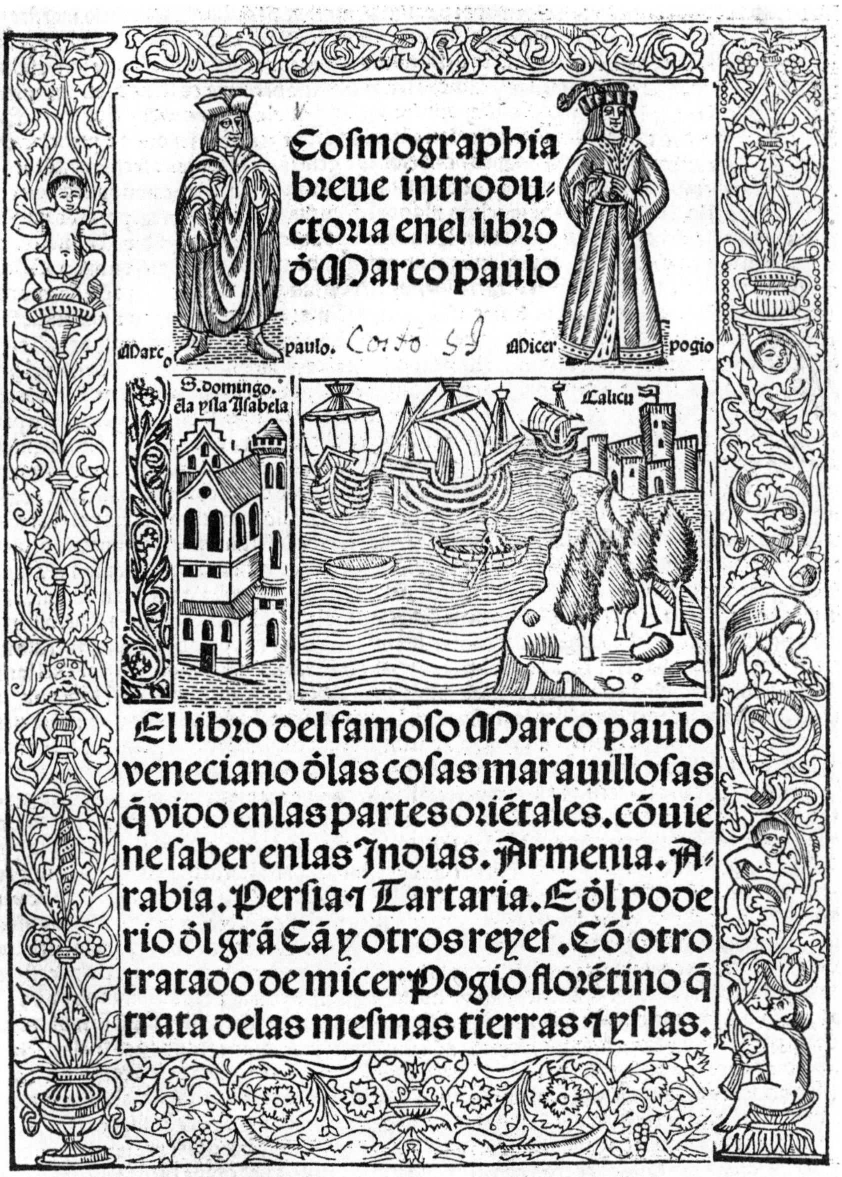

2.1 A compilation of Marco Polo's and other travels to India, with Columbus's colony Santo Domingo on the cover. Frontispiece, woodcut on paper. *El libro del famoso Marco Paulo veneciano*, trans. Rodrigo de Santaella (Seville, 1503). New York, Hispanic Society of America library. The title page of Santaella's translation shows "Marco Paulo" (Marco Polo) and "Micer Pogio" (Poggio Bracciolini), authorities on the Indies, above port scenes of "Santo Domingo en la ysla Isabela" (the island commonly known as Hispaniola) side by side with "Calicut" on the Malabar coast of India.

in the East all the way to the lands of the Great Khan (where already your powerful name begins to resound), where lie the very noble provinces of Tenduch, Mangy, Tanguth, etc., the beginning of which, according to my limited knowledge, was discovered by the most honorable gentleman Gaspar Corte-Real."[5] Tenduch (Tenduc), Mangy (Mangi), and Tanguth were all places visited by Polo in eastern Asia. Understanding Corte-Real's and Polo's Indies to be one and the same, Fernandes depicts an Amerasian Portuguese empire.

A year later, in 1503, Rodrigo de Santaella, a Spanish humanist and cleric, produced a Castilian translation of Polo and Bracciolini/de' Conti.[6] Basing himself on Fernandes's text though not translating directly from it, Santaella argued that Columbus's and Polo's Indies were not the same and that Spanish and Portuguese voyages had landed in different parts of the world. Santaella remarks that he had translated Bracciolini's/de' Conti's text on India in order to support and confirm Polo's descriptions. Making no reference to "newness" or "new worlds," Santaella presents the Indies as Asian lands with no connection to the lands recently explored in the western Atlantic. Whereas the "common people" think that Antilla and those islands recently discovered by commandment of the Spanish king and queen are the Indies, "they are deceived if they call these lands by the name of *Indias*. Since on Hispaniola or in New Spain they find gold, some say this is Tharsis or Ophir or Sethin, from which in the time of Solomon they brought gold to Jerusalem. By thinking this way, they accrue errors upon errors." Thus, Santaella's aim is "to kill this cancer, so that it creeps no more nor engenders greater errors."[7] He invents an etymology for the Antilles as the "Ante-India, which means counter India, much as Anti-Christ is contrary to Christ . . . so that it cannot be named India," concluding that Asia is "in the East and Antilla Hispaniola in the West, in place and condition much different."[8]

Santaella was unable to kill the Amerasian cancer. Even the design of Santaella's title page goes some way to undermining the polemic contained within, as it shows the figures of Polo and Bracciolini above port scenes of Santo Domingo on Hispaniola and "Calicut" in India (fig. 2.1). For the reader coming upon this volume, Polo and Bracciolini's accounts of India are presented as guides to new or newly discovered lands at the extremities of the earth. The figure of Polo, the great source of information about Asia, is visually aligned with the Spanish new world. The relation between Santo Domingo and Calicut is set out for consideration; they are juxtaposed, neither neighborly nor antipodal. While his polemic argued for difference and distance, the publication itself continues to put these parts of the world into the same discursive context, a dialogical relation broadcast by the frontispiece layout. Designed to appeal to contemporary audiences interested in the expansion of European contact with the wider world, Santaella's book in fact sustained the Amerasian conversation, which asked repeatedly how the farthest reaches of the earth connect to one another and thus relate to Europe. The following decades of publications, maps, and visual representations continued to investigate the unresolved relations set forth by Santaella's frontispiece.

As seen in chapter 1, Columbus's news incited much debate about the location of the lands he had explored and their potential relation to Cathay and India.[9] While Santaella denied that Columbus had landed in Asia, a variety of other commentators on the Columbian voyages who have been cast as skeptics in modern scholarship in fact also saw an Amerasian continuity even as they trumpeted the discovery of new lands. Often presented as naysayers, famous figures such as the compiler Peter Martyr d'Anghiera, the navigator Amerigo Vespucci, and the mapmaker Martin Waldseemüller turn out to be quite as involved in the Amerasian worldview as Christopher Columbus. An approach that begins by recognizing the extent and logic of the Amerasian phenomenon will be able to make more sense of the period sources, including those voices that appreciated and insisted on the newness of the discovered lands.

Columbus himself, for all his insistence on being in or near Asia, in fact avowed at certain moments that he had reached an unknown land or a "new world." On his third voyage of 1498, he coasted along a vast landmass to the south of the islands of Cuba and Hispaniola that later would be called America, then South America. In a 1499 letter to Ferdinand and Isabella reporting on the results of this voyage, Columbus describes the powerful waters of a river called Orinoco rushing into the Gulf of Paria, indicating that a previously unknown continent, "an immense tract of land situated in the south, of which no knowledge has been hitherto obtained," lay inland.[10] Similarly, in a letter from 1500 to Doña Juana de Torres, the nurse of prince John, the son of Ferdinand and Isabella who had accompanied Columbus on his second voyage, Columbus refers to having undertaken "another voyage to the new heavens and new world" (*nuevo cielo y mundo*) and that he had "subdued another world" (*otro mundo*) and added it to the empire of the Kings of Spain.[11] However, even as he entertained the idea that these were "new lands," he proposed that the southern landmass contained the earthly paradise of biblical tradition, a goal on his mind since his first voyage.[12]

New Worlds East and West

Columbus's pattern of seeing both new and old in the lands he encountered was shared by a number of other early reporters on the voyages of discovery and conquest. The humanist Peter Martyr d'Anghiera, who during his service as chaplain to the Spanish court became famous as a compiler of recent travel reports, often referred to the western lands discovered by Columbus and others as a "new world." In a letter to Cardinal Ascanio Sforza on November 1, 1493, he speaks of "Columbus the discoverer of a New World" (*Colonus ille Novi Orbis repertor*), an expression that has, more than any other, grounded modern understandings of Columbus as the discoverer of America.[13] Martyr famously used the same term, *Orbis Novus*, in the title of his collection of reports, the first three volumes or "Decades" published under the title *Decades of the New World* (*De orbe novo*) in 1516. According to the historian Edmundo O'Gorman, Martyr offers the "best illustration" of skepticism that Columbus had found Asia, and many historians have followed O'Gorman in presenting Martyr as a doubter of Columbus's claims.[14] What else could his embrace of the term *new world* mean if not that he rejected the idea that the newly discovered lands across the Atlantic had anything to do with Asia? It has been hard to shake the idea that Martyr recognized the newness of America for what it was. Yet, as we saw in chapter 1, the humanist was able to combine the idea of a new world with the idea that Columbus had reached the Indies. Newness and Indian extension were not contradictory claims for him.

Recent scholarship has shown that the term *new world* in fact carried a wide application in the period. It was used to refer to newly discovered lands both to the west and to the east, leaving open the question of how the various new worlds conjoined. This wide semantic field makes it possible to hear the Amerasian resonances in Martyr and in many other period voices—even those, such as Vespucci, that have been taken as bedrock for the modern view that the discovery of America had nothing to do with Asia.

New meant above all that these lands were until then unknown. Unknown could mean never known, even to the ancients, but it could also mean now known firsthand and in-depth, or conquered, colonized, and converted for the first time. Even before his own Latin publication of the *Decades*, an Italian vernacular translation of some of Martyr's early reports was included in a frequently reprinted collection of travel accounts from East and West entitled *Paesi novamente retrovati et novo mondo da Alberico Vesputio Florentio intitulato* (The newly discovered lands and new world so named by Amerigo Vespucci), which was first published in 1507. The term *retrovati* in the title, in the immediate vicinity of the term *novo mondo*, hovers in a field of meanings including "discovered" and "rediscovered" or "newly discovered."[15] The volume includes the journeys of Vasco da Gama and Alvise Cadamosto (who, writing in the middle of the fifteenth century, referred to the western coast of Africa as "another world"), showing how the term *new world* referred to any or all lands that were now newly accessible to European navigators, colonizers, merchants, and missionaries.[16] Decades later, Simon Grynaeus and Johann Huttich's *Novus orbis* (Paris, 1532), whose full title was *New World of Regions and Islands Unknown to The Ancients*, collected travel accounts from all over the world, and not only the Americas, into what became the standard collection of travel literature in Protestant Northern Europe. (For more on how these accounts were combined and compiled in publications of the period, shaping patterns of travel-through-reading, see chapter 6.) As the historian Giuseppe Marcocci has observed, "the discovery of America was part of a more general and complex cultural reorientation that resulted from a changed [European] relationship to the whole world, and not just with one part alone."[17]

Reviewing the early modern travel-writing genre, the historian Joan-Pau Rubiés observed that the idea of the new world "included most of Asia, no less than America, given that much of the East had been equally 'newly found' by European navigators."[18] In his world map of 1538, Gerardus Mercator first placed the word *America* on what are today North and South America, yet the older understanding of new worlds persisted in maps, cosmographies, and histories even into the seventeenth century; indeed, in Mercator's own even more influential 1569 map the term *America* disappears from the new landmasses, replaced by *India Nova* (see chapters 11 and 12).[19] In his 1604 account of the Portuguese voyages around the coast of Africa to the Malabar Coast of India and on to Malacca, China, and Japan, the Italian Jesuit Giovanni Pietro Maffei uses the term *new world* to refer to India.[20] Similarly, the Venetian Doge Leonardo Donà (1536–1612) catalogued accounts of both American and Asian travels under the title *Del Mondo Nuovo*.[21] In his *Discours de la nature et des parties du monde* (1587), the French poet and philosopher Pontus de Tyard explicitly defines the "new world" as any and all lands unknown to the ancients. With some originality, he gives the lands ranging from Labrador above the arctic circle through New France (Canada), Florida, New Castile (Mexico), Panama, Brazil, and Peru down to the strait of Magellan the label "new Asia" (*la nouvelle Asie*), which extends across the South Sea to the China Sea, where the "old Asia" begins.[22] The automatic identification of the term *new world* with America, which one finds throughout the modern scholarship on the "Age of Discoveries," is in fact rare to find in the sixteenth-century sources.

In his treatise *The Marvels of the World* (*Des merveilles du monde*, probably 1553), the Orientalist Guillaume Postel offered a thoughtful deliberation on the matter of new world terminology. He found it suitable to use two terms, *monde nouveau* and *monde renouvelé*, sometimes together. The southern part of Africa and Asia, he explains, was known until recently more by hearsay than in truth, and "for that reason I call it *monde nouveau renouvelé*, just as the ancients had conventionally called both one and the other part India, due to the Indian color, olive and somewhat ashy, common to all or most of the inhabitants there." The *monde nouveau* proper, by contrast, was the territory to the West discovered fifty or sixty years earlier, but even this was rediscovered (*retrouvé*) since the ancients, in particular Plato, had suspected its existence in their legends of Atlantis. Postel proposes to call this land *Japéthie* after Japethus, the giant father of Prometheus and Atlas, identified by Postel also with Japheth, the son of Noah. Thus Postel terms newly encountered parts of Africa and Asia *nouveau monde* but *renouvelé*, and he calls America a *nouveau monde* but *retrouvé*—both are new and not new.[23]

From the first, the term *new world* was used as often to describe discoveries in Asia as in America. To return to the early years of the sixteenth century, a 1507 oration delivered by the papal preacher Egidio da Viterbo before Pope Julius II and the College of Cardinals proudly proclaims the Asian exploits of the Portuguese king as a new world discovery, even though many of the Indian ports reached by the Portuguese had been known to Mediterranean cosmographers since antiquity. He tells the pope that "the King of Portugal had under your auspices enlarged the bounds of your most sacred empire even to the Indies, thus ushering in a golden age in that recently discovered new part of the world" (*in novum terrarum orbem inuentum*).[24] Egidio's long oration never mentions America or the new lands to the west; here, the framework is that of the Portuguese encounters with lands and peoples in Asia, and it is a *novum orbem*.

Egidio's 1507 oration came in response to a letter published in 1506 (and reprinted thereafter) from the Portuguese king to the bishop and cardinal of Lisbon, Jorge de Costa, celebrating Francisco de Almeida's expedition (March 25, 1505–May 23, 1506) to India, Ethiopia, and "other oriental lands."[25] On the frontispiece, a hand-colored woodcut shows male and female inhabitants of these eastern parts (fig. 2.2). The long-haired woman's nakedness is covered only by a small branch, while the ruddy long-haired and bearded male wears a feather headdress, feather skirt, and leg ornament (the colorist made sure to show the different colors of the feathers) and brandishes a bow. Although the letter only describes travels along the African coast and to India, narrating the destruction of Mombasa and the battle at Cochin among other achievements, this new world Adam and Eve correspond to depictions of the Tupi people of Brazil encountered by Pedro Álvares Cabral and Vespucci a few years earlier (fig. 2.3 and chapter 3). Da Viterbo, who very likely held this publication in his hands, could only imagine an Amerasian new world based on images like these.[26] (For more on visions of the new world in Julius II's Rome, see chapter 4.)

Vespucci's Amerasian Visions

No two names have been more celebrated for having recognized and indeed branded the newness of America than Amerigo Vespucci the navigator and Waldseemüller the cartographer. Both specialized scholarship and popular histories have given the explorer and the mapmaker major roles in heralding a break with the past and announcing the advent of

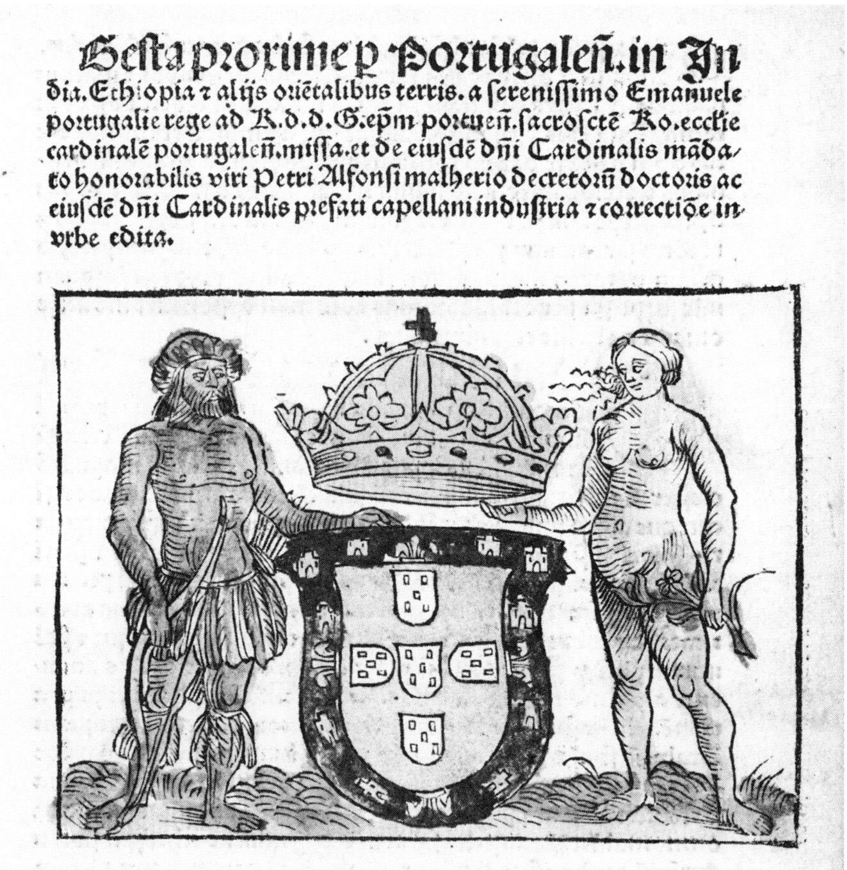

2.2 The merging of Brazilian and "oriental" new worlds. Frontispiece, hand-colored woodcut on paper. *Gesta proxime per Portugalensis in India, Ethiopia, et alijs orientalibus terris...* (Nuremberg, 1507). Washington, DC, Library of Congress.

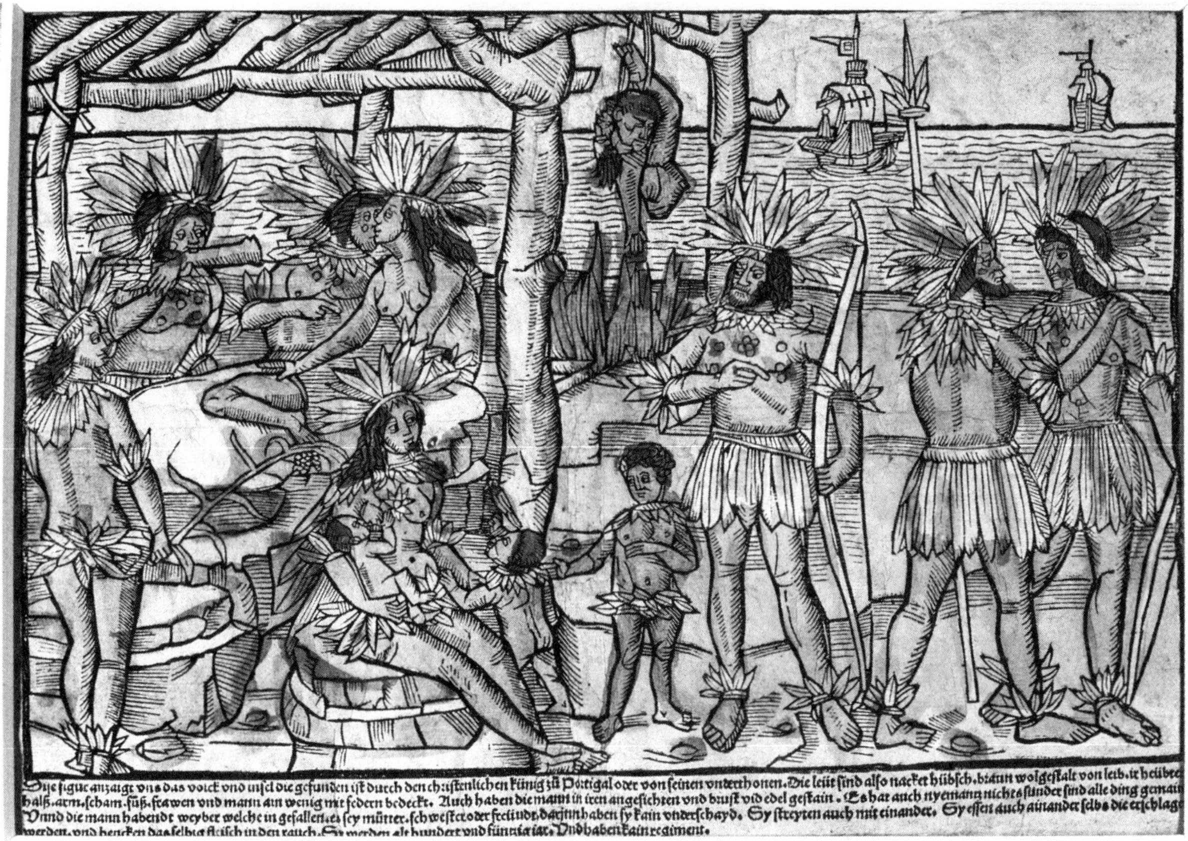

2.3 A 1505 visualization of the Native peoples described by Vespucci. Broadsheet, hand-colored woodcut on paper, 22 × 33.3 cm (Augsburg, 1505). New York Public Library.

the modern world on the basis of Europe's discovery of a new world. This story has obscured the evidence of the documents themselves, a close reading of which reveals that their publications were imprinted with Amerasian thinking, and in fact gave shape to an Amerasian understanding of the world that was to dominate the rest of the century. A letter published under Vespucci's name describing the navigator's third visit to the coast of present-day Brazil in 1501–1502, was first published in Latin in 1503 without a title, and then reprinted with the resounding title *Mundus novus* or *De mondo novo* in many editions and languages over the following years. The *Mundus novus* letter was repeatedly pirated, excerpted and adapted, as in the broadsheet published by Johann Froschauer in 1505, showing the "naked, handsome, brown" cannibals described in Vespucci's letter, with a long caption that excerpts some of its most lurid details: they go naked but for some feather coverings and the studs of precious stones in their faces and chests, they do not know private property or government, they are sexually licentious, eat people, and live for very long, some to 150 years old (see fig. 2.3).

The first lines of the *Mundus novus* letter itself famously proclaim that "those new regions . . . can be called a new world, since our ancestors had no knowledge of them and they are an entirely new matter to those who hear about them."[27] The *Mundus novus* letter was soon followed in 1505 by another Vespucci publication in Italian, the *Letter to Piero Soderini*, also widely read. When Waldseemüller published his world map in 1507, the accompanying commentary, entitled *Cosmographiae Introductio*, featured a Latin translation of Vespucci's *Letter to Piero Soderini* and gave credit to Vespucci for having discovered a fourth part of the world, beyond Europe, Africa, and Asia, "which since Amerigo discovered her could be called Amerigen or perhaps the land of Amerigo or rather America."[28] Accordingly, on his accompanying 1507 map, Waldseemüller delineates an independent (if narrow) landmass not far to the east of "eastern India" (*India orientalis*) and labels it America, as we will see. It would seem that within a few years, Vespucci (through the letters published under his name), Waldseemüller (the baptizer of America), and Martyr (the compiler of *De Orbe Novo*) had overcome and laid to rest Columbus's confusion, opening the way for the clear-eyed appreciation of a new world separate from Asia and unknown to previous Europeans.

In fact, an Amerasian context is woven into the claims made in these important period documents and built into the framework within which they were understood at the time. In the same *Mundus novus* letter, Vespucci at moments sounds rather like Columbus: "certainly, if anywhere in the world there exists an earthly paradise, I think it is not far from those regions."[29] As Alessandro Scafi has explained, while the Hebrew word *Eden*—the garden where Adam and Eve lived in a blissful state of perfection—means "delight," early translators of the Septuagint often understood it as a proper noun that designated a specific place on earth and "chose to give the expression . . . spatial meaning, stating that God planted paradise in the east."[30] The vast majority of medieval cartographers and cosmographers mapped paradise at the eastern extremity of Asia, beyond India, in that same *India extra Gangem* that, according to Martyr and others, Columbus had reached when he arrived on Cuba (see chapter 1). While sometimes on a mountaintop, paradise was at other times located on a remote island at the eastern end of the earth, connected to the inhabited regions of the earth by its four rivers.

Vespucci's eastern orientation pervades his writings, as when he notes in his first letter (this one autograph and not published in his lifetime, though it grounded and informed the *Mundus novus* and *Letter to Soderini* published under his name) that the Brazilian coast must be near the cape of Cattigara, understood by Ptolemy to be at the southeastern limit of Asia, the most distant port of the known world (see chapters 6, 9, and 11).[31] This basic orientation explains why, both in the *Mundus novus* letter and the *Letter to Soderini*, lions are observed among the fauna of Brazil, gold is in evidence and said to be found in rich supply in the interior, people are said (in the *Mundus novus* letter) to live to the age of 150, thus associating them with the long-lived races that Pliny and Lucian among others had placed in India and other eastern lands, and they are said (in the Soderini letter) to "have broad faces somewhat reminiscent of the Tartars."[32] The entire description given in the *Mundus novus* letter of Natives who go naked, have no notion of private wealth, keep women in common, and eat human flesh, corresponds point for point with John Mandeville's late medieval description of the inhabitants of the island of Lamory, not far from Java.[33]

Vespucci was inclined to see and present the Brazilians in terms drawn from descriptions of the most remote peoples of Asia. Vespucci's orientation toward Asia was confirmed in the reception of Vespucci's writings, where we see readers, compilers, and later authors contextualizing Vespucci in an Amerasian understanding of the world. The most famous of Vespucci's interpreters, possibly, was Thomas More, whose *Utopia* of 1516 took inspiration in the basic depiction (though not in the details) of an antipodal culture that turns European institutions upside down. As will be discussed in chapter 5, More directly attached his dialogue to the Vespucci accounts by casting his main narrator as one of Vespucci's men, left behind in Brazil, who traveled westward from there and eventually reached the island of Utopia, an Amerasian civilization far older than Europe's cities, where the inhabitants speak a language not far from Persian.

We noted earlier that the *Mundus novus* letter's claim that the Native peoples live to be 150 years old, reported in the broadsheet illustrated in figure 2.3, associated them strongly with an ancient tradition that located long-lived peoples in the Far East. A treatise on *Macrobii*, or long-lived humans, attributed to the ancient writer Lucian notes that "the so-called Magi, a prophetic caste consecrated to the gods, dwelling among the Persians, the Parthians, the Bactrians, the Chorasmians, the Arians, the Sacae, the Medes and many other barbarian peoples, are strong and long-lived."[34] The longest-lived of all are the silk-producers or Seres (that is, the Chinese), who live to be three hundred years old.[35] In about 1515 the Roman humanist Fabio Vigile translated Lucian's treatise into Latin, and in his prefatory letter updated Lucian in light of the recent discoveries. Vigile claimed that the recently encountered new world peoples offered clear ethnographic evidence for Lucian's fabulous accounts of long-lived Asians. In his dedication to Cardinal Raffaele Riario (a patron of Michelangelo, also portrayed by Raffaello Sanzio da Urbino in the Vatican Stanze), Vigile explains:

> I was leafing through the *Dialogues* of Lucian the Syrian . . . and I fell upon a book in which that precise question seemed to be treated that was discussed at your house after dinner the day before you left, namely regarding the age and life of those who live in the islands that were recently discovered beyond the Canaries under the auspices of the most invincible kings of Spain. He gives the name "*Macrobii*" to them, that is "long-lived."[36]

"He gives the name *Macrobii* to them." For the Roman humanist, the long-lived people recently discovered beyond the Canaries are not *like* the long-lived nations of Lucian; these *are* the very people described by the ancient writer! This identification is set up by Vespucci himself, who could not after all have known for certain that people there lived 150 years. Vespucci brought with him ancient stories about far eastern peoples of long life and then applied it to the people of Brazil, and in turn his account was taken as eyewitness confirmation of the ancient tradition that until then had been based on hearsay. For Vigile, the new world reports resolve the "knotty question" of the long-lived peoples: Europeans have now met the ancient (and eastern) *Macrobii* in the flesh.

Vespucci is proud of having traveled so much farther south than previous navigators had done, allowing him to observe and describe constellations until then unavailable to Europeans. Toward the end of the *Mundus novus* letter, Vespucci calculates that he has sailed one quarter of the circumference of the earth (or ninety degrees) southwards, and he illustrates this fact with a right triangle that puts the tropical Indians of Brazil (*illi*, "they") into a perpendicular relationship to Europeans (*nos*, "we") (fig. 2.4).

Vespucci's triangle was famous. Stephanie Leitch has observed its use on the frontispiece of a much less read 1506 account of a voyage of battle-hungry German merchants around the coast of Africa and to India.[37] Here the triangle is flipped to the right, reflecting the fact that these fortune-seekers had traveled east rather than west. Also, now the triangle hovers over a landscape with figures, a European on the y-axis and an Indian on the x-axis (fig. 2.5).

Described in bare lines, the landmass can be read both from the side, a cross-section of the earth, as the triangle suggests, and also from above, like a map. At the northwest corner of the Eurasian continent is a European soldier in armor and at the southeastern corner is an Indian from "Kallakuth" with his longbow, representing the *illi* who stand at a

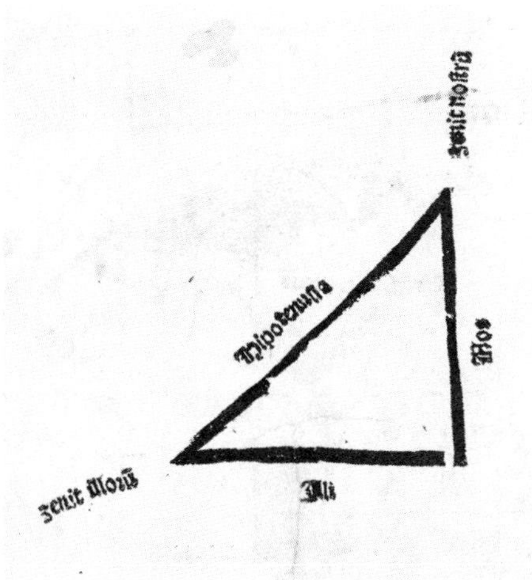

2.4 Vespucci's triangle showing the perpendicular relation between "us" and "them." Woodcut on paper. Amerigo Vespucci, *De novo mundo* (Rostock, 1505). Rostock, University Library.

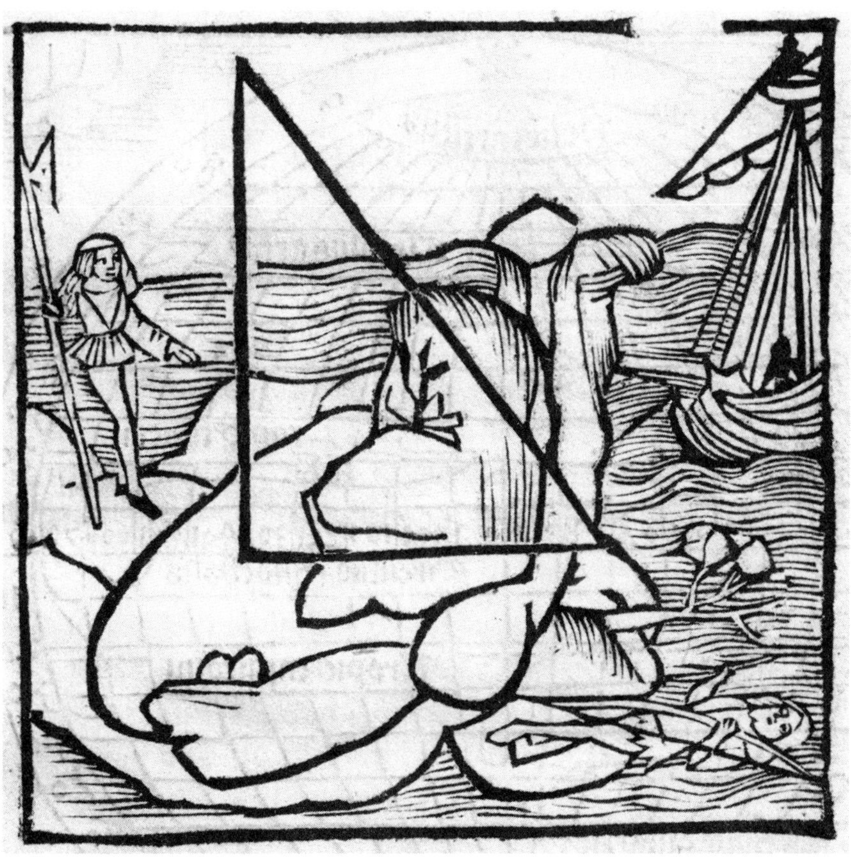

2.5 Vespucci's new world triangle is flipped rightward and eastward, diagramming a voyage to India. Frontispiece, woodcut on paper. Anonymous, *Den rechten weg ausz zu faren vo[n] Liszbona gen Kallakuth* (Nuremberg, 1506).

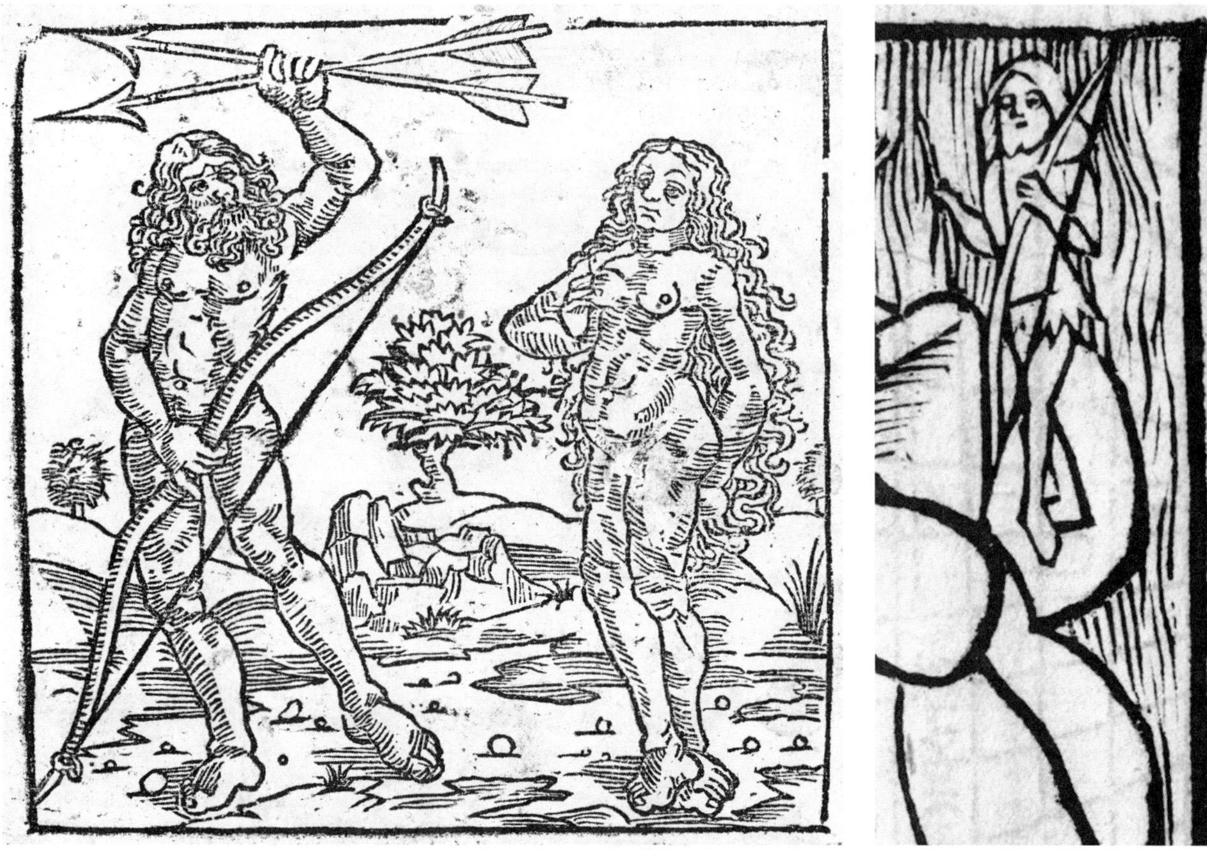

2.6a–b The Indians in Vespucci's new world and in Calicut are a common type. On the left is the frontispiece of Vespucci's *Mundus novus* letter showing Brazilian Indians, and on the right an Indian from Calicut (a detail of figure 2.5, flipped ninety degrees).

right angle to nos. Both stand on land and are profiled against the water. Though cursory, the single landmass with various articulations epitomizes the *oikoumene*, the common inhabited earth surrounded by the ocean sea as described by the ancient cosmographer Ptolemy.

What is the relation between these two triangles, one pointing west (in the *Mundus novus* letter) and one pointing east (in the German *Voyage to Calicut*)? If we were to place these two triangles not on the flat surface of a map but on a globe, where would the vertices land? Are the "they" in the two cases separate western and eastern Indians, or are they the same Indians, reached by sailing west in one case and east in the other? If the Indians to the east and west are different, are they culturally and climatically associated, as they appear to be? Many of the images in this book, some of them from as late as the end of the seventeenth century, suggest a persistent belief in a commonality of climate and culture connecting Indians to the east and west. That belief was first formed through these images of the first years of the sixteenth century. (For the wide field of application of the terms "India" and "Indian," see chapter 12).

If we turn to the frontispiece of the *Mundus novus* letter, we find a shaggy Indian to compare to the Indian in the *Voyage to Calicut* (fig. 2.6a–b). Both are long-haired and bearded, one entirely naked while the other is barely dressed, and both wield longbows. They appear to be the same people, or at least of similar rough stock. After Europeans encountered the impressive civilizations of Mesoamerica and Peru in the 1520s and 1530s and also learned more about Asian societies throughout the sixteenth century, the basis of association changed but the association itself continued—Indians both East and West boasted elaborate trade networks, impressive built monuments, advanced traditions of textile craft, and developed systems of astronomical knowledge (see chapters 8, 11, 12, and 17). But here, in the first decade of the sixteenth century, both Indians are hairy, naked or nearly naked, bow-and-arrow-wielding warriors.[38] East and West Indians are either assimilated in a shared primitivism or are understood to be the same people.

Waldseemüller's Amerasian New World

The idea of Amerasia actually gained traction over time as it assimilated new geographical knowledge, contravening a progressivist narrative that expects and finds a steady clarification of the geographical and ethnographic picture in modern terms. If there is a significant development between Columbus and the moment of Vespucci and his first readers, it is that new world places were less identified with Asian locales than expanded into an Amerasian configuration, new and yet connected by land or proximate by sea to Asia—extensions or satellites of Asia.

This expanded view was offered by Waldseemüller's 1507 map of the world, where we see the newly discovered lands to the west interpreted as a series of islands, with the most southern province named America, after Amerigo Vespucci (fig. 2.7). Although Waldseemüller proposed that the new lands be considered a fourth part of the world, he noted that this part was different in nature, for whereas Europe, Africa, and Asia were continents, this fourth was an island.[39] So far from pushing Asia farther away, Waldseemüller's map in fact populates the maritime gap with an archipelago that brings Asia within reach, just beyond the newly discovered islands: less than ten degrees of longitude separate Parias, where Columbus encountered the mouth of the Orinoco River, from Zipangri or Japan on the other side of the map. "The point about this new island," notes Surekha Davies, "was not its separation from east Asia but

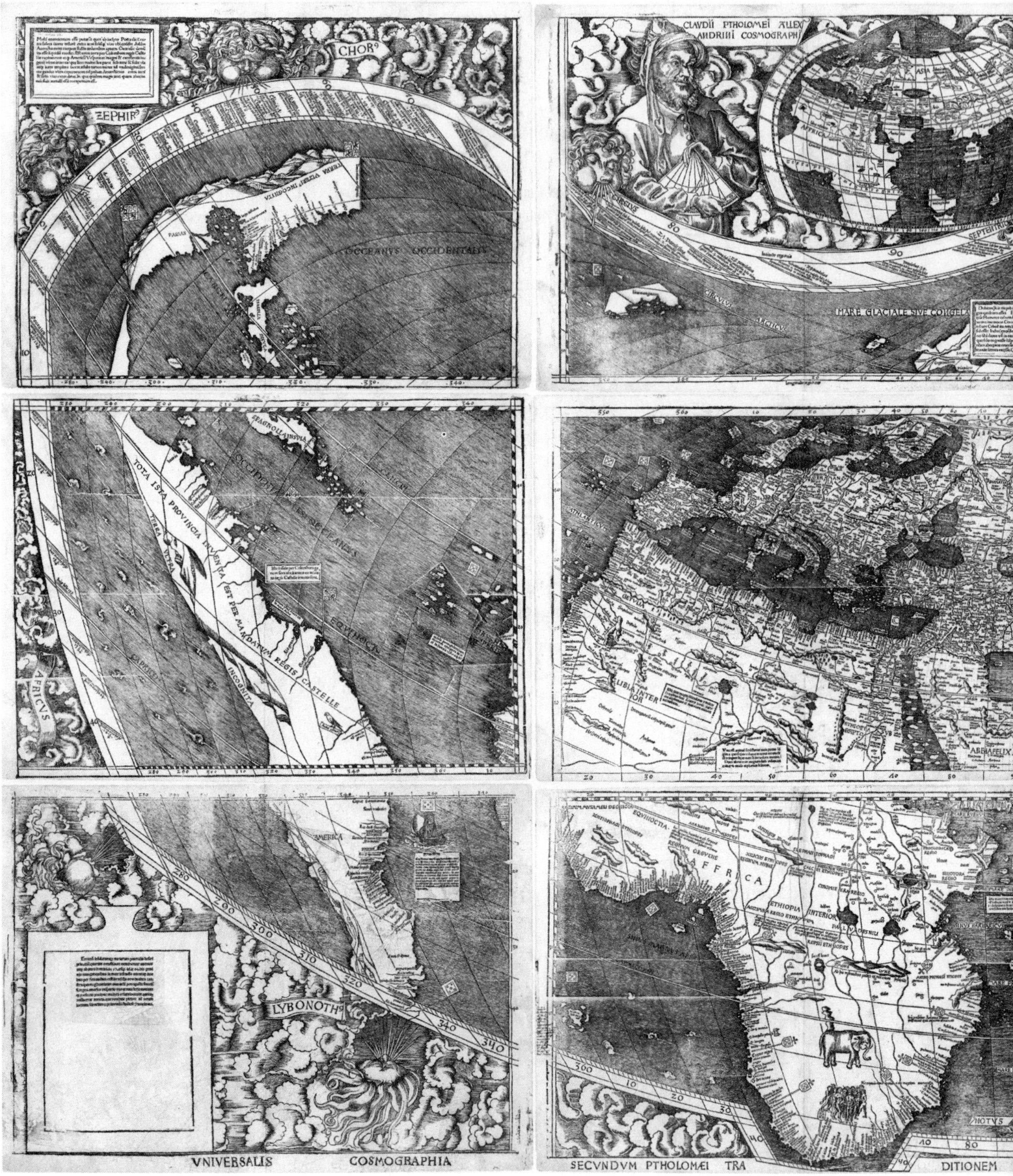

2.7 "America" is named for the first time, and imagined as a stepping stone to Asia. Woodcut on paper in twelve sheets, each measuring approximately 46 × 62 cm. Martin Waldseemüller, *Universalis cosmographia secundum Ptholomaei traditionem et Americi Vespucii alioru*[*m*]*que lustrationes* (Strasbourg, 1507). Washington, DC, Library of Congress.

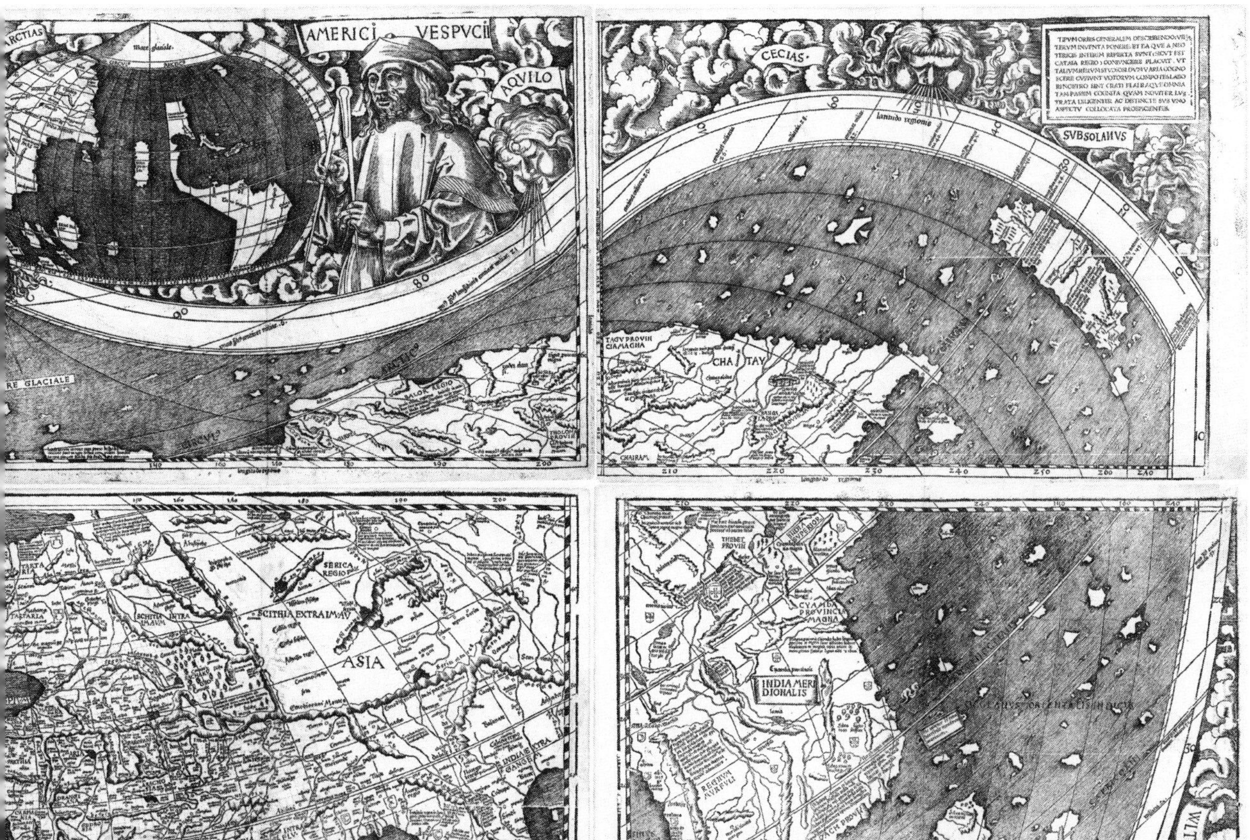

AMERICI VESPUCII
AQUILO
CECIAS
SUBSOLANUS
CHATAY
ASIA
SERICA REGIO
INDIA MERIDIONALIS
SINUS GANGETICUS
OCEANUS INDICUS MERIDIONALIS
MADAGASCAR
SEYLAN
IAVA MAIOR
EURONOTUS
AUSTER
ET AMERICI VESPUCII ALIORŪ QUE LUSTRATIONES

its similarity to it as part of a longer island chain associated with spices and anthropophages."[40] The new world, here, comes as an expansion of the traditional view that imagined a system of significant islands off the coast of Asia, as it would later for Sebastian Münster in his 1540 map, *New Islands* (see fig. 8.3). In space exploration, the parallel to what is being announced here would be a previously unrecognized sizable moon around Jupiter, so sizable some might call it a planet—a significant discovery, to be sure.

The idea of an Amerasian new world is clarified at the top of the map, where two insets recapitulate the world map in projections showing the earth in two hemispheres (fig. 2.8). The two halves are clearly laid out as old and new. Ptolemy is shown on one side with the traditional half of the world extending from Spain to India, and Vespucci is on the other side with the parts now in the news: East Asia, the islands of Java and Japan, as well as the islands newly discovered by Columbus and the land visited by Vespucci, here labelled not America but *Terra Incognita*. The division between old and new corresponds to the layout of the inscription that runs across the bottom of the map (see fig. 2.8) where the first half, "The Whole World according to the Tradition of Ptolemy," lands on the map's left side and the second half, "and the Voyages of Amerigo Vespucci and Others," lands on the right, matching the division shown in the two hemispheres at the top of the map. For Waldseemüller, the new world explicitly encompasses East Asia together with the islands discovered and described by Columbus and Vespucci. He named America, but his conception of the new world was Amerasian.

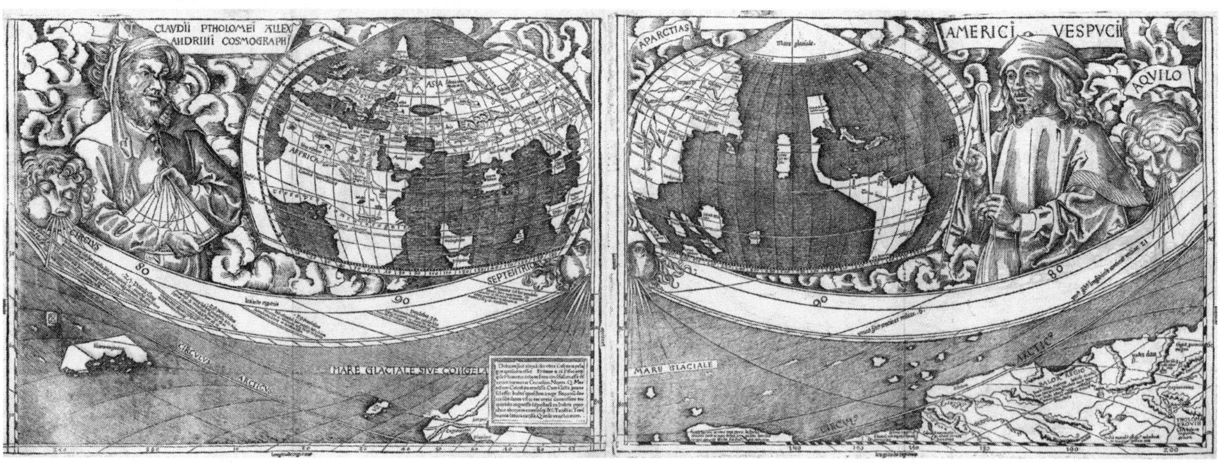

2.8 The new world extends from East Asia to Terra Incognita. Detail of figure 2.7. Washington, DC, Library of Congress.

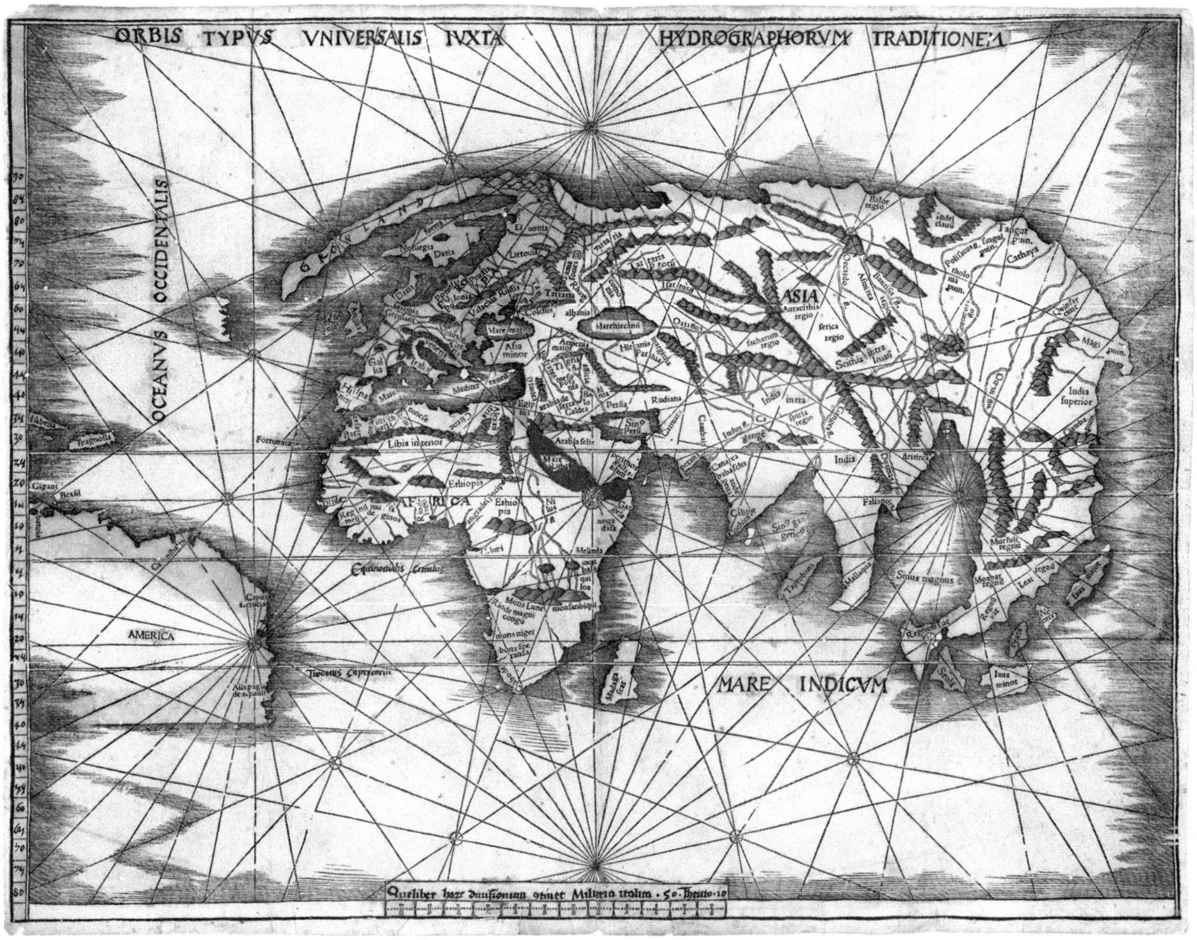

2.9 Waldseemüller brings America and Asia closer. Hand-colored woodcut on paper, 54 × 48 cm. Attributed to Martin Waldseemüller, *Orbis typus universalis iuxta hydrographorum traditionem* (Nuremberg, 1513 or earlier). Providence, RI, John Carter Brown Library.

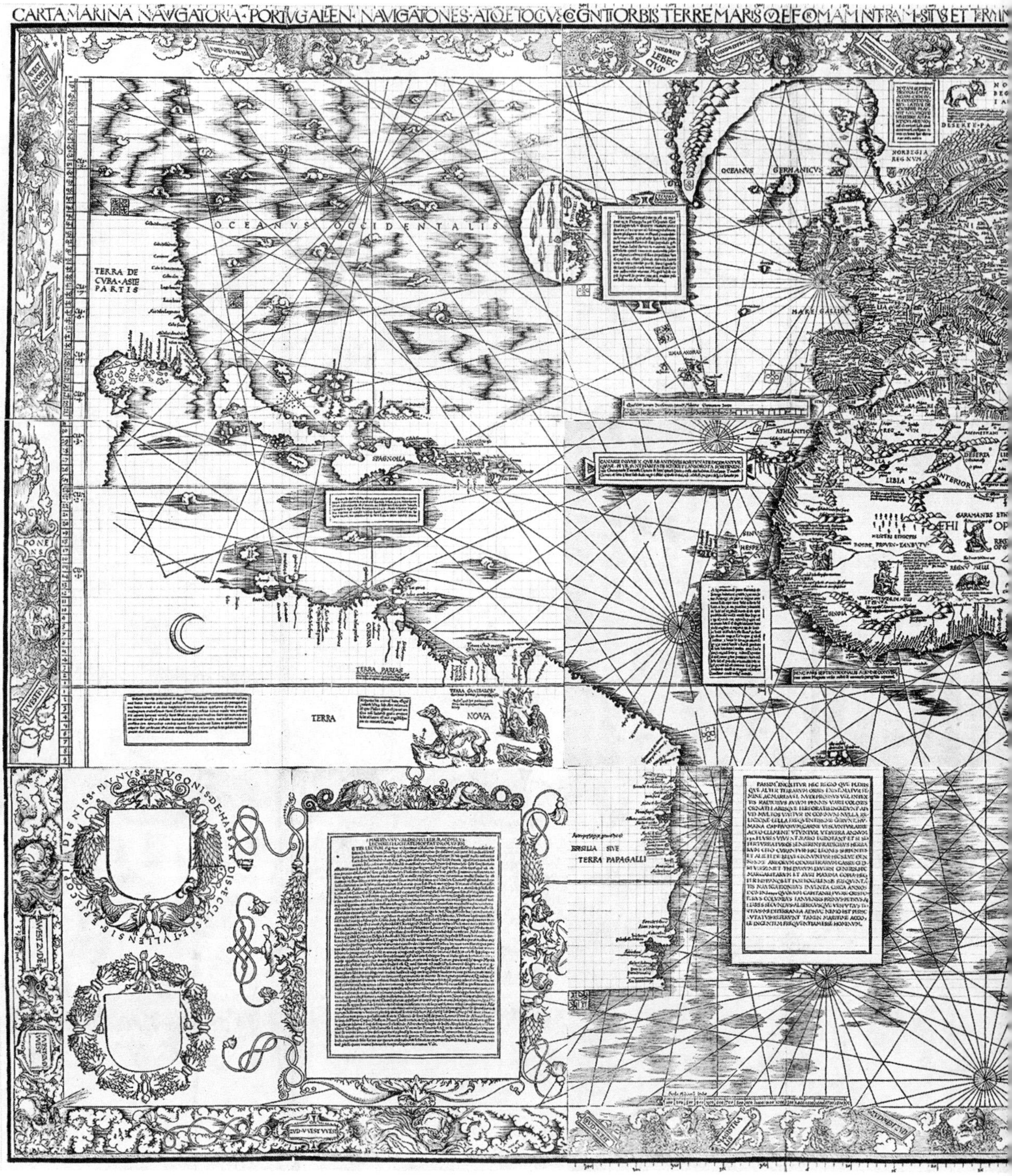

2.10 America is Asia. Woodcut in twelve sheets, each measuring approximately 45.5 × 62 cm. Martin Waldseemüller, *Carta marina* (Strasbourg, 1516). Washington, DC, Library of Congress.

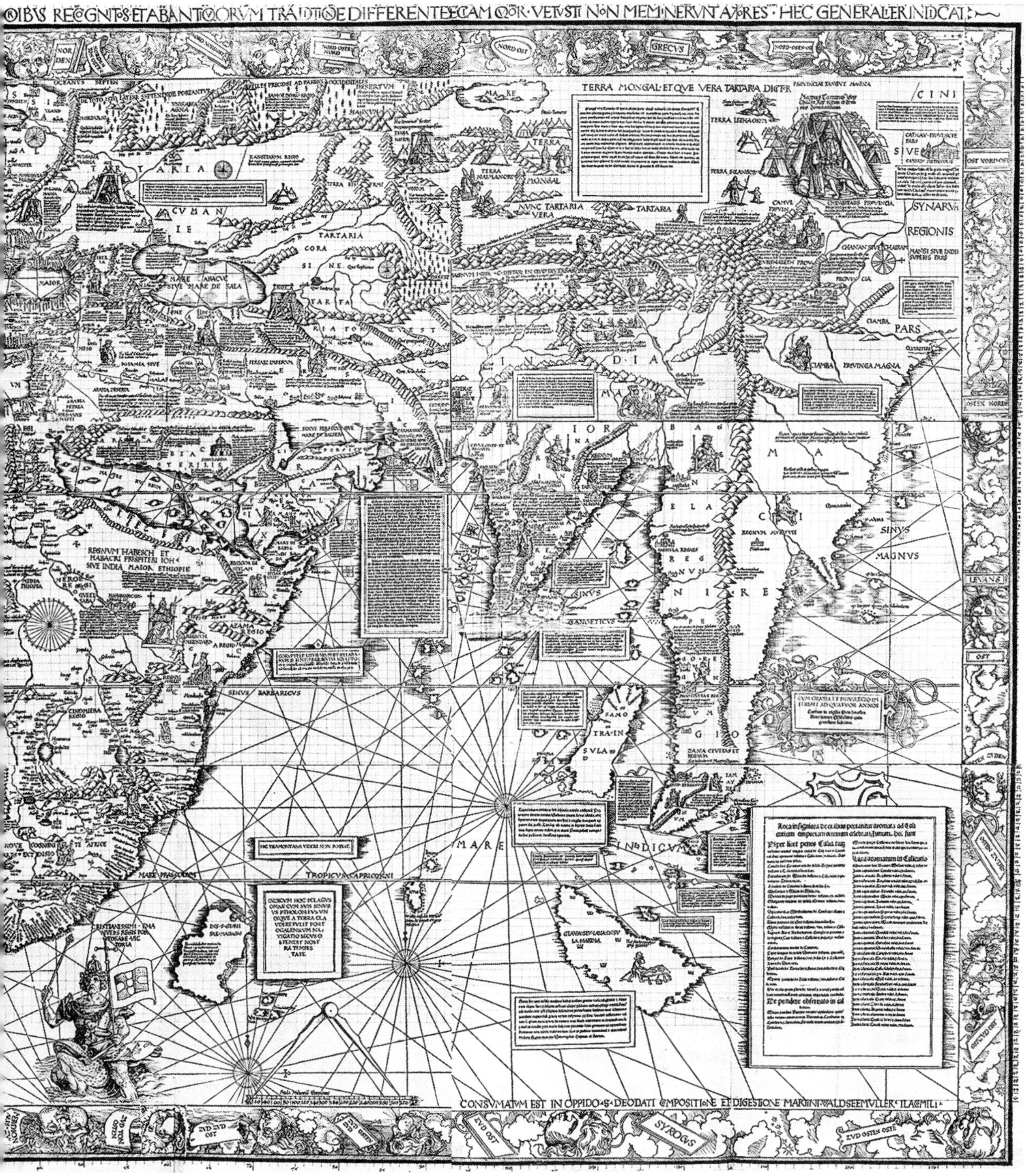
TERRA MONGAL ET QUE VERA TARTARIA DICITUR
TARTARIA
CUMANIE
NUNC TARTARIA VERA
MONGAL
CINI
SYNARUM REGIONIS
INDIA
SINUS PERSICUS
SINUS BARBARICUS
REGNUM HABESCH ET HABACAT PRESBITERI IOH SIVE INDIA MAIOR ETHIOPIE
SINUS MAGNUS
MARE INDICUM
TROPICUS CAPRICORNI
TAPROBANA
NORD OST
GRECUS
LEVANS
OST
ZUD OST
SYROCS
ZUD OSTEN OSTE
CONSUMATUM EST IN OPPIDO S. DEODATI COMPOSITIONE ET DIGESTIONE MARTINI WALDSEEMULLER ILACOMILI

Waldseemüller elaborates and affirms the Amerasian conception in later maps, such as a 1513 map associated with Waldseemüller that retains the southern landmass labeled AMERICA, but no longer shows the islands north of America labeled PARIAS in his 1507 map (fig. 2.9).[41] The island of Japan, present on the 1507 map, is also gone, a notable absence that raises the question whether it is now to be identified with Columbus's Hispaniola (*spagnolla* on this map), as the cartographer Johannes Ruysch had proposed in 1507 (see chapter 4). Now America is unbounded on its western edge, leaving open the question of its ultimate extent and thus its relation to Asia, which is shown not very much farther west of there (on the other side of the map), labeled with the regions of Upper India and Cathay. Easternmost of all, on a peninsula pointing downward toward the islands of *spagnolla* and *isabella* on the other side of the map, is the "province of the Magi." (For the migration of the Magi into America, see chapter 3.) The map all but promises that Europeans will soon grasp the connection between Columbus's lands and the eastern extremities of Asia.

Shortly thereafter, Waldseemüller's *Carta marina* of 1516 abandons the word America altogether, shows no body of water off the western coasts of these lands, and in doing so suggests that this landmass is joined with Asia (fig. 2.10). Here, the cartographer adopts an expansive vision that merges the lands discovered by Columbus with what was known of Asia.[42]

Like many other documents of the period, Vespucci's *Mundus novus* letter and Waldseemüller's 1507 map, naming a new land after Amerigo, in fact understood "new worlds" to include parts of Asia or connect to Asia. There was no question that the discoveries across the Atlantic were new and beyond what Ptolemy and other ancient cosmographers had known, yet the dominant view remained that the new islands, as they were most commonly understood, lay far closer to the known Asian islands, such as Japan and Java, than to Europe. As cartographers and scholars gathered more information about the newly discovered lands in the following decades, they in fact found more reason to imagine the new world as an Amerasian expanse across land and sea, as we will see in the following chapters. Contradicting a progressivist narrative that would chart the dispelling of Columbus's confusion and an ever-clearer separation of new world and old, the Amerasian view in fact developed and expanded over the sixteenth century, as the expeditions of Hernán Cortés, Magellan, and other Europeans who followed produced more encounters and generated new accounts.

• • •

Bulletin: Cortés Conquers China

As we saw in figure I.1, a handwritten note on one copy of Vespucci's *Mundus novus* letter reported the exciting news that the Spanish captain Cortés's had conquered the Chinese capital. Directly under Vespucci's triangle, the pamphlet's owner reported Cortés's 1521 conquest of *Temixtitam* (Tenochtitlan), a city the annotator identifies with the "most famous trading capital of eastern Asia," the Chinese city of Quinsay or the City of Heaven (today Hangzhou), the great Southern Song capital and trading center of many bridges and bustling traffic admiringly described by Polo in the thirteenth century. For this educated reader of the 1520s, Cortés had revealed that Columbus's and Vespucci's new world was connected to the great Chinese Empire.

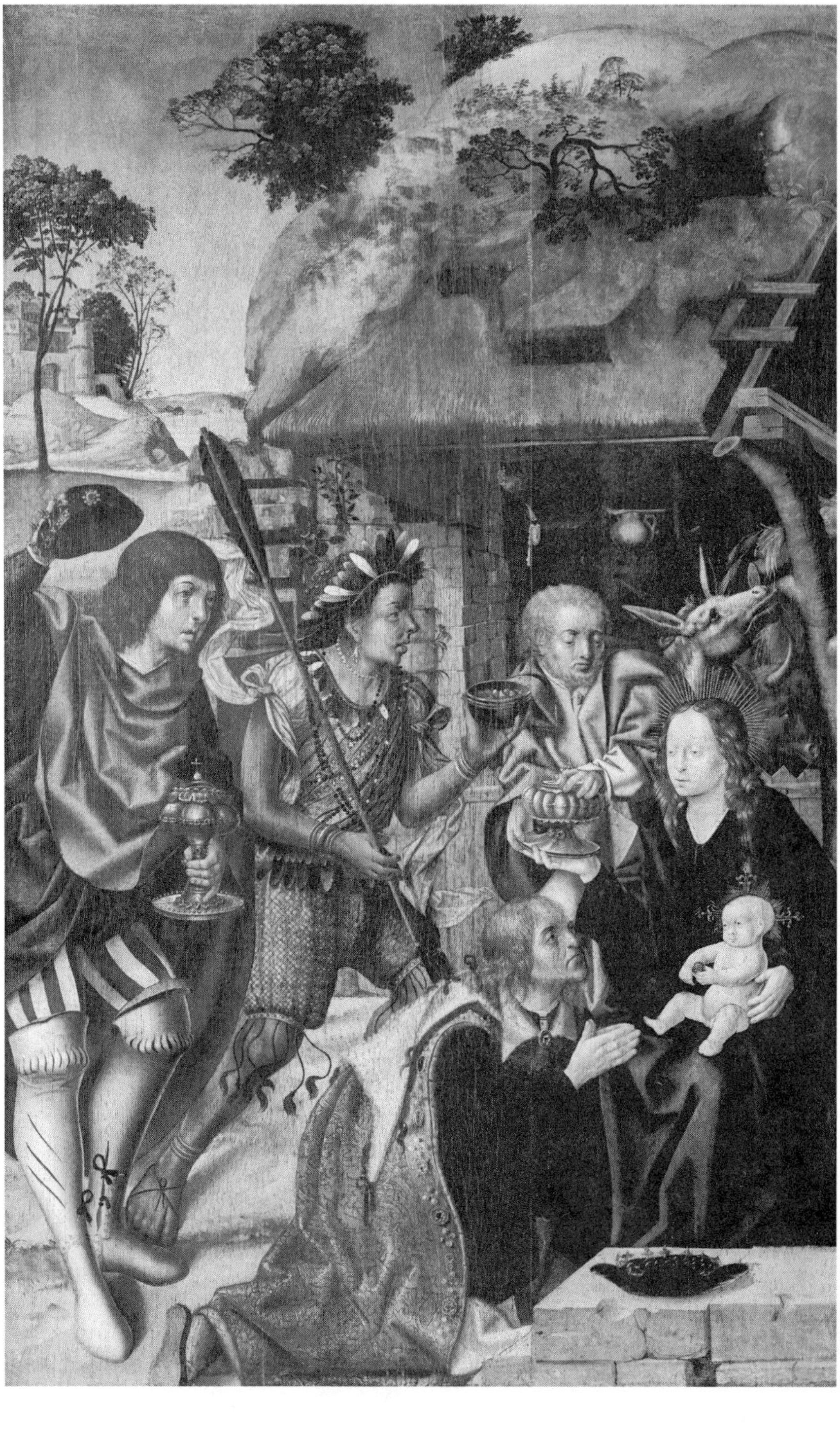

3.1 An Amerasian expansion of the Magi's range. Vasco Fernandes, *Adoration of the Magi*, oil on panel, 131 × 81 cm (ca. 1502–1506). Viseu, Museu Nacional Grão Vasco. (See color plates.)

THREE

Amerasian Magi

A panel painted by the Portuguese artist Vasco Fernandes between 1500 and 1506 depicts the arrival of the Magi to worship the baby Jesus, recognized by them as a divine king (fig. 3.1). The eldest magus, kneeling at the child's feet, has doffed his crown and offered his gift of gold, which is now being handed back to Joseph by Mary. The youngest king, still holding his gift, has removed his crown and is beginning to bend a knee. The child's gaze is turned upward toward the center of the painting, where the dark-skinned middle king is shown still striding forward, a crown of feathers on his head, an arrow in one hand, and a bowl of incense in the other, by far the most animated figure in the scene.[1] Vasco's feather-adorned king has been linked by virtually all commentators to the encounter in the year 1500 between Portuguese explorers and Tupi Indians on the coast of what is now called Brazil, an event soon reported all over Europe.[2] As we will see below, the dark middle king combines Tupi elements with features of people from the western coast of India, in particular the so-called "king of Calichut," also encountered and described on this expedition.

Brazil, Passage to India

Rather than an incongruous bit of American reportage in an otherwise traditional painting, Fernandes's new world king represents an Amerasian extension of the Magi story. In chapter 2, we considered a letter from the Portuguese king describing military exploits in Africa and India, with a woodcut frontispiece showing mostly naked Native peoples in feather garments and with a bow, as the Brazilians had been described by Vespucci and others (see fig. 2.2). Within a few years of the Portuguese landing on the Brazilian coast, the imagery of Indigenous Brazilians was being used to depict Asians. This pattern took hold in part because the Americans were themselves initially seen in Asian terms, as Vespucci did when he modeled his description of cannibalistic Brazilians on a widely read late medieval account of the completely naked, polyamorous, and cannibalistic Native peoples of the far-eastern island of Lamory (sometimes identified with Sumatra) in the *Book of Sir John Mandeville* (see chapter 2).

Vasco's panel of the Magi is one of eighteen that formed the wings of an altarpiece made for the cathedral of the Portuguese city of Viseu, which was the ancestral home of the family of Pedro Álvares Cabral, the naval captain who on April 22, 1500, reached the coast of what was soon to be called Brazil on a voyage bound for India.[3] He dispatched a supply ship back to Lisbon to bring news of this newly discovered land to King Manuel I, news that came primarily in the form of a letter written on May 1, 1500, by the fleet's chief scribe, Pedro Vaz de Caminha, which recorded the first contact between Europeans and the Tupiniquim. Cabral called this new territory Land of the True Cross (*Terra da Vera Cruz*), because the constellation of the Southern Cross, not known to inhabitants of the Northern Hemisphere, had been clearly in view to the crew for several days before landfall and because the ships had reached land not long before the feast of the Invention of the True Cross. (The location of Cabral's landing is now designated *Santa Cruz Cabrália.*) The title Land of the True Cross or, as it soon came to be known, Land of the Holy Cross (*Terra da Santa Cruz*), registered the southerly nature of the territory and its divinely ordained revelation to Christians.

Yet there were other designations for this territory that reinforced its Asian associations. The Venetian ambassador to Portugal, Giovanni Matteo il Cretico, reporting to the Venetian authorities on the return of Cabral's fleet in June 1501, called the new land the "Land of the Parrots" (*terra de papagaios*), due to the colorful enormous macaws—"an arm and a half in length"—that Cabral had seen there, some of which he had brought back.[4] Apart from parrots, another notable feature of the place was a red wood useful for dyeing, called *ibira-pitanga* by the locals. Until then this type of wood had been available only from Asian sources (Marco Polo praises the brazilwood of Ceylon and Sumatra). In medieval sources it was called *bresilium* or *brexilium* or (in Italian) *verzino*, a term whose derivation remains a matter of speculation, perhaps an adaptation from the Arab term for the red wood, *bakkam*, or perhaps because the red of the wood was thought to resemble embers (in Old French *brese*, in Spanish *braza*, in Portuguese *brasa*).[5] When the Portuguese found a red wood very much like *bresilium* in the newly discovered land across the Atlantic, they named the new land after the Asian wood, resulting in the Amerasian toponym Brasil. Confirming the promise of direct access to Asian riches that motivated the voyage, Cabral's discovery gave Europe a source of *bresilium* without the need for Levantine intermediaries.

When Cabral left Lisbon in March 1500 intending to go east, repeating

Vasco da Gama's voyage to India from two years earlier, he inadvertently ended up going west and in April landed in what he named the Land of the True Cross, "a stopping-place," as Caminha says, "for this voyage to Calicut."[6] While Caminha does not clarify exactly where this new landmass was in relation to Asia, he associated it with travel to the east, an association that persisted. A 1514 account by an anonymous German merchant similarly describes the coasts of southern Brazil as "not . . . more than six hundred miles [from] Malacca," a major commercial entrepôt on the Malay Peninsula in Southeast Asia.[7] After landing in Brazil, Cabral in 1500 did continue on to India, even claiming to have found the body of Thomas, which he brought back to Lisbon.[8] Thus, there was every reason to associate the Brazilian stopover with the overall India-bound direction of the voyage. Within just a few years of Cabral's first encounter with Brazil and its people, they were entwined in the Portuguese and European imaginary with India and Indians, an association that persisted for well over a century (see chapters 5, 12, and 17).

The connections between Brazil and India are embodied in Vasco's dark middle king. He certainly bears many of the features of the inhabitants of the land of parrots and brazilwood;[9] yet elements of his dress go beyond what was observed about the dress and manner of the Tupi locals, as Kathleen Christian has noted: "What is certainly exaggerated, however, is his jewellery, including his prominent earring, the pearls and beads around his neck, his gold bracelets and ankle bracelets."[10] We propose that these fabulous elements derive from additional observations made on the Indian leg of Cabral's expedition, in particular the description of the Indian "king of Calichut" offered later in Caminha's account of Cabral's voyage, an expedition that did in fact attain its goal of reaching India after the initial Brazilian stopover. Vasco's figure thus emerges as an Amerasian composite, though for Portuguese contemporaries he would have come across less as a strange mixture of disparate elements than synthetically as "new world" or as "Indian."

Let us begin with the Brazilian elements in the figure. Caminha's account describes the locals encountered there as naked and carrying bows and arrows. One of them wore a hat of parrot feathers, which he offered to the captain together with "a large string of very small beads, which look like seed pearls."[11] Ten leagues up the coast, Caminha describes the inhabitants as "dark, somewhat reddish, with good faces and good noses, well-shaped," noting that the men pierced their lower lip with bone, wore their hair well trimmed, with a feather headdress that was firmly applied to the hair with a waxlike material. Once aboard the ship, these people pointed to the captain's gold collar and then to the land, doing the same with a silver candlestick, gestures taken to mean that gold and silver could be found inland. One of them took up some white rosary beads, playing with them and putting them around his neck and then around his arm.[12] Almost immediately, accessories were being exchanged, indexing the resources of the homelands of the two communities encountering each other for the first time. Caminha's account describes an active two-way exchange of information.

Vasco's king—a spirited figure with reddish skin and a dignified, well-shaped face—assembles features of the Tupi people described in Caminha's account, yet he also exhibits extra-Brazilian features. Whereas the inhabitants of the land of the parrots went naked, this exotic king is dressed in a gold-ornamented shirt, vest, and breeches, with gold earrings and bracelets, regalia here combined with the adornments the Tupi were seen to wear—the feather ornaments, the pearl-like beads strung together into a necklace, the sash and head ornament, and the prominently displayed arrow that was perhaps based on an actual Tupi weapon. To account for the additional features of Vasco's king, we need only read on in Caminha's account to descriptions of the men of India, in particular the amazing apparel of the "king of Calichut" himself, who is described wearing a cloth of very fine white cotton "worked in gold" wound around him, with two belts of gold "full of rubies" over the cloth, earrings of gold, rubies, diamonds, and pearls, bracelets of gold inlaid with precious stones, and a ring on one of his toes encrusted with a ruby of great value.[13] Could one find a better living model for one of the Magi? (For Hans Burgkmair's nearly simultaneous visualization of the "King of Cochin," see fig. 15.6). While not all features correspond precisely, Vasco's magus does wear impressive earrings, bracelets, and sashes, and his beautiful cotton shirt is indeed worked in gold. Whereas for centuries the Magi had been the stuff of legend, known visually through a tissue of image traditions, now Europeans were coming face-to-face with real kings from the farthest reaches of the world, bringing back eyewitness reports and relics of their fantastical trappings, rituals, and retinues. Vasco's Amerasian magus was an effort to incorporate these observed *realia* into the regalia of traditional Magi iconography. Combining features of Brazil and India, Vasco's magus embodies a newly extensive Amerasian new world.

The Magi as Cosmic Vectors

Incorporating a magus from the new world, or multiple new worlds, into the story of the Magi was an extension of the border crossing and interchange that mark all of Christian history, a cultural process paradigmatically dramatized by the journey and arrival of the Magi. As Richard

Trexler has observed, the very nature of the gifts of gold, frankincense, and myrrh brought by the Magi imply the ever-present activity of a social group almost never shown in the scene—the traders and merchants who made people and materials move around the world.[14] It is probably not coincidental that the theme of the Magi flourished in Europe from the thirteenth through the fifteenth centuries in tandem with a new global system of trade.[15] The adaptation we see in the middle king, with elements of Brazilian and Indian dress woven into the shirt, vest, and breeches familiar to Europeans—or perhaps the other way around, familiar features of European dress rendered unfamiliar by the incorporation of exotic elements—is in fact an extension of the thematic dynamics of Magi imagery generally, which continually threaded together foreign and familiar elements. The eldest king kneeling before the child in Vasco's painting is, after all, also a mix of familiar and strange, his fabulous gold mantle closed by a familiar type of brooch and covering a European-style *camicia*. Likewise, the mantle, striped leggings, slashed boots, and long hair of the youngest king at left riff on the latest European fashions, to the point of outlandishness.

The painting asks Christians to look back at this event and recognize their own relation to these faraway people encountering other faraway people. Foreigners from the farthest reaches of the world, crossing many lands in order to worship an unlikely king, the Magi are the first Gentiles to whom Christ was revealed, and thus, as parishioners all over Europe were repeatedly told, the Magi are *our* precursors, precursors to all Gentile converts who came after them. All Christians come from a distance to worship Christ, whether or not they travel on a physical pilgrimage to the Holy Land. To contemplate the Magi, who crossed boundaries and allowed their worldview to be upended, was to internalize a model for one's own piety. These Magi, the painting proposes, represent a remote pole of our own history, a reminder that something of ourselves is in them and something of their foreignness is in us. According to some scholars, Vasco brought these dynamics of identification to a head by giving the eldest king the features of the captain Cabral himself, a fitting association for a voyager across worlds and a giver of gifts, notably the donation of this altarpiece itself.[16]

Like other renderings of the *Adoration of the Magi,* this painting is based on a short passage from Matthew, the only one of the four gospels to mention the event: "After Jesus was born in Bethlehem in Judea, during the time of King Herod, Magi from the East came to Jerusalem and asked, 'Where is the one who has been born king of the Jews? We saw his star when it rose and have come to worship him'" (Mt 2:1). The passage describes a quest of voyagers who reached Bethlehem with the aid of the stars. It also stresses the distant origins of the voyagers, for the Latin Vulgate translation, used throughout Western Christendom, says the Magi came *ab oriente*, and that they had seen his star *in oriente*. The idea that the Magi came "from the East" dominated the geographical understanding of the figures in Western Christendom. The alternate notion—much repeated in art-history textbooks—that the Magi represent Europe, Africa, and Asia, the three parts of the known world, is in fact only fairly rarely attested in period texts and images.[17] Innumerable Latin accounts, hymns, and liturgical texts describe the Magi as "oriental" or "from the Orient."[18] Accounts of eastern travel from Marco Polo to Odoric of Pordenone to Giovanni de' Marignolli concur in searching for the origins of the Magi in Asia, whether in Persia, India, or China; John of Hildesheim's widely read fourteenth-century account of the Magi identifies them as kings of India, Chaldea, and Persia.[19] In a poem describing the frontispiece to Abraham Ortelius's world atlas, first published in 1570 and in many editions thereafter (see fig. 16.1), the figure of Asia is said to hold incense and myrrh in her golden censer, encapsulating the three Magi's gifts as Asian attributes.[20] Occasionally, the provenance of the Magi was expanded in a southerly direction, as when John Mandeville locates the homeland of one of the kings in Ethiopia. Yet even the Ethiopian black king carried eastern associations, since Ethiopia was sometimes considered part of greater India (*India occidentalis*). The occasional Ethiopian derivation of one of the Magi, together with the increasing commerce with Africa, informed the rise of the figure of the black magus in European art of the last decades of the fourteenth century and throughout the fifteenth century. A correlate index of the association between Ethiopia and India was the legendary Christian ruler Prester John, sometimes considered a descendant of one of the Magi, who was progressively relocated from India to Ethiopia in the fourteenth and fifteenth centuries.[21]

From the present participle of the Latin *orior*, to rise, related to the Greek verb *orino*, to rouse or move, which is not far from the Sanskrit *aruh*, to set in motion, the word *oriens* suggested an action of rising or moving and making move. When the Vulgate Latin translation of Matthew says that the Magi came *ab oriente*, it is casting them as oriental in this deeper sense, as embodiments of the dynamic principle of a rising movement out of the East. Matthew sets the Magi into a cosmologically ordained vector, moving westward in accord with the movement of the heavens. In a foundational passage, Aristotle (*De Caelo*, 2.2.284b) wrote that the universe moves from right to left, from east to west, as confirmed (in a nonheliocentric view) by the daily course of the sun and stars.

Many Aristotelian commentators drew the further implication that the direction of the universe also dictated the course of human history. The twelfth-century theologian Hugh of Saint Victor eloquently articulated a well-established idea when he cast historical progress as a movement westward. "Divine providence," he observed, "seems to have arranged things so that what was made to be at the beginning of time was also made to be in the east—at the beginning, so to speak, of the world. And then, as time proceeded towards its end, the center of events would have shifted to the west." In this way, "the world nears its end in time as the course of events reaches the extremity of the world in space."[22]

In the Christian view of the world, the Magi were signal agents of this movement westward. The advent of the new child king in Palestine brought the Magi forth from the East, following "his" star as it rose in the east and moved west. Their travels, conversion, and obeisance to him signaled an epochal transfer of power from East to West and from old to new. From its Holy Land nativity, Christianity then spread in all directions. The Apostles Thomas and Bartholomew were believed to have preached in India (then extended to America; see chapter 13), and Thaddeus in Armenia. Matthew was believed to have been martyred in Ethiopia, and several apostles preached in Greek lands. The Bible attests to Paul's presence in Rome, and later tradition affirmed that Peter, too, had traveled to Rome. In *Paradiso* 6:1–3, Dante observes that the first Christian emperor Constantine turned *backward* by moving the Roman capital east, against the course of the sun. For Dante, the natural course of the Roman empire is westward; Aeneas had also traveled west from Troy to Rome to found the Roman Empire, as did Paul from Jerusalem to Rome, the New Jerusalem in the West. The implication is that going even farther west will lead to the apocalypse, the return to Eden (in the East), and the coming of an even newer Jerusalem.[23]

The many explorations across the Atlantic in the wake of Columbus signaled to some Europeans a further epochal step in the divinely ordained progression westward of Christianity. In an account of Jacques Cartier's second voyage up the Saint Lawrence River in 1535, the author writes that God "in his divine goodness" had allowed these new world discoveries as a fulfillment of the predestined movement of Christianity from east to west, following the course of the sun. The Christian religion had originated in the Holy Land, "in Asia to the east of our Europe, and afterwards by succession of time it has been carried and proclaimed to us, and at length to the west of our Europe, just like the sun, carrying its light and heat from east to west, as has already been shown."[24] (For more on Cartier, see chapter 9.) The movement of Christianity from Holy

Land to new world was, for Cartier and others, more than a progression westward; it was a conclusive world-historical grasping of the limits of the earthly sphere and thus a revelation of the shape of history. Peter Martyr d'Anghiera reported that upon landing in Cuba, Columbus called it Alpha-Omega because he believed that "there lies the boundary of our orient, since the sun sets there, and of our occident, since it rises there."[25] To come full circle where West ends and East begins, or the other way around, must signify not just a next historical phase but a concluding of history altogether. In the widely read *Mundus novus* letter published under the name of Amerigo Vespucci, discussed in chapter 2, the discovery of unknown lands and people is naturally placed in an apocalyptic frame: "We found in those regions such a multitude of people as nobody could number (as we read in the Apocalypse), a people I say gentle and amenable."[26] (The reference is to *Revelations* 7:9, "After this I looked, and behold, a great multitude that no one could number, from every nation, from all tribes and peoples and languages, standing before the throne and before the lamb.") Columbus wanted to convert the Great Khan of China, turning him into a new magus/king who would rise up *ab oriente* and descend on the Holy Land, thus bringing to fulfillment the process of worldwide conversion the Magi had initiated. The closing of the circle meant a return to the orient/origin, and thus a final and global Christian victory (for more on this theme, see chapter 7).

Charting the Magi in an Expanded India

Cabral's Brazil landing is pinpointed in a famous Portuguese map of 1502 that shows at lower left a coastline populated by a number of beautifully described and colored parrots set against a verdant expanse that fades off to the west, its limits unknown (fig. 3.2). An adjoining inscription explains that it was named Land of the True Cross by Cabral: "On the way to India, he came across this land here, which he thought to be mainland, in which land there are many people, men and women going about as their mothers gave birth to them, naked. They are more white than brown and have very smooth hair. The land was discovered in 1500."[27] Here in a land pullulating with a breed of bird traditionally located in the most eastern lands in the world live a people who seem as close to the origins of humanity as they can be, "going about as their mothers gave birth to them, naked." The Asian coast known from ancient geography is shown on the far right of the map, opposite this land but not far from it if one were to bring the two ends of the map together into a continuum. The burning question around 1500—where is the Alpha Omega where westernmost meets and crosses into easternmost?—was both newly urgent and newly mysterious,

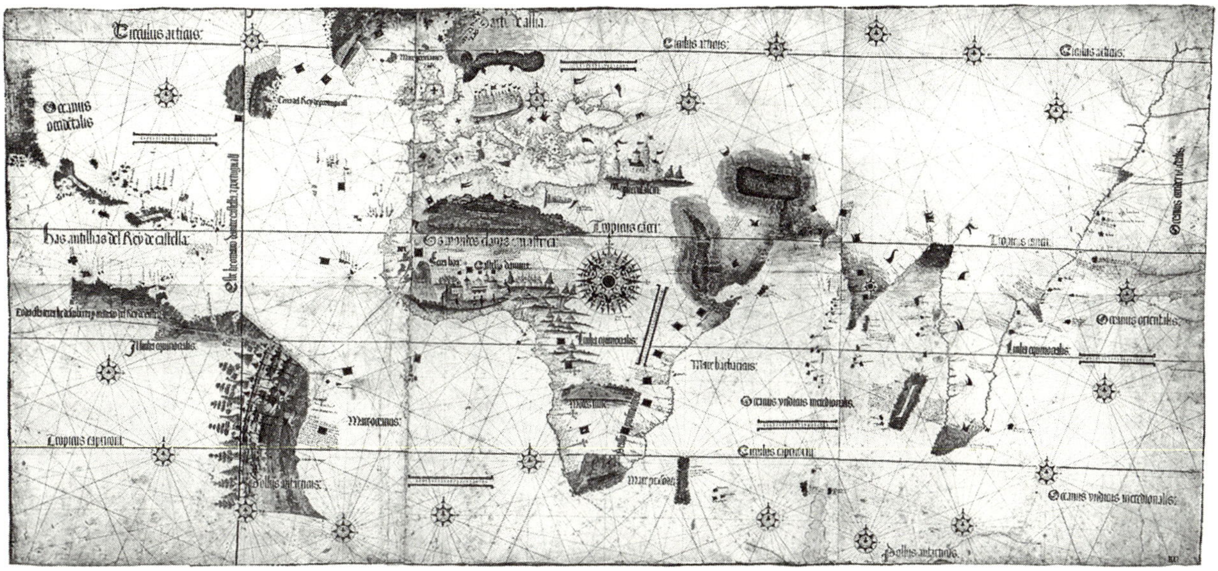

3.2 How and where did East and West meet? World map (so-called "Cantino Planisphere"), hand-painted parchment, 220 × 105 cm (1502). Modena, Biblioteca Estense.

and this map leaves the question unresolved. Yet the organizing identity of the lands across the ocean to the west is made clear by the title inscription on the back of the map, which labels it a "Navigational chart for the lands newly discovered in the parts of India" (*Carta de navigar per le Isole nouam[ente] tr[ovate] in le parte de India: dono Alberto Cantino al S. Duca Hercole*). "Newly discovered" they may be, but these lands are in the extreme parts of India, whose extent and contours are as yet unknown.[28]

Vasco's painting of the Magi, like its cartographic counterpart the Cantino map, expands the Asian imaginary to encompass Brazil. In the previous centuries, the Magi's exotic accoutrements had undergone fairly elaborate iconographic codification, but in this painting, as in the Cantino map, the idea and look of what comes *ab oriente* is being radically reshaped under the impact of the most recent accounts and imports. New data—reports, specimens of flora and fauna, as well as human Native peoples—were arriving from the extremities of the known world, and Fernandes, working in the city of the explorer Cabral, had privileged access to it. No longer needing to rely only on received conventions for representing the Magi, the painter could incorporate the latest information about the inhabitants of the lands across the ocean; the magus with the feather headdress and jewels appears here as an exhibit of the recently encountered inhabitants of the "parte de India"—both Brazil and Calicut.

If that is indeed Cabral's portrait in the first king, then he is the one who ushers the new world Indian magus to the Virgin and Child.

When Vasco's Magi panel was installed in its altarpiece, it was possible to imagine that the strange figure of the middle king could be incorporated into the subject, expanding rather than disrupting it. The theme and iconography are stretched to include the new information, just as the prevailing geographical schema was being expanded and adapted in contemporary maps, as when the Cantino map describes the newly discovered islands as being in the "parts of India." In later centuries, when these lands were newly understood to be separate from Asia both geographically and culturally, it became harder to see this unusual painting of the first years of the sixteenth century as anything other than an assemblage. Rather than an *Adoration of the Magi* incorporating exciting information from the latest discoveries in the "parts of India," it became a document of multiple and incompatible purposes: a traditional representation of the Magi that was also a new world ethnography exhibit, a biblical legend interrupted by a current event.

The question of where Asia reached its farthest extent was raised whenever the three Magi came to mind, and the Magi were often on the minds of the European explorers. The search for the Magi in America began as early as Columbus's first landfall. He learned from the Native peoples of the island he had named Hispaniola that a land of gold lay nearby on the same island, called Cibao. Columbus knew that Polo had described Japan, which Polo had called Zipangu, as the place of origin of the magus who brought gold to the Christ child. As discussed in chapter 1, Columbus decided that Cibao must be Cipangu/Japan, the famous island some miles off the coast of China.[29] The identification of Hispaniola with Japan was confirmed in one of the most famous and widely known maps at the time documenting the new world discoveries, Johannes Ruysch's world map designed to be included in a new edition of Ptolemy's *Geography*, published in 1507 in Rome (see chapter 4). At the mouth of the Orinoco River on his third voyage, Columbus believed he was at the outlet of one of the rivers of paradise. Also on his third voyage, Columbus noticed people on Trinidad wearing "a cotton cloth elaborately patterned in colors, which I believed to be *almaizares* [head-dresses of the type worn by Muslims in Spain]" and a few pages later, notes that Indigenous peoples "wear woven cloths round their heads, which look from the distance like silk and resemble, as I have said, Moorish scarves."[30] On his second voyage of 1493–94, Columbus became certain that Cuba, called Sobo by the Native peoples, was the land of the Sabeans, from whom frankincense was obtained; this would then logically be the native land of the second magus. On his fourth voyage of 1502–1504, Columbus affirmed that the gold mines of the land that he christened Veragua (on the Panamanian coast) were those of the city of Ophir, celebrated in the Old Testament as a source of gold. He now contended that this was the homeland of the eldest magus, the one bearing gold. Columbus's search for biblical sites in the new world would be pursued by many others for well over a century (see chapter 13).

In a 1513 map attributed to Martin Waldseemüller, discussed in chapter 2 (see fig. 2.9), on an easternmost peninsula of the Asian continent, jutting out into the ocean and virtually pointing to America, there is a "province of the Magi." As reports of inland deposits of gold started coming back both from Columbus's voyages and from Portuguese voyages to Brazil, it was not a great leap to imagine that that easternmost province from which one or more of the Magi came was in close association with the newly discovered lands to the west.

In 1497, just before Fernandes's *Adoration of the Magi* was made, the Venetian Republic did in fact receive a visit from a new world king, a gift to the Venetian Doge from the king of Spain. A contemporary account describes him as a *re saracino*, a Saracen king, describing him as not quite black but brown-skinned, like the people from the Canary Islands but in fact "from those islands newly discovered by the King of Spain." The Venetians were informed that this brown-skinned king had been baptized but did not know how to speak any Western language. The "Saracen king" arrived with several parrots of different colors, an avian entourage that would have confirmed his eastern provenance. It was said that he had two thousand people under his rule, that in his country they ate the human flesh of executed criminals, and that "together with six other kings, he was brought to Castile by the caravels and troops of Spain, who went to conquer the lordship of the said islands; and it is said, that before they were captured, these chiefs made a stout defense." The account makes it clear how the Amerasian framework came to embellish new world news and people with hints of Asian fabulousness, not very different from Mandeville's account of the island of Lamory near Java: here was a cannibal king, one among many from these lands who was vanquished after a worthy battle. The Venetian authorities discussed what to do with their Saracen king from across the Atlantic, some of them considering that he would make an excellent gift for Isabella d'Este, marchioness of Mantua, known for her interest in collecting black-skinned specimens from Africa as household slaves.[31] But instead he was packed off to Padua, where he was made to participate in the Corpus Christi procession of 1497, in which he was given a position of honor in front of the Doge. The last we know of him is that he had been given lodgings (and funds for his clothing, as needed) in the Palazzo del Capitano, where "it seemed to him that he was in Paradise."[32]

Magi in the Expanded Field

If the dark king in Vasco's *Adoration* could assimilate Tupi trappings, if a Taíno ruler was anointed a Saracen king once he landed in Europe, if indeed Asian islands and territories were considered a "new world" as much as the newly discovered lands to the west (see chapter 2), if the gold of Ophir was now rumored to be discoverable in the islands to the west, and if Mexico was eventually understood as a province of China (see chapters 2, 9, and 11), then the expansion of reference became a pervasive and irreversible part of the story of the Magi in the sixteenth century. It is not just that American iconography occasionally finds its way into Magi scenes; those instances are an index of a larger shift whereby the Magi were now generally reframed in a new world context. For example, an unattributed early sixteenth-century Bolognese *Adoration of the Magi* tondo in a private collection shows at least two feather-ornamented figures in the crowded retinue of the Magi, even as the Magi themselves retain the by then conventional African and Asian features.[33] The new world frame of reference now potentially invested *any* Magi-associated figure, whether or not they actually wore a crown of feathers identifiable to modern scholars as Native American, for the simple reason that the category "Native American" did not yet have its modern contours, and the concept of the new world carried Asian and African associations as much as American ones. All representations of the Adoration of the Magi after 1492 should be reviewed in a new world light.[34] Even Magi in "traditional" eastern garb, with no feathers or Tupi clubs in sight, might now read as new world figures, just as Adam and Eve in the earthly paradise now reverberated with new world associations whether or not artists chose to include a new world macaw in their surroundings, as Albrecht Dürer did in his famous 1504 engraving of *Adam and Eve*.[35]

A later *Adoration of the Magi* in Freixo de Espada á Cinta, attributed to a follower of Fernandes, shows a clearly identifiable African king in the second position, the same position as the Tupi-Calicutish king in Vasco's Viseu altarpiece (fig. 3.3). Here, too, the painter has made an effort to study actual artifacts and people, offering a portrait-like rendering of the African king's face and a careful portrayal of his striped cape. Modern viewers can easily distinguish this king as African and the one in the Viseu Altarpiece as American in derivation, but could period viewers do the same? Most likely both portrayals would have been called eastern, or

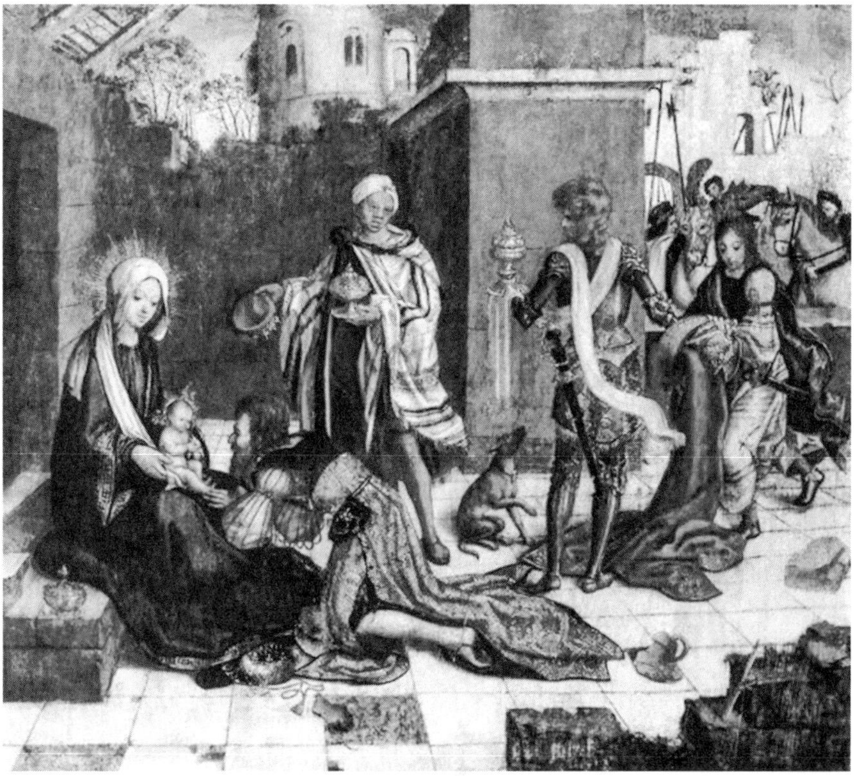

3.3 A carefully described Ethiopian middle king gives specificity to the range of India. Follower of Vasco Fernandes, *Adoration of the Magi*, oil on panel, 77.5 × 75.7 cm (ca. 1525). Freixo de Espada á Cinta, Church of São Miguel.

Ethiopian, or (as the Venetians did with the king they received) Saracen, or "from the new world"—or, indeed, they could have called them both Indian (see chapter 12).

Likewise, in an *Adoration of the Magi* of about 1525 in a book of hours for Portuguese King João III, again not far from the world of Vasco's Viseu altarpiece, we see an attendant in the foreground who is carefully portrayed as a dark-skinned though not African figure in a white turban and dhoti, gold slippers, and elegant body jewelry (fig. 3.4).[36] To a modern viewer the trappings clearly read as Indian in the strict modern sense (i.e., from the Asian subcontinent), and it is indeed likely that the painter was working with information from one of the Portuguese voyages across the Indian ocean. But would it have been possible for a viewer in the 1520s to distinguish this figure—mostly naked, with long straight hair, outlandish yet impressive, clearly obeying a code of dress and behavior—from Brazilian peoples that had received similar portrayals in both texts and images?

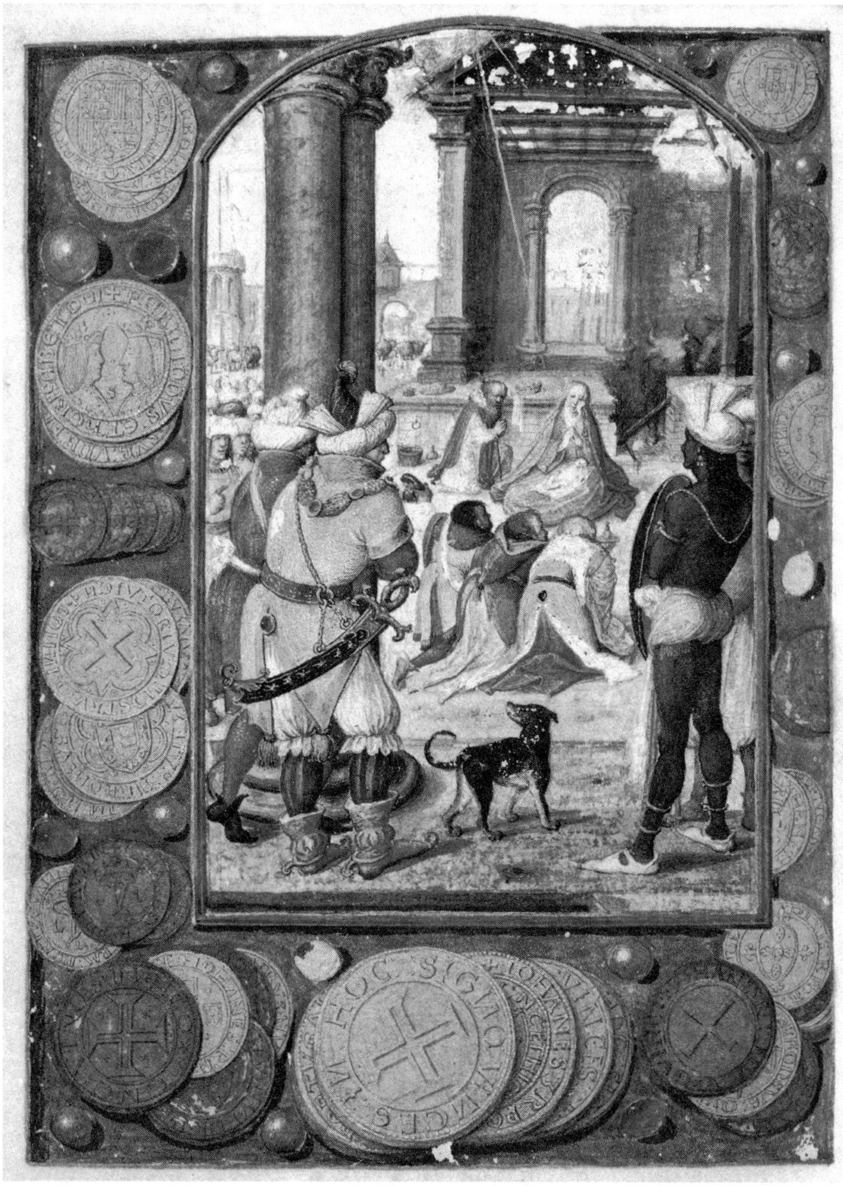

3.4 An expanded India under the sign of the Portuguese king. Vasco Fernandez, *Adoration of the Magi*, *Book of Hours of King João III*, tempera and gold on parchment, 14 × 11 cm (ca. 1525). Lisbon, Museu Nacional de Arte Antiga, fol. 87v. The Portuguese coins shown in the margin of the miniature, minted under royal authority from gold sourced in Sudan, put the impress of the Portuguese king on the scene—a worthy successor to the Magi, crossing the world under divine guidance. Several of the coins take up the motto of the first Christian emperor, Constantine, *in hoc signo vinces*: "by this sign [the cross] you shall conquer."

The main development here, as in the central magus of Fernandes, is the specificity of observation. In all three Portuguese renderings of the Magi scene considered here, the theme is being enhanced by the incorporation of observed details from far-off regions that had been legendary for centuries but that now, fairly suddenly, were coming under actual observation. Whether the details in fact come from Indian, African, or American sources, the premise is the same: the peoples newly encountered through Portuguese expansion allow us to imagine anew the lands and figures of the Magi.

• • •

Postlude: Inca Magus

Even as the distance between America and Asia grew, the search for evidence of the Magi and other biblical figures in the new world persisted. On his march from Sinaloa to the Seven Cities of Cibola, Francisco Coronado noted in 1540 that he was searching for the homeland of the Magi, not because he had decided to move the home of the Magi to the new world, but because he believed himself to be on the path to China (see chapter 8).[37] The Quechua historian Guaman Poma de Ayala proposed in his *Nueva corónica* of about 1615 that the apostle Bartholomew (whom the Andean peoples called Tunupa) had preached in the Andes long before the arrival of the Spanish, and that an Inca chief was one of the three kings who had gone to Bethlehem. He speaks of "the king-magus Melchior an Indian [by which he means an American], Balthazar a Spaniard, and Gaspar a black."[38] Also in the early seventeenth century, the Augustinian friar Antonio de la Calancha wrote that the apostle Thomas had taught in eastern Peru, and that the descendants of those who first admitted him to the region, the Chriguano Indians, still wear their hair long in the back with crowns on their heads, a memory of their discipleship.[39] Yet the Christian teachings did not take root, or became perverted by the devil, requiring the more recent campaigns of conversion, a campaign long anticipated by Christ himself, who faced west on the cross, turning his back on Jerusalem (and the Jews) and embracing the peoples to the west.[40] Christ facing west on the cross was an entrenched if postbiblical idea, and it was often invoked to orient the connection between European Christians and the source of their salvation: Christ faced west on the cross, toward Christians in the West. Calancha extends the idea in light of recent events, asserting that Christ was facing west on the cross not only to embrace the future expansion of Christianity to Europe, but also in the foreknowledge that Christian history would extend into America.

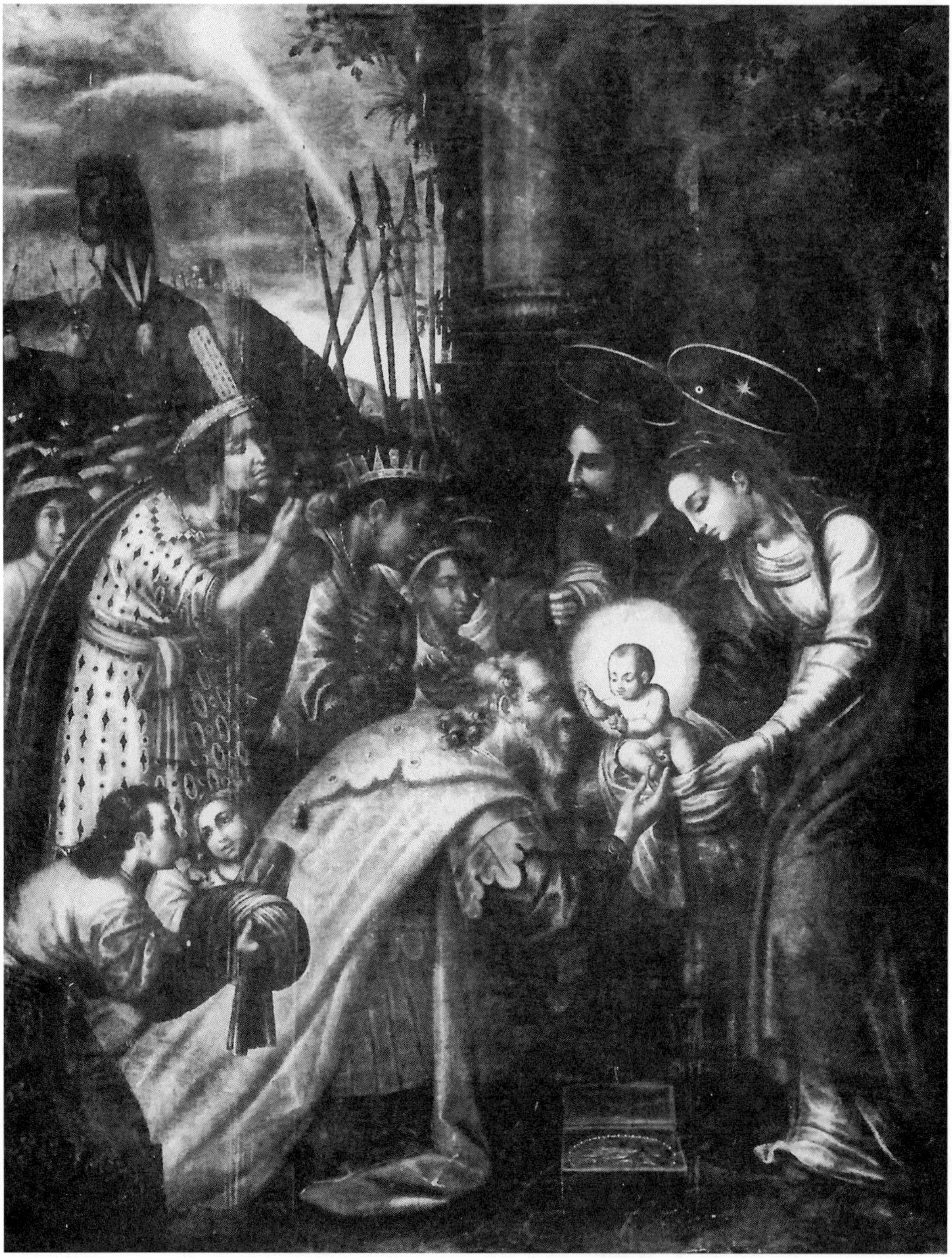

3.5 The Indian magus in Inca-derived dress. Diego de la Puente, *Adoration of the Magi*, oil on canvas (1650s). Juli, Museo Templo Nuestra Señora de la Asunción.

As if putting Guaman Poma's ideas into visual form, the Flemish Jesuit painter Diego de la Puente, who lived and worked in Peru from at least 1620 until his death in 1663, produced a scene of the *Adoration of the Magi* in which one of the kings wears the regalia of an Inca king (fig. 3.5). The eldest magus, representing traditional Asia, has removed his turbaned crown, the African magus wears a crown of gold, and the Indian magus wears a diadem adorned with two feathers and cloak ornamented with patterns that suggest Inca derivation even if they are not entirely accurate.[41] The inclusion of the Incan magus both acknowledges the conversion of this population to Christianity and recognizes the legitimacy of the Inca as a great kingdom of the world.[42] Now, over one hundred years after Vasco's painting, the pre-Columbian cultures were being studied by historians and ethnographers in a context that also included the study of Roman, Greek, Jewish, Egyptian, and different forms of Asian antiquity (see chapters 13 and 14). If Vasco's Tupi-Calicutish magus comes on the scene as a sudden arrival, Diego's Incan magus takes his place among the biblical worthies as if by ancient birthright.

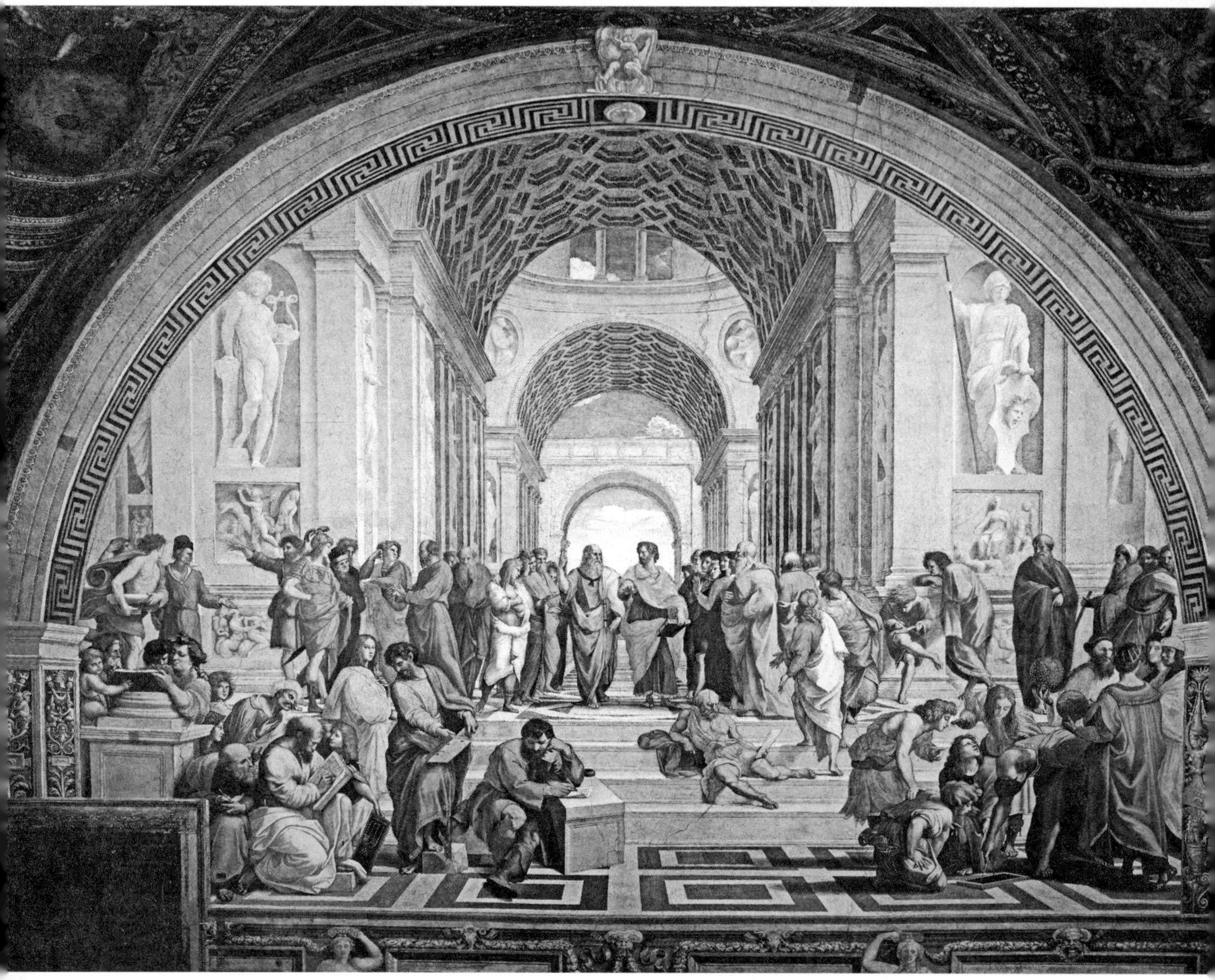

4.1 A global assembly of philosohers. Raphael, *Philosophy*, fresco (ca. 1510). Vatican City, Vatican Palace, Stanza della Segnatura.

FOUR

Raphael's Global Philosophy

Directly upstairs from the apartments of Pope Alexander VI decorated by Pinturicchio (discussed in chapter 1) are the apartments of Alexander's successor, Pope Julius II, now known as Raphael's Vatican Stanze. On the same wall as Pinturicchio's *Resurrection*, though on the other side of it and one flight up, is Raphael's fresco *Philosophy*, painted in about 1510 in what was then Julius II's library (fig. 4.1).[1] Since an authoritative description was offered in 1695 it has erroneously been called *The School of Athens*,[2] but in fact it shows philosophers from different lands and schools (and times) conversing in clusters of philosophical inquiry.

The Philosophical World

Of the figures that are more or less identifiable, Socrates, Pythagoras, Plato, and Aristotle were Greek, though not all from Athens; Diogenes was from Asia Minor, Archimedes from Sicily, Ptolemy was Egyptian. The turbaned figure behind Pythagoras is often identified as Averroes, a Muslim from Córdoba. And though we may not agree that the figure holding the celestial globe is Zoroaster, as Giorgio Vasari says, it is telling that he believed a Persian philosopher belonged in the assembly.[3] From a European point of view, the fresco attempted a global sweep of philosophical wisdom.

Although this chapter focuses on the *Philosophy* fresco, it proceeds from the premise that it is impossible to understand any element in isolation from the decorations throughout the room as a whole. We propose that the new world explorations were essential to the conceptualization and design of Raffaello Sanzio da Urbino, or Raphael's, *Philosophy* fresco and its relation to the room it decorates. A basic feature of the fresco's conception was a spherical and, in all senses, global understanding of the nature of philosophical inquiry, in the context of which the expansion of the known world, the emerging knowledge of the world in its rotundity, was a major philosophical event. Raphael, it turns out, was keenly aware of the latest cartographic developments, in particular the famous 1507 world map designed and engraved by Johannes Ruysch. In presenting an

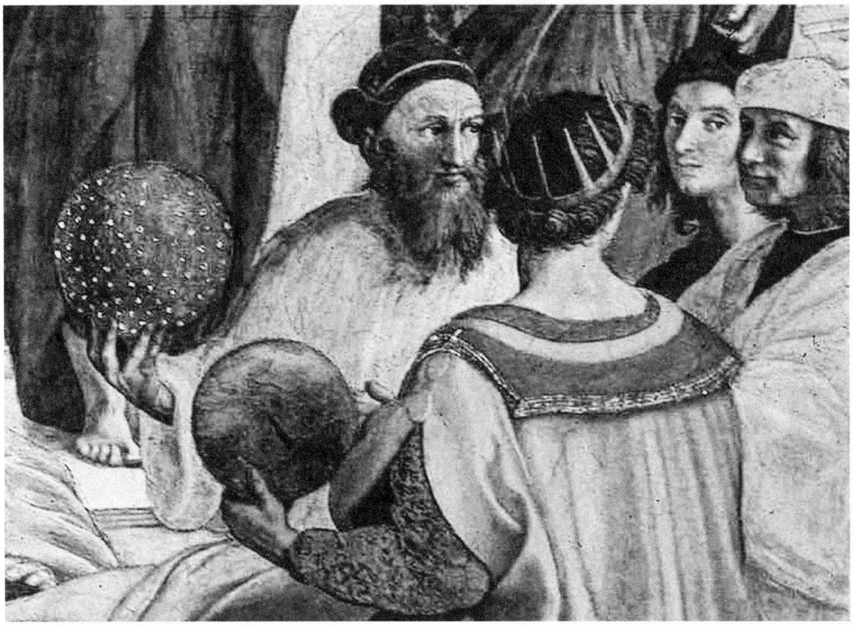

4.2 Ancient cosmographers consult their modern heirs. Raphael, *Philosophy*, fresco, detail of figure 4.1.

Amerasian new world, this map doubled the size of the inhabited world known to Ptolemy and other ancient cosmographers.

Toward the right side of the fresco we see the figure of Archimedes of Syracuse bent over his chalkboard delineating a diagram on a slate tablet. Not far from this geometrical demonstration are two philosophers holding globes, a cosmographically oriented philosophical assembly (fig. 4.2). A bearded man holds a celestial orb with the fixed stars; the other, who wears a crown on his head and is seen from behind, holds a terrestrial globe. Most figures in the fresco have proven difficult to identify with certainty, but in the case of this crowned philosopher there is no doubt that it portrays the ancient geographer Ptolemy, who was mistaken in late medieval texts and images as a member of the royal lineage of the Ptolemies of Egypt and thus is shown here as elsewhere wearing a crown. The philosopher across from him holding a celestial globe, identified as Zoroaster by Vasari, is more likely the cosmographer Strabo from Amasya in Asia Minor.[4]

The two ancient philosophers holding globes are turning toward two counterparts at the extreme right edge of the fresco, one of them a self-portrait of Raphael, then twenty-six or twenty-seven-years old, who looks out of the picture toward us. These contemporary portraits were late additions to the fresco, perhaps the last elements to be painted on this wall. The full-scale cartoon for the composition in the Ambrosiana in Milan reaches its limit at the two philosophers with globes at its right edge; Raphael and his companion are not shown, yet the cartoon does show the two globe-carrying philosophers turning toward the right, as they do in the final fresco, implying that figures beyond the cartoon's right edge were intended at this stage. The man in white next to Raphael, who is also shown in contemporary clothing, has not yet been securely identified. It has been proposed that he is the painter Sodoma, who worked in this room, or the painter Timoteo Viti, an associate of Raphael's, but there is simply no evidence to support these claims. Presently we will offer evidence to identify this personage as Raphael's colleague, the Flemish painter and cosmographer Ruysch, who is also known to have worked in this room.[5] In this corner of the painting, the vision of ancient philosophers meets the world of the artist and opens onto the world of its many viewers.

The visible half of the terrestrial globe shows what Ptolemy and cosmographers after him called the *oikoumene*, the inhabited world as known to the ancient philosophers of the Greek-speaking world. At the left edge we see the Iberian peninsula and Africa, then the Mediterranean extending to the east from there, with a prominent Red Sea and an expansive Asia spreading across the right edge of the globe. The fact that we see none of what we term the new world might seem a bit surprising, even disappointing. After all, Rome and in particular the papacy and the court of cardinals were well informed and in the flush of enthusiasm over news of the expeditions of Christopher Columbus, Vasco da Gama, Pedro Álvares Cabral, Amerigo Vespucci, and others. As we saw in chapters 1 and 2, papal preachers and prominent cardinals celebrated these exploits as a turning point in history, heralding the triumph of Christianity around the globe. Raphael's globe does register recent information about the shape of Africa, obtained through Bartolomeu Dias's and then da Gama's voyages around the Cape of Good Hope, thus correcting the prevailing Ptolemaic view of an Africa that extended eastward and closed off the Indian Ocean.[6] The earlier shape of Africa can be seen in a painting of *Heraclitus and Democritus* by Raphael's compatriot Donato Bramante (fig. 4.3).[7]

Beyond correcting the shape of Africa, Raphael's globe suggests an open Indian ocean, both land and sea extending without any clear limit around the right edge of the globe—a new idea, though Raphael's handling of the eastern part of his globe leaves the question unresolved. It may or may not be a response to the latest discoveries, since, after all, the eastern limits are also left unresolved in the globe in Bramante's painting, which was most likely painted before 1492. Raphael's globe makes adjustments within the traditional range of the Ptolemaic *oikoumene*, keeping the globe centered on the Near East and recalling medieval Jerusalem-centered

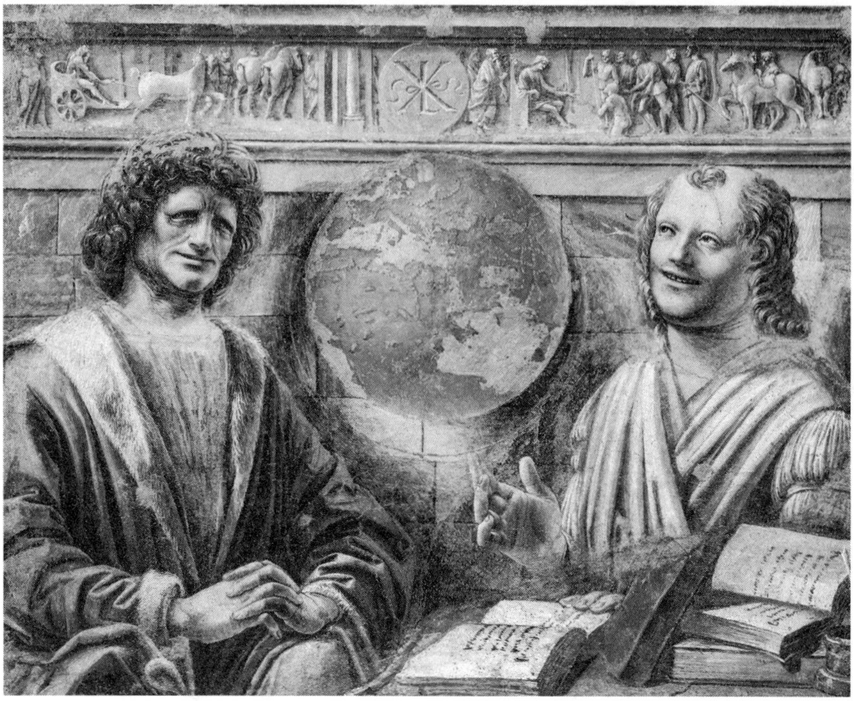

4.3 An earlier globe. Donato Bramante, *Heraclitus and Democritus*, 102 × 127 cm (ca. 1485), fresco transferred to canvas. Milan, Pinacoteca di Brera.

mappaemundi.[8] Whatever hints it gives of recent discoveries, nowhere does Raphael's globe show the territories and islands to the west of Europe discovered by Columbus, Cabral, Vespucci, and others. Was Raphael uninterested, or simply uninformed?

The Sphere as a Figure of Philosophy

Various pieces of evidence show that Raphael was both interested and informed. Let us begin by examining the globe in Ptolemy's hand not as an isolated bit of cartographic information, but in relation to the thematic and formal workings of the fresco and the room as a whole. Above the group with Ptolemy, Raphael depicted a relief in the architecture with a figure of Astrology/Astronomy, or possibly Reason, enthroned on clouds, with a segment of the band of the zodiac circling beside her head. Working under the aegis of the statue of Athena, goddess of wisdom, this cosmological figure presides over the assembly of cosmographically oriented philosophers below her. The zodiac, figuring astral constellations that run along the ecliptic, the path of the sun, diagrams a swath of the complete starry sphere held by Strabo directly below.

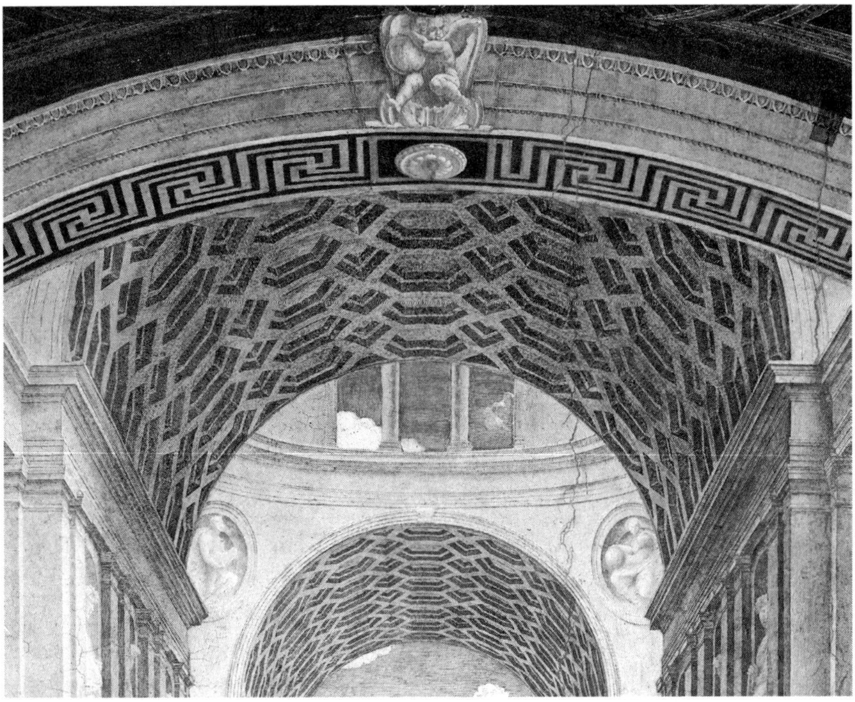

4.4 Spheres abounding. Raphael, *Philosophy*, detail of figure 4.1.

Also on this side of the painting, filling a circular niche in the pendentive zone under what we understand to be the building's crowning central cupola, is a robed woman holding a globe, as yet unidentified, who seems to look straight down at us. In the corresponding pendentive to the left a bearded man plays a harp while looking upward, suggesting that we have here Music and Astronomy, each positioned over the part of the assembly below that corresponds to them—Music above the statue of Apollo and the philosopher Pythagoras, who is shown writing as the table of harmonic proportions is propped before him, and Astronomy above Minerva and the cosmographers. Extrapolating from these two roundels, we can imagine the two unseen facing pendentives across the drum carrying corresponding roundels with Arithmetic and Geometry, the other subjects of the *quadrivium,* the four mathematical disciplines within the seven liberal arts. Here as elsewhere, the fresco invites us to think all the way around a round form, only part of which can be seen from a given position.

Then, outside of the scene altogether, a fictive keystone crowning the lunette carries a putto grappling with a large sphere (fig. 4.4). This is not a generic keystone decoration throughout the room. The putti in the keystones on the other walls hold not spheres but items relevant to the faculties of those walls: the putto above *Jurisprudence* carries a cornucopia, like the one in the scene below; the putto above *Disputa (Theology)* holds a dove, again like the one within the scene; and the putto above *Parnassus (Poetry)* holds branches of laurel, like the ones on the laurel tree in the scene below. The putto above *Philosophy* handles a large globe that appears especially mobile and hard to handle in the small child's hands. The turning orb, a challenge to human comprehension, was evidently Raphael's emblem for the faculty of philosophy.

We find still more globes directly below the main wall fresco in the monochrome frescoes painted by Raphael's pupil Perino del Vaga in the lower zone of the room (fig. 4.5). Under the left side of Raphael's fresco, one of Perino's panels shows a hooded philosopher in a pose of contemplation, an echo of the mantled, downward-looking allegory (of Astronomy?) in the pendentive roundel of the fresco above. Following from this lone philosopher is another scene of a group of wise men in debate around a globe, pointing at it from different directions, an echo of the discussion around globes in the fresco above. Throughout the room, Perino's *basamento* scenes are carefully keyed to Raphael's frescoes above. For example, the other two scenes further to the right on this wall, directly below the Archimedes-Ptolemy group in Raphael's fresco, depict the accomplishments and death of

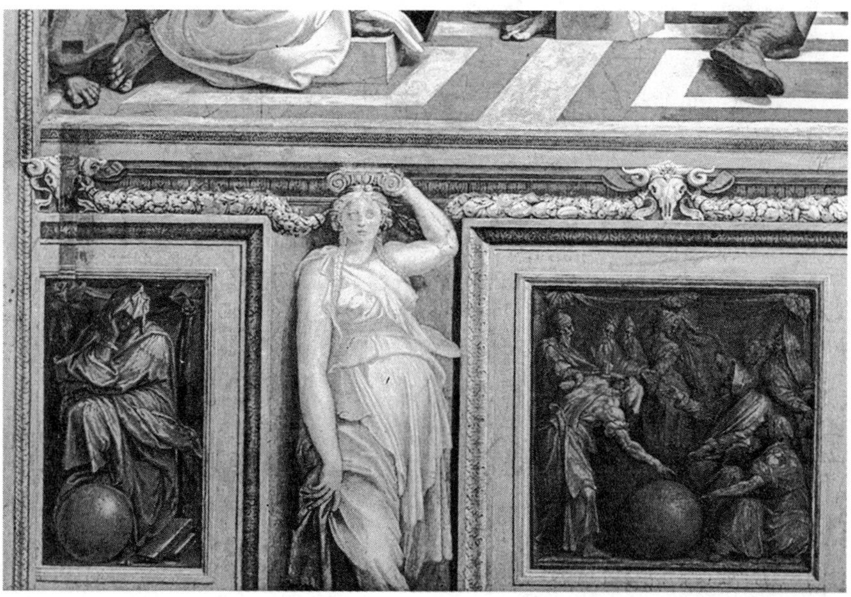

4.5 Philosophers and their spheres. Perino del Vaga, part of the *basamento* under Raphael's *Philosophy* fresco, early 1540s.

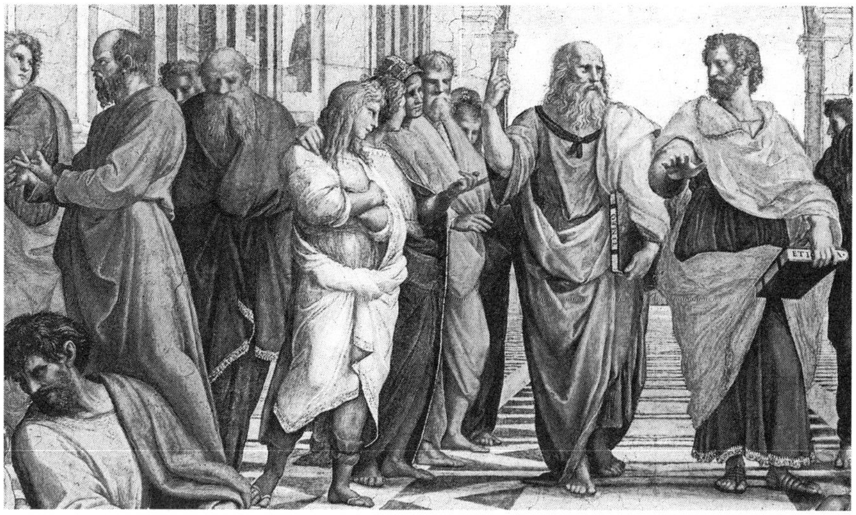

4.6 The new model, great men in dialogue. Raphael, *Philosophy*, fresco, detail of figure 4.1.

Archimedes in Syracuse. Under the Justinian and Pope Gregory the Great on the *Jurisprudence* wall, Perino portrayed the lawgivers Solon and Moses, and under the *Disputa (Theology)*, Perino's panels show a pagan sacrifice, a legendary scene from the life of Saint Augustine, the Tiburtine sybil revealing the Virgin and Child to Augustus, and a figure identified as Theology.[9] Only the two panels under the *Philosophy* fresco depict globes. By the time the lower zone of monochrome frescoes was painted, in the early 1540s, the room no longer functioned as a library, yet Perino remembered and respected the program put into place by his one-time boss Raphael, casting the sphere as an attribute and occasion for philosophical inquiry.[10]

The Sphere as a Motor of Dialogue

Beyond the evidence of the pictorial staging, the most relevant philosophical context confirms that at the Vatican in about 1510, philosophy was global philosophy, an idea that was fundamentally Platonic in inspiration. Plato is shown in the center of the scene holding his *Timaeus*, a dialogue celebrating cosmic order and beauty, which begins with an account of creation (fig. 4.6). Plato says that in imitation of the spherical form of the cosmos humans were given a spherical body, "which form we now call the 'head,'" and then that sphere was placed on a vehicle composed of torso and arms and legs, whose job it is to hold up and convey the orb of the head, the part of us that is connected to divinity. The addition of the body with its limbs gave a front and back to the human form, and so the sphere of the head was given a face with eyes set into one side of it, imposing one-sided vision on what had been a head with fully spherical potentiality. Among humans, philosophers are distinguished by their understanding that these are merely physical limitations that can be overcome by using the mind, the part of the human that remembers its divine origin, to contemplate the revolutions of cosmic order and to relate them to the "revolvings of the reasoning that is within us."[11]

Philosophers never forget that their heads are spheres, modeled on the spheres of the cosmos, and through this anamnesis they learn to govern their own unstable natures. Look at Socrates to Plato's right, our left, with his impressively round head, rounder even than Plato's, engaging the circle of disciples around him. Look at the beautiful round head of Pythagoras below, hearing the music of the spheres, with two philosophers behind him, one with a remarkably globular bald pate and the other with an impressive round turban circling his head. It is probably not a coincidence that the figure of Archimedes just next to the Ptolemy group has a particularly spherical head, positioned right next to the globes of the earth and heavens held by the cosmographers (fig. 4.7).[12] Unlike the rest of humanity, philosophers do not just look and think straight ahead; they think "spherically" and are helped in doing so by entering into dialogue with other minds, as the dialogues of Plato themselves demonstrate. The

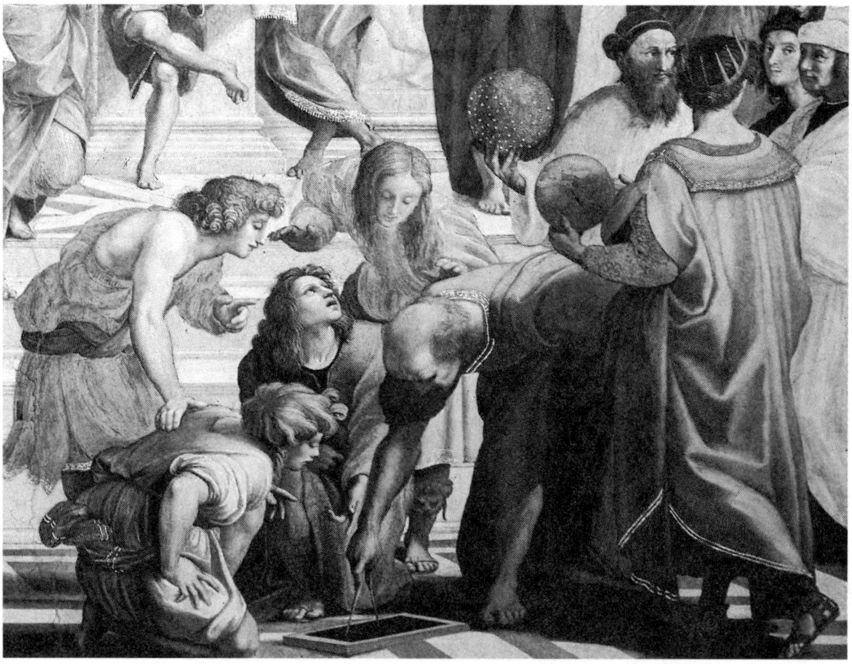

4.7 Raphael, *Philosophy*, detail of figure 4.1.

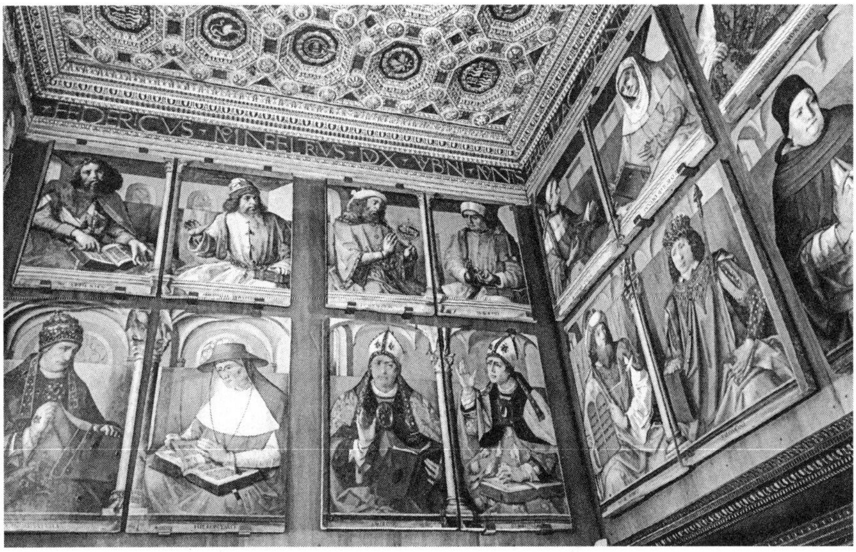

4.8 The old model, great men in compartments. Studiolo of Federico da Montefeltro, Urbino, Ducal Palace, 1470s. Ptolemy, with blue cloak, turban, crown, and armillary sphere, is in the upper row.

diagram of intersecting triangles Archimedes is making—a demonstration that has never been properly identified or understood—is patently made to be observed from multiple points of view, as evinced by the pupils who move into varying positions to gain views of it from different vantages.[13] Raphael, included in the assembly of philosophers among geometers and astronomers, those who give visual form to cosmic truth, extracted from Plato's sphere-based philosophy a principle of spatial dynamism and bodily engagement. He produced a choreography of actors, bringing together philosophers from different times and places into multisided and present-tense conversation, a participatory conception that extends to the way the figures inhabit shared conditions of light and color that articulate complex groupings.[14] As Heinrich Wölfflin described the fresco, "Raphael's rendering of movement in individual figures is a lesser achievement than the skill with which he builds up his groups and there is nothing in earlier art which can in any way be compared with this polyphony."[15]

Raphael's commitment to the choreographic idea led to a dramatic departure from earlier conventions for decorating studies or libraries, which displayed the heroes of knowledge statically in rows and in isolation from each other. In Raphael's hometown of Urbino, for example, Federico da Montefeltro's library was decorated with portraits of illustrious thinkers, each in its own compartment and identified by an inscription (fig. 4.8). This is a rational solution, respecting the differences among the various thinkers, and their separation in space and time. By contrast, in Raphael's frescoes for the pope's private library, the figures representing each faculty are made to interact, and the identifying inscriptions are jettisoned (thus giving later scholars much work to do). Raphael does include a memory of the earlier form of organization by adorning the great vaulted hall behind the philosophers with statues of the gods, each to a niche—the statues of Apollo and Athena on the front of the building and then twelve more on either side of the building's main hall. By contrast, the philosophers in vibrant color who inhabit this forecourt embody the truth that knowledge happens through dialogue and dispute. In book seven of Plato's *Republic*, Socrates describes how reason is cultivated through rational discussion and dialectic as "the discipline that will enable them [students] to ask and answer questions in the most scientific manner"; therefore, "no other higher kind of study could rightly be placed above [dialectic]."[16] The diachronic, mediated form of this activity is textual commentary, a protracted, scholarly form of dialectic.[17] Plato, a writer, translated Socrates's live dialectic into textual form in his own dialogues, part of an epochal shift from orality to literacy that soon produced the cultural institution of libraries, such as the one in this room. Using the visual resources of painting, Raphael reverses the cultural shift from orality to literacy by staging live dialectic among philosophers, theologians, jurists, and ports from different eras, a "virtual arena of orality" one level up from the room's lowest zone filled by the library's bookshelves.[18] The frescoes in the room translate into the terms of live conversation what are in fact a series of imaginary conversations, the kind of conversations that happen when scholars sit in a library, consult various books, and compare them to one another, sparking a conversation in their minds among the various opinions that they are reading, a dynamic that ultimately includes the readers themselves, whether or not they are actually writing a commentary on one or another text. Beyond the content of the various philosophies, Raphael is interested in the mechanisms of philosophical knowledge, and that focus on modality is the motor of his pictorial conception.

Unlike the *Disputa* fresco across the room, which shows God the Father, Christ, and the dove of the Holy Spirit arrayed along a vertical axis, emphasizing a single descent of divine presence invested in the host on the altar,[19] the assembly of *Philosophy* is a horizontal spread bifurcated at its very center into two philosophers who embody an implicit dialogue: Plato on one side pointing upward to the heavenly spheres and Aristotle with his arm extended over the surface of the earth. The relation between the earth and the heavens is the implicit theme of the whole fresco, one embodied in the architecture itself, which rises from straight forms to a domed vault echoing the vault of heaven, a form invisible to the viewer of the fresco but imagined soaring above the pendentive zone.[20]

Among dwellers on earth, philosophers are the best able to articulate earth's own relation to the cosmos, and the sphere, engaging multisided dialogue, is the implicit or explicit motor of such inquiry—explicit in Perino's dispute of the philosophers around a globe in the *basamento*, implicit in the entire scene of *Philosophy* above. Nowhere is the "global" nature of philosophical conversation more clearly in evidence than in the cosmographical assembly at the right. Ptolemy, a columnar and fluent form turning on the axis of his right foot, activates conversation in an especially eloquent way. His face is hidden, but we can easily imagine it, animated as he turns toward his interlocutors to make a point or possibly ask them a question. His left hand holds up the globe for demonstration, while his right hand, seen only in part but eloquent enough in its gesture, is pointing to the globe—more precisely, to the *other* side of the globe, the side we cannot see, and that Ptolemy himself had not seen. Like his own head, turned so that we lose sight of his face, the globe, too, has a face we cannot see. Ptolemy is appealing to another point of view, a view from another side and also from another time. Seeing the globe as held and presented by the turning body that supports it, we realize that this earth is not a static body but is in this very moment rotating as it is being shown and discussed. Ptolemy and other ancient cosmographers knew very well that the inhabited parts known to them, the *oikoumene*, constituted only a fraction of the surface of the globe. Ptolemy admitted that the inhabited world was "bounded on the east by the unknown land which borders on the eastern races of Greater Asia"[21]—in other words, that its boundaries were as yet unknown. The laws of geometry dictate that when we look at a sphere from a given point of view we see exactly one half of it—180 of its full 360 degrees—and what we see on this side of Ptolemy's globe is the 180-degree span that he had projected and described in his *Geography*.

The question about what lay beyond and what beings if any lived there was left notoriously open for later natural philosophers to resolve. Plato himself, also in the *Timaeus*, tells the story of a great island named Atlantis, beyond the Strait of Gibraltar and bigger than Africa and Asia combined, a great and ancient civilization that was submerged into the sea.[22] What was there now? In the period after 1492, the inhabitants of Europe were starting to get some answers about the rest of the world, calling it a "new world" (*mundus novus* or *novus orbis*). This new world was not necessarily far from India, or even separate from it, but possibly a hitherto unknown extension of Ptolemy's India beyond the Ganges. As Peter Martyr d'Anghiera, the humanist chronicler of the recent voyages, wrote to Cardinal Luis of Aragón in Rome in 1501, "the cosmographers have left the boundaries of the Gangean India undefined, and many are of the opinion that the shores of India are not far from the coasts of Spain."[23] Here, in Raphael's Vatican fresco of about 1510, Ptolemy wants to talk with his colleagues from the future about what they see on the far side of the earth. Raphael, who can see, and in fact has seen, is looking out of the painting toward us. This corner of the picture is a conversation that emphatically mobilizes multiple points of view, including our own.

The Room as a Compass

The *Philosophy* fresco depicts a world, but it is also very much designed to interact with the world of the viewer and reorient the viewer in the world and the cosmos (fig. 4.9). Rather than a capsule floating in isolation from the world, this room is a compass, responsive to the cardinal directions established by the earth's polarity and relation to the sun. The *Philosophy* scene, which is on the east wall, is lit from the right, a fact that requires explanation, since the conventional lighting for paintings is from the left. The room contains two windows, one to the left of the painting (shown boarded up in the photo) and one to the right, and either one could have been taken as the source of light for the scene Raphael painted. The northern window, to the left, gives onto a view of the Vatican hill, and above this window in the fresco representing *Poetry* we see Apollo presiding over Mount Parnassus. The Vatican hill was believed by the humanists in Raphael's milieu to be sacred to Apollo, and Raphael appropriately places the god above the relevant hill seen through that window.[24] The lighting of the *Philosophy* fresco is, however, aligned with the most powerful source of light, the opposite south-facing window to the right. Across the room, the *Disputa* (*Theology*) fresco is on the west wall, and it depicts Western theologians, in counterpoint to the Greek and Eastern philosophers assembled in the *Philosophy* fresco. Like the papal Roman churches of Saint Peter's and the Lateran, as well as the Sistine Chapel, the altar and cloudy apse of the *Disputa* is disposed toward the west, whereas we look down the great temple-like structure of the *Philosophy* fresco in an easterly direction.[25] Ptolemy strides into the picture at its southernmost point, perhaps an allusion to his Egyptian origins. His shadow is cast by light from the south, or rather the southwest, an afternoon light. The other side of the globe, the side Ptolemy is pointing out to his interlocutors, is the eastern side, while we in the room see the known western face of the globe.

What did Raphael know of the other side of the world? Our best evidence is a map designed by Ruysch, made in 1507 or 1508 to be included in a new edition of Ptolemy's *Geography* (fig. 4.10).[26] The 1508 edition, dedicated

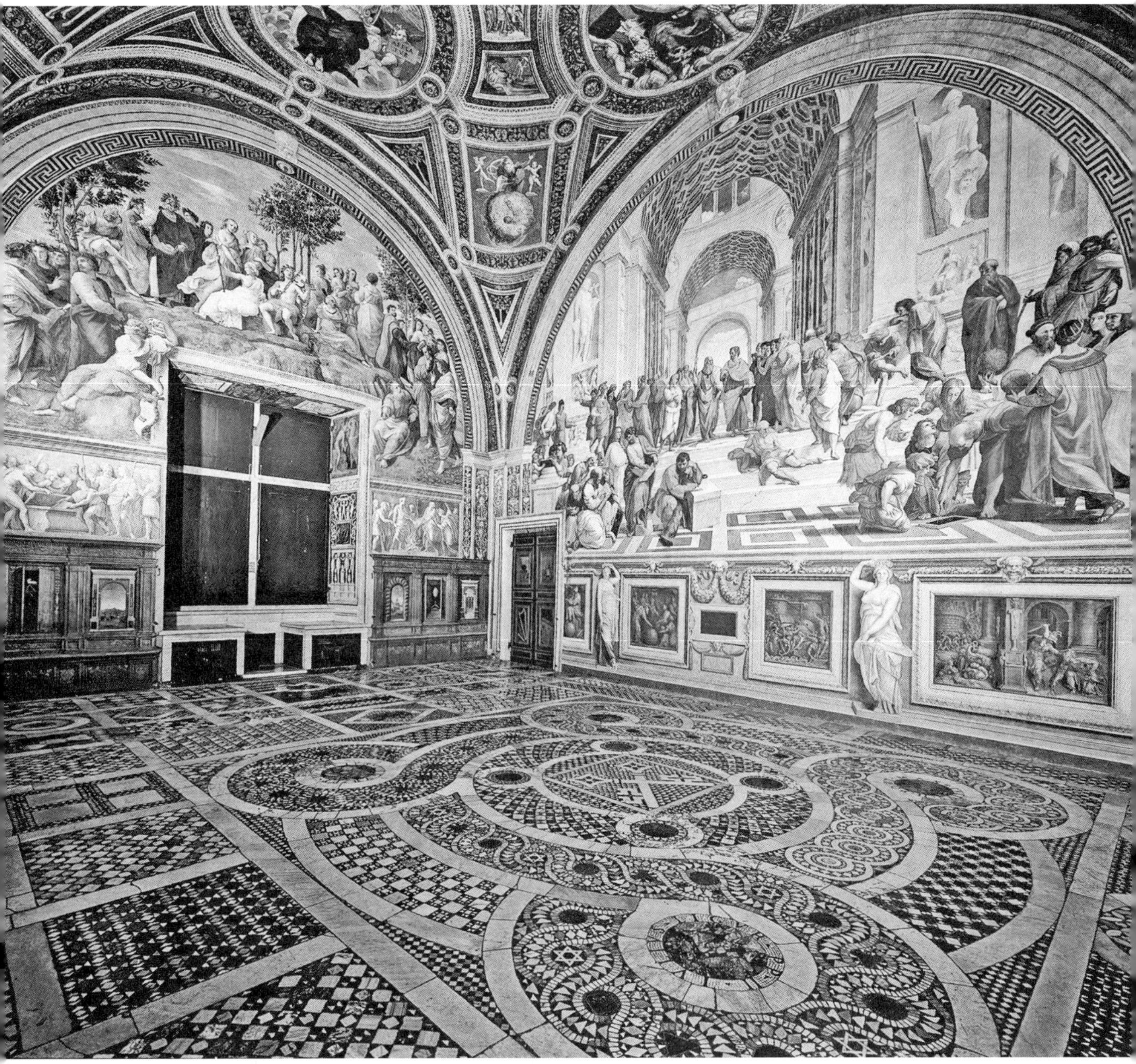

4.9 A compass, not a capsule. Vatican City, Vatican Palace, Stanza della Segnatura.

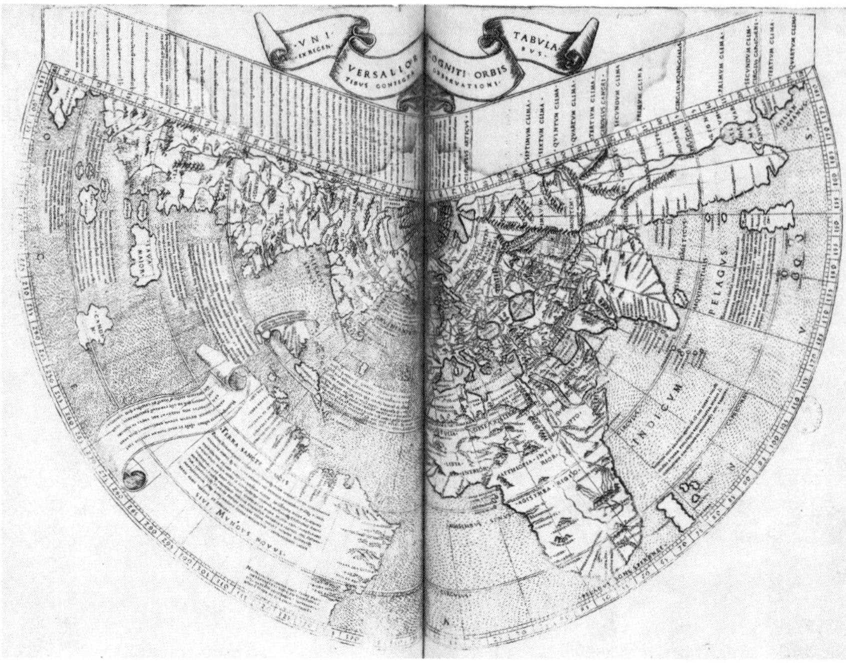

4.10 The world in 360 degrees, half old and half new. Ptolemy, *Geographia* (Rome, 1508), plate 2. Paris, Bibliothèque Nationale.

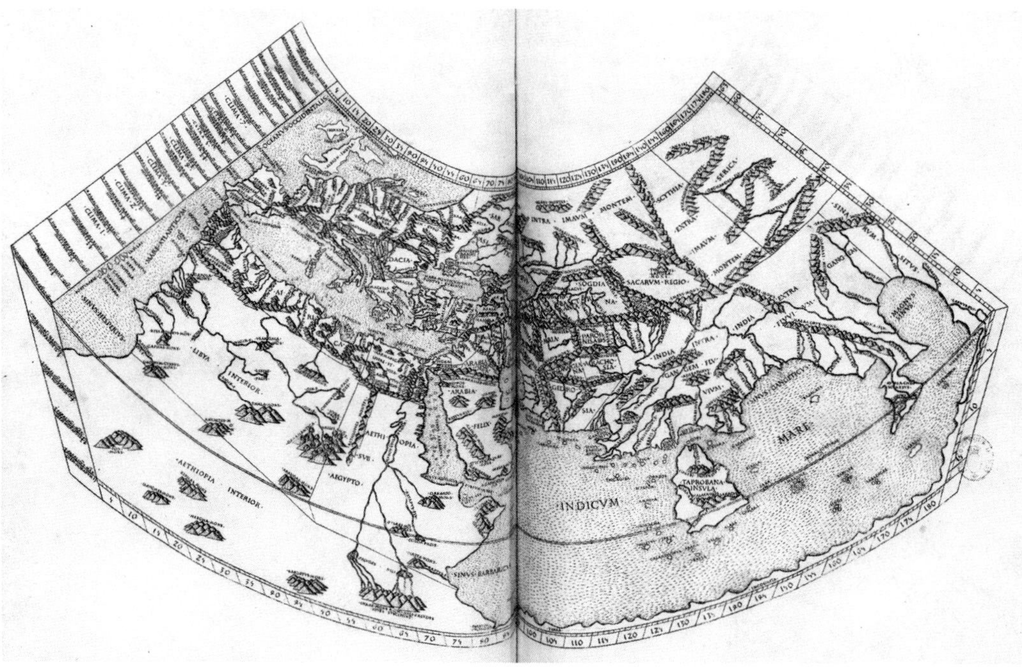

4.11 The 180 degrees of the old world. Ptolemy, *Geographia* (Rome, 1508), plate 1. Paris, Bibliothèque Nationale.

to Pope Julius II, presented the traditional tables of Ptolemy as handed down in the manuscript copies of Ptolemy's treatise, but added new information about the recent discoveries and a new map of the world, which was deemed necessary in light of the previous fifteen years of explorations. Julius, who saw the new discoveries as an opportunity to expand the global reach of the Roman Church, was interested in Ptolemy and in any expansion beyond the world known to the great Alexandrian geographer. A profile portrait of the pope, dated 1507, appears in a manuscript of Ptolemy's *Cosmographia* (an alternative title for the *Geographia*) that was part of the papal library housed in the Stanza della Segnatura, presumably in the shelves directly under Raphael's *Philosophy* fresco.[27] Ruysch's map updating Ptolemy's world picture is a conical projection of the world north of the Tropic of Capricorn; the top left edge is meant to meet the top right edge to produce a continuous and complete flat projection of the earthly globe. It is printed on a full folio sheet folded into the volume's gutter, its two sides starkly emphasizing the proportion of old knowledge to new knowledge by placing left of the gutter everything new or newly understood, and leaving the right side for the known Ptolemaic world. Our knowledge of the world's extent, the map proclaims, has doubled in the last fifteen years.

In order to bring the contrast home as clearly as possible, Ruysch's new map is immediately preceded in this edition by a corresponding two-page map of the old Ptolemaic world, with its closed Indian Ocean (fig. 4.11). Confirming the point about the doubling of the known world, Ptolemy's map is shown with its 180 degrees longitude, half of Ruysch's 360. The contrast between plate 2 and plate 3 is a figurative caveat, announcing the limitations of all the illustrations that follow, which present Ptolemy's now outdated tables.

On its new-world half, Ruysch's map identifies the large landmass to the west of Africa called Land of the Holy Cross (*Terra Sancte Crucis*), following the name given by the Portuguese navigator Cabral, as we saw in chapter 3 (fig. 4.12). In a nod to Vespucci, the inscription continues *sive Mundus novus* (or the new world). The western edge of this landmass, a banderole helpfully explains, is as yet unexplored and uncharted. Above this large land are two sizable islands as well as many smaller ones. One of the big ones is named Spagnola, Columbus's Hispaniola, the first island to receive a Spanish colony. Close by Spagnola is Cuba, which Columbus considered to be attached to the Asian mainland, and there a banderole wrapped around its western edge explains that the Spanish kings' ships got as far as here, implying that the shape of this landmass was also as yet unclear.[28] North of Cuba, in a notably accurate rendering, is the coast of Terra Nova, Newfoundland. To the west of Cuba we have an Asian landmass, marked with

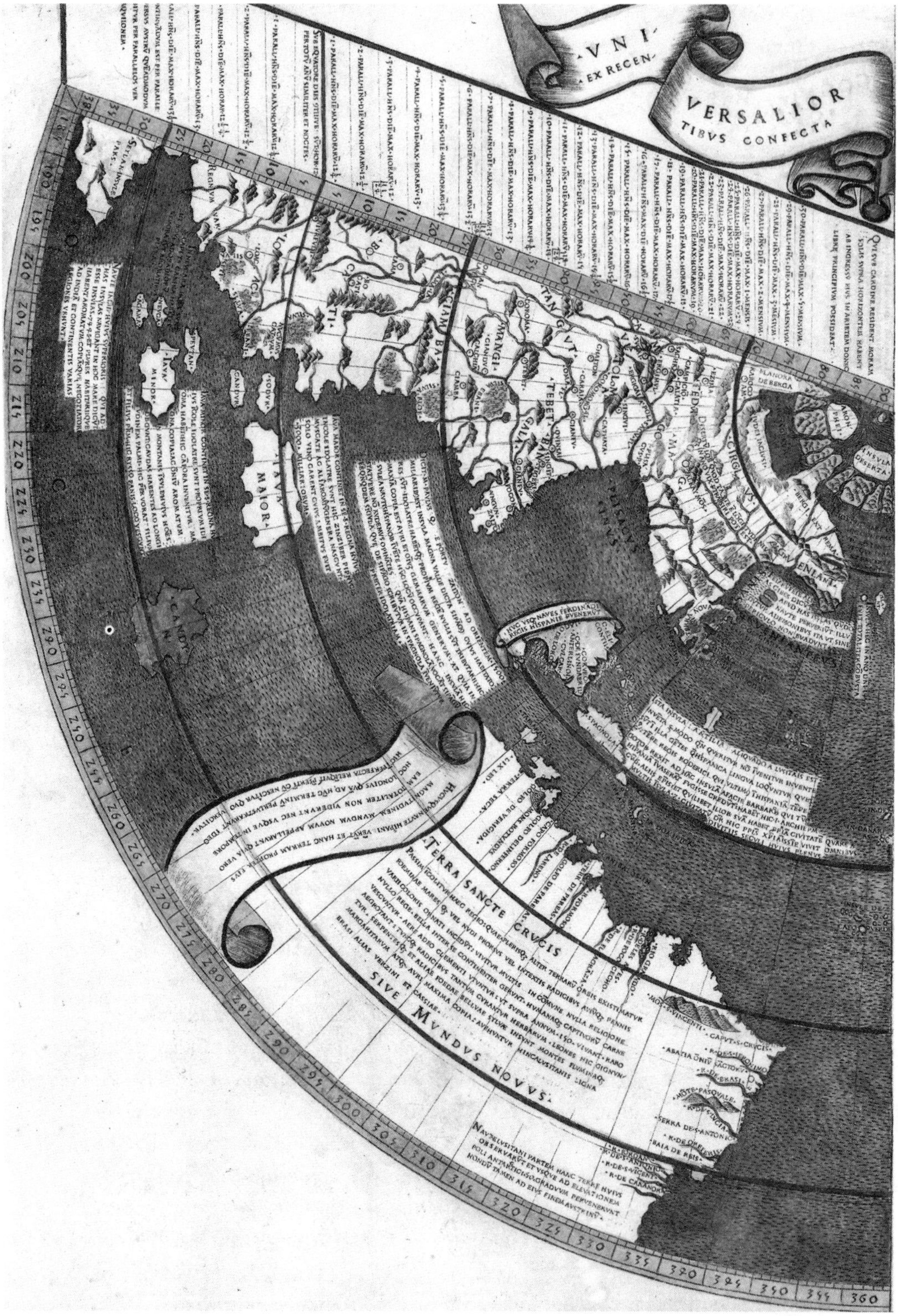

4.12 The new-world half of Ruysch's map in a hand-colored impression (1507). Washington, DC, Library of Congress.

the well-known place names of Mangi, the term used for southern China during the Mongol period, north of which is the western Chinese province of Tangut, and, to the east, Bangala and Tebet. Near the coast is Quinsai, the great city now called Hangzhou, described in effusive terms by Polo. An inscription in the waters off the coast of Asia explains that Polo had said that Japan, Sipangu, was 1,500 miles off the coast of Asia, and that therefore the fabled Asian island is to be identified with the island of Spagnola discovered and colonized by Columbus. The map shows not only that East had been extended eastward and West westward but also that one crossed over into the other: Spagnola is in fact Sipangu. (For the shifting position of Japan in period maps, see chapter 11.) Ruysch's map is the strongest cartographic expression from these years of a new world conceived as an Asiatic extension occupying a recently discovered hemisphere.[29]

The 1508 edition of Ptolemy's *Geographia* includes a text by the Celestine monk Marcus Beneventanus, entitled "New Description of the World" (*Nova orbis descriptio*). The text was introduced just before the sequence of plates in order to explain what was new on Ruysch's map. Beneventanus informs us that the "most learned Ruysch, who was also most expert in depicting the world, to whose aid in this little work I am indebted," was not only a cosmographer but also an experienced sailor. He reports Ruysch's own account "that he sailed from the South of England, and got as far as the fifty-third degree of north latitude, and on that parallel sailed west through the angle of night [*per angulum noctis*] toward the shores of the east [*ad ortus littora*], and observed many islands."[30] The cosmographic term *angulus noctis* refers to the place on the horizon where the sun sets, which is to say that Ruysch reached the east by sailing west.[31] On Ruysch's map, the fifty-third parallel indeed leads straight from England to an accurately described *Terra Nova* or Newfoundland, suggesting to several scholars that Ruysch had made one of the voyages in the later 1490s from England, traveling beyond the setting sun.

Ruysch was not only a navigator, cosmographer, and printmaker but also a miniaturist and painter, having illuminated manuscripts in his native Utrecht.[32] He was brought to Rome for his cartographic knowledge, no doubt, but also for his talents as a painter. As it happens, Ruysch painted under Raphael in the Vatican and likely in the very same Stanza della Segnatura, as we know from not insubstantial payments to him for painting work there alongside the painters Sodoma and Lorenzo Lotto.[33] There is no question that Raphael knew Ruysch's map of the world that accompanied the 1508 edition of Ptolemy, showing lands that Ptolemy had not known but that Ruysch himself had seen firsthand. Raphael was as well informed about the new discoveries as anyone in Rome could be.

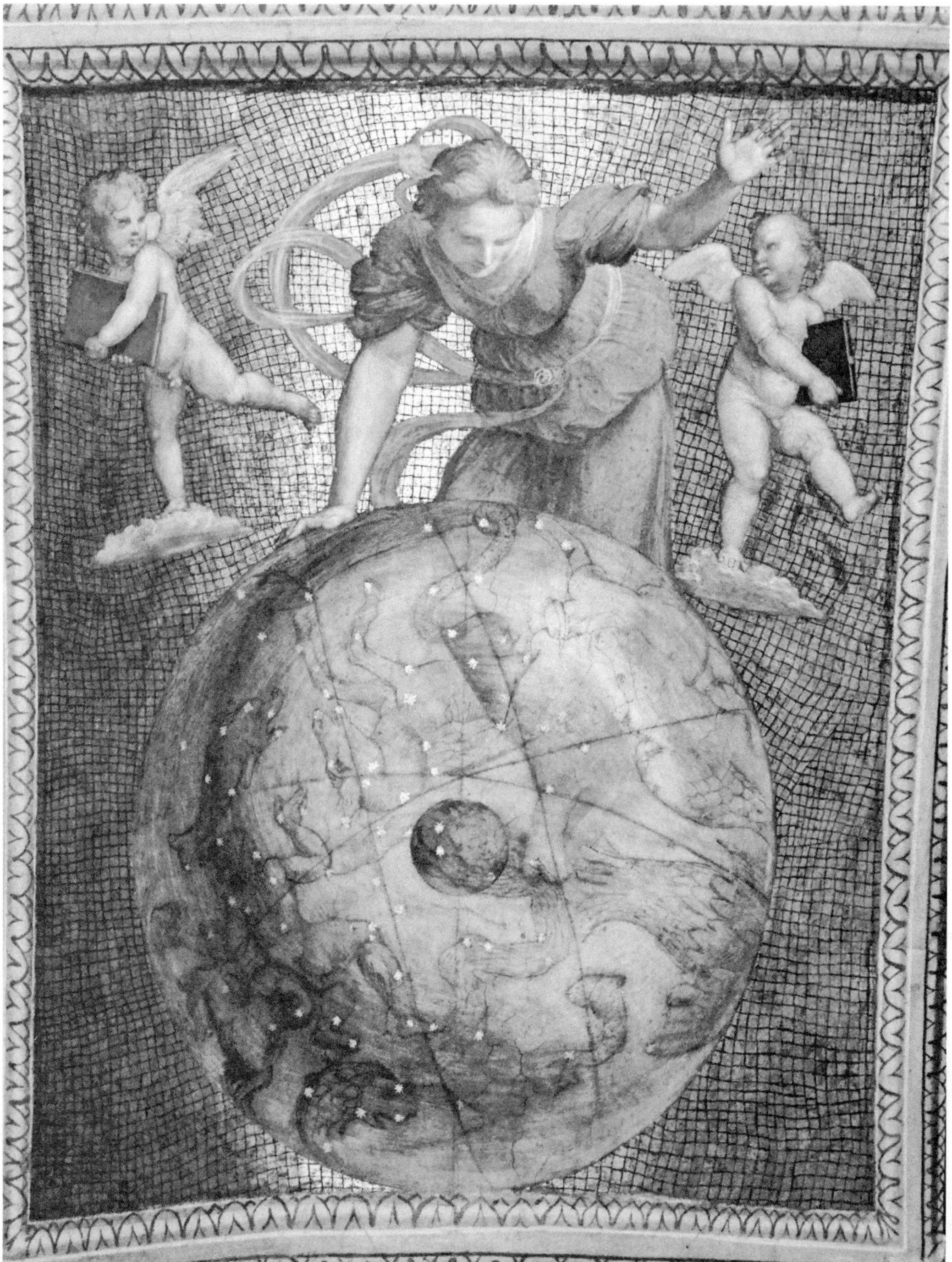

4.13 The cosmos in motion. Raphael (and Johannes Ruysch?), *Astronomia, or Urania*, fresco (ca. 1510). Vatican City, Vatican Palace, Stanza della Segnatura.

Most scholars agree that among the tasks given to Ruysch in this room was the design if not the painting of the vault panel with the figure sometimes identified as the astronomical muse Urania, or as an allegory of Astronomy herself, just above and to the left of the *Philosophy* fresco (fig. 4.13, and see fig. 4.9).[34] She is shown setting in motion the crystalline sphere of the stars, the outermost encircling orb of the Ptolemaic cosmos, beyond which is the Prime Mover of all creation. Thus, we have yet another sphere, or rather a set of spheres, associated with *Philosophy.* The sphere of the stars is transparent, allowing us to see through it to *Astronomia, or Urania*'s left leg and foot on the other side; as in the *Philosophy* fresco below, we are prompted to think about seeing spheres from more than one side. The crystalline sphere is marked by the celestial equator, an evenly balanced arc around the globe, as well as the ecliptic, crossing the equator at an angle. The starry constellations are arrayed in relation to the ecliptic more or less in their correct positions, though slightly pushed out of the way to make visible the small gem at the center of the spherical cosmos, the earth.[35] This really is an earthly globe, with formations of green land and blue sea visible on its surface, a companion to the one in Ptolemy's hand, yet no sustained attention has been given to it (fig. 4.14). The earth at the center of the cosmos is shown with landmasses that are

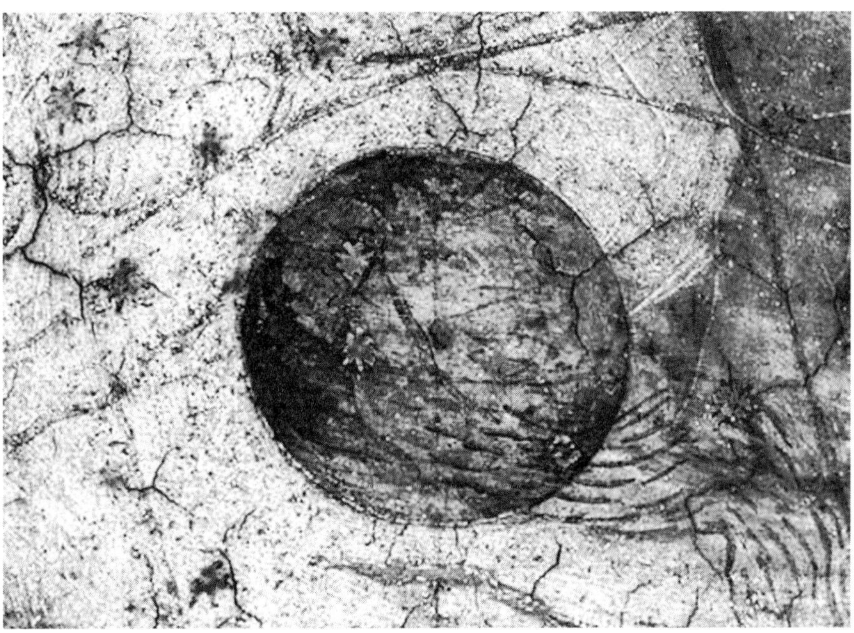

4.14 The earth from another point of view. Raphael (and Johannes Ruysch?), *Astronomia, or Urania*, fresco (ca. 1510). Vatican City, Vatican Palace, Stanza della Segnatura.

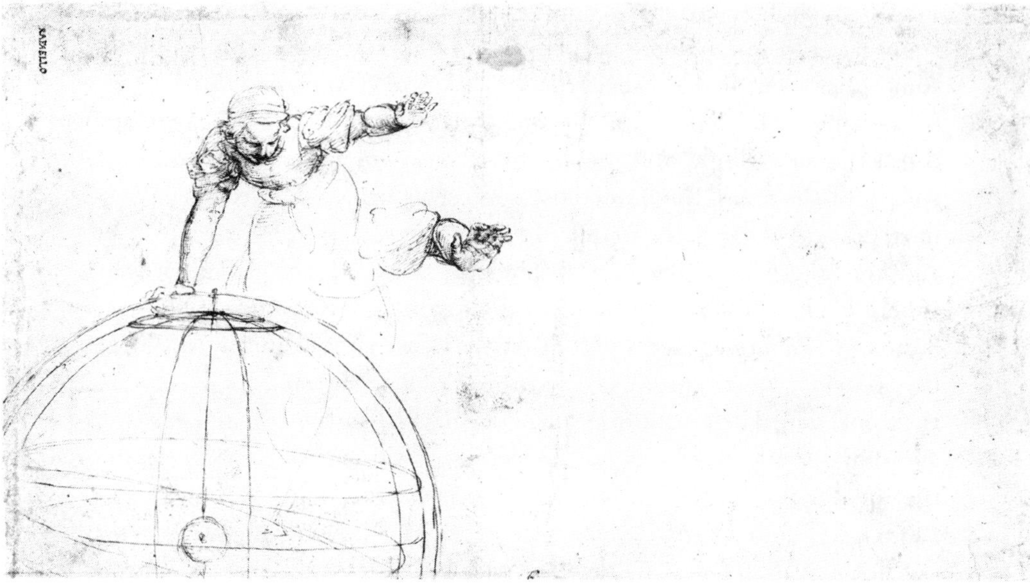

4.15 An earlier conception for the universe. Raphael, study for *Astronomia, or Urania*, 23.5 × 40.9 cm (ca. 1510), pen and ink over metalpoint on paper, Vienna, Albertina Museum.

not immediately recognizable from maps of the Ptolemaic world, yet it is unlikely that Raphael, or especially Ruysch, would have decorated it with arbitrary oceans and landmasses. (The dark repeated lines over the bottom right of the earthly globe, like the gold stars here and there, do not belong to the globe but describe constellations in the outer sphere of the cosmos—the lines here belonging to the tail of Cetus—that partially occlude the view.)

Perhaps what is unfamiliar here is the viewpoint. The celestial equator is shown as an arc rising toward the middle, a clear indication that we are seeing the entire cosmic machinery from below. This was a deliberate decision, since the only preparatory study we have for this fresco shows the concentric universe seen almost on the level: the rings of the tropics and the equator are shown in the form of an armillary sphere, almost dead-on but seen slightly from above so that they are visible in their full circumference (fig. 4.15).[36] Here as well, *Astronomia/Urania*'s foot is visible through the structure, landing nearly level with its equator.

By contrast, in the fresco (as realized by Ruysch?), the universe is shown as a celestial entity seen from below. It is possible that Raphael, and perhaps Ruysch, altered the viewpoint when considering that the painting was for the vault, and that it would in fact be seen from below. All of this means that the earth, too, is being presented to us *dal di sotto in sù* (from below looking up), an unusual view from the southern hemisphere, but one that was newly entering European consciousness as a result of the rounding of Africa and the exploration of Brazil and Patagonia. We look at it from below just as we do the spheres in the hands of the pendentive figure of *Astronomia/Urania* and the putto-keystone of the *Philosophy* fresco just below. To concretize this view onto the earthly globe in the context of contemporary global projections, we can compare it to the nearly contemporary Hunt-Lenox globe in the New York Public Library, a copper ball made of two hemispheres whose join represents the equator (fig. 14.16).[37] Tilting the Hunt-Lenox globe upward so as to see it at an angle corresponding to that indicated by the arcing equator in the *Astronomia/Urania* globe, and rotating it so that the Atlantic region is visible, we find here some similarities to what we see in Raphael's fresco: a landmass to the left (labeled *Mundus Novus* on the Hunt-Lenox globe) with islands called Isabel (for Cuba) and Spagnolla (for Hispaniola) floating above it, and another large curving landmass across the ocean to the right, corresponding to Africa. There is no reason for these two configurations to be identical, since the Hunt-Lenox globe was made in a different cultural and cartographic context (more informed by Portuguese sources), and the shape of both Africa and especially the new southern landmass called *mundus novus* by Vespucci were open to differing interpretation in maps of the period.

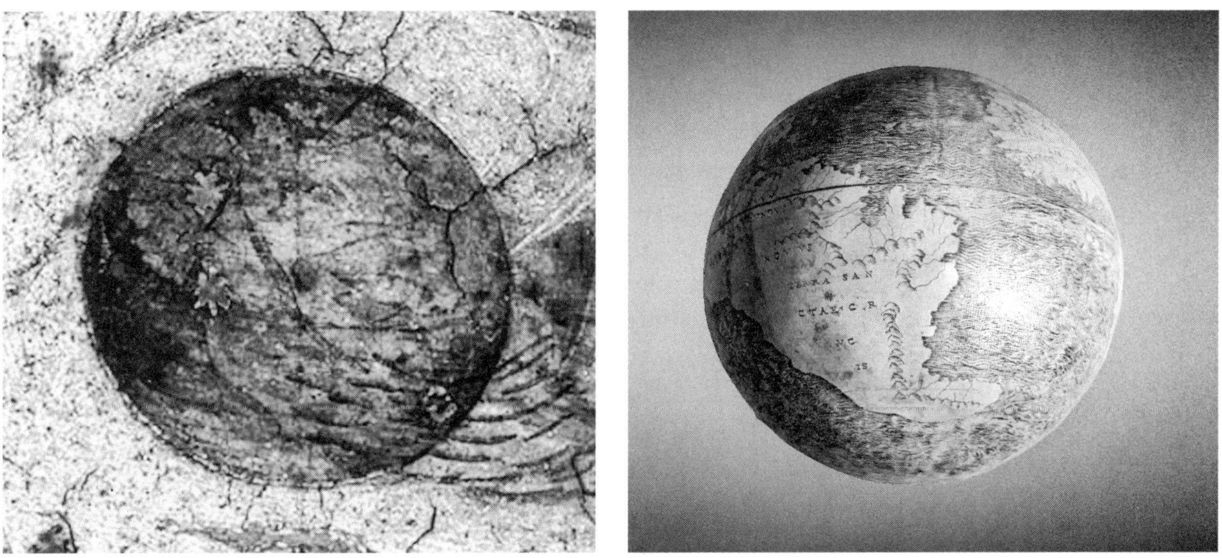

4.16 The globe in the *Astronomia/Urania* fresco and a from-below view of the Hunt-Lenox globe. 11.2 cm in diameter (ca. 1510), cast copper. New York Public Library. (See color plates.)

The best point of reference for what we see on the earthly globe shown at the center of *Astronomia/Urania*'s cosmos is Ruysch's own map for the Ptolemy edition (see figs. 4.10 and 4.12). Ruysch's conical projection offers almost the opposite view, looking down from the North Pole, and showing the world only as far south as a little below the Tropic of Capricorn. Nonetheless, if we were to place this information onto a globe and then visualize it from below, we might find something close to what we see in the vault fresco. The equator as drawn by Ruysch passes across the newly discovered land to the south, whose shape is quite similar to that of the continent on the left in the *Astronomia/Urania* fresco. Above that landmass, we see two islands, possibly Cuba and Hispaniola, and to the east would be Africa, with the equator running under its widest part, as it does in the Ruysch map. From this angle, significantly, Europe, lost over the horizon to the northeast, is not visible. A view from below gives us a new view of the world as well as a view of the new world, with the viewer's own position lost to view. It is a post-Ptolemaic globe.

• • •

Counterview: Looking up at the Earth

To return to the contemporary personage in a white mantle standing next to Raphael in the *Philosophy* fresco—is this Ruysch, the geographer and navigator who worked in this room? He was about two decades older than Raphael, and so this figure seems to be (see fig. 4.2). Most important, he was a cosmographer, a legitimate participant of this part of the scene.[38] Both Strabo and Ptolemy would thus be turning toward their successor, "the most learned Ruysch, who was also most expert in depicting the world," as Beneventanus described him in the 1508 Rome edition of Ptolemy, the one containing Ruysch's world map. Ptolemy would thus be pointing out the other side of the earth to Ruysch, who had in fact traveled there. Strabo, too, holding his celestial globe, seems to be specifically looking toward the figure in white. Significantly, however, Ruysch does not meet their gazes. He looks with faraway eyes over the heads of the ancient worthies addressing him, a simple and strange fact that has never been explained. If we simply follow the direction of his gaze, we find that it leads to *Astronomia/Urania* on the vault (see fig. 4.9), possibly painted by Ruysch himself and embodying Ruysch's view of the universe and of the earth at its center.

In Ptolemy's hand is a globe where we, standing in front of the fresco, see the known world. Raphael is shown the new world but he looks at us. Ruysch looks up toward the crystalline cosmos, at the center of which is the earth seen from a new point of view. The earth in motion, now coming into view in its full rotundity, cannot be seen except through images, a multiplicity of them captured at different times and from different viewpoints and then relayed to viewers who combine them and recombine them in their imaginations.

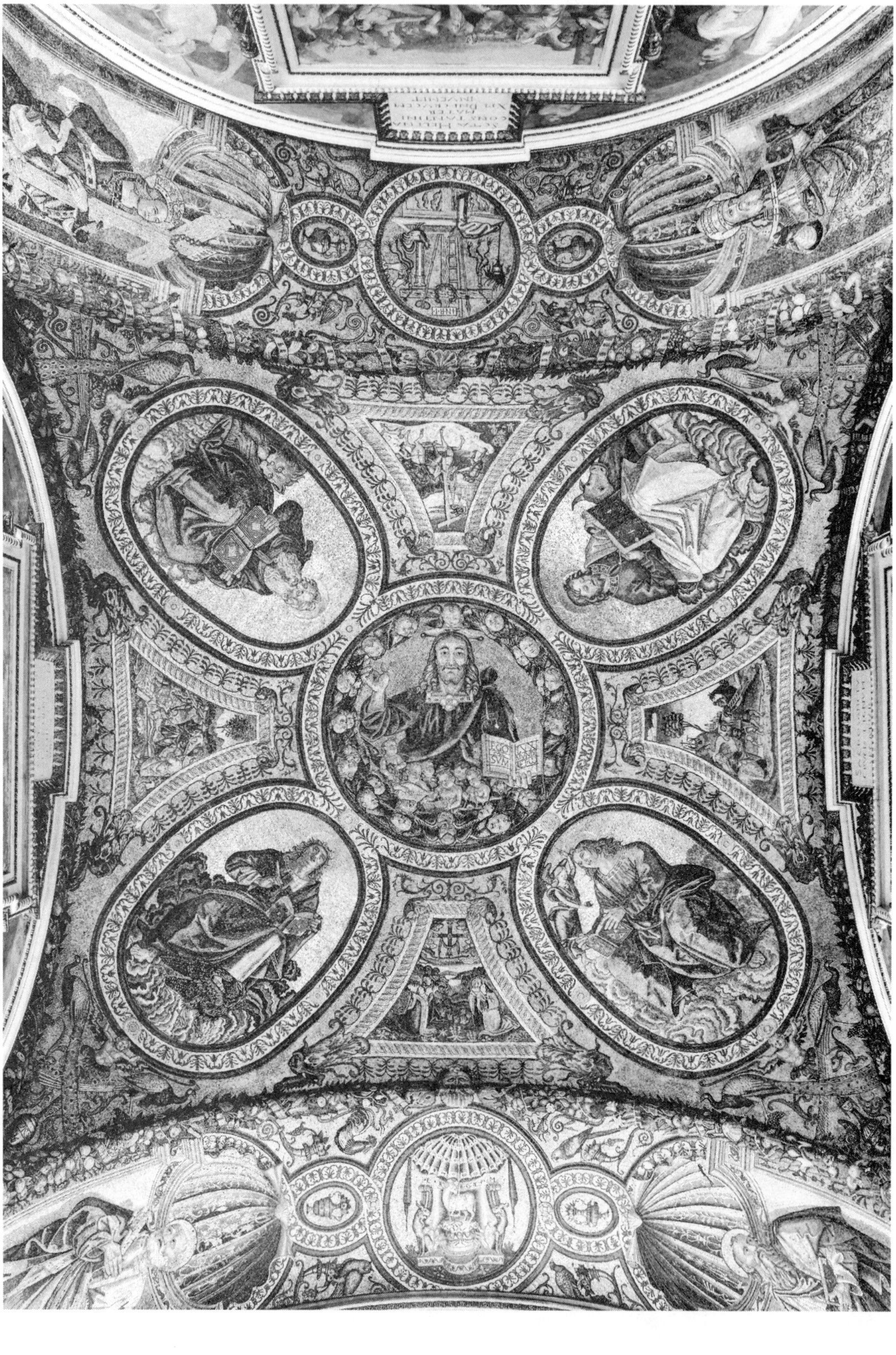

5.1 The end of time meets the new world. Helena Chapel, Santa Croce in Gerusalemme, vault, mosaic (probably before 1503).

FIVE

Utopia at the Extremities of the Earth

New World and Paradise at the End of Time

The vault of the chapel of Saint Helena in the church of Santa Croce in Gerusalemme in Rome was commissioned by the Spanish Cardinal Bernardin de Carvajal and finished probably before 1503 (fig. 5.1). It immediately gained renown as a major work in mosaic, a medium associated with the great palaces and churches of antiquity in Rome and throughout the Mediterranean.[1] There is a strong similarity between the compartmentalized organization of the vault in the Helena chapel and that of the Raphael-designed ceiling of the Stanza della Segnatura, discussed in chapter 4, which was begun in 1508. Although the ceiling of the Stanza della Segnatura is painted, its backgrounds simulate the tesserae of mosaic, suggesting that the model of the Helena chapel vault was almost immediately imitated or at least rivaled.[2]

The Helena Chapel vault's program is a treatise on the dissemination of the Christian message and of Christian dominion over the world. A half-length portrait of a blessing and beatifically smiling Christ surrounded by angels occupies the center. Radiating diagonally from the central roundel are the four Evangelists, figuring the spreading of Christ's message. Between the Evangelists' compartments are four scenes that tell the history of the relic of the cross after Christ's crucifixion: its loss immediately after the removal of Christ's body, its excavation by Helena in Jerusalem three centuries later and the testing of its authenticity, the return of the cross to Jerusalem by Heraclius in the seventh century, and then a scene of the Exaltation of the Cross at the end of time. Pieces of the cross were held in this very chapel, which had been (so legend had it) a room occupied by the early fourth-century empress Helena in a palace built by her son Constantine, the first Christian emperor. A majolica inscription placed in the corridor leading to the chapel, installed by the same patron, Cardinal Carvajal, explains that Helena had placed in this chapel various relics of the Passion besides those of the cross, giving the

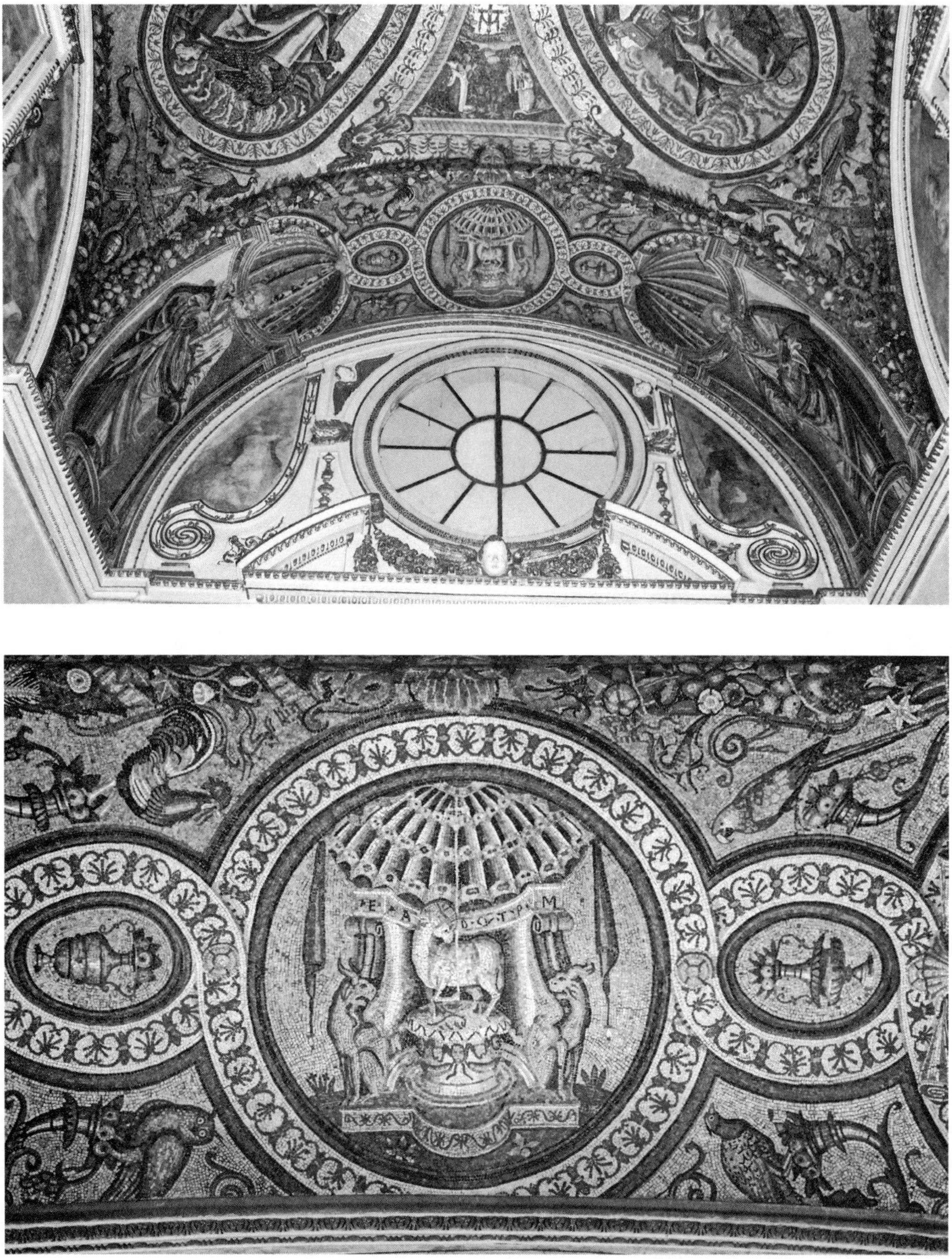

5.2a–b The arch over the altar, with elements from the new world, and the apocalyptic lamb standing over the four rivers of paradise. Helena Chapel, Santa Croce in Gerusalemme, vault, mosaic (probably before 1503).

church that was eventually built on this site the name of Santa Croce in Gerusalemme. Grounding the various relics placed in this room/chapel was a large quantity of soil alleged to be from the site of the crucifixion—earth "soaked with the blood of Christ," says the inscription—that Helena had transported to Rome from Jerusalem. The floor of the chapel was thus a literal tract of the holy land in Rome. For pilgrims, this was the site in Rome most identified with Jerusalem and in common parlance was known as Chapel Jerusalem.

On either side of the central vault are two barrel vaults, also decorated in mosaic, one carrying images of Helena and of Sylvester, the pope reigning in Helena's and her son Constantine's day, flanking a composite image of the various symbols of the Passion, and the other, directly above the chapel's altar, showing Saints Peter and Paul, the Apostle martyrs who brought the Christian religion to Rome, flanking a scene of the apocalyptic lamb flanked by lions on an altar from which flow the four rivers of paradise.[3] Above the lamb are the letters E.A.D.Q.T.P.M, an anagram for *Ecce Agnus Dei Qui Tollit Peccata Mundi:* behold the lamb of God who removes the sins of the world (fig. 5.2a–b). The mosaic program thus marks out almost the full extent of the known world, from paradise to Rome in the Mediterranean. The idea is traditional, but now, in the early sixteenth century, the extent of the world has been expanded, and that expansion was being understood in apocalyptic terms. As we saw in chapter 2, Christopher Columbus, amazed by the force of the Orinoco River on his third voyage, believed that such a river could only have come from a great height, and that its source must be paradise, not far inland, and Amerigo Vespucci, in Brazil, land of the parrots, also imagined paradise could not be far away.

In the Helena Chapel, we see in the vicinity of paradise some of the earliest representations of flora and fauna from the new world, connecting them to the old. On the barrel vault near the lamb and across from a peacock we see an American macaw, and among the fruits collected together in the mosaic pergola decorating the vault we see pineapples and new world maize, rising up close to the parrot's tail.[4] Probably based on study of a living specimen, the Helena Chapel's scarlet macaw, native to South America, translates the bird's brightly colored feathers into an astonishingly faithful tessellation of white, yellow, red, and blue pieces of glass and stone (fig. 5.3). One single row of lapis lazuli cubes forms the characteristic long blue feather along the edge of the parrot's tail. The person who placed this bird before the artist was most likely the cardinal funding the decoration, Cardinal Carvajal, who was in a position to receive such a specimen.

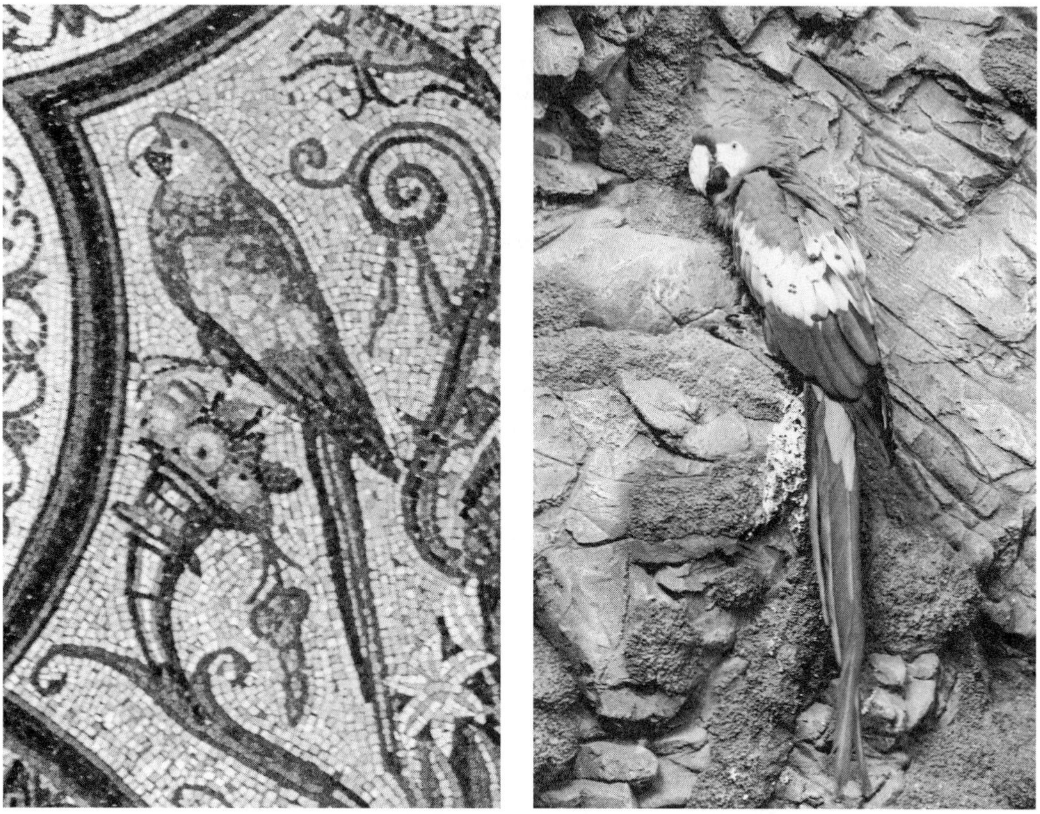

5.3 An American macaw near paradise. Helena Chapel, Santa Croce in Gerusalemme, vault, mosaic (probably before 1503), detail of 5.2a–b, scarlet macaw, and a living specimen.

Carvajal was one of the earliest recipients of letters on the new world voyages written by Peter Martyr d'Anghiera, an Italian humanist residing in Spain who established himself in the 1490s and early 1500s as one of the foremost chroniclers of the recent discoveries. As early as 1493, as we saw in chapter 2, Martyr had written: "The parrots brought from there and many other things show that these islands taste of the soil of India, either because of their proximity or because of their natural properties."[5] Colorful parrots were signs of tropical life and strongly suggested Far Eastern derivation.

Near the parrot, at the springing of the vault next to the figure of Saint Paul, we see ears of maize (fig. 5.4). Modern botanists have determined that this was a new world crop hitherto unknown to Europeans. The best-informed sources of the sixteenth century, however, understood maize as an Asian variety of grain. The Spanish naturalist Gonzalo Fernández de Oviedo identified the maize he himself had seen cultivated

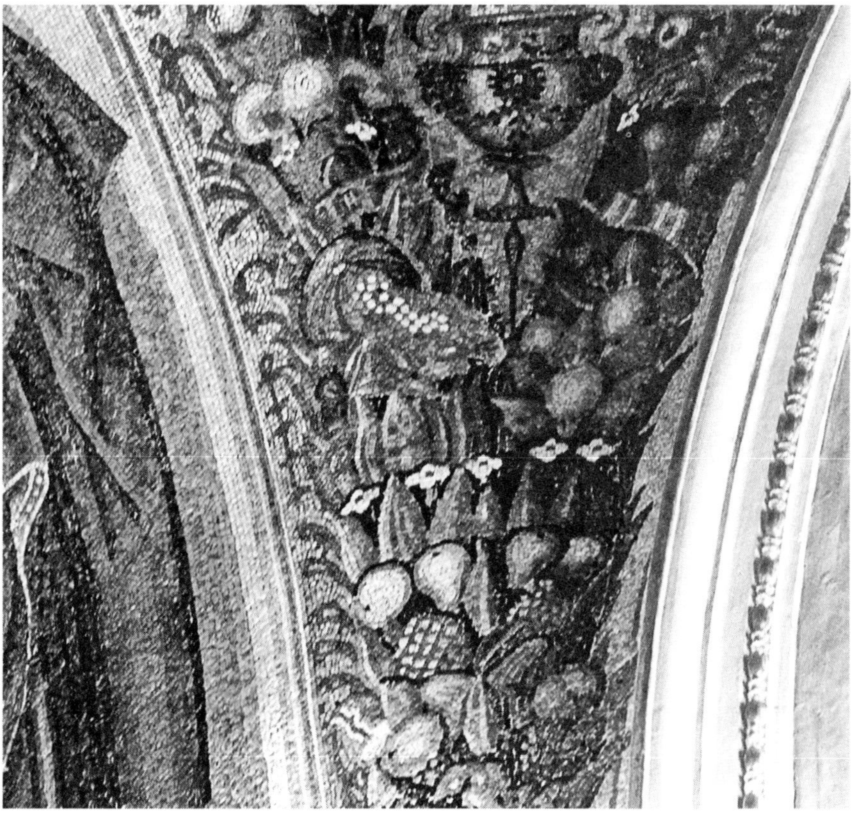

5.4 Maize and pineapples flourish near paradise. Helena Chapel, Santa Croce in Gerusalemme, vault, mosaic (probably before 1503), detail of 5.2a–b, of springing of the vault.

in Mexico with the millet of India described by Pliny, pointing to the correspondence of color, size, propagation capacity, and the shared climatic conditions preferred by the crops.[6] Following suit, treatises throughout the sixteenth century described maize as an Asiatic or Turkish grain: *Triticum bastianum Plinii*, *Milico indico pliniano*, *Frumentum turcicum*, *Tritticum turcianum*, *Frumentum asiaticum* (fig. 5.5).[7] The elements of the Amerasian new world on this vault "taste of India" but also go beyond what was known of Asia. In 1496, Martyr wrote directly to Cardinal Carvajal himself, the Helena Chapel's patron, about Columbus's second voyage, pointing to evidence that the navigator's "new world" extended from the outer reaches of Asia to the unknown: "Our Admiral Columbus brought from the new world's shores which he traveled southward, six degrees from the equator, great many necklaces of oriental pearls; he thinks that these regions are contiguous and border Cuba. And so, since both would be of the same continent as India of the Ganges, he sailed on for many days also

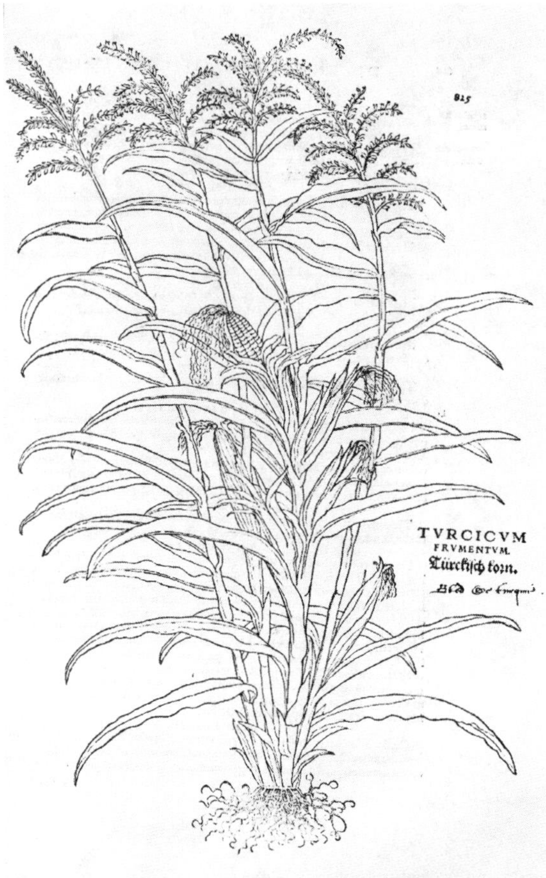

5.5 An accurate rendering of maize is labeled *Turcicum frumentum*, or Turkish grain. Woodcut on paper. Leonhart Fuchs, *De Historia Stirpium Commentarii Insignes* (Basel, 1542).

along these shores and confesses of not seeing either the end nor any clue of the end of this land."[8]

Beyond representing Christ, the Evangelists, two Apostles, Saints Helena and Sylvester, and various scenes from the history of the cross relic, Cardinal Carvajal's vault in the Helena Chapel figures and thus completes the time of human history. The Christ at the center figures the second coming, directly below him is the image of the Exaltation of the Cross at the end of time, and directly below that is the apocalyptic lamb. The new world is also old, a temporal Alpha Omega. Its discovery was not merely a great achievement, though it was certainly celebrated as such throughout Europe; for many, including this chapel's patron, it was a signal that history was coming to its culmination and the end times were at hand. Cardinal Carvajal, a primary candidate for the papal throne in the early sixteenth century, gave a sermon in 1508 before Emperor Maximilian I (grandfather of Charles V and his precursor as Holy Roman Emperor) in which he presented the recent victories of the Portuguese and the Spanish as a sign that the ultimate fulfillment of history in Christian victory was within grasp.[9] This victory, a temporal and geographical closing of the circle, is visualized in the mosaic vault of the Helena Chapel, where it comes to a head in the area around the apocalyptic lamb, surrounded by exotic flora and fauna.

The pineapples represented in and among the ears of maize on the Helena Chapel vault were widely celebrated as a fruit utterly new to the eyes of Europeans. There was simply no relation to old world flora, only comparisons of form, which led Columbus to call it *piña* for its visual resemblance to a pinecone. The naturalist Oviedo speaks of it in glowing terms, claiming that for its visual beauty, gentleness of scent, and excellent flavor there "was no equal to it anywhere in the world."[10] Although the mosaic gives an "Indian" atmosphere to the zone near paradise, that does not mean every detail corresponds to previously known Asian features. The earthly paradise, traditionally located in the easternmost part of the earth, had been visited by no traveler, and so might well contain surprises beyond the known world.[11] Amerasia was by its nature a composite of old and new, made up of Asian features together with a quantum of the previously unknown—a new variety of Asian grain called maize, parrots of a size never before seen, or the completely new pineapple, surpassing any known fruit. The mosaic of the Helena Chapel is designed to lead the viewer from a world already known and a historical trajectory already traveled to a reality never before seen and ultimately (in the Christ of the Second Coming) beyond time and space. At the end of time we return not to the earthly paradise but to its heavenly prototype and successor.

Amerasian Utopia

Beyond generating reports about new and old places and the relations among them, the Amerasian new world reached Europe as the promise of an ultimate knowledge, a knowledge of the full rotundity of the earth, revealing finally the configuration of the world and thus the shape of historical time. The maximally distant, and the related idea of a zone where East meets West, were by definition antipodean ideas, mobilizing oppositional relationships. These were not merely faraway and different places but alternate worlds in which Europe could see itself mirrored and possibly inverted and thus acquire new bearings for its own place in the world and in history. Thomas More's *Utopia*, published in 1516, delivered a report from the other side of the world that offered an antipodean mirror to Europe's mores and institutions. The dialogue informs us that the Utopians call Europeans "Ultraequatorials," since Europe is on the other side of the world in terms not only of longitude but of latitude. The narrator, one Raphael Hythlodaeus (Greek for "professor of nonsense"), explains that he was a mariner left behind from Vespucci's final voyage in the land Vespucci's most famous letter had called a *mundus novus* (see chapter 2). He then traveled westward from there, eventually landing on the island of Utopia, where they worship Mithras and speak a language not far from Persian. The island of Utopia is thus located toward Asia from Brazil; otherwise it is unlocatable.[12] Hovering between America and Asia, it can assume a literally utopian (literally, no-place) position, the better to serve as a space of reflection for Europeans considering and reconsidering their own institutions and histories. A map of the island, without coordinates that might set it into relation to the rest of the world, formed the frontispiece of the book (fig. 5.6).

On the facing page is an explanation of the Utopian alphabet and language. Verses in the Utopian language, transliterated word by word into Latin letters, and then translated for meaning, read:

> The commander Utopus out of a non-island made me an island.
> I alone of all lands, without philosophy,
> have figured for mortals the philosophical city.
> Freely I impart my benefits; without reluctance I accept what is better.

In the transliteration from Utopian, the words are all unknown, and nyone reading them aloud makes unrecognizable sounds, with two significant exceptions. The Utopians pronounce the words "philosophy" and "philosophical" *gymnosophaon* and *gymnosophon*, summoning the *gumnosophistai,* or "naked philosophers" of India, described by Plutarch, Strabo, Philo, Clement of Alexandria, and other ancient Greek sources known to More.[13] Alexander the Great was reported in various histories to have encountered Brahmins in Taxila who lived together in a commonwealth of virtue.[14] As Donald Lach summarizes, More's Utopia "can be seen as an effort to reproduce from classical, medieval, and contemporary sources an ideal society similar to but more credible than the serene and sinless world of the Gymnosophists [of India]."[15] Right at the outset of the book, even before the account begins, the first description of More's *Utopia* associates it with the society of the wise men of India known since antiquity.

Beyond its Asian references, More's Utopia is also marked as a new world phenomenon in the tract's very title, which calls it *nova insula Utopia.* The island and its society were not new, having been founded long ago by Utopus, who in a remarkable feat of engineering removed natural land bridges that connected what was originally a peninsula to the mainland, thus producing an island out of a non-island. And yet it is marked as new. In this tidy allegory of the malleability of geography in human

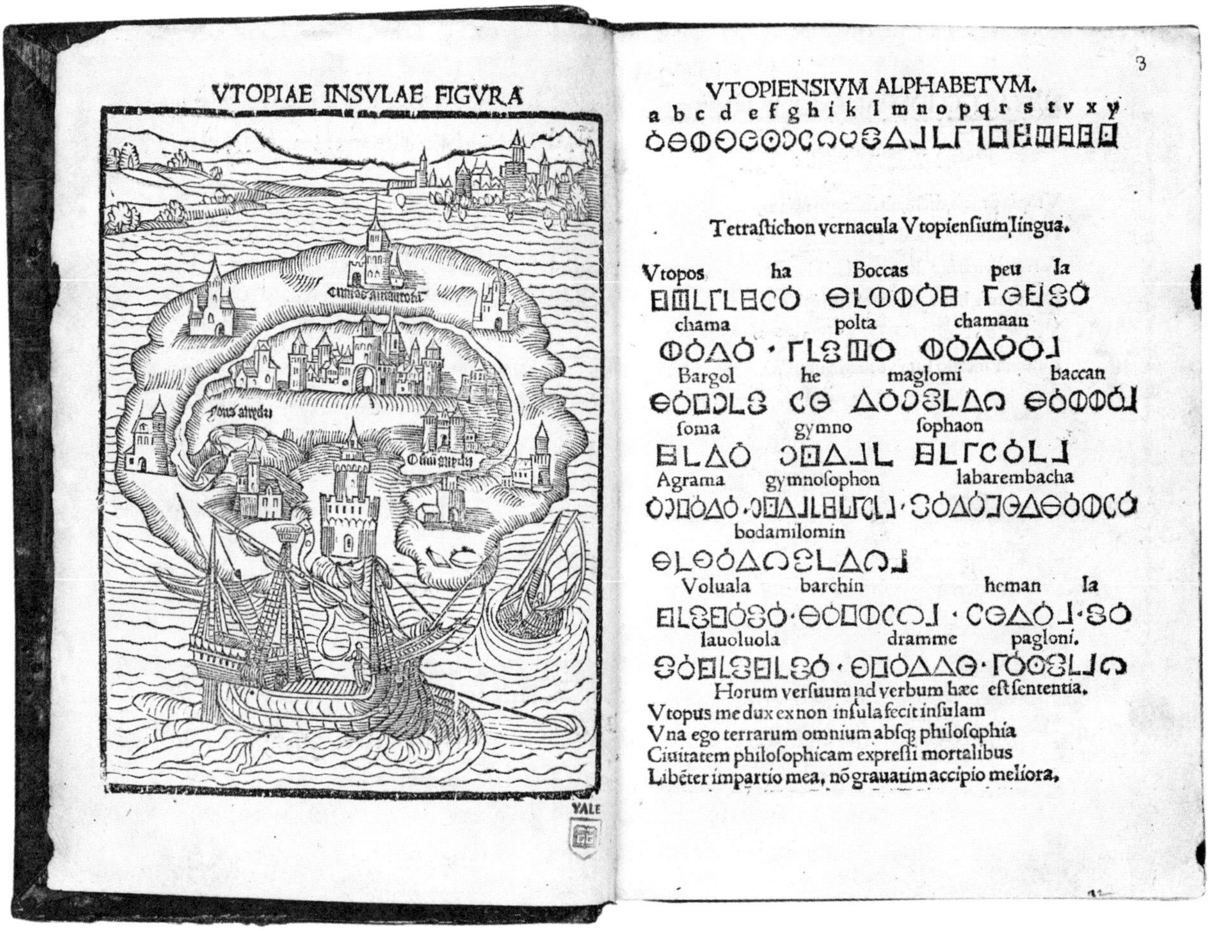

5.6 The location of the island of Utopia, floating somewhere between Brazil and India and Persia, remains unclear. Woodcut and type on paper. Thomas More, *Libellus vere aureus nec minus salutaris quam festivus de optimo reip. statu deq; nova insula Utopia*, frontispiece, woodcut (Louvain, 1516).

hands, More reflects an evident dynamic of the geographical imagination of his time, which was constantly redrawing the relation between water and landmasses, visualizing new islands or identifying them with ancient Asian ones, sometimes carving islands off from mainlands, as in the case of Florida, Yucatán, and California, or attaching them, as in the case of Cuba or indeed America itself (see chapters 2, 8, and 11). Thus, the *nova insula Utopia* of More's title recognized its layered newness—geologically new, newly discovered, and newly imagined. Its status as an island, emblematized in the frontispiece and elaborated in the text, powerfully contributed to an emergent discourse that imagined the new world as a galaxy of islands (see chapters 6 and 8).

The fact that the narrator Raphael identifies himself as one of the men left behind in Brazil by Vespucci concretizes the connection to new world description and mapping. Martin Waldseemüller's 1507 map, which named America after Amerigo Vespucci, came packaged together with an accompanying *Introduction to Cosmography*, probably authored in part by Waldseemüller's collaborator the humanist Matthias Ringmann, in which Vespucci's so-called *Letter to Soderini* is included in its entirety. It was probably Ringmann's idea to name the new landmass America after Vespucci, and also for the wordplay that it offered: "I do not see why anyone should rightly prevent this [part] from being called Amerigen—the land of Amerigo, as it were—or America, after its discoverer, Americus, a man of keen temperament, since both Europe and Asia received their names from women."[16] But there is more to it than a reference to the famous navigator. *Ge* means "earth" and *meros* means "place" in Greek, so *A-merigen* can translate as no-place-land, a suitable name for a place whose location and relation to the rest of the world was as yet undetermined.[17] It is very likely More knew Waldseemüller and Ringmann's *Introduction to Cosmography*.

Vespucci's *Letter to Soderini,* inserted into the *Introduction to Cosmography,* is in fact the Vespucci-related document that most clearly anticipates More's *Utopia* in depicting a society that inverts European institutions and values. Vespucci describes a people without a king or lord who "live in their own liberty," noting that they have no judicial system or system of punishment—yet "rarely or never did we observe a quarrel among them." They appear to speak simply yet "are very cunning and clever in the matters that concern them." Above all, Vespucci describes a society blissfully free of the notion of wealth that burdens European civilization:

> Their wealth consists of birds' feathers of many colors, and strands of beads they make out of fish bones or white and green stones, which they hang from

> their cheeks and from their lips and ears, and many other things which we do not value at all. They do not engage in commerce, neither buying nor selling; in short, they live and content themselves with whatever nature gives them. The wealth to which we are accustomed in this Europe of ours and in other parts, such as gold, jewels, pearls, and other riches, are of no interest to them, although they have them in their lands, they neither labor to procure them, nor prize them.[18]

Vespucci's account certainly differs in details from the Utopian state as described by More, which although without a king certainly has a judicial system, and whose citizens can hardly be described as simple. Yet, even so, More's narrator insists that there is very little crime and punishment on Utopia, and describes inhabitants who are simple in the sense that their minds and social relations are admirably free of complication and conflict. Above all, like the society described by Vespucci, Utopia is remarkable for the absence of a notion of private property and for its lack of interest in gold. Inspired by the early reception and cartographic elaboration of reports from the lands discovered to the west that had been famously and resonantly named *Amerigen* by Waldseemüller and Ringmann, More drew from them the fundamental idea that the Amerasian new world offered an antipodean contrast and correction to the gold-and-possession-obsessed, and thus litigious and conflict-ridden, culture of Europe.

More's *Utopia* charts a continuity between the gymnosophists of India and Vespucci's new world, presenting Utopia as the Amerasian island par excellence, a mirror to Europe from the other side of the world. More's narrator describes a community that worships Mithras and speaks a language not far from Persian, clearly Asian features, yet the imprint of the newly discovered Amerigen-America is also strong. The priests of Utopia, we learn, wear "multi-coloured vestments, magnificent in workmanship and design," but rather than being woven in gold or with rare gems, as Europeans might expect of liturgical robes, "they're merely decorated with the feathers of various birds." So great is their workmanship, however, that their value is "far greater than that of the richest material in the world. Besides, the feathers are arranged in special patterns which are said to symbolize certain divine truths, and the priests are careful to teach the meaning of these hieroglyphics."[19] There is no question that More had knowledge of the feather garments from Brazil, for earlier in the dialogue Peter Gilles invokes Vespucci's letters, and in Vespucci's letter to Soderini, the very one reprinted by Waldseemüller and Ringmann in their *Introduction to Cosmography* of 1507, he says of the inhabitants of Brazil that "their wealth consists of birds' feathers of many colors," as we saw earlier.[20] More wove such accounts into his image of a Utopian society that prizes ingenuity over the glitter that counts for wealth in Europe. Like other texts and images of the period, More's *Utopia* adapts the feather garments of the Native populations encountered by both Columbus and Vespucci into features of an expanded Asian iconography.

Entangled Amerasian Iconographies

Almost immediately, European reports and images attached the particular forms of feather ornament found in the western islands and Brazil to depictions of Asian people, creating an entangled Amerasian imagery that was to last well over a century. For example, in woodcuts by Jörg Breu that accompanied the 1515 German publication of Ludovico Varthema's account of his (real) travels in India and beyond, the inhabitants of Sumatra are shown wearing feather headdresses and carrying clubs of the sort first encountered among the Tupi people of Brazil (fig. 5.7). The spread of such iconography reinforced the idea of an Amerasian new world extending from the known parts of Asia to the newly discovered lands across the ocean to the west. Six years before Ferdinand Magellan's voyage around the world, More's *Utopia* depicted a (non)place that connected Vespucci and Varthema's real voyages to the west and to the east.

The idea that the farthest reaches of the world meet in a joining of America and Asia is put on spectacular display in the final three woodcuts made by Hans Burgkmair in the late 1510s for a vast procession of 139 woodcuts representing the peoples of the world as they come to pay homage to the Holy Roman Emperor Maximilian I (fig. 5.8a–c). Far from being generic depictions of exotic foreigners, the last three woodcuts in the series represent the tail end of a clearly organized and labeled procession of all the known populations in the world. Concluding the procession, these three scenes bring into view the inhabitants of the remotest lands, the lands of India—the "people of Calicut," as Maximilian himself describes them in his instructions for the series.[21]

The first of the three woodcuts shows an elephant ridden by an Indian from Calicut, who wears a turban, followed by five Indian warriors with long hair wearing loincloths, perhaps meant to depict dhotis (fig. 5.8a). The second woodcut shows more male warriors, led by a long-haired and dhoti-clad Brahmanic figure holding a lance, perhaps a wise man or gymnosophist, followed by soldiers wearing feather headdresses and feather skirts and wielding clubs of a sort observed and collected by travelers to Brazil (fig. 5.8b; see also fig. 2.3, the famous broadsheet by Froschauer). Already in the 1515 woodcut by Breu illustrating Sumatrans encountered by Varthema, just discussed, these feather ornaments were transferred to Asian

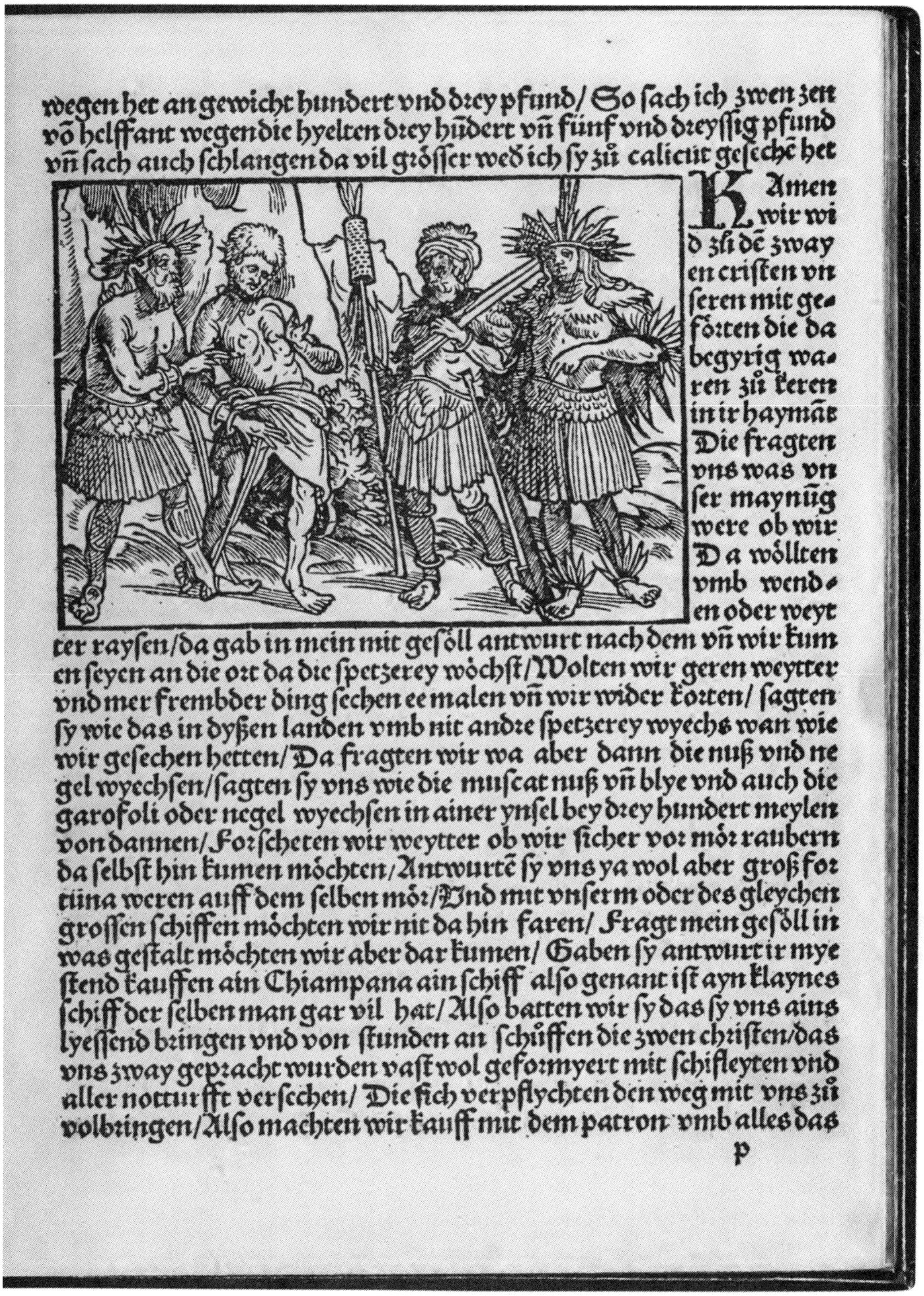

wegen het an gewicht hundert vnd drey pfund/ So sach ich zwen zen vō helffant wegen die hyelten drey hūdert vñ fünf vnd dreyssig pfund vñ sach auch schlangen da vil grösser wed ich sy zů calicut gesechē het

Kamen wir wider zů dē zwayen cristen vnseren mit geförten die da begyrig waren zů keren in ir haymāt Die fragten vns was vnser maynūg were ob wir Da wöllten vmb wenden oder weytter raysen/ da gab in mein mit gesöll antwurt nach dem vñ wir kumen seyen an die ort da die spetzerey wöchst/ Wolten wir geren weytter vnd mer frembder ding sechen ee malen vñ wir wider korten/ sagten sy wie das in dyßen landen vmb nit andre spetzerey wyechs wan wie wir gesechen hetten/ Da fragten wir wa aber dann die nuß vnd negel wyechsen/ sagten sy vns wie die muscat nuß vñ blye vnd auch die garofoli oder negel wyechsen in ainer ynsel bey drey hundert meylen von dannen/ Forscheten wir weytter ob wir sicher vor mör raubern da selbst hin kumen möchten/ Antwurtē sy vns ya wol aber groß fortūna weren auff dem selben mör/ Vnd mit vnserm oder des gleychen grossen schiffen möchten wir nit da hin faren/ Fragt mein gesöll in was gestalt möchten wir aber dar kumen/ Gaben sy antwurt ir myestend kauffen ain Chiampana ain schiff also genant ist ayn klaynes schiff der selben man gar vil hat/ Also batten wir sy das sy vns ains lyessend bringen vnd von stunden an schůffen die zwen christen/ das vns zway geprächt wurden vast wol geformyert mit schifleyten vnd aller notturfft versechen/ Die sich verpflychten den weg mit vns zů volbringen/ Also machten wir kauff mit dem patron vmb alles das

p

5.7 Brazilian Tupi feathers and weapons on Sumatra. Woodcut and type on paper. Jörg Breu, "Inhabitants of Sumatra," in Ludovico Varthema, *Die ritterlich uñ lobwirdig Rayss* (Augsburg, 1515). Providence, RI, John Carter Brown Library.

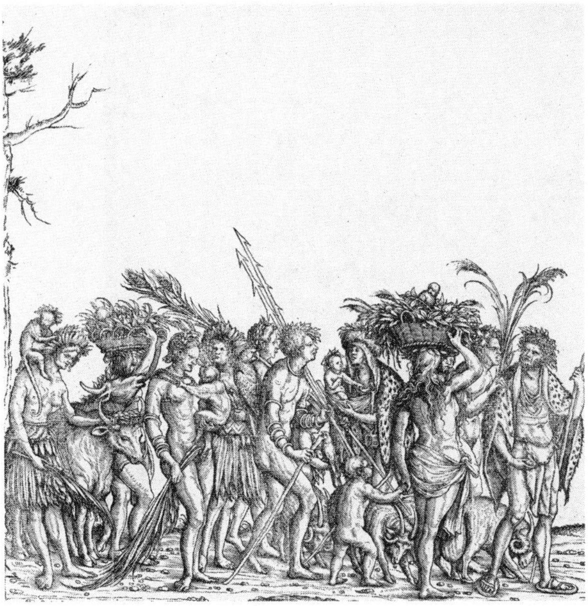

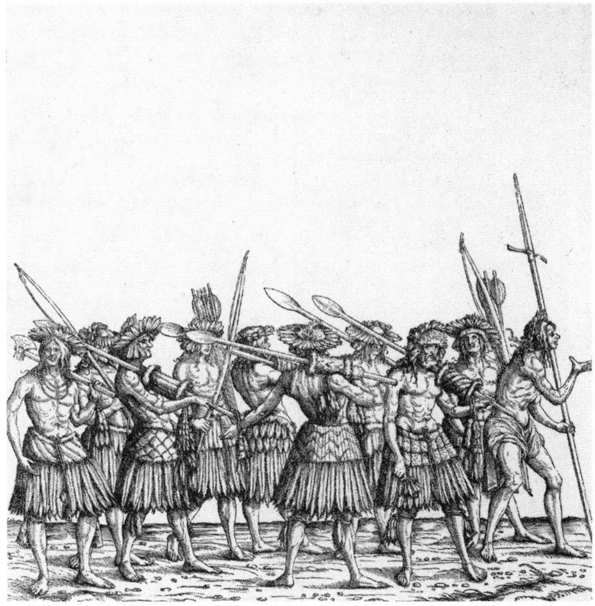

populations encountered by traveling east. This entangled Amerasian iconography soon became irreversible and indeed grew only more imbricated throughout the sixteenth and seventeenth centuries (see chapters 12 and 17). In Burgkmair's procession, the feather-clad warriors clearly come as an extension of Indian peoples, marking the easternmost extremities of the territory known as India beyond the Ganges (see chapter 1). The warriors are followed by the final scene of the entire 139 in the series, which represents the people of Calicut more broadly, shaggy-haired men and women either naked or barely dressed, several wearing animal skin (fig. 5.8c). Some of them wear feather headdresses, and one of them hoists ears of maize. More than one parrot appears in the scene—American or Indian, or both.

Burgkmair's procession shows a mingling of American and Asian features, all encompassed by the notion of the "people of Calicut." As Christian Feest explains, "Calicut was then thought to be a place which could be reached by sailing either to the east or to the west."[22] Rather than call this a confusion, as if one thing has been mistaken for another, the very structure of Burgkmair's parade of the peoples from the farthest reaches of the world offers an alternative and more helpful modeling of these relationships, a model of extension. The three scenes of the people of Calicut figure a lateral extension across a tropical zone connecting the Indians of America and Asia into a continuum. As the final "embassy" of the peoples of the world, the people of Calicut represent the extremities of the world,

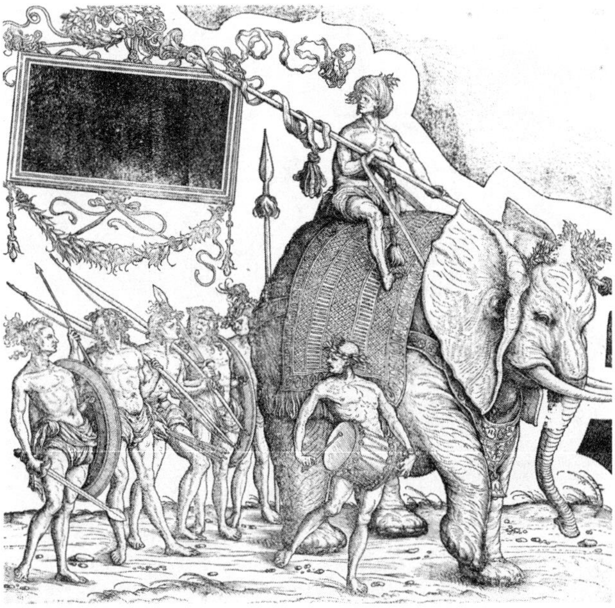

5.8a–c The "people of Calicut" figure a tropical Amerasian extension. Hans Burgkmair the Elder, *People of Calicut*, from *The Triumphal Procession of Emperor Maximilian I*, woodcut on paper, 38 × 38 cm (designed 1516–18); (a–b) from the second edition, 1777, Vienna, Albertina Museum, (c) from the first printed edition, 1526, London, Victoria and Albert Museum.

and also a return to a beginning, a golden age civilization of simplicity and natural abundance, made evident by the teeming harvests, animals, and people carrying offspring in the final scene.

The New-Old World

The golden-age quality of the new world—new, fertile, abundant, simple, revealing humanity still at its beginnings—introduced a temporal element into the antipodal contraposition with the "old" world. It is not so much that one is cast as old and the other as new, but that the terms continually flip as they interact, since the old world emerges through this encounter as modern—advanced and thus both recent and belated, beset by a thirst for resources that drives greed and conflict—whereas the new world emerges as old in the sense of primordial, archaic, a resetting of the world clock back to its golden-age beginnings.[23] In his 1521 Italian translation of the treatise on architecture by the ancient architect Vitruvius, the Milanese Cesare Cesariano illustrates Vitruvius's famous account of the beginnings of human civilization, the discovery of fire and the first dwellings, with woodcut illustrations that bear a strong family resemblance to early depictions of the new world and its naked inhabitants (fig. 5.9). And in fact, Cesariano glosses the description of these early humans by comparing them not only to the Troglodites described by Pliny but also to "the new peoples discovered in the islands of Tabrobane or Calicut by

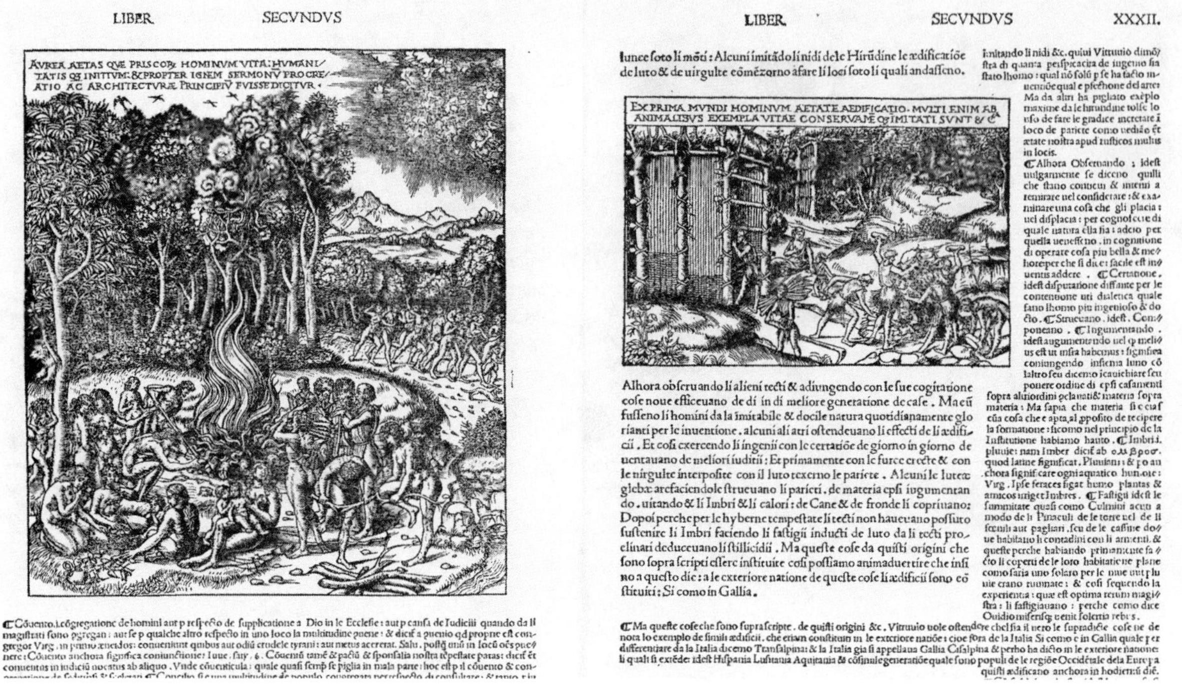

5.9 Vitruvius's description of the first human societies and dwellings, with imagery drawn from reports of new worlds East and West. Cesare Cesariano, *Di Lucio Vitruuio Pollione De architectura libri dece* (Como, 1521), fols. XXXIv–XXXIIr. Woodcut and type on paper.

the navigators of the Spanish king similar to those discovered by the Portuguese king, from which places have been drawn infinite riches of great value and delight and other useful things for our human Christian political life."[24] The switching of the destinations of the Spanish and Portuguese expedition is commonly seen in period responses, as is the idea that the peoples in the two places were "similar."

Cesariano's description and the accompanying illustrations of the first humans and their dwellings correspond fairly well to the account of Pedro Álvares Cabral's voyage to India, discussed in chapter 3, where the inhabitants are said to live in dwellings made of wood, "covered with leaves and branches of trees, with many wooden columns. In the middle of the said houses and from the said columns to the wall they hang a net of cotton, which holds a man. And between the nets they make a fire."[25] It is likely that Cesariano derived his vision of first humanity from such accounts, perhaps from this very description of the Cabral voyage, available to him in Italian translation in the widely distributed *Paesi novamente retrovati* (which was reprinted, after the Vicentine 1507 edition, in Cesariano's city of Milan in editions of 1508, 1512, and 1519.)[26] Cesariano's accompanying woodcut illustrations show the houses of wood covered in thatch, the fire (though not inside the houses), and, sure enough, in one of the houses in the distance we find a woman nursing her child, sitting with one leg crossed over the other on a hammock. The hammock, a netted hanging bed described by Cabral and Vespucci in Brazil, was soon to become a defining attribute of the new world. For modern scholars, it is clear that the Cabral account is describing inhabitants of Brazil, but contemporary readers were presented with it as one stop on a voyage to India, and would have had little sense of how the route mapped geographically. Cesariano himself does not appear to draw clear distinctions between the islands discovered by the Spanish and Portuguese, calling all the newly encountered people *novi popolazioni*.

As discussed in chapter 3, prevailing notions of historical time since Aristotle had associated eastern territories and generally Asia with the beginning of the human story on earth, whose origin was identified by Christian commentators as paradise in the easternmost part of the earth, and whose history then tracked a movement westward over the course of time. Europe thus understood its own entry onto the world stage as the latest phase of human history and the discovery of a new world to the west that ultimately joins with Asia as a culmination and conclusion of history itself. On this model of temporal geographics, the Amerasian new world is characterized by the paradoxical quality of being the oldest and newest of places, older and newer than Europe. As Thomas More's narrator says of the island of Utopia toward the end of book 1: "There were cities there before there were people here [in Europe]." In the European Utopian discourse that followed More, this combination of old and new is occasionally literalized, as when Tommaso Campanella in *City of the Sun* (1602), Francis Bacon in *New Atlantis* (published posthumously in 1627), and Margaret Cavendish in *The Blazing World* (1666) describe the inhabitants of their respective Utopias treating themselves with a special balm or bath that initiates a process of rejuvenation.[27] The new world and its inhabitants are both ancient (a return to some form of antiquity) and recent (newly discovered, but also new in the sense of innocent or primal), both late and early, both old and young, and occasionally they enact in their own bodies the return from old to young. Europe is configured by this encounter as middling, neither ancient nor new, and in this sense by nature undefined and restless, seeking definition through encounter and insatiably curious about both the ancient and the new.

The island of Utopia, a discovery of the recent voyages, is meant to offer Europe a lesson and a correction of its abuses, corruption, and injustices, before it was too late. It offers a counter to the evident fact that the new world voyages had been motivated in the first place by greed and desire for conquest. The newly discovered lands allow Utopia to come into view, stabilizing for a moment a fragile possibility of self-reflection and reform. But soon enough the forces driving the whole process would bring about what the Spanish friar Bartolomé de Las Casas was to call "the destruction of the Indies." In the following decades, More's *Utopia* came to haunt accounts of the actual colonization and conversion of the Native populations, but rather than the discovery of a Utopia that could stand as a mirror to Europe, now we are presented with accounts of Utopia torn apart by the depredations of the Europeans. In a 1541 tract entitled *Folly* (*La pazzia*), attributed by some modern scholars to Ortensio Lando, the first translator of More's *Utopia* into vernacular Italian, the *indie occidentali* are presented as an example of a society that was happy "without laws, without letters, without wise men, valuing neither gold nor jewels, not knowing greed or ambition or any art, nourishing themselves on the fruits that the earth produced without cultivation, having as in Plato's Republic all things in common . . . just as in that fortunate and truly golden age of Saturn in ancient times," a golden age that was then "interrupted and disturbed by the ambitious and avaricious Spaniards, who, arriving in those regions . . . have filled these people with a thousand kinds of troubles and evils."[28]

If there was to be a new world Utopia, now it would have to be deliberately constructed out of the reality of the encounter of Europeans and Native populations. For the reformer Vasco de Quiroga, writing from Mexico in 1535, Thomas More had done nothing other than prophesy the existence of the communities he was working with in Michoacán, who did not know greed and cared little for superfluities: "They are pure and prudent and most simple; they look at us in amazement when they see our restlessness and anxiety."[29] Without having seen it, Quiroga affirms, "[More] puts it there, depicts it, and describes it in such manner as makes me admire it repeatedly. Because it seems to me it is as if by revelation of the Holy Spirit suited to the order that would be convenient and necessary for this New Spain and New World."[30] In order for them to achieve Christian understanding, Quiroga allows, they needed the arrival of the Spaniards, but at the same time Europe and Christianity needed the new world, which "it seems God disclosed at the end of the aging Church" (*que parece Dios descrubrió fine jam senescentis Ecclesiae*). The new world is aptly named, says Quiroga, not because it was newly discovered, but "because in its people as in everything it is like that which existed in the first age, the golden age, which already by the malice and greed of our nation has become the iron age or worse."[31] Hence, it is not a matter of making these people conform to European laws and customs (such as slavery), but of adapting European laws to that of this new world and of its Native peoples. There was, of course, no question for Quiroga that the Indigenous populations needed to be Christianized and reorganized, yet it was just as important not merely to import and apply corrupt European social models.[32] His model for the new society that would be produced out of this meeting of old and new, of familiar and strange, was instead More's *Utopia*, a critique of European society from the vantage of an imagined new world ideal. Quiroga produced a translation of More's dialogue for the benefit of the Spanish governors to whom he addresses his plea.

What had remained the unstated and implicit premise in More—that Utopia did not exist but was the fictional projection of a European writer in response to reports of new worlds, written in order to provoke self-reflection by Europeans about Europe—becomes explicit in Quiroga: any utopia would now need to be deliberately constructed through the interaction of Europeans and the people or *naturales* of the new world, each adapting to the other so as to produce a tempered mixture of old and new, advanced and primary, decadent and innocent, gold and iron. This would indeed be an unprecedented reality. In the hospital city he founded at Pueblo Santa Fe, followed by others in Michoacán, Quiroga established the common holding of goods, the alternation of rural and urban work, the six-hour working day, the employment of women, the just distribution of the fruits of communal labor, the refusal of luxuries, and institutions of elective office.[33] Quiroga's efforts to create something new out of the encounter—a Christianized new world, but also a reformed and rejuvenated European culture receptive to Indigenous ways of being in the world—remained an exceptional experiment amidst the destruction of the Indies.

• • •

Coda: Hell is for White People

A painting of *Hell* in Lisbon, nearly contemporary with More's *Utopia*, offers a different kind of antipodean vision: a torrid underworld where monstrous races torture concupiscent, greedy, and gluttonous Europeans. Naked arrivals from our world tumble into the picture through a circular opening at top right, their features immediately blurred by rising heat and smoke (fig. 5.10). Below, various bodies are being put to the flames, a traditional punishment for those consumed by lust in their lifetimes. A screaming man deeper in the flames is bound to a woman, her genitals clearly on view, who is being prodded toward the flames by a bearded, hook-nosed devil with pendulous breasts and curved spikes sprouting from his armor. Under the naked couple, we see the tops of two heads,

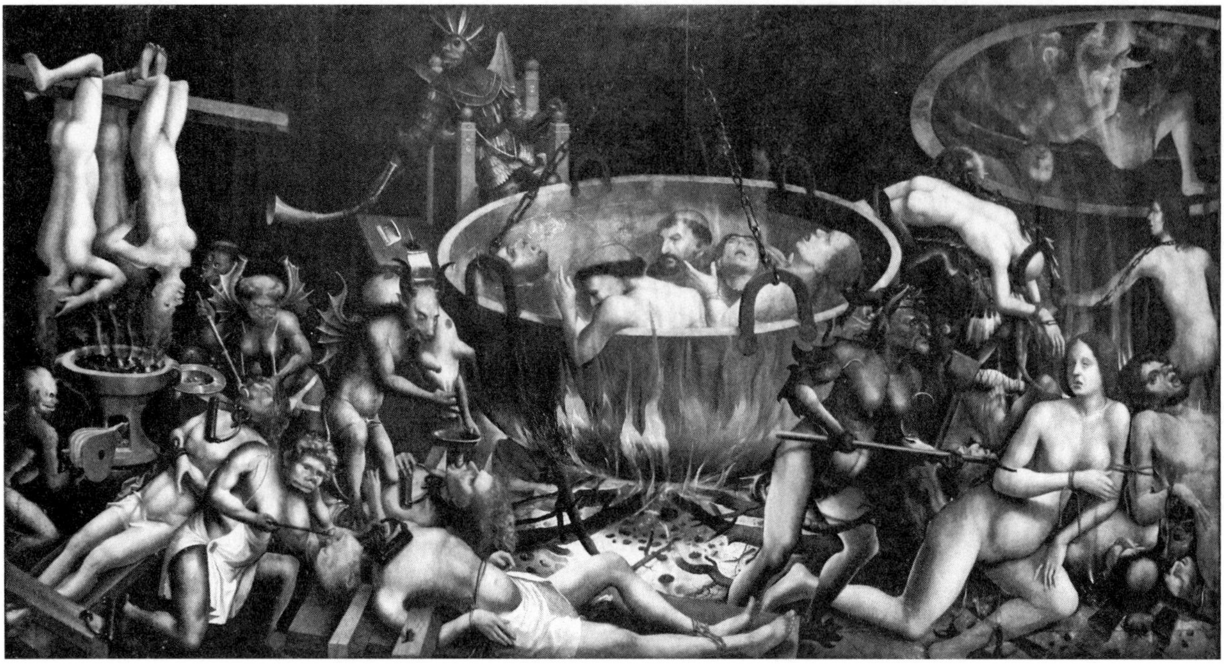

5.10 A new type of hell. Cristovão de Figueiredo (?), *Hell*, oil on panel, 119 × 217.5 cm (ca. 1515). Lisbon, Museu Nacional da Arte Antiga. Photo by Alexander Nagel. No one knows who painted this new world-informed depiction of hell, or who asked for it to be made, or even what purpose the large panel served. Several of the strange motifs—the figure with bent knee on a crutch, the pig orifice, the spurting fire, the beak-nosed figure, and the albino monster—are closely drawn from a triptych of *The Temptation of Saint Anthony* by Hieronymus Bosch that was in Portugal (probably in the Portuguese royal collection) in the early sixteenth century. The facial types resemble those of the royal painter Cristovão de Figueiredo, who died in 1525.

one of them tonsured like a monk or friar, their bodies lying flat on tinder that is catching. Between their heads, the flames coalesce into a glowing masklike figure, inviting us to bend forward to try to get a visual grasp on it—is it flame or face or mask? Above the bound couple, a demon carries one body over his shoulder and leads another by the hand, though the prisoner is already chained around the neck. Taking his two captives from the flames toward fresh tortures in the center of the picture, the demon's rodent-like face looks left, a rictus revealing sharp teeth, his backside ending in a tail, and his left leg in a cast, bent at the knee, resting on a crutch. Prosthetics come naturally to these creatures. He is covered in feather-decorated armor, or maybe the feathers just belong to him. He wears a helmet made of a ferret-like animal looking backward and apparently vomiting blood, or maybe he just has two faces, front and back.

In a cauldron at the center—matching in size the oculus at upper right, as if they were fitting pieces that have slid apart—three friars and two women languish in bubbling and steaming liquid, a traditional punishment for greed, here notably applied to three men who belong to religious orders. The basin hangs on three chains, descending from an unknown vault above; three of the five figures look up toward this height as they struggle to breathe. Below them the fire crackles, sending sparks into the air. Presiding over the scene, the devil sits on a throne possibly based on African models, his masklike face with wide-open eyes turning toward his right, our left, as does his right hand, which brandishes an ivory horn similar to ones that had already reached Portugal from West Africa.[34] The devil wears an elaborate suit of feather armor, as well as a feather headdress that strongly resembles those of the Tupi of Brazil, already famous in Europe for their reputed cannibalism, free sexuality, and open social structure, without hierarchy, marriage, or money. Around the devil's shoulder is a purse with red and white decorations, and on his left knee is a folded piece of paper, while on the table to the right is an inkwell with a pen and two paper scrolls with indecipherable writing on them, accounts of a sort that we will never understand. This devil is a foreigner, an amalgam of the peoples encountered (and dominated) on recent Portuguese voyages. But here he's in charge.

Below the table, a horned, goat-faced demon with a bird's beak for a penis and red dragon wings with black and white decorations holds a pig's skin over his shoulder, emptying some kind of powder (spices?) or liquid into a funnel placed firmly in the mouth of a prisoner with long flowing blonde hair who is shown gagging, due punishment for gluttony. Below him, another prisoner is being fed a lump of metal (gold?) by an androgynous demon with breasts and hand-like feet, wearing a sort of toga. Another victim is shown being force-fed Portuguese coins of the era, making it clear that he is not a member of generic humanity but specifically a greedy Portuguese merchant/explorer being given his due punishment (fig. 5.11).

To the left, another prisoner is being fed coins at the hands of a tonsured, bearded demon with trumpets growing out of his/her breasts, and two more trumpets serving as armature for his wings, while a ragged jockstrap fails to hold a testicle. The coins going into the prisoner's mouth are identifiable as Portuguese gold ten-cruzado coins of the period of Emmanuel I (1495–1521), with their characteristic crosses and platter-like borders inscribed with the now-ironic motto "by this sign [the cross] you shall conquer" (see fig. 3.4). Behind is a three-eyed beak-nosed demon, apparently without a body, who stares at three prisoners hanging upside down with triplicate rapt eyes (perhaps drawn from Hindu images recently

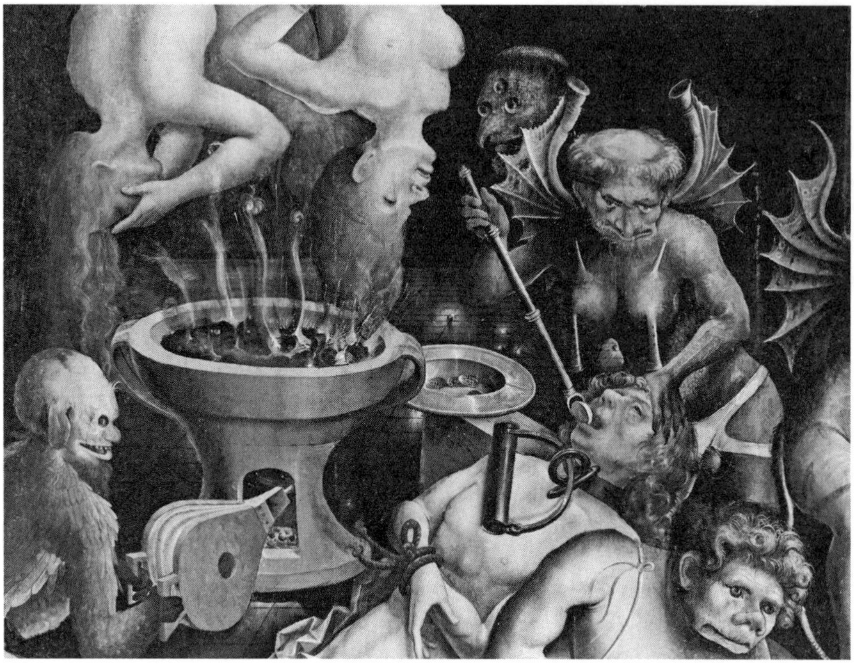

5.11 Cristovão de Figueiredo (?), *Hell*, detail of figure 5.10. (See color plates.)

encountered by Portuguese navigators?). The hair of one of the hanging women is being consumed by the fire, while another tries in vain to protect her eyes from being burned out. These women are suspended over a sort of altar with glowing fiery coals that is being stoked from below by an albino demon with a natural monochrome coat of feathers, who plies the bellows while laughing and turning truly haunting eyes toward us. Embers spit out from this altar and land on the pavement behind.

Hell is big, requiring a very large rectangular painting, one that does not fit clearly into any category of picture known at the time. It is an independent panel, not a scene in a fresco cycle that gains meaning from the larger program. Not an altarpiece nor a typical private devotional image, its oblong shape suggests it was not part of a larger structure, as in triptychs by Hieronymus Bosch and others, where hell might occupy a compartment, one part of a larger statement about human life and the world. This is a big stand-alone painting of a subject that normally did not stand alone. The painting lowers you right down to the sub-basement of hell and lets you look. The looking begins as voyeuristic fascination and then settles into self-reflection.

Does the painting demonize the peoples of Africa and America and possibly Asia by associating them with the devil's domain? Possibly. But it also shows white Europeans receiving due punishment, clearly identifying them as white Europeans. Paintings of hell made in earlier periods routinely showed people, often resembling the people for whom the paintings were made, undergoing various punishments for their sins. But this painting no longer represents generic humanity. Here, the tortured are marked as white Europeans, being punished by mostly swarthy monsters with distinctly exotic trappings drawn from the newly encountered inhabitants of the farthest ends of the world—all the way down the African coast, all the way across the (Atlantic) Western Ocean, and possibly as far as India. The punishments appear to concentrate on the bad behavior unleashed by the European expeditions, the sins of rapaciousness: lust, gluttony, and greed. The monks and friars who accompanied these expeditions, tacking missionary work onto mostly commercial exploits and rebranding them as spiritual enterprises, are emphatically included among the damned. This version of hell systematically unmasks the myths of conquest.

The painting is full of upendings that unsettle orientation, and doublings and triplings that set off a viral logic of proliferation, presenting figures as multiples or versions of each other—the three hanging women, the several prone men, the repeated tonsured friars, etc. The viewer walks back and forth in front of it, taking in the sickening details, never quite putting it all together as a picture. An uncontained quality, enhanced by its unusually large size, makes it less like a picture than an infectious atmosphere or a fever dream. Turning the colonial gaze back on the colonizers, the painting presents the hairstyles of the Europeans, such as the tonsures, in the manner of recent European reports and images depicting the strange hair and stylings of outlandish Indigenous peoples. Here, Europeans themselves go naked, just as best-selling accounts were then describing the inhabitants of America, Africa, and India. Here, white people are the rapacious specimens, the lust-filled Native peoples, the defeated and damned population.

Two faces, the albino monster to the left and the flame mask to the right, turn toward us as if to say, yes, I know you're enjoying watching this, and have you considered this might be you? Viewing here is not distanced but self-involving, seeing becomes seeing oneself seeing.

Some images from the period—just a few—show the costs of subjection and colonization for the Indigenous populations of America, Asia, and Africa. Virtually none prod their viewers to imagine the costs for the colonizers themselves. Depicting Europeans as Europeans, this painting challenged its original viewers to ask: Is this my tribe? And of its future viewers it asks: Who was this tribe, and what is my relation to it?

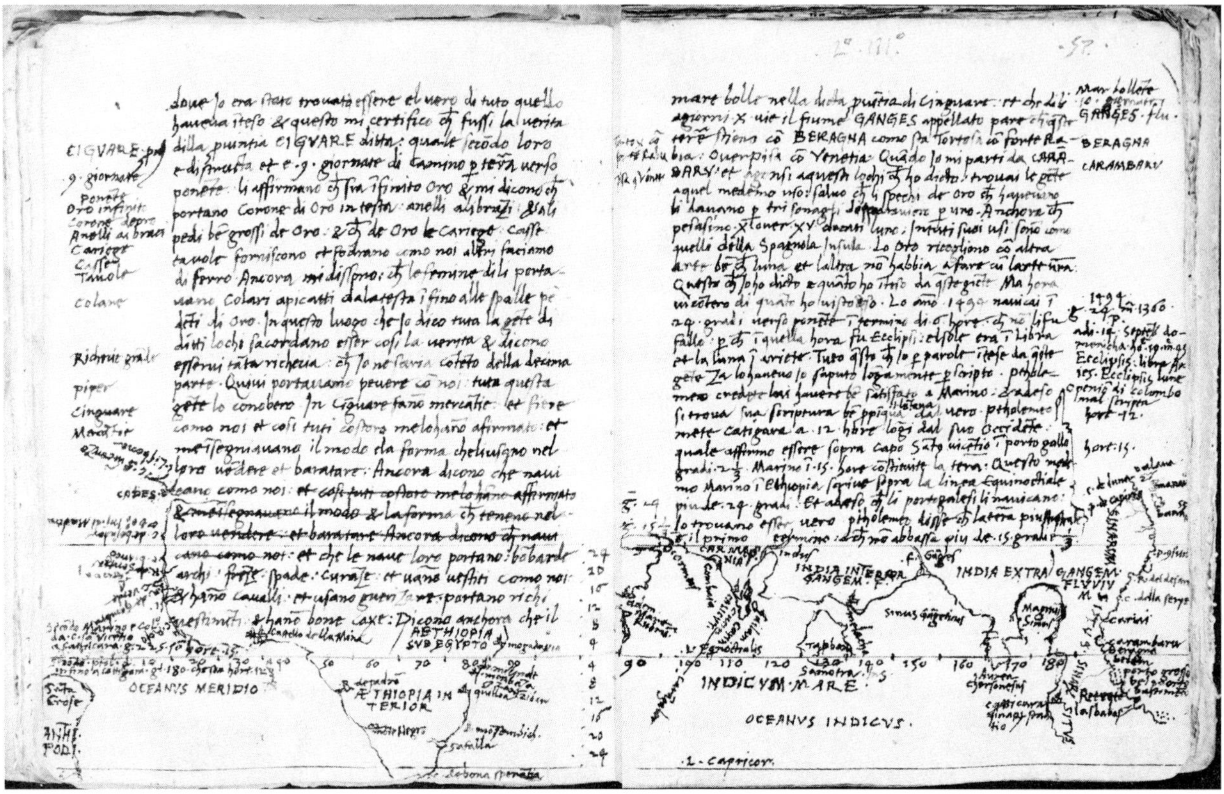

6.1 How does East rejoin West? Alessandro Zorzi, Codex Alberico (ca. 1517–38). Florence, Biblioteca Nazionale Centrale, MS Banco Rari 234, fols. 56v and 57r.

SIX

Columbus Meets Polo, or the Logic of Elliptical Continuity

When voyages were rendered in writing, and then combined with other accounts into compilations, distances were reconfigured into itineraries. Far-flung voyages unfold over a number of pages, perhaps eliding vast ocean crossings, or passing over time-consuming overland travel with a few words, while the locales at either end of a trajectory are described in full color and brought into new proximity, like beads on a necklace. A visual image based on such accounts, such as Vasco Fernandes's *Adoration of the Magi* (see fig. 3.1), gathers elements observed in different locales into a single composite figure, an editorial configuration. In the encyclopedic collections formed by European scholars and princes, objects from different places were set into new adjacency, suggesting relations across unmarked gaps. This chapter focuses on the logic of what we call elliptical continuity in books and manuscripts, from anthologies of travel accounts to cartographic atlases, leaving other formats, such as image programs and collection displays and their inventories, to later chapters.

A Venetian Editor Unfurls Amerasia

Marginal sketches drawn by the Venetian editor Alessandro Zorzi in a manuscript now in the National Library in Florence reveal a European observer grappling with new geographic knowledge and in the process imagining an Amerasian new world (fig. 6.1). Zorzi's manuscript consists of a collection of notes and transcriptions from recent travel reports, apparently in preparation for a published compilation of travel literature. On the pages here reproduced, Zorzi transcribes Columbus's Letter from Jamaica, where he was marooned for almost a year. Sometimes called his *Lettera Rarissima*, it was written to the Spanish monarchs on July 7, 1503, during his fourth voyage. Zorzi sketches a map in the lower margin, focusing on the band between the Tropics of Cancer and Capricorn and unfurling it across almost the whole of the world's circumference.

Compared to his celebratory letter to Santángel announcing the joyous news of his first voyage (see chapter 1), a decade later Columbus is exhausted and in a state of desperation, describing himself as a broken man. He recounts traveling south from Cuba and landing in a variety of harbors along what we today call the Central American coast: places he called Cariay, Ciamba, and Carambaru. He equated the people of Cariay and Carambaru in particular with those of Marco Polo's Ciamba or Cochin China.[1] In Carambaru, local informants told him about the province of Ciguare, which lay inland nine days' journey to the west, where there was "a vast quantity of gold" (*infinito oro*), a place where "all are acquainted with red pepper . . . the custom is to trade in fairs and markets . . . and [was] ten day's journey away from the river Ganges" (*quivi portavano pevere con noi: tuta questa gente lo conobero . . . fanno mercantie et fiere . . . et che di li a giorni X vi e il fiume Ganges*). Sailing south from Carambaru, Columbus reflects on Ptolemy's placement of the Asian port of Cattigara, the most eastern and southerly known land, musing that "the world is not so very large" (*il mondo non e tanto grande*) and that six parts of it are land, suggesting it would make sense that he was now close to the extremity of Asia as Ptolemy had understood it. He then went on to explore other places along this coast that he called Bastimentos and El Retrete, and was forced to leave one of his rotten and worm-eaten ships in another harbor he called Belporto. From there, his two remaining ships soon arrived "at the province of Mago, which borders on Cathay, and from there set out to Hispaniola" (*agionsi in la provintia di Mago, laquale parte con quella dil Cataio, e di quivi mi parti per la Spagnola*). He describes navigating around dangerous shoals and through stormy seas, losing anchors, and feeling as if "the world were coming to an end" (*che pareva essere il fine del mondo*). Though his ship was riddled with holes and his crew exhausted, he managed to return to Jamaica eight days later, making the trip from Cathay to Jamaica—as Christopher Columbus understood it—a journey of a little more than a week.[2]

Zorzi's map, accompanying this account across the two-page spread, presents Africa, Asia, and a bit of the new world in one extensive sweep. Beginning on the bottom left with the new world (*Santa Croce*, an alternative name for Brazil), from which one crosses a narrow ocean to Africa (*Aethiopia sub Aegypto* and *Aethiopia Interior*), and then, on the right-hand page, shown in detail in figure 6.1b, Zorzi redraws Ptolemy's eleventh map of Asia (see fig. 1.4), crossing from the Red Sea to India on this side of the Ganges (he initially wrote INDIA INTERIOR and then corrected it to INDIA INFRA GANGEM F[LUVIUM]) and on to India beyond the Ganges [INDIA EXTRA GANGEM FLUVIUM]. At the extreme right edge, Zorzi momentously maps Columbus's findings onto this extremity of Asia.

Columbus's Cariay, Carambaru, Veragua (which Columbus calls Beragnia or Beragna), Bastimentos, Retrete, and Belporto here appear on the easternmost coast of Asia, on the far side of what Ptolemy (see fig. 1.4) called the *Sinarum Sinus* and Zorzi adapts as *Sinarum Situs*, believed by modern historians to correspond to the present-day Malay Peninsula.

Across two pages, Zorzi's map unspools one continuous tropical expanse spanning the recent discoveries of the Portuguese and Amerigo Vespucci in Brazil, or Santa Croce (at the extreme left edge) to the recent discoveries of Columbus's fourth voyage (at the extreme right edge). Europe, north of the tropical zone, is not figured on the map, except by the one city of Cades (Cádiz), from which Columbus had set sail May 9, 1502, on his fourth and last voyage. The map reveals Cádiz to be close to the new world and by implication also close to farthest Asia.

A few pages later, Zorzi added a third sketch that zooms in on the span between Spain and the west coast of Africa on one side and the new world and Asia on the other (fig. 6.2a–b).[3] Offering the final segment of the tropical tour of the world offered in figure 6.1, this sketch map lays out the expanse between the lands discovered by Columbus and Spain and Africa (fig. 6.2a). Here "Silk Mountains" (SERICI MONTES, fig. 6.2b) extend southward into the "Region of China" (*Sinarum Situs*, the present-day Malay Peninsula), again populated with the places Columbus visited on his fourth voyage. In this part of the world, Zorzi cobbles together new places with Indigenous names such as Beragnia (Veragua, in present-day Panama) with a series of regional names derived from ancient maps by Ptolemy, such as "Land of Silk" (*Serica*) all within the greater region of Asia. Extending eastward from there is the MONDO NOVO, in the region of Parias corresponding to the mouth of the Orinoco River, which led Columbus to believe that inland from there was the earthly paradise (see chapter 2). In both maps, Cattigara, the Ptolemaic port believed to be at the southeasternmost point of the known extent of Asia, forms a hinge to the lands explored by Columbus. (For more on the shifting position of Ptolemy's Cattigara in maps of the new world, see chapter 11.) Zorzi's pen was one of the first to unfurl an Amerasian expanse that would be variously imagined and populated by Europeans for over two centuries. The pages of Zorzi's manuscript and the format of the book itself work to bring these distant places into an imaginable continuity.

A little-known Venetian intellectual active in the late fifteenth and early sixteenth centuries, Zorzi was the author of two manuscript compilations of travel literature, one in Florence and the other in Ferrara.[4] The sketch maps just discussed are from the Florentine manuscript, the longer and more inclusive of the two compendia, which consists of four volumes

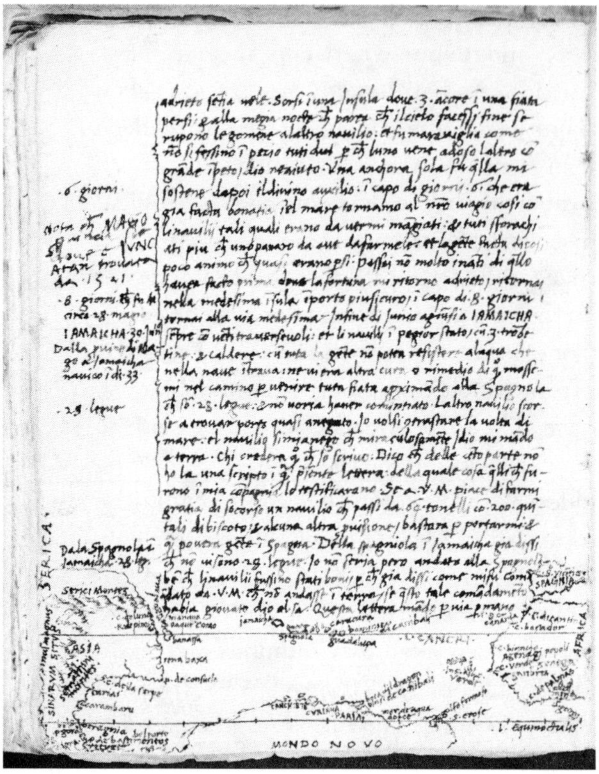

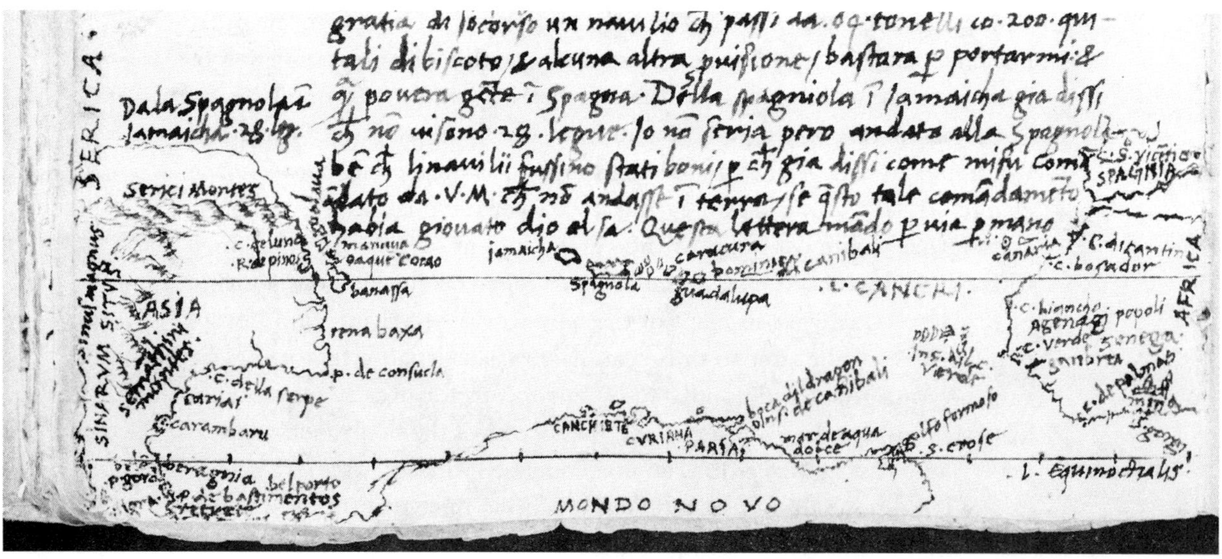

6.2a–b The port cities explored by Columbus line the coast of Asia. Alessandro Zorzi, Codex Alberico (ca. 1517–38). Florence, Biblioteca Nazionale Centrale, MS Banco Rari 234, fol. 60v.

of material dated between 1470 and 1538. Combining pages ripped from printed books with Zorzi's own handwritten notes and annotated with extensive marginalia like this map, Zorzi's compilations were multimedia scrapbooks from the first global age, glossed with the compiler's imaginative and informed reflections on a great variety of new worlds. They offer a stark physical epitome of the way information about the recent discoveries was mediated, processed, stitched together, and passed on.

Zorzi's compilations work through an Amerasian understanding of the known world, and at the same time work with older sources of knowledge for the extremities of the known world. Zorzi almost obsessively sketches groups of islands, often labelling them with the words "infinite islands" (*insule infinite*) or "many islands" (*insule molte*), showing how Zorzi's geographical imaginary was informed by the vast archipelago of Southeast Asia depicted by countless late medieval and early modern cartographers (see chapters 8 and 11).[5] In addition, the marginal notes regularly associate Columbus with Zorzi's Venetian compatriot Marco Polo. Those marginalia are a reaction to book four, chapter ninety-two of the *Paesi novamente retrovati*—in a section of the text that describes parrots, cannibals, an island inhabited by women, and amazons, all corresponding to accounts in Polo's *Travels*. Near the island of Bunchema (referring to Borinquen, the Taíno name for Puerto Rico), Zorzi prominently writes "archipelago," likening the lands in the western Atlantic to late-medieval understandings of a galaxy of islands off the coast of Asia.

In the margins of his Ferrara compilation, among passages describing Columbus's landing in Cuba that mention "two serpents that were eight feet long in the form of crocodiles" (*doi serpenti di otto piedi lungo... ala forma di cocodrilli*) and "serpents tied to trees with cords" (*serpenti ligati ad arbori cum cordi*), Zorzi draws large, crocodile-like figures tied to trees and a close-up of a single claw, with an annotation comparing these "serpents" to ones described in Pope Pius II's treatise on Asia, as well as to serpents seen by Polo at the court of the "Great Khan" (fig. 6.3).[6] Zorzi sees Columbus's Cuban animals in Asian terms, and regularly mentions Polo, Cipangu (Japan), Kublai Khan, and spices (*spezie/speterie*) in the margins of Columbus's voyages.[7] For Zorzi, Columbus's travels converged with those of Polo and Conti; Cuba and Jamaica come as a continuation of Asia.[8]

It was no accident that Zorzi's Amerasian imaginings were incubated in Venice. As one of the most prolific printing centers in Europe, Venice was a hub for the production of knowledge about new worlds in the first half of the sixteenth century. Polo figured prominently in a variety of Venetian printed texts about the lands in the western Atlantic which were, for Zorzi and many other Venetians, an extension of Polo's Asia.

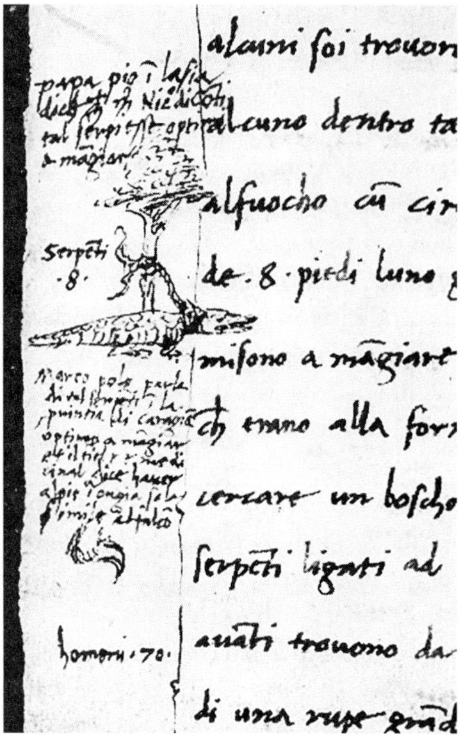
alcuni foi trouon
alcuno dentro ta
alfuocho cu cir
de. 8 piedi luno
misono a magiart
ch erano alla for
cercare un boscho
serpeti ligati ad
auati trouono da
di una rupe grand

6.3 Cuban crocodiles as Asian serpents. Alessandro Zorzi, Ferrara Codex (ca. 1506). Ferrara, Biblioteca Comunale Ariostea, MS. cl. II. 10, fol. 20v.

For instance, the Venetian mapmaker Giacomo Gastaldi regularly grafted Polo's Asian toponyms of Anian, Tolman, and Pegu directly onto his maps of the northern part of the American continent (see chapter 11). In addition, in his *Navigations and Travels* (*Navigazioni e viaggi*) (1550–59), a major early collected history of global exploration, the Venetian cosmographer Giovanni Battista Ramusio included a new translation of Polo's *Travels* (1559), a modern edition that provided the basis for the texts's wide dissemination for centuries to come.[9] Defending Polo's continuing relevance for understanding the world, Ramusio lamented that medieval texts and translations had corrupted Polo's work and caused it to be discredited; many had come to consider it an untruthful exaggeration until the Portuguese encountered "many cities and provinces in India and many islands with the same names our author [Polo] had used." The time had come, according to Ramusio, for a properly researched and philologically correct edition of Polo's narrative, for "even though there are written in [Polo's] book many things that seem fabulous and incredible, they are no less worthy of belief than the other things he narrates that are true, nor [should we] accuse him of committing a large error, for he reports what he was told."[10] Strabo, Pliny, Herodotus, and Columbus, he argued, had all reported marvels beyond belief, so that while Polo may have reported incredible things, they remained no less worthy of credence Columbus and Vespucci's news from the western Atlantic. The wonders of Quinsai were as believable as those of Tenochtitlan, and Ramusio wanted to remind European audiences that it had been Polo who had first introduced most Europeans to the wealth of the Indies.

Even outside of Venice, Polo was a touchstone for European ideas about the new world. As we have seen, Columbus read and heavily annotated his personal copy of Polo's text. When he went in search of a Northwest Passage as *piloto mayor* for the Spanish crown, the explorer Sebastian Cabot similarly consulted Rodrigo de Santaella's Spanish translation of Polo's text (1503) to produce a world map.[11] European explorers and conquistadors—including Francisco Coronado, Jacques Cartier, Giovanni da Verrazano, Samuel de Champlain, and countless others—saw the world through his text and were inspired to search for China, or routes to it, in the lands to the west of the Atlantic (see chapters 8 and 9). Columbus's son Ferdinand Columbus linked the Columbian voyages to Polo in the seventh chapter of his biography of his father, entitled "The Second Reason That Encouraged the Admiral to Seek to Discover the Indies." Arguing that Polo's journeys to eastern lands implied that "India bordered on Africa and Spain," he sustained his father's speculations about traveling west to arrive in the East.[12] In the last quarter of the sixteenth century, mapmakers such as Gerardus Mercator and Abraham Ortelius continued to draw on Polo's narrative in their maps of the world, and as late as 1611, Jodocus Hondius the Younger's world map consulted Polo to establish the location of Java Minor (see chapter 11).[13] Polo's Asian travelogue informed the exploration and understanding of new worlds, including those in the western Atlantic, well into the seventeenth century.

Compilation as a New World Logic

Zorzi's manuscripts are an early contribution to a vogue of travel compendia that overtook Europe in the sixteenth century.[14] These anthologies, which compiled firsthand travel accounts into one or several volumes, sustained Amerasian imagery for decades to come, both in their content and in their construction and form. Such compilations regularly combined texts from America with accounts of discoveries in India and East and Southeast Asia. In passing from one sentence or page to the next, readers stepped across continents and oceans. Both compilations and single-authored travelogues elided distances and gaps (such as sea passages) by producing an overall rhetorical effect of swift passage. The very form of the printed book, a regular succession of pages filled with text of consistent typeface, imposed a logic of elliptical continuity across gaps on the accounts of distant worlds, an effect of formatting—in books, but also in images—whereby faraway and far-apart things are embraced in one continuous vision, creating contiguity and propinquity at the level of the page. Printed compilations of travel accounts from newly discovered parts of the world (or scrapbooks like Zorzi's, still in manuscript form but intended for print) were primary exhibits of elliptical continuity.

A highly successful early compilation, *Paesi novamente retrovati et novo mondo da Alberico Vesputio Florentio intitulato* (The Newly Discovered Lands and New World So-Called by Amerigo Vespucci) (1507)—a publication glossed by Zorzi—was one of the first compendia of contemporary literature on European navigation and exploration. It contained travel narratives dating between 1454 and 1501 divided into 142 chapters over six books. The sequence of chapters include an account of Alvise Cadamosto's 1455–56 voyages to Senegal and Gambia, together with Cadamosto's description of Pedro de Sintra's 1462 expedition to what is today Sierra Leone (book 1), Vasco da Gama's 1498 voyage to India (book 2, and continuing into book 3), selections from Peter Martyr d'Anghiera's *Decades* (book 4), Vespucci's *Mundus novus* letter describing his third voyage to South America in 1501–1502 (book 5), and various letters of Venetian ambassadors and merchants between 1501 and 1502 concerning the Portuguese voyages to India, Gaspar Corte Real's voyage to America, and Pedro Álvares Cabral's voyage to Brazil and India (book 6).[15] The notably popular *Paesi novamente retrovati* was reprinted at least eight more times in the next fifteen years and in fifteen editions overall during the sixteenth century, including editions in Latin, German, and French.[16] The collection distributes the parts of the world zonally, into books focused on Africa, India, and the Americas, placing them all under the title of "Discovered Lands."

Led around the world from one description to another, virtually no reader of the *Paesi novamente retrovati* would have been clear as to whether vast or small distances separated the parts described by the various accounts. Even within individual accounts, itineraries connect rather than separate America and Asia. For example, the *Paesi novamente retrovati* reproduces an anonymous report by one of the crew on Pedro Álvares Cabral's 1500 voyage to India, which included the unexpected discovery of Brazil (discussed in chapter 3). To the modern commentators who have reconstructed Cabral's voyage, and to the navigators themselves, it was clear that Cabral's ships had been carried westward across the Atlantic, stopped on a new shore, and then proceeded to round Africa, travel up the African coast, and finally reach India. But to the armchair reader of the *Paesi novamente retrovati*, the Brazilian account is folded into book 6, which covers Portuguese voyages to "Calichut," and specifically describes Cabral's voyage as that of an armada sent by King Manuel of Portugal "per le parte de India," which indeed it was. The account begins with the encounter with the people of Brazil, but there is no mention made of having been blown off course or having crossed an ocean. After landing on the Canaries and Cape Verde, this is the next land sighted, a newly discovered land "very abundant in trees, and there were people there going along the shore of the sea."[17] The account proceeds to describe the colorful and very large parrots of this land and the hats and bonnets worn by the inhabitants that were made out of the feathers of these birds. These people, the account says, go naked without shame, wear their hair long, noting that the women are beautiful of body. They eat a bread made out of the root called *igname*, "which is the bread the Arabs eat," and live in dwellings made of wood with roofs of branches and leaves, in which they hang hammocks.

The important point for our purposes is that this account, as presented in the *Paesi novamente retrovati* (and in turn republished in Simon Grynaeus's *Novus orbis* and in the first volume of Ramusio's *Navigazioni e viaggi*), did not locate these lands and people clearly in America or Brazil. Most contemporary readers would have naturally connected these people and this new land to "the parts of India" that make up the rest of the voyage, as Cesare Cesariano seems to have done when he glossed descriptions like this, if not this very description, in his account of the first humans and their dwellings (see chapter 5). As noted in chapter 3, the new world magus who makes an appearance in Vasco's *Adoration of the Magi*, a painting connected to Cabral's patronage and informed by Cabral's voyage, is in fact an epitome of a voyage to both Brazil and India, an amalgam of Tupi and south Indian elements. Like Cesariano's first humans, Vasco's magus is a visual distillate of the elliptical continuity of accounts such as this one.

Additional examples of travelogues from the first quarter of the sixteenth century, in manuscript form, offer additional instances of the generative power of elliptical continuity. A manuscript compilation of Venetian travel literature dated between 1518 and 1520 describes the lands of Calicut, turns to the Columbian voyages, Hispaniola, and the travels of Vespucci, and then returns to descriptions of India, the headless *blymmes* that inhabited those lands, and the Great Khan of China.[18] The Florentine Codex Vaglienti, composed and compiled before 1514, proceeds according to a similar logic.[19] It begins with a retracing of Polo's travels through Asia, followed by excerpts from John Mandeville's travels focused on the Holy Land, and then on the next page offers the first "familiar letter" written by Vespucci to Lorenzo di Pierfrancesco de' Medici. This letter of

Vespucci, related to but not the same as the more famous *Mundus novus* letter often published under his name in the sixteenth century (see chapter 2), states that it was composed on his return from the "islands of India" (*isole d'India*). In it, Vespucci speculates as to whether he had been close to paradise and how it relates to the known parts of the world, finally deciding that these new lands were on the Asian mainland, given the presence of "lions, deer, wild boar, and rabbits, all animals known to inhabit not islands but *terra ferma*."[19] Vespucci's first letter is followed by the letter of Bartolomeo Marchionni on the first voyage of Pedro Álvares Cabral, then by Vespucci's second and third familiar letters, a letter by Piero Rondinelli concerning Vespucci, another report on Cabral's first voyage (in which the inhabitants of Brazil are called *mori*, or Moors, a term signifying "dark-skinned" and used most often in this period to refer to the Muslim populations of the Mediterranean basin), several letters on the voyages to India of da Gama, a report on the travels of Giovanni da Empoli to India, a brief account of Prester John, a eulogy of King Manuel of Portugal, a letter on the kingdom of Congo, Vespucci's letter to Piero Soderini, a letter on Tristão da Cunha's expedition to India, several more reports from India, followed by several texts on the history of Florence, a translation of excerpts from the Koran, an account of the Ethiopian embassy to Pope Eugenius IV of 1441, and finally a report on the Fall of Negroponte to the Turks in 1470. The compilation is overwhelmingly oriented toward the Levant and Asia, fitting Vespucci's new world travels into that orientation.

A bit later in the century, Simon Grynaeus and Johann Huttich's *New World of Regions and Islands Unknown to the Ancients* (*Novus orbis regionum ac insularum veteribus incognitarum*) (1532) became the standard collection of travel literature in Protestant northern Europe. Here, as in many other texts of the period, "new world" includes Asian as well as American destinations (see chapter 2). In 1534, Michael Herr produced a German translation of Grynaeus and Huttich's work that published these accounts from around the world under the title *Die New Welt* (*The New World*). Using a somewhat different logic, Giovanni Ramusio, in his highly successful *Navigazioni e viaggi*, organized the globe according to routes of trade and the degree to which Venetian merchants and travelers had infiltrated other parts of the world. For instance, volume one of Ramusio's three-volume collection combines travel narratives associated with the history of the spice trade, compiling the journeys of Leo Africanus and Alvise Cadamosto to Africa, Vespucci to America, da Gama to India, and Antonio Pigafetta around the world, among others, associating here the Near and Far East, Africa, and America. Sixteenth-century travelogues such as these did not understand the world according to the traditional "parts" of the world, not to mention the modern continents (see chapter 16), or by thinking of it in terms of East and West. If they grouped the lands of the world at all, they did so according to forms of organization that reflected patterns of trade, or climate, or by collecting descriptions of places that they categorized as new, which included lands reached by sailing east or west.

Elliptical Expansions of Ptolemy

The one subset of cosmographic texts that did tend to group information by parts and regions of the world were editions of Ptolemy's *Geographia*. Ptolemy organized knowledge of the world into the parts of Europe, Africa, and Asia, in that order; sixteenth-century editions followed this tradition, and a variety of texts about travel and global geography followed suit.[20] As news and information about the Americas began to filter into Europe, early modern editions of Ptolemy tended to attach the newly discovered lands in the western Atlantic to the end of the Asian section, admitting them as a kind of appendix to Ptolemy's text. Ptolemy's discussion of Asia ran from west to east, beginning with Asia Minor (book 5, chapter 1) and ending with the region of India beyond the Ganges (book 7, chapters 2–4). As we saw in chapter 1, "India beyond the Ganges" was an extensible formation of the least-known part of the world whose limits were famously left undetermined by Ptolemy and his many successors, prompting modern cosmographers to see the new lands to the west as one of its extremities.

Sebastian Münster's *Cosmographia* (1544)—a Ptolemaically organized text that saw thirty-five editions in Latin, German, French, Bohemian, Italian, and English—does exactly this. Rather than depict America as a fourth part of the world, Münster's highly popular work of descriptive geography (and the many subsequent translations of it) present the Americas as an appendage of Asia (see also chapter 8). This way of treating the Americas "constituted a reasonable model even half a century after the Columbian discovery of America."[21] In texts of cosmography that followed this tripartite Ptolemaic organization, the Americas did sometimes appear as one or more parts of the world from the later sixteenth century, eventually forming discrete and final sections of the texts after Asia.

Yet even when America is identified as a part in its own right, Amerasia persists. Johannes Boemus's *The Manners, Laws, and Customs of All the Peoples* (*Omnium gentium mores, leges et ritus*) (Augsburg, 1520) for instance, arguably the most widely cited and reprinted cosmography of its day, considered the cultures of Europe, Africa, and Asia, presented in a traditional Ptolemaic ordering. While Boemus's original edition did not include a discussion of

America, later editions and translations did. The first French translation, *Recueil de diverses histoires* (1539) considered only Europe, and later translations up through the middle of the century only replicated Boemus's original three continents; the English translation, *The Fardle of Factions* (1555) also considered only Europe, Africa, and Asia. The Italian *I costumi le leggi, et l'usanze di tutte le genti* (1558/1564) included the Americas in a fourth and separate book. However, these Italian translations placed the islands of Borneo, the Moluccas, and the Philippines (Zebut) in the Americas—sandwiched in between discussions of the Straits of Magellan and Cuzco, revealing that the Pacific was not the dividing line.[22] In addition, Francisco Tamara's Castilian translation and revision of Johann Boemus's cosmography, *El libro de las costumbres de todas las gentes del mundo, y de las indias* (Antwerp, 1556), incorporated Spanish texts absent from Boemus's original and reordered Boemus's text so that the volume moves from most to least civilized, in the order of Europe, Asia (Asia Minor, Persia, and Tartary), and Africa. It is in the final book on Africa that we find the Amerasian configuration of the Americas, including Hispaniola, Mexico, Peru, etc., grouped with India, including Calicut, Cathay, and Japan. Beginning in chapter 6 of book 3, this sequence is titled a "Summary and brief relation of all the Indies and lands newly discovered by the people of Spain, in the west as well as in the east, and on the manners and customs of the Indians and inhabitants of those lands." Given the anthropological orientation of the treatise, a climatic rather than continental model might have been uppermost in Tamara's mind, given the dominant belief in the determining role of climate on the nature of local populations. For Tamara, perhaps, an association with the tropics—where the weather is hot and the people least clothed—attaches the people of what he calls "all the Indies" (*todas las Indias*) to the people of Africa.[23] The textual structures of travelogues and cosmographic literature confirmed a tendency to bring far-apart places into proximity and to facilitate movement among them while minimizing the reality of the expanses or oceans separating them, the vastness of which were after all known only to the relatively few who had marched or sailed across them. In the historian Paolo Giovio's *Dell'historie del suo tempo* (1552), Ferdinand Magellan moves from the western coast of South America to the island of Java in one sentence.[24]

The logic of elliptical continuity applies not only in compilations, where accounts from different parts of the world jostle in neighborly fashion, but also in single-authored accounts, such as navigational logs or *derroteros* (a Spanish term for navigational itineraries, also used for the texts recounting the voyages, or for texts composed as if recounting a voyage). The reader is made to hop from coast to coast and part to part, just as the viewer does in map cycles where the world is presented in a series of tables. For example, an entirely typical manuscript *derrotero* in the Huntington Library, written in 1576, takes the reader around the world. Toward the end it reaches the limit of Asia, which starts to mingle with territories such as Florida and Newfoundland.[25] Not far from the Indonesian port of Malacca is a province with cannibals named Caribes. In Cipangu, or Japan, there are also cannibals/Caribes. Then the reader reaches "Gatigara," the limit of Ptolemaic Asia, where there are unicorns, and the author proposes that this is where paradise can be found. The sequence ends in the province of Catayo, Cathay, the last habitation of the East, which is believed to be "una con la Florida y terranova que son al occidente"—one with Florida and Newfoundland, which are in the west—and then proceeds to the newly discovered lands. On the same page, from one sentence to the next, we pass from Asia to America. East flows into West, in the logic of Martyr's Alpha Omega. It is a continuous narrative that leaves a lot of elements out, among them the Pacific Ocean. Decades after Magellan had crossed the Pacific, narrative forms such as this offer little or no registration of the ocean that might separate America and Asia.[26]

Elliptical continuity is also clearly in evidence in multi-table atlases, where the world is cut up into pieces of land presented in one panel or one page after another, with the connections and gaps between left implicit or simply unexplained. In a fairly typical example of a later sixteenth-century manuscript portolan atlas, almost exactly contemporaneous to the *derrotero* just discussed and also made in Spain, possibly Mallorca, we see a full-page spread of the southern part of the South American continent, tipped on its side, followed by a detail of the coastline near the Rio de la Plata, followed by a map of the northern part of South America up to and including Florida, followed by a map of the northern coast of America, followed by a map showing the ocean between the west coast of Africa, the west coast of Iberia, and a bit of England on one side, and, on the other, a bit of Newfoundland and a bit of South America.[27] This is followed in turn by a map of Arabia and Persia on either side of the Red Sea, a map of the Indian Peninsula, and a map of the Moluccas, in East Asia. Turning the pages from spread to spread, the reader/viewer is taken from one place to another, leaving out elements that fall between them. The Pacific is nowhere to be seen in this atlas. These intervening expanses are not represented, but also not denied. There is a certain logic to the sequence from new world in the west to the farthest reaches of Asia, but the manuscript leaves open the question about how the two ends of the earth connect.

• • •

Appendix: Durian and Guanabano on the Same Page

Such thinking also emerged in the work of European botanists, connecting the world in new ways. For instance, fearing the growing power of the Portuguese Inquisition, the Portuguese Sephardic Jewish physician and naturalist Garcia de Orta left Portugal and settled in Goa in 1538, where in 1563 he published his voluminous and wide-ranging *Conversations on the Simples, Drugs and Materia Medica of India* (*Colóquios dos simples e drogas he cousas medicinais da Índia*), the first European publication to catalogue Indian medicinal herbs in their native environment. The Dutch Latinist and botanist Carolus Clusius acquired de Orta's text in Lisbon in 1564 and produced a Latin translation of it in 1567, which became a standard reference text on medicinal plants in Europe. Clusius introduced several significant changes to de Orta's original and in doing so, generated his own compilation of botanical literature. Clusius reorganized de Orta's list of flora to range, in Clusius's new edition, from the most to least "recognizable" in a European context. Clusius also added an alphabetical index, and perhaps most important, included his own commentaries on de Orta's

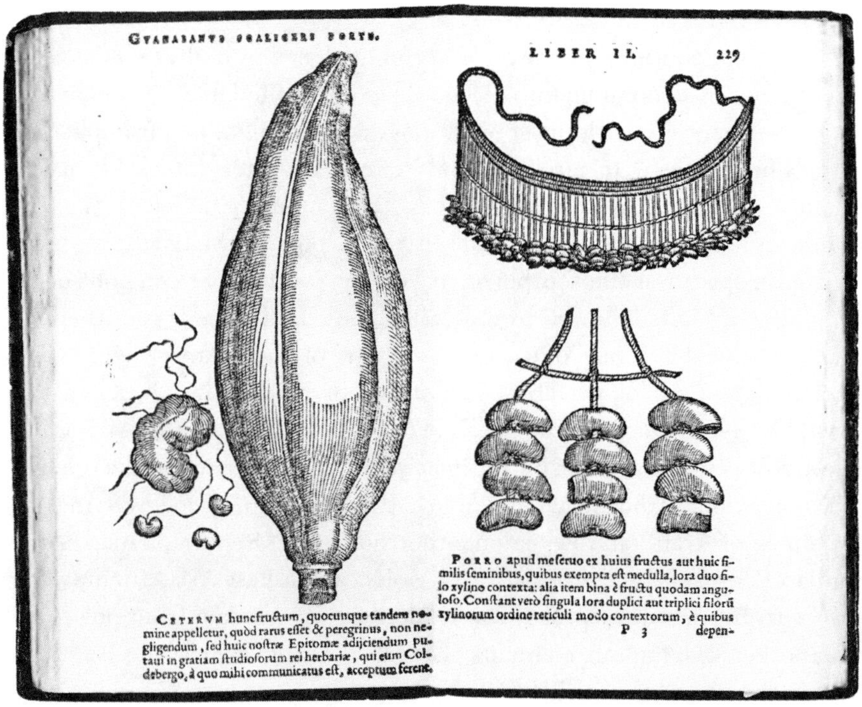
LIBER II. 229

CETERVM huncfructum, quocunque tandem nomine appelletur, quòd rarus esset & peregrinus, non negligendum, sed huic nostræ Epitomæ adijciendum putaui in gratiam studiosorum rei herbariæ, qui eum Coldebergo, à quo mihi communicatus est, acceptum ferent.

PORRO apud me seruo ex huius fructus aut huic similis seminibus, quibus exempta est medulla, lora duo filo xylino contexta: alia item bina è fructu quodam angulosо. Constant verò singula lora duplici aut triplici filorũ xylinorum ordine reticuli modo contextorum, è quibus

P 3 depen-

6.4 Asian and American fruits on facing pages. Garcia de Orta/Carolus Clusius, *Aromatum, et simplicium aliquot medicamentorum apud Indos nascentium historia: ante biennium quidem Lusitanica linqua per dialogos conscripta* (Antwerp, 1567), pp. 228–29.

work, as well as printed illustrations of some plants. In editing de Orta's text about durian—a large, spiny, green, and malodorous fruit native to Borneo and Sumatra—Clusius's annotation compares the durian to the guanabano and *higüero* plants, fruits native to the American tropics. For Clusius, the shiny, oval-shaped gourd of the durian fruit bore similarities to the maracas used in Tupinamba religious rituals, as noted by the Franciscan explorer André Thevet. Clusius added to de Orta's description of durian an illustration of a guanabano fruit from the natural history of the Italian physician Julius Caesar Scaliger, as well as prints of the decorative beads worn by the Tupinamba as described by Thevet, rattles made by joining the dried fruits, filled with seeds, together with wood fibers into necklaces and anklets that resonated when the Tupinamba wore them to dance (fig. 6.4).

Clusius concluded his discussion of durian by remarking that the higüero gourd—similar to durian—"was common to Hispaniola, and so it seemed, in many other islands, and all the lands of India."[28] Living on the ground in India, de Orta understood Goa as an important center of Asian trade, one that he, writing in Goa, did not evidently feel the need to connect to the lands described by Columbus and Oviedo. From the more distant vantage of a Latin translation and more compendious publication produced in Europe, Clusius depicted Goa and its plants as part of a tropical continuum, connecting the Spanish and Portuguese colonial worlds in Asia and the Americas into "the Indies."[29] Other naturalists would connect geographies in similar ways, including those of ginger (see chapter 9) and cinnamon (see the Epilogue).

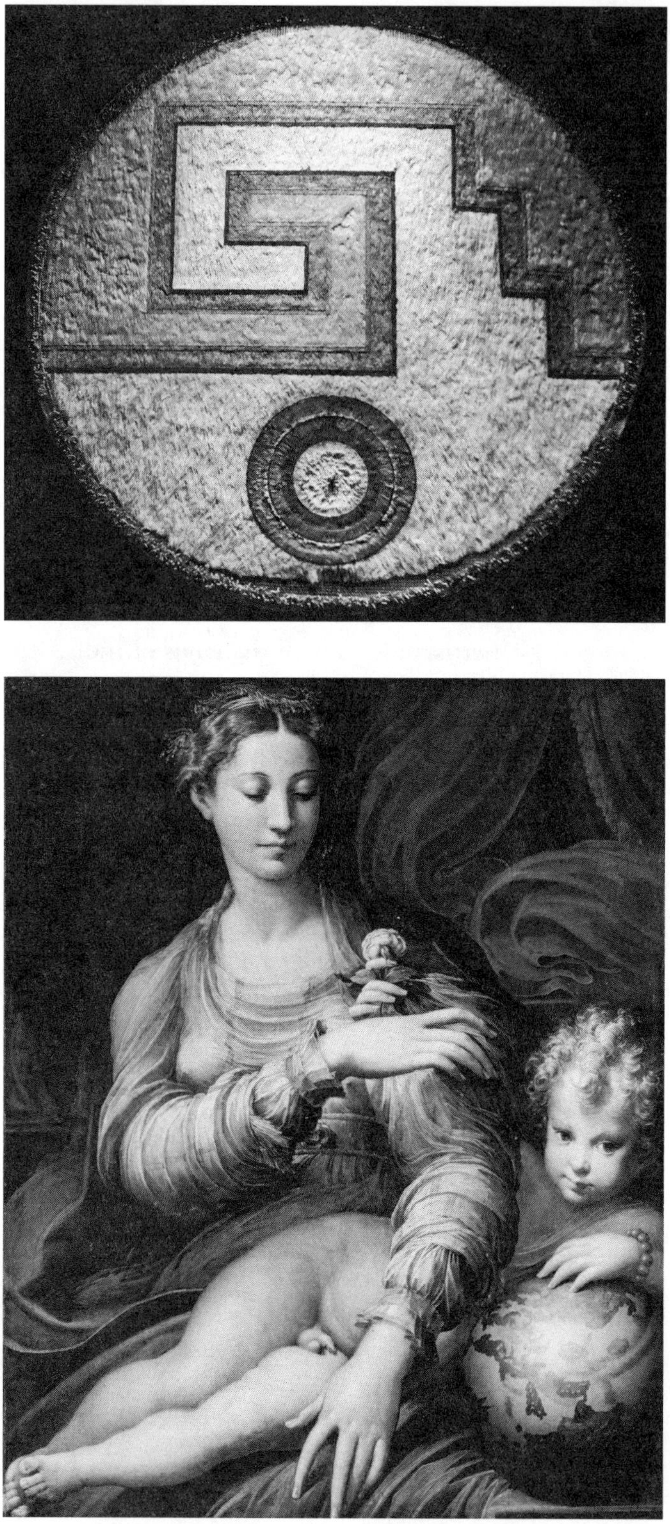

7.1a–b Spirals and circles. (a) Feather shield with "twisted gourd" (*xicalcoliuhqui chimalli*) motif and concentric circles, wood, cane, fleece, feathers, and rawhide, 71 × 75.5 cm (ca. 1520?). Stuttgart, Landesmuseum Württemberg. (b) Parmigianino, *Madonna of the Rose*, here called *Madonna of the Earthly Globe*, oil on panel, 109 × 88.5 cm (1529–30). Dresden, Gemäldegalerie. Photo: Hans-Peter Klut, Art Resource. (See color plates.)

SEVEN

The Revelation of the Earth: Parmigianino's *Madonna of the Earthly Globe*

A featherwork mosaic shield now in Stuttgart was one of the first Mexica objects to arrive in Europe after Cortés's siege of Tenochtitlan in the Spring and Summer of 1521 (fig. 7.1a). Specialists now identify the stepped and turning central motif to be *xicalcoliuhqui*, "twisted gourd," a widespread motif in Indigenous cultures of what we now call Mesoamerica.[1] The Mexica-controlled provinces sent ceremonial shields like this to Tenochtitlan, a form of tribute to the capital, trophies of sorts within the Mexica empire even before they became trophies for Europeans.[2] Complicating the question, this shield might not be a pre-Cortés relic of Aztec culture but a product of the contact itself. While the twisted gourd motif on the Stuttgart shield is traditional, the motif of concentric circles is not, at least not in this combination (target shield designs did exist, but on their own and with not as many circles).[3] Could it be that this shield was made by Hernán Cortés's Mixtec allies for him in appreciation for his successful campaign against their Mexica enemies?[4]

Without knowledge of Indigenous cultures, the Europeans who first saw this shield in the 1520s and later would have relied on their own sense of these forms, a stepped spiral formation at top and a target-like design of concentric circles at bottom. From Christopher Columbus's first arrival on Haiti, European viewers speculated about whether works made by the newly encountered Indigenous communities were made as beautiful ornamentation or as symbolic imagery related in some way to a ritual function.[5] The objects landing in Europe as a result of Cortés's exploits in Mexico evoked riches and great civilizations coming under the aegis of Christian empire, still unintelligible messages now becoming available, possibly suggesting a divine plan hidden until now and revealing itself in these times.

Reciprocal Anthropology

The shield's pattern is not very different from that of a *Madonna and Child* by the Italian artist Parmigianino (fig. 7.1b). Parmigianino's spiraling forms were new in western art, but the motif of concentric circles was long familiar to Europeans. A diagram used in a widely read European cosmographic treatise, showing the earth at the center of an onion-like cosmos, was well known in an array of media and formats (fig. 7.2).

To European eyes, a luxury object like the feather shield, with its exotic yet not entirely unfamiliar forms, might well have suggested that this new and still unknown world shared deep origins with their own world. (On the possible biblical or Egyptian cultural origins of new world peoples, see chapters 13 and 14). Rather than approach the painting in a European framework of inquiry—as an interesting moment in the career

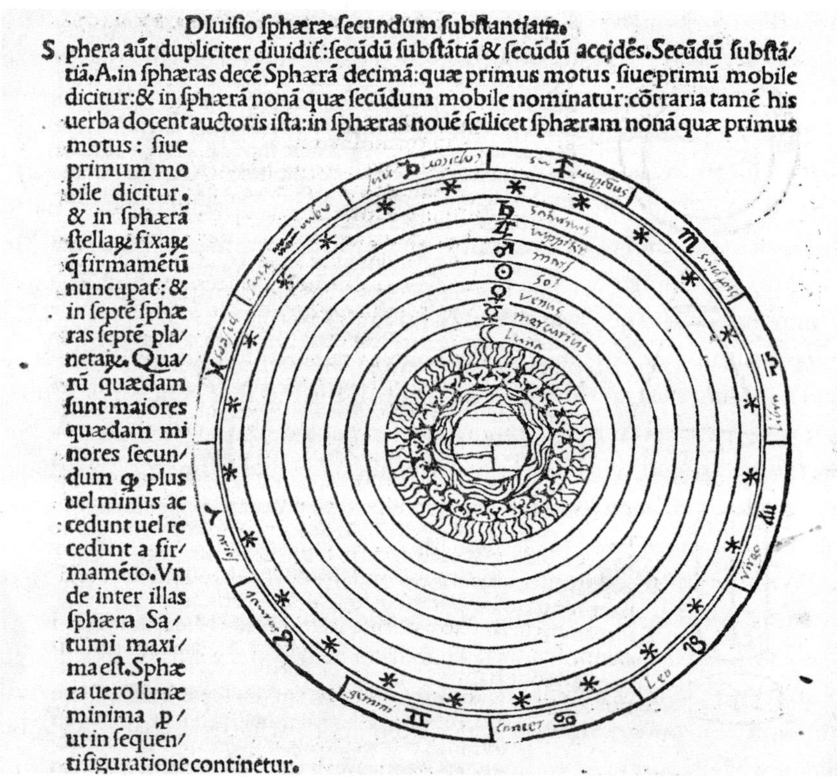
Diuisio sphæræ secundum substantiam.
Sphera aũt dupliciter diuidit̃:secũdũ substãtiã & secũdũ accidẽs.Secũdũ substã/tiã.A.in sphæras decẽ Sphærã decimã:quæ primus motus siue primũ mobile dicitur:& in sphærã nonã quæ secũdum mobile nominatur:cõtraria tamẽ his uerba docent auctoris ista:in sphæras nouẽ scilicet sphæram nonã quæ primus motus: siue primum mobile dicitur. & in sphærã stellarum fixarum q̃ firmamẽtũ nuncupat̃: & in septẽ sphæras septẽ planetarum. Quarũ quædam sunt maiores quædam minores secundum q plus uel minus accedunt uel recedunt a firmamẽto. Vnde inter illas sphæra Saturni maxima est. Sphæra uero lunæ minima ꝓut in sequenti figuratione continetur.

7.2 The cosmos as a series of concentric spheres focused on earth. Johannes de Sacrobosco, *Sphaera mundi* (Venice, 1490), unpaginated. Providence, Brown University Library. Earth is at the center, surrounded by the wavy waters, the cloudy puffs of air, and the tongue-like flames of fire—the four elements of the sublunar sphere. Above our atmosphere, helpfully labeled by an early user of this book, are the Moon, Mercury, Venus, the Sun, Jupiter, and Saturn, then the crystalline sphere of the stars and the zodiac. Beyond that, in the emptiness of the white paper, is God, the *primum mobile*.

of the artist, as an example of Mannerism, as a bid for the patronage for the pope, etc.—we can view it in the mirror of the ceremonial feather shield, an artifact inviting a reciprocal anthropology. The painting, as we shall see, landed before the Pope's feet, in Bologna in 1530, together with magnificent objects from the new world, including shields like this one. If the shield traversed worlds, the painting was a response to the encounters with new worlds. Putting the earth under the hand of the Christ child, it figures the recent global developments as a question—what does it mean that the earthly orb in its fullness is being revealed now?—and it suggests that the answer to the question is imminent.

Like the shield, Parmigianino's painting is a design shaped to a format. A large woman's head reaches to the top of the painting, her form spreading downward across the composition's lower boundary, as the child's body extends from one edge to the other. The child's hand threads knowingly under the woman's left arm to offer her a rose, while her right hand passes across his to receive it, a crossing of limbs that draws attention to the picture's center, exactly marked by the woman's left nipple. The child looks out of the picture with a sharp gaze as he rests his hand on a globe, a feature defined the picture for its early commentators, who consistently noted that this was a Madonna that included a terrestrial map, a *mappamondo*.[6]

A rhythmic pattern generates repetition and resonance through the painting's forms. The child's arm resting on the globe rhymes with the upward swell of the curtain above. The parting of the curtains top right, suggesting an opening canopy, finds an echo in the parting of the woman's veil to either side of her head, and in the general downward spread of the her form. Striations and twisting lines course through the painting with dizzying consistency and variety. Yet, for all their swirling, the draperies and the bodies are strangely still. There is no consistent wind moving the drapes around, yet they spiral. The limbs of the figures are in movement—the child offering the rose and the woman lifting one hand to receive it while putting out a protecting arm in front of the child—yet there is something still about these limbs.[7] The globe, too, combines movement and stillness. It offers a cartographic exhibit—we see the Iberian Peninsula at the orb's left edge, with Africa below and Asia extending across to the right—and yet one feels the energy that animates it as a cosmic body. It seems to want to rotate on the axis delicately but unambiguously marked by the landing of the child's pinkie on the North Pole.[8]

The emphasis on pattern and rhythm and the paradox of stillness in movement intensify in the rose, a layered and repeated unfurling of forms, an image of cosmic order, the full view of which is being offered not to us but to the woman. (This is probably a damask rose [*Rosa x phoenicia*], a hybridization of *Rosa gallica* and *Rosa phoenicia* produced in Asia Minor and distributed throughout the Near East and Middle East, then brought to Europe by crusaders in the twelfth and thirteenth centuries and christened with the Damascus provenance.[9]) The woman gazes down at the flower and through the flower towards the child, who is turned toward us. His hand resting on the globe emerges from a bracelet composed of miniature red coral globes polished to a shine, following one another around his wrist and disappearing from view—like the rose, a sequence of forms repeated into circular infinity. The ambidextrous child presents the unfurling rose to her and the swirling earth to us.

The painting's emphatic enclosure strengthens the impression of allover ornamentation. The patterning and striations that make up the layered forms constantly curl and turn, suggesting that all ornament is other-sided, that by following the course of any surface the opposite side of it will be revealed.[10] The figures reach to the edge of the picture field, turning gyrating draperies into a sort of ground for pearlescent bodies. There is a partial view of what appear to be bedclothes at the left, but they are of the same color as the draperies, so we are offered not so much a view into space as an undulating red field fading into shadow toward the top left corner. The resulting impression is that this is not an excerpt from our world, not even a scene in the earthly life of mother and child. The woman's golden sash carries at its center a large crystal, receiving light from all sides, an embedding that is repeated fractally throughout the painting. The scintillating form of the woman—Parmigianino's twisted gourd—shimmers against the backing of wine-red draperies and in turn becomes the setting for the body of the child.

To put this now in the terms of European art history, the ornamental emphasis is a clear "no" to the last one hundred years of space-describing paintings and arguably a call to an earlier mode of Christian *ars sacra* based in the cosmic principle that all aspects of a work of religious art, both ornament and figuration, participate in its sacred meaning, just as all elements of creation participate in God's design. Whereas in conventional painting of the period figures and objects are placed in a rendition of worldly space, what is called a setting, here we have a different relation of figure and ground, with the multicolored earth set against the picture's layered forms like a precious stone against a foil—a setting not in the pictorial but in the jeweler's sense. The earth is nestled against the white body of the child, which is in turn set against the striated gold of the Virgin-matrix-foil, in its turn placed against the dark and sumptuous red bole-like field of draperies. The earth here is a gem of creation, or perhaps it is a cosmic toy, under the playful and delicate hand of a child god who seems to know exactly what he is going to do with it. The painting thus reverses the traditional relation between world and picture: this is not a picture of a portion of the world but a cosmic setting for the earthly sphere itself.

If the picture contains the world and not the other way around, then scale is radically open to question. These figures could be sitting in a room, or they could be set out of time and earthly space altogether. The globe under the child's hand could be a mere model of the earth, like a desktop globe a scholar might keep in his study, or it could be a vision of the planet earth presented to those who live on earth. Raphael's vault fresco of *Astronomia/Urania* puts us outside of the spheres of the cosmos, looking through the crystalline sphere of the fixed stars to a diminutive earth at the center of the universe (see fig. 4.13). Parmigianino's painting also dislodges us from human-scaled reality, but without setting the earth into the traditional cosmological armature of planets and stars, as we see in Raphael's fresco and Sacrobosco's astronomy book (see fig. 7.2). Instead, the earth is a living organism under the hand of a strangely wise child enthroned on a vast ornamented earth mother. This is a cosmogonic image, an insight into creation, or rather a final unfolding of the destiny of creation now being offered to us by its creator. The painting captures the sense of a gathering excitement that is now coming to a head. Everything is in transformation. The coral beads on Christ's wrist hover between the categories of mineral, vegetal, and animal.[11] They are a succession of potential worlds, shown in proximity to the realized earth, the first draft of creation, populated by God's fallen humans.

A Global Summit in Bologna, 1530

In his *Lives of the Artists* of 1550, Giorgio Vasari tells us that Parmigianino's painting was offered to Pope Clement VII when he came to the city of Bologna in late 1529 and early 1530 to meet with and crown the emperor Charles V. Then, in his second edition of 1568, Vasari says that the artist originally intended the painting for the writer Pietro Aretino and only in a second moment gave it to the Pope. We will probably never know the true story, but the preparatory drawings for the painting do suggest an important change occurred at an advanced stage in the process, suggesting a redirection of purpose. In none of the existing several preparatory drawings for the painting do we see the rose or the globe, suggesting that these elements came into play after a whole earlier development of the composition. Late-stage additions, the globe and the rose are mutually interdependent symbols of cosmic order that suit a newly elevated papal reception for the painting. In any case, it is highly likely that Parmigianino finished the picture in late 1529.

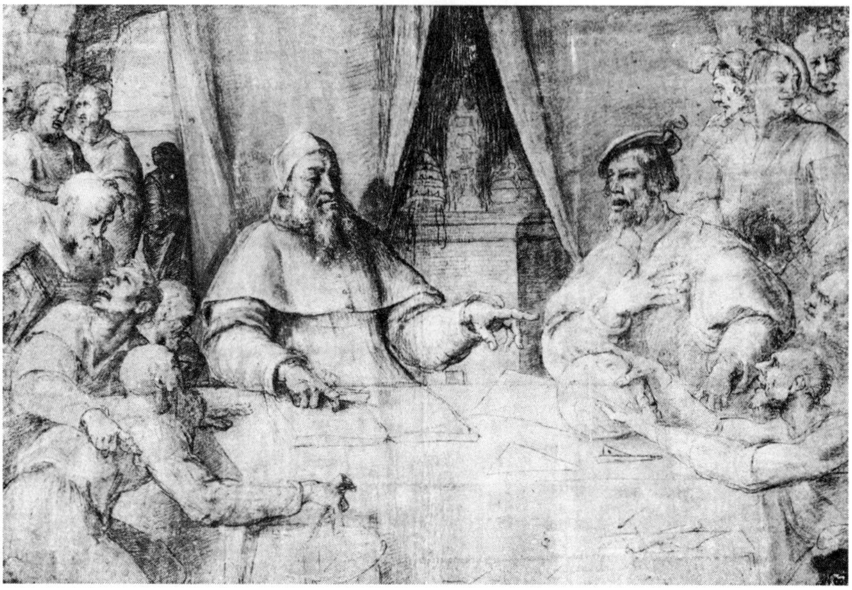

7.3 Sebastiano del Piombo represents Emperor and Pope in animated discussion over a globe, at Bologna in 1530. Black and white chalk on gray prepared paper, 30.9 × 46.3 cm (1530). London, British Museum.

In a bull of March 1, 1530, announcing the coronation of the emperor at Bologna, we read that in the ceremony at the church of San Petronio on February 24, Pope Clement VII had bestowed on the emperor the various insignia of his rule, placing a ring on his finger, a sword at his hip to be used "against the enemies of the faith," and on his head the golden crown of empire. He then offered the emperor the scepter in one hand and in the other hand a "globe representing the image of the entire world" (*globum totius mundi imaginem repraesentans*).[12] After the coronation ceremony, these insignia were carried in triumph through the city, as we see in engravings by Nicolaas Hogenberg commemorating the procession, in one of which we see the golden globe and other insignia carried by knights of the realm, clearly showing that it was not a cartographic globe but an abstract orb mounted by a cross.

The artist Sebastiano Veneziano (later del Piombo), who traveled to Bologna in the pope's retinue, produced a drawing of the papal-imperial summit possibly for a never-executed painting (fig. 7.3). Between the two potentates under a canopy is a monstrance with the host consecrated in the papal mass, the pope's tiara on the left (Evangil) side of the monstrance and the newly bestowed imperial crown on the right (Epistle) side. After the fanfare of the coronation, the two potentates have sat down to confer in Christian harmony. On the table before them, all attention is drawn to the spherical *mappamundi* charting the earth's landmasses and seas, which is being presented with some excitement by a cosmographer, whose instruments are strewn over the table in attestation of the ingenuity and labor that went into the making of the globe that is the object of discussion. The pope points to the globe even as the emperor, hand on chest and mouth open, offers his own opinion. Apart from the impending Turkish threat, the principal geopolitical issue under discussion at this meeting was the Christian empire's global expansion over the previous decades, marked by a succession of world-historical events: Christopher Columbus and Amerigo Vespucci sailing west and landing in hitherto unknown reaches of the earth's inhabited lands; the Portuguese king's wildly successful expeditions around Africa and onto the farthest known islands of Asia; Cortés's conquest of Mexico in 1519–20; and then, making it possible that it could all be tied together, the complete circumnavigation of the globe by Ferdinand Magellan's crew in 1519–22. A golden globe mounted by a cross may have been sufficient as a symbol of global power to be displayed in ceremonies and processions, but at the actual summit world domination was on the table as a political reality, and that meant the abstract imperial orb needed to be supplemented by the accurate mapping of the world, incorporating the latest geographical information obtained from the recent spectacular campaigns in far kingdoms East and West.

Europe was abuzz with reports on these events. On September 24, 1522, the Venetian ambassador Gasparo Contarini, who was to be a prominent participant in the negotiations at Bologna in 1530, wrote to the Venetian Doge Andrea Grimani from Valladolid in Spain with a description of Cortés's conquest in Mexico and the gifts sent by the conqueror to the emperor Charles V, which may have included the feather shield discussed earlier. Contarini reports that Cortés had discovered "various and diverse cities and castles, inhabited by men more civilized than those that had been discovered until now." He tells of Cortés having reached the city of "Scaltezza" (probably Tlaxcala, which had allied itself with Cortés against the Mexica), and then reaching "Temisitam" (Tenochtitlan), saying that the prince there was held in "great veneration" (*gran veneratione*) and that the inhabitants, though they sacrificed humans to their idols, were "very civilized" (*molto civili*) their dwellings well adorned, even with cotton textiles. He continues,

> They have a great deal of gold, but they do not use it for money, instead appreciating it and using it in various ornaments.... They live on bread made of the grain of India [*frumento d'India*, an early designation for maize; see chapter 5] and on meat; they ingest a beverage similar to beer; they don't have characters

> for letters, but write the more necessary things using figures of animals and other things, in the way that the Egyptians did in antiquity.

Seeking to understand where this land, with all its seeming connections to Asia, is to be located in relation to the known world, Contarini turns from the account of the Mexican conquest to the recent voyage of Magellan and his crew in search of the Moluccas, the fabled Spice Islands. Excerpting a letter that one of Magellan's mariners, Juan Sebastián (or del Cano), had sent to Charles V describing the hardships suffered by the crew and the death of Magellan, Contarini celebrates the fact that Magellan and then after his death del Cano managed to reach the Spice Islands and encircle the earth all the way around (*et così hanno girato la terra a torno a torno*). Contarini's letter, combining the news of the Mexican conquest with that of the Magellan expedition's passage through the American strait and on to the Spice Islands before returning to Europe, strongly suggests that Spanish exploration westward had opened a western passage to Asia.[13] The same hope of access to Asia animated Cortés and his followers in their various westward and northward ventures of the 1520s, 1530s, and 1540s, as will be discussed in the following chapter.

Contarini's excitement chimes with verses of the poet Ludovico Ariosto, who in the 1532 edition of his *Orlando furioso* (that is, after his d'Este patrons had shifted allegiance from the French to the imperial side in the wake of the emperor's coronation in Bologna in 1530) inserted a prophecy of future world discovery into his medieval epic:

> I see Hernán Cortés, who put
> new cities under imperial edicts,
> as well as kingdoms in the East so remote,
> that we, who are in India, do not know of them.
>
> *Veggio Hernando Cortese, il quale ha messo*
> *nuove cittá sotto i cesarei editti,*
> *e regni in Orïente sí remoti,*
> *ch'a noi, che siamo in India, non son noti.*[14]

For Ariosto after 1530, Mexico opens a misty vision of kingdoms so far to the east that even those in India don't know them.[15]

Misty as those places were in the European imagination, beautifully painted books and stunning artifacts from those regions were now arriving in Europe. The questions about these places and people—their riches, their extent, the nature of the people who inhabited them, the problem of their governance—were hotly discussed in this period generally and in

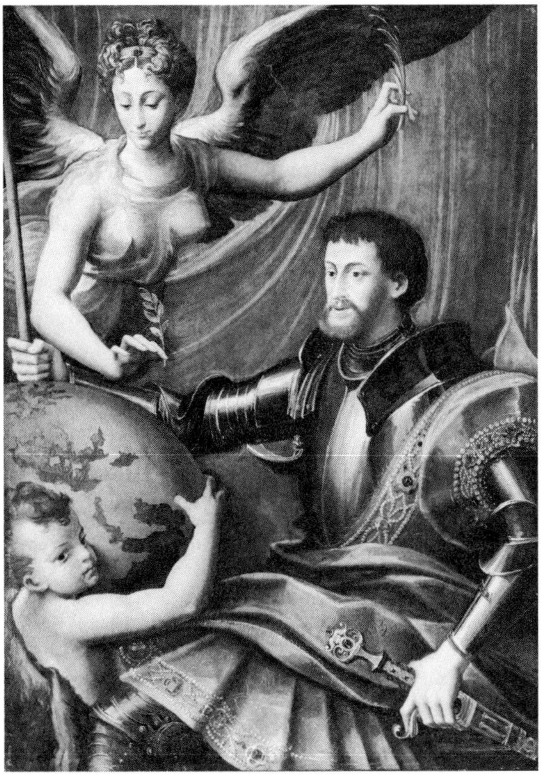

7.4 The imperial motto *Plus ultra*, nowhere inscribed in this allegorical portrait of emperor Charles V, is everywhere expressed in it. Parmigianino, *Charles V and the World,* oil on canvas, 172.7 × 119.4 cm (1530). New York, Arader Gallery.

Bologna particularly. What was the nature of the peoples who lived there? How did these places relate to the known world? Were they capable of being converted? Among these questions was the basic and unresolved question of how and where East met West on the other side of the globe and how the world should be divided: were the Spanish territories across the Atlantic part of a continuum with Asia, thus putting eastern Asia under Spanish rule, or were the Asian territories separate and under Portuguese dominion? In negotiations at Badajoz in 1524 and at Zaragoza in 1529, the Spanish and Portuguese vied over which power had claim to the Moluccas, the Spice Islands celebrated since antiquity for their coveted aromatic produce.[16]

The question of the extent of Christian dominion on earth motivated another painting made by Parmigianino at the time of the Bologna summit (fig. 7.4). If the *Madonna of the Earthly Globe* was for the pope, this one was made for Charles V, showing the emperor with one hand on his sword and the other holding a staff or lance. This second "summit painting" by Parmigianino also prominently features a cartographic globe, presented to the emperor by a young Hercules, with the winged figure of Glory or Fame above holding a laurel branch in one hand and the palm of victory in the other. In what has been described as the first allegorical ruler portrait made in Europe, Charles is shown as master of the earth's geographic totality.[17] As in the *Madonna of the Earthly Globe*, we see only the most familiar part of the earth: the Iberian Peninsula on the left, the northern coast of Africa, and a vast Asia extending eastward, its limits nowhere in sight.

What about the rest of the globe? What about the recent discoveries beyond the previously known world? Not shown, they are nonetheless very much in play. Charles's left hand grasps a sword whose scabbard is embellished with two columns, a reference to the columns of Hercules, placed by the mythical hero at the mouth of the Mediterranean Sea on either side of the Strait of Gibraltar to mark the westernmost limit of the known world, a geographical frontier here shown at the left edge of what we can see of the globe. Those reaches beyond the Strait of Gibraltar had long been a subject of speculation and myth. In the *Timaeus*, Plato told the legend of the lost realm of Atlantis, which lay beyond the columns of Hercules until it was submerged by the waters to the west of Africa and Europe. As early as Pindar and in the writings of several medieval authorities, the columns were interpreted as a warning to the prudent not to navigate beyond this limit. In the *Inferno* (26, 104–108), for example, Dante says that with the columns, Hercules had placed a warning "that man should not go farther beyond" (*dov'Ercule segnò li suoi riguardi / acciochè l'uom più oltre non si metta*). Charles V proudly proclaimed that this limit *should* be surpassed and had been on his own initiative. On his imperial insignia, the device of the columns was often accompanied by the motto *Plus Ultra*—"farther" or "beyond"—in open defiance of the ancient and medieval warning, a call often associated in period sources with the Spanish/imperial explorations and conquests in the new world.[18]

In Parmigianino's portrait of the emperor the new world is not visible to us, but it is fully available to the figure of Glory, who looks down onto the globe from the other side as she offers a branch of victorious laurel, her hand hovering just above Charles's right arm, which is shown passing around the far, unseen side of the globe as if to stake a claim there. Confirming and mirroring the emperor's world-embracing reach, Hercules's right hand extends eastward past Arabia while his left hand, undepicted but clearly implied, can only be reaching westward beyond the picture's edge—*Plus Ultra*—toward the new world on the globe's far side. The words *Plus Ultra* do not appear in the picture for they have been translated into visual terms: the portrait as a whole is the motto's figure.

The far side of the globe was very much on the emperor's mind in the years around 1530. Shortly before the Bologna summit, the Flemish cartographer and globe-maker Franciscus Monachus published his *The Position and Description of the World* (*De orbis situ ac descriptione*) under an imperial privilege, a symbolic form of copyright protection significant mostly as a sign of imperial approbation (fig. 7.5). The pamphlet publishes a letter from the cartographer to Jean Carondelet, the archbishop of Palermo and one of the most important advisors to Charles V during the debates with Portugal over the division of the world into two dominions. Its frontispiece presents a woodcut world map divided into hemispheres, one of which (captioned "this hemisphere of the globe falls to the king of Portugal") corresponds to the known world extending from the Iberian Peninsula to Asia, and the other marking out the new world ("this hemisphere of the globe falls to the king of Spain," meaning Charles I of Spain, or emperor Charles V). These woodcut hemispheres are an abbreviated projection of a three-dimensional terrestrial globe, reportedly produced by Monachus, now lost, and the world picture they convey would frame the European understanding of the shape of the world for generations.[19] Carondelet and Charles V found in Monachus's small treatise a geographical vision that placed farthest Asia, from the Spice Islands eastward, in

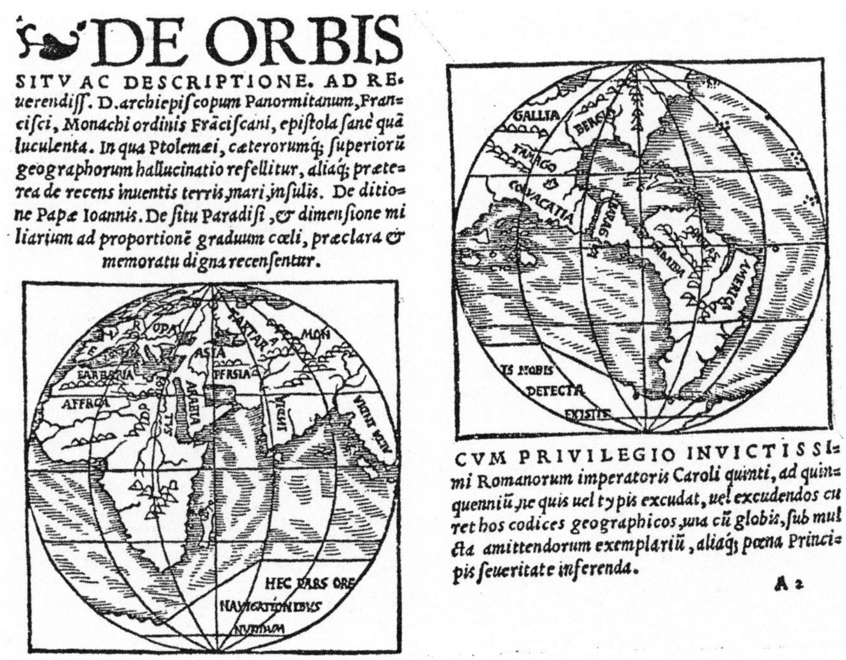

7.5 America as a remote region of an Asian landmass of which Mexico was always a part. Franciscus Monachus, *De orbis situ ac descriptione*, frontispiece woodcut, ca. 14 × 11 cm (Antwerp, possibly 1529).

the Spanish hemisphere, a view promoted by the Spanish in various forms throughout the sixteenth century (see chapter 11).

For Franciscus, America was an appendage of Asia, and the travelers to distant Asia of previous centuries could now be understood to have reached America.[20] "According to Hernán [Cortés]," he asserts, "in Culua or the province of Culuacana [Mexico] lies the residence of the eastern emperor, called Cathay in other travel accounts."[21] He points out that the names of various Asian cities observed by earlier writers such as Polo, Mandeville, and Odoric of Pordenone "coincide with the words and account of Ferdinand [Cortés]."[22] After reaching Java and Borneo, the early fourteenth-century missionary-explorer Odoric had traveled to the port of Zaiton on the eastern coast of China, and then came to Mangi, or southern China, which Franciscus now identifies with Mexico: "I think that presently the name [of Mangi] is Messigo, as Ferdinand Cortés recorded it; thereafter [Odoric] made for the city Themistetan [Tenochtitlan]."[23] According to Monachus, Sypangus or Cipangu (Japan) was now known as Hispaniola, Mansus or Mangi was Mexico, Cathay was Culiacán, Quinsay was Themistetam (Tenochtitlan), Tangut was Tamago, and Bergia was Polo's Bargu in the northeastern extremes of Cathay.[24]

On Monachus's New World hemisphere—one that directly informed Charles V's understanding of the globe—very little is in fact new. America is here not a part of the world but a region at the easternmost edge of a newly extensive Asia. Cosmographers working in the orbit of the emperor Charles V around 1530 were actively bringing into view the far side of the globe, with its Amerasian territories.[25] A Franciscan friar, Franciscus saw the rounding of the globe in his times as nothing short of a divine revelation accorded to Christians:

> In our time God marks out truly extraordinary and marvelous things, such as have never appeared in any historical chronicles or memorials. Has one ever heard since the creation of the world that a fleet has circled the whole orb? Yet this has been granted by the superior powers under the auspices of the Emperor Charles. The Antarctic pole, unknown lands, seas, people beyond the Equator, the very existence of whom was not long ago a matter for continual debate, all of this has come into view [*videre contigit*, literally, visually reached]. And so by the explorations of our Caesar a huge part of the world has opened, bared, and revealed itself.[26]

The Fullness of the Earth

Although it is not visible in either of Parmigianino's summit paintings, the far side of the globe is powerfully present in both. In Parmigianino's

Madonna of the Earthly Globe, the newly discovered lands are as yet hidden, nestled against the child's body, a kind of arcane knowledge. The marbled world pivots under the little finger of its creator, unsettling scale without resetting it. In Bologna in 1529–30, the basic project of painting as a description of the world is upended even as the shape of the world itself—its continents, its peopling, and its history—was newly and radically opened to question. Are we on the brink of uncovering what God's plan has been all along? The unnerving gaze of the child, who clearly has more knowledge than we do, suggests that the disclosure is imminent, and that this will be no mere addition to existing knowledge but the opening of a seal, upending what humans thought they knew.

To imply that a meaning hidden since the beginning of the world is being revealed—apocalypse means, literally, uncovering—is to deal in prophecy and its fulfillment, a common enough mode of European response to the new world discoveries in the sixteenth century.[27] In Vespucci's so-called *Mundus novus* letter, a widely read text, the large number of inhabitants found in the newly encountered lands was framed as an apocalyptic vision: "We found in those regions such a multitude of people as nobody could number (as we read in the *Apocalypse*), a people I say gentle and amenable."[28] (The reference is to *Revelation* 7:9: "After this I looked, and behold, a great multitude that no one could number, from every nation, from all tribes and peoples and languages.") Egidio of Viterbo, a prominent theologian in Rome in the early sixteenth-century Rome, proposed that in the tenth and final age, in which the world now finds itself, "all secrets will be revealed, those of the divine and eternal world through the cabbala and those of the creative world by voyages of discovery. Mankind will be brought into an intellectual and religious unity under the papacy."[29] In his last work, *Scechina*, dedicated to emperor Charles V and written in 1530—thus exactly contemporary with Parmigianino's painting—Egidio noted that whereas the apostles had conquered only the smallest part of the world, through Charles V Christians were now preparing to conquer it in its entirety.[30] The Spaniard Cardinal Bernardino de Carvajal, a highly influential ecclesiastic and a primary candidate for the papal throne in the early sixteenth century, gave a sermon in 1508 before Maximilian I where he presented the recent victories of the Portuguese and the Spanish as a sign that the ultimate fulfillment of history in Christian victory was at hand.[31] As discussed in chapter 5, Cardinal Carvajal went on to commission an elaborate mosaic in a principal church of Rome, where new world flora and fauna complete a vision of Apocalypse.

Something of the spirit of Cardinal Carvajal's address to the Emperor Maximilian appears to have been taken over into a page of the prayerbook

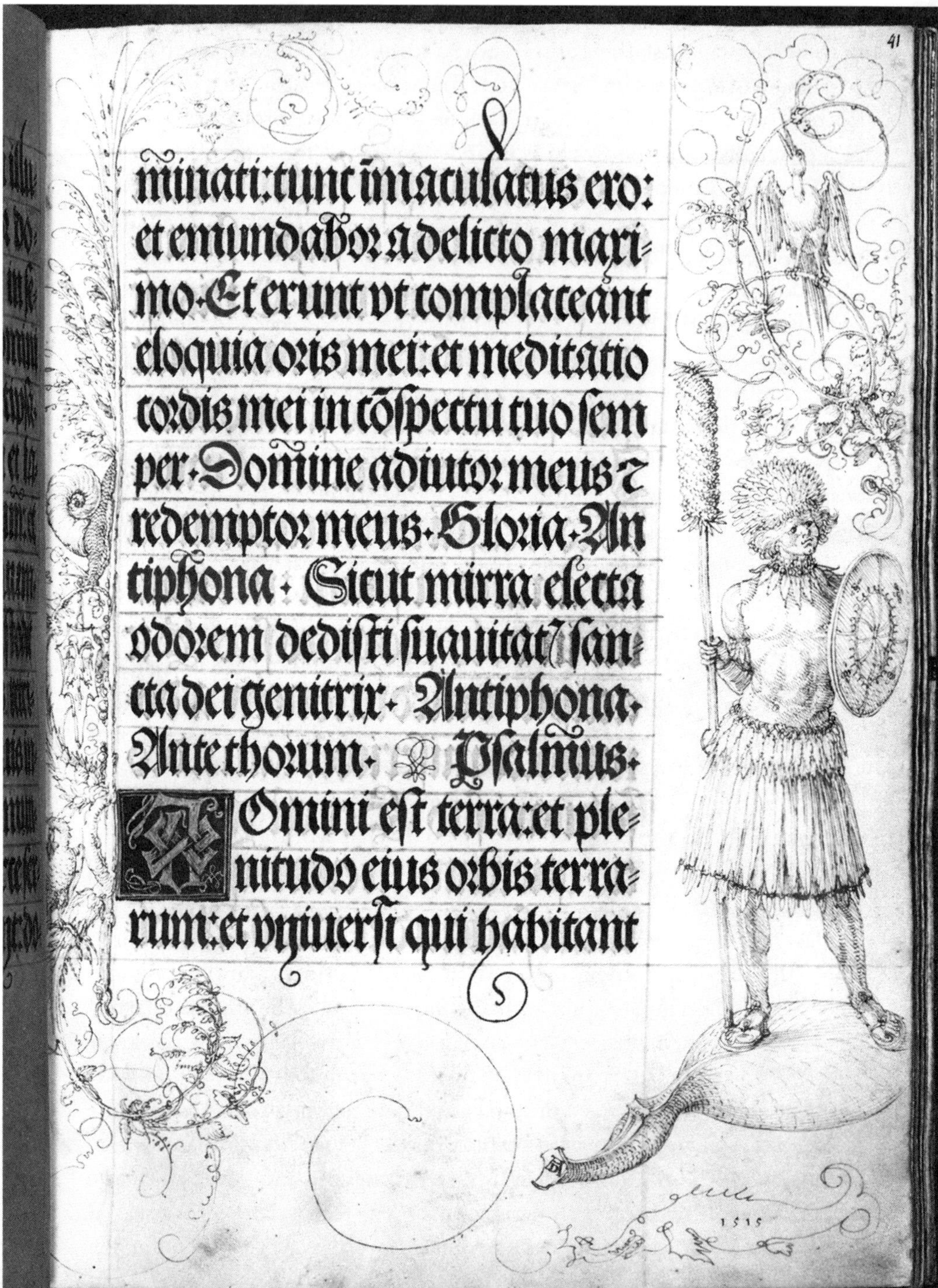

minati: tunc ĩmaculatus ero:
et emundabor a delicto maxi-
mo. Et erunt vt complaceant
eloquia oris mei: et meditatio
cordis mei in cõspectu tuo sem
per. Domine adiutor meus ⁊
redemptor meus. Gloria. An
tiphona. Sicut mirra electa
odorem dedisti suauitat⁊ san
cta dei genitrix. Antiphona.
Ante thorum. Psalmus.
Domini est terra: et ple-
nitudo eius orbis terra-
rum: et vniuersi qui habitant

7.6 "The earth is the Lord's, and the fulness thereof; the world and they that dwell therein." Albrecht Dürer, *"Calecutisch" man*, *Prayerbook of Maximilian I*, typeface and ink on paper (1515). Munich, Bayerische Staatsbibliothek, f. 19.

the same Maximilian had illuminated by the great German artist Albrecht Dürer in 1516 (fig. 7.6). On the right margin of this page we see a figure with a round shield (like the one discussed earlier) and an exotic club, naked above the waist, with a feather-adorned collar as well as a feather skirt. Dürer's depiction is particularly close to a woodcut of 1516 by Jörg Breu illustrating the account of a voyage to farthest Asia by the Italian merchant Ludovico Varthema, where we see the feather skirts and headdress as well as the clubs, based on Tupi clubs imported from Brazil, decorating the bodies of the inhabitants of Sumatra (see fig. 5.7).

Given the use of feather garments and club were to typify inhabitants of Asia as well as America at this time, it is in fact unclear what population Dürer was describing on this page of the Maximilian prayerbook. Is this an Indian warrior, as encountered by Portuguese expeditions eastward into the Indian Ocean, or is it one of the fierce combatants described in the lands discovered by Columbus and Vespucci to the west? Or did that come to the same thing for Dürer? Dürer's own response to recent imports from far-flung places suggest that he made little distinction among these lands and peoples. In 1520, when travelling in the Netherlands, Dürer saw and acquired a "*calecutisch* wooden shield," "several feathers, *calecutisch* things," "2 *calecutisch* ivory salt cellars," "*calecutisch* cloths, one of them of silk," and a "small *calecutisch* target, made of a fishskin, and two gloves for their fighting."[32] As Christian Feest has observed, "While the shields and cloths were probably Asian and the salt cellars Afro-Portuguese, the feathers could have come from Brazil."[33] For all of them Dürer uses the designation *calecutisch*, a descriptor derived from Calicut, the western term for *Khozikode* in India and by extension for the region of the western or Malabar coast of India, which had been reached and then colonized by the Portuguese from 1498. Given Dürer's own liberal use of the term, the fairest description of Dürer's warrior on the margins of Maximilian's prayerbook is that he is a specimen of *calecutisch* folk, in exactly the sense that Hans Burgkmair applied it in his nearly contemporary woodcuts for Maximilian I's triumphal procession, where the "people of Calicut" (so they are described in Emperor Maximilian's instructions for the scene) combine figures and features from both India and Brazil (see fig. 5.8).

Dürer's antipodean Amerasian warrior illustrates the prayers on the page, which invoke the peopling of the world and the extent of God's dominion. At the top of the page we read the ending of Psalm 19, "May these words of my mouth and this meditation of my heart be pleasing in your sight, Lord my helper and my redeemer." Earlier the same psalm reads, "The Heavens declare the glory of God, the skies proclaim the work

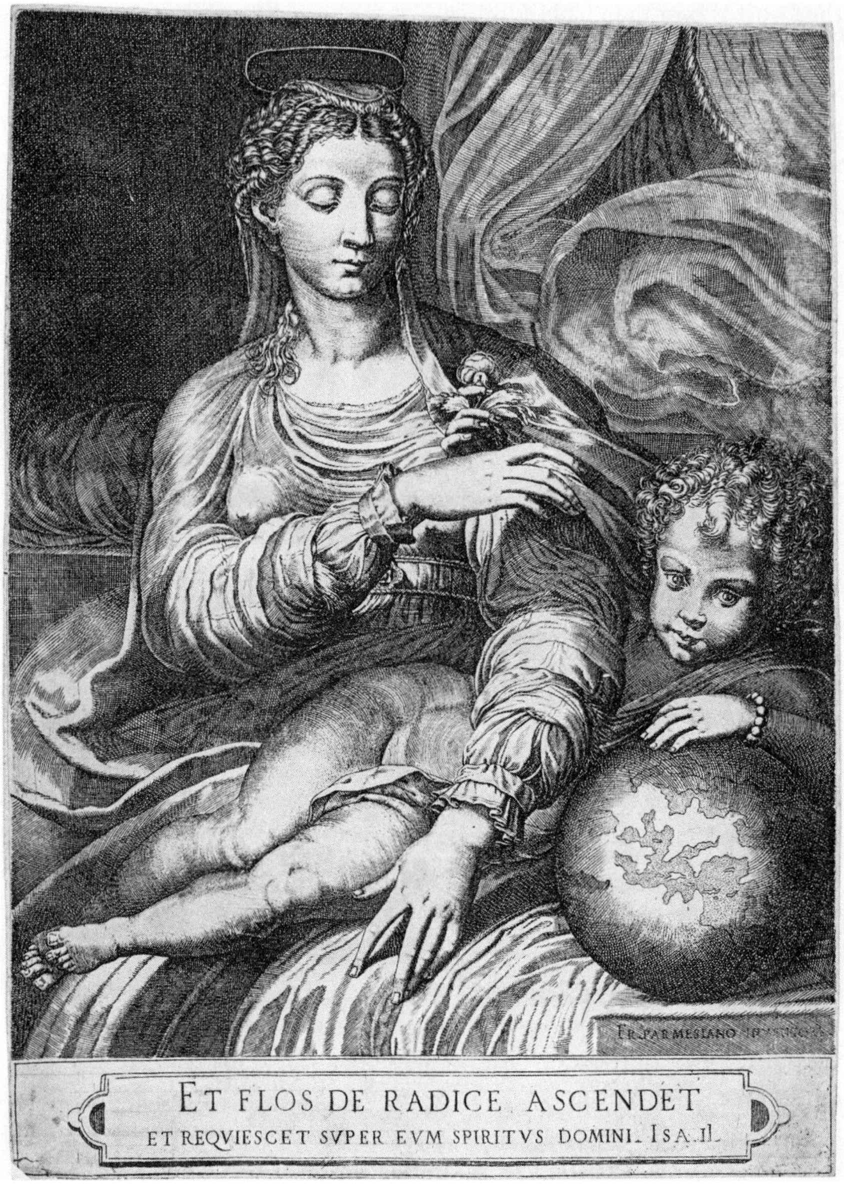

7.7 A print publishes a famous painting and prompts its interpretation in a global-prophetic key. Domenico Tibaldi, engraved reproduction of Parmigianino's *Madonna of the Earthly Globe*, also called *Madonna of the Rose*, 47.5 × 38.8 cm (1560s). New York, Metropolitan Museum of Art.

of his hands. Day after day they pour forth speech, night after night they reveal knowledge. They have no speech, they use to words; no sound is heard from them. Yet their voice goes out into all the Earth, their words to the ends of the world." On the page decorated by Dürer, the end of Psalm 19 is followed by pieces of two hymns to the Virgin, in turn followed by the beginning of Psalm 24: "The earth is the Lord's, and the fulness thereof; the world and they that dwell therein" (*Domini est terra et plenitudo eius orbis terrarum et universi qui habitant*). This is the passage illustrated by Dürer's *Calecutisch* man, who is there to represent the fact that the fullness of the earth is the Lord's—all of it, and everyone who dwells in it, to the extreme ends of the world.

In the wake of Magellan, the idea of end-times was bound up with the complete rounding of the globe.[34] There had to be a reason that of all the periods of human history this was the one in which its fullness was being revealed, and revealed to Christians, who were now trying in real time to assimilate the ongoing revelation into Christian understanding. Beyond biblical interpretation, there was also a basic cosmological counterpart to this quest and its questioning. As we saw in chapter 3, an ancient idea stemming from Aristotle and developed throughout the Middle Ages coordinated the movement of the stars and the sun from east to west with the course of history. Human history begins in the East, in paradise, and over time progresses westward, an idea that was applied freely in the early sixteenth century to the latest explorations, now seen as a furthering of the progressive movement westward of human history.

Soon enough, Parmigianino's often-copied painting was contextualized in global and prophetic terms. An engraving of the 1560s after Parmigianino's painting by the Bolognese Domenico Tibaldi glosses the painting with a biblical inscription from Isaiah 11:1–2 (fig. 7.7). Here are the two verses in their entirety, with the parts not quoted in the print placed in brackets: "[And there shall come forth a rod out of the root of Jesse,] and a flower shall rise up out of his root, and the spirit of the Lord shall rest upon him, [the spirit of wisdom, and of understanding, the spirit of counsel, and of fortitude, the spirit of knowledge, and of godliness.]" Christian interpreters had long read these verses as a prophecy of the advent of Christ, but here the text is excerpted in reference to the flower that Christ offers the Virgin in the painting. The excerpt then cues up the rest of Isaiah 11, which applies well to other aspects of the painting, in particular the earthly globe. A few verses down (Isaiah 11:10–12) we find a prophecy of a new era of the Lord's dominion over the whole earth:

> And it shall come to pass in that day, that the Lord shall set his hand the second time to possess the remnant of his people, which shall be left from the

> Assyrians, and from Egypt, and from Phetros, and from Ethiopia, and from Elam, and from Sennaar, and from Emath, and from the islands of the sea. And he shall set up a standard unto the nations, and shall assemble the fugitives of Israel, and shall gather together the dispersed of Juda from the four quarters of the earth.

Tibaldi's print glosses Christ as the new shoot, with one hand bringing forth the flower of wisdom and with the other "setting his hand to possess the remnant of his people . . . from the four quarters of the earth." The implication is that Isaiah's prophecy is coming to pass now, as the fullness of the earth and Christ's dominion over it are finally being revealed.

• • •

Aftermath: Apocalyptic Painting and Divinatory Book

If it is true that Parmigianino's painting was offered to Clement VII, the Pope didn't keep it. According to Vasari, it came into the hands of Dionigi Zani of Bologna, and it was seen in the Zani palace in Bologna by Vasari and other lovers of art for over two centuries until it was sold in the middle of the eighteenth century and went to Dresden, where it is today. In 1657, the Bolognese writer Francesco Scannelli located Parmigianino's painting in the Zani palace, then in the possession of Count Valerio Zani, a scholar and compiler of travel accounts from around the globe and owner of curiosities from faraway parts of the earth, including one famous manuscript that arrived in Bologna from the new world in 1533 or possibly earlier. Like Parmigianino's painting, the manuscript, a Mesoamerican screenfold, had been presented to Pope Clement VII, and like Parmigianino's painting it remained in Bologna and ended up in the Zani palace, where Count Zani named it a *Libro della China*, a title later changed to *Libro del Messico* (see chapter 14 and figures 14.1–5). Zani believed it to be a Chinese book either because he was mistaken regarding its provenance or because the earlier idea that Mexico was a province of China, expounded by the cosmographer Franciscus Monachus and several others in the sixteenth century, had continued into Zani's time, perhaps with some adaptations. The idea that Mexico was attached to China persisted for decades (chapters 8 and 11), and the idea that a cultural commonality connected China, Japan, and Mexico took various forms well into the seventeenth century.

Both Parmigianino's painting and the Cospi Codex were works of religious art intended for the use of priests—in the case of Parmigianino the pope, high priest of the Catholic Church, and in the case of the manuscript a diviner and celebrant equipped to use it as a ritual instrument, opening and manipulating the screenfold to use in divinatory and propitiatory ceremonies. (Even if no European at this time understood how the manuscript worked, they ascribed it a high religious function in identifying it as a collection not merely of pictures but of hieroglyphs—literally, sacred inscriptions—an archaic form of priestly writing known primarily from Egyptian monuments and held in the highest regard by European scholars.) Yet both the painting and the book were dislodged from their original functions and audiences, set on unexpected itineraries, and finally brought together at the palace of a prominent Bolognese family. Count Zani thus held in his family's collection two signal works of art inherited from the previous century, a vibrantly colored hieroglyphic manuscript from a newly discovered part of the world and a jewel-like painting by Parmigianino of the Virgin with a Christ Child manipulating an earthly globe. Each work in its own way set the earth and earthly time into the movements of a cosmos driven by not always gentle divine forces. However he interpreted them, the connoisseur and armchair traveler Count Zani was in a position to appreciate them together, possibly in the same room. Gazing at Parmigianino's painting, Zani knew that his *Libro della China* came from that part of the world that the Christ Child is keeping close to his chest.

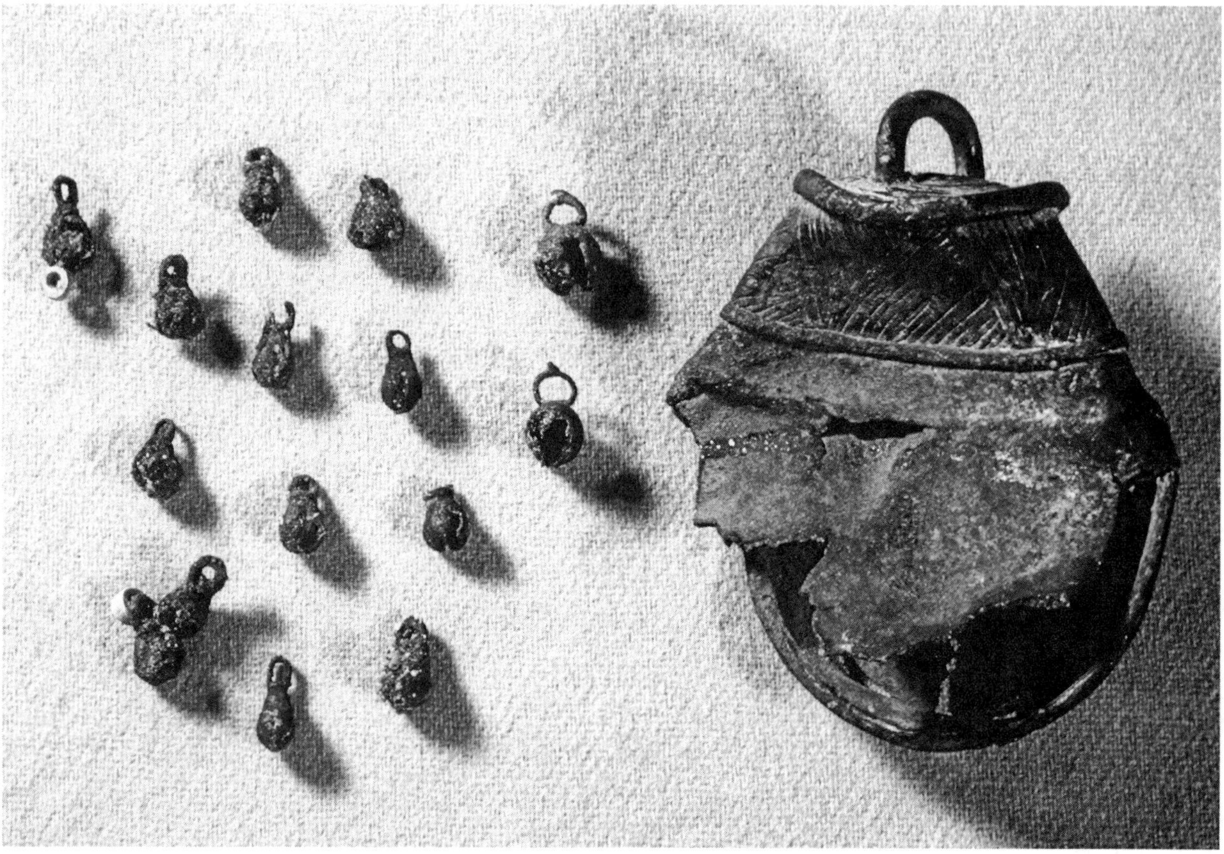

8.1 Copper bell and rattles from village sites in southeast Arizona. 12 × 9.5 cm (bell), copper alloy. Tucson, Arizona State Museum.

EIGHT

Copper Bells:

The Search for Asia North of Mexico

In 1527, Pánfilo de Narváez led an expedition sponsored by Emperor Charles V to explore and settle La Florida, a region extending from the Florida Peninsula to the north and west. After landing on the Florida coast, the original party of about three hundred (made up mostly of soldiers, together with some women and enslaved Africans) suffered repeated misadventures as they traveled westward along the northern coast of the Gulf of Mexico. Reduced numbers landed near the island called Auia by the Indigenous population, now called Galveston, and only fifteen survived the winter of 1528–29. Taken into servitude by the Han and Capoque tribes, after a period of a year or two, four men escaped and continued traveling westward across land: Álvar Núñez Cabeza de Vaca, Alonso del Castillo Maldonado, Andrés Dorantes de Carranza, and "Estevanico the Black," from the Moroccan city of Azemmour, who had come over as a slave of Dorantes's and now acquired a new, not-quite-defined status as co-refugee and companion. Together, they survived and eventually thrived, because Cabeza de Vaca and his companions gained an increasing reputation as medicine men, healing people along the way. After each stop, an embassy from the local tribe would lead the group of foreign healers on to the next locality, smoothing the path with reports of their abilities.

The astonishing story of the group's survival and wanderings westward from one community to another along the Rio Grande and farther west during the early 1530s is known from an account or *Relación* by Cabeza de Vaca, published after having found his way back to Mexico and then to Spain. The *Relación* captures a brief interval of the Spanish presence in the Americas where Spaniards play the role of refugees looking for acceptance in successive regions across the expanse north of Mexico. For six years, Cabeza de Vaca and his three mates walked these territories not as conquerors, colonists, and missionaries but as servants and then healers dependent on local hospitality for their survival. If in the published account, dedicated to Emperor Charles V, Cabeza de Vaca is sure to point out his efforts to spread Christian forms and faith through the land, the bulk of his narrative in fact documents his and his companions' extraordinary sensitivity to the environmental intelligence, social rituals, and medicinal knowledge of their successive Indigenous hosts. When, in 1536, the long-haired, sun-baked Cabeza de Vaca again encountered fellow Spaniards near Culiacán on the western coast of Mexico, they did not recognize him as a Spaniard.

A Bell from Far Away

Somewhere in northern Mexico and not far from the Rio Grande, probably in the region of Coahuila, Cabeza de Vaca and his companions arrived at an encampment of forty houses inhabited by people whose language they had not heard before, and who presented them with a large copper bell of some value:

> And among other things they gave us, Andrés Dorantes received a thick and large bell, made of copper, and on it was figured a face [*rostro*], and they demonstrated that they valued it greatly. And they told them that they had obtained it from other people who lived nearby. And asking them where those people had obtained them, they said that those people had brought it from toward the north, and that there was more of it there, and it was valued greatly. And we understood that from wherever it had come, there was a foundry and that they made it by casting.

After another day's travel, they arrived in a further community with many permanent houses set on a very beautiful river, where Cabeza de Vaca extracted an arrowhead from a man's chest and stitched him expertly, causing him to be celebrated by the inhabitants. He turned to them for more information about the bell:

> We showed them that bell we were carrying, and they told us that in the place from which it had come there were many plates [*planchas*] of that material in the ground, and that it was a thing they valued highly, and that there were permanent houses there. And this we believe to be the South Sea since we always had understood that that sea is richer than the one of the North.[1]

From these reports, the travelers learned that the bell had come from far away in the north, from a wealthy place perhaps bordering the South Sea. For Cabeza de Vaca and his contemporaries, the South Sea was the common designation for the Pacific, the North Sea for the Atlantic. The episode was also recounted by the widely read naturalist Gonzalo Fernández de Oviedo in his *Historia general y natural de las Indias* (1535), where we learn that Cabeza de Vaca and his party had also received cotton mantles together with the bell, and that those who bestowed the gifts "told them that it had come from toward the north, crossing the land in the direction of the South Sea."[2]

The copper bell—likely similar to the large one shown in figure 8.1, which along with several rattles was found in Arizona but did not come from there—offered direct proof of mining, metalworking, and significant centers of trade, providing material evidence of a civilization more advanced than any Cabeza de Vaca had encountered during his journey across the lands to the north and northwest of the Gulf of Mexico. Finally arriving in Mexico City in 1536, Cabeza de Vaca and his companions presented the bell to the viceroy of New Spain, Antonio de Mendoza, who was captivated by this artifact of a rich civilization up the coast of the South Sea toward the north and west.[3] Dozens of Spanish expeditions to the north and west were launched over the next century in response to the call of Dorantes's bell.[4]

The region north and west of Mexico inspired European visions of Asia perhaps more than any other part of the world. In the 1530s and 40s, authoritative maps by Oronce Finé, Caspar Vopel, and others realized these visions by merging China and India with the newly discovered Mexico (see chapters 9 and 11). In his *Historia*, Oviedo identified "these our Indies" with the Hesperides of ancient lore, admitting that it remained an open question whether they were connected to Asia, which would be the case "if the farthest extreme of Asia, farther on from the kingdom of China, or if some other land farther east were connected to the westernmost part of the mainland of these our Indies."[5] Although he cast doubt on the idea—"my opinion . . . gives me more the suspicion that it is not part of Asia"—Oviedo's skepticism was no match for the lure of the great possibility, which inspired generations of Spaniards to funnel money and resources into successive expeditions north and westward in hopes of spectacular discoveries and great reward.

The expeditions launched from Mexico northward to the *Tierra Nueva* entered into and disrupted the Indigenous networks of trade, diplomacy, and communication that had held the greater Sonoran Desert together for centuries. Sometimes welcomed peaceably by the Native communities they encountered, the Spanish fortune-seekers also regularly provoked violent clashes, leaving a trail of murder, rape, pillage, and destruction along their path, occasionally documented in detail by the Spaniards themselves.[6] The inhabitants of the region were, however, not only victims, and the Amerasian vision was not simply a European blueprint imposed on a passive land and people that had no conception of the wider world. The Indigenous communities already inhabited a wider world and were active in the development of emergent geographical ideas, which they deployed with strategic intelligence.[7] Asked to function as regional informants for a new species of invaders, they drew on Native knowledge systems and then delivered the information with a discretion tempered through centuries of regional trade as well as conflict.

Some communities preserved themselves from the European threat by adapting to and deploying the ways of Amerasian signaling, for example by sending the expeditions onward with accounts of cities and rich resources. These accounts may occasionally have been fabricated in order to fool the invaders, as seems to have happened in the case of the Coronado expedition, which was led from the Rio Grande region to present-day Kansas, where the fabled cities of Quivira lay, according to a Plains Indian whom Coronado had dubbed "El Turco." According to some accounts (yet disputed by others), El Turco was trying to get back to his homeland and at the same time lead the Spanish troops far astray, so that ultimately his own people could do away with the bedraggled soldiers who had survived the journey.[8] Even on occasions when local informants offered truthful reports drawn from their understanding of the larger environment, these communities knew that the arrival of yet another Spanish expedition meant they would be asked again where the gold and silver were, or where this or that item came from. They learned to provide information tailored to the expected questions, and to do so in a way that would keep the Spanish on the move and their own communities as much as possible free from harm. As the expeditions succeeded one another, a sedimentation of references formed between the Spaniards and a wide range of Native communities, a routine of signposting that integrated, interfered with, and contributed to the trade and cultural networks that had already existed among those communities. Soon enough, Amerasian visions became entangled with Indigenous practices, legends, and ways of imagining the land and moving through it, just as European techniques and products entered into dialogue with regional customs and trade pathways.[9]

Most copper bells in the northern regions were in fact Mesoamerican products, which had been traded for centuries before the arrival of the Spanish. The bell that Dorantes received most likely came not from the north but from western Mexico, Michoacán or Sinaloa, and had traveled to northern centers through Indigenous trade routes. Since examples of west Mexican production have been found as far north as present-day Arizona and New Mexico (see fig. 8.1), it is possible that Dorantes's bell had traveled from western Mexico to the northern lands, and then in a further move traveled southeast toward Coahuila near the Gulf of Mexico, where

Dorantes received it—a staggered, clockwise route.[10] By the time Dorantes received it, the memory of the artifact's foreign origins remained, possibly adding to its value, yet its exact provenance and meanings may well have become something of a mystery to its Coahuila keepers. In saying that it came from the north and west, they switched its provenance (from southwest to northwest) or perhaps truncated it, remembering it only as far as the final major leg of its trajectory. Cabeza de Vaca notes that this large bell had a face (*un rostro*) on it. It is likely that this figure, whatever it was, meant something different to the producers of the bell than to its later recipients, despite the fact that connections between Mesoamerica and northern and Pueblo cultures had intensified in the period before the arrival of the Spaniards.[11] Confronted with their outlandish visitors, one of them African, the keepers of the highly valued and exotic bell—exotic for them—might well have felt that this was an appropriate occasion to pass it on. As the latest recipients of the artifact, Dorantes and Cabeza de Vaca were given a role within a larger system of communication and trade that they were striving to coordinate with their own understanding of world geography. From the moment of Cortés's conquest and the further expeditions it launched, Amerasian views gained new depth and texture through interaction with Native practices, trade networks, cosmovisions, and origin legends.

The idea of a land-based expanse from Mexico northward to China was one major effect of the interaction with Indigenous communities in the *Tierra Nueva* north of Mexico from the time of Cabeza de Vaca onward. Over the sixteenth century, this conception developed in tandem with an island-based, maritime model.[12] The idea of a proximate maritime relationship between New Spain and Asia appears as early as the romance novel *The Adventures of Esplandián* (*Las sergas de Esplandián*, 1510), a chivalric tale popular in sixteenth-century Europe, where Garci Rodríguez de Montalvo first described the legend of California. "Know that on the right hand of the Indies there is an island called California very close to the side of the Terrestrial Paradise; and it is peopled by black women, without any man among them, for they live in the manner of Amazons."[13] For Montalvo and his readers, California was an Asian island, not far from the earthly paradise that Vespucci had been searching for. Ruled by Queen Calafia, the island was home to Amazon-like women who entertained men once a year to perpetuate their race. With this image, Montalvo established an imaginary frame for the region that informed the expeditions of Francisco de Ulloa and Hernando de Alarcón to what are today the Sea of Cortez and the Baja Peninsula and what they called the "island" of California, in search of the Strait of Anian.[14] The island-based

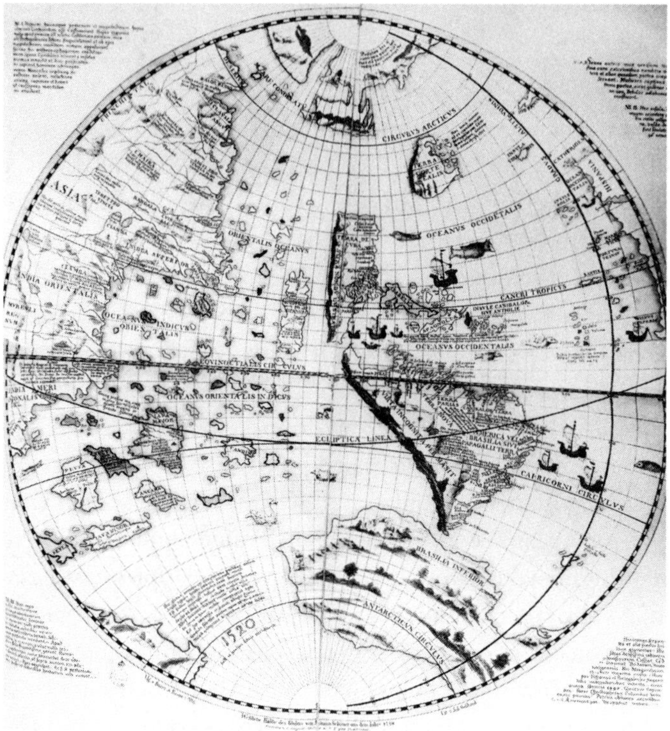

8.2 For Johannes Schöner, the new world belongs to a system of islands. Projection of the Western Hemisphere of Schöner's 1520 globe (original globe 57 × 35.5 cm), from Friedrich Wilhelm Ghillany, *Geschichte des Seefahrers Ritter Martin Behaim* (Nürnberg, 1853).

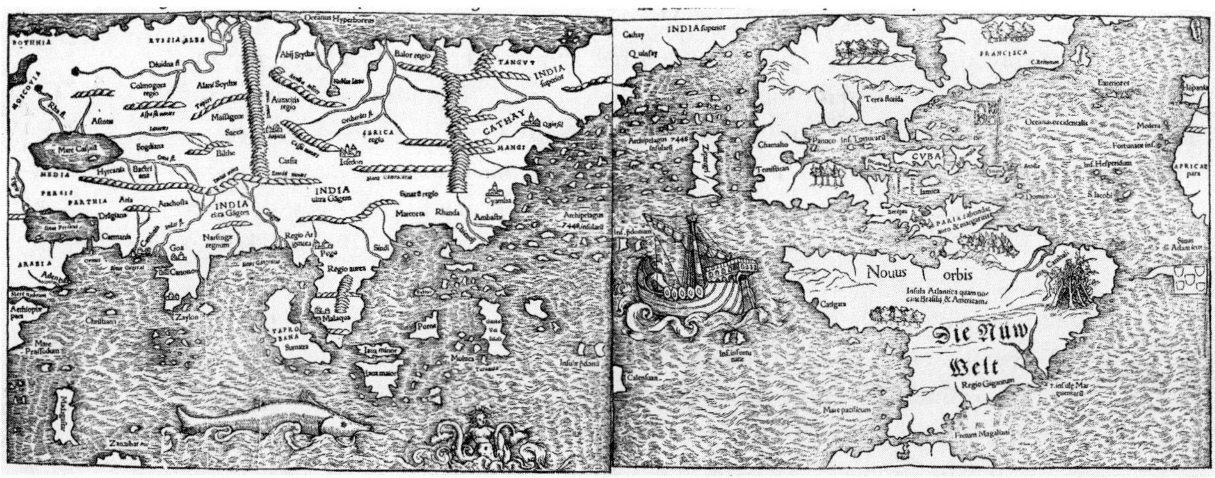

8.3 The new world as an Asian archipelago. Sebastian Münster, *Geographia*, woodcut, ca. 51 × 68.2 cm (Basel, 1540). Two maps in Münster's 1540 publication of Ptolemy's *Geographia*, the *Tabula orientalis regionis* and *Tabula novarum insularum*, are often considered separately. When joined together, it becomes clear that the new world or *Novus orbis*, described here as "the Atlantic island which is called Brasil and America," is understood as the largest in what the map labels an "archipelago of 7,448 islands" off the coast of Asia.

model persisted through the century. Francisco de Vargas, a sailor on Juan Rodríguez Cabrillo's expedition along the California coast (1542), claimed in the 1560s that Cabrillo had been on his way to the Spice Islands ("he was very near Moluco and the spice country and in the neighborhood of China") when he suffered an untimely death.[15] In 1597, a letter written from Pueblo de los Angeles (corresponding to modern Los Angeles) described the islands of California rich in "very fair Oriental pearls," indicating the persistence at the end of the century of an Asian island of California, with dreams of Asian wealth intact.[16]

In 1517, before Cortés's invasion of Mexico, Francisco Hernández de Córdoba led an expedition to the Yucatán and named it the Wealthy Island (*Isla Rica*); likewise, Juan de Grijalva believed he had discovered a new island when he sailed along the Yucatán's coasts in 1518.[17] The explorer Juan Díaz, who was under the command of Grijalva, additionally reported in 1518 that from the island of the Yucatán "they cross over to trade with the mainland of India."[18] Numerous maps in subsequent decades depicted the Yucatán similarly, including the Diogo Ribeiro map (1528), the Verrazano world map (1529) and Giacomo Gastaldi's highly influential *Universale* (1546); the cosmographer Joannes Myritius Melitensis still described the Yucatán as an island in 1590.[19] Indeed, the idea of endless Indian islands dominated the visions of Cortés's contemporaries. The explorer Juan Ponce de León reported his discovery of the "island" of Florida in 1513 and 1521, as did his successor Lucas Vázquez de Ayllón in 1526.[20] Alessandro Geraldini, a humanist at the Spanish court who eventually became Bishop of Santo Domingo, confirmed in his *Itinerary*, addressed to Pope Leo X on March 19, 1522, that the land of America (corresponding to what was then known of southern landmass including Paria and Brazil) was an island larger than Europe and Asia, and that by crossing it at its narrowest point (in present-day Panama) and beginning to build ships in the "other Ocean," Gil González Dávila was now in a position to discover "the 11,000 islands which are described by Aristotle, and then put the island of Hispaniola in contact with Bactriana [in present-day Afghanistan], the Nabatheans [an ancient kingdom whose capital was Petra, in present-day Jordan], the Golden Chersonese, India, the island of Taproban beyond the Ganges, Persia, Arabia, and the whole of Asia and Africa."[21]

At the time of the Cortés expedition, this insular vision of Mexico and its surroundings aligned neatly with other cartographic models of the world. Johannes Schöner's 1515 and 1520 globes (fig. 8.2), as well as Sebastian Münster's *Novae insulae* of 1545 (fig. 8.3), depicted Yucatán as an island and, more significantly, the Americas as a whole as an insular appendage of Asia, an understanding that surely had its roots in earlier geographical accounts, such as John Mandeville's description of the five thousand islands that comprised India, or Polo's estimate of the thirteen thousand islands in the Sea of India and more than seven thousand in the sea surrounding Japan.[22] As the historian and archaeologist Richard Flint put it, "European cosmographers and cartographers still conceived of the islands and land masses that Columbus had seen nearly fifty years earlier as eastward appendages and the periphery of Asia."[23] Schöner accompanied his 1515 globe with the explanatory treatise *A Most Lucid Description of All Lands* (*Luculentissima quaedam terrae totius descriptio*), in which he explains, "America, and the other islands belonging to it, [is] the fourth part of the world. In this way it may be known that the earth is in four parts and that the first three parts are continents, that is, *terra firma*, but that the fourth is an island, for it is seen to be surrounded everywhere by the seas."[24] Insular maps like Münster's and Schöner's cast the Americas into a noncontiguous yet associated relationship to Asia. This basic orientation explains why, for example, the 1558 Venetian edition of Johann Boemus's *The Manners, Laws, and Customs of All Nations*—one of the most popular sixteenth-century texts on geography and ethnography—placed the islands of Borneo, the Philippines, and the Moluccas in its fourth book on the "West Indies or New World" (see chapter 6).[25]

The Amerasian vision gained traction with the successful siege of Tenochtitlan and the advance of Cortés's troops through the Mexican mainland. Following these successes, Cortés immediately wanted to press on to the Asian South Sea on Mexico's far coast. "All those who have some learning and experience in the navigation of the Indies," he wrote in his third letter of 1523, "are quite certain that once the route to the South Sea has been discovered we shall find many islands rich in gold, pearls, precious stones and spices."[26] He made preparations for expeditions into the South Sea believing that it was just a matter of time before he could find a sea passage connecting the Caribbean to the Moluccas.[27] He organized a 1527 voyage to the South Sea that he delegated to his cousin Álvaro de Saavedra Cerón, instructing him to be prepared to translate Latin letters entrusted to him either into Arabic or into Indian languages. To this end, Cortés arranged for "a native Indian from Calicut" to accompany the voyage in order to facilitate translation on the ground once Saavedra reached the Spice Islands.[28] He gave Saavedra Mexican printed cottons to exchange for live clove trees, hoping to bring about a Southeast Asian botanical transformation in Mexico. Cortés also hoped to transplant spice trees to New Spain, and he commanded Saavedra to educate himself as much as possible about these matters.[29] Cortés also organized the import of mulberry saplings and silkworms, and by the 1530s the production of silk had become well established around Oaxaca.[30] Building on the developing trade, the Franciscan missionary Toribio of Benavente (or Motolinía) believed that he would be able to extend his missionary activity directly from central Mexico to Asia; in 1532–33, he moved to Tehuantepec, a Zapotec city in southern Mexico on the Pacific coast, where for seven months, he and other friars waited for ships from Cortés that would take them to China, which he perceived to be not far off the west coast of Mexico.[31] Rather than dissolve with advancing geographic knowledge, the idea of Amerasia took new shape as explorations expanded, commercial networks grew, and botanical and animal species were transplanted.

Spanish Expeditions into the Tierra Nueva

When received in Mexico City by the Spanish authorities, Dorantes's bell came packaged with a legendary provenance from distant lands to the north and west, opening up a vista of northward expansion toward Asia to accompany the maritime quest unleashed by Dávila and Cortés. Viceroy Antonio de Mendoza's geocultural interpretation of the bell propelled successive expeditions into the *Tierra Nueva* in the decades that followed, and the many accounts they produced yielded a cumulative record of the quest to reach China, or at least a significant outpost of Chinese civilization, from Mexico. The Franciscan friar Marcos de Niza was sent by Mendoza himself to search for the walled towns described by Cabeza de Vaca. De Niza had been a missionary on Santo Domingo, in Guatemala, and in Peru, and so came to his expedition with copious experience in the Americas. He wrote an official report describing how between March and September of 1539, he departed from Culiacán and traveled along the upper Rio Grande. He was accompanied by a priest named Honorato, and "Estevanico the Black," the same servant who had traveled with Cabeza de Vaca and Dorantes and was therefore familiar, to some degree, with some Indigenous customs and languages. While it has long been debated whether or not de Niza actually completed this trek to the north, he reported having sighted from a distance the wealthy city of Cibola (or the present-day Zuni pueblo in what is today west-central New Mexico), believed to be one of the legendary seven Cities of Gold, which he estimated to be as large as Mexico City.[32] Estevanico had learned of Cibola from Native informants (its name was perhaps related to an Indigenous term for buffalo) and reported it to de Niza, so that once again, as in the narrative of Cabeza de Vaca and Dorantes, larger systems of Indigenous information on the ground informed Spanish expeditions.

Upon his return in the fall of 1539, the friar's stories generated a stir in Mexico City and as they spread, the Asian promise of the *Tierra Nueva* grew to fantastical proportions. On October 18, 1539, Rodrigo de Albornoz, the treasurer of New Spain, wrote a summary of de Niza's journey for his superior the royal treasurer in Spain, reporting that de Niza had visited a land populated by camels, elephants, and people wearing camlet, a luxurious fabric made from a combination of silk and camel hair that according to Marco Polo came from the city of Kalacha in what is now northwestern China.[33] On October 9, 1539, the Augustinian friar Gerónimo Ximénez de San Estéban reported that he had heard de Niza describe the inhabitants of Cibola wearing "silk clothing down to their feet" (de Niza's relation had only mentioned cotton) as well as temples with walls "covered with precious stones. I think he said they were emeralds. They also say that in the country beyond there are camels and elephants."[34] Even de Niza's barber, it seems, became caught up in the excitement, reporting that while he was shaving the friar, de Niza told him that on his journey he saw "women [who] were accustomed to wear golden necklaces, and the men, belts made of gold" (de Niza only reported seeing turquoise on his journey).[35] According to Flint, additional pieces of the de Niza narrative, such as his visit to a place named Marata (a town in the interior of the Arabian Peninsula, according to Ptolemy's *Geographia*) contributed to "the popular conviction of the day that North America was an extension of the Orient."[36] A decade and a half later, in 1556, the Venetian cosmographer Giovanni Battista Ramusio produced an Italian translation of de Niza's *Relación* in his *Navigazioni e viaggi*, altering the report to make Cibola sound wealthier than it was. Ramusio describes Cibolans using "drinking cups made of gold and silver. They employ [these metals] more often and in greater quantity than [they do] in Peru."[37] Extant, original Spanish copies of the *Relación* omit the passage and make no reference to gold or silver when speaking of Cibola, suggesting that Ramusio added it on the basis of rumor. Everyone who heard about de Niza's travels, it seems, added to the speculation about the lands to the north and the potential nearness of Asian lands.[38]

The geographical implications of these ideas filtered back to Europe. On the Genoese cartographer Battista Agnese's vellum painted world map, one of several high-end atlases for armchair travelers he made in the 1540s, we see the old world (Europe, Africa, and known Asia) to the right and the new world to the left (fig. 8.4). Connecting them like a ribbon is Magellan's route around the world. As was common on sixteenth-century maps, the words *MUNDUS NOVUS* mark the southern landmass across the Atlantic. The northern landmass has no label, with the borders undefined, flirting with the idea that it is an extension of the "province of Cathay." Mexico is identified solely by the city Tenochtitlan (*Temistitan*), shown as an elaborate construction on a lake. To the west is a reddish sea

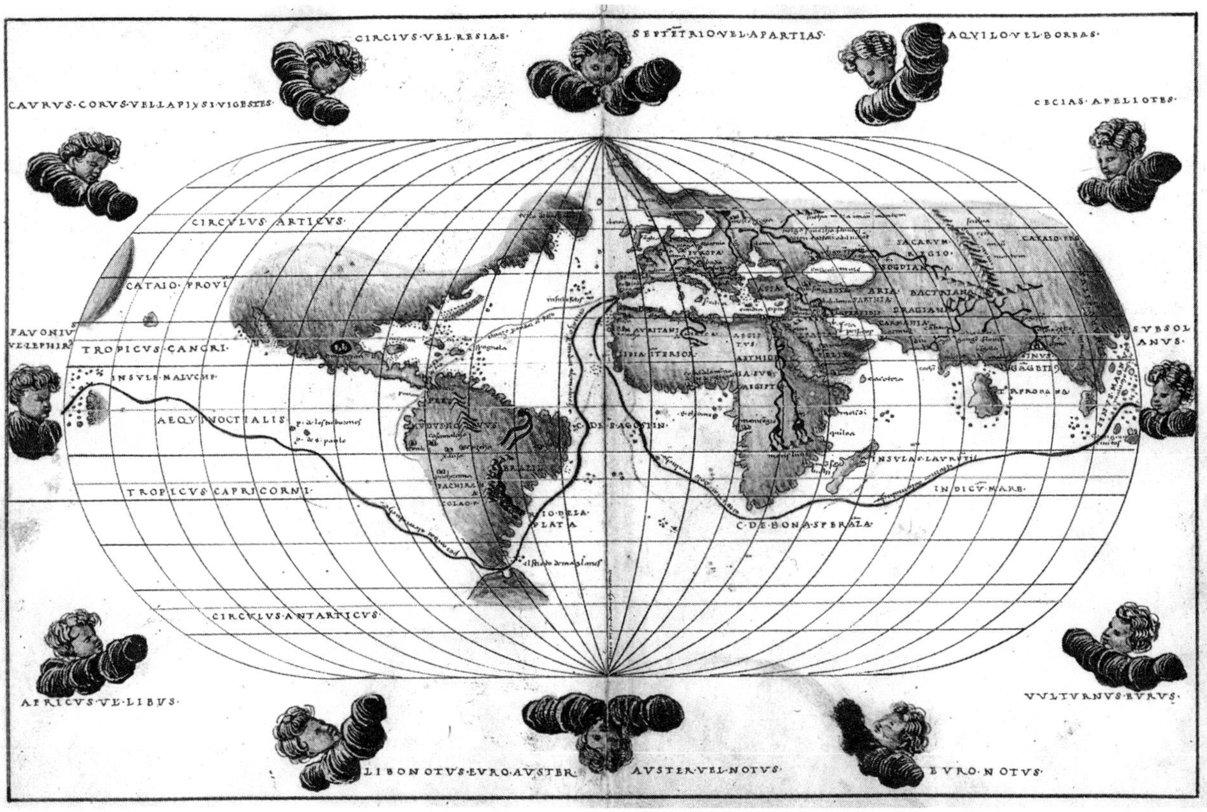

8.4 The convergent world of the 1540s. Battista Agnese, *Portolan Atlas*, pen-and-ink and watercolor on vellum, 21 × 29 cm (1544). Washington, DC, Library of Congress.

that Francisco de Ulloa had called the Sea of Cortés in 1539 in honor of his patron. North of this gulf the green land fades away into the water, an admission of the limits of geographic knowledge, and to the west, not far away, the eastern coast of Cathay appears as a curving continent at the western edge of the map. In the body of water between this end of Asia and the new land still being explored are the words CATAIO PROVI[NTIA], a repetition of the designation at the right edge of the map, making clear that this is an extension of Cathay back around the west. By placing the words in the watery space between the eastern land and the not fully understood extent of the lands north of Mexico, he suggests that the province of Cathay crosses the water. Furthermore, on the western edge of the map and to the south, inside the tropics, Agnese places the Moluccas, by implication putting them in Spanish territory. The map endorses the current Spanish conviction that Mexico was a gateway to Asia, certainly by sea and possibly by land.

Contrary to what one might expect, subsequent Spanish expeditions northward by land from Mexico appeared to bring China even closer. Based on the tentative but firsthand knowledge gleaned from de Niza, Mendoza was certain that subsequent explorations would reach either Cathay or some equally wondrous eastern territory. He therefore organized in late 1539 a two-pronged expedition to the north, by land and by sea, sending ships up the Gulf of California with Hernando de Alarcón to carry supplies and seek a harbor where they could rendezvous with a land party led by Francisco Vázquez de Coronado. While stationed in Tiguex (near modern Albuquerque), Coronado was presented with an Indigenous man not local to the region but from the "interior land" to the east. "They called the Indian Turco because by his appearance he seemed like one"—a Turk, that is. He recounted that his home country, named Quivira, was rich, with large cities, where common people ate from plates and bowls worked in silver and gold. The land had a wide river with fish as big as horses, and the lord of the land took his siesta under a tree hung with golden bells, because it "gave him pleasure." His imagination fired, Coronado followed El Turco's directions, traveling eastward and northward over many weeks and the increasing grumbling of his soldiers, eventually arriving in what is today central Kansas, the farthest point in his journey. Disappointed by what they found, some of Coronado's men concluded that El Turco had lied and led them astray, putting him to death before returning on the long route back to Mexico City.

An accompanying soldier and chronicler of the Coronado expedition of 1540–42, Pedro de Castañeda de Nájera, insisted that El Turco had led them in the wrong direction, holding instead to the dominant belief that the route to Asia lay to the north and west, and in doing so described a geographic extension connecting New Spain and Asia: "Just as this land of Nueva España is a [continuous] landmass with El Perú, so is it also with Greater India or China, unless there is a strait in that direction which divides it."[39] Castañeda described the Pueblo Indians as a constellation of communities centered on Tiguex, proposing that these people had come "from that part of Greater India, the coast of which lies toward the west of this land. They may have descended through that region, crossing those mountain ranges, coming downstream along that river [Río de Tiguex], and settling in the place that seemed best to them."[40] All the Spaniards needed to do was reverse the migratory path that had brought the Indians themselves to their present location: "If the lands from which those people originate were entered, magnificent news would probably be obtained. [That is] because, according to the direction, [that land] is the beginning of Greater India, although [in] remote regions, unfamiliar and unknown."[41]

Recording the site of a recent burial and a cross made of twigs tied with cotton thread, he hypothesized that these people "in some way . . . possess some knowledge of the cross of Christ, Our Redeemer. It could be by way of India, from where [the Indians] originate."[42] Castañeda puts China and India into extended continuity with Mexico in an Amerasian continent, much the way the maps of the Venetian cartographer Gastaldi depicted it two decades later (see chapter 11).

Castañeda's Amerasian interpretation of the evidence applied contemporary Spanish ideas that could be found in various forms in writings about the new world. For example, the Dominican friar Bartolomé de Las Casas, who spent years in different parts of the new Spanish colonies, including Guatemala, Oaxaca, Chiapas, and Mexico City, asserted that "all of our Indies are the last part of what was called the Indies in antiquity."[43] (For further discussion of Las Casas's conception of India, see chapter 12.) Yet Castañeda was also giving texture to the developing Spanish worldview through the experience of a new terrain and with whatever evidence he could gather from Indigenous sources—not only their knowledge of the wider geography but also possibly their origin legends. Pueblo origin tales, as reported by anthropological investigations of the twentieth century, tell how the first people were two women, sisters, who emerged from inside the earth somewhere in the north and then initiated a migration southward.[44]

There were of course those among the Spanish who rejected the idea of a joined Mexican-Chinese landmass, yet even they still saw possibilities for imminent contact with China by traveling northward. In his 1552 *Historia general de las Indias*, Francisco López de Gómara duly reported that "many believe that the land up there unites with China . . . and for that reason one should sail along the coast in the area that remains unknown, even if it is at the cost of our king, because there is so much there, and the one who follows through would have a lot to gain." Yet he himself held to the view that "they will not join, since Asia, Africa, and Europe are islands, as we said at the beginning."[45] He expected that further explorations would eventually find an upper Pacific coast filled with ports already well traveled by Chinese ships, and he applauded the expeditions of de Niza and Coronado in search of the new passageways to China, even as he adapted those reports to suit his maritime vision. The original account of Coronado's spoke of the boundless riches that could be found in this Quivira, where "there was a river in a plain two leagues wide. . . . And [there were] a great many exceedingly large canoes with more than twenty rowers on each side, which also carried sails. The lords traveled on the poop, seated beneath awnings. On the prow [there was] a large eagle of gold."[46] López de Gómara offered again this account but introduced a significant change of location from inland river to ocean coast: "They saw on the coast ships which had pelicans of gold and silver on their prows, with merchandise that they thought to be from Cathay and China, because they made signs that they had sailed thirty days."[47] By moving Quivira from the plains to the coast, Gómara retroactively corrected Coronado's misbegotten inland venture.

The new image of a port of Quivira on the ocean, with large vessels arriving from Cathay, was then consolidated and embellished by the many editions, adaptations, and translations of Gómara's highly popular account. In his 1584 "Discourse of Western Planting," Richard Hakluyt's translation of Gómara's passage offered even more information about the great port of Quivira.

> Againe, when he [Coronado] was afterwards at the towne of Quivira, which is scituated by the sea side in the latitude of 40 degrees, he founde there shippes with maryners, which had the picture of a birde, called Alcatrazzi [albatrosses], in silver upon their bonnetts and on the forepartes of their shippes, which signified that they were thirtie daies sailinge to that place whence it is saied that they muste nedes be of Cathaio or China, seinge that there is none but Spanishe shippinge upon all the coaste of the backside of Noua Spania.[48]

Just as de Niza's audience in Mexico City fired the imaginations of his influential listeners, the spreading retellings of Coronado's journey transformed the inland capital of Quivira (located by modern scholars in Kansas) into an active Amerasian port harboring Chinese ships.

The two ideas—a territorial and a maritime extension to China—continued to intertwine in the Spanish imagination throughout the sixteenth century and beyond. Coronado and Viceroy Mendoza in Mexico City believed Asia to be to the north and west of New Spain, yet Mendoza was well aware this might involve sea travel. In a letter to Oviedo, Mendoza declared that the expedition was guided by two missions: "One to reconnoiter the coast of this *Nueva España* and another which was to travel to the west in search of the Lequios [clusters of islands off the coast of China, today believed to be around Okinawa] and Cathay."[49] The two-pronged approach marked expeditions to the west and north of New Spain right through the sixteenth century. In 1573, King Philip II sent a copy of his *Ordinances for the New Discoveries, Conquests, and Pacifications*—a guide to the legal principles governing Spanish territorial expansion—to Juan de Oñate, who was appointed to explore and settle lands on the northern frontier of New Spain, eventually leading to the founding in 1598 of the province of *Nueva México* (an area much larger than the present-day state of New Mexico). The king requested that Oñate undertake a survey of this territory's coastline and harbors, indicating the continued Spanish belief—even after the firm establishment of the Manila galleon trade—that these lands lay perhaps not far from China.[50] Oñate in fact requested permission to take shipbuilders on his expedition.[51] Later, in October 1598, having heard reports of pearls and having seen their shells, Oñate traveled west across the Rio Grande and led a detachment of mounted soldiers to search for the South Sea "whose trade with Peru, New Spain, and China should not be underestimated."[52] He launched an additional expedition in 1604 to search for the Golden Fleece, in ancient mythology located in Colchis in Asia, but now believed to be near the Gulf of California.[53] In 1602, Rodrigo del Rio de Losa, Knight of the Order of Santiago and governor of Nueva Galicia, a coastal province of Mexico, wrote to the Viceroy of New Spain describing the lands to the north in "Indian" terms: "We may well believe that in a new country [*Tierra Nueva*] of such vast proportions where it is said that there are people who bear a metal crown like our kings, there are walled towns and houses of five, six, or seven storeys . . . and silver and gold as in other lands and in the Indies. For the greed of these riches, we Spaniards came to these parts."[54]

Gaspar Pérez de Villagrá's epic poem narrating the Oñate expedition, the *Historia de la Nueva México* (1610), echoes Castañeda's earlier account of the Coronado expedition in suggesting the Asian origins of the people of New Spain. Having garnered information from the oldest Indigenous inhabitants (*naturales*) of the region concerning the "ancient origins, arrival, and settling of the Mexicans," he asserts, "in my view, all who live in what we call the Indies came from the great China."[55] The widely reported "sightings" of Chinese ships off the western coast of the *Tierra Nueva*, as well as the remarkably civilized and well-resourced societies encountered along the way, suggested to readers in New Spain and Europe that an Amerasian network in fact existed before the arrival of the Spaniards and was only now being understood and developed.[56]

The expeditions from Coronado to Oñate were applying a geocultural model not far from that of the great Vopel map, studied in chapter 11, a Spanish/Habsburg vision of the world produced in the 1540s and propagated in succeeding decades, where Mexican place names mingle with East Asian ones in a vastly extended "Greater Asia." Or perhaps their model was closer to other maps of the period that show China at some distance from Mexico yet still connected to it by a broad land bridge bordering a great South Sea gulf populated by islands. (A representative array of different models is studied in chapters 9, 10, and 11.) In this unresolved geographical imaginary, both routes—overland and maritime—were possible, and might even join on the other side.

The copper bell of Coahuila was probably generations if not centuries old when it was bestowed on Dorantes in the 1530s. Yet it had never settled as a local heirloom for its Indigenous owners, who had received it from another locality nearby, who in turn remembered that it had come from lands to the north. The communities of Coahuila may or may not have known for certain which deity's face was cast into one side of the bell. By putting it into the hands of their highly exotic visitors, one of them called "el Negro" for his skin color, the most recent keepers of the bell were ensuring that it would continue to travel, perhaps farther than ever. For them, the bell had always sounded an identifiably foreign tone, an echo of faraway lands. And so it did for the Spaniards, who inherited the origin story as well as the bell.

• • •

Postscript: Mexico Writes the Book of China

Given the Chinese orientation of the European experience of Mexico and of the further encounters with the communities and cultures of the *Tierra Nueva*, it is not a surprise that the earliest history of China written by a European was composed in sixteenth-century Mexico. *The History of the Great and Mighty Kingdom of China and the Situation Thereof* (*Historia de las cosas más notables, ritos y costumbres del gran reyno de la China*), written by the Augustinian friar Juan González de Mendoza (c. 1540–1617), was first published in 1586, to be followed by a plethora of translations and further editions in the years to follow and over the next century. Mendoza came into contact with numerous transpacific travelers whom he interviewed when they passed through his convent in Michoacán. His main informants were Franciscan missionaries returning to New Spain from China and the Philippines, and his history of China is largely a compilation of their accounts.[57]

Mendoza's history begins with a lengthy discussion of Chinese culture, including descriptions of marriage and burial practices, clothing, architecture, language, the provinces of China, its government, and the Chinese use of both artillery and printing, drawing on the accounts of a variety of travelers to Ming China in the 1580s to do so. Toward the end of his volume, Mendoza turns to the account of Antonio de Espejo, a wealthy explorer from Mexico City who traveled in 1582–83 to the villages along the northern frontier of New Spain, yet another expedition to *Nuevo México*.[58] Even though Mendoza's entire book is a testament to the missionary activity and cultural exchange opened up by the regular crossing of the Pacific by the Manila galleon trade that began in 1565 (see chapter 17), the Espejo expedition into the northern Mexican hinterland follows the well-established pattern of imagined land-based continuities between America and Asia. Near the meeting of the Conchos River and the Rio Grande, Espejo encounters Jumano Indians who remembered the encounter with "three Christians and a negro" long before, which Espejo recognizes must be a memory from fifty years earlier of Cabeza de Vaca and his three mates.

As was the case for Cabeza de Vaca and his companions and for the many expeditions northward that followed, Espejo encountered along the way examples of local handiwork that seemed to promise Asian proximity. For example, along the Rio Grande the local *Indios* possessed "many curious things made of feathers of different colors, and many mantles made of cotton, barred with blue and white, like those that are brought from China to trade for other things." When Espejo asked about the origin of these products, the locals replied that "five days' journey from there, towards the north-west, there was a great quantity of these goods." They also showed the Spaniards "stones of rich metal," and again the locals said that the stones came from a place five days' journey to the north and west.[59] Further north along the Rio Grande, in a province called Quires, above the thirty-seventh parallel, Espejo noted "a magpie in a cage, as is the use in Spain, and parasols (*tirasoles*), like those that are brought from China, and painted on them the sun and the moon with many stars."

Further north still they came to the town of Cia, where the dwellings were well painted, the surroundings rich in minerals, and where the people seemed to have greater dignity and better government than any seen so far. Finally they arrived in the large town of Zuni, "which the Spanish call Cibola," where they saw some inhabitants practicing forms of Christian worship, a holdover of the missionary work of the Coronado expedition from decades earlier, as well as a few Spaniards left there who had almost forgotten their native language. There they learned that sixty days farther on there was a great lake with several towns around it, a land full of gold where the Native peoples wear gold bracelets and earrings. Coronado had tried to get there, Espejo notes, but had run out of water and had had to turn back.[60] In a venture in that direction before heading back, Espejo finds communities more civilized than any he had encountered before, as well as strong evidence of silver and gold in the area.

Mendoza's China compendium is based on accounts of friars who had sailed to the Philippines and the islands near China and then returned through Mexico, people who knew first-hand the rigors of the long transpacific crossing. Yet in his text, the Espejo venture into *Nuevo México* from the early 1580s still holds out hope that the lands north of Mexico and their inhabitants were independently connected to China through overland trade and cultural exchange. Espejo's account is itself a loop interpolated by Mendoza into an *Itinerario del Nuevo mundo*, a voyage of the friar Martin Ignacio from Spain to Mexico and on to Asia and then back to Spain through Persia and the Levant. Yet—in a typical instance of elliptical continuity—the sea passages hardly register in Ignacio's voyage. In contrast to the extended description of Espejo's travel into the north country, which vividly depicts a long march northward and westward with many pit stops over dozens of pages, the swift Ignacio travels across Mexico to Acapulco and then overseas to the Mariana Islands and Guam (Islas de los Ladrones) in a matter of paragraphs. Mendoza himself admits that "there are different opinions of the leagues between the port of Acapulco and those islands, for until now none have understood how to measure them with certainty, since this is an east-west navigation and no one has yet been able to measure the degrees of longitude."[61] (He concludes that it must be 1,700 leagues, not far off from the actual figure of 2,200.)

For a reader of Mendoza's volume, it would have been difficult to judge from internal evidence just how far Espejo traveled northward and westward on his long march, and thus how his overland route might relate to Ignacio's sea route, which involved a stop in the Philippines before proceeding northward toward China. The land-based model is coiled inside the sea-based model, as if to correlate them, in Mendoza's final book, called an *Itinerario del Nuevo mundo*. For Mendoza, just as for Columbus, Vespucci, Martin Waldseemüller, and Johannes Ruysch at the beginning of the century, the term *new world* encompassed all the lands newly encountered westward by the Spanish and eastward by the Portuguese and that went under the name Indies. The concluding chapters of the book describe Malacca, Sumatra, Taprobane, Calicut, Coromandel, Cochin, Goa, and Ormuz, all of which are announced in the corresponding chapter titles as "kingdoms of the new world."

NINE

The Swelling Earth: French Navigations in the Amerasian Imaginary

Amerasia found iconic cartographic expressions in the cordiform (heart-shaped) maps of the French cosmographer, geographer, and mathematician Oronce Finé (1494–1555). Finé's *Recens et integra orbis descriptio* (Paris, 1534), a woodcut map with additions of watercolor, shows toponyms from China overlapping and interweaving with ones from Mexico (*Messigo*), and Chinese rivers flowing into a body of water bounded on the south by a land of cannibals and on the east by the lands of Florida and the islands of *Yucatán* and *Cuba* (fig. 9.1). Asia borders the waters of the sea that contains Cuba and Marco Polo's toponyms of Mangi, Tangut, and Catay sit in close proximity to Tenochtitlan and the Panuco River (fig. 9.2). Finé knew of Ferdinand Magellan's voyage—the strait named after the navigator is clearly labeled on his map—yet he minimizes the expanse of water on the far side of Mexico, showing a narrow Mare de Sur that spans only ten degrees of longitude between the Moluccas (*Moluce*) and Mexico. Timor and Java (*Iava)* hover nearby, also on the western half of the map. The banderoles on either side of the globe labeled East (*Oriens*) and West (*Occidens*) do not correspond to Asia and America respectively. Though hard to make out amid all of Finé's details, instead the four letters of the regional label "Asia" extend across the top of the map—that is, across both sides of the cordiform—spanning the geographic space from the Ganges River and the Caspian Sea to Khanbalik (*Canbalu*) and Tenochtitlan (*Temistitan*), a single vast landmass that occupies both hemispheres. In the southern part of the Western Hemisphere, there is a large area named America, yet in the northern part of the same landmass Florida and Mexico are part of Asia.[1] As in many other maps, treatises, and travelogues of the sixteenth century, the toponym *America* is folded into an Amerasian view of the world.

As Tom Conley has noted, Finé's momentous career "mirrors the fortunes of the French nation" during the reign of Francis I. The cartouche

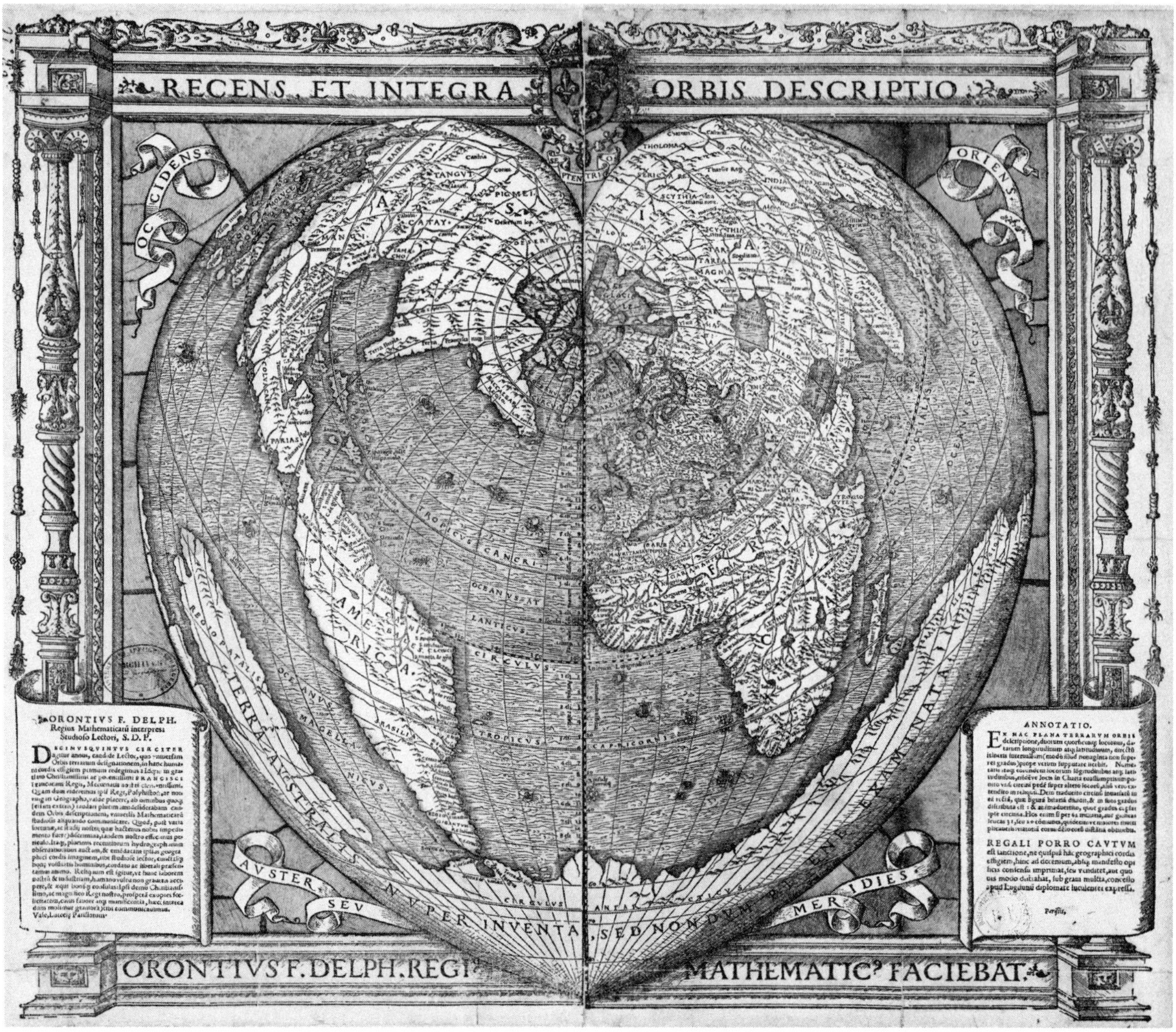

9.1 Asia encompasses Mexico. Oronce Finé, *Recens et integra orbis descriptio*, woodcut with watercolor, 57 × 51 cm (1534). Paris, Bibliothèque Nationale de France, Cartes et Plans, Rés. Ge DD 2987 (63). Though hard to make out amid all of Finé's details, the four letters of the regional label *asia* extend across the top of the map—that is, across both sides of the cordiform—spanning the geographic space from the Ganges River and the Caspian Sea to Khanbalik (*Canbalu*) and Tenochtitlan (*Temistitan*). (See color plates.)

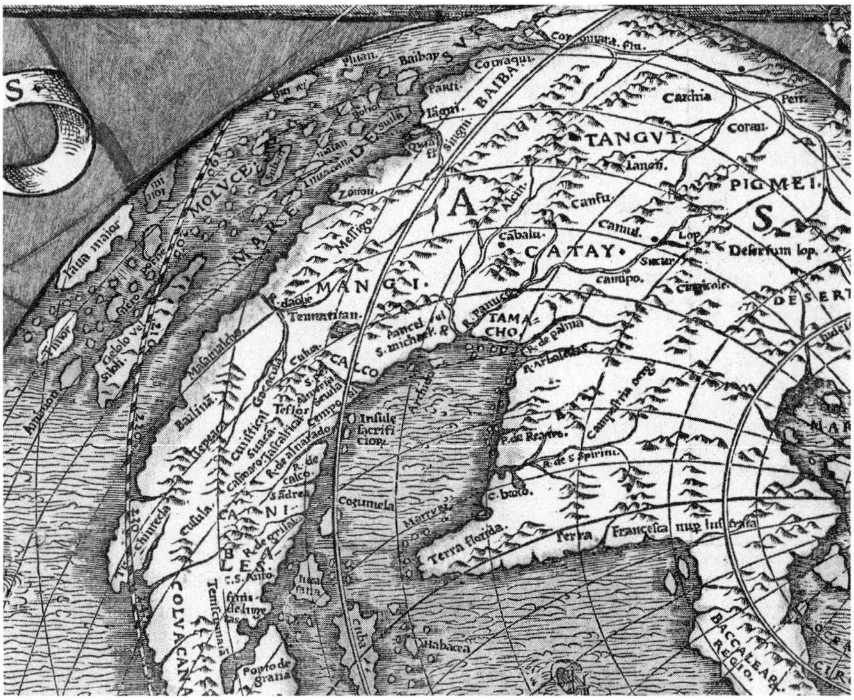

9.2 East Asia and the New World. Oronce Finé, *Recens et integra orbis descriptio*, detail. The Spice Islands or *MOLUCE* are not far from *Messigo*, itself part of southern China or *MANGI*, directly south of *CATAY*, indicating that the information supplied by the survivors of Magellan's voyage did not translate into a separation between America and Asia.

in the left corner of Finé's map proclaims that Finé had conceived of his projection "in the shape of a human heart, this universal map of the world, in gratitude to the Most Christian and Most Mighty Francis, King of the French." Finé first made use of the shape of the heart in a single cordiform map executed for Francis I in 1519, a form that was also employed during the French king's participation in a variety of triumphal entries in the first quarter of the sixteenth century.[2] At this time, the king's theatrical architects designed panels and textual diagrams in the shape of hearts based on Paul's letter to the Corinthians and the Song of Songs, lessons in evangelical humanism promoted under Francis.

Heart-Shaped World

A projection designed to render an orb on a two-dimensional surface while retaining a sense of its rotund shape, Finé's cordiform world gives tactile form to a vision of cosmic totality. As the eye follows the curving shape of the projection, writes Conley, "the viewer loses a sense of vertical grounding in respect to a picture seen at a distance, while the map is held in a square surround."[3] In fact, the cordiform exceeds its frame, spilling out in front of the borders at top and bottom and casting a shadow onto the lower part of the tabernacle that cannot quite contain it. Projecting even farther beyond the frame than these contours is the protuberant heart's center, where the meridian crosses the tropics, which swells forward from the background to meet the corresponding orb of our eye. The tabernacle with its cracked red marble background resolves conceptually as a human-made structure functioning optically as the framing background for what is in fact a floating planetary body of incommensurable scale. Close to the projecting center of the cordiform is Finé's France, or Gallia, which together with the rest of Europe is presented with little distortion. As we move from this part of the globe, closest to our eye, to the other parts of the world, our vision is torqued by the curving cordiform, the longitudes arcing into descending loops and the latitudes spiraling upward. The earth's extremities are strange not only because they are unknown but because our eye always grasps them as extremities that can only be seen obliquely, never in their true shape. Rounding the upper left lobe at the edge of our vision is the Amerasian extension connecting China to Mexico and America. Here is the expanse that French navigators, cosmographers, and writers of the sixteenth century explored and expounded in imagining the relationship between Europe and the extremities of the earth.

Finé derived his cosmography from the German mathematician and cosmographer Johannes Schöner, whose globes indeed bear a striking resemblance to Finé's projection (see chapters 8 and 11).[4] Finé was also well informed about the travels of Giovanni da Verrazano, sponsored by Francis I in an effort to compete with and counterbalance the expanding Habsburg presence around the globe, recently trumpeted by Magellan's much-publicized rounding of the globe in 1521–22. Declaring his intention "to reach Cathay and the extreme eastern coast of Asia," as he noted in a letter to the French king, Verrazano arrived in early 1524 on the northern coast of what was then known as Terra Florida.[5] There Verrazano encountered an inlet, in modern times called the Pamlico Sound, which he reported was the beginning of the Pacific Ocean, leading to the known parts of Asia.

For Verrazano, this coastal territory was para-Asian, separated by water from the known continent of Asia. He wrote to the French king in July 1524 that "all this land or New World which we have described above is joined together, but it is not linked with Asia or Africa (we know this for certain)," yet the navigator's descriptions of the people and fauna in the lands he explored are rife with Asian associations. He describes the Indigenous peoples of the region as having "big black eyes, and an attentive and open look. They are not very strong, but they have a sharp cunning, and are agile and swift runners. From what we could tell from observation, in the last two respects they resemble the Orientals, particularly those from the farthest Sinarian [i.e., Chinese] regions." He noted that "some have other hair arrangements such as the women of Egypt and Syria wear, and these women are older and have been joined in wedlock. Both men and women have various trinkets hanging from their ears as the Orientals do." Noting the sweet fragrance of local trees, Verrazano proposed that "they belong to the Orient by virtue of the surroundings, and that they are not without some kind of narcotic or aromatic liquor."[6]

When the Verrazano voyages started to inform maps, this association of the environment and inhabitants of the territory showed up as Amerasian mingling of locales. The so-called Verrazano globe at New York's Morgan Library shows the Asian emporium of Cattigara, which Ptolemy had placed in the southeasternmost part of Asia, in Peru, a detail Finé retained in his map. Here as elsewhere, Asia extends across the waters to the newly discovered lands to Europe's west. Similarly, the 1527 Paris Gilt or De Bure Globe located in the Bibliothèque Nationale in Paris—among the first to incorporate information from Verrazano's 1524 voyage—joins the lands in the western Atlantic to Asia. This globe is believed to be a reflection of the globe described by Franciscus Monachus in his small but influential treatise on the organization of the world, discussed in chapter 7.[7] The Gilt Globe depicts the land of Florida (*terra florida*) and the land of France (*terra francesca*) as eastern extensions of China and the south American landmass as an appendage that extends southeast from Asia. Following this model, Finé places Tenochtitlan (*Temistitan*) in the southern Chinese region of Mangi and makes *terra florida* an extension of Asian territory.

Cinnamon in Canada and the Northwest Passage to Asia

A decade later, in 1534, Francis I sent Jacques Cartier to explore what he soon called Canada, with the continuing objective to discover a passage to the riches of Asia.[8] During this first voyage, Cartier noted, "I am rather inclined to think from what I have seen that there is a passage [to Asia] between Newfoundland and the [Cape] Breton's island."[9] On his second voyage, 1535–36, Cartier repeatedly invokes Iroquois reports of a place called Saguenay, one month's voyage north of the St. Lawrence river, where cinnamon and clove grow in abundance, noting that there are "immense quantities of gold, rubies, and other rich things, and that the men there are white as in France and go clothed in woollens."[10] Cartier was told of this place by the chief Donnacona as tensions were rising between the French and the Iroquois; it is possible that the Iroquois chief offered this enticing lure to the French as a scented dose of their own Amerasian thinking, in an effort to get them to move on. By this point the Iroquois leaders had a clear sense of what the French wanted to hear, for after his first voyage Cartier had taken two sons of Donnacona back to France with him, returning them to their homeland on his second expedition.

The failure to find the Northwest Passage to Asia only stoked enthusiasm for further expeditions. In commissioning Cartier's third voyage on October 17, 1540, King Francis I took the continental extension of Canada into Asia as a premise, noting that "we had sent there our dear and beloved Jacques Cartier, who had discovered a great country in the lands of Canada and Hochelaga, forming one extremity of Asia on the West."[11] Another document, an order from Francis I to investigate a series of hindrances that had been preventing Cartier's departure, similarly describes the lands of Canada as "forming one of the extremities of Asia."[12] On this third voyage (1541–43), Cartier traveled up the Saint Lawrence River again to Stadacona and Hochelaga (close to what are today Québec City and Montreal), and embarked for Saguenay, but the account remains unfinished. A much later letter of 1587 by Cartier's nephew Jacques Noel appended to the original document of Cartier's third voyage describes a map with annotations in Cartier's hand noting the location of "the land of Saguenay, which is rich and wealthy in precious stones," where the explorer had written, "'here in this Countrey are Cinamon [*sic*] and Cloves, which they call in their language Canodeta.'"[13] A fourth expedition undertaken in 1542–43 by Jean-François de la Rocque de Roberval, who had served as pilot on Cartier's third voyage, was directed towards reaching Saguenay, and again the unfinished account falls short of the goal. Yet, the mysterious Saguenay was now firmly ensconced in the French new-world imaginary, and is represented on Pierre Desceliers's 1546 world map, where inland from the St. Lawrence river Roberval and his army are shown reaching "Le Sagnay," represented by a solemn ritual gathering, with several devotees kneeling before a throne on which sits a venerable bearded figure with arms outstretched, all of them light-skinned. In this vignette from the Canadian hinterland, Asia seems not far off.

The legend of Saguenay and related ideas about the nearness of Asia also feature in the writings of Jean Alfonse de Saintonge (also known as Jean Fonteneau), a renowned Portuguese navigator who accompanied Roberval and Cartier.[14] His *Cosmographie* (1544) describes the places he had traveled over the previous decades, including those seen on Cartier's third voyage, writing that the Saguenay River in Canada "seems to be an arm of the sea, for which reason I think that this sea goes into the Pacific or to that of Cathay."[15] Alfonse collected his own experiences and hearsay from other pilots, copying freely from the work of other cosmographers. He was aware of Spanish reports of the exploration of the valley of the Rio Grande, in particular, the recent accounts of Fray Marcos de Niza and Coronado, animated by the idea that these lands were a possible Asian frontier (see chapter 8).[16] Alfonse combines his own knowledge of New France with Spanish reports and observations to build a vision of the new world that extended to the extremities of Asia. As a result, Alfonse positions Peru within a system of far eastern islands rich in gold and spices. After describing Java and Jakarta, where he says there is "much gold and silver, and elephants and monkeys as in Barbary," as well as Dorfy (Ophir), "the name of the place from which it is written that Solomon had gold transported to make the temple." He estimates that "from here to Peru, in the East, it is 900 or 1000 leagues at most," at which point he resumes his discussion of the Moluccas and other nearby Pacific islands.[17] Alfonse understands that Peru is farther on from Java and Indonesia, yet it remained, for him "in the East," part of an Asian galaxy of dazzlingly wealthy lands and islands.

Verrazano and Cartier were soon followed, parodically, by the giant Pantagruel and his sidekick Panurge, whose fanciful voyage across the ocean was described by François Rabelais in the *Fourth Book of Pantagruel* (1547). They leave from the port of Olonne on the French Atlantic coast in search of the Oracle of the Holy Bottle, which "lay near Cathay, in Upper India." They are clearly navigators of the Northwest Passage to China made famous and real for French speakers by the reports of Cartier's voyages. (From the early seventeenth century, readers affirmed that Rabelais had met Jacques Cartier and that the geography of his fourth book was directly informed by Cartier's voyages.[18]) In chapter 2, they reach the island of Medamothi (Greek, for "nowhere"), encountering a great fair populated by the richest and most famous merchants of Africa and Asia, where they buy unicorns, typical of Asia, as well as a tarande, an animal as big as a bull with the head of a stag and branching horns and with the chameleon-like ability to change color with its environment. The source for all these details is the *Natural History* of the ancient authority Pliny, who places the tarande in Scythia, a northern province of Asia; Pantagruel himself in a later chapter calls the animal Scythian.[19] Later in the book Pantagruel arrives on the island of the "macreons," literally the long-lived people, noted by Pliny in Ethiopia, India, China, and Mount Athos.[20] The idea had been transplanted to the newly discovered lands as early as the widely read letter on the new world published under the name of Amerigo

Vespucci, where it is noted that the inhabitants of Brazil lived to the age of 150, earning them the designation *longaevi* (see chapter 2 and fig. 2.3).[21]

In 1550, the French king Henry II commissioned the navigator and cartographer Guillaume Le Testu, whom he had named *Pilote Royale*, to create a map of the Americas. Le Testu's maps were well known for their sophistication and detail, informing generations of cartographers to follow. His *Cosmographie universelle selon les navigateurs, tant anciens que modernes* (1556), which contained hand-drawn maps based on his expeditions, showed cynocephalics, or dog-headed men—traditionally located by ancient and medieval writers in Africa or India—in the lands explored by Cartier in New France (fig. 9.3).[22] Yet the question of the Asian-ness of the transatlantic world remained a matter of debate. The French cartographer Desceliers declared in a cartouche at the top of his 1550 world map: "Some cosmographers have conjoined Asia with Florida, the continent of New Spain and America, and say that this is part of Asia, but their opinion is not to be followed since it does not appear to be true, neither according to experience nor according to reason." It sounds like a clear break with his great precursor Finé. Yet even Desceliers placed Asian elements in the region he labeled Canada, including the toponyms Tangut and the Desert of Lop, both of which come from Marco Polo's description of Asia.[23] He also gave scalloped borders to northern Canada and northern Asia at the eastern and western edges of his map, his way of signaling uncertainty as to their true extent, and left very little water off both coasts, implying that though they occupy opposite ends of the map no great ocean separated them.

On Cannibals, Amazons, and Indians in America

After the colonization of what is today Canada, French interests in the Americas shifted south, to Brazil. While most explorers and cosmographers who reported on this part of the world saw it as separate from Asia, Amerasian themes colored their understanding of the place and the people who lived there. André Thevet a loquacious, seagoing Franciscan friar who traveled as the aumônier or chaplain of Nicolas Durand de Villegaignon on his voyage to Brazil in 1555, published his *The New Found World, or Antarctica* (Les singularitez de la France Antartique), one of the earliest illustrated French books on the new world, on his return in 1557. Thevet differentiates clearly between Asia and America: "Why [America] should be called India I do not know; the Eastern part of the country that is called India has taken its name from the notable river Indus, which is very far from America. It will therefore suffice to call it America, or France Antartike."[24] His text described many new world plants and animals for the first time to French and Europeans audiences and enjoyed

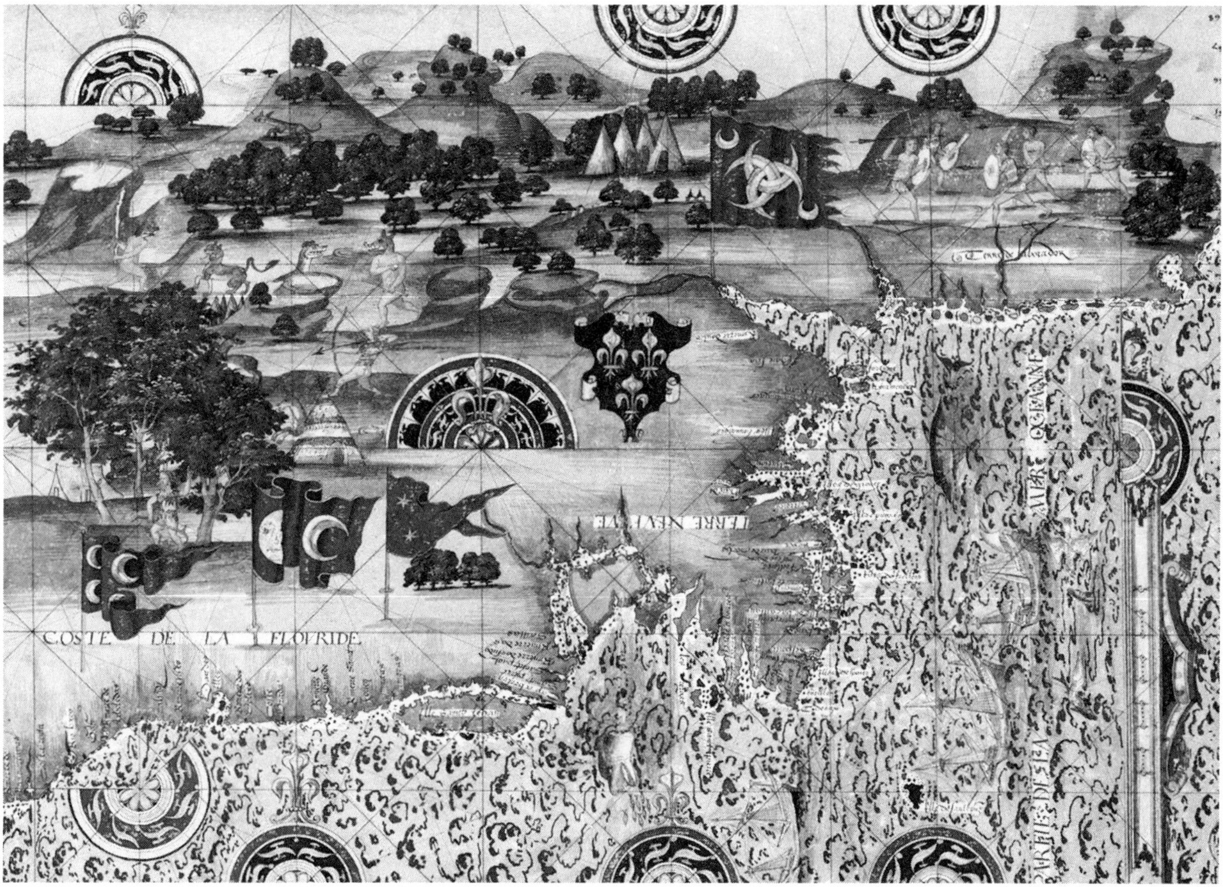

9.3 Dog-headed men in Canada. Guillaume Le Testu, *Cosmographie universelle selon les navigateurs tant anciens que modernes*, illuminated paper, ca. 55 × 40 cm (Le Havre, 1556). Paris, Bibliothèque Nationale de France, Service Historique de la Défense, MS D.1.Z14, fol. 58. Older European travel accounts, such as Marco Polo and John Mandeville, had reported the existence of spice-growing dog-headed men on islands in Southeast Asia.

a great popular success, even if the author failed to gain the esteem of contemporary scholars and cosmographers. The fame of his publication won Thevet the position of royal cosmographer to four French kings at the Valois court (Henry II, François II, Charles IX, and Henry III).[25] In his *Singularitez*, Thevet felt compelled to address the issue of Amazons in South America at length: "Some might say that these are not real Amazons, but for myself I believe they are, seeing that they live just as the ones in Asia did." After offering an extensive account of Scythian Amazons based on ancient sources, he asks how Amazons had arrived in the Americas, recounting that some say they came after the War of Troy, others that they left Greece or Africa, chased by some cruel king. A review of the different accounts leaves him unresolved as to the relation between the American and Asian Amazons.[26]

After *Les Singularitez*, Thevet began his most ambitious work, his *Universal Cosmography* (*Cosmographie universelle)*, finally published in 1575. A compendium of geographic knowledge that aimed to describe and define every part of the known world, it relied heavily on the accounts of Cartier, an acquaintance of Thevet's. A collaborator on the project, François de Belleforest, quarreled with Thevet, left his employ, and published his own *Cosmographie universelle*, also in 1575, a translation and reprinting of Sebastian Münster's *Cosmographia* (1544), receiving a royal privilege, an early form of copyright protection. Disagreeing with Thevet, Belleforest held out for an Amerasian continuity. Introducing the seventh and last book, a translation of Münster's section on the new world, Belleforest asks first how these newly discovered lands related to existing knowledge of the world, noting that at their western extent they are not far from China (they are "only separated from Quinsai by a sea channel, which is not very wide"). On the question of the naming of the territories, Belleforest reports that commentators have generally settled on calling them the Indies, just as the ancients did when they designated the entire extent from the Indus River to the Eastern Ocean under the term *India*, since customs are shared by people throughout this vast Asiatic region. Justifying the extension of general term *Indies* and *Indians* to the new territories, he hypothesizes that in the past there must have been fairly frequent contact between Asian India and the Indies in America across "the short distance of sea," though in the present time these interactions seem to have been much reduced. Nonetheless, he notes, there remain notable similarities in the customs of the two populations, such as their sun-worshipping religion and other ceremonies.[27] Belleforest ultimately rejects the blanket term *Indian*, proposing that the discoverers of any new lands should name them as they see fit; nevertheless, his discussion explains how the use of the terms "India" and "Indian" in the Americas was supported by the evidence of a similar and possibly shared culture, an idea that we will encounter again in chapter 12.[28]

Belleforest, a man of letters who never traveled to the new world, made his reputation with his *Tragic Histories* (*Histoires tragiques*), a best-selling compendium of tales drawn from the Italian novelist Matteo Bandello and other sources, published in multiple volumes between 1566 and 1583. Among his distinguished readers were William Shakespeare, who drew elements of *Hamlet* from Belleforest's rendition of the story, and Michel de Montaigne, who was inspired by Belleforest's story of a brave Taíno cacique resisting Spanish dominance on the island of Hispaniola in the 1520s, a tale that appeared in the fifth volume of the *Histoires tragiques*, published in 1572. Montaigne's essay "Des cannibales," published in his first volume of *Essais* in 1580, defends the valor and virtue of so-called cannibals, seeing in theirs a culture of honor in many ways more developed than that of their European conquerors, a defense not far in tone and language from Belleforest's glowing description of the brave and high-minded Taíno cacique.[29]

In his story, Belleforest was describing the situation on Hispaniola, in the Gulf of Mexico, but in his *Cosmographie*, also evidently read by Montaigne, Belleforest has more to say about Brazil, Montaigne's main focus in "Des cannibales." In fact, Montaigne's understanding of the larger geography of the new world, as sketched in the opening paragraphs of "Des cannibales," corresponds almost point for point to what Belleforest describes in the *Cosmographie*—a fact not yet noted. Montaigne understands the larger territory in which Villegaignon had set up his colony in the 1550s as a newly discovered land, a humbling reminder that we do not yet understand the world: "I'm afraid our eyes are bigger than our bellies, and that we have more curiosity than capacity; we embrace everything but grasp nothing but wind." Yet the new territory, vast as it is, does border what is known of the world: "Modern navigations have almost discovered it to be no island, but rather terra firma, and connected with Oriental India on one side, and elsewhere with the lands under the two poles; or if it is separate it is by so narrow a strait and interval, that it does not deserve the name of an island for that."[30] As we saw above, this is almost exactly what Belleforest writes in his introductory essay for the seventh and last book of the *Cosmographie*, on the new world, where he describes a landmass that reaches close to the poles north and south and that is separated from China on the west by nothing more than a narrow sea channel.

For Belleforest, the neighboring relation to Asia is not only geographical but cultural, given that the populations in the two areas "seem to conform to each other in their mores." Likewise, Montaigne in "Des cannibales" consistently finds parallels for the hardy valor and innate sense of honor of the new world peoples in stories of the Scythians, formidable warriors from northern Asia described by ancient sources. Noting the abstemious eating and drinking habits of the so-called cannibals, Montaigne notes that Souidas (the legendary author of a tenth-century Byzantine lexicon) ascribes similar habits to "some other peoples of the Orient" (*comme Suidas dit de quelques autres peuples d'Orient*). Basing himself on Belleforest, Montaigne sees the Brazilians as a warrior culture best understood by comparison to "other peoples of the Orient."

While Belleforest's *Cosmographie* clearly enjoyed a wide readership, Thevet's 2,000-page *Cosmographie*, also published in 1575, was not nearly as successful as his *Singularitez* had been; Belleforest's *Cosmographie* seems to have stolen Thevet's thunder, and by this point many had come to regard Thevet's scholarship as dubious if not fraudulent. (Thevet in turn claimed that Belleforest had stolen much of Thevet's material.) Contrary to Belleforest, Thevet's *Cosmographie* continued to defend the idea that Cathay was distant from the Americas, decrying the "false maps" that represented what is today the Gulf of Mexico as the Sea of Cathay, and declaring that any attempt to find Asia in or near the Americas "was all in vain, since it was not the way to the Indies, nor to Cathay either."[31] Thevet's anti-Protestant tone was a provocation to the Huguenot Jean de Léry, who also traveled to Brazil and in 1578 published his *History of a Voyage to the Land of Brazil* (*Histoire d'un voyage fait en la terre du Bresil*), where he criticized Thevet repeatedly, especially his inconsistency in the naming of the lands across the Atlantic.[32] "Although in his *Cosmography* he [Thevet] vehemently attacks those who call this land of America West India, and claims that he wants it to keep its name of 'Antarctic France,'" Léry retorted, "he has nonetheless himself in several places called it 'American India.'"[33] Like other Orientalists at the time, Léry believed that Saint Thomas had proselytized in Brazil, and that the Americans were the descendants of Noah, most likely through his son Ham, since according to Léry, they were "a people accursed and abandoned by God."[34] Any reader trying to make their way through this thicket of debates could only come away thinking there was little consensus among the experts, and even a good measure of inconsistency within any writer's own arguments.

Most French writing about the lands to the west of the Atlantic from Cartier to Léry was ethnographic in nature, focusing on Indigenous war customs, hunting methods, medicinal knowledge, religious beliefs, and clothing styles. Larger speculations about global geography are rare, yet the basic premise of Verrazano and Cartier—that the New World was a passage to Asia—remains in place even in later accounts, especially when describing lands in the northern hemisphere. Even Thevet, who tended to believe that Asia and America were widely separate, related in his *Singularitez* that the "great land of Florida is very dangerous to those who sail in the direction of Cathay, Cambalu [Beijing], Panuco, and Themistitan [Tenochtitlan], for in seeing it from afar you would guess that it was an island in the middle of the sea," thus suggesting that such a passage was viable to the prudent.[35] Later, in his discussion of Mexico in the *Cosmographie*, Thevet says that when one leaves the kingdom of Xalisco and heads west, "you can go to the oriental kingdom of China [and] to the Indies subject to the Great Cham of Tartary. According to the calculations of pilots and good mariners, the distance between this cape and China is some thousand leagues: and if the mainland is continuous, as some hold, you could go from this cape [from what is today California] to Asia and India."[36] At times for Thevet, as for many of his contemporaries in New Spain, Asia lay just to the west of the new world, and might even be reached overland. Similarly, in another late work, Thevet's *Great Book of Islands and Piloting* (*Grand insulaire et pilotage*) (1588), the cosmographer claimed that in the region north and west of Mexico, "there is a great city named Sebolla [Cibola] which is at thirty-five degrees. The houses of this city and temples of their idols are covered with gold and the others with silver. According to these inhabitants, these lands abut against oriental Tartarie, which is Asiatic according to the roundness of the world."[37] Thevet in fact remained unresolved about how Asia and America were related.

Lachine, the People of the Sea, and the Migration of Ginseng

About eighty years after the first French transatlantic expeditions, Samuel de Champlain continued to explore "the feasibility of discovering the passage to China without the inconvenience of the ice of the north or the heat of the torrid zone."[38] The terms of the original commission for exploration that he received from King Henry IV in 1603 state that he should seek "a route easy to traverse through this country to the countries of China and the East Indies, or elsewhere, as far as possible."[39] Traveling along the Saint Lawrence River in 1603 in search of China, Champlain was forced to turn back at a series of unpassable falls. There, he heard reports from local Algonquin-speaking people of a large lake that lay beyond these falls, identifiable as today's Lake Huron; though they had not seen it for themselves, they conveyed reports that many rivers fed into it, and that its waters were "very bad, like that of the sea." Champlain inevitably concluded that "this makes me think that [this lake] is the South Sea, given that it is salty as they say."[40] Fifteen years later, he proposed his stopping point by the falls as the location for a riverside customs house that would tax the goods passing to and from China and Europe. Wishfully, the town that developed near these rapids, as well as the rapids themselves, were named Lachine, now the name of a borough in the city of Montreal.[41]

Even after the French had been established in North America for decades, the search for a northern passage to Asia continued. On his *Universal Hydrographical Chart* (1634), the French cartographer Jean Guérard noted in the blank space beside Hudson Bay that "it is believed there is a passage from there to Japan."[42] According to the reports of Jesuit missionaries compiled by Barthélemy Vimont, the French explorer Jean Nicolet, an emissary of Champlain's, was sent in about 1632 to the far side of the Great Lakes to treat and make peace with "the nation called People of the Sea" (*la nation appellée des Gens de mer*). After his initial gifts were well received, he was conducted into their presence wearing a Chinese silk robe embroidered with flowers and birds (*revestu d'une grande robbe de damas de la Chine, toute parsemée de fleurs, & d'oyseaux de diverses couleurs*). The robe may well have been obtained from Jesuits who had spent time in China. He had brought it back around the world in the other direction for the purpose of this first entry, perhaps thinking it appropriate attire for meeting the peoples of the Northwest Passage.[43]

The quest for the passage persisted into the eighteenth century. Father Pierre Jartoux, a Jesuit missionary stationed in Beijing, was one of the first Europeans to witness the Chinese collection and medicinal preparation of ginseng. Working as a cartographer to the Kang-Hsi emperor, he compiled an atlas of China that required a journey to Manchuria, near the Chinese border with Korea. To fortify himself after these exertions, Jartoux took to consuming ginseng root, which flourished in the forests of the region, and wrote a letter about the curative powers of the plant, dated April 12, 1711, to be distributed to Jesuit missions throughout the world.[44] Including a printed image of the Asian plant taken from a careful drawing, Jartoux's letter described how generations of Chinese medicine men had learned to extract the essence of the root through boiling and had come to revere the plant for its medicinal properties.[45] Even though Jartoux had never been to Canada, he surmised that based on the plant's habitat in the cool shady forests and thick woods of northern China, "if it be in any other part of the world, it must be chiefly in Canada, where the mountains and woods, as those who have lived there report, do much resemble these here."[46]

Jartoux's report activated an Amerasian Jesuit network. The Jesuit missionary Joseph-François Lafitau, working among the Iroquois in New France at the time, set himself to look for the plant in the forests bordering the Saint Lawrence River between Montreal and Ottawa, near the mission to the Mohawk at Kahnawáke/Sault Saint Louis, where Lafitau resided between 1712 and 1717. Using Jartoux's detailed illustration as a guide, Lafitau was drawn to the bright vermillion fruit of a plant growing close by a mission lodge, recognized by an Iroquois healer as a remedy. Penning a description, Lafitau sent it along with preserved specimens to Quebec, and eventually to Paris, where the Académie Royale des Sciences looked skeptically on the idea that the Chinese and Canadian plants were the same. (In fact, American and Chinese ginseng represent different species of the genus *Panax*, thus are related but different.) Undaunted, Lafitau published his *Memoir Presented to His Royal Highness the Duke of Orléans... Concerning the Precious Plant Ginseng from Tartary, Discovered in Canada* (*Mémoire présenté à Son Altesse Royale Monseigneur le duc d'Orléans . . . concernant la précieuse plante du gin-seng de Tartarie, découverte en Canada*) (Paris, 1718), a letter gathering linguistic, anthropological, medical, and botanical evidence to argue that "the plant that I have discovered is the true ginseng," the same plant Jartoux had seen in China.[47] The linguistic similarity was made plain in the title of the engraving included with the letter (fig. 9.4): "Aureliana of Canada, in Chinese gin-seng, in Mohawk

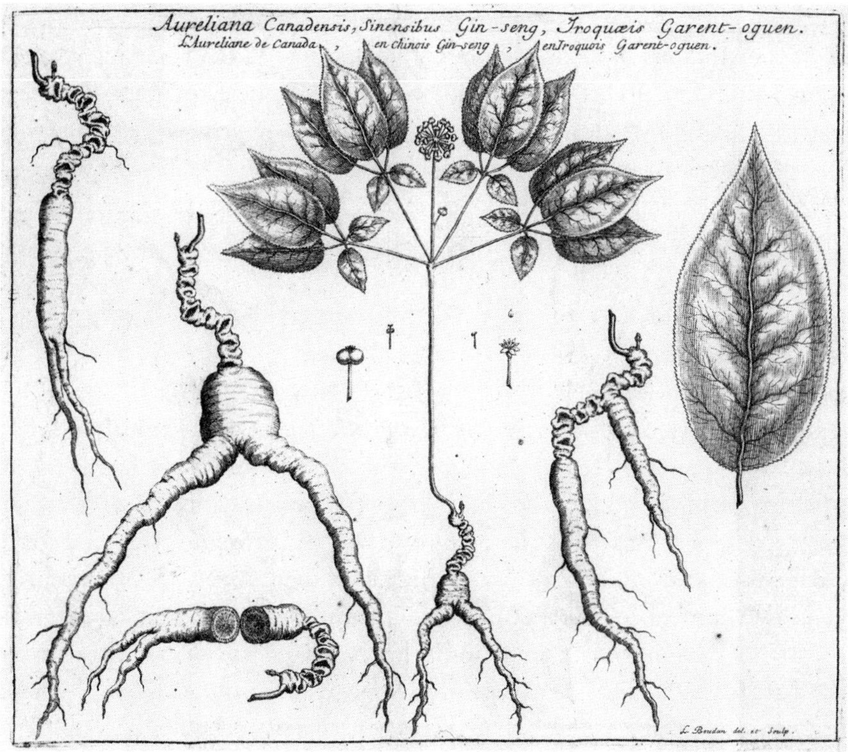

9.4 "Aureliana of Canada, in Chinese gin-seng, in Mohawk garent-oguen." Joseph-François Lafitau, *Mémoire présenté à Son Altesse Royale Monseigneur le duc d'Orléans... concernant la précieuse plante du gin-seng de Tartarie, découverte en Canada par le Pere Joseph-François Lafitau* (Paris, 1718), p. 19.

garent-oguen" (*l'aureliana de Canada, en chinois gin-seng, en iroquois garent-oguen*).[48] To the botanical evidence Lafitau added ethnographic arguments, pointing out that the Chinese and the Iroquois used the root in the same way, usually in the form of a tea, whether to cure a loss of appetite or to fight dysentery or fever.[49] If not entirely convincing to European botanists, his text had real-world consequences, prompting a wave of ginseng collection in the Americas, intended for international export. By 1720, American ginseng hunters had yielded enough supply that a French trading firm, the Company of the Indies, was exporting it to China.[50] The Chinese embraced Canadian ginseng immediately, since the habitat for wild ginseng in China had long been destroyed, forcing the Chinese to obtain it farther afield, from Manchuria, from Korea and now, through overseas commerce, from Canada.

The story of American ginseng reveals the lively application and adaptation of Amerasian ideas well into the eighteenth century.[51] Whereas Jartoux had imagined that the plant might be found to be growing spontaneously in Canada by virtue of environmental commonality with regions of Asia, Lafitau took its presence in New France as evidence of ancient human interaction between the two worlds, proposing that the Iroquois and other Indians had come from China and had taken their plant remedies with them.[52] This was an ethnobotanical application of the theories of Lafitau's Jesuit precursor José de Acosta, who had posited Asian origins for the American Indians in his widely read *Natural and Moral History of the Indies* (see chapter 13). The long tradition of Amerasian histories then came full circle—and became real—when Canadian ginseng passed into use in Chinese medicine and culture.

• • •

Revision: Lévi-Strauss and the Transpacific "Lost World"

In his 1955 memoir *Tristes Tropiques*, the anthropologist Claude Lévi-Strauss, who had conducted fieldwork in Brazil and saw himself as an heir to de Léry, mused on the many transpacific crossings that occurred during the period that preceded the arrival of the Europeans. These European newcomers, he wrote, had fallen into "the error that consists of thinking that for twenty thousand years America had been cut off from the rest of the world, on the grounds that it was cut off from western Europe during that time." Reviewing then-recent archeological, anthropological, and botanical findings, he pointed out the many connections among pre-Columbian cultures across North and South America, often involving water travel along the Pacific coast in the period before the rise of the Inca in Peru and the Aztecs in Mexico. To envision this longer history also brings into view, he noted, the connection between Indigenous American and Asian cultures, not only in their genetic origins but also in their ongoing interaction over millennia, an interaction suggested by the botanical record alone, which reveals dozens of vegetable species with the same chromosomic composition found both in pre-Columbian America and in Asia.[53] We are now able to imagine, wrote Lévi-Strauss, a "lost world" of transpacific traffic, an arcing northern pathway of communication across Siberia and Canada that reached down on both sides, to southern Asia and down through the American continent, explaining why anthropologists have recorded myths in Borneo that are found nowhere else but in North American Indian cultures—all of it pointing to a powerful cultural interactivity over thousands of years. "In contrast to the total silence of the Atlantic, a humming as of a swarm of bees sounded all around the periphery of the Pacific."[54]

In light of these mid-twentieth-century musings, which have developed into a whole field of research in the twenty-first, the idea that America and Asia were disconnected until the globalization of the early modern era starts to look like an artifact of a relatively brief phase of European colonial thought. Imposed by modern European geographical models, the continental division of the world, which set America and Asia far apart, was then reinforced by the rise of the modern European university system, with field studies organized according to continents and subregions. "American" studies, arising long after the development of the "Orientalist" disciplines, was understood to represent a separate universe of investigation, a premise that is only now being revised. But before this separation there was a long history of connection, and for two centuries or so after Columbus, Europeans themselves had no trouble hearing the beelike buzzing of a millennial Amerasian history.

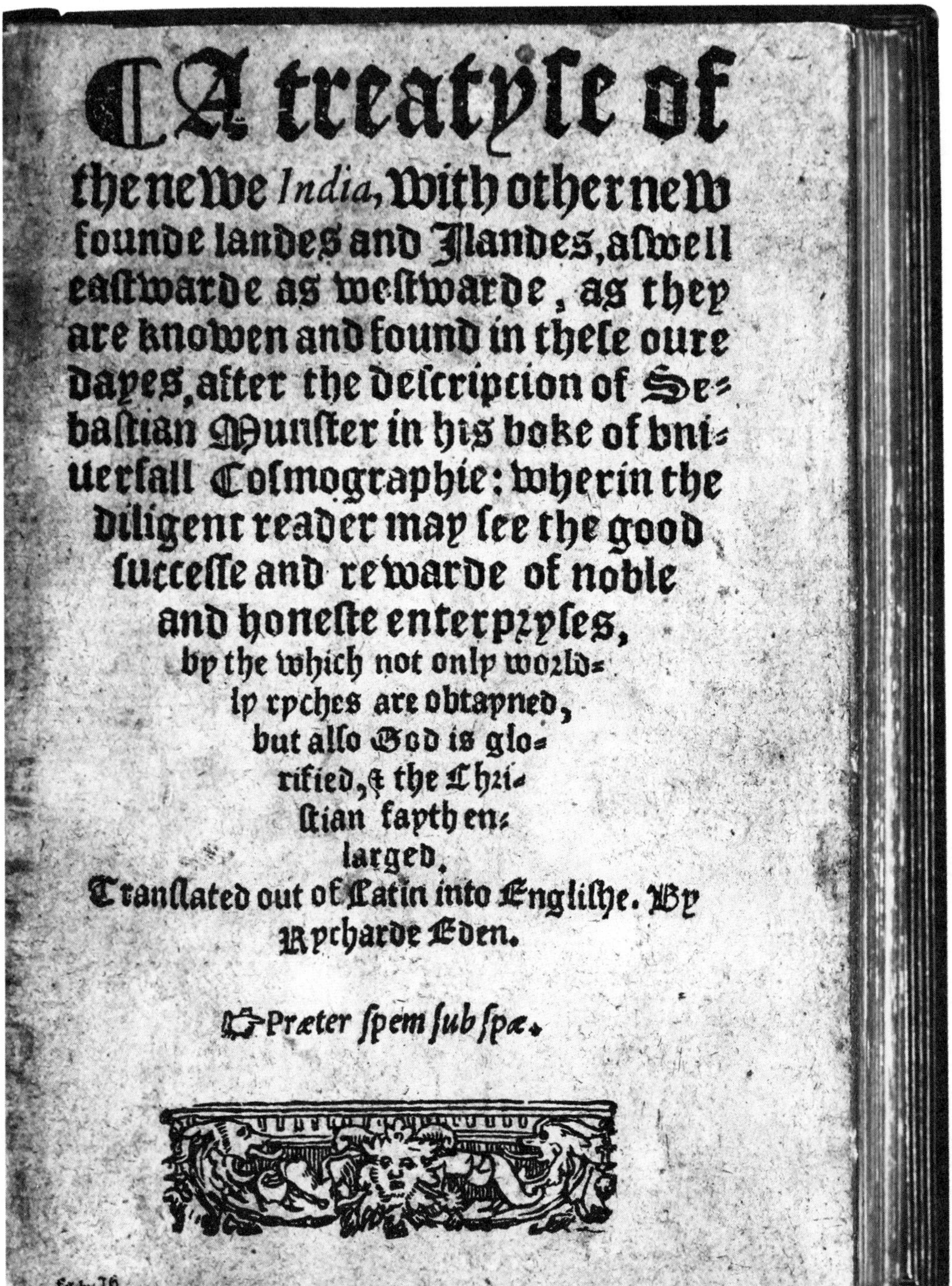

A treatyse of
the newe *India*, with other new
founde landes and Ilandes, aswell
eastwarde as westwarde, as they
are knowen and found in these oure
dayes, after the description of Se-
bastian Munster in his boke of uni-
versall Cosmographie: wherin the
diligent reader may see the good
successe and rewarde of noble
and honeste enterpryses,
by the which not only world-
ly ryches are obtayned,
but also God is glo-
rified, & the Chri-
stian fayth en-
larged.
Translated out of Latin into Englishe. By
Rycharde Eden.

Præter spem sub spe.

10.1 "New India" encompasses East Asia and America. Title page of Richard Eden, *A Treatyse of the Newe India, with other new founde landes and Ilandes, aswell eastwarde as westwarde*... (London, 1553).

TEN

English Reflections of Amerasia

Richard Eden's 1553 *A Treatyse of the Newe India* was the first printed English text to offer extended consideration of the voyages of Christopher Columbus and Amerigo Vespucci, sixty years after they had occurred (fig. 10.1).[1] There had been a number of notable expeditions into the new world undertaken from English lands with English backing, such as the Newfoundland voyage of John Cabot (1497–98), who believed he had reached China, the voyages across the Atlantic sponsored by Robert Thorne and Hugh Elyot (1502 and 1504), John Rut's attempt to find a Northwest Passage (1527), as well as Richard Hore's venture to Cape Breton and Newfoundland (1536). And yet English publishers evidently did not think accounts of any of these expeditions would find a market, until the dam broke in the middle of the century. Thomas More's *Utopia* of 1516 was finally published in English translation in 1551, followed by Eden's compilation of two years later, heralding a new era of English publications and armchair travel during the Elizabethan period.

Mediated Amerasia

The primary template for early modern travel writing in England was the venerable figure of John Mandeville, the name under which a collection of accounts of travels to the Holy Land and farthest Asia had appeared from the fourteenth century on. Richard Pynson produced the first printed English version of Mandeville in 1496, three years after Columbus had returned from his first voyage to great fanfare. Three more editions of *The Book of Mandeville* would be published in England before the appearance of Eden's *Treatyse*.[2] Later, the English piggybacked on the new world–inflected popularity of Marco Polo's *Travels*, which saw no fewer than twenty-four editions throughout Europe during the sixteenth century. The first English edition in 1579 by the Elizabethan translator John Frampton was by most measures a success.[3] One English reader applauded Polo as a precursor to "our Mandeville" and the one who "opened the world" for the more recent explorers such as Columbus, Vespucci, and Hernán Cortés.[4] Since Polo and especially Mandeville dominated the imaginary of global travel in England, Asia—a rather fantastical Asia—remained the primary framework for understanding all new world discoveries, whether the news came from East or West. In England, as elsewhere, Atlantic voyages fueled interest in Asia, making it easy to understand America through the lens of China and India and the fabled islands off the Asian coast, and that also meant that information gathered in America steadily informed images of Asia, producing a sedimented Amerasian imaginary, an effect compounded in England by the fact that much of their new world news in the form of translations of prepackaged European sources. The news did not, in fact, come from East or West but from the continent, in a steady Amerasian flow.

Eden's treatise was itself a translation of (part of) the *Cosmographia universalis* of Sebastian Münster, a highly successful publication first printed in German in 1544 and then, to reach a wider European readership, in Latin in 1550. Münster's 1550 Latin edition, one of the most successful and popular descriptions of the world in the sixteenth century, was followed by countless editions over the next hundred years in Latin, French, German, Czech, Italian, and English, diffusing its vision of Amerasia everywhere it went, especially in the translations of François Belleforest (*La cosmographie universelle de tout le monde* of 1575; see chapter 9) and Eden.[5] Whatever these translators' intentions, they passed Amerasian knowledge on to an expanding readership, sealing graphic ideas into authoritative knowledge.[6]

The English embraced a secondhand approach to new world matters, beginning with More's *Utopia*, which presented itself as the account of a member of Vespucci's crew, who had stayed behind in the new world and eventually reached the Amerasian island of Utopia (see chapter 5). English writers, publishers, and explorers came into the discussion on the basis of previously published sources, and they reflected (on) the news. Like the Venetians, they generated and explored the new world through printed media, though the English got in on the enterprise somewhat later, with more printed material already in existence. When they finally plunged into empire building, in the era of Francis Drake and Sir Walter Ralegh, it was necessarily a belated effort, focused on making incursions into the existing transpacific new world empire of Spain and setting up satellite colonies at its margins, with the dreamy hope of one day overtaking and dominating the Amerasian trade flow that the Spanish had already established. Working with a largely mediated new world, the reflections of English writers, publishers, and readers acquired a processed and combined quality, whether they took the form of ironic mirroring (More), fantastical world-making (Edmund Spenser), skeptical remove (Richard Hakluyt and Samuel Purchas), satirical inversion (Williams Shakespeare), or metaphysical meditation (John Donne).

The pattern begins with Eden's 1553 publication, whose long title announces a "Treatyse on the newe *India* with other new found lands and Ilands, aswell eastwarde as westward, as they are knowen and found in these our dayes." The word new is used twice, to assure readers that here, in this volume, they will get up to speed on all the discoveries that had been announced here and there. The main focus is "newe India," together with some other new-found lands and islands, a fairly wide yet defined canvas ranging from China to Cuba and Brazil. The title then declares that this treatise is itself drawn from an authoritative source ("after the descripcion of Sebastian Münster in his boke of Universall Cosmographie"). Finally, the title announces its purpose: "wherein the diligent reader may see the good success and rewarde of noble and honeste enterpryses by the which not only worldly ryches are obtayned, but also God is glorified, and the Christian fayth enlarged."

Münster's was a *Universal Cosmography*, valuable because it purported to cover the whole world. Eden excerpted from Münster's treatise only that section that corresponded to what most European sources had labeled the "new world," namely the easternmost parts of Asia and the lands discovered across the Atlantic (see chapter 2). In other words, Eden frames off the newsworthy new world, training English attention on this zone of greatest opportunity, where good reward and "worldy ryches" will be rightfully obtained and through which God's empire on earth will triumph.[7] That zone was Amerasia, evidently also the greatest opportunity for a publisher hoping to generate excitement for a book on geography. Münster's book 5, ranging from Arabia to America, offered a paradigmatic Amerasian view of the newly discovered territories East and West.[8] In his *Treatyse*, Eden reshaped his source, leaving out Münster's descriptions of western Asia (largely Asia Minor, Cyprus, Armenia, Palestine, Arabia, Persia, and Afghanistan) and focusing only on Münster's descriptions of easternmost Asia and America. This is what Eden calls "newe India," in which America appears as part of an archipelago that stretches from Hispaniola to the Moluccas. Importantly, the "newe India" was not a new, western counterpart to the old India of Calicut and Bengal—it was not the West Indies as opposed to the previously known East Indies. Rather, it was a newly extensive India, stretching from Madagascar in the Indian Ocean through India, China, Java, Sumatra, Japan, and so on (that is, what Ptolemy knew as *India infra Gangem* and *India extra Gangem*, India west and east of the Ganges), all the way to the newly discovered lands of America and its many newly discovered islands near it. "Newe India" was not an addition to old India but a reconfiguration of all of India in light of the new discoveries.

For Münster and his expanding multilingual audience, the Americas existed at the extreme east of India, and all the lands grouped together under the banner of Asia Maior (greater Asia) were the "newe India." As Eden explained, "the hole globe of the world . . . hath been sayled about, by the West into the East, as doth more largely appeare in this boke in the navigacions of Magellanus, who from Spayne sayled Westward to the Ilands of Molucca being in the East sea, farre beyond ye furthest partes of East India, and the portugales came to the same Ilands from Spayne sayling Eastward."[9] Either route, in any case, took travelers to the same place, the "newe India," which Münster had visually underscored in his *Cosmographia* by using the same printed illustration of cannibals to illustrate daily life in both Java and the islands discovered by Columbus. In Eden's treatise, this means it is not unusual to find Asian and Mexican place names in close proximity. On a single spread of his *Treatyse*, for instance, the reader learns about Portuguese colonies in Malacca and Goa and negotiations with ambassadors from other Indian kingdoms and then, with no paragraph break, reads of the king of Spain's colonies in Cuba, Yucatán, and Cozumel (fig. 10.2).

Eden quickly followed his *Treatyse* with a second work, *The Decades of the Newe Worlde, or West India* (London, William Powell, 1555), an anthology of translations from the first three decades of Peter Martyr d'Anghiera's *Decades* (also called *De orbe novo*), selections from Gonzalo Fernández de Oviedo's *Historia general y natural de las Indias*, Francisco López de Gomara's *Historia general de las Indias*, and cosmographical material from Sebastian Cabot, as well as accounts of the East, Russia, and Africa. As his title indicates, Eden here carves up his material in a less Amerasian way by focusing only on "West India," raising the question of what the term meant for him. It could mean "the other India in the west," or "the west part of India," since both options were on the table in the middle of the sixteenth century. Here he appears to be moving toward the growing idea of the West Indies, meaning another India in the Western Hemisphere, and yet that did not mean that the separation of the Indies was established from this point forward.

The prefaces of both his *Treatyse* and *Decades* reveal Eden's understanding of the relationship between America and Asia, in particular through his discussions of Ophir and Solomon's wealth. In the preface to the *Treatyse*, Eden suggests a connection between the gold of the new world and the world known to King Solomon.

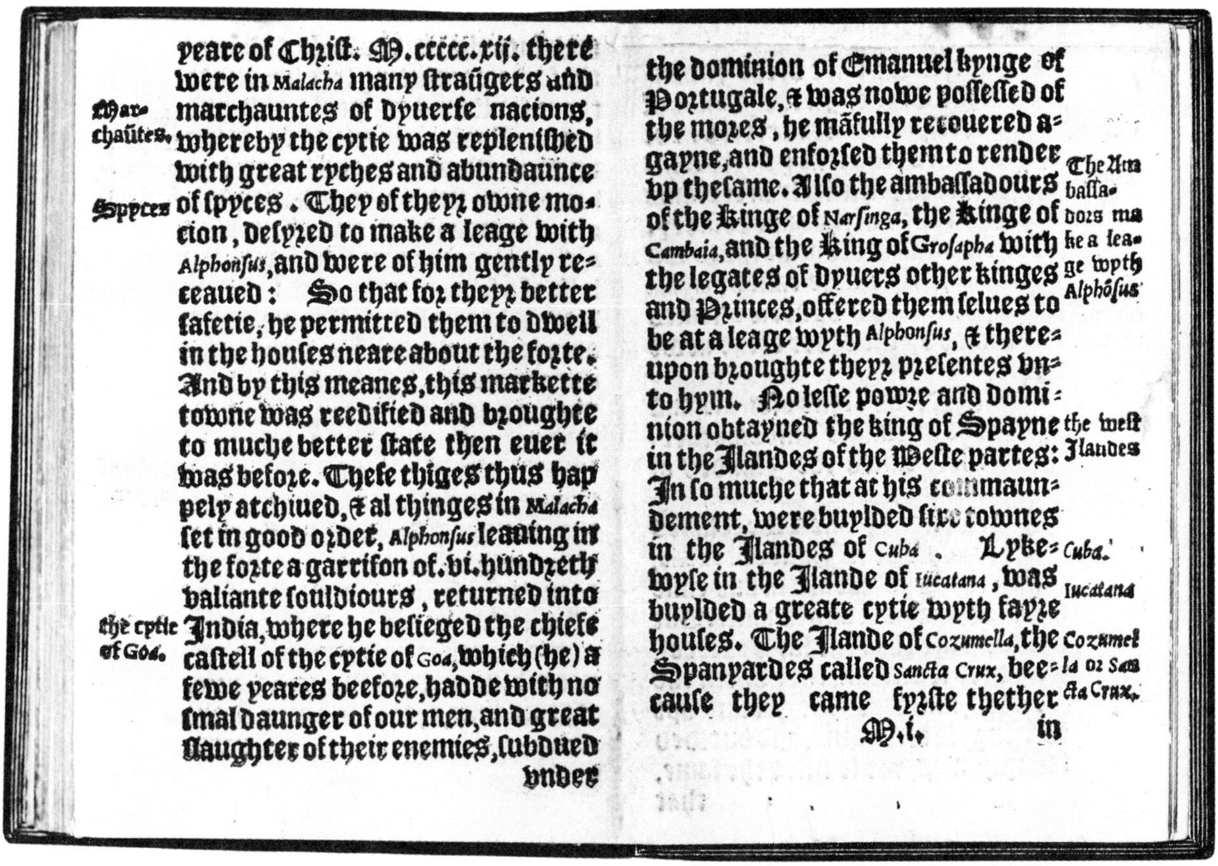

yeare of Christ. M.ccccc.xii. there
were in *Malacha* many straũgers and
Mar-chaũtes. marchauntes of dyuerse nacions,
whereby the cytie was replenished
with great ryches and abundaunce
Spyces of spyces. They of theyr owne mo-
cion, desyred to make a leage with
Alphonsus, and were of him gently re-
ceaued: So that for theyr better
safetie, he permitted them to dwell
in the houses neare about the forte.
And by this meanes, this markette
towne was reedified and broughte
to muche better state then euer it
was before. These thiges thus hap
pely atchiued, & al thinges in *Malacha*
set in good order, *Alphonsus* leauing in
the forte a garrison of. vi. hundreth
valiante souldiours, returned into
the cytie of Goa. India, where he besieged the chiefe
castell of the cytie of *Goa*, which (he) a
fewe yeares beefore, hadde with no
smal daunger of our men, and great
slaughter of their enemies, subdued
vnder

the dominion of Emanuel kynge of
Portugale, & was nowe possessed of
the mores, he mãfully recouered a-
gayne, and enforsed them to render The Am
vp the same. Also the ambassadours bassa-
of the Kinge of *Narsinga*, the Kinge of dors ma
Cambaia, and the King of *Grosapha* with ke a lea-
the legates of dyuers other kinges ge wyth
and Princes, offered them selues to Alphõsus
be at a leage wyth *Alphonsus*, & there-
upon broughte theyr presentes vn-
to hym. No lesse powre and domi-
nion obtayned the king of Spayne the west
in the Ilandes of the Weste partes: Ilandes
In so muche that at his commaun-
dement, were buylded sixe townes
in the Ilandes of *Cuba*. Lyke- Cuba.
wyse in the Ilande of *Iucatana*, was Iucatana
buylded a greate cytie wyth fayre
houses. The Ilande of *Cozumella*, the Cozumel
Spanyardes called *Sancta Crux*, bee- la or Sã
cause they came fyrste thether cta Crux.
M.i. in

10.2 An example of elliptical continuity. Richard Eden, *A Treatyse of the Newe India* (London, 1553).

> Therefore wheras thou shalt reade of the great abundance of gold, precious stones and spices, which the Spaniardes and Portugales have brought from the south partes of the worlde, as from the newe founde lands and Ilandes, the sodeyn straungenes or greatnes of the thing shal not so much amase thy wittes, and gender in thee incredelitie, yf thou consider the saying of wyse Salomon, who affyrmeth yat there is no new thing under the Sunne, and that the thing that hath been cometh to passe again.[10]

Eden recounts how Solomon's ships had traveled to Tharsis and Ophir, "and brought Gold, Silver, Apes, Peacockes, and Elephantes teeth. Which words surely seme so to confirme such things as are spoken of in the navigacions wherof this boke entreateth."[11] Eden then speculates that "this Tharsis . . . from whence Salomon had so great plenty of Gold and Iverie, were rather some other countrey in the south partes of the world, than this Tharsis of Cilicia," implying that Tharsis may not have been in the Middle East or the Mediterranean, but could have been in the newly discovered Indies.[12] While Eden's own preface did not explicitly place Ophir in the transatlantic islands or in Peru, as Columbus and Oronce Finé had, by offering a translation Martyr's *Decades* into English Eden conveyed Columbus's conviction that Hispaniola was Ophir, as well as the idea that "these Ilandes [in what we today call the Carribean were] parte of India."[13] Maintaining editorial neutrality, Eden himself only reflected that "Summe wryters connecte this lande [Mexico] to the firme lande of Asia, but the truth hereof is not yet knowen."[14]

"Even from Persepolis to Mexico"

After Eden, as information about new worlds began to pour in, Amerasia blossomed in the English imagination. In his 1559 *The Cosmographical Glasse*, the first original work on cosmography in English, William Cunningham conflated the Portuguese and Spanish voyages, relaying that Vespucci and Columbus had traveled to Calicut, and placing the islands of the "Yucatán," Cuba, and Jamaica squarely in Asia (fig. 10.3).[15] Richard Willes, who continued Eden's work after his death, placed Japan "beyond all Asie" in the ocean between China and the West Indies.[16] For Willes, as for Münster and Eden, the islands of Asia flowed directly into those of the Gulf of Mexico. A year before the publication of the *Treatyse*, in 1552, Eden had become secretary to the English statesman William Cecil; his Amerasian vision served English commercial aspirations and mercantile interests by bringing the Far East closer to home.

Eden's midcentury Amerasian conception of the world is comparable to

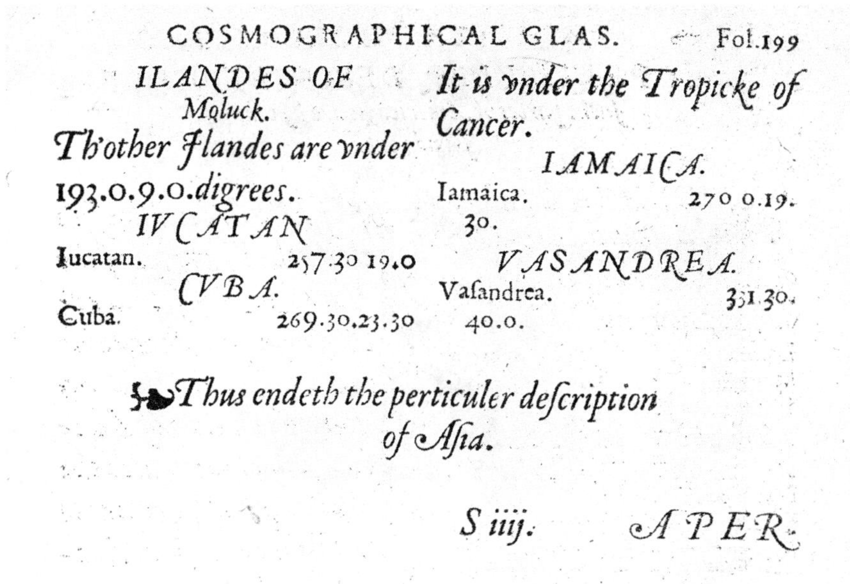

COSMOGRAPHICAL GLAS. Fol.199

ILANDES OF Moluck.

Th'other Ilandes are vnder 193.0.9.0.digrees.

IVCATAN

Iucatan. 257.30 19.0

CVBA.

Cuba. 269.30.23.30

It is vnder the Tropicke of Cancer.

IAMAICA.

Iamaica. 270 0.19. 30.

VASANDREA.

Vasandrea. 331.30. 40.0.

Thus endeth the perticuler description of Asia.

S iiij. APER.

10.3 Asia extends to include Mexico, Cuba, and Jamaica. William Cunningham, *The Cosmographical Glasse* (London, 1559), p. 199.

the 1544 world map of Sebastian Cabot, son of the famous navigator John Cabot (fig. 10.4).[17] Though produced in Nuremberg at a time when Cabot was residing in Spain, Cabot had intermittently entertained the thought of returning to England to undertake new expeditions, and the map was clearly an advertisement for such an enterprise.[18] The territory north of Mexico, occupied by a large tigerlike creature, fades out toward the west, allowing the mapmaker to leave its relationship to China undecided. In the watery interval, the Great Khan sits on his throne. Directly beneath his figure is a lengthy description of Cipangu (Japan) drawn from Polo, as if implying that while Columbus had never actually reached the golden-roofed land of Japan as described by Polo, perhaps Cabot still could.[19]

Whereas Münster and Eden connected Asia and America through the chain of the islands of the Indies, Cabot suggested a continental convergence. For Münster, America was an Asian island; for Cabot, China is a maritime empire extending toward Mexico. These continuities, convergences, and imagined chains across oceans connecting America and Asia were powerful stimulants to the imagination, as well as to financial investments. Around the time of Eden's publications, the English became focused on developing new international markets for woolen cloth, leading to quests for a Northwest Passage undertaken by the voyages of Humphrey Gilbert, Martin Frobisher, and John Davis, among many others.[20]

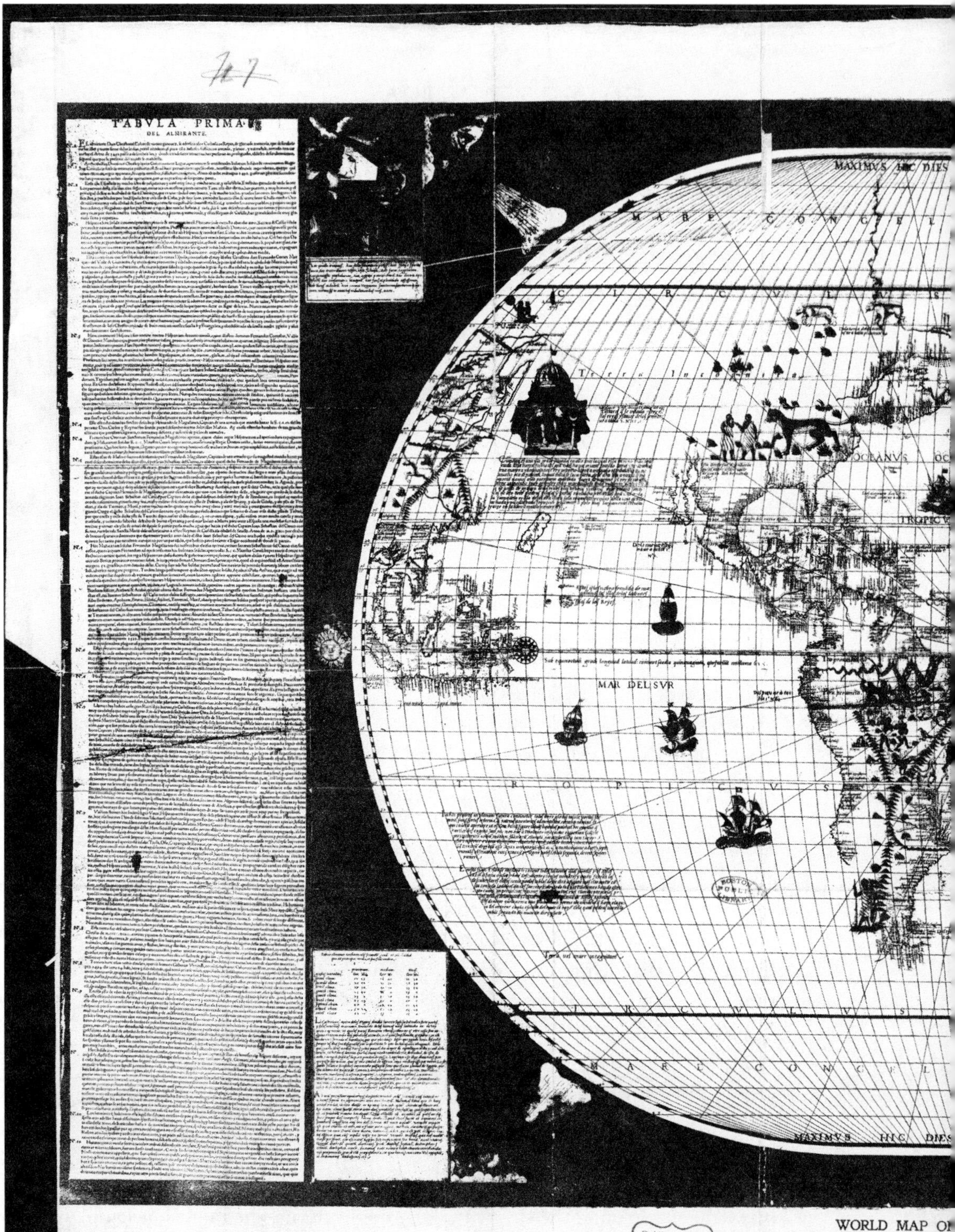

10.4 The Cabot Map refrains from labeling the transatlantic lands America and leaves the relationship to China undecided. Sebastian Cabot, world map, copper engraving, 220 × 125 cm (1544). Paris, Bibliothèque Nationale de France, Département Cartes et Plans.

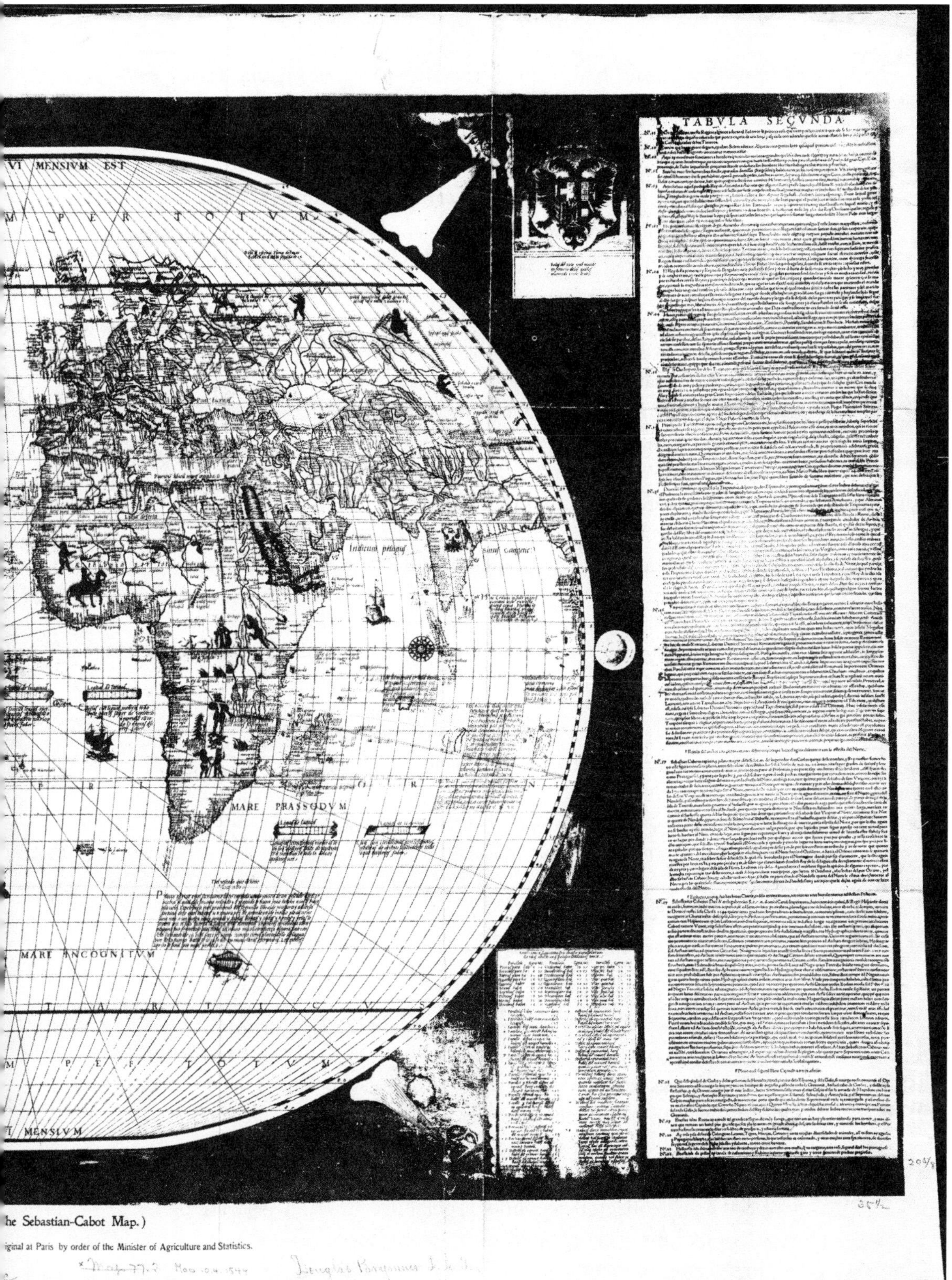

he Sebastian-Cabot Map.)

iginal at Paris by order of the Minister of Agriculture and Statistics.

Spenser's Faeryland, described in his 1590 epic *The Faerie Queene* as an empire set in remote reaches of the world encompassing an expanse from India to America, was woven out of these threads of cartographic projection and geographical commentary.[21] And so it seems was the world of Christopher Marlowe's *Tamburlaine*, who imagines a near future in which his Persian fleet "Sailing along the Orientall sea, / Have fetcht about the Indian continent: / Even from Persepolis to Mexico, / And thence unto the straightes of Jubalter."[22]

Hakluyt's *The Principal Navigations, Voiages, Traffiques and Discoueries of the English Nation* (1589; 2nd ed. 1598–1600), a three-volume anthology of primarily English travel narratives, recorded and publicized many of the voyages, firing the imaginations of English readers, cartographers, and poets. Hakluyt was among the most influential promoters of English colonialism and one of the most significant collectors and editors in the history of travel, building on a trend that had already begun to shape the publishing industry throughout Europe (see chapter 6). Eden had depicted Spain as a colonizing example to be emulated; Hakluyt argued that Spain's power had run its course and would soon be overtaken by more devout nations. In his 1589 dedicatory epistle, Hakluyt gives a tour of the world accomplished by English navigators, with full due given to the "mighty breadth of the South Sea."

> What English shippes did heretofore ever anker in the mighty river of Plate? Passe and repasse the unpassable (in former opinion) straight of Magellan, range along the coast of Chili, Peru, and all the backside of Nova Hispania, further than any Christian ever passed, travers the mighty bredth of the South Sea, land upon the Luzones [the Philippines] in despight of the enemy, enter into alliance, amity, and traffike with the princes of the Moluccas and the Isle of Java, double the famous Cape of Bona Speranza, arrive at the Isle of Santa Helen, and last of all returne home most richly laden with the commodities of China?[23]

This is a maritime itinerary detailing a series of stops along a route, a proud description of a nascent English commercial presence around the globe, rather than a geographical map. He does not use the term Pacific, nor does he specify exactly how large the South Sea is or would need to be in order to separate Asia from America, especially as the two could remain connected even with a large sea between them, as some maps show (see chapter 8). Yet he gives it a "mighty bredth."

Many of Hakluyt's collected accounts proclaimed the land separation of America from China, yet stopped short of calling it a new part of the world, preferring to call it an island, the terminology of the modern continents not having come into regular use before the eighteenth century. A discourse by Sir Humphrey Gilbert, the half-brother of Ralegh and ardent supporter of the search for a passage to Cathay, describes the land across the Atlantic as "an iland environed round about with sea," like Plato's Atlantis, "now called America."[24] According to Gilbert, if Asia and America were connected, animals would pass between them, "but there hath not any time bene found any of the beasts proper to Cataia, or Tartarie in America, nor of those proper to America, in Tartarie, Cataia, or any part of Asia. Which thing proveth America, not onely to be one Island, and in no part adioyning to Asia, but also that the people of those countreys, have not had any traffique with each other."[25] In contrast to the ideas of the German cosmographer Johannes Schöner (1533) or the Dominican chronicler Gregorio García (1607), who both believed that Polo had traveled to Tenochtitlan, Gilbert asserts that Polo had never come to America, and that neither Verrazano nor Coronado "ever found entry from thence by land to Cataia, or any part of Asia."[26] The English editor of travel literature Willes similarly proclaims "that Asia and the West Indies be not tied together by any isthmus or straight of land, contrary to the opinion of some new Cosmographers, by whome doubtfully this matter hath bin brought in controversie."[27] Many of the accounts in Hakluyt's volumes demonstrate a clear awareness of the Manila galleon trade, which annually traversed the vast distance between East Asia and the Americas.[28] Other widely read English new world narratives from the end of the sixteenth century, including Thomas Harriot's *Brief and True Report* and Walter Ralegh's *Discovery of Guiana*, make similar assertions.[29] Hakluyt and his contemporaries, it would appear, left Eden's *Newe India* behind, as America, China, and India became far-apart places.

Yet even Hakluyt entertained in 1599 the idea that America contained a rich inland, an idea he had gained by having insider access to Spanish accounts of a search for Chinese riches in America (see chapter 8). Leaving out the references to "Upper India" and to China that pepper the Spanish accounts, Hakluyt keeps in place the lure of rich lands to the west of Virginia,

> the In-land whereof is found of late to bee so sweete and holesome a climate, so rich and abundant in silver mines, so apt and capable of all commodities, which Italy, Spaine, and France can affoord, that the Spaniards themselves in their own writings printed in Madrid 1586, and within few months afterward reprinted by me in Paris [he is speaking of Antonio de Espejo's voyage, described in chapter 8], and in a secret mappe of those partes made in Mexico the yeere before for the king of Spaine . . . as also in their intercepted letters come unto my hand, bearing date 1595 acknowledge the In-land to be a better and richer countrey than Mexico and Nueva Spania it selfe.[30]

Supplementing the idea of inland riches inherited from the Spanish expeditions, there was the ever-present belief in the Northwest Passage, a route that it was hoped would take English merchants around the island of America to the north to reach Asia. When Martin Frobisher crossed the Atlantic in the 1570s in search of the Northwest Passage, he took with him a copy of Mandeville, still a standard guide to eastern Asia.[31] In an account included in Hakluyt's collection, the chronicler George Best described Frobisher's entry into the inlet that is now called Frobisher's Bay in Baffin Island, which Frobisher hoped was a strait, noting that "that land vpon his right hand as he sailed Westward he iudged to be the continent of Asia, and thereto be diuided from the firme of America, which lieth vpon the left hand ouer against the same."[32] For Frobisher as reported by Hakluyt, Asia was in fact a strait's distance from America, and the Inuit are "like Tartars." Michael Lok, an investor in the expedition, described an Inuit captive that Frobisher brought back to England as a Chinese man: "Now, when Martin Frobisher returned home again, in October 1576, with his strange man of Cathay, and his great rumor of the passage to Cathay, he was called to the Court and greatly embraced and liked of the best."[33] To document the finding, the Flemish painter Cornelis Ketel was commissioned to make portraits of the man, none of which have survived; meanwhile, Frobisher claimed reimbursement for "apparell for the strainge man of Cathay or new land India."[34] Frobisher returned from a later voyage with another Inuit man and an Inuit woman with her child, and again Ketel was called in to make portraits, which even a century later, in a royal catalogue of the 1680s, were entitled "A Cataia, or Island Man" and a "Cataia Woman."[35]

Elephants in America and the Northwest Passage

After his death, Hakluyt's manuscripts and papers came into the possession of the Reverend Samuel Purchas, chaplain to the Archbishop of Canterbury, who reedited Hakluyt's documents in his *Hakluytus Posthumus, or Purchas His Pilgrimes* (1625). Like Hakluyt, Purchas often emphasized the distance between Asia and America, and the maps by Jocodus Hondius that illuminate his volumes show them as clearly separate landmasses. However, Purchas also often circled back to Eden's Amerasian understanding of the world. In his preface to readers, for instance, he describes his text's organization: "First, we have divided the world in our method into the old and new, allotting to each his own tome," with the the first half of his collection dedicated to "the Elder World, that is Asia, Africa and Europe" and the second half to the new world. Yet, this is still an Amerasian new world, including any parts farther east than ancient navigations had reached: "Now for the New World, we begin it at China, which the Ancients knew not, and take all the East and North parts of Asia from the Caspian Sea, the Arctoan Regions, all America and Terra Australis, comprehending all in that New Title."

Like Eden, Purchas begins his text with a discussion of King Solomon and Ophir, including a chapter pointedly entitled "Peru why and whence so named. It was not Ophir."[36] Purchas argues that while many Europeans, in particular orientalist scholar Benito Arías Montano, had hitherto believed that Ophir existed somewhere in the Americas, they were wrong, for it would have been too long a voyage for Solomon's ships to navigate to the Americas to obtain gold, and these lands could not have been reached without a compass, which Solomon did not have. Arías Montano and others had conflated Peru with Ophir based on the similarity between the two names, focusing on the Hebrew passage "the gold he used was gold of Parvaim" (*aurum erat de loco Paruaim*, 2 Chronicles 3) indicated the source of Solomon's gold. As we will see in chapter 13, Arías Montano argued that Paruaim was the plural of Ophir, making Paru or Peru the singular; over time, Ophir had become Opir, and then Opir became Piru or Peru. None of this impressed Purchas, who retorted that there was no etymological relationship between these words, and if the word Peru resembled biblical names, it was not because it had evolved from them, but only a coincidence resulting from miscommunication between two cultures barely capable of communicating with one another to begin with. "Thus the name which they would make as old as Solomon, began but *Anno* 1515 at the most, and that which is extended to New Spain and Peru, was known in neither, nor in any place else of the world." And then there was the evidence from natural history: "Peru could not be Ophir if we conceive that Solomon brought thence ivorie and peacocks," he argued, for "an elephant could not live in Peru, but by miracle. For the hilles are cold in extremitie, and the valleys, till the Incas made artificiall rivers, were without water, it never rayning there. Whereas the elephant delights in places very hote and very moist."[37]

Hakluyt and Purchas would seem to have put an end to Amerasian speculation in England. Hakluyt had essentially ignored this conception of the world, as if it existed for him no longer, and for Purchas such discussions were no more than shadow-boxing: "But I deserve blame to fight with elephants in America, which is with less than a shadow, and to lay siege to castles in the aire." Yet, the debate was not over, as Walter Ralegh had engaged the question shortly before,[38] and Purchas's own wrangling had the effect of reviving the discussion. As the historian Richard Trexler noted, "well into the eighteenth century, there were those who still sought magi, apostles, Ophir, and the variously spelled Tarsis in the Americas."[39]

Amerasian ideas were not just a misty projection from England but an active concern in the colonies on the ground. In 1606, the Jamestown settlers were charged with finding a "passage toward the East India Sea."[40] Francis Magnel, an Irishman who had been to Jamestown shortly after the colony was founded in 1607, returned to Spain to tell of English activities in their settlement on the James River, reporting that local Powhatans knew of three reliable routes to the ocean and had offered to take the settlers to them. These Indians "assure them that on the other side of Virginia by the South Sea there is a land where the natives wear long silk robes and red buskins"—unmistakable signifiers of Chinese courtly culture—and that these people had "a great deal of gold." As in the case of Andrés Dorantes's copper bell (see chapter 8), which was bequeathed to him by Indigenous communities who themselves reported having received it through trade pathways connecting to richer civilizations to the north and west and possibly to the South Sea, the Powhatans presented the English with knives and other things that they had reportedly acquired from traders that had traveled back from these western lands. Accordingly, Jamestown settlers planned to build forts along the river leading to the sea in order to claim control over this potential trade route. Their goal was to "make themselves lords of the South Sea, so as to have their share of the riches of the Indies, and to be in the way of the traffic of the King of Spain, and to seek other new worlds for themselves."[41] Despite having failed to produce real results, the quests of Francisco Coronado and others, studied in chapter 8, had been publicized in tantalizing accounts that seemed to confirm each other as they spread from edition to edition and language to language. In their new role as global rivals to Spain on American soil, the English, too, contracted a fairly serious case of Coronado syndrome.

Tantalizing evidence of an Indigenous-China trade continued to be reported. In 1619, John Pory, secretary to the governor of Virginia, traveled south and confirmed the English navigator Harriot's accounts of rich silkgrass and other commodities on the Carolina coast. According to Pory, Indians there had told the colonists of a nearby copper mine, and at the house of one Indian king these settlers had seen a "China box" acquired in trade with Indians who lived on the other side of the Appalachians, "neare the Sea." These colonists had acquired the box from men who came in ships "and weare clothes, and dwelle in houses, and are called Acanackchina."[42] Once again, as in the case of Dorantes's bell, multidirectional trade flows were taken to confirm dramatic global narratives of connectivity between Asian and American lands. In fact, fine Chinese porcelain wine cups have been excavated from seventeenth-century sites along the James River, prestige objects proudly owned by local colonial elites. As along the northern frontier of New Spain at exactly the same time, colonial households were populated with Asian items obtained through maritime trade even as the prospect of reaching Asian territory by traveling westward overland remained an imagined possibility (see chapter 17).[43] In his *New English Canaan* (1637), a devastating critique of the current model of English colonialism informed by familiarity with the Indigenous populations as well as the natural environment of Massachusetts, the colonist Thomas Morton admitted that the geographical question was unresolved: "what part of this mane continente may be thought to border upon the country of the Tartars it is yet unknowne."[44] Purchas's geographical reasonings and biblical criticism did not necessarily carry weight with those who had a ground-level understanding of the American land and the cultures that thrived there.

An Elizabethan Vogue for Globes

In the preface to the first, 1589 edition of his *Principal Navigations*, Hakluyt announced the intended publication of the first terrestrial globe made in England by Emery Molyneux, an Elizabethan maker of mathematical instruments and ordnance. Molyneux eventually made this globe in 1592, as well as an additional terrestrial globe in 1603. Paired with celestial globes, each set was presented and dedicated to Queen Elizabeth I, who surely saw them as symbols of her terrestrial empire and spiritual mission.[45] Today, these early English globes are preserved in Petworth House in Sussex (1592) and in the Middle Temple Library in London (1603). Molyneux used the most up-to-date reports and charts to make his globes, and he indicated the speculative nature of geographical theories he considered unproven, as when he drew the coastline of a hypothetical southern continent. Molyneux designed these globes, with royal arms emblazoned across the north American landmass, in part to inspire Elizabeth's ambitions for imperial expansion; the globes track the circumnavigations of Drake (1577–80) and Thomas Cavendish (1585–88) and show Ralegh's Roanoke colony in detail. The production of these globes was accompanied by Robert Hues's *Tractatus de globis et eorum usu: A Treatise Descriptive of the Globes Constructed by Emery Molyneux, and Published in 1592*, which also clearly separates the Americas and Asia.

Yet even here we see Amerasian traces. On Molyneux's 1603 globe, the North American landmass is called *America sive India Nova*, America or New India, and in the part of the world that is today called Mexico there is a region curiously named *Calicutan* (fig. 10.5). While toponyms on early modern maps can be notoriously difficult to decode and often appear unlinked to any known geographical names or places, many of the ones in this part of the globe are identifiable: *Marata*, *Coana*, *Petatlan*, and *Culiacan*, for instance, all represented Indian "kingdoms" visited by Coronado, and *Astatland* to the north surely refers to the land of Aztlán, the ancestral homeland of the Aztecs. *Calicutan*, by contrast—not one city among many but a regional label in larger letters placed at an angle to cover a broad swathe of territory—does not correspond to any previously known Mexican place. It is difficult not to read this as a kind of Mexican *Calicut* (or *Calecut*, as it is indicated on the Indian subcontinent, on the other side of Molyneux's globe), representing an Amerasian persistence, or an ongoing fusion of Mexico, New Spain, and India, that continued subtly but steadily to inform English visions of commerce and wealth gleaned in the West.

Very few people had access to Molyneux's globes to inspect for themselves the delineation of landmasses and the breadth of its oceans, yet they were immediately famous, entering the popular imagination and sparking new "global" talk at various levels of society in the 1590s. It is possible that the decision in 1599 to rename Shakespeare's theater "The Globe" came in response to the new popularity of the idea.[46] For those interested in the details of the famous globes, printed sources made them available to a wider public, and, interestingly, these printed renderings—both in text and image—bring Amerasia into view far more than the globes themselves had. Edward Wright flattened the 1592 terrestrial globe using a Mercator projection, for publication in the greatly expanded second edition of Hakluyt's *Principall Navigations* (1599–1600) (fig. 10.6). Whereas the globe gives hard edges to a separated America and Asia, this engraved version leaves the landmasses unbounded above a shared latitude. Before fading out, the

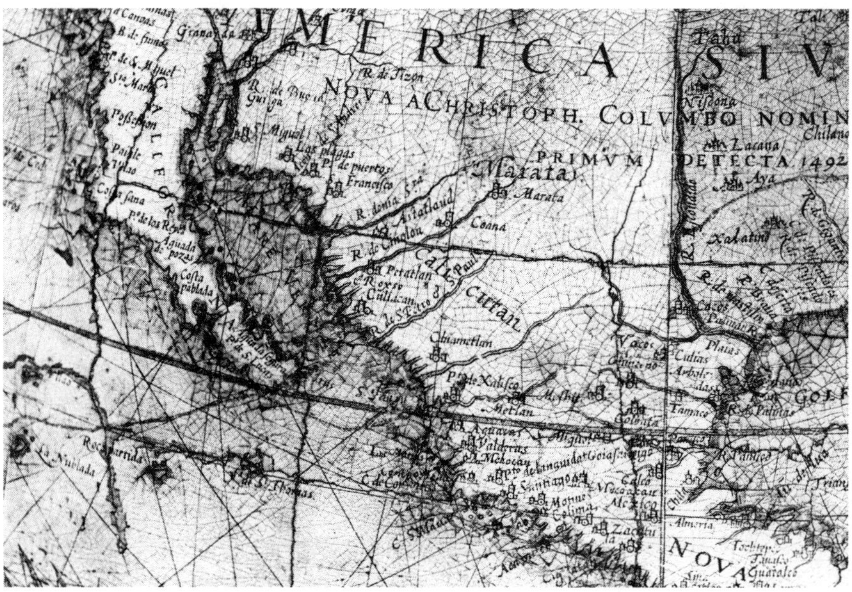

10.5 Calicut still finds a place in Mexico. Emery Molyneux, terrestrial globe, detail (1603). London, Middle Temple Library.

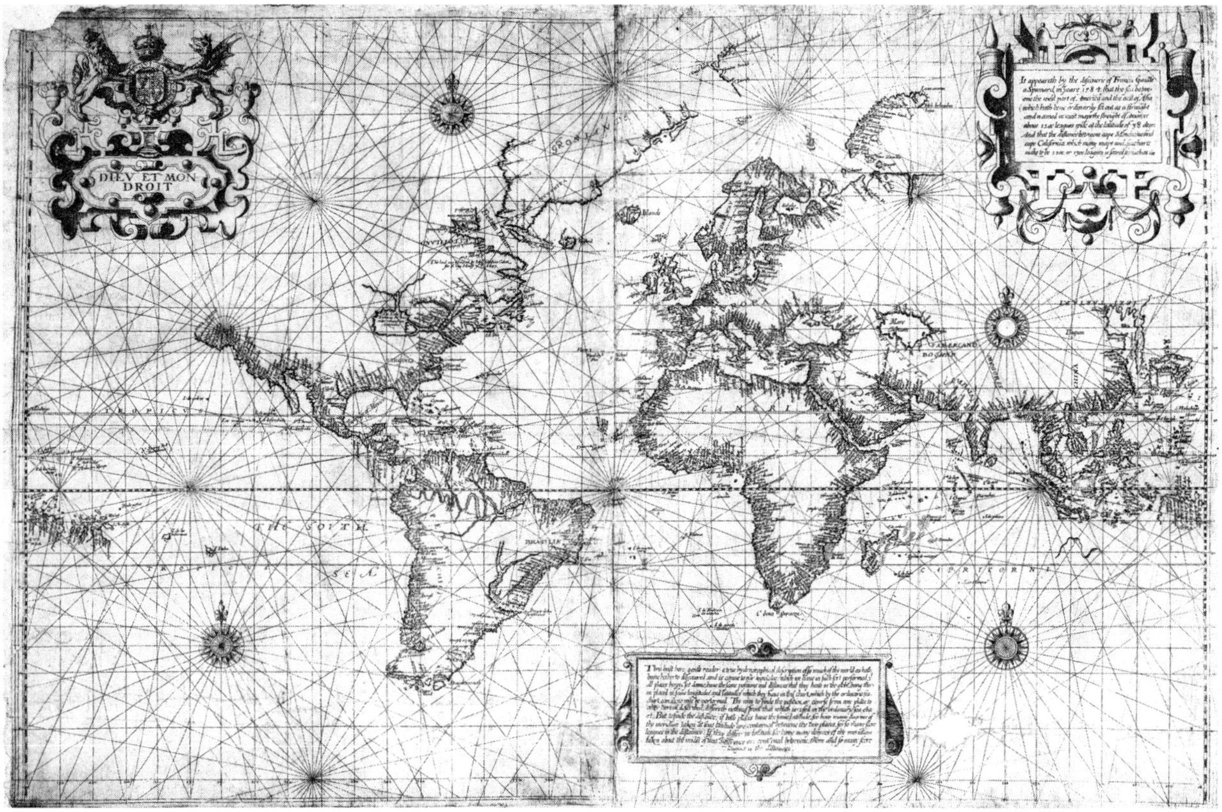

10.6 A flattening of the Molyneux 1592 globe. Edward Wright, *A true hydrographical description of so much of the world as hath beene hetherto discovered*, engraving on paper, 43 × 64 cm (1599). University of Oxford, Bodleian Libraries.

Asian coastline trends northeast and the American coastline northwest, leaving open the question of the degree of their nearing at higher latitudes.

Without explicitly joining them, the Wright-Molyneux map shows America and Asia in staggered overlap. South of the last point on the American West Coast, in the South Sea, is Isla de los Tiburones, the so-called Unfortunate Isles (Puka-puka in present-day French Polynesia), and a bit west of there is San Cristoforo (San Cristóbal) at the eastern end of an archipelago (now called the Solomon Islands), and further west of there is Guinea (Papua New Guinea). On the left side of the map, America fades out just as Asia emerges out of the sea once again, in the form of a long ellipsis of islands, much like those discussed in chapter 8. Shakespeare scholars largely concur that Maria's comment about Malvolio's smiling face in *Twelfth Night* (III, ii)—"He does smile his face into more lines than is in the new map with the augmentation of the Indies"—is a reference to none other than the famous 1599 Wright-Molyneux map with its many rhumb lines.[47] If so, then the most notable thing about this projection of the world for Shakespeare was its "augmentation of the Indies."

A hundred or so years after Columbus, the map still grapples with the same question that Columbus had raised on his arrival to Cuba—the location of the Alpha Omega convergence where the West reaches its limit and the East begins, and vice versa (see chapter 1). Europe's advance westward followed the movement of the sun, which rose from the east and fell toward the west, the cosmic predicate of historical time. Throughout the sixteenth century, the complete circling of the globe back to its eastern beginning was understood as a momentous revolution in the order of time, a geographical conclusion that was also a fulfillment of human history on earth (see chapters 3 and 7). What does it mean to pass through the end back to the beginning? The geographical data that would resolve these questions, left tactfully incomplete on many maps we have reviewed, touched on fundamental mysteries concerning creation and humanity's place in it, provoking the poet Donne's emblematic gloss,

> As west and east
> In all flat maps (and I am one) are one
> So death doth touch the resurrection.[48]

Molyneux's 1592 terrestrial globe was also described in printed texts. In a 1594 volume of treatises on the art of navigation, intended for wide readership, the mathematician Thomas Blundeville offered a tour of Molyneux's globe as a mapping of the voyages of Drake and Cavendish. He describes how Drake sailed up the western coast of America farther than anyone before, to a place he named Nova Albion (exactly the northernmost point on this coast as shown in the Wright-Molyneux map). Not wanting to go farther northward, Drake returned back down the coast, and "from thence he sayled in a manner right Southeast to the Iles Moluccas."[49] Applying the logic of elliptical continuity (see chapter 6), Blundeville reduces the distance between the American coast and the Spice Islands to one sentence, and also changes the direction from the expected southwest to the southeast. He is not generally confused about direction since he then says that Drake sailed southwest from the Moluccas to Java. Turning to the voyage of Cavendish, once again the passage from the American coast to the Spice Islands spans a sentence, and once again he proposes the curious idea that the ship sailed southeast and east to do so. From Puerto San Lucas on the Baja California Peninsula, Cavendish "sayled in a manner Southeast about 320 leagues and then he directed his course Eastward towardes the Moluccas."[50] Rendered by Blundeville in the form of two famous itineraries, Molyneux's famous globe is understood to chart a swift if somewhat disorienting Amerasian passage.

• • •

Endpiece: Shakespeare's Amerasian Globe

The year 1594 also saw the premiere of the *Comedy of Errors*, one of Shakespeare's most popular plays, which offered an amusing bit of "global" talk in the parodic form of a lover's admiration for the rotundity of the "kitchen wench" who had claimed his heart. Description of her parts becomes a charting of her globe, reaching even "America, the Indies," the only non-European destination on the tour.

> *Dromio of Syracuse.* No longer from head to foot than from hip to hip: she is spherical, like a globe; I could find out countries in her.
> *Antipholus of Syracuse.* In what part of her body stands Ireland?
> *Dromio of Syracuse.* Marry, in her buttocks: I found it out by the bogs.
> *Antipholus of Syracuse.* Where Scotland?
> *Dromio of Syracuse.* I found it by the barrenness; hard in the palm of the hand.
> *Antipholus of Syracuse.* Where France?
> *Dromio of Syracuse.* In her forehead; armed and reverted, making war against her heir.
> *Antipholus of Syracuse.* Where England?
> *Dromio of Syracuse.* I looked for the chalky cliffs, but I could find no whiteness in them; but I guess it stood in her chin, by the salt rheum that ran between France and it.
> *Antipholus of Syracuse.* Where Spain?
> *Dromio of Syracuse.* Faith, I saw it not; but I felt it hot in her breath.
> *Antipholus of Syracuse.* Where America, the Indies?
> *Dromio of Syracuse.* Oh, sir, upon her nose all o'er embellished with rubies, carbuncles, sapphires, declining their rich aspect to the hot breath of Spain; who sent whole armadoes of caracks to be ballast at her nose.
> *Antipholus of Syracuse.* Where stood Belgia, the Netherlands?
> *Dromio of Syracuse.* Oh, sir, I did not look so low.

America is the Indies altogether, encrusted with gems. On Shakespeare's globe, Amerasia glitters, even if upon the carbuncled nose of a kitchen maid.

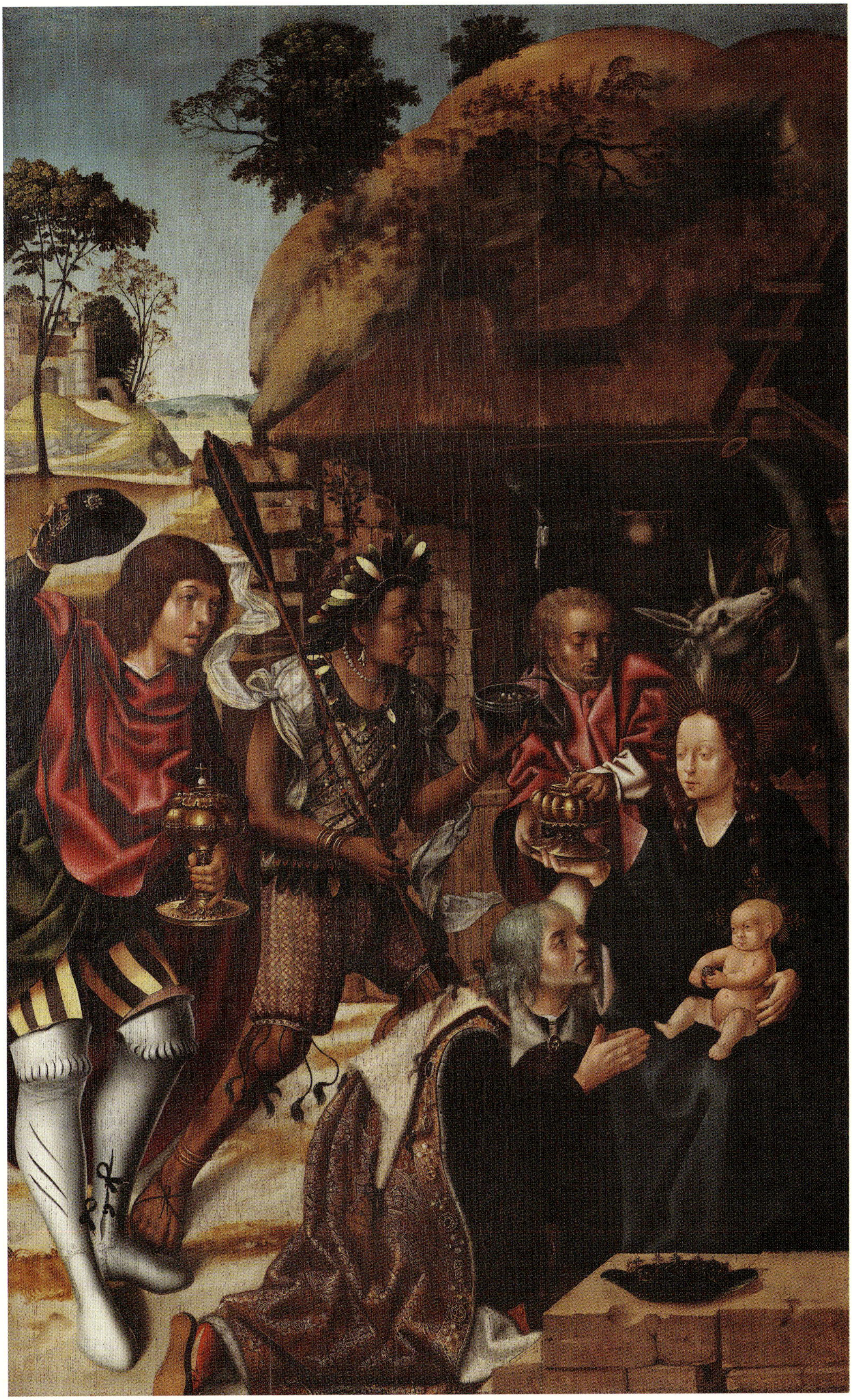

Plate I An Amerasian expansion of the Magi's range. Vasco Fernandes, *Adoration of the Magi*, oil on panel, 131 × 81 cm, ca. 1502–1506. Viseu, Museu Nacional Grâo Vasco. (See chapter 3.)

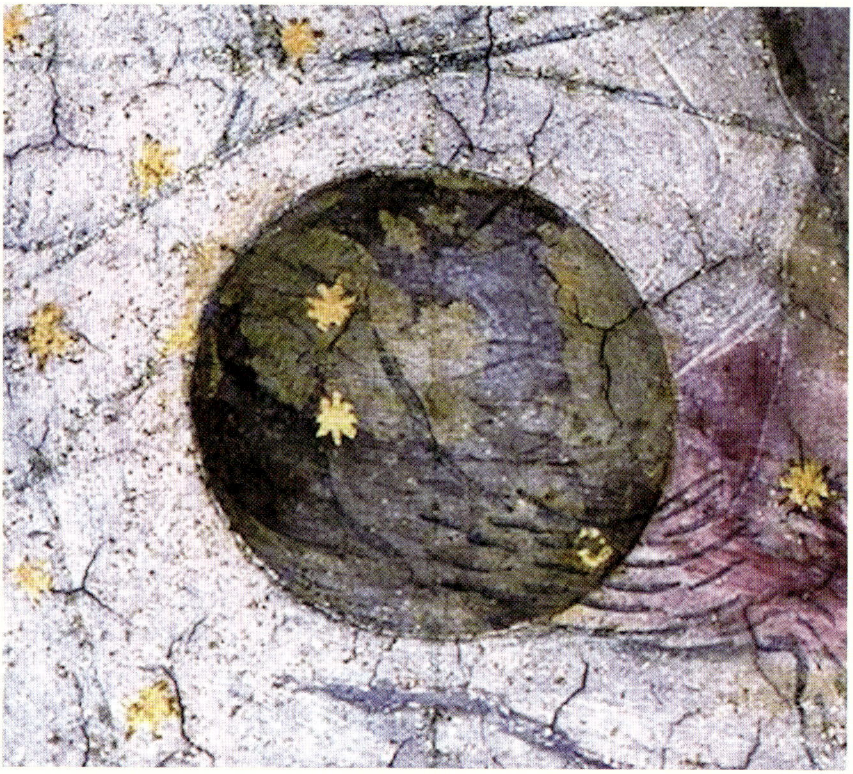

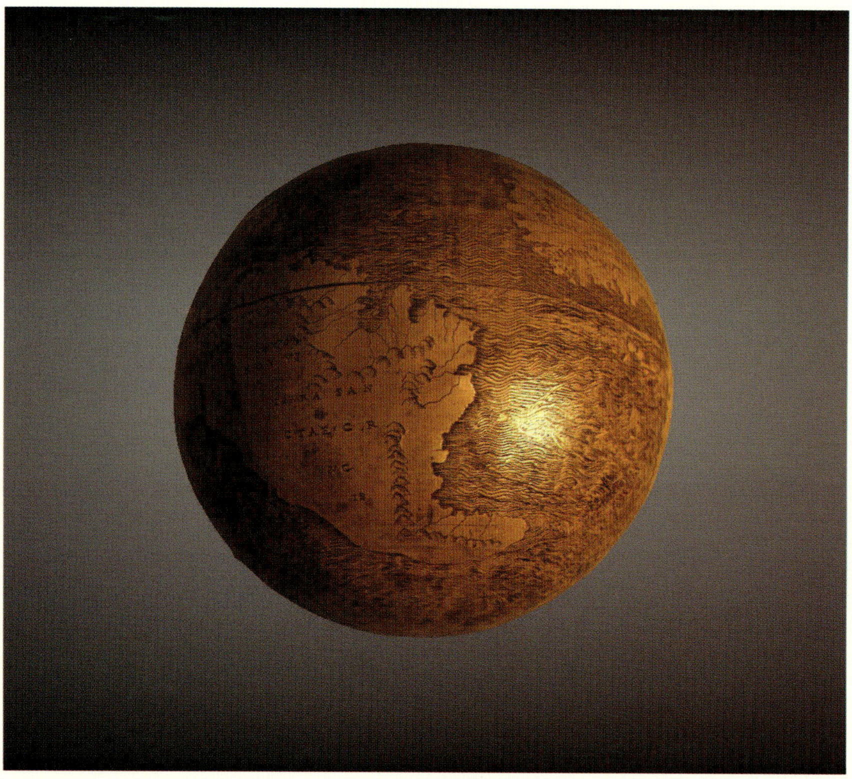

Plates II and III Two views of the earth from below. Raphael (and Johannes Ruysch?), *Astronomia/ Urania*, ca. 1510. Vatican City, Vatican Palace, Stanza della Segnatura. Hunt-Lenox globe, ca. 1510. New York Public Library. (See chapter 4.)

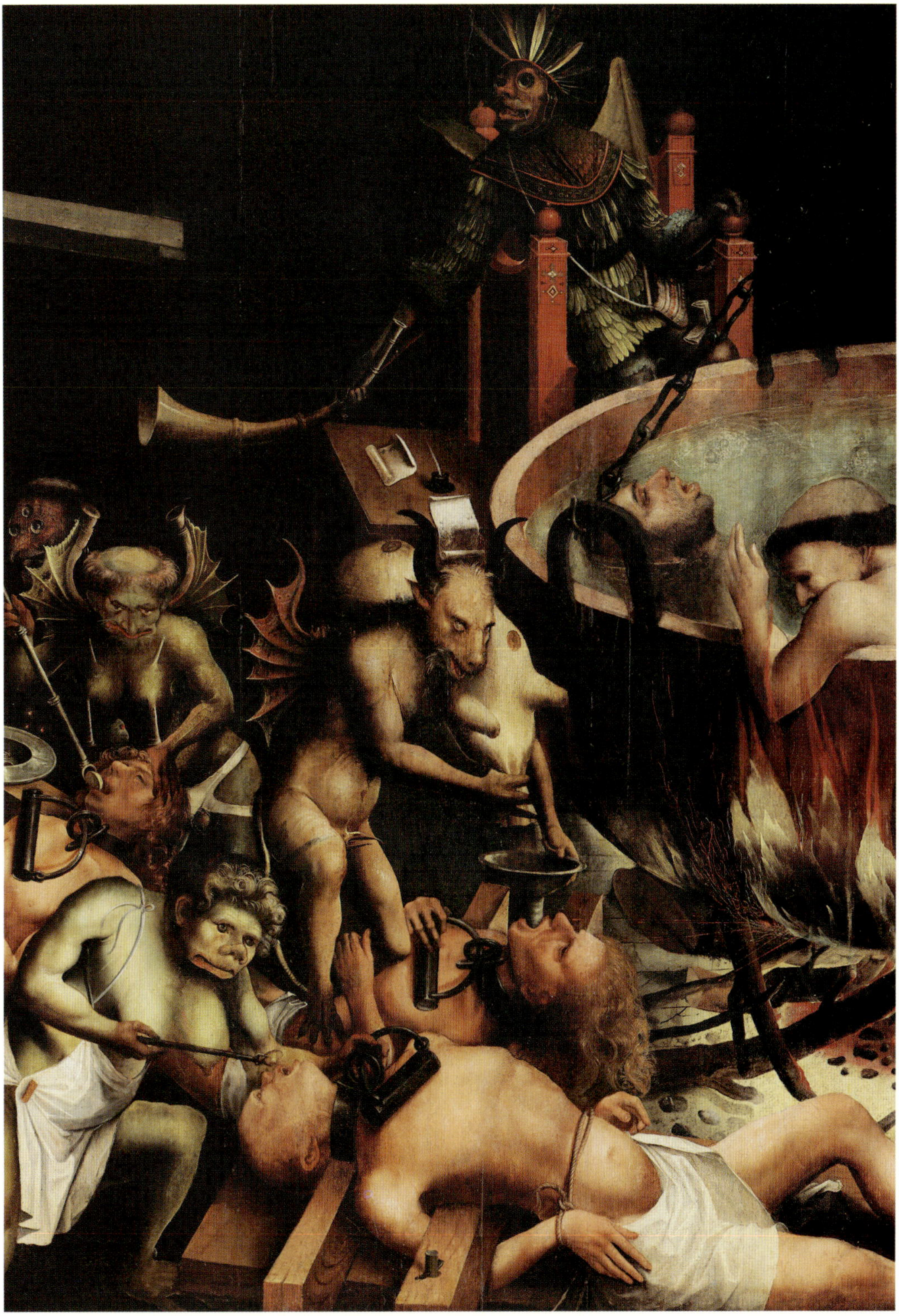

Plate IV The devil, wearing Brazilian Tupi feather headdress, wields an ivory horn from West Africa. Cristovão de Figueiredo (?), *Hell*, ca. 1515. Lisbon, Museu Nacional de Arte Antiga. (See chapter 5.)

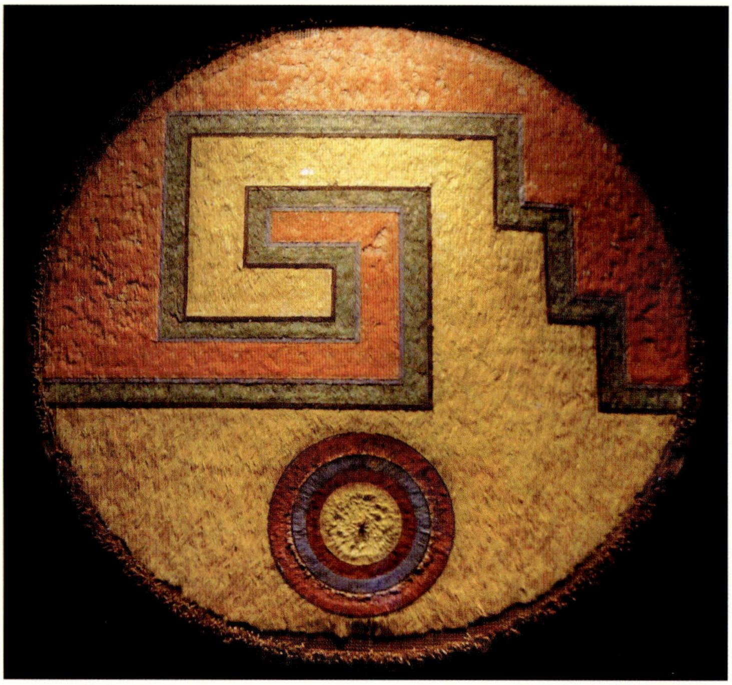

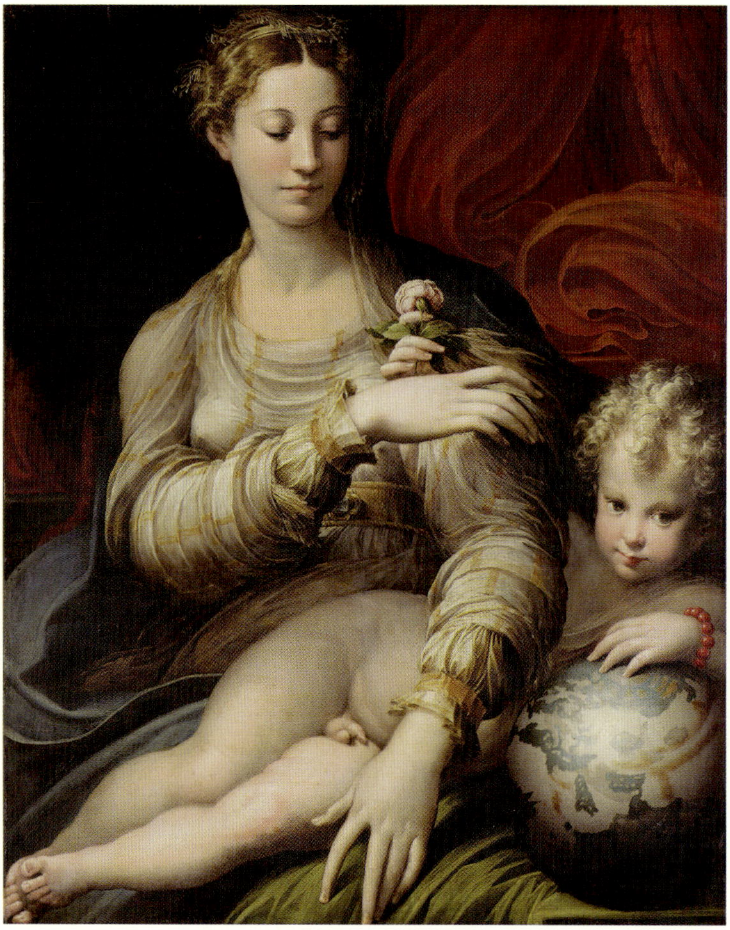

Plates V and VI Two cosmic images. Mexica culture, feather shield, ca. 1520?, Stuttgart, Landesmuseum Württemberg. Parmigianino, *Madonna of the Rose*, here called *Madonna of the Earthly Globe*, 1529–30, Dresden, Gemäldegalerie. (See chapter 7.)

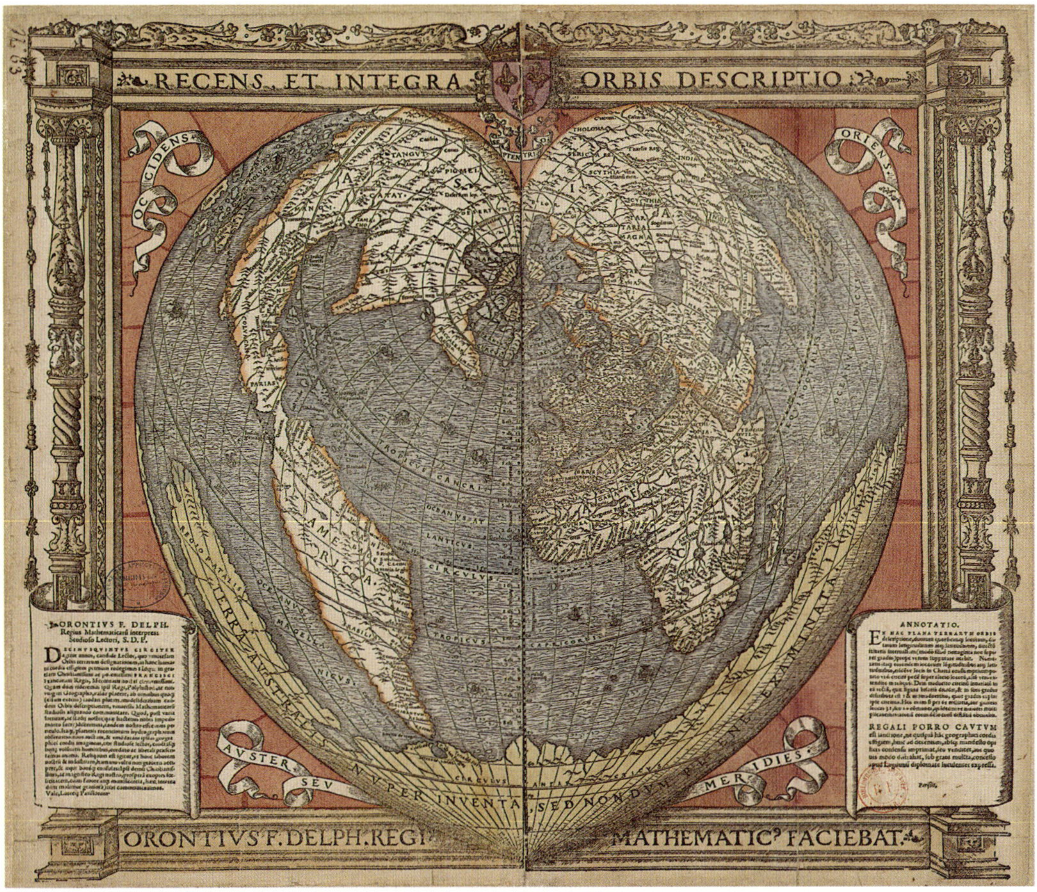

Plate VII The heart-shaped world swells beyond its frame. Oronce Finé, *Recens et integra orbis descriptio*, 1534. Paris, Bibliothèque Nationale de France. (See chapter 9.)

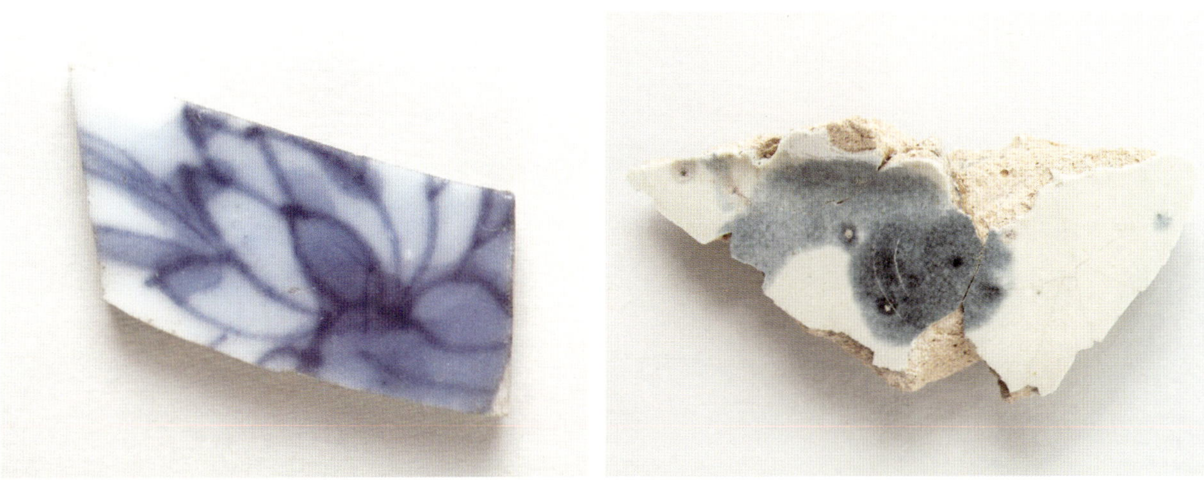

Plate VIII Fragments of Ming blue-and-white porcelain and its Mexican imitation in maiolica. Both found at San Gabriel de Yunque, 1598–1610. Albuquerque, Maxwell Museum of Anthropology, University of New Mexico. (See chapter 17.)

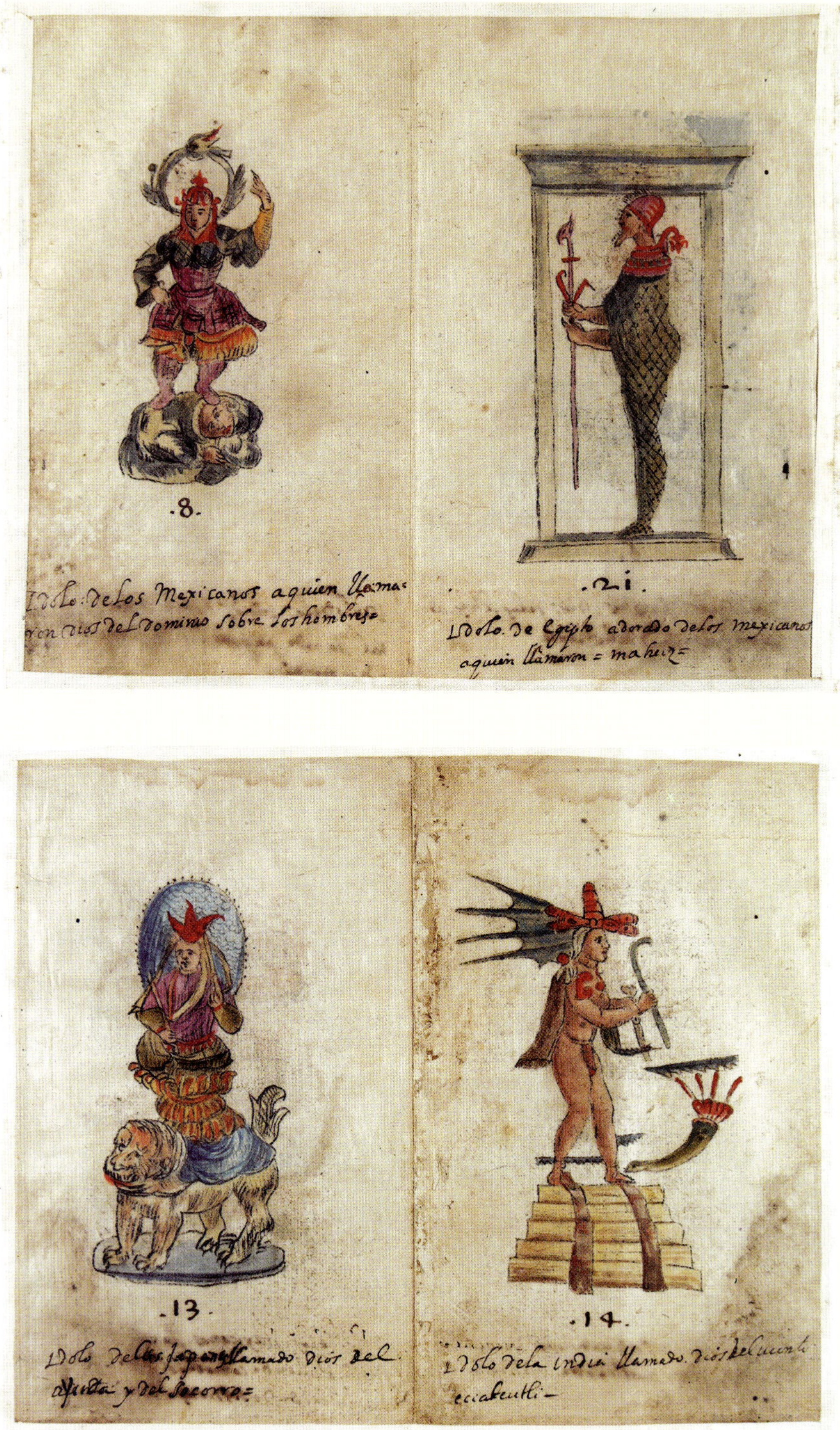

Plate IX Gods from Mexico, Japan, China, and Egypt mingle and merge in an accordion manuscript made in Rome on Asian paper. *Icones coloribus ornatae idolorum mexicanorum, Aeguptorum, Sinensim, Japanorum, Indorum*, 1615–26. Rome, Biblioteca Angelica. (See chapter 14.)

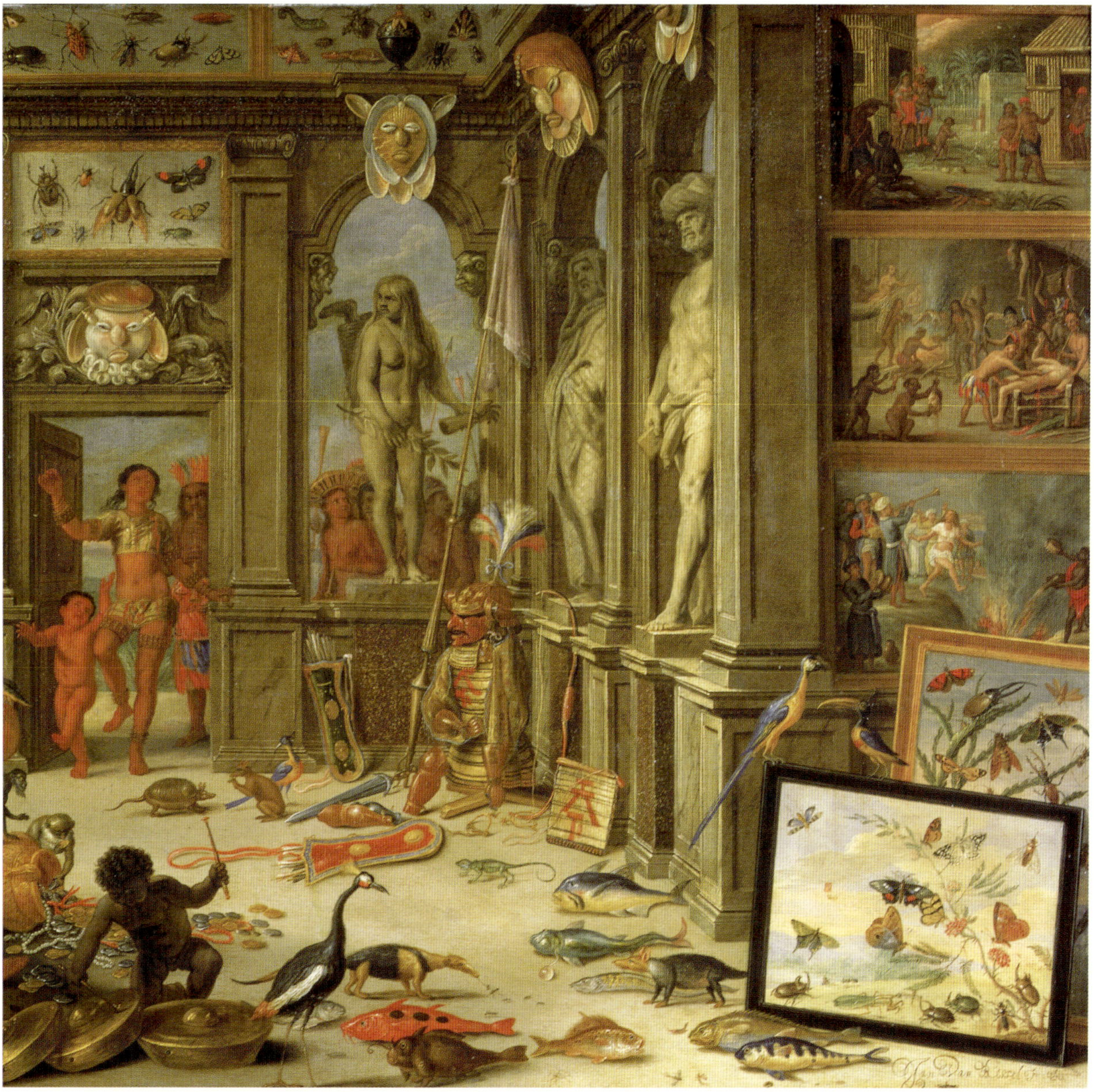

Plate X A scene representing America is populated by figures from India and samurai armor from Japan. Jan van Kessel, *America*, 1664–66. Munich, Alte Pinakothek. (See chapter 16.)

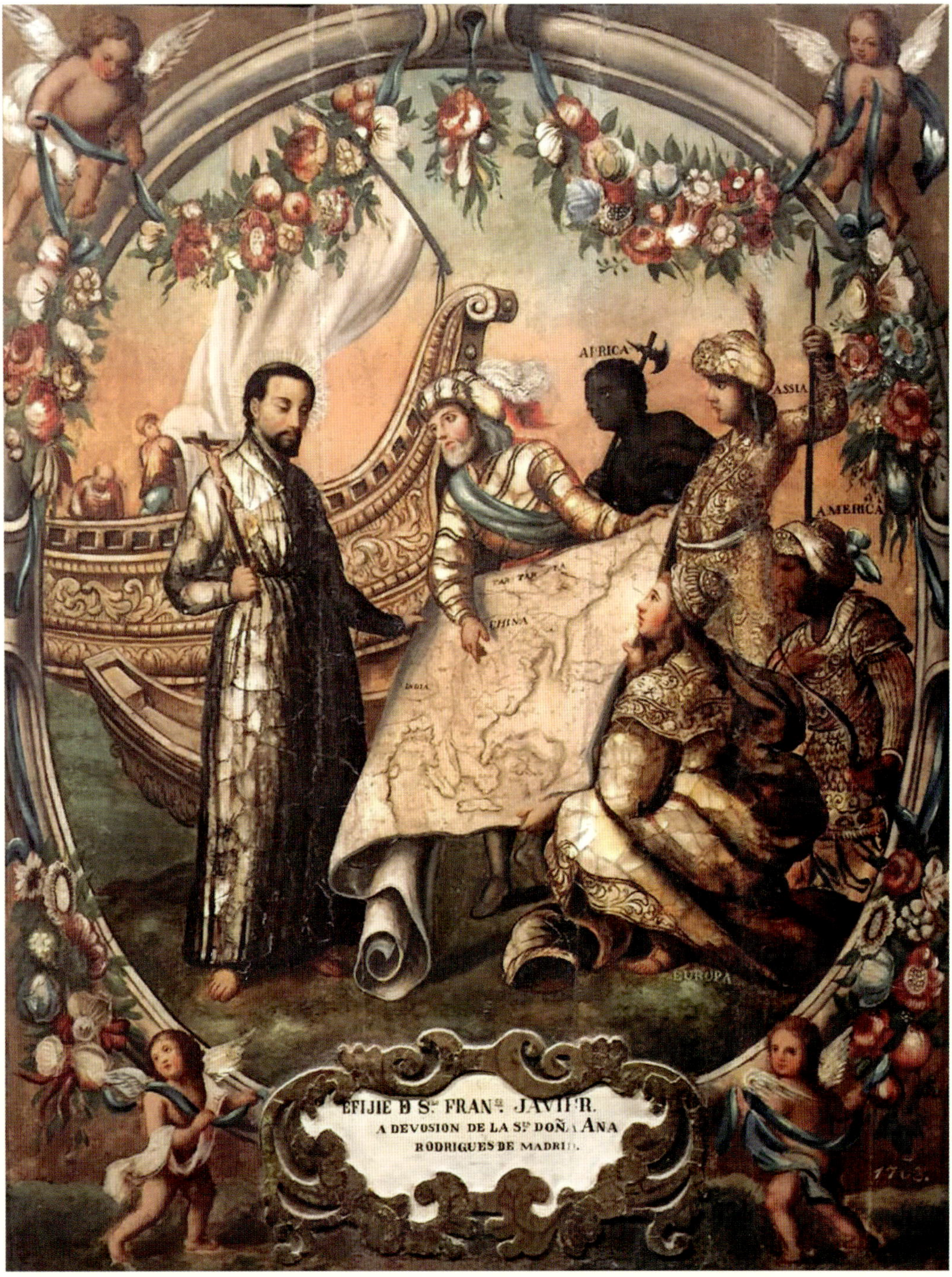

Plate XI Saint Francis Xavier presented with a map of Asia, as visualized in America. Juan González, *Saint Francis Xavier Contemplating His Missions*, 1703. Mexico City, private collection. (See chapter 17.)

ELEVEN

Moctezuma the Great Khan: Caspar Vopel's Global Vision

Making Amerasia visible often requires teasing out its latent presence by reading between lines of a text or scrutinizing details of an image in order to bring out background concepts and coordinates. Occasionally, however, Amerasia reveals itself in a brilliant and dazzling flash, as it did in an influential and large-scale printed wall map of 1545 by the cartographer Caspar Vopel that is known through a 1558 copy by the Venetian mapmaker Giovanni Andrea Vavassore (fig. 11.1).

Amerasia by and for the Emperor

Framing the Habsburg coat of arms, the title at the top reads *A New Complete and Universal Description of the Whole World, according to the Modern German Tradition*, and an introductory cartouche at the right affirms that the map—made of twelve large sheets—was informed by the geographical knowledge of the Emperor Charles V, on the basis of the latest reports from "the newly discovered lands." On the Vopel/Vavassore map, American places are not simply added to legendary Asian ones; instead, they merge and mingle into an Amerasian extension of Asia, with Chinese and Mexican toponyms mixed together, and lengthy texts explain the geography and culture of parts of the world that Europeans were only recently attempting to control, both conceptually and materially.[1]

The map depicts both Eastern India and New Spain (India Orientalis and Hispania Nova), including Mexico, as regions of Greater Asia (Asia Magna) (fig. 11.2). In this projection, the latitude lines bend around the curving form of the globe, bending East/West relations from horizontal to vertical as one reaches the map's edge. The Tropic of Cancer, marked as a red line, curves upward at the two edges of the map, as does the equator, marked in a line of alternating black and white. We find Tenochtitlan (*Temixtitan*, "discovered by Cortes in 1521") just east of Mangi, or Manzi, the derogatory term used by the Mongols and Marco

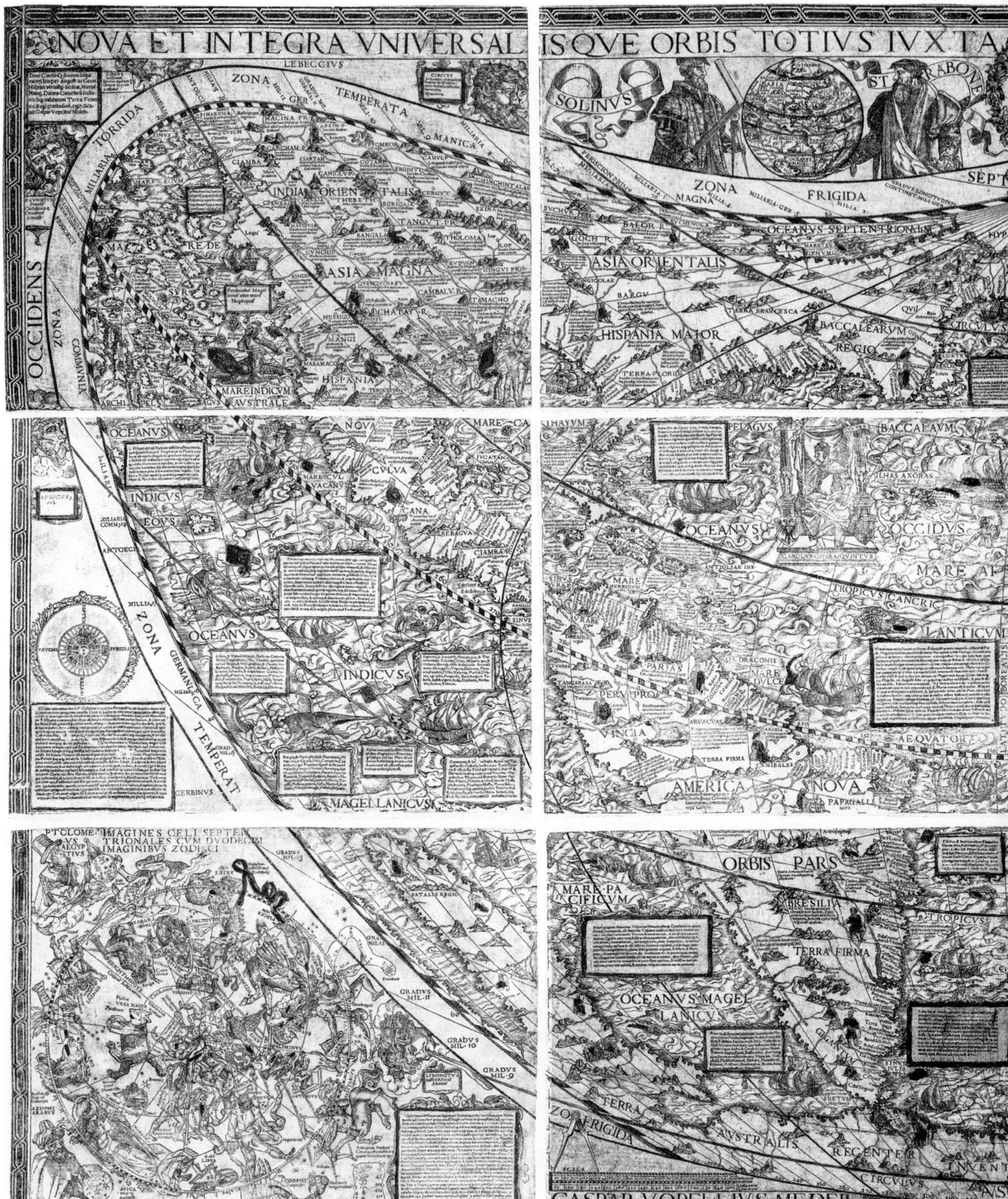

11.1 Amerasia as an imperial vision. Caspar Vopel, *Nova et integra universalisque orbis totius... descriptio*, 12 sheets, copper engraving, 194 × 112.5 cm (Venice, 1558). Cambridge, Harvard University, Houghton Library.

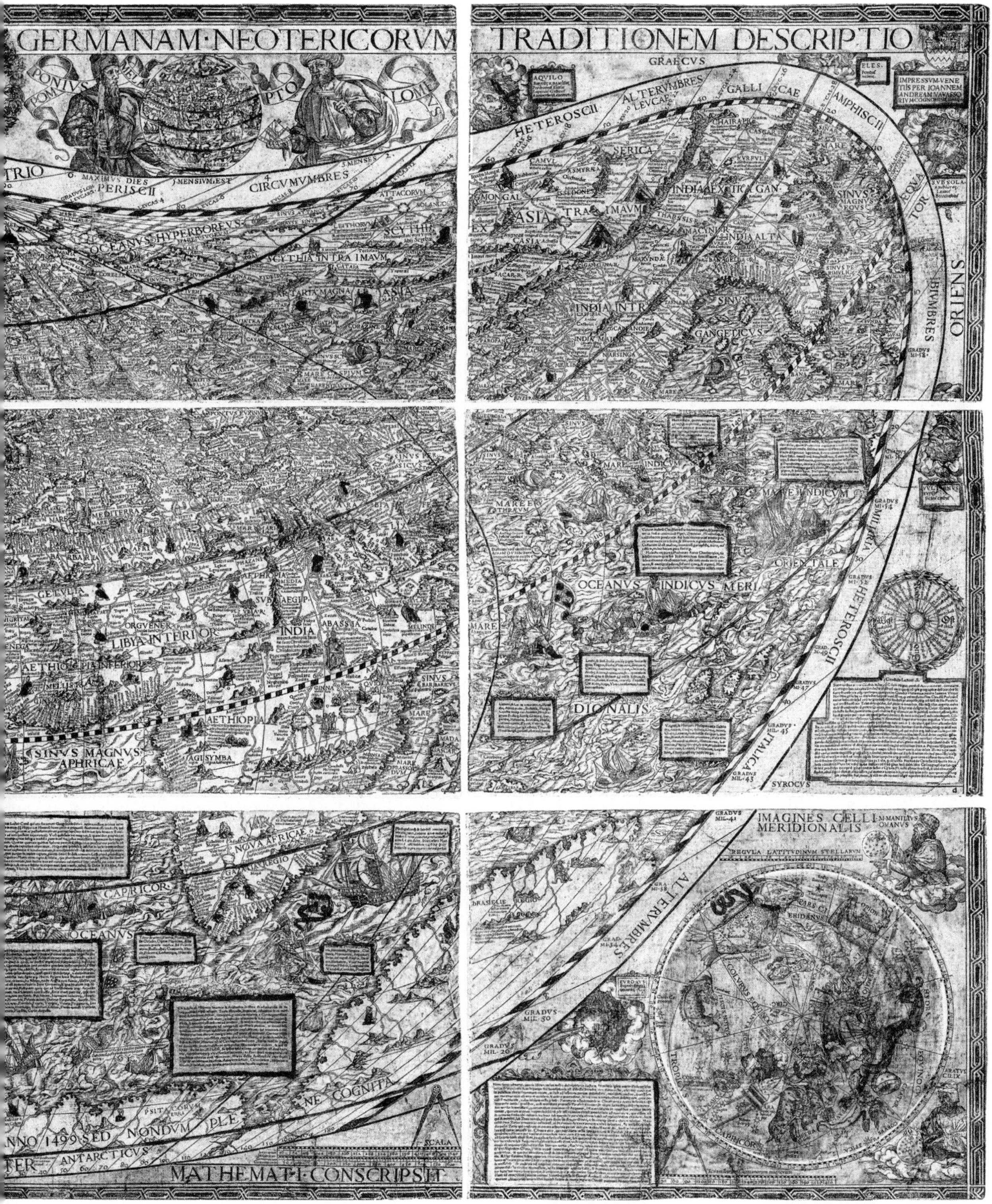
GERMANAM·NEOTERICORVM
TRADITIONEM DESCRIPTIO
GRAECVS
ALTERVMBRES
HETEROSCII
AMPHISCII
SERICA
INDIA EXTRA GAN
ASIA
INDIA ALTA
SINVS GANGETICVS
INDIA INTRA
ORIENS
BIVMBRES
OCEANVS HYPERBOREVS
SCYTHIA INTRA IMAVM
CIRCVMVMBRES
PERISCII
LIBYA INTERIOR
AETHIOPIA INFERIOR
AETHIOPIA
INDIA
SINVS MAGNVS APHRICAE
MARE INDICVM
ORIENTALE
OCEANVS INDICVS MERI
DIONALIS
HETEROSCII
SYROCVS
NOVA AFRICAE
CAPRICOR
OCEANVS
NE COGNITA
ANNO 1499 SED NONDVM PLE
ANTARCTICVS
SCALA
MATHEMATI·CONSCRIPSIT
IMAGINES CELLI MERIDIONALIS
REGVLA LATITVDINVM STELLARVM
ALTERVMBRES
IMPRESSVM VENETIIS PER JOANNEM ANDREAM VAVASSORIVM COGNOMINE

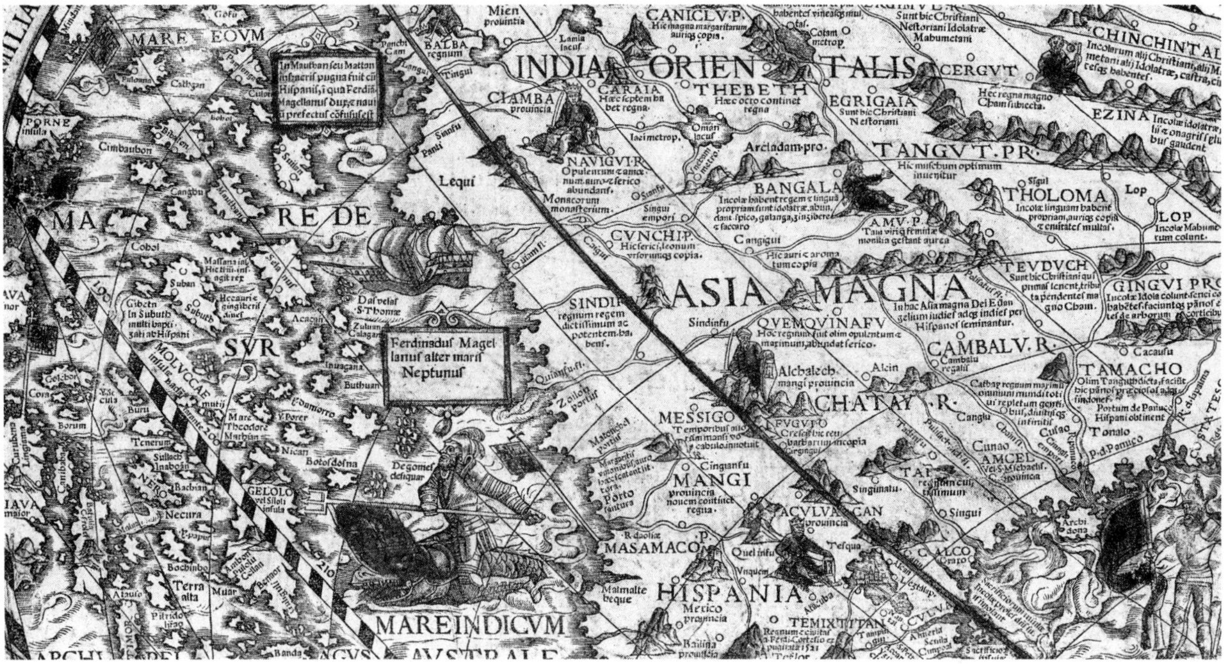

11.2 Tenochtitlan as the Capital of China. This detail of figure 11.1 shows the upper left corner of the cordiform projection, where the lines of longitude curve into near-horizontal parallels.

Polo alike to describe the barbarians of southern China. Just north and west, we can see Quemquinafu, a Latinization of Quanzhou, called Zaiton/Zayton by Polo, the port in eastern China where Polo discovered porcelain and from which he departed to travel back to Europe by boat (though here, in its Amerasian location, it is shown not anywhere near a coast).[2] A bit further east, just north of the Tropic of Cancer, we see Chatay or Cathay, the kingdom of China, and north of there Cambalu, referring to Kahnbalik, the Mongol capital and today modern Beijing. Farther west is Bangala or Bengal, as well as Tangut, the ethnicity or kingdom of Xixia in northwestern China, the Chinese province of Tholoma, and Lop, the Uyghur word for lake. South and east of all of this is Messigo, positioned just west of Mangi, or southern China.[3] We see the figure of Ferdinand Magellan ("another Neptune of the sea") taking off from an Amerasian coast toward the Moluccas.

The newly discovered kingdoms of America are not a mere appendage to these Asian locations. The inscription at Messigo explains that "in the time of our ancestors, Messigo was known by the term Mansi," thus asserting identity, not just propinquity, with the nearby Mangi. A cartouche not far away explains that the Mexica capital Themixitan

(*Tenochtitlan*), found just to the south of Mangi on the map, is to be identified with Quinsai (present-day Hangzhou), the vastly populated and rich city full of waterways and bridges effusively described by Polo. Moreover, the cartouche continues, the ruler at Themixitan is to be identified with the Great Khan of China ("referred to by Hernán Cortés conversely as Monti Zuma"). The great gulf of water to the east of these locations, populated by the islands colonized by Columbus, is described not as the Gulf of Mexico but as the Sea of Cathay. In this worldscape, America fully merges with what was known of Asia.

This depiction of Amerasia is stunning, but just how unusual was it? From the beginning of the sixteenth century, mapping newly encountered lands to the west presented a series of problems for European cartographers that persisted for over a century after 1492. Was the mainland to the west of the newly discovered islands an extension of Cathay? Or did it contain water passages that would lead to Cathay? In the first half of the sixteenth century, only a handful of maps, including the *Cantino Planisphere* (1502), and maps by Martin Waldseemüller (1507), Benedetto Bordone (1528), Gerardus Mercator (1538), and Sebastian Münster (1540) represented the new world as separate from the easternmost parts of Asia. And as we have seen, separation by water was not in itself a contradiction of the Amerasian view, for an ancient tradition had held that Asia fanned out at its eastern edge into a galaxy of islands (see chapters 2, 4, 6, and 8). While the vast majority of sixteenth-century cartographers showed America and Asia on one and the same landmass, with America as an eastern province of Asia, many of those that showed a water separation between Asia and the newly discovered lands maintained an island-based Amerasian view that understood Asian culture to extend across water.[4]

There were good reasons for imagining that the new lands were part of Asia or connected to it by trade and cultural exchange. This would explain the biblical origins of new world peoples, as well as how the ten tribes of Israel could have crossed an Asiatic continent and arrived in the Americas (see chapter 13). An understanding of Spanish possessions in the New World overlapping with Asia would always be in the interest of the Spanish/Habsburg crown, especially after losing the Moluccas in 1527 and as they lobbied to maintain their rights in the Philippines.[5] As Ricardo Padrón has demonstrated, the cartographic rhetoric of Habsburg imperialism worked to place New Spain in closer proximity to the wealth of Asia by describing a narrow Pacific and by collapsing East and West.[6]

Though certainly bolstering Habsburg claims, Vopel was advancing a well-established view not restricted to Habsburg circles. As discussed in chapter 9, in the French ambit, the Paris Gilt or De Bure globe (c. 1528) in the Bibliothèque Nationale in Paris shows Cathay, New Spain, and Mangi (southern China) vertically on the same line of longitude, placing New Spain in central China, and Mexico to the west of all of these Chinese lands. On this globe, the port city of Zaiton, the port from which Polo returned home by sea, is on a coast facing west. The Nancy Globe (1530–40?) in the Lorraine Museum in Nancy resembles the Gilt globe in placing Mexico and New Spain directly south of Greater Asia, and all of these lands just to the west of the Sea of Cathay, which is bordered by Florida and Cuba in the east. As we have seen in chapter 9, Amerasia found one of its most iconic cartographic expressions in Oronce Finé's *Recens et integra orbis descriptio* (Paris, 1534), where in a similar depiction, Chinese toponyms interweave with Mexican ones, and Chinese rivers flow into this same body of water.

In the Venetian sphere, we have seen that Alessandro Zorzi understood the Americas as an outcropping of Southeast Asia (see chapter 6). Others like the Venetian cartographer Giacomo Gastaldi built on this idea by experimenting with depictions of New Spain and Florida as part of an Asian landmass connected to Labrador by a narrow land bridge to the north. Gastaldi shows this configuration in his *Carta marina nova tabula*, published

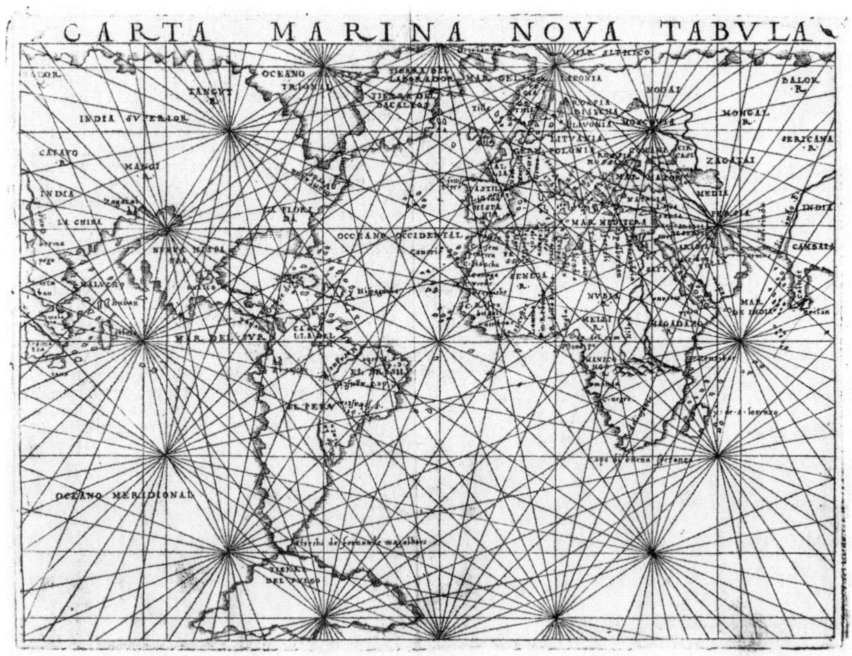

11.3 Gastaldi shows two American appendages to Asia, one in the north and one in the south. Giacomo Gastaldi, *Carta marina nova tabula*, copper engraving, 17.8 × 12.8 cm, published in Giacomo Gastaldi, *Geographia* (Venice, 1548).

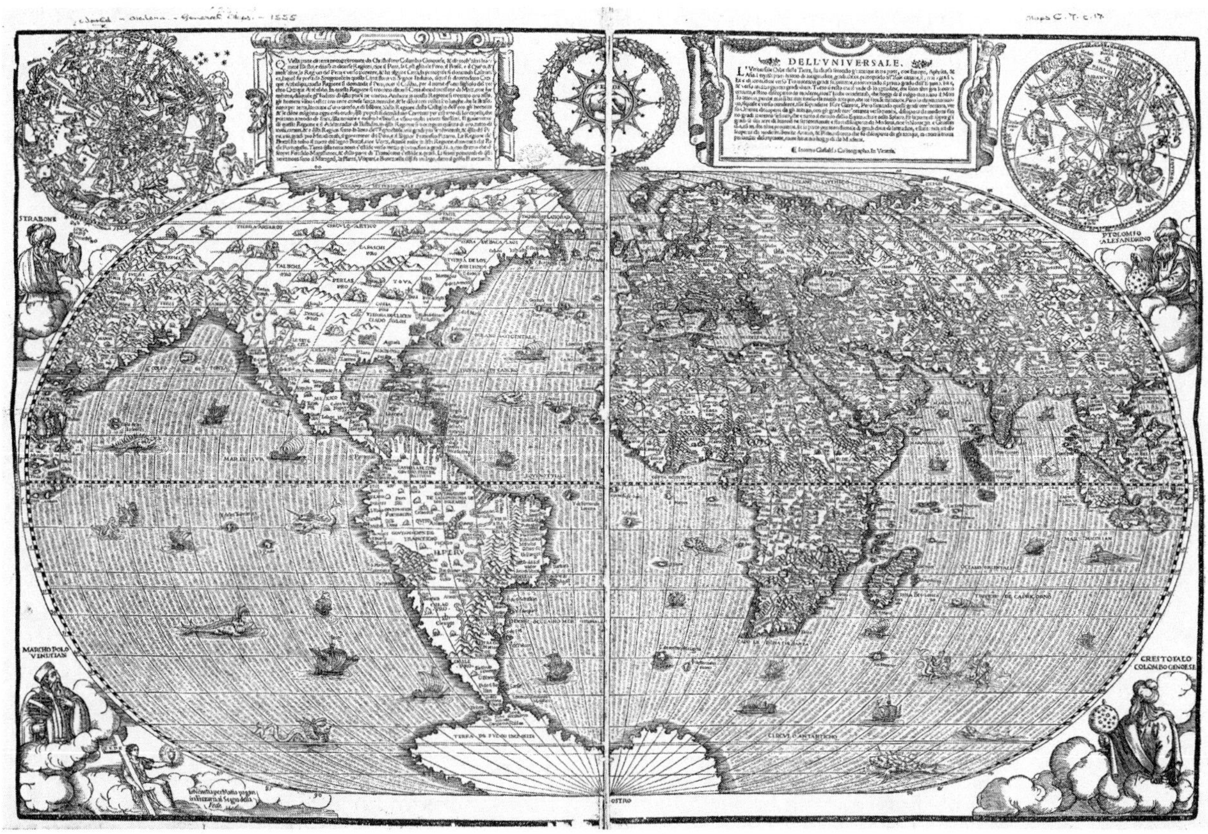

11.4 Lions and elephants populate Gastaldi's Amerasian continent. Giacomo Gastaldi, *Dell'universale,* woodcut, 77 × 51.5 cm (Venice, ca. 1550). London, British Library.

in the 1548 Venetian edition of Ptolemy—three years after Vopel's original 1545 world map—which connects South America to Asia through what is today the Malay peninsula (fig. 11.3). Gastaldi's 1550 *Dell'universale* (fig. 11.4), in which figures of Columbus and Polo are positioned in the bottom corners, underscoring their relationship to one another in the exploration of new worlds, labeled this land bridge between America and Asia Arsarot, in Hebrew Asrareth, literally "other land," the land "where never mankind dwelt" that was reached by the exiled ten tribes of Israel, according to the apocryphal book of Esdras (2 Esdras 13:40–48).[7]

Japan, Cattigara, and Mexico as Amerasian Shifters

To return to Vopel's map, let us examine the location and description of the juncture points of Japan, Cattigara, and Mexico, which knit the Amerasian view together. In their explorations of the islands across the ocean to the west of Europe and the landmasses called by them Mexico, New Spain, and La Florida, Cortés and his contemporaries believed the South Sea to be dotted with innumerable Asian islands (see chapter 8). Accordingly, the left edge of Vopel's map, where we find Java, Timor, Borneo, and the Moluccas, shows many more islands, yet this is not the only island-filled Asian sea here. There is also the Sea of Cathay to the east of Messigo and Mangi, populated by islands long since colonized by Europeans. There we find the island of Cuba, and east of there Hispaniola Zipanga, Columbus's first colony in the New World, here identified with Japan. The historian Lawrence Wroth calls Japan "the shuttlecock of cartographers," a mobile link between East and West and a key to a given cartographer's larger worldview.[8] Until the Portuguese arrival in Japan in the 1540s, the location of Japan off the coast of China was entirely derived from Polo's description of it and could only be conjectured. Waldseemüller (1507) and Martin Behaim (1492) placed Japan near the coast of Asia, the Paris Gilt Globe (1528) and the Nuremberg Globe Gores (1535) equated Japan with the "island" of Yucatán (visible on Vopel's map west of Cuba), and European maps through the second half of the sixteenth century continued to place Japan in a wide variety of locations, in positions close to Asia, midocean, or close to America.[9]

A series of prints in Theodor de Bry's *Americae*—the Flemish engraver and publisher's encyclopedic collection of translations and prints that gave many Europeans their first visual representations of North America—suggests that the nearness of Japan to the Americas persisted into the seventeenth century. In his Latin translation of José de Acosta's *Historia Natural y Moral de las Indias* (1590) in his *Americae* volume 9 (1602)—a text almost entirely focused on Mexican and Peruvian history—de Bry included a print illustrating "The Miraculous Way in which the Japanese Confess." The Jesuit missionary Acosta himself had often drawn the peoples of the Indies into comparison (see chapters 12 and 13). During his years as a missionary, Acosta had lived primarily in Peru, but also resided briefly in Mexico in 1586, where he received information about Asia from other Jesuit missionaries returning to Mexico from the Philippines. De Bry's illustration of Japanese confession comes from Acosta's book 5, chapter 25, "Of The Confession and Confessors Used by the Indians," where Acosta describes how in Peru, "they believed that all adversities and illnesses came from the sins they had committed and had recourse to sacrifices in order to atone for these." In this ritual, individuals confessed and received penance from *ichuiri*, or Peruvian sorcerers, who administered both corporal punishment and ritual baths as a part of this Indigenous Peruvian ceremony of confessing secret sins. Having described this practice, Acosta notes that "because it is to the point here, I will speak of the remarkable use of confession that the devil brought to Japan," where near Osaka, from the tip of a cliff, the Japanese lower "a sort of balance whose pans are so large that a man can sit in one of them." The man's weight tips the scales entirely to one side, and demons, called *goquis*, "call out for the man to confess and speak all his sins," the scale leveling out when the sinner's weight is lightened by his confession. Through these comparative accounts, Acosta observes that "the devil has tried to usurp divine worship for himself by turning the confession of sins that the Savior instituted to save men into a diabolical superstition intended for their greatest harm, no less among the heathens of Japan than in the province of Collao in Peru."[10]

At the end of his *Americae* volume 9, de Bry's plate 9 shows "Another Indian Sacrificial Rite" in Mexico, in which we see a sacrificial victim being flayed alive, (illustrating Acosta's book 5, chapter 21), plate 10 depicts the practice of confession in Japan, and plate 11 illustrates "Indian Dances and Festivities" in Mexico (illustrating Acosta's book 5, chapter 28) (fig. 11.5a–c).[11] Building from one passage of Acosta comparing Japan to Peru, de Bry gives visual form to the similarity, adorning his Japanese and Mexican figures with the same feathered headdresses, and places the scenes into a sequence, thus strongly encouraging the reader to associate Japan with Mexico.

To return to Vopel in 1545, by placing Japan just south and east of Terra Florida at the mouth of the Mare Cathayum, and by equating it with Hispaniola, his map continued in the tradition of the Ruysch map of 1507 (see fig. 4.12) and the Finé map of 1534 (see figs. 9.1–2). For Ruysch, Finé, and Vopel, as well as all those like Vavassore who reproduced Vopel's map, Hispaniola was at the same time Hispaniola and Cipangu, just as Mercator calls what is today Mexico both India and New Spain (see fig. 11.8). This tendency to double the names of places, letting new and old designations stand side by side, can be found in many sources. Peter Martyr d'Anghiera notes, for example, that Columbus "sent thirty men in different directions to explore the region of Cipangu [Japan], otherwise Cibao."[12] Writing to Domenico Malipiero in 1501, the Venetian ambassador to Lisbon Angelo Trevisan thought that Jamaica was Java: "Columbus arrived at an island called by its inhabitants Jamaica, but, as he says, cosmographers call it Java Major."[13] Trevisan didn't rename Java as Jamaica; as his language clearly states, Jamaica was Java, both a new and an old place, or a place that had two names. Likewise, Vopel lets Messigo stand next to Mangi even as he asserts that they are two terms for the same thing. We can often explain this as part of the practice of Christian renaming; for instance, when on his first voyage, Columbus recorded that "the big island, which these

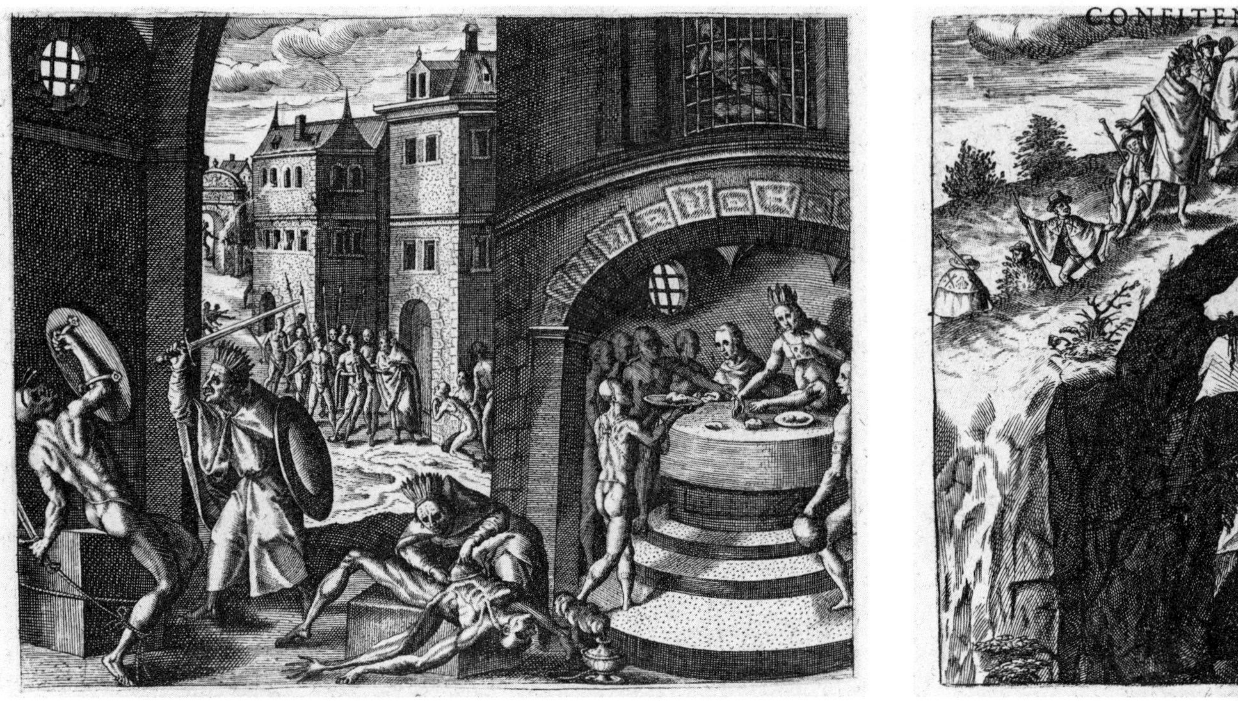

11.5a–c Reading de Bry, we travel from Mexico to Japan and back again. Theodore de Bry, *Americae*, 27 vols. (Frankfurt: Matthew Becker, 1602), copper engravings, vol. 9. (a) plate 9; (b) plate 10; (c) plate 11.

people from San Salvador . . . have named Samaeto . . . I gave the name Isabela."[14] Yet many instances suggest a facility for double-seeing, allowing a place and a people to be seen in more than one way, or in two ways at the same time, a facility not so different from the "medieval pattern of 'double-think,' or, better, 'multi-think'" observed by the art historian Richard Krautheimer in the European tendency to see churches as both local foundations and Holy Land prototypes.[15] As with a Rubin vase, where we flip between face and vase, early modern Europeans saw both Japan and Hispaniola, allowing them to shift back and forth while holding the same book or map in their hands.

Cattigara, the most southeasterly port as understood by western geographers since antiquity, was a received name for a Southeast Asian emporium that represented a limit point of Asia. The Egyptian geographer Ptolemy (c. 100–c. 170 CE) gave the precise location of this port considerable attention in his *Geographia*, placing it on the coast of the Magnus Sinus, or what is today the Gulf of Thailand, on the Golden Chersonese or the Malay Peninsula. For Ptolemy, Cattigara was part of Sinae,

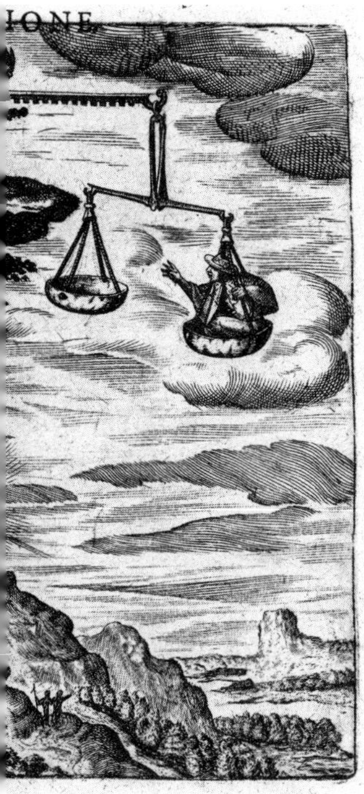

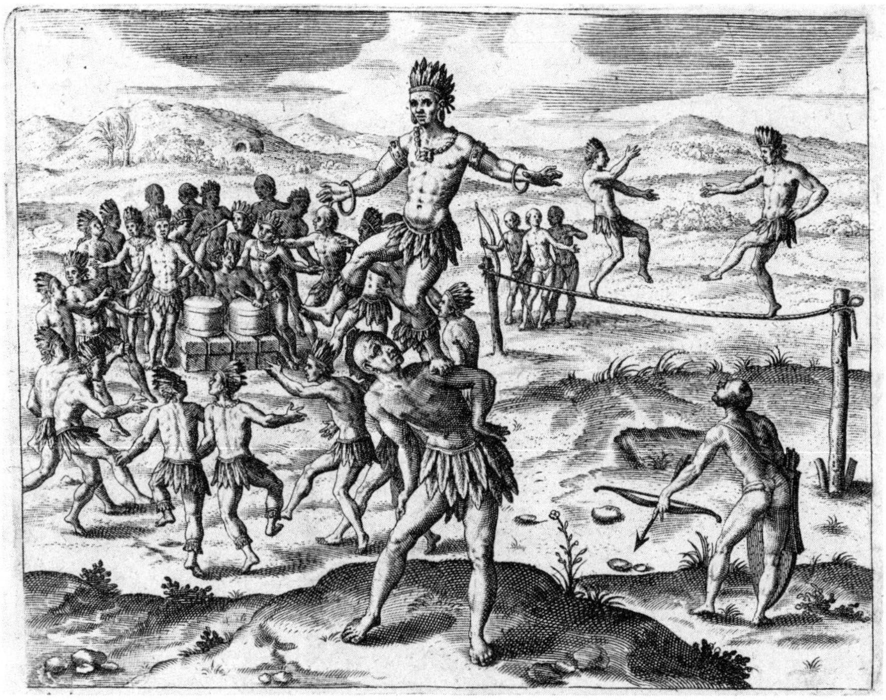

or southern China (see fig. 1.5).[16] For all of these ancient geographers, Cattigara was of indeterminate location, and so was manipulated and moved into a great variety of locations by early modern mapmakers. A variety of sixteenth-century Europeans, including Magellan, sought out the mythical entrepôt of Cattigara, tending to move it eastward, effectively extending Asia in that direction.[17] Several European cosmographers moved it to South America on the coast of Peru, as did Vopel and his followers.[18] In 1588, the Venetian cosmographer and mapmaker Livio Sanuto continued to locate Cattigara in Peru.[19]

Amerasia comes into focus perhaps most clearly on the Vopel map in and around the toponym of Asia Magna, which encompasses both Mexico and China, not in itself a novel idea. Finé's map, for instance, shows Messigo and Temistitia as regional names in the province of Mangi or Southern China. The Vopel map is innovative above all in the number of toponyms it shows and the extent to which it explains and justifies the meaning and placement of them. Legends and cartouches assert in no uncertain terms that Mexico and China are one and the same place, as on the large cartouche on the far-right edge of the map, where Vopel notes how he scrupulously sought to understand the relationship between Asia and the newly discovered lands to the west by refusing to go to press with his map until he could quell the rumors about whether or not a strait separated the continents of America and Asia. To this end, knowing that Charles V received up-to-date reports on these lands, Vopel managed to arrange a meeting with the emperor while he was visiting Cologne. According to Vopel, the emperor confirmed that Mexico and China were one, and that,

> those aforementioned countries were in no way separated by the interval of a sea, but rather connected to the eastern lands. He continued, saying that earlier the Spaniards had again and again gone west exploring from Tenochtitlan, the famous city of the Great Khan, also called Montezuma, and had not been able to find for him an end to the huge land. This would be sufficient proof that the western country reaches to the Chinese region and to the people of China, and make it certain that they belong in the sphere of the Castilians. This information he had received from Indians who had fought in wars with the unconquerable Ferdinand Cortés in New Spain.

Along similar lines, the large legend to the west of what is today Central America, just below the equator, explains that Tenochtitlan is Polo's Quinsai (the Chinese Hangzhou):

> For modern writers, Themixitan [i.e., Tenochtitlan] or Thenostica[n], is what Marco Polo the Venetian previously called Quinsai, insofar as it means "city of heaven," whereas Oderico [of Pordenone] called it Themistan. And this is nearer the truth, in concordance and agreement with the tradition of authorities, both in terms of the wealth of the same region and in terms of its power, for indeed earlier accounts revealed that the town of Themixitian is situated on a salt lake and that it far surpasses the city of Venice in splendor and size: here are the palace of the eastern emperor sometimes called the Great Khan (referred to by Hernán Cortés conversely as Monti Zuma), very magnificent houses, [and] sovereignty over all the neighboring peoples and regions. What writers report of the greatness and wealth and dominion of this [region] and the emperor and the city is marvelous and almost beyond belief. Some of the inhabitants are idolaters and others Christian, for Christ's Gospel is always planted by the hands of the brothers of the Order of Saint Francis not only in Themixtitan but also throughout Greater Asia. More [on these matters is to be found] in the writings of Hernán Cortés.

In fact, Cortés had never declared he was in China or that Moctezuma was the Great Khan. Asian ambitions were at the heart of Cortés's enterprise, which was to open a portal to the great riches of Asia, the pursuit of which in further travels westward and northward occupied him and his followers in the 1520s and 1530s (see chapter 8). Reporting to the Venetian senate on Cortés's conquest, Gasparo Contarini in 1522 did not outright identify Tenochtitlan with any Asian capital, though he made a point of describing the advanced nature of the civilization encountered by the Spanish, their splendid buildings and their writings, which resembled, he wrote, the hieroglyphs of the Egyptians (see chapter 9). The Venetian Bordone's well-known *Libro di Benedetto Bordone* (1524)—an *isolario* that translated parts of Cortés's Second Letter (originally written to Charles V on October 30, 1520)—described Mexico in similar tones. Although he made no claim that these were eastern lands, Bordone delighted Italian readers with his lavish description of the glittering cities of Mexico, where like Polo, Cortés encountered cities of more than five thousand houses with public baths and markets, where more than thirty thousand people gathered to "sell gold, silver, and precious stones."[20] With such descriptions, Bordone provided the raw materials for future convergences of Mexico and Cathay. In the decades after Cortés, Mexico came closer to Asia.

A clearer association of Mexico with China began to crystallize toward the middle of the 1520s. As we saw at the very beginning of this book, a manuscript note from the 1520s on an early edition of Amerigo Vespucci's *Mundus novus* letter offered a new world update, reporting that Cortés had laid siege to Quinsai, "also known as Temixtitam or the City of Heaven, most famous trading capital of eastern Asia" (see fig. I.1). Another early move toward the "sinification" of Mexico came from the Flemish cartographer and globe-maker Franciscus Monachus, whose *Position and Description of the World* (*De orbis situ ac descriptione*), probably of 1529, identified Mexico as among the East Asian territories visited by Odoric of Pordenone, Polo, and Mandeville, and identified Cipangu (Japan) with Hispaniola, Mansus or Mangi with Mexico, Cathay with Culiacán, Quinsay with Themistetan (Tenochtitlan), Tangut with Tamago, and Bergia with Polo's Bargu, a Tartar region in the northeastern extremes of Cathay. The frontispiece of Monachus's pamphlet included a woodcut world map in two hemispheres, a summary flattening of the globe described in the treatise (see fig. 7.5).[21] There he depicts a continuous landmass connecting China and Mexico, a geographical formation that became standard in maps of the middle sixteenth century. The Vopel map of 1545, with its hundreds of toponyms, detailed notation, and dense geographic description, fleshed out Monachus's sketch of global geography from the later 1520s, and, in fact, imported extended passages from the text of Monachus's pamphlet.[22] He took over several of Monachus's toponyms, such as Tamago, which Monachus tells us is the modern word for Tangut; Vopel places the toponym Tamacho just to the right of Cathay on his map, explaining that "Tamacho was once called Tangut." Similarly, the Monachus map contains the toponym Coluacana, indicating the province of Colhuacan in Mexico; the Vopel map labels Mexico with the regional name, Hispania,

Nova Culuacana, which, following Monachus's text, indicates an overlap between Cathay and the Nahuatl-speaking city state in the Valley of Mexico, founded by the Toltecs. Bergia on the Monachus map represents Polo's Bargu in the northeastern extremes of Cathay; the Vopel map identifies Bargu, noting that "they are subject to the Great Khan, whom Don Ferdinand Cortes calls Montezuma."[23]

Vopel's conflations of the Mexica emperor with the Great Khan and Tenochtitlan with Quinsai reveal the active role Marco Polo's account continued to play in the sixteenth-century imagination. The idea that Marco Polo had discovered America in his farthest Asian travels persisted in accounts of the new world through the seventeenth century.[24] Even as Europeans began to question this idea, skeptical voices could not undo a well-established tradition. In the eighteenth century, the second edition (1729) of the Dominican missionary and chronicler Fra Gregorio García's *Origin of the Indians of the New World and the West Indies* (*Origen de los indios del Nuevo Mundo e Indias Occidentales*) actually adds the assertion that Polo and other medieval travelers in China had traveled overland as far as Mexico before Cortés, a claim that García did not make in the 1607 original edition.[25] As the literary scholar Michael Householder has noted, accounts of medieval journeys to the east remained authoritative sources of geographical information well into the sixteenth century, "even after the publication of eyewitness accounts of the extraordinary but real kingdoms of Mexico and Peru."[26]

Besides relying on Monachus, Vopel also benefited from the widely seen printed globes and publications of the German cosmographer and cartographer Johannes Schöner, who revised his earlier view into a newly assertive Amerasian vision in his *Opusculum geographicum* of 1533. In his section "On the general divisions of the earth," Schöner connects Vespucci's discoveries to Polo's:

> Sailing along the coasts of Upper India from Spain to the west, Amerigo Vespucci believed that this part, which is connected to Upper India, was an island, which he decided would be called by his own name. However, more recent hydrographers discovered that this land and others beyond it make up the continent of Asia, for they even arrived thus at the Molucca Islands of Upper India. We gather that this continent of Upper Asia is a part beyond [the knowledge of] Ptolemy, explored before our time by Marco Polo the Venetian and many others.[27]

According to Schöner in 1533, Vespucci had not discovered an island, as Schöner himself had earlier believed, but a remote extension of Asian territory. Schöner notes that "there is a land which is called Mexico and Temistitan, in upper India, which previous people called Quinsay, which is the city of heaven in their own tongue."[28] Later, in his section "On the Regions Beyond the Description of Ptolemy," he confirms that "after [what was known by] Ptolemy, however, beyond 180 degrees toward the east, many regions were discovered by the man Marco Polo the Venetian and others, but now they have been discovered by Columbus the Genoan, and Amerigo Vespucci, landing only there on the coastal regions from Spanish [territories] through the Western Ocean."[29] For Schöner, the "many regions" of this part of the world, including "Bachalaos . . . the great kingdom of Bergi, the land Florida, the desert Lop . . . the province Thamacho, Sucur, Sampa (or Zampa), Cauul, Tangut, Cuschin, Cathay (which is also Chulmana), the province of Saint Michael, Messigo (which is also the region Mexico, in which the great city Temistita[n] is situated in a great lake, but among older generations was called Quinsay)." All of these, writes Schöner, were a part of "the continent of Upper India, which is part of Asia."[30] Like Finé (see chapter 9), Vopel was deeply influenced by Schöner's developing understanding of the globe, newly revised to project an Amerasian landmass.

Amerasia by Sea or by Land

Our review of the Vopel map and its sources illustrates the notably non-progressive development and spread of European understandings of the world during the early modern period, similar to what we find in Qing China, as Timothy Brook shows in the Afterword to this volume. Far from being steadily dismantled as knowledge of the new world increased, the idea of Amerasia actually grew over time as it assimilated new geographical knowledge; as Ricardo Padrón puts it, the Amerasian visions of Europeans are marked by "discursive exchange rather than progress."[31]

Far from an isolated case, Vopel's map offered a detailed picture of an emergent Amerasian vision, and then continued to speak to audiences long after it was first printed. Besides Vavassore's 1558 reprinting in Venice, a frescoed version (c. 1550) adorns the Palazzo Besta in Teglio, Valtellina.[32] It was also reproduced in Amsterdam by the mapmaker Jerónimo Girava in 1556 in a one-sheet reduction of Vopel's original, of which no copy survives, and by Bernard van den Putte, who recut Vopel's map in Antwerp in 1570.[33] The Dutch merchant Jan Huygen van Linschoten, who lived in Goa for over five years, offered a careful description of the Manila galleon trade, including in his *Itinerario* (1596) detailed maps of Asia by none other than Petrus Plancius—one of the founders of the Dutch East India Company, for which he drew over 100 maps. Yet even the Asianist Linschoten continued to call the body of water between the lands of Florida and the Yucatán the Mare Catayum.[34]

Vopel's Amerasian vision, expressing a Spanish imperial view, was also adapted into the terms of Portuguese conquest. In his *Tratado dos diversos e desvairados caminhos* (Lisbon, 1563, with an English translation by Hakluyt in 1601), António Galvão, a Portuguese administrator and chronicler in the Moluccas, argued that America was an ancient Chinese colony. At the outset of his treatise, he proposes that the Chinese, rather than the Greeks, Egyptians, or Phoenicians, were the first sailors. They came to inhabit India (and here he means India in the large sense; see chapters 1 and 12), all the islands of the Pacific, "and besides this, New Spain, Peru, Brasil, [and] the Antilles, with all the rest joined to them, as we can see by the fashions and manners of the men and women and by their proportions, having small eyes, flat noses, and other similar proportions."[35] While the Spanish view of the Amerasian continent in Vopel's map is land-based, Galvão offers a Portuguese counterpart to Vopel's ideas, a maritime vision that stages the Chinese as the first major explorers who traveled far and wide and in this sense the great precursors to the Portuguese of the present day.

Amerasia was built not only on the idea of continuous landmasses of the sort shown by Monachus, Schöner, Finé, and Vopel and their many followers. Even after cartographers in the later sixteenth century more regularly introduced a water separation between the Eurasian landmass and the territories to the west being colonized by the Spanish, French, and English, the Amerasian view persisted, thriving on water as much as on land. The Verrazano globe in the Morgan Library (1530) as well as Münster's *Novae insulae* (1540) (see fig. 8.3) place the Asian emporium of Cattigara in Peru, even as a body of water separates a North American continent from the lands of Cathay, in effect declaring that the Asia of Ptolemy extended to the New World.

The Venetian cartographer Gastaldi, emending the continuous landmass depictions we have been considering, inserted a narrow body of water, which he called the Strait of Anian (first noted in the Ramusio edition of Polo's *Travels*) in the middle of Asian lands in the east in his world map *Cosmographia universalis* of about 1561 (fig. 11.6). Here, we are tempted to say that the strait exists "between America and Asia," yet this would not quite describe it, since Gastaldi shows the Asian toponyms of Tolman, Agama, and Pagul on the "American" side of the strait. When he had been sent to travel west by the Great Khan, Polo visited Tolman on his return voyage after passing through Tibet, reporting that it was near India and rich in gold.[36] Polo scholar Paul Pelliot associated Agama with "Andaman" or the Malay name of the Andaman Islands, and placed Toloman in the northeast part of Yunnan.[37] Pegu (Pagul), finally, was the capital of Burma.

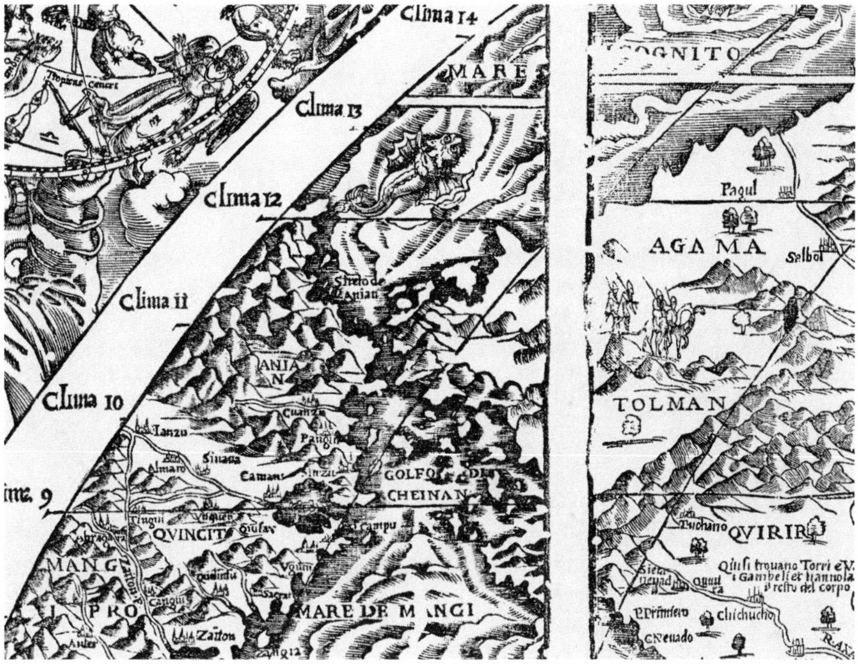

11.6 Mongols on camels making their way towards the lands of Mexico. Giacomo Gastaldi, *Cosmographia universalis*, 10 sheets, woodcut, 182 × 90 cm, detail (Venice, ca. 1561). London, British Library, BL Maps C.18.N.1.

In sum, Gastaldi's Strait of Anian does not define continents; it only introduces some water between landmasses. The divide cannot contain Asia, which carries across it without difficulty, populating the land that continues into Mexico with Asian peoples, fauna, and locales.

Mercator's 1569 world map *New and More Complete Representation of the Terrestrial Globe Properly Adapted for Use in Navigation* (Nova et Aucta Orbis Terrae Descriptio ad Usum Navigantium Emendate Accommodata) ushered in a new and more navigationally reliable technique for translating a spherical reality onto a flat plane, the so-called Mercator projection (fig. 11.7).[38] This map shows at the two edges of the map a narrow water separation between the Asian landmasses and the newly discovered lands to the west of Europe, yet here, too, India bridges the separation by water. In a large cartouche at the bottom, Mercator explains that in showing the Ganges River flowing into the Bay of Bengal, traditional mapmakers have mistakenly placed it far too far to the west, arguing that the Ganges is to be identified with the Cantan River at the extreme east of Asia. That means that locations far to the east of Bengal, such as Pegu, Çampa, Sian, and Malacca, are now part of *India intra Gangem*, India before the Ganges.

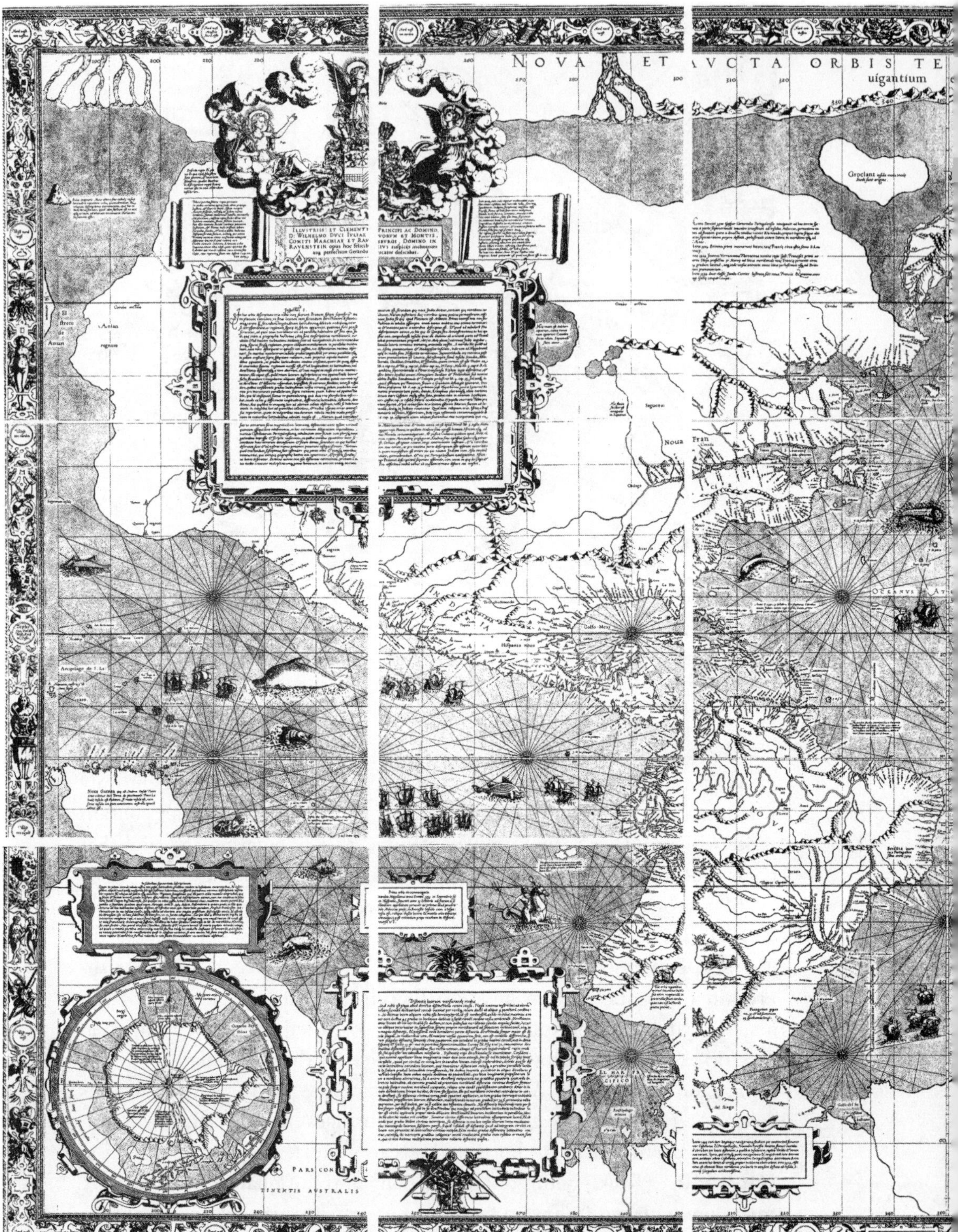

11.7 Mercator's highly influential 1569 world map. Gerardus Mercator, *Nova et Aucta Orbis Terrae Descriptio ad Usum Navigantium Emendate Accommodata*, 18 sheets, copper engraving, 202 × 124 cm (Duisberg, 1569).

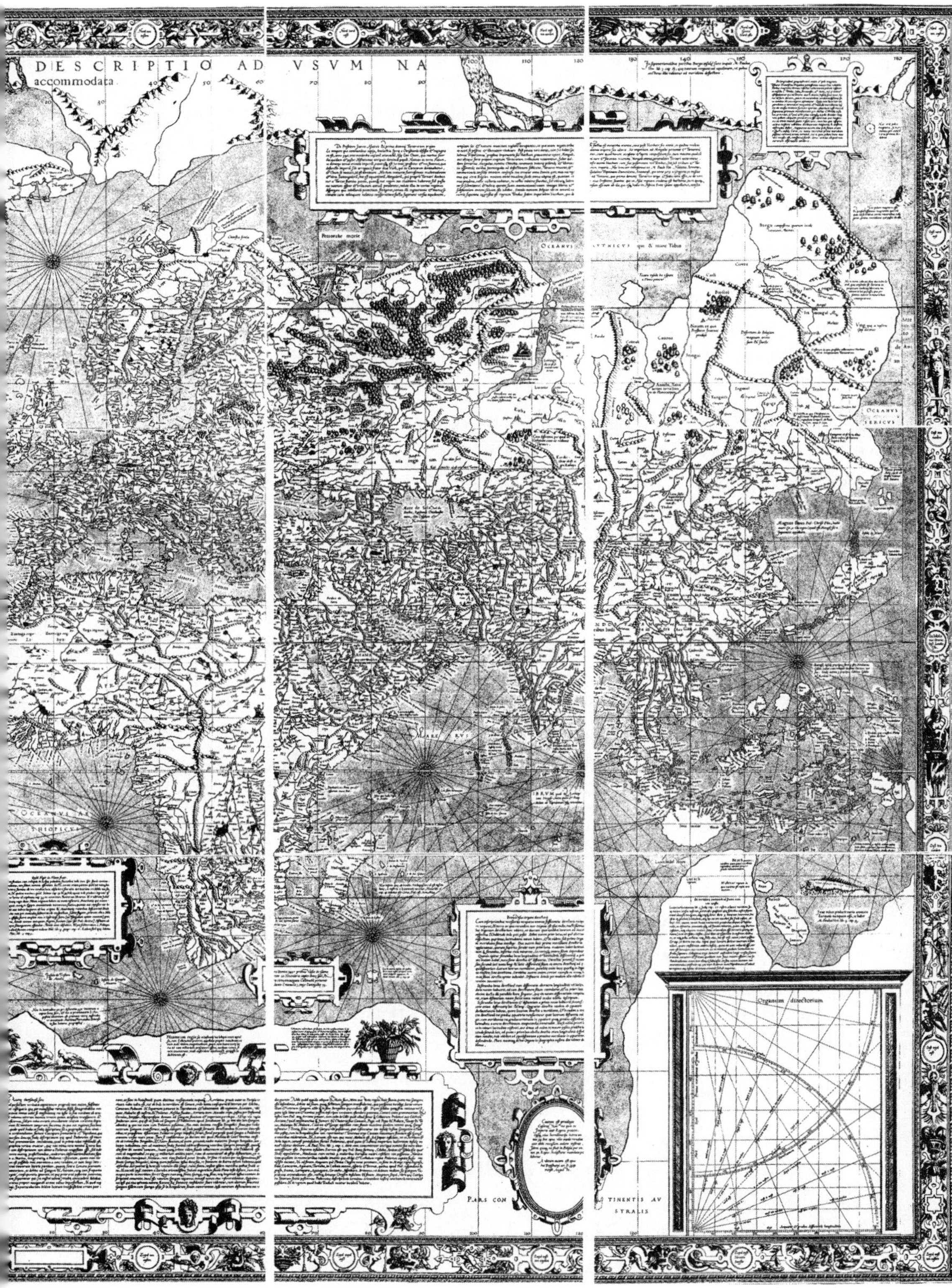
DESCRIPTIO AD VSVM NA
accommodata
Organum directorium
PARS CON TINENTIS AV STRALIS

As for *India extra Gangem*, Mercator suppresses it—or, rather, he transforms it and renames it. Across the water, on the other side of the map, we find the new territories discovered by the Spanish described as India Nova, with the word India hovering in the region between California and Golfo Mexicano and Nova extending below the equator toward Bresilia (fig. 11.8).

On the one hand, he explicitly asserts, in the large cartouche top left, that India Nova does not form a continuous landmass with Asia, rejecting the view embodied in the Vopel map and other maps, yet on the other hand he does not label it *Mundus Novus* or America but rather India Nova. His point in the cartouche is that this was completely unknown to Ptolemy; hence his suppression of *India extra Gangem* and adoption of the new term (for more on the extensions of India, see chapter 12). Yet the logic of India Nova is not in fact that different from the logic of India extra Gangem. The western side of the map is in fact not without its far eastern elements, as it shows the Archipelago de S. Lazaro (the Philippines) as well as the island of Nova Guinea, both not far off the coast of India Nova. Toward the north, Mercator makes a point of showing just how close India Nova comes to Asia, by repeating an Asian promontory found at the extreme right of the map (here labeled the extremity of Asia, Asie extremum), showing that the two are separated by only a few degrees of longitude and making it clear that the island of Japan on the other side of the map is only about twenty degrees away from Quivira, about which tantalizing reports were coming back from Spanish expeditions north of Mexico (see chapter 8). India Nova may be strictly speaking a separate landmass, but it was still understood in Indian terms, and its realities were not far from Asian realities.

In another Amerasian convergence, the Venetian cartographer Giovanni Francesco Camocio's wall map of the Americas of about 1570 displays Tuchiano, one of the American pueblos visited by Francisco Vásquez de Coronado during his journey into New Mexico between 1540 and 1542, on both the Asian and American sides of the divide.

Variations on this pattern, where water separation does not conclusively separate Asia and America, can be found in other prominent maps of the period. In his 1570 *Typus orbis terrarum*, the Netherlandish cartographer Abraham Ortelius separates the landmasses by representing a wide Pacific even as he continues to populate the American side of the divide with Asian toponyms such as Anian and Tolm, places known from Polo's *Travels*. For Gastaldi, Mercator, Camocio, Ortelius, and many others, Amerasian continuities were not dependent on a continuous Amerasian landmass.[39]

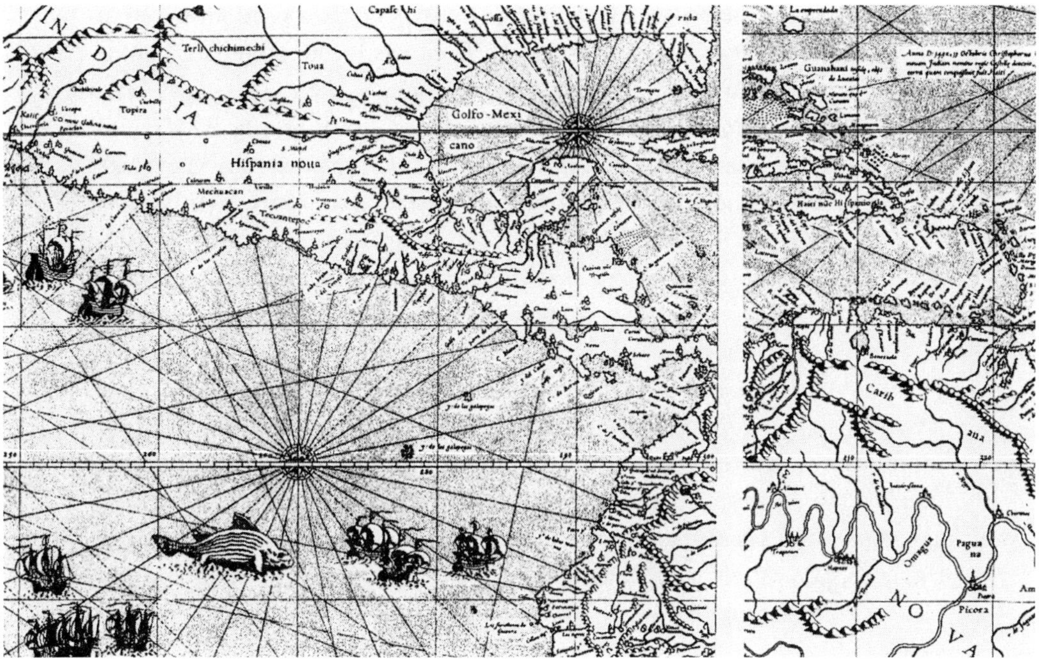

11.8 Mercator's India Nova, his substitute for India Extra Gangem. Gerardus Mercator, *Nova et Aucta Orbis Terrae Descriptio ad Usum Navigantium Emendate Accommodata*, detail of figure 11.7.

A review of European world maps of the sixteenth century reveals that Magellan's circumnavigation of the globe in 1519–22, with the long crossing of the Pacific chronicled in Antonio Pigafetta's account, did not confirm the separation of America and Asia once and for all. Instead, for many Europeans Magellan's voyage demonstrated the world's connectedness, proving that one could in fact get to Asia by sailing westward. According to a logic of elliptical continuity (see chapter 6), long ocean crossings were routinely abbreviated in textual accounts focused on the succession of ports and landfalls. Magellan's achievement in fact informed and enriched Amerasian world visions such as Vopel's, and indeed Vopel portrays the circumnavigating Magellan, labeled a "second Neptune," triumphantly taking off from this Amerasian coast, with a mingled China and Mexico at his back. For one of Vopel's sources, Schöner's *Opusculum geographicum*, Magellan's circumnavigation came as confirmation that America and Asia were in fact the same place.[40] Most scholars agree that old ideas were slow to die in the face of discoveries like Magellan's; occasionally, as in this case, new information actually gave new life and new shape to the Amerasian picture.

Even Ortelius and Mercator did not simply establish a new consensus followed by all reasonable people after them. Most historians concur that the view of the world elaborately drawn by Vopel in fact predominated in the minds of most sixteenth-century Europeans.[41] The connected landmass of Amerasia continued to appear in later maps, such as Joannes Myritius's *Universalis Orbis Descriptio*, published in Ingolstadt in 1590. This could be seen as a regression, but in fact, in a further nonlinear twist, Myritius's map separates American toponyms from Asian ones more firmly than the water-divided worldscapes of Gastaldi, Mercator, and Camocio had, where an active interchange of American and Asian peoples, animals, and locales is shown crossing the divide. Vopel's map and the entire sequence of maps of the later sixteenth century studied here do not fall into a progressive history that leads from Amerasian confusion to geographical clarity along modern lines. Instead, they present us with the persistent and fertile interpenetration of the ideas of China, India, Mexico, and America in developing European visions of the world.[42] The sinification of Mexico and the North American continent was a late development; it started in the 1520s, and as news about new worlds became assimilated, Amerasian visions were dramatically enhanced, resulting in spectacular Amerasian exhibits like the Vopel map. For European audiences, America and Asia were more separated in the early sixteenth century than they were in the middle of the century.

TWELVE

India as a Semantic Field

In Jost Amman's 1577 etching of the costumes of the people of the world, Europa is central and dominant, presented in an oval above the other peoples and populated by exhibits of its diverse regional dress: Spaniards, Venetian, French, Poles, Hungarians, Greeks, and various German regions (fig. 12.1). Below Europe on the left is Africa with its Moors (*Moren*), Arabs, Ethiopians, Berbers, and Gypsies (*Zigeuner*), all presided over by Prester John. At the lower right is Asia with its Muscovites, Tatars, Persians, and above all Turks. There, in the center, directly below Europe, adjoining it as its southern antipode, is *India oder America*—not India and America, not East Indies and West Indies, but rather Indians *as* Americans. The *Indianer* are presented next to the *Presilianer*, the cannibal Brazilians described by the navigator Amerigo Vespucci, whose name gave this land its additional title, America (fig. 12.2).

The India Continuum

The *Indianer* are as a whole marked by American signifiers—featherwork, bows and arrows, cannibalism—or at least signifiers that a modern scholar can confidently identify as American. The iconography of feather ornaments seen here in elaborated form originated in the Brazilian encounters of Cabral and Vespucci and others at the beginning of the sixteenth century. Yet, European artists almost immediately applied them to people of eastern Asia from India to Java, irreversibly entangling American and Asian and sometimes African imagery for two centuries to follow (see chapter 2 and 5). Cannibalism had been attributed to the inhabitants of East Asian islands in the widely read late medieval text of *The Travels of John Mandeville* and so was expected and found in the new Indies, as discussed in chapter 1, and then its American incarnation was reexported back to Asia over the next decades, becoming another crisscrossing Amerasian feature.

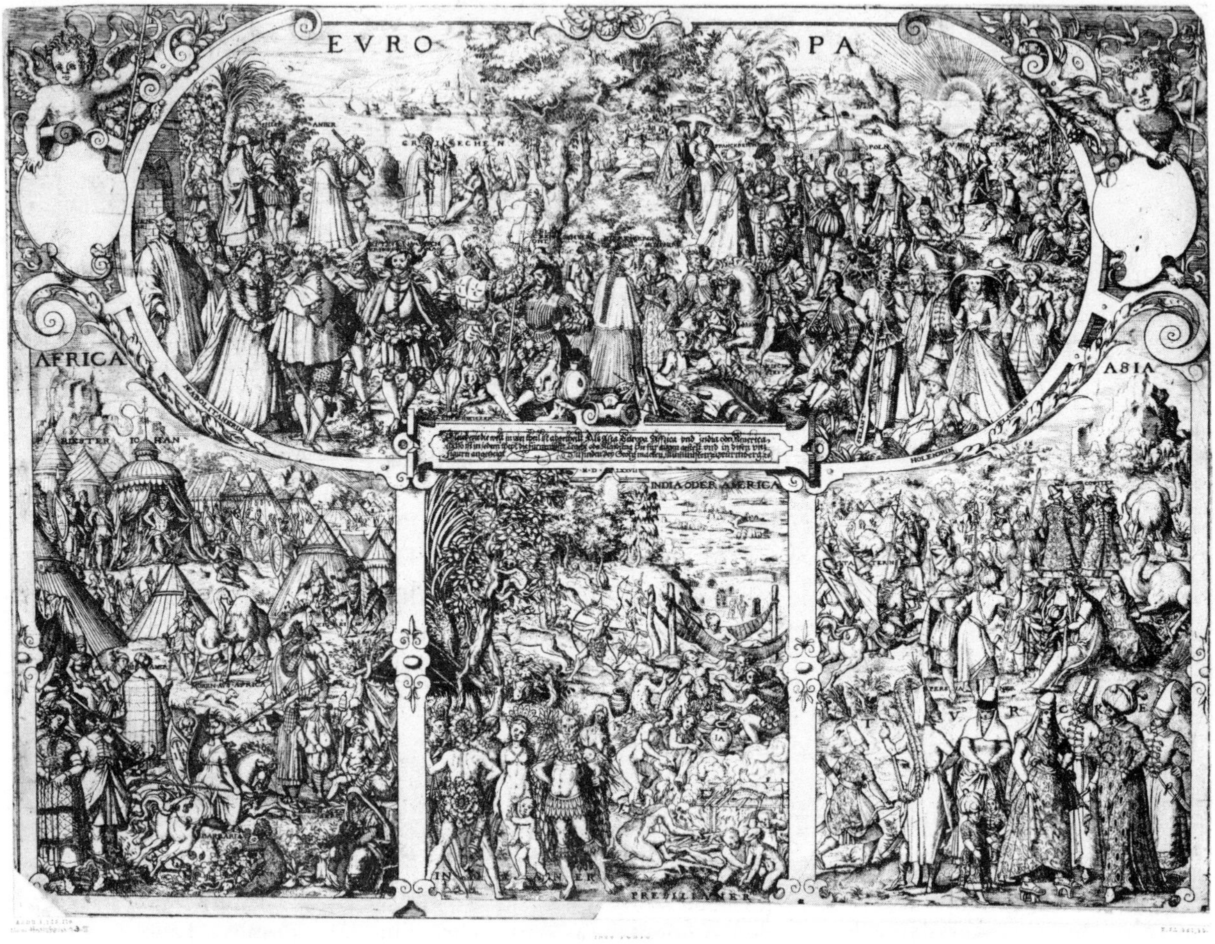

12.1 The world in costume. Jost Amman, *Costumes of the Nations of the World*, etching on paper, 34.5 × 45 cm (1577).

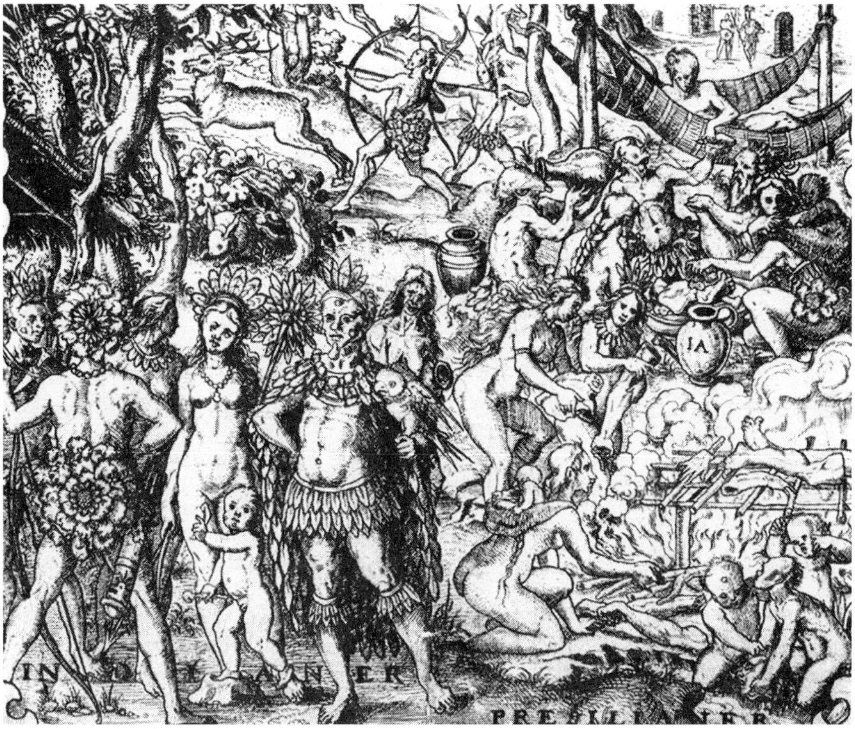

12.2 "India or America." Jost Amman, *Costumes of the Nations of the World,* detail of figure 12.1.

Near-nakedness as such is not exclusive to India here, since a few individual figures in the adjoining Africa panel go with little clothing, but Amman's "Indians-or-Americans" are defined across the board as lightly clad: fantastic headdresses, skirts, and leg ornaments woven of feathers. One Indian archer seen from behind wears a bonnet and skirt made of feathers that take the form of large flowers, an image borrowed from illustrations in André Thevet's 1575 *Cosmographie universelle*, discussed in chapter 9. In a nod to hierarchical order, the central figure who holds a parrot on his arm adopts a kingly pose, with a feather diadem and cape, confidently striding forward as he gazes directly at the viewer.[1] Whereas Thevet's 1575 *Cosmographie* depicted these feather ornaments in a section specific to South America, Amman's print once again universalizes feather ornamentation as the primary signifier of India in general, while presenting the cannibalistic *Presilianer* next to them as their less civilized cousins, bearing a diminished form of the more splendid feather gear of the *Indianer. India oder America* is an epitome of an extensible Indian cultural expanse that reaches a near degree-zero of civilization at its extreme eastern limit in Brazil.

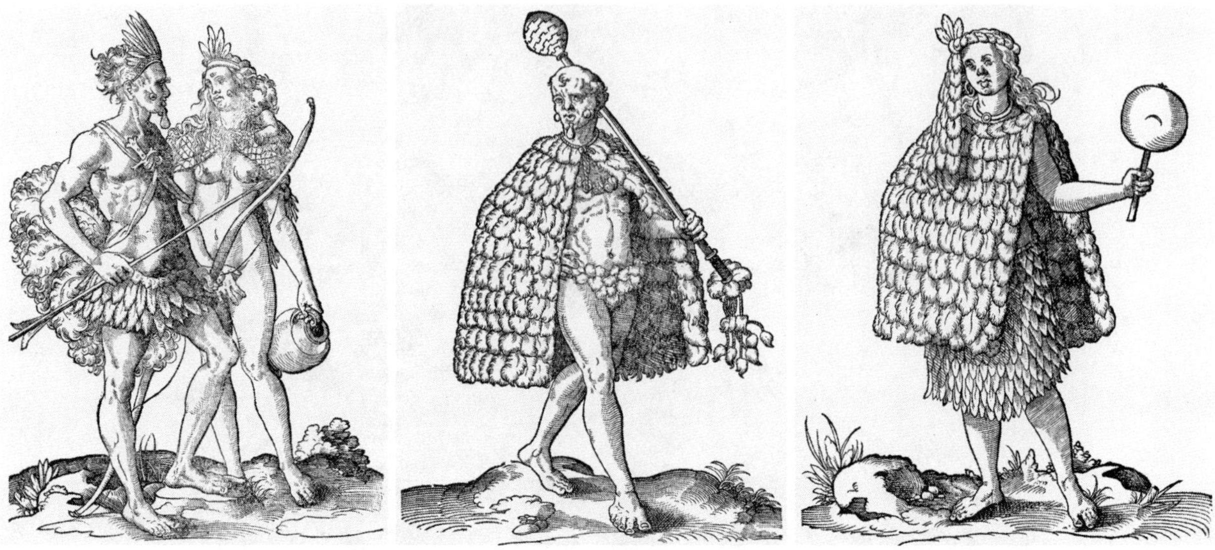

12.3 Indian and Brazilian cousins. Jost Amman, *Brazilians Who Live in Peru, Brazilians from America, and the Apparel of Women in India*, woodcut on paper, 30.1 × 20.1 cm. From *Habitus praecipuorum populorum, tam uirorum quam foeminarum* (Nuremberg, 1577), plates 181, 182, and 183.

The joining of India and America is neither a fluke nor a conflation resulting from having to compress all the peoples of the world onto one sheet. In the more than two hundred illustrations Amman produced for Hans Weigel's 1577 book on the clothing of the peoples of the world, well over a hundred detail the costumes of the various European localities before the book turns to other regions. The 180th plate shows an Ethiopian wife, which is followed by three related exhibits of Brazil and India: an image of two Brazilians "from the new Islands" with their feather gear and bows and arrows, a "Brazilian from America," dressed for battle with a feather cape and a club in hand, and finally a plate labeled *Ornatus foeminae in India*, or apparel of a woman in India, which shows an *Indianische Fraw* with a feather cape holding what the text identifies as a *Tammaraca* or tamaraca (fig. 12.3). Modern scholarship understands this as a term for a Tupi rattle of divination, making it easy to say with confidence that this woman is a Brazilian being called an Indian. But the matter was not so decided for a sixteenth-century reader, for these Tupi words were part of the soundscape of an expanded understanding of India and Indian as such. The *Indianische Fraw* is the only figure in the entire book who is labeled as Indian, which is to say that her feather-adorned figure represents the geographical and cultural category of India altogether. After this sequence the book continues with an image of a male Ethiopian "from Barbaria" and then concludes with a long series of images mostly of Turkish dress. Again, India/Brazil/America is understood as a continuum on the far side of the world, their inhabitants feather-wearing cultural cousins.

The India continuum is in stark contrast to the split usage of the word Indian in modern language. "Taíno Indians" and "Indians of Gujarat": the words are spelled the same, but in present-day usage they are two different words, confused by no one; they are no more than homonyms. By contrast, during the two centuries after Christopher Columbus, India was one word. The historical examples and episodes brought together in this book show that the lexical divorcing—one spelling "Indian" for two descriptors that point to realities universally recognized to be distinct—was a surprisingly recent development. One can hear the word coming apart during the eighteenth century, yet this was no sudden splitting. In the 1768 entry on *Indes* in the French *Encyclopédie*, the scholar Louis de Jaucourt railed against the confusion the term had engendered. He dates the American extension of the term to the Portuguese discovery of Brazil around 1500, "and since they did not clearly know at that time the relation between it [Brazil] and the Indies, they baptized it with the same name," a nominal conflation with fateful consequences: "Then they improperly extended the name to all of America; and by a new abuse, which it is no longer possible to correct, in published accounts the term Indians is used to mean Americans."[2]

Clearing away the ignorant confusion that has reigned for centuries and calling for a newly clarified, enlightened understanding of the world, the entry on *Indes* could stand as an epitome of the entire project of the *Encyclopédie*. As an historian and realist, Jaucourt understood that lexical confusion does embed itself in lived experience through usage, making it nearly impossible to root out. Try as he might to clarify the historical error, he knew the term *Indian* would continue to name Indigenous Americans for a long time to come. Yet even he could not have predicted that over two hundred years later, at the beginning of the next millennium, an American nation founded on Enlightenment ideals would enshrine the usage in a National Museum of the American Indian.

As Ricardo Padrón has observed, Spanish sources of the early modern period rarely use the term *América*, preferring to describe the landmasses as a *nuevo mundo* or, more commonly, *Tierra firme*. In the vast majority of texts relating to the Spanish empire, the lands we call America were designated by the more encompassing term *las Indias*, "which referred to something broader, in some ways more ambiguous, but always more inclusive than what others called America."[3] During the sixteenth and seventeenth centuries, the terms *India/Indian* was not yet split; a family of related terms such as *India*, *indiano*, *dell'india*, or *all'indiana* (or in German *Kalikut* and *kalikutisch*) occupied a common semantic field that indicated an imagined extension—geographic, climatic, or cultural, or all three—connecting Asia and the lands to the west of the Atlantic, and sometimes also Africa. Drawing together some of the materials already discussed as well as some further evidence, this chapter lays out a number of different forms of imagining the Indian expanse, from projections of common Amerasian landmass, as in the Vopel map (see chapter 11), to an imagined transpacific Indian range marked by climatic similarity or cultural affinity, and eventually to a number of cultural and genetic mixings produced by trade and migration activity, as will be explored in the remaining chapters.

The idea of an extensive India is a difficult idea to hold in mind, especially in the face of the more familiar view, widely accepted in the scholarly literature, that the term *Indian* was used by Europeans rather arbitrarily to refer to anything foreign or exotic, as well as the view that it was often used in error, out of geographical confusion or ignorance. We may address the question of error first by turning to Pierre Schneider's thorough study of the persistent "confusion" of Ethiopia and India in ancient Greek and Roman sources, where he found that error was less often a factor than it might appear at first glance. If an ancient authority refers to an Indian giraffe, it looks like there must be an error either in his understanding of the habitat of giraffes or in his understanding of the geography of India; however, if the writer understands eastern Africa to be a part of an extended India (*India occidentalis*), Schneider points out, then "Indian giraffe" is not a mistaken designation.[4] Likewise, if Mexico is understood as part of China in greater Asia, as we saw in chapter 11, then there is a logic to calling a Mixtec manuscript Chinese (see chapter 14). There are also, certainly, cases of downright error, as when Cesare Cesariano writes that the Spanish rather than the Portuguese king had discovered the "new peoples of Taprobane or Calicut" (see chapter 5). But the examples discussed in this book show that many instances of apparent error were in fact logical applications of prevalent geographical and ethnographic ideas.

Like the idea that the terms *India/Indian* were simply used in error, the idea that it was used arbitrarily as a catchall for anything exotic underestimates the effective presence of early modern geographical conceptual armatures. The defining feature of India since antiquity, as we have seen, was its multi-part, expansive nature, and the semantic field of the term was accordingly expansive and expandable (see chapter 1). The cosmological framework of the climatic zones, moreover, led Europeans to expect and find strong commonalities among the flora, fauna, peoples, and cultures of the tropical zones across wide spans of longitude from Africa to America (see especially chapters 3 and 6).[5] Since ancient authority and many modern maps designated Ethiopia as western India (*India occidentalis*) and China as upper India (*India superior*), the semantic fields of the term *new world* and India overlapped to a considerable extent. The family of India-related terms apply specific axes of association, in turn leaving strong patterns in the sources, axes and patterns that speak to the application of a consistent set of concepts. These associations are affirmed again and again in the documents—in letters, in cartographic materials, in treatises of natural history, in inventories of collections, in ethnographic accounts, and in images. Yes, there was fuzziness and sometimes downright sloppy use of terms, but that should not obscure the fact that more often than not the use of the terms was governed by logical applications that are now unfamiliar to us.

The word "exotic" was almost unknown in the sixteenth century, coming into more frequent use in the seventeenth century as a technical and scientific term to designate non-native species. Only at the very end of the seventeenth century and more commonly in the eighteenth century was it employed in the modern sense.[6] Yet the apparent mixing of provenances of foreign items in European collections and representations has suggested to many scholars that a culture of European exoticism arose with the new world discoveries. For Peter Mason, feather headdresses and other such items are not to be taken as signifiers of America but as indicators of an exotic taste for foreignness that was not particularly concerned with provenance.[7] We share his skepticism about assigning a strict American location or origin to such features as feathers and maize, or for that matter a strict Asian association for tigers and elephants, but we do not accept his claim that such reassignments bespeak an indifference to provenance. In the "pre-exoticist" model proposed here, the origins of a person or object were regularly assigned according to consistent early modern geographic and cosmographic premises that organized multiple levels of cultural practice, from maps and globes, to representations of new world flora and fauna, to the narrative structure of travel accounts, to the organization and inventorying of European collections. Perhaps later notions of exoticism were gradually layered on top of representations of Amerasia, in the end eclipsing the Amerasian idea altogether.

The word *India* originates in an association with the Indus River, whose name is itself derived from the Proto-Indo-Iranian *sindus* and the Sanskrit *sindhu*, which means river or body of water; the Indus is the river of water, fed by Himalayan glaciers and snows, known to flood its banks and occasionally to deviate from its course. People of the Indus, the Indians are the people of the waters. Ancient Greek and Roman cosmographers knew that India was vastly extensive, encompassing many subidentities, spanning seas, and that its limits were not known with certainty. Already in antiquity, India was associated with limitless variety and multitudes. The Greek historian and ethnographer Herodotus declared that "there are many Indian nations, none speaking the same language," and centuries later the Roman natural historian Pliny affirmed that India contained an incalculable number of peoples (*multitudinem populorum innumeram*).[8] As knowledge of the world expanded in antiquity, so did the extensiveness of India in Greek and Roman accounts. By the second century CE, Greco-Roman traders had reached harbors beyond Malacca, developments known to the second-century geographer Ptolemy, who made famous the notion of an *India extra Gangem*, or India beyond the Ganges, that extended to the ends of the known world, a conception taken into the Christian tradition and inherited by Columbus and other navigators of the modern period.[9] Even as its expanse grew, the eastern limits of India remained a matter of speculation. In book 7, chapter 5 of Ptolemy's *Geographia* India is said to extend toward unknown lands to the north, east, and south. The multiplicity and extent of India as imagined by Greco-Roman authorities was developed by the later European Middle Ages into an India of many parts. India became the Indies, divided into subregions variously named *India Major* and *Minor*, *Prima*, *Secunda*, *Tertia*; *Superior*, *Inferior*, and *Media*; *Ultima* and *Ulterior*; *Intra* and *Extra Gangem*.[10] Even with all of India's parts, the idea that the ultimate boundaries of India or the Indies were unknown persisted right through to the period of the modern European navigations. Shortly after Columbus's first voyage, the new world chronicler Peter Martyr d'Anghiera observed that "the cosmographers have left the boundaries of the Gangean India undefined," making it possible that Columbus had discovered unknown reaches of India (see chapter 1).[11]

The discourse of an expansive and expandable India informed expectations and thus representations of the new world, which then rebounded on the imagery of Asia in a feedback loop throughout the sixteenth and seventeenth centuries. Fauna that America had in common with India, like parrots, came as evidence of its Indianness, and by the same logic what was learned on the ground in Hispaniola, Cuba, Brazil, and eventually Mexico and Peru came to inform images and conceptions of the entire Indian complex. The king with cape and diadem in Amman's broadsheet, who epitomizes the expanse of India, comes especially close to a large early sixteenth-century woodcut showing a powerful warrior dressed

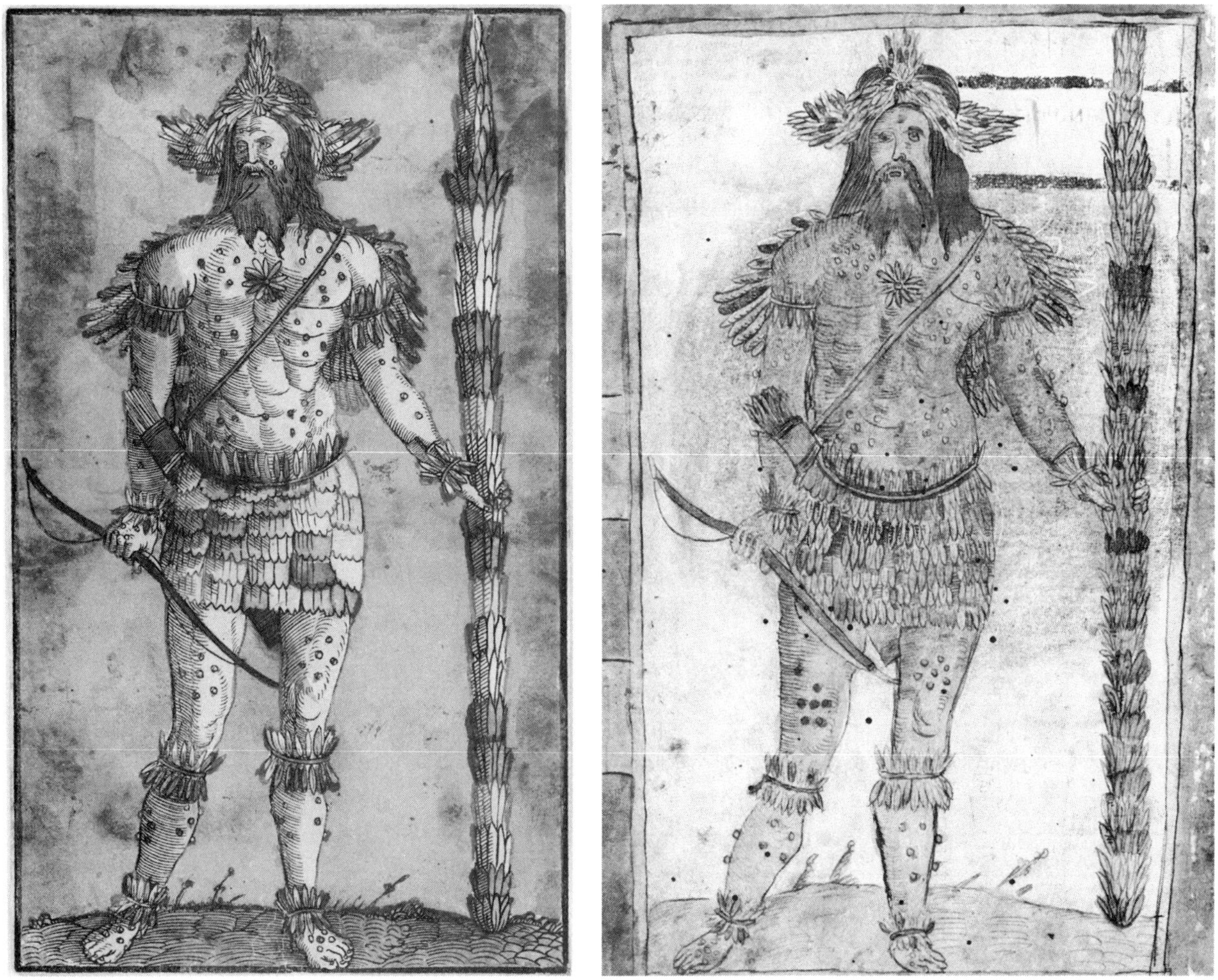

12.4a–b The "People of Calicut" persist through the sixteenth century. (a) *Feather-clad Warrior*, hand-colored woodcut, 31.6 × 18.1 cm (ca. 1510). Berlin, Staatliche Museen zu Berlin, Kupferstichkabinett. (b) Adriaen Coenen, Drawn copy of the woodcut from his *Visboek* (fol. 409v), pen and watercolor on paper, each page 31.7 × 21.5 cm (ca. 1579). The Hague, Royal Library.

in feather ornaments and holding a feather-decorated staff (fig. 12.4a). In a manuscript devoted to sea creatures, the Dutch fishmonger Adriaen Coenen carefully copied this print by hand in the 1570s and, with remarkable confidence and specificity, identified the image as one of the "noblemen of Calicut, usually called Naeri," that is, a member of the Nayar ruling class of the Malabar coast in India (fig. 12.4b).[12]

Like Amman, Coenen carried this feather-clad pan-Indian imagery into the later sixteenth century and beyond. By the end of the seventeenth century, when the geographical separation of America and Asia was clearly established, the feather gear came to be attributed more consistently to Asian Indians than American ones (see chapter 17).

The Nature and Societies of the Indies

The notion of an expansive India and its Amerasian implications come through clearly in a number of natural-historical and ethnographic writings during the sixteenth century. In 1532, a pamphlet was published in Bologna that presented letters from Franciscan missionaries written in Mexico, describing activities there, yet the letters are described as having come "from the extreme ends of the world, from the Indies in greater Asia." Mexico was not the Indies in some vague sense; it was the Indies in Magna Asia.[13] A letter to Pope Paul III, printed in 1537, from the first bishop of Tlaxcala, the Dominican friar Julián de Garcés, speaks of the propagation of Christianity "in the fertile ground of this India," making it clear that that "this India" was understood to be in Asia: "With so much more keen a spirit and greater ardour, may we strive to gather the idolaters of Asia under the banners of our faith."[14] The conceptual grounding for this view was laid out by the Spanish reformer and cleric Bartolomé de Las Casas in his *Apologética historia sumaria de las gentes de estas Indias*, composed over the second quarter of the sixteenth century. Marshaling the tools of traditional cosmography and ethnography to argue for the rationality and dignity of the Indigenous inhabitants of New Spain, he grounded his defense in part on the presumed commonality between these Indies and the India known and celebrated in ancient sources. "Our Indies are the last part of what in antiquity was called India," Las Casas observed, pointing to the many similarities between the one and the other. He invoked one of the most authoritative texts of the Middle Ages, Isidore of Seville's seventh-century *Etymologies*, which in book 14, chapter 3 describes an India of salubrious earth and abundant populations, trees that don't lose their leaves and offer their fruits twice a year, a land rich in minerals and gems and home to colorful parrots, known, as Isidore says, only in India—"all of which," writes Las Casas, "we see in these Indies."[15] Las Casas placed the Indies of New Spain at the extreme end of "the India they call *extra-Gangem*," which the ancient cosmographers agreed to be of vast extent. These lands are not just like India but are an extremity of India, explaining the many shared features as well some obvious differences from India, such as the absence of elephants, as well as a more temperate climate and people than those of India: "The people [in these Indies] have better coloring, and are more perfectly balanced between the two extremes of white and black than any of the peoples living in the celebrated and renowned [land of] India."

Las Casas was carefully charting a geographical and cultural extension of India as traditionally known, observing similarities and differences over an extended range. This reasoning, based on familiar ancient sources and applying widely held climatic models, was not unusual but mainstream. It is no doubt true that there are certain early modern sources that do not proceed on such a reasoned basis, sources where the term *Indies* "could mean almost anything."[16] Yet, with surprising and underappreciated frequency, the use of the terms *India/Indies/Indian* was grounded in an understanding of the nature and extent of India, an understanding that was not the rarefied preserve of a few scholars but rather a generally held view of the world. In its new applications after Columbus, the term affirmed that the Indigenous peoples of the Americas, whom Las Casas and others called *Indios* and also *naturales*, were not savages but rather some of the "infinite populations" of greater India as antiquity had known it, natives of a land blessed with greater fertility, beauty, and temperateness than any other part of the world. For Las Casas, their Indianness was the fundamental ground for defending their right as humans not to be enslaved.[17]

More than a ready-made Spanish concept imposed on a passive Indigenous population, the identity *Indio* was an ongoing creation woven out of an irreversible history of engagements and conflicts.[18] As Irene Silverblatt has shown in a study of Spanish colonization in the Andes, the Spanish term *Indio*, a by-product of the colonizing process, was also capable of galvanizing Andean communities that had been mortal enemies during the Inca period and that now claimed common identity as *Indios* against the Spanish in campaigns to reaffirm Native cultural and religious practices.[19] Indianness was without doubt a racialized category of subjection;[20] at the same time, the ideological foundations of the term gave it wide-ranging applicability, allowing it to be used by Europeans about provincial communities within Europe, and even about one European power in relation to another.[21] It was a middle term, in many ways a shifter, susceptible to different uses—from subjugating to self-affirming—depending on context. It was a term that could be used to advance antislavery polemics as well as claims to cultural and political autonomy and justice. This is in clear contrast to the Spanish term *negro*, which carried unremittingly negative connotations, justifying dehumanization and enslavement. There was no counterpart to Las Casas defending the dignity of the *negros*.

Perhaps the most influential of all sixteenth-century publications in shaping European visions of India and its new world expansion was Sebastian Münster's *Cosmographia universalis*, first published in German in 1544 and in Latin in 1550, and over the next eighty years published in no fewer than eighteen further editions in German, four more in Latin, six in

Indorum mores.

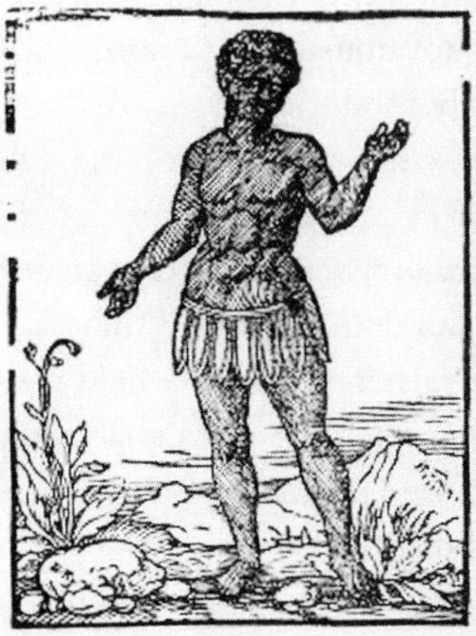

EST Indis omnibus promiſſa cæſaries, cultus præcipuus cum gemmis, habitus diſcrepantiſſimus: alij laneis, alij lineis peplis ueſtiuntur, pars nudi, pars obſcœna tantū amiculati, plurimi etiā flexibilib. libris circundati. Niger uulgo corporis color, in materno utero tales fiunt ſeminis diſpoſitione, quales ipſi ſunt qui genuere. Genitale ſemen ut Aethiopibus nigrū. Statura procera ac ualida. In uictu frugales ſunt, & à furtis magnopere abſtinent: Literas nō norunt, ſed omnia memoriter adminiſtrant, & propter ſimplicitatē ac uitæ parſimoniam omnia eis proſpere ſuccedunt. Vinum non niſi in ſacrificijs bibūt, potū ex oriza conficiūt & hordeo. Cibus magna ex parte oriza ſorbilis eſt. In cultu corporis nimij: nam & aurum geſtant & lapillis ornātur, & ſindonem candidiſſimam induunt, umbellasq; ſecum portant. Nam pulchritudinem excolentes omnia faciunt, quæ ad decorandam faciem pertinēt. Aetati ſenum prærogatiuā nullā tribuunt, niſi prudentia excellāt. Multas nuptas habent, quas à parentibus accipiunt, pari boum emptas, alias obediētiæ gratia, alias prolis ac uoluptatis & niſi caſtas eſſe cogant, fornicari licet. Qui falſus teſtis deprehenditur, extremis decurtatur digitorum articulis. Qui membro aliquo quempiam orbauerit, non modo talionis pœnam ſubit, ſed etiam manu truncatur. Quod ſi quis artifici manum oculum'ue ademerit, capitale eſt. Regi interdiu dormire non licet. Si qua mulier regem ebriū occiderit munus habet ut cum illius ſucceſſore iungatur.

Senes prudentes honorātur.

Septem ordines Indorum.

Philoſophi in primo gradu.

VNiuerſa gens Indorum olim in ſeptem ordines diuiſa fuit, quorū primus philoſophorum erat, qui cæteris numero pauciores, honore & dignitate apud reges longe anteibant. Hi ab omni opere immunes, neq; ſeruiunt cuiquam neq; imperant, recipiuntq; à priuatis ea quibus ſacra dijs faciant & curam habeant defunctorū tanquam chari dijs, & quæ fiunt apud inferos præcipue norint: propterea dona plurima honoresq; eis impenduntur. Multum enim proſunt Indorum uitæ. Nam anni principio unà conuenietes, ſiccitates, pluuias, uentos, morbos prædicunt, cæteraq; quorū cognitio poſſit eſſe utilis. Qui autem philoſophus falſa prædixerit, nullam præterquam quod perpetuo ſilet pœnam ſubit. Secundus ordo eſt agricolarum, qui multitudine ſuperantes cæteros, à bello reliquoq; opere liberi, ſolis agris colendis tempus impartiunt. Nullis hoſtis eos laceſſit neque ſpoliat, exiſtimans illos in communi utilitate uerſari, ideo ab omni iniuria abſtinet. Itaq; ſoluti metu agricolæ terram'q; libere colentes, rerum afferunt ubertatem. Viuūt autem in campis cum uxore & liberis, neque in urbes cōmeant, dant regi tributū, nulli priuato licet agros poſsidere abſq; tributo. Quintam autem fructuū partem regibus impendunt. Tertium ordinem conficiunt omnis generis paſtores, qui neq; in ciuitatibus neq; in uillis morantur. Vtuntur tabernaculis, uenatu ac retibus, tutas à feris auibusq; regiones reddunt. Quartū locum artifices tenent, quorū pars armis, pars ruſticis inſtrumētis, alij alijs utilibus rebus fabricandis uacant. Hi non ſolum immunes à tributo ſunt, ſed frumentū inſuper à regia percipiunt. Quinto ordine milites ſed numero ſecundi, belli diſciplina exercentur omnis ea multitudo armis dedita, tum equi elephanti'que bello apti ex regia uictum habent. Sextus eſt ordo Ephoro-

Agricolæ in ſecundo gradu.

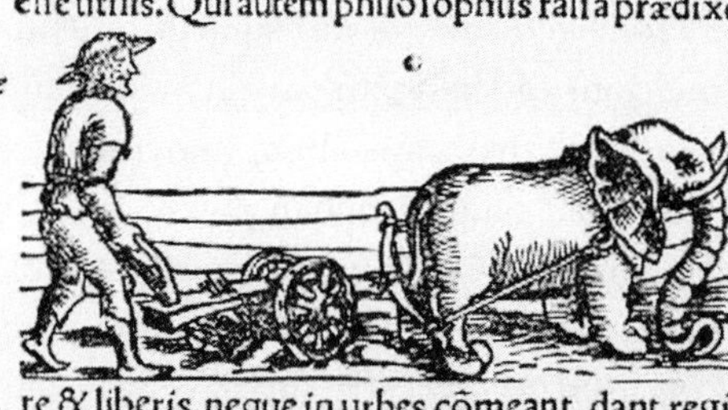

Paſtores.

Artifices.

Milites

Præfecti.

12.5 The nature and society of the Indians. Type and woodcut on paper. Sebastian Münster, *Cosmographiae uniuersalis lib. VI*... (Basel, 1550), p. 1,066.

French, two in Italian, and one in Czech. As we saw in chapter 10, its book 5 deals with Asia, which includes a section on India beyond the Ganges followed by a discussion of *India Nova*, where the provinces of America are grouped with those of East Asia. In Münster's coverage of India beyond the Ganges, a chapter on the "customs of the Indians" describing their eating and kinship practices as well as their dress is followed by a chapter describing the seven orders of their society—philosophers, farmers, shepherds, artisans, soldiers, prefects, counselors—though with a caveat that since India is so vast and its peoples' languages so many, customs vary widely, ranging over diverse populations, some dedicated to veganism and others practicing cannibalism. After these observations on the orders of Indian society, Münster includes a chapter on the customs and features of the Brahmins. Illustrating these passages on the nature of the Indians we see a by now familiar nearly naked figure with a feather skirt, in fact at variance with the accompanying textual description of Indians wearing pure white loincloths (*sindonem candidissimum induunt*) (fig. 12.5). Adorned with feathers, this Indian is dark-skinned with tightly curled hair and thus appears similar to Münster's representations of Africans. This amalgam of features epitomizes the range of India described in Münster's book 5, stretching from the islands of the Indian ocean, including Madagascar, to what Münster calls *India Nova*, that is, America.

Since Münster's *Cosmographia* had such a wide influence, let us traverse the full range of his India as he charts it in book 5. The figure of the feathered Indian is followed by information about Indian elephants and several accounts of Alexander's exploits in India. Proceeding beyond *India extra Gangem* to *India Nova* (which—oddly, to our eyes—begins with a map of the Indian subcontinent) the text describes the rhinoceros, illustrated by a close copy of Dürer's famous 1515 woodcut, followed by an account of "the most famous emporium" *Calechut*, and then proceeds to East Asian islands such as *Pego*, *Taprobana*, *Borneo*, and *Gyava* (noted as a place where cannibals live). Münster continues with discussions of *Cathay* and *Tangut* and then moves on to the new islands discovered by Columbus, where there are more cannibals (illustrated by the very same image used for the cannibals of Java). He then offers an account of Portuguese explorations to the Spice Islands known as the Moluccas, followed by the third voyage of Columbus to *Paria* in present-day Venezuela and Vespucci's voyages to Brazil, finally bringing book 5 to a close with visits to Madeira and the Canary Islands.

An arbitrary-seeming jumble to a reader working from modern geographical coordinates, Münster's book 5 in fact offered an eastward progress through the newly expanded Indian expanse. For all the variety of place names he includes in India, Münster's itinerary is a tropical itinerary; the commonality of the Indian range is imposed by latitude rather than longitude. The same point was made with great visual economy in Jost Amman's images of the costumes of the world discussed earlier, with their sequences of related Indians and Brazilians wearing feathers and little else. And the same expectations are explicitly articulated in a 1598 Italian edition of Ptolemy's *Geographia*, which in the manner of Münster offers an account of America appended to its section on Asia, explaining that while some call it *America* after Vespucci it is also called *Atlantica* and *India Occidentale*, "because it was discovered at the same time that the Portuguese were exploring Oriental India, or better, due to the resemblance of the inhabitants to the Indians of Asia, as the ones like the others go totally naked."[22] Here as in Münster zonal tropicality is a primary organizing principle, since nakedness responds above all to shared climatic conditions.

The point is not that everyone subscribed specifically to Münster's conception of India, influential as it was, but that common conceptual underpinnings yielded an array of Amerasian applications. For example, a rigorous application of the zonal/climatic model in a 1585 treatise on painting by the Milanese artist Gian Paolo Lomazzo yields Amerasian axes different from Münster's even as they proceed on a similar conceptual basis. In a section instructing the painter how to depict the clothing, customs, and flesh color of people from different parts of the world, "so that right away they [the depicted figures] are recognized distinctly as Indian, Moor, German, or whichever other nation you like," Lomazzo explains that in the tropical zone near the equator people are black, with tightly curled hair and fierce disposition "due to the nearness of the sun," yet he does not confine them to Africa. This type of people can be found in the entire range of Mali, Tambutù (Timbuktu), Caragola (Carangola in Brazil?), Guinea, Borno (in present-day Nigeria), and Barnagasso (Ethiopia) where Prester John lives, as well as Calicut, Cananor, Narsingia, and Bisnagar, where Saint Thomas is buried, Zeilan, Malacca, the Moluccas, Tabrobane, Java Major and Minor, and the Philippines, "from which one passes to" Mexico, Yucatán, Cuba, Hispaniola and finally to Cape Verde. This is a tropical band—African, Asian, and "new Indian" (Lomazzo does not use the term American)—circling the world. Drawing a diagonal Amerasian axis through this band, he notes a particular similarity between the Peruvians and the Chinese: "the inhabitants of the new Indies, especially in Peru, and those of the great emperor of China are without beard, with one single hair on the chin, and both the men and the women go naked, except that the married women wear a cotton band around their private parts, and in many places they eat each other."[23]

Despite a clear understanding of the distance between East and West Indies and growing interest in the features of specific cultures and customs, the zonal logic applied by Münster, Lomazzo, and others yields sudden conjunctions that diminish the Pacific and bring into view Amerasian continuities and resemblances. India remained a continuous reality, if extended to include the new world, giving the India-related terms a shared semantic field through the sixteenth century and beyond. This may explain why in Theodor de Bry's popular volumes illustrating various parts of the world the very same woodcuts of Indians in colonial Jamestown in the *America* volumes reappear to illustrate Mughal India in the *India Orientalis* volumes.[24] It may of course have been a cost-saving measure, yet it was one justified and underwritten by a well-established pattern of assimilating Indians East and West.

Collecting Indian Amerasia

These various axes of Amerasian association form the background for the European practices of collecting and assembling artifacts and *naturalia* from remote parts of the world. For the purposes of this chapter, we focus on the category "Indian" and its attributions in the inventories of the period, such as those of the Medici family, which regularly identify Mesoamerican objects as well as Asian objects as *indiano* or *dell'India*.[25] We can identify for example two masks that are listed as "having come from India" (*venuta d'India*) in a 1553–54 Medici inventory with the two famous mosaic masks in the Museo della Civiltà in Rome and now identified as "Mixtec," yet the modern identification of the piece does not settle the historical questions raised by the language of the inventory.[26] For the Medici and the visitors to their collections, the mask was not Mixtec but Indian, an identity that set these objects into a constellation of other artifacts, including some from what is today considered the Indian subcontinent and also from other parts of Asia, as well as from other parts of America, that all configured the cultural identity "Indian." In their study of Medici and Habsburg inventories, Jessica Keating and Lia Markey propose that in the course of the sixteenth century "'India' had come to refer to a non-specific place of abundance and was equated with our modern notion of exoticism." They propose that it served as "a generic signifier for anything non-European," a view close to that proposed by Mason discussed earlier.[27] Yet, when examining the Medici inventory that lists each of the Mixtec mosaic masks as *venuta d'India* and catalogues them among jewelry that includes "eight Indian emeralds" and "three Indian animals, one of amethyst and two of agate," Keating and Markey allow that "perhaps the shared Indian provenance of these works, whether New World or South Asian, was significant to the cataloguer or collector."[28] We consider this instance, where a shared Indian provenance spanning America and Asia is "significant" rather than arbitrary, to be the norm rather than the exception.

The textual, cartographic, and iconographic materials brought together throughout this study suggest that the terms *India/Indian* did have meaning, even if their semantic field was broad. Inventories are frustratingly reticent documents, but they can be understood in light of more discursive texts, such as the letters of the Florentine merchant Filippo Sassetti written from India to his Medici patrons, which throw clear light on the various usages of the terms *Indian* and *Indies* in the cultural world of Medicean Florence. Writing in 1585 from his perch in Cochin on the Malabar coast, Sassetti explains to a colleague in Pisa that the Portuguese viceroy commands "all of India from Mozambique to Malacca" (*Un vicerè commanda all'India tutta da Mozambique sino a Malacca*), a clear expression of the idea that India begins in eastern Africa and extends to the eastern ocean.[29] It is a large expanse for one viceroy, he acknowledges, yet all of it is India.

And yet this is not India's full extent, as we learn in a letter of Sassetti's from the following year, 1586, to his patron Cardinal Ferdinando de' Medici, in which he calls the lands of New Spain governed by the Spanish king "those other Indies" (*quell'altre Indie*) or "those . . . western Indies" (*quelle sue Indie occidentali*).[30] He is not saying that those other western Indies are not really Indian, only that they are in the domain of another European king and that they are across the ocean. For Sassetti as for many other commentators, India was by nature modular and extensive. One extent of it spans Mozambique to Malacca, to which should be added this other extent, more recently discovered. That a new part of India has been discovered in recent times may be spectacular news, but it does not contradict the logic of a vast, mostly tropical India of many parts with many subcommunities speaking many different languages, whose full extent was not known by ancient geographers.

A similar logic informs the 1572 inventory of a gift of Florentine Grand Duke Francesco de' Medici to Duke Albrecht V of Munich, where American, African, and Asian items are all called Indian and a gray parrot (native to equatorial Africa) is even said to "speak Indian."[31] In a 1598 inventory of Duke Albrecht's Kunstkammer containing some of these objects, two chests from "India" are listed with various items inside, such as combs, rings, and other small objects. The chests still exist in the Munich treasury, and have been identified by modern scholars as coming from present-day Sri Lanka, an Asian provenance that accords with the fact that they had arrived in Munich through Portuguese channels in 1567. Thus, in this case "Indian" chests really do correspond to the region of India as understood by modern geography. Yet the 1598 inventory also lists a gold ring that has been identified by modern scholars as Mixtec. Probably not originally in the chests that arrived from Lisbon, the ring may have been placed in the "Indian" chest by Albrecht V himself, who thus would have grouped it together with the other *Indianische Ientilesas*, or little heathen gifts from India, in the collection.[32] Modern curators and scholars would never put a piece of Mixtec jewelry and a Sri Lankan comb into a common case, but for Albrecht and his heirs they went together naturally as Indian artifacts.

Inventories of the Habsburg family confirm the pattern, regularly showing that American objects, virtually never called American but rather "Indian," mingled with Asian and (sometimes, though less frequently) African ones. Sometimes it is simply impossible to tell from the inventories where an object comes from, a result not so much of sloppy terminology as of the fact that America and Asia were not clearly separated provenances. Well into the seventeenth century, Aztec and Mixtec manuscripts were classed as Oriental manuscripts in Western collections, or specifically as books from India or China, which was often termed *India superior* (see chapter 14). Conforming to the pattern, the Spanish Habsburg collections at the Escorial, the Alcázar, and the royal convent of the Descalzas Reales assembled American and Asian objects together, often labeling both as *indiano* or *de las Indias*.[33] The nuns of the Descalzas Reales had no knowledge of the modern field categories; rather, they understood these objects collectively as Indian—a real category for them, just as "African" remains a real category in modern academic and museological discourse, even if it is an enormous expanse containing a great diversity of people and cultural productions.

With few exceptions, modern scholars study such inventories in an effort to reposition the materials collected in early modern Europe into the categories established by modern field definitions. Excellent studies have been devoted to what the Medici or the Spanish Habsburgs knew about the Americas and what Americana they collected, despite the fact that the category "American" carried virtually no organizing force in these cultures. Anthropologists and ethnographers comb the early modern sources in order to learn something about specific Indigenous communities—Inuit, Nahua, Javanese, and so forth—a worthy enterprise, but not one that will have much to say about the shape of the world as configured by early modern European collections and inventories. To circumscribe the data set from the start by applying the modern field designations is to bracket out the early modern armatures of European maps, books, and display rooms in order, presumably, to gain an understanding of the objects themselves. And if those objects are somehow understood to be essentially identified by the modern designations, they can only seem misplaced or hopelessly jumbled together in early modern collections. Yet the modern field categories are themselves a relatively recent development, having arisen initially in nineteenth- and twentieth-century European and North American academic culture, and then more prominently in the area studies developed during the Cold War.[34] What has been lacking is a sustained inquiry into the taxonomies and underlying armatures used by the early modern collectors and cosmographers themselves.[35]

In sum, it seems impossible to think outside of modern field boundaries without defaulting to the view that "Indian" is a virtually meaningless term for anything exotic to Europeans. It is also difficult to keep in mind that the use of modern-sounding designations in early modern sources does not necessarily imply that they carry the modern meaning. For example, when early modern European writers identify an object as "Mexican," that is not conclusive proof that it was dissociated from the Indian matrix, given that in several important European treatises and maps Mexico counted as an Indian province, part of greater Asia, as we have seen earlier in this chapter and in chapter 11, and will see again in chapter 14. Yet these difficulties are not insurmountable. That materials should be put into sometimes unwieldy larger groupings is hardly an unfamiliar idea, since contemporary academic life is also regularly organized by vast and untenable yet institutionally efficacious macrocategories. Every year the Association of Asian Studies conference gathers scholars whose interests range from Persian literature to Malaysian theater to Japanese art. Is this conception of Asia and Asian studies, a category created by European culture, any less arbitrary than the expansive notion of India we are tracing? No one at the Association of Asian Studies conference is deluded as to the differences among the various subfields, yet the macrocategory of Asian studies allows these materials to be considered together and in their interrelations. "Asian" is not a mere catchall; it organizes academic study and structures dialogue in the field. In the next decades we will probably see increasing prominence given to associations and conferences dedicated to transpacific and Pacific Rim studies, a different macroframe that brings other sets of relationships into view. In the early modern period, even as it was possible to see differences among subregions, the common designators *dell'india* or *indiano* carried similar organizing force, allowing the early owners and admirers of "Indian" objects to see commonalities and relations among them at the level of materials, functions, and form. The field designations institutionalized in the nineteenth and twentieth centuries have come under withering critique as scholars rethink the boundaries that have structured the traditional academic fields; the early modern sources studied here promote that rethinking in unexpected ways.

A Long Way from Indian to Indian

The ancient and medieval idea of India—that it was vast and varied, that its limits were unknown, and that it extended across bodies of water, even encompassing islands big and small far to the east of mainland Asia—found clear and resonant confirmation in the modern European encounter with a still farther and previously unknown "new India," which shared many climatic, ethnographic, and botanical features with the realms of India known since antiquity while also presenting previously unknown features as well as a host of internal variations. The adaptation is clear in Mercator's epoch-making 1569 map, discussed in chapter 11, where East Asia is placed at the right edge and then shows up again at the left edge to show just how narrow a strait separates it from India Nova, which contains New Spain, making it clear that the regions explored by the Spanish north of Mexico, as discussed in chapter 8, were not far from the Philippines, New Guinea, and Japan (see fig. 11.7). Mercator's modern world map certainly understands the newly discovered territory west of Europe to be a separate landmass and unknown to ancient geographers, yet presents it in Indian terms: it is *India Nova*; the word *America* appears nowhere on it.

The Jesuit priest José de Acosta (1540–1600), writing from Peru in the later sixteenth century, was clear that the name *India* had been applied to this territory on the model of the Asian India, "because for the ancients India was the remotest place on earth and it was believed that it constituted the limit of the earthly globe" (*fines orbis terrarum claudere putaretur*). Originally from Medina del Campo in Spain, Acosta lived in Peru with visits to Mexico between 1570 and 1587, during which time he collected copious information about Inca and Mexica customs and history. Acosta understands the transatlantic new world to be a separate and distinct land, yet at the same time he routinely understands the Peruvian and Mexican Indians in relation to the Asian ones. When he asserts that the "natives of America are very varied and diverse, and very different from one another as much in climate, environment, and dress as in intelligence and customs," he is applying a lesson from the "old" India, echoing Herodotus and others on the many languages and cultures encompassed by the expanse of India. Moreover, he places the diversity of new world Indians into a shared range with the Indians of Asia, "for although we use the name Indian for all the barbarians discovered in our days by the

Spanish and Portuguese, . . . nonetheless not all of them have the same characteristics, and there is a long way, to say it with humor, from Indian to Indian, and some barbarians far outpace others."[36] Seeing distinctions among Indians East and West, as well as variations among Indians within larger subregions, was not a contradiction but a confirmation of the idea of an extensive India, one that in antiquity extended all the way from Ethiopia to Java, and now from Java into America.

• • •

Reverse: What Remains of India

In 1562, the medalist Gianpaolo Poggini wrote from Madrid to the Medici Duke Cosimo de' Medici to announce to his Florentine patron that he had created a new medal for the Spanish king Philip II with his royal portrait on the obverse and a new and interesting invention for the reverse for the figure of India (fig. 12.6). The reverses of portrait medals, often allegorical or emblematic, were an arena of notable artistic conceits, and Poggini, eager to make the Florentine Duke aware of his abilities, explains that he had created for the Spanish king "a reverse for India, [in] which I have dressed the men and women in the clothes they wear in Peru, as you see; and that animal that resembles both a camel and a sheep I have portrayed from one that is alive here [in Madrid] . . . and I have shown it burdened with bars of silver."[37] Poggini thus makes a point of having depicted features of clothing, animal life (the llama or alpaca), and resources (the silver) that are particular to Peru and rarely if ever represented before, all of them informing this newly conceived image of India. As he goes on to say, "The woman who carries the half-globe as an offering is figured as the province of India, as Signor Gonzalo Pérez would have it. But I identify her as Fortune or Providence, according to his [Pérez's] motto."

Poggini is advertising to the Florentine Duke Cosimo that he is in active intellectual exchange with one of the most powerful men of the Spanish empire, Gonzalo Pérez, King Philip II's secretary of state, a man widely admired for his humanistic learning. Pérez's motto, which combines the two allegorical ideas mentioned by Poggini (India and Fortune/Providence), reads at the top "Reliquum Datura" and at the bottom "India," meaning, "The rest shall be given (by her)—India." Poggini observes that the female figure is shown in the act of offering a half-globe (*la donna che porta a offerire il mezo mondo*). What is she offering and what remains to be rendered? How does the image relate to the motto?

The medal shows more than Poggini saw fit to describe in his brief letter. We see the figure of India-Fortune-Providence offering a schematic

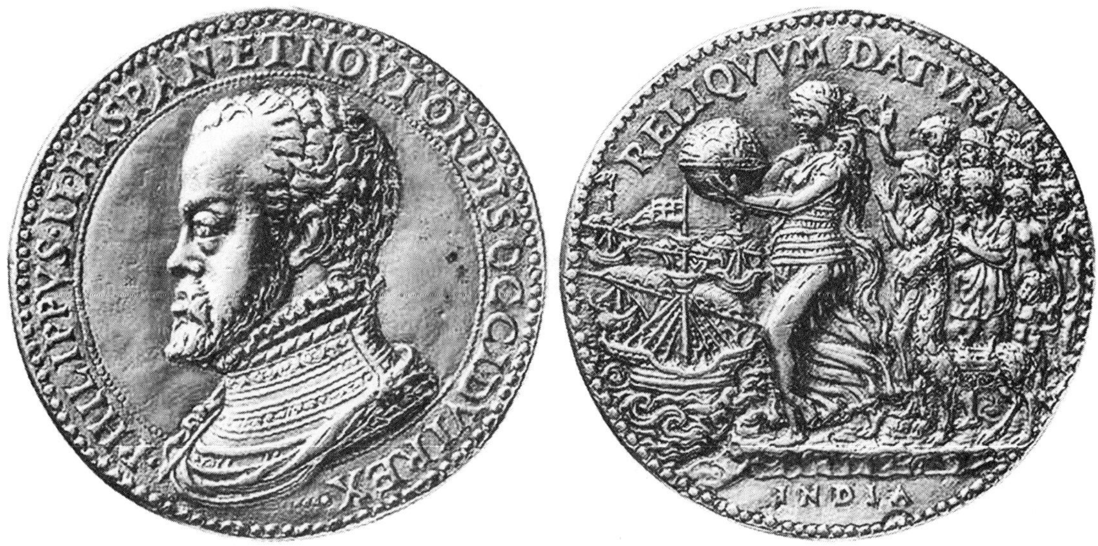

12.6 Philip II, King of India. Gianpaolo Poggini, *Medal of Philip II* (obverse and reverse), silver cast with gilding, diameter 4.1 cm (1562). Madrid, Museo Arqueológico Nacional.

celestial globe, with the band of the ecliptic (the path of the sun and zodiac) set at an angle to the celestial equator. The globe's bottom half is smooth, uncharted, suggesting that more remains to be known about the unfamiliar southern heavens visible from the southern part of the world. India stands at a coastline and holds the half-globe aloft, directly below which we see ships afloat on a churning sea. Behind the figure of India are a number of *Indios*, one of whom backs the offering of the globe with a prayer while another points up at the motto, adding emphasis to the affirmation that the rest shall be given, here underwritten by the llama loaded with bars of silver. Directly above the camelid is a portrait of a bearded and barefoot Indian man with hands across his chest, perhaps one of the miners who has brought this wealth out of the ground and now watches it being given over to the ships, India's offering to a newly interconnected world. Behind him is a naked woman with her child, part of a grouping of *Indios* representing India's raw fertility and abundance. All the figures look left, west from Peru across the ocean toward the various emporia of Asia, whose economies were in fact being transformed by the arrival of Peruvian silver during these decades.

"The rest shall be given by India" is a prediction admitting an element of the unknown, recasting the traditional notion of India's abundance and fertility in a world that is being remade by the discovery of India's hitherto unknown reaches and riches. The effigy of the Spanish king is cast

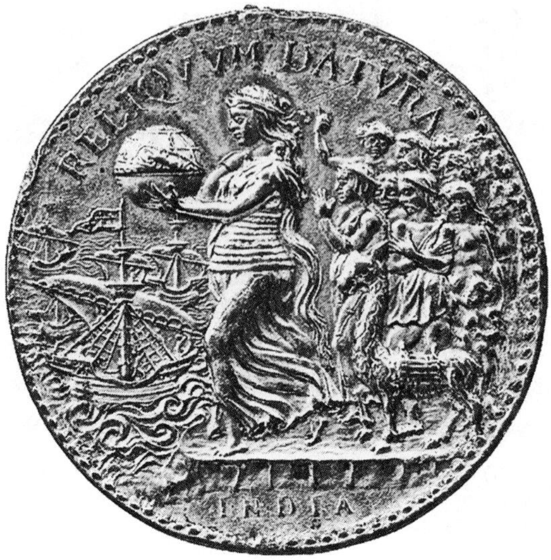

12.7 A harsher cast. Gianpaolo Poggini, *Medal of Philip II* (reverse), copper alloy cast with gilding. New York, Frick Museum.

from the very Peruvian, or rather Indian, silver that is newly connecting and configuring the world. The smooth bottom half of the globe symbolizes a world as yet unknown, but it also puts on display a gleaming orb of precious metal offered up as a prize. The silver that makes up this medal is covered by gilding, a sublimating treatment that lifts the item out of the material world it represents: made of the material of this province, it glitters with higher meaning and promise.

Though Poggini was the artist and Acosta the man of religion, the priest turns out to have been the realist. He, too, saw Peru as a land of exorbitant native fertility, but seventeen years after Poggini's medal, in his 1579 treatise on the *salus* (salvation, or well-being) of the Indians, he sounded the loud warning that the Spanish depredations were leaving Peru depleted and denatured, no longer resembling fabled India in any sense: "Not only has the native Indian population been decimated, but moreover their lands of exuberant fertility are drying out, the production of gold and silver is diminishing, the articles of first necessity are in decline. With one voice, the judgment of all those lamenting the matter consider the Indian state of affairs deplorable, fallen from its ancient prosperity."[38]

Acosta's account upends the idea that this land was originally isolated and needed the arrival of the Europeans in order to be brought to fulfillment and prosperity by being reconnected to the rest of the world. In Acosta's view, the land's native fertility and abundance—the quality that most connected it to India as traditionally understood—has been artificially and quite suddenly drained by the greed of the Spaniards, and thus it is the Spaniards who have cut off America from its "ancient prosperity." Ancient in its abundance, Peru has been made "new" by being stripped and violated; twice in one sentence Acosta uses forms of the verb *lapsare* to describe Peru's fallen condition. In barely two generations, the European presence has managed to bring this world out of its pristine abundance (with every attribute of a golden age, though Acosta doesn't quite say that) and into Europe's grim and rapacious age of iron. This view, in a treatise dedicated to Philip II, comes as a corrective to the assertion of Indian abundance offered in Poggini's medal for the same Spanish king. Or rather, Acosta's report on the sudden Anthropocene visited by the Spanish on Peru casts the medal in a harsher light, less triumphant than bracing and premonitory. Only tilt the medal in your hands at a different angle, or look at another cast of the medal with a different material history (fig. 12.7), and Poggini's *Indios* begin to look rather gaunt, their faces downcast, their gestures more pleading than prayerful, the bars of silver in fact few, the ground quite bare, the waters in turmoil. In light of Acosta's biting realism, the motto "The rest shall be given by her" acquires a less positive ring. *Reliquum* can mean "the rest" but it also means "the remainder." *Datura* can read "shall be offered by her," but also "shall be surrendered" or simply "shall be paid." We are not very far from: "She will give over what remains." Intended to invoke overspilling abundance spontaneously yielded, *Reliquum Datura* also clearly sounds a familiar language of coercion—the centuries-long echo of resource-hungry empires extracting tribute from colonies, boots planted firmly on their necks.

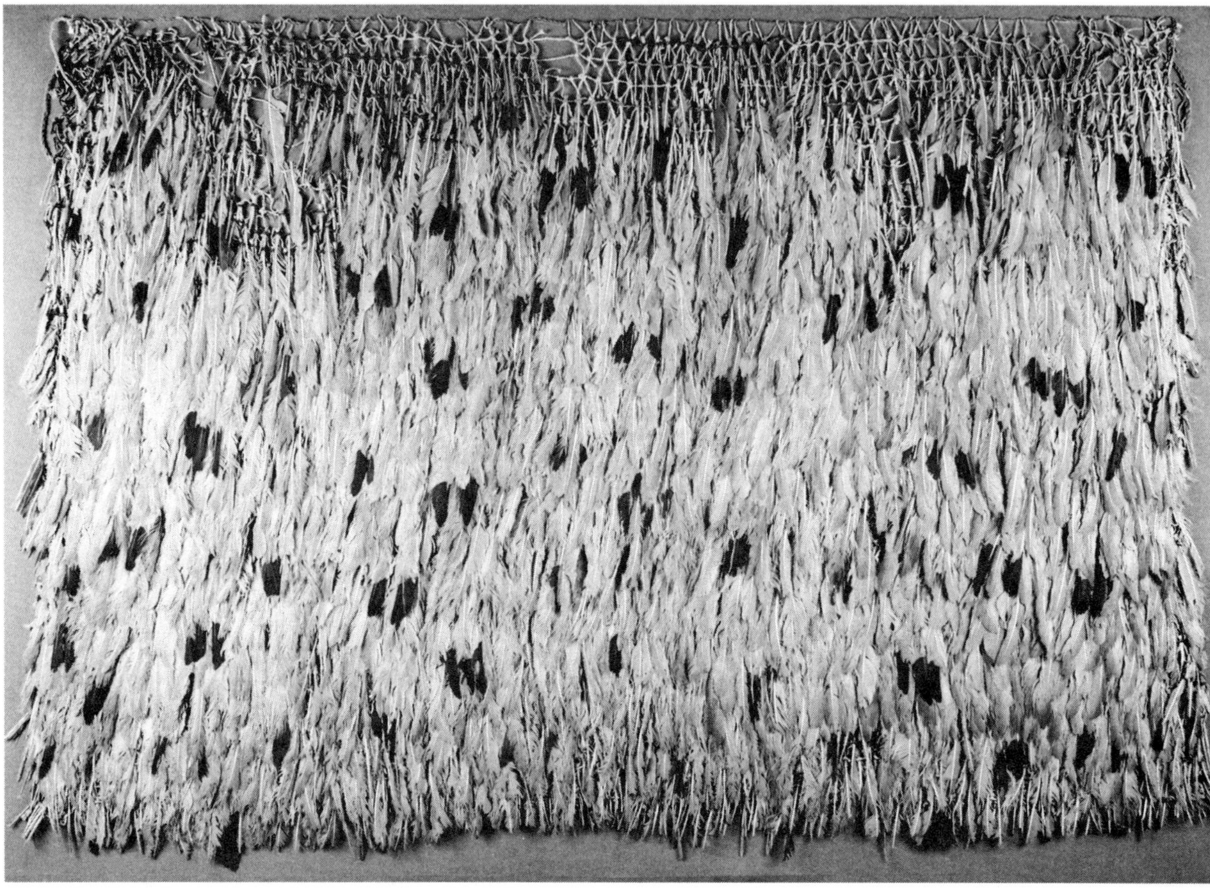

13.1 Biblical art in the new world? Mantle made of feathers of red ibis on reticulated cotton fibers, height 110 cm, width of top edge 141 cm, of bottom edge 151 cm, Tupinamba people, Northeast Brazil, sixteenth century (in the Medici collection by 1618). Museo di Antropologia ed Etnologia, Florence.

THIRTEEN

The Biblical New World

Sixteenth-century Europeans regularly expressed great admiration for artifacts arriving from the new world, including books, masks, carvings, and especially works in feather and obsidian. Almost immediately, they hypothesized biblical origins for the crafts of new world peoples.

Mosaic Featherwork, Solomonic Gold, and Judaic Obsidian

On March 3, 1533, Domingo de Betanzos, a Spanish missionary and the founder of the Dominican province of Santiago de México, offered to the Medici Pope Clement VII gifts from the new world, including Mixtec codices and examples of featherwork. In his *History of Bologna* (Bologna, 1548), the Dominican friar and humanist Leandro Alberti described the items that Betanzos had presented to the pope, including "two bed covers made and woven out of blue, green, black, and yellow parrot-feathers, which looked like velvet" as well as other featherwork items that he believed to be for liturgical use specifically as stoles and maniples.[1] It is possible that the items he described as stoles, or liturgical shawls, are to be identified with the feather mantles now in the Museo di Antropologia ed Etnologia of Florence, which are documented in the Medici collection by the middle of the sixteenth century (fig. 13.1).[2]

"We may recognize here," Alberti writes, "what is written in Scripture describing the apparatus of the tabernacle of God where it is commanded that it be ornamented with featherwork."[3] Alberti is referring to a passage from Exodus 26 where Moses is commanded to make the curtains of the tabernacle out of blue, purple, and scarlet yarn. In the Latin Vulgate, used throughout the Middle Ages, it reads that these curtains are to be woven "with the work of feathers," *opere plumario*, an ablative form that Alberti maintains in the original Latin in his description of the new world featherwork: "Onde parvi di conoscere quel che habbiano nella scrittura descrivendo l'apparato del tabernacolo de Iddio over comandava che opere plumario se dovesse ornare."

For Alberti, these mysterious objects were portals into biblical antiquity. They had come from "the New Indies or the New World" (*dalle Nuove indie ovvero dal Mundo Nuovo*), and yet they preserved traditions of handiwork that Christians could read about in their Bibles but had never seen in their lives—until now. The shimmering, effulgent patterns produced by the expert weaving of the feathers of exotic birds spoke of an ancient, somehow unbroken tradition. Alberti says the feathers are primarily from parrots, a bird strongly associated with paradise and the easternmost parts of the world (see chapter 1). It was not only that West met East in the new world, an idea we have encountered repeatedly, but that the new world delivered back to Europeans evidence of the oldest world. Soon, Indigenous featherworkers or *amantecas* were put to work applying the technique to Christian furnishings such as miters and altarpieces, as if to reconnect Christian liturgical art with its roots in ancient biblical craftsmanship.

A back-and-forth about the Israelite origins of American featherwork runs through the sixteenth century. In his *Apologética historia sumaria* (1550–55, but begun decades earlier), the Dominican friar and longtime resident in the new world Bartolomé de Las Casas cast doubt on the already widespread theory that American featherwork was to be identified with the *opus plumarium* of the biblical tabernacle, as he could not imagine that featherwork curtains could have withstood the constant movement that the tabernacle had undergone. Yet the mestizo businessman and historian Diego Muñoz Camargo reaffirmed the Israelite thesis, arguing in his *Descripción de Tlaxcala* (1581–84) that some Indigenous inhabitants "come from those people and tribes of Israel," who "used the work of woven feathers in their tabernacles, for God ordered that there be patterned curtains woven of feathers with which to decorate the tabernacle, as is evident in Holy Scripture." He goes on to specify what a rare craft survival this is: "which work we read that no nation in the world, until today, had had or used or known how to do, because of its difficulty, unless it is these Mexican Indians and their nations. From which one infers that really these are Jews because they served their gods in their temples with this decoration."[4]

In addition to the featherwork, Domingo Betanzos's new world gifts for Pope Clement VII included "some stone knives that cut like razors, which they used for shaving." Once again, Alberti gives them a biblical gloss. "By these knives, we recognized the kind of knives of which the bible speaks when the Lord says 'Make me the stone knives to circumcise.'" A somewhat later account, the *Descrittione dell'India occidentale*, published in Venice c. 1556 and probably authored by Juan de Córdova, a Dominican friar active among Indigenous communities in Oaxaca, lists a variety of items that he transported back to Italy, including "black porphyry razors which they used to circumcise as the Jews used to do."[5]

When obsidian tools, featherwork items, gold ornaments, and densely illustrated manuscripts began to arrive from Mexico after 1520, it was clear to all Europeans who encountered them that these works were equivalent in functional complexity and meaning to anything produced in the West. In August 1520 the German artist Albrecht Dürer saw some Mexica objects recently brought to Brussels, including "a sun all of gold a whole fathom broad, and a moon all of silver of the same size, also two rooms full of armor of the people there, and all manner of wondrous weapons of theirs, harness and darts, very strange clothing." They inspired in him the confounded awareness that these objects spoke a language at once universal and unfamiliar: "for I saw amongst them wonderful works of art, and I marvelled at the subtle *Ingenia* of men in foreign lands. Indeed I cannot express all that I thought there."[6] Dominican friar-scholars such as Alberti and de Córdova, reeling from a similar recognition, found in these impressive cultural expressions not just an analogous cultural achievement but a distant branch of the same biblical tree. To make sense of them, they applied a form of typological analysis, a familiar strategy of biblical interpretation, to find connection across dissimilarity.

If traditional typological reading had been developed to find the transhistorical fulfillment of Old Testament events and phenomena in Christian history, parallel forms of interpretation were also adapted to find Christian meaning in pagan mythology. The news of the new world launched a hermeneutics that wavered between one and the other: while some found distant connections between the new world Indians and the Israelites, thus applying biblical hermeneutics, others, to be studied in chapter 14, connected the language and material culture of the new world Indians to the forms of ancient knowledge found in ancient Asian cultures, sometimes collecting them all together into a cultural diaspora emanating from Egypt in remote antiquity. The operating premise in all these efforts of interpretation was that these cultures contained a message encoded in ancient times that was surfacing now, a provocation to European understanding. Perhaps in some instances the artifacts of the new world were just exotic curios. But in many cases, works from the new world were understood to carry eloquent and powerful messages that Europeans themselves knew they could only partially read, messages in a sense intended for them, since it was the Europeans who had produced the fateful encounters in the first place, acting, so they believed, as agents of an inevitable Christian triumph and revelation.

As we will see, these encounters prompted scholars and missionaries to engage in ethnographic study of the cultures of the Indigenous populations, with all the expected misunderstandings and cultural impositions and just-so stories. Associations between the lands in the western Atlantic and the books of the Hebrew Bible date back to the Columbian voyages, as when Peter Martyr reported in 1493 that Columbus had claimed "that while he steered his ships eastward he discovered the island of Ophir," and in 1501, Martyr again referred to "Hispaniola, which [Columbus] claims is the Ophir about which one reads in the third book of Kings."[7] Ophir, famous for its wealth, was the port and region from which King Solomon received a cargo of gold, silver, sandalwood, pearls, ivory, apes and peacocks every three years (1 Kings 10:22). Jewish tradition associated Ophir with a place in India and claimed it was named for one of the sons of Iektan (sometimes also called Ioktan, or Joktan), the second son of Eber, a great-grandson of Noah's son Shem.[8] It was this Indian location that allowed Ophir's placement to shift into the Americas, according to a well-established logic of Indian new world extension. Several decades after Martyr, in his *De orbis situ* probably from 1529, the Belgian cosmographer Franciscus Monachus argued that Peter Martyr d'Anghiera was wrong, that Ophir was in Ethiopia.[9] When Álvaro Mendaña became the first European to land in the Solomon Islands in the South Pacific in 1568, he named them as such because he believed them to be Ophir.[10]

Following these early discussions about Ophir, European chroniclers began to wonder about how new world peoples related more generally to the accounts of the Hebrew Bible. Such speculations became a favorite subject of early American colonial chroniclers and early modern European orientalist scholars who linked Asian sites to the Americas through tales of migration.[11] A short manuscript in seven folios that circulated in the 1540s in Peru and New Spain written by a "Doctor Roldán" offered one of the earliest substantive arguments for the Israelite heritage of Indigenous Americans.[12] The Roldán manuscript analyzes descriptions of the Israelites' return to Zion following the Babylonian captivity taken from the fourth chapter of the book of Ezra in the Hebrew Bible: descriptions that loom large in European discussion about the discovery of America and the Israelite origins of Native Americans.[13] Based on a rate of twenty miles a day as described in Ezra 4, Roldán calculates the distance the Israelites would have traveled from the Mesopotamian city of Nineveh until they reached the lands inhabited by the American Indians. Roldán emphasizes the prophet Hosea's description (Hosea 1:10) that "the children of Israel would be as many as the sand and the sea," and describes "Indians" in both Asia and America—as one of the largest "nations" on earth in geographic and demographic terms. Roldán also asserts that many American words had Hebrew origins. The islands of the Caribbean, for instance, had been given their names by their first *caciques*, the tribal leaders of the Israelite nomads who had traveled from Assyria into what is today the Gulf of Mexico. In a striking instance of "acoustemological" resonance (see chapter 1), he argues that the name Haiti was an echo of the Hebrew noun *Aith*, the name of the Hayna River on the island of Hispaniola an echo of the Hebrew *Hain* for spring, and the word *cacique* carried the memory of the Hebrew *Acasin* (or *Katsin*) meaning leader or judge, among many others. It was clear for Roldán that the Indian practices of circumcision, ablutions, not touching the dead, and polygamy were derived from those of the Israelites.[14]

The never published Roldán manuscript appears to have come into the hands of the Dominican friar Diego Durán, who developed an even more elaborate theory of the Hebrew origins of new world peoples. Durán lived and worked in both Mexico City and Oaxaca, becoming fluent in Nahuatl and developing close associations with the people he was attempting to convert. In the first chapter of his ethnohistory of the Mexica, *The History of the Indies of New Spain* (1581, though published only in the nineteenth century), Durán argued that Mexica ceremonies, rites, superstitions, and idolatrous practices ("strange ways, conduct, and lowly actions") were much like those of the ancient Israelites.[15] They "burned incense, killed their sons and daughters, sacrificed them, and offered them as victims to their gods. They sacrificed children, ate human flesh, killed prisoners and captives of war. All of these were also Hebrew rites practiced by those ten tribes of Israel."[16] In his *Book of the Gods and Rites* (written between 1574 and 1576, also unpublished until the nineteenth century), a description of Mexica rituals, Durán noted that their elders "preached words regarding the law and ritual, similar to the Ten Commandments," including directives to fear and honor the gods, honor feast days, and not to kill, commit adultery, steal, or bear false witness.[17] If the biblical East had the Tower of Babel, the Americas had the lofty Pyramid of Cholula, and pagan priests at Huexotzinco maintained an ark filled with holy objects, a version of the Ark of the Covenant of the Israelites. Both cultures purified themselves by bathing and were subject to dietary prohibitions. Listening attentively to their origin myths, Durán recognized in their legends a history of a chosen people that endured perilous pilgrimages in order to reach their promised land, the Valley of Mexico, their equivalent of Canaan.[18] On the basis of 2 Esdras 13:40–47, which describes how the Ten Tribes of Israel were transported to a remote region beyond the Euphrates, Durán argued that from there, through Tartary, they came to the lands of Mexico, correlating Mexica accounts of their origins in the northern region of Aztlán with what could be extrapolated from biblical history. Durán thus formulated an Amerasian vision of a migration eastward from the holy land into the new world.

Ophir in Peru

As in numerous other cases, the relative position of India played a role in Durán's understanding. If the Apostles had gone forth to spread the word of God to all parts of the world, which one of them had reached Mexico? Certain details about the life and personage of Topiltzin-Quetzalcoatl, the mythological ruler of the Toltecs (not to be confused with the Meso-american plumed serpent deity, Quetzalcoatl) were taken as blurry traces of the Apostle Thomas, who was known to have proselytized in India.[19] According to Mexica tradition, the Toltecs had maintained control over the central valley of Mexico in the centuries before the Mexica arrival, and the Toltec ruler Topiltzin had originally come from a foreign land. He had performed miracles, had been revered as a holy man, had fasted and abstained from eating meat, had built shrines and knelt before them, and had been followed by a group of disciples. After being persecuted in Mexico, he left the land in the direction of the eastern sea. For Durán, this was a hitherto unknown episode in the Indian mission of Saint Thomas:

> [God] cannot have left [the Mexica] without a preacher of the Gospel. And if this is true, that preacher was Topiltzin, who came to this land. According to the story, he was a sculptor who carved admirable images in stone. We read that the glorious apostle Saint Thomas was a master craftsman in the same art. We also know that this apostle was a preacher to the Indians, but that, having become discouraged there, he asked Christ . . . to send him wherever He wished except to the Indians.[20]

To confirm his hypothesis, Durán sought out documents said to have been bequeathed to the local population by Topiltzin himself at the time he had passed through the region; Durán was told, however, that such evidence, illegible to the Indians, had been burned. "I was sorry to hear this, because the manuscript could have shed light on our suspicion that [they] might have been the Holy Gospel in Hebrew."[21]

Durán was not alone in developing such theories. The cosmographer Johannes Schöner noted that the inhabitants of Brazil had "put the name of Thomas in their books," and the idea of a Brazilian mission of Saint Thomas persisted through the sixteenth century.[22] The American residence of Saint Thomas was built on the idea that the range of the earliest biblical history extended to include the new world. In Deuteronomy and other books from the Old Testament, God told his people to multiply; he predicted that a punishment would befall them because of their wickedness and idolatries, and unleashed a scourge upon them "while others were to take possession of their estates." The American peoples' long migration, followed by their propagation, idolatry,

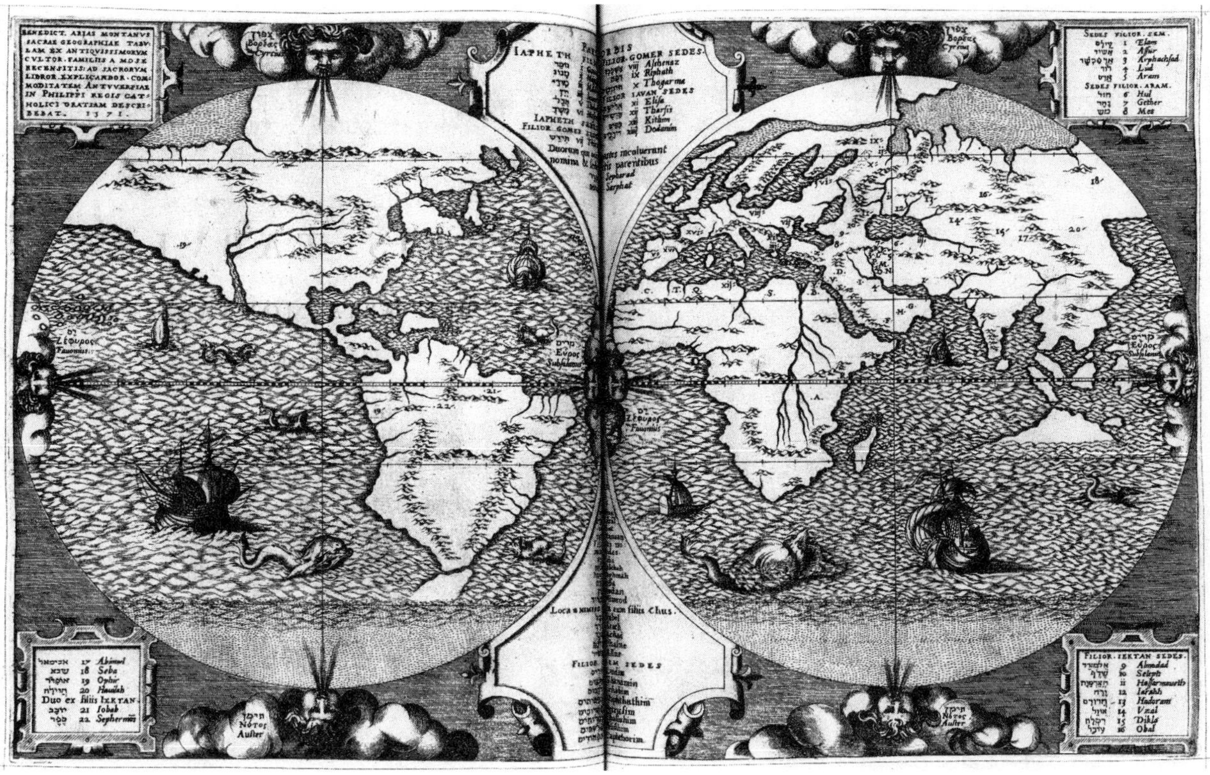

13.2 Did Ophir, the descendant of Noah through the ancestral line of Shem (as described in Genesis 10:29), eventually settle in Peru? Benito Arias Montano, *Sacrae geographiae tabulam ex antiquissimorum cultor*, copper engraving, 53.3 × 32 cm (Antwerp, 1572).

and subsequent punishment by the Spanish (and in particular Cortés) all offered "sufficient proof that these Indians descend from Hebrews."[23]

Around the same time that Durán became intrigued by the many similarities between the Mexica and the ancient Israelites, his contemporary, Benito Arías Montano, expressed a similar understanding of biblical history in a map that depicted the Israelite migrations around the globe.[24] Arías Montano, eminent among biblical scholars, antiquarians, and orientalists in sixteenth- century Spain, was appointed as the first director of the Escorial Library by King Philip II, who sent him to Antwerp in 1568 to be the chief editor of the *Biblia Regia* (1569–73), otherwise known as the Plantin Polyglot Bible, an eight-volume edition of the Hebrew Bible and New Testament in their original languages. Volume eight contains a double-hemisphere world map entitled *Sacrae geographiae tabulam ex antiquissimorum cultor* (1572) that depicts the postdiluvian repopulating of the earth by the descendants of the three sons of Noah, Shem, Ham, and Japeth (fig. 13.2). Arías Montano's map, like many sixteenth-century European maps, shows a land bridge between Asia and America; the cartouches in the center and corners of the map indicate where the lineages of Noah's sons ended up as they traveled around the world, including those who arrived in what are today the Americas.

Arías Montano identified the gold-bearing region of Ophir with Peru, a claim for which he found direct philological proof in the account of the building of the Jewish temple in 2 Chronicles 3:6, which states that the temple's gold "was the gold of Parvaim." Parvaim had traditionally been translated to mean "a mark of high quality" (*probatissimum*), but Arías Montano identified the word with Ophir, the source of Solomon's gold as described in 1 Kings 9:28 ("They sailed to Ophir and brought back 420 talents of gold, which they delivered to King Solomon"). In addition, he proposed that parvaim meant "double Peru" or "the dual of Peru," thus interpreting 2 Chronicles 3:6 to mean that the gold of the temple in Jerusalem "was the gold of Peru and Peru." Such an understanding allowed for the placement of two Ophirs on his world map, the map's number nineteen, located on the western coasts of what are today North and South America.[25]

As Arías Montano's cartouches tell us, Ophir was both a place and a person; it is both the location of Solomon's mines and one of the sons of Iektan (Joktan) from the line of Shem as described in Genesis 10.[26] He argues that the three sons of Iektan—Ophir, Havilah, and Iobab (numbers nineteen, twenty-one, and twenty-two on the map, listed in the bottom left cartouche)—traveled much farther east across Asia than the other progeny of Shem, eventually reaching what is today South America. Thus, it was possible to argue for the presence of the lands later labeled New Spain in biblical history by following the ancestral line of Noah's son Shem. Taking up this influential line of thought, the Franciscan missionary Bernardino de Sahagún claimed in his *Conquest of New Spain* (1585) that "now it is held to be certain that the fleet of King Solomon reached Peru, and also at the island of Santo Domingo, to gather gold for the building of the temple."[27]

Not all were convinced by this association of Ophir and Peru. The Flemish cartographer Abraham Ortelius, for instance, found the connection tenuous at best, and the Dutch philologist and the historian Joseph Scaliger judged Arías Montano's arguments "completely stupid."[28] The Jesuit missionary and naturalist José de Acosta's *Natural and Moral History of the Indies* (Seville, 1590) offered a sharp refutation of Arías Montano's ideas. As noted in chapter 12, Acosta insisted on differentiating between America and Asia, regularly using the terms America, East Indies, and West Indies to indicate their separateness.[29] According to Acosta, Peru could not be Ophir; the riches of the Americas had "nothing worthy of the praises written in the scriptures. Nor do I think it accurate to believe that Solomon should have sent his fleets to this farthest land, leaving behind the riches of the East Indies." Instead, for Acosta, the name of Peru most likely derived from the Spanish interpretation of the name of a local river.[30] Acosta clearly grasped the vastness of the body of water separating the continents: "Solomon's fleet could not have come here without crossing all of the East Indies, all of China, and another infinitely broad sea."[31] In addition, according to Acosta, a variety of cultural dissimilarities argued against the thesis; the ancient Israelites, for instance, used writing, whereas in his estimation, "among the Indians there is no trace of this" (see chapter 14). The Israelites had used money, which American Native peoples did not, nor was there evidence of circumcision in the Americas.[32]

However, Amerasian thinking persists in Acosta's understanding of the people and nature of the Indies, East and West. Acosta likens the maize of Peru to millet from India, compares plantains in the Americas to those in Italy and Spain, which had come "from Greece, and to Greece from Asia" (noting that plantains "require a great deal of humidity and a very hot climate"), and observes that grains are used to make fermented beverages in the lands stretching from China and the Philippines to Peru.[33] Along similar lines, Acosta describes the production of cotton as "one of the best things in the Indies, for it serves the inhabitants for clothing in place of linen and wool; it grows in hot places, much of it in the valleys and on the coasts of Peru, in New Spain, in the Philippines and China."[34] Describing the Peruvian worship of a supreme creator of heaven and earth named Viracocha, he remarks that "the same belief exists, after their fashion, in the Mexicans and the Chinese."[35] As discussed in chapter 12, despite his clear understanding of the separation of the continents and though he was skeptical of any biblical connection to the Americas, Acosta continually emphasizes the commonalities of the Indies. For Acosta, calling them all the Indies was not a merely arbitrary common designation.

European cosmographers and antiquarians continued to consider the origins of the Indigenous peoples of the Americas for centuries to come: discussions that often reflected and constructed persistent strains of Amerasian thinking. Gregorio García's *Origen de los indios del Nuevo Mundo e Indias Occidentales* (1607), widely read well into the eighteenth century, offered an encyclopedic summary of all the then current hypotheses about the origins of Indigenous new world peoples, and Samuel Purchas continued to refute the arguments of Arías Montano in his *Purchas His Pilgrimes* (1625).[36] The Flemish cartographer Jodocus Hondius the Elder's 1608 world map *A New and Accurate Geographic and Hydrographic Description of the World* (*Nova et exacta totius orbis terrarum descriptio geographica et hydrographica*) argued that it was "more plausible that this region [the Americas] began to be populated from the northern parts of Europe or Asia (with which America is contiguous or at any rate separated from them by a narrow strait)."[37] The new migration theories expanded the inhabited earth beyond the ancient *oikoumene* and also imagined vast voyages by land and sea in deepest antiquity. Early modern biblical scholars and antiquarians, much like cartographers of the period, employed a variety of Amerasian configurations to make the Americans part of the same order as other humans. The lands inhabited by American Indians, for Durán, Acosta, and others, must be an extension of the known, human world rather than an *orbis alterius*, simply another world. Such an understanding allowed discussions of theories of the universal origins of humanity to proliferate well into the seventeenth century. Even when observers only established analogies between the ancient Hebrews and Indians, as in the case of the feather capes that began this chapter, this worked to locate Indians in a particular place along the path to salvation. Indians were idolaters, but once baptized they could be saved.

• • •

Excursus: The Grand Overland Migration

Although he rejected the idea that the American Indians were descendants of tribes of Israelites, Acosta accepted and carefully argued the theory that they came to America in a momentous overland migration from Asia. No doubt encouraged by the many sixteenth-century maps that show a land bridge between Asia and the New World (see chapter 11), he imagined "that one part of the earth and the other must join and continue, or at least they come very close," and in that case "we would have to say that they crossed not by sailing on the sea but by walking on land. And they followed this way quite unthinkingly, changing places and lands little by little, with some of them settling in the lands already discovered and others seeking new ones, so that in the course of time they arrived and swelled the lands of the Indies with many nations and peoples and languages."[38] More than a century after Acosta, the Danish navigator Vitus Bering discovered the strait that now bears his name in 1728 and eventually twentieth-century research showed that a land bridge in that region, now known as Beringia, was exposed during the last ice age due to falling water levels produced by the emergence of great ice sheets, allowing people to cross over.[39] More recent findings show that the land bridge became passable only about 12,600 years ago, long after evidence of settlements farther south, suggesting that the first migrations as well as later ones occurred by coastal, water-based movement around the Pacific Rim.[40]

The consequential difference between Acosta's theory and the theories being argued over in the last years is that for Acosta and the other sixteenth-century commentators the Amerasian migration did not happen in a vastly remote Upper Paleolithic but within the biblical frame of postdiluvian antiquity. Whatever their origins, these people inhabited the world of antiquity and carried some of that world with them into the new Indies. Of course, theorists differed as to how connected these remote migrants were to the more advanced forms of ancient civilization. The Jesuit Bernabé Cobo, who worked in Peru in the first half of the seventeenth century, emphasized the barbarity of American Indigenous life and its distance from any ancient knowledge,[41] while the defendants of the Israelite theory posited quite a bit of baggage filled with traditional wisdom and ritual knowledge. Moderates like Acosta saw in various practices of the Indians an inheritance of aspects of East Asian culture carried over through the migration. Writing in the early eighteenth century, Joseph-François Lafitau, Acosta's Jesuit heir, embraced the theory of overland migration and proposed a further hypothesis of ancient connectivity by pointing out would-be traces of ancient Greek culture in certain aspects of Iroquois and Huron life.[42]

By the eighteenth century, the modern view had come to prevail that the first peoples in America had migrated overland from Siberia. Yet this history of migration was now understood to be even more recent, part of a history of cultural diffusion that might have brought Christian ideas and images to Mexico in the first Christian centuries. Noting Christian-seeming elements in Mexica cosmogonies, Alexander von Humboldt in 1810 still deliberated over the long-held view that Saint Thomas may have left traces in the Mexica figure of Quetzalcoatl, and with more confidence he proposed that Christian ideas and rituals may have reached America in the early medieval centuries as a result of the spread of Nestorian ideas through northeast Asia, eventually reaching Mexica culture through "the inhabitants of that northerly region from which the Toltec emerged, and which we must consider as the *officina virorum* [smithy of men] of the new world."[43]

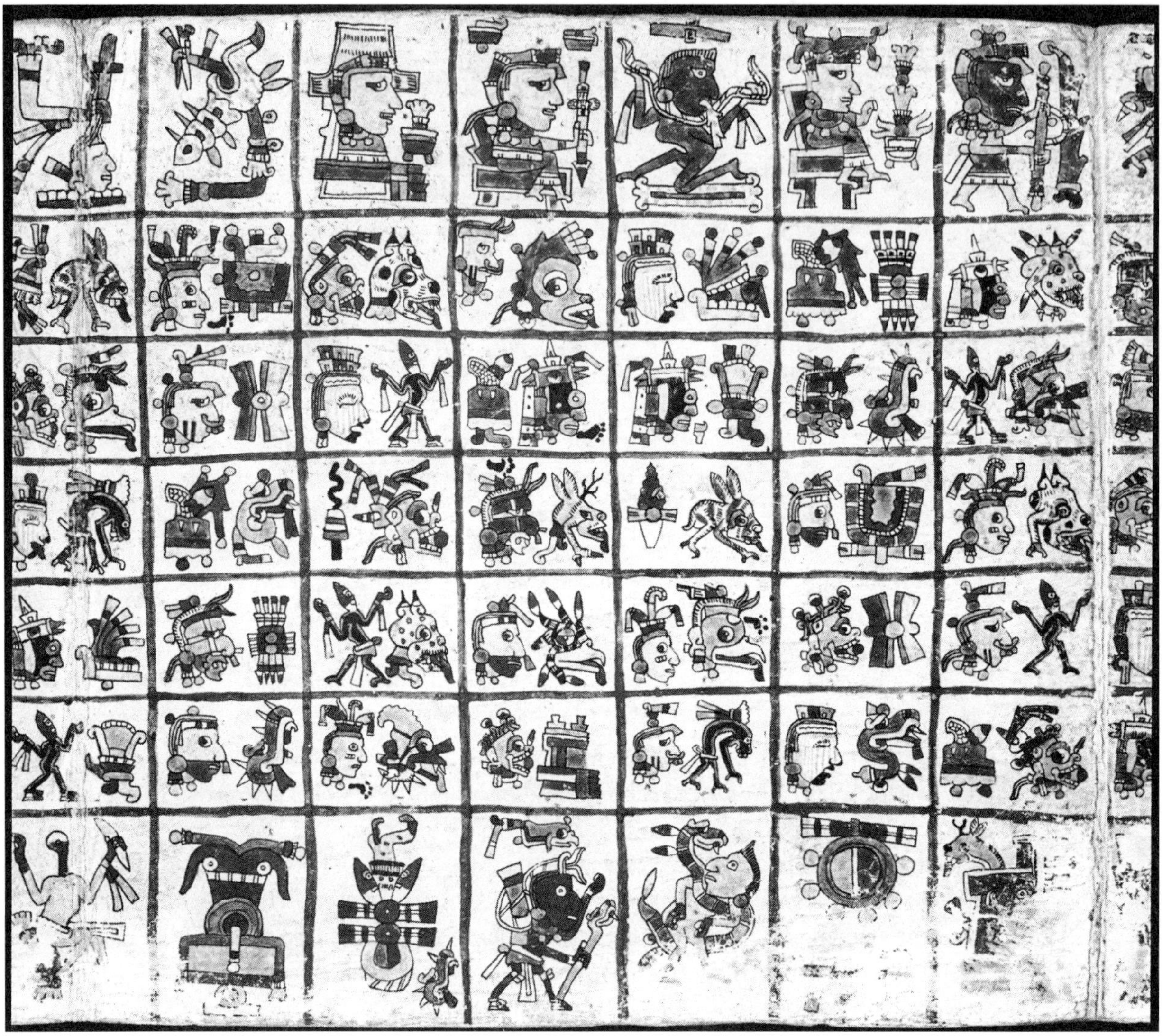

14.1 The Cospi Codex: painting, writing, or primordial language? Biblioteca Universitaria of Bologna, MS 4093. Painted on animal skin (probably deer) prepared with gesso, 18 × 18 cm, probably made in the region of Puebla and Tlaxcala (1500?).

FOURTEEN

Amerasian Hieroglyphics

A Book from China Becomes a Book from Mexico

A painted screenfold from the new world arrived in the Italian city of Bologna, probably in 1533 but possibly earlier, and it remains there today. An instrument of divination and an aid to ritual meant to be read aloud, the manuscript begins with a *tonalpohualli* ("Count of the Days"), or 260-day divinatory calendar (fig. 14.1). This is followed by a section representing five nefarious aspects of Tlahuizcalpantecuhtli ("Lord of the House of Dawn"), or Venus as Morningstar, shown in skeletal form after having spent time in the underworld and now throwing arrows at five successive targets: the maize god Cinteotl, the water goddess Chalchiuhtlicue, a water mountain (signifying community), a throne (signifying royal power) (fig. 14.2), and a jaguar holding a human heart (signifying the young warriors), all with devastating effects on the fabric of society. The third section shows four gods burning incense at temples (fig. 14.3), with omens specific to the twenty days tabulated at the page's left margin. The reverse side of the screenfold, painted by another hand and probably later and in a different locale, presents a series of gods, prescribing the nature and number of offerings to be made to each.[1]

In the mid-seventeenth century, long after its arrival in Italy, the manuscript was rebound with a parchment cover and inscribed with the record of a Christmas gift: "Book of Mexico given by Lord Count Valerio Zani to Lord Marquis Cospi the day xxvi December MDLXV" (fig. 14.4). Count Valerio Zani was a member of Bologna's premiere literary academy, the Accademia dei Gelati, and also an editor of travel writings from around the world.[2] Ferdinando Cospi, who received the manuscript, was an antiquarian and naturalist then collecting material into his Museo Cospiano, later to be given to the city of Bologna. Zani's precious gift was meant to go into his friend's Museo, a compendium of naturalia and artificialia from different parts of the globe.

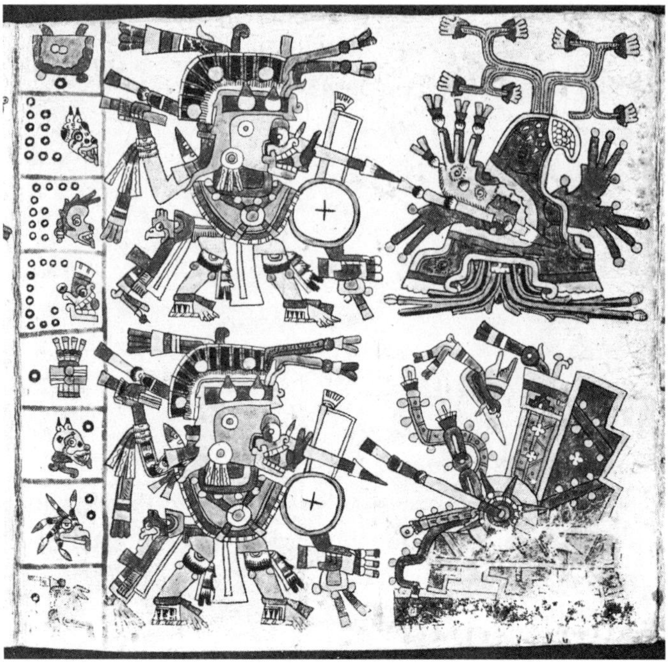

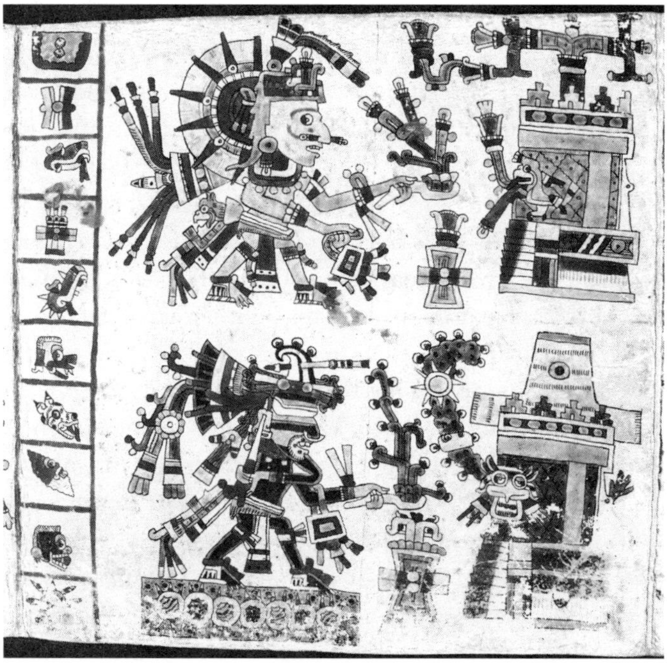

14.2 and 14.3 The Cospi Codex: Venus rising wreaks havoc on rulers and resources; and gods burning incense at temples. Biblioteca Universitaria of Bologna, MS 4093. Photo: Luca Sgamellotti—© Biblioteca Universitaria di Bologna.

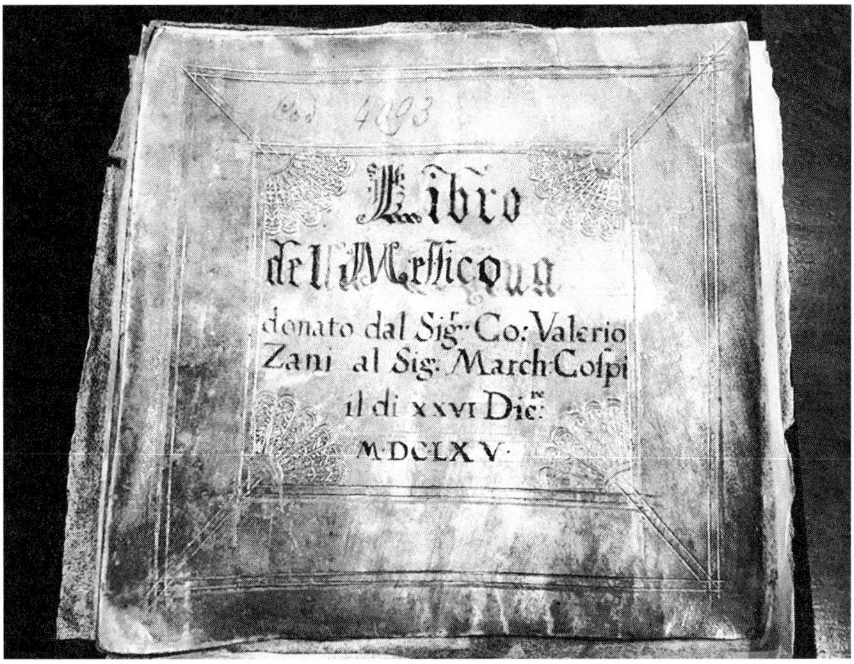

14.4 The Cospi Codex. The European parchment cover carries the inscription "Libro del Messico donato dal Sig[no]r Co[nte] Valerio Zani al Sig. March[ese] Cospi il di xxvi Dic[emb]re MDLXV." Photo: Alexander Nagel.

The inscription on the cover is a bit messy, with overwriting that suggests some hesitation about what title to give the book. As can still be seen with the naked eye, originally it read *Libro della China*. Using digital means, we can reconstruct the process by which the book from China became a book from Mexico (fig. 14.5):

In 1667, two years after the gift of this "Book of China" was made, a preliminary catalogue of Cospi's collection lists it as "a book come from China, with various hieroglyphs." It was only ten years later, in 1677, that the antiquarian Lorenzo Legati produced an expanded catalogue, now describing the book's contents as "hieroglyphs from Mexico" (fig. 14.6).[3] In it, the codex is illustrated by the scene of Tlahuizcalpantecuhtli attacking the throne (see fig. 14.2), but in the 1677 publication the god is shown in reverse (as might be expected in a printed format) yet the throne is re-reversed into its original orientation. Europeans did not understand these images. The smaller vignette embedded in the text at left is from the manuscript's earlier section, the *tonalpohualli* (visible in one of the compartments of figure 14.1). In any event, 1677 is probably the moment when it was decided that the title on the cover needed to be rubbed out

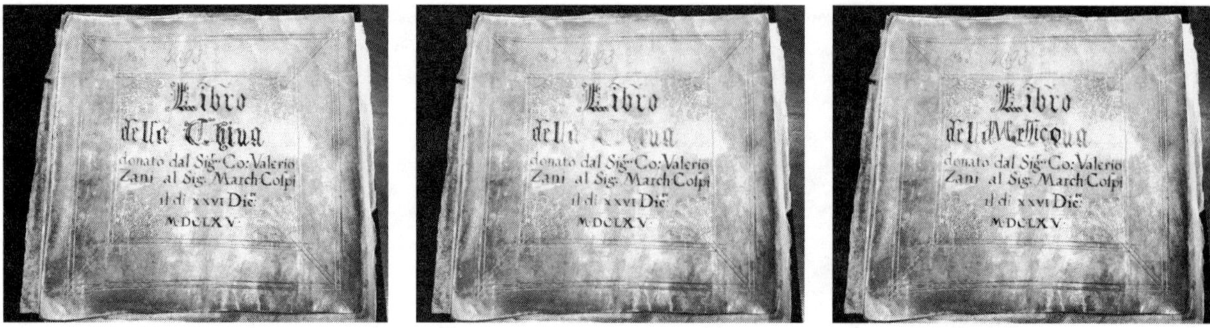

14.5 ***A Libro della China*** **becomes a** ***Libro del Messico.*** Digital reconstruction of the original and erased state by Amelia Saul on the basis of a photo of the codex by Alexander Nagel.

and reinscribed. Yet the original provenance, *della China*, was never fully erased. It remains a hovering identity.

The idea that such books originated in Asia was longstanding and hard to shake. Another Mesoamerican manuscript, now known as the Vienna Codex, was given to Pope Clement VII sometime in the 1520s and was described not long after (between 1537 and 1557, by Johann Albrecht Widmanstetter, formerly secretary of Clement VII) as "a book of hieroglyphs from South India . . . with little bells, also from India, and a coverlet made of parrot feathers."[4] When Widmanstetter says the Vienna Codex is from India Meridionalis, he does not mean southern India in our sense—the southern end of the subcontinent corresponding roughly to the provinces of Kerala and Tamil Nadu—but rather a much farther and mostly imaginary peninsula at the extreme limit of Asia, beyond even the Golden Chersonese or Malay Peninsula. On Martin Waldseemüller's 1507 map, India Meridionalis, which hosts Cattigara, Ptolemy's most remote Asian port, is shown as a peninsula at the extreme east edge of the world, in fact not many degrees of longitude away from the newly discovered land he famously labeled America on the map's western edge (see fig. 2.7). Alessandro Zorzi's early sixteenth-century map drawings position localities encountered by Columbus on his fourth voyage (Veragua, Cariai, etc.) on the Atlantic coast of a peninsula that carries Cattigara on its Asian side (see fig. 6.1a–b), an Amerasian isthmus-hinge.

In the next decades, several maps and globes pushed Ptolemy's south Indian port of Cattigara farther into America, to the coast of Peru (see chapter 11). To imagine in the 1530s, therefore, that the parrot feather-covered Vienna Codex came from India Meridionalis was in fact not very far off from placing it in America, because at that time India Meridionalis charted an extremity where India, China, and America converged. A

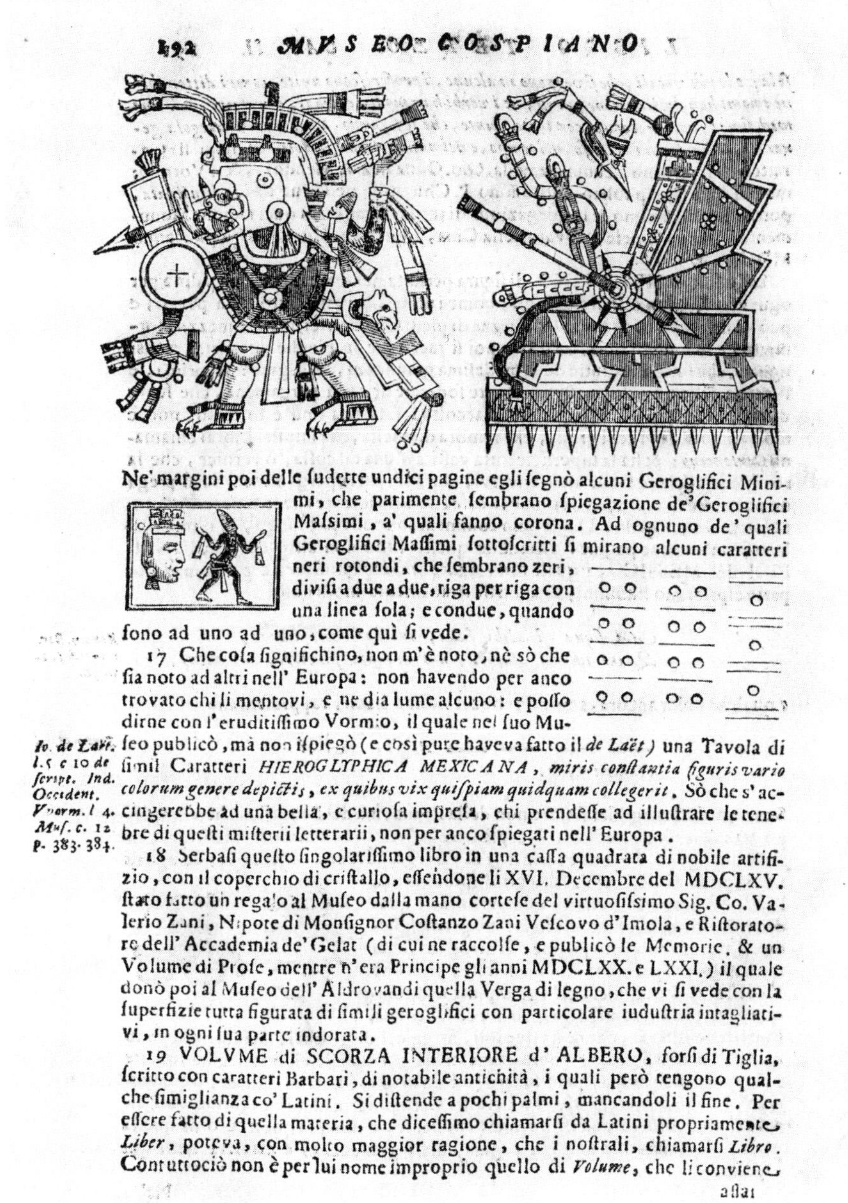

192 MUSEO COSPIANO

Ne' margini poi delle ſudette undici pagine egli ſegnò alcuni Geroglifici Minimi, che parimente ſembrano ſpiegazione de' Geroglifici Maſsimi, a' quali fanno corona. Ad ognuno de' quali Geroglifici Maſſimi ſottoſcritti ſi mirano alcuni caratteri neri rotondi, che ſembrano zeri, diviſi a due a due, riga per riga con una linea ſola; e condue, quando ſono ad uno ad uno, come quì ſi vede.

17 Che coſa ſignifichino, non m'è noto, nè sò che ſia noto ad altri nell' Europa: non havendo per anco trovato chi li mentovi, e ne dia lume alcuno: e poſſo dirne con l'eruditiſſimo Vormio, il quale nel ſuo Museo publicò, mà non iſpiegò (e così pure haveva fatto il *de Laët*) una Tavola di ſimil Caratteri *HIEROGLYPHICA MEXICANA*, *miris conſtantia figuris vario colorum genere depictis, ex quibus vix quiſpiam quidquam collegerit*. Sò che s'accingerebbe ad una bella, e curioſa impreſa, chi prendeſſe ad illuſtrare le tenebre di queſti miſterii letterarii, non per anco ſpiegati nell' Europa.

Io. de Laët. l. 5 c. 10 de ſcript. Ind. Occident. Vorm. l. 4. Muſ. c. 12 p. 383. 384.

18 Serbaſi queſto ſingolariſſimo libro in una caſſa quadrata di nobile artifizio, con il coperchio di criſtallo, eſſendone li XVI. Decembre del MDCLXV. ſtato fatto un regalo al Muſeo dalla mano corteſe del virtuoſiſsimo Sig. Co. Valerio Zani, Nipote di Monſignor Coſtanzo Zani Veſcovo d'Imola, e Riſtoratore dell' Accademia de' Gelati (di cui ne raccolſe, e publicò le Memorie, & un Volume di Proſe, mentre n'era Principe gli anni MDCLXX. e LXXI.) il quale donò poi al Muſeo dell' Aldrovandi quella Verga di legno, che vi ſi vede con la ſuperfizie tutta figurata di ſimili geroglifici con particolare induſtria intagliativi, in ogni ſua parte indorata.

19 VOLVME di SCORZA INTERIORE d' ALBERO, forſi di Tiglia, ſcritto con caratteri Barbari, di notabile antichità, i quali però tengono qualche ſimiglianza co' Latini. Si diſtende a pochi palmi, mancandoli il fine. Per eſſere fatto di quella materia, che diceſſimo chiamarſi da Latini propriamente *Liber*, poteva, con molto maggior ragione, che i noſtrali, chiamarſi *Libro*. Contuttociò non è per lui nome improprio quello di *Volume*, che li conviene

aſſai

14.6 The Cospi Codex in print. Lorenzo Legati, *Museo Cospiano annesso a quello del famoso Ulisse Aldrovandi e donato alla sua patria dall'illustrissimo signor Ferdinando Cospi* (Bologna, 1677), p. 192.

further reason for associating the Vienna Codex with an as yet unknown extreme fringe of Asia was that it had come to Pope Clement VII (probably when he was Cardinal Giulio de' Medici) as a gift from king Manuel I of Portugal, the modern king most renowned for explorations to the eastern Indies. Later, in 1598, the manuscript was described more briefly as a "book that opens on the front and back with all sorts of Indian figures, not unlike hieroglyphic writing."[5]

Living Hieroglyphs

The idea that these painted books from the new world originated in Asia goes back to the earliest moments of their European reception. As we saw in chapter 7, in 1522 the Venetian ambassador Gasparo Contarini, reports from Spain to the Venetian Doge of Venice on Hernán Cortés's discovery of great cities inhabited by people who were "*molto civili*" (despite being idolaters and eating their enemies) and who "do not have characters for letters, but write the more necessary things using figures of animals and other things (*scriveno qualche cosa più necessaria con figure di animali over altro*), in the way the Egyptians did in ancient times."[6] Whatever his understanding of the geography, his framework for understanding this culture was Asian, and in this his approach was fairly typical.

In 1539, the famed scholar of Oriental languages Ambrogio wrote of having visited Bologna and of having seen there "a book that had come from India, covered with tiger skin, in which several figures of men (and if I remember correctly) various other things as well as figures of animals were depicted"—almost certainly the Cospi Codex. As a specialist in Syriac and other near Eastern languages, Ambrogio believed, unusually for his time, that the manuscript displayed at least in part an alphabetic language, not hieroglyphs. He noted subsidiary characters near the depictions (visible in figures 14.2 and 14.3) that he believed were letters. (Sounding a complaint familiar to scholars the world over, he claimed that if the owner hadn't denied him the opportunity to make a copy of it, he "would have been able to construct a new alphabet."[7])

Since this was almost certainly the Cospi Codex, Ambrogio was describing its original animal skin cover, before Zani in the seventeenth century gave it a new parchment cover with his dedicatory inscription. That he considered it tiger skin (it was probably jaguar) is of a piece with his understanding that it was "from India." If read by the conventions of modern metageography, according to which America has nothing to do with India, then Ambrogio was making a mistake about both the skin and the provenance, as tigers are not native to what we call the Americas. If, however, we read Ambrogio within the prevalent geographical model of the period as reviewed in chapters 11 and 12, according to which the land discovered by Cortés was an extension of *magna Asia* not fully understood, then Ambrogio did not err in calling it tiger skin. Moreover, he was not aware of the modern taxonomy according to which jaguars, leopards, tigers, and lions are distinguished as species classed under the genus of *Panthera*; it is possible that for Ambrogio and for others at the time *tygris* was the generic, encompassing term. For example, when the historian Paolo Giovio described a book with "hieroglyphic figures" from the territory conquered by Cortés as a volume "made of large sheets folded back, and bound in a tiger-skin cover [*indanaiato di tigre*]," he was probably also using the term *tigre* generically.[8] In the 1612 first edition of the dictionary of the Accademia della Crusca, the term *indanaiato* is used to describe "the skin of an animal that is spotted with small round spots, like those of the lynx, the leopard, or the tiger"[9]—or the new world jaguar, often enough called tiger in the period. The term *indanaiato* meant literally "Indianed," given the strong associations of these large cats with India. For the Orientalist Ambrogio and the historian Giovio in the 1530s, these books—with their tiger-skin covers and their picture-based language—were *indanaiati*, culturally and materially connected to India, an expansive India recently expanded farther than antiquity had known.

The Bolognese humanist and historian Leandro Alberti similarly described books and other spectacular transatlantic items brought to Pope Clement VII in Bologna on March 3, 1533. He mentions pieces of ceremonial clothing woven of multicolored feathers, perhaps the very feather cape that remained in the Medici collection and is now a centerpiece of the Museo di Antropologia ed Etnologia of Florence (see fig. 13.1), and also "some very finely painted books, which looked like hieroglyphic figures, by which they communicate with each other as we do through letters."[10] Most scholars believe the Cospi Codex was one of these, though it could also have arrived earlier. Alberti mentions that these spectacular items were brought by a Dominican friar "who came from the New Indies or rather the New World." This might sound as if Alberti sees these as Mexican or American objects rather than Asian ones, but in fact these terms were not necessarily mutually exclusive.[11] As we have repeatedly seen, the term "new world" carried Asian associations as much as American ones, and the place name New Indies or New India was understood in the middle decades of the sixteenth century as an extension of a highly expansive and multipartite India that reached and included America. That is, one could use the term Mexico or even America and yet consider these to be subregions of an Asian macroregion, whether Magna Asia or India Nova or simply India (see chapters 2 and 12).

Around the time that the Cospi Codex arrived in Bologna, a 1532 pamphlet published in the same city of Bologna presented letters written by Franciscan missionaries in Mexico, describing them as having come "from the extreme ends of the world, from the Indies in greater Asia (magna Asia)" even as they are clear they are writing from the city of "Messico" in "HUKETAN sive nova Hispania (Yucatán or New Spain)."[12] Both the pamphlet and Alberti's account are referring to a newly discovered world at the limit of the known world, placing it in a not fully understood extension of the larger Indian expanse. To be at the limits of the known world was what defined the new world. That Alberti understood this new world to be connected in some way to the old is clear from another part of his account, where he interprets Mesoamerican featherwork and stone knives as guides to the physical appearance of the tabernacle of Moses and the flint knives that Moses proposed for use in circumcision, associations with the Exodus story that match the Egyptian associations of the hieroglyphs found in the books arriving from New Spain (see chapter 13).

To call the images in these books hieroglyphs—literally "sacred inscriptions"—was to acknowledge that they were not just pictures to be looked at but symbols to be deciphered and read. Even Ambrogio, who did not see them all as hieroglyphs, was convinced that at least some of the images formed parts of an alphabetic language. Like his contemporaries, Ambrogio understood that these images could not be merely pictures; they had to be a language. The determination on the part of Europeans to see these recognizable depictions of human figures, animals, and objects as forms of language, and as a primordial or at least ancient language at that, speaks to a powerful ideological commitment to see the newly revealed lands in both ancient and Asian terms.

European culture understood hieroglyphs to be a lost form of language, developed in ancient Egypt and then spread through the Asian world, a language not based on the conventions of humans but on the forms of nature, the God-imprinted "book of the world."[13] The European scholarly world was thus excited by the discovery in 1419 of a late antique manuscript by a certain Horus Apollo (condensed into Horapollo) that purported to explain Egyptian symbolic writing, a treatise that was soon disseminated and eventually published in printed editions.[14] When, a century later, Europeans began to encounter hieroglyphs in the new world—and made by living people!—the remote past became suddenly present.[15] Like the featherwork items that sometimes accompanied them, these brightly painted books, worn at their edges by repeated and recent ritual use, were spectacular material evidence of the present-tense antiquity of the new world. To call their images hieroglyphs was to confirm that they belonged to an ancient and, as we will see, Asian lifestream that had survived in the new world, which thus revealed itself to be a very old world. During the same decades that European collectors and scholars marveled at these books from Mexico, some of the first Chinese texts also arrived in Europe, prompting comparison between them.[16] New worlds East and West mingled and sometimes merged in the scholarly conversations of Europe in the sixteenth century.

The correspondences between Asian and American hieroglyphs preoccupied commentators for well over a century, yielding among other things Count Valerio Zani's 1665 inscription naming his Mesoamerican manuscript *Libro della China*. Writing in the later sixteenth century, the Jesuit José de Acosta distinguished between cultures that use letters and writing, such as we find in Latin, Greek, Hebrew, and "in many other nations," where the signs refer to words, and those that use either pictures or characters (or what he sometimes calls ciphers), where the figures refer to things. Remarkably, he notes, all the recently encountered cultures of "Indians" (and here he brings together Peruvian, Mexican, Chinese, and Japanese) belong to the second category: "no nation of Indians that have been discovered in our time uses letters or writing but rather use the two other modes, images and figures, and I mean this not only for the Indians of Peru and New Spain but also in part as well for the Japanese and Chinese."[17] For Walter Mignolo, "Acosta is unique in his efforts to draw the peoples of the East Indies into a comparison and classification with the Inca and the Aztecs."[18] Acosta is indeed singular in the subtlety and rigor of his thinking, yet the evidence shows that in seeing similarities across difference among the "Indians" of America and Asia he conformed to a larger European tradition (see chapter 12). Nuanced in his assessment of the relation, never simply identifying East and West Indians, Acosta's authority then ensured that the basic framework of Amerasian comparison would persist through the seventeenth century. Several decades later, the polymath Athanasius Kircher, also a Jesuit, built on Acosta's analysis, observing that there were three cultures still in existence that used hieroglyphs in something like the way the Egyptians had done in antiquity: the Brahmanic culture of India, the Chinese, and the Mexican.[19] Despite the vastness of the Pacific ocean, there was in his view a cultural commonality extending from Asia to Mexico, one rooted in antiquity. The new worlds both East and West were something close to living relics of the ancient world.

The comparable cultural developments of Asia and America could be seen as independently arising phenomena, remnants of different ancient lifeworlds that could be compared, but most scholars of the period preferred to take the comparability as evidence of cultural diffusion in antiquity, an Egyptian influence that reached through Asia to America. Writing in the 1630s, Kircher imagined a history of sweeping dissemination, contending that "the Indians and other Asians received their wisdom from the Egyptians, as demonstrated by the common worship of heavenly bodies and animals in ancient Egypt, India, China, Japan, Tartary, Cathay, and even America."[20] The idea that "even America" was known in the ancient world was not a new one. In his widely read treatise of 1590, Acosta reviewed in several early chapters the most salient Greco-Roman and biblical evidence for ancient contact with the western Indies.[21] For many sixteenth-century commentators, the American new world was not in fact new, but, like Asia, newly encountered in modern times.

New World as Egyptian Diaspora

The most carefully developed theory of ancient Egyptian diffusionism through Asia and to America came from the Paduan antiquarian Lorenzo Pignoria, who published in 1615 a treatise "On the Images of the Indian Gods," which came as an addendum to Vincenzo Cartari's popular guidebook *The Images of the Gods of the Ancients.* Invoking the widely discussed theory of Arías Montano that biblical Ophir was to be identified with Peru (see chapter 13), Pignoria asserted that, like the Israelites, the enormously powerful Egyptians must also have had knowledge of these lands. He thus set out to find traces of Egyptian culture in Chinese, Japanese, and American artifacts in the cabinets of friends and patrons.[22] For the Mexican gods, he had figures copied after a sixteenth-century manuscript in the Vatican, the Codex Ríos, an important early compilation and explanation of Mexica iconography of the 1560s (fig. 14.7a–b).[23] Pignoria draws his image and explanation from a page describing the god Ometeotl in the aspect of Tonacatecuhtli in the Codex Ríos, where the god is placed in his originary residence Omeyocan (*Homeyoca*), though Pignoria misunderstood the place name at the top of the page in the Ríos manuscript to be the name of the god. Unlike his source, Pignoria includes in his illustration smaller, oval, gemlike images of the Egyptian god Osiris, in order to show the derivation of the Mexican god from the Egyptian one. Pignoria's 1615 new world addendum to Cartari's popular guidebook, expanded in a second edition of 1626, was included in successive editions, such as this one from 1647, making it a highly influential account of Amerasian diffusionism.

He occasionally notices Christian elements in the Mexican gods, for example in the figure of Quetzalcoatl, who is shown with ornaments that include crosses, evidence that the merciful Lord had "made a wide path to prepare the way for the Gospel in some of these lands."[24] But he then returns to his theme of Egyptian influence. Occasionally, Pignoria

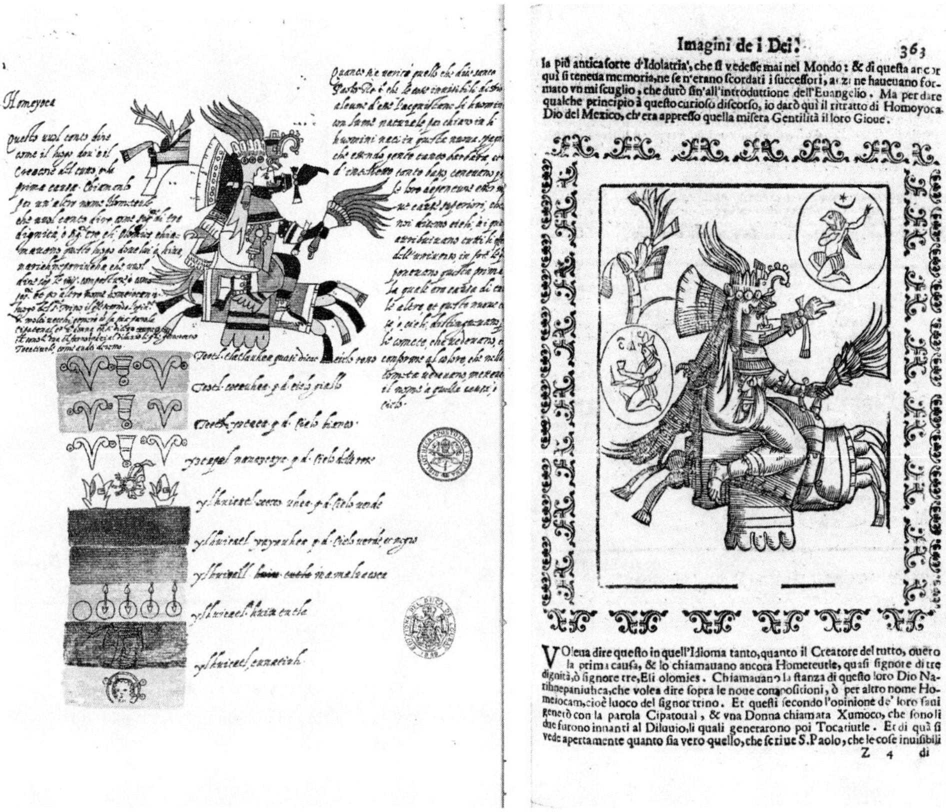

14.7a–b "Homeyoca," the Osiris of Mexico. (a) Codex Ríos, Vatican, Biblioteca Apostolica, Vat. lat. 3738, fol. 1v, after facsimile edition (Graz: Akademische Druck, 1979), 46 × 24 cm (after 1566). (b) Lorenzo Pignoria's *Aggionta all'Imagini del Cartari*, with woodcuts by Filippo Ferroverde, in Vincenzo Cartari, *Imagini delli Dei de gl'Antichi* (Venice, 1647), p. 363.

gets confused about provenance, for example calling a mask from Florida an "idol from Mexico," which he then compares to an Egyptian figure (fig. 14.8a–b). That the mask is not from Mexico is demonstrated by its similarity to the idol "Kivvasa" shown in an engraving by Theodore de Bry illustrating an account of the Indians of Virginia. In fact, the engraving probably derives from a drawing by Jacques le Moyne made in Florida.

The turn from exposition of Mexican gods to Asian ones happens without a page break or even a paragraph break, but within one sentence: "In sum, throughout this entire new world, so called, both in the west and in the east [*per tutto questo che chiamano novo Mondo, tanto nell'Occidente quanto nell'Oriente*], I have found such great conformity between the Egyptian superstitions and those of the particular locale, that I have at times marveled at it."[25] This transition is immediately followed by a report from

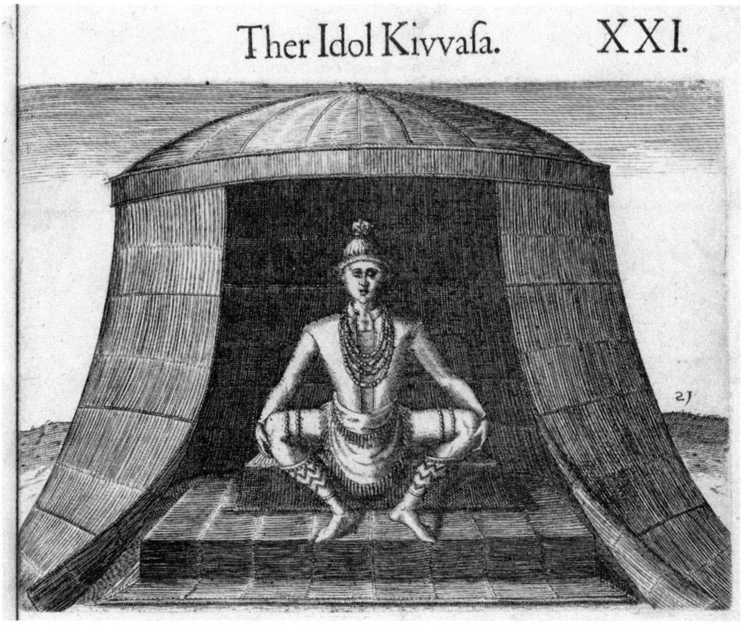

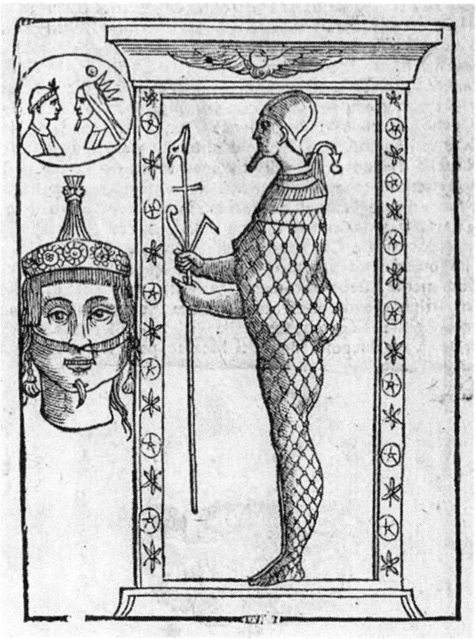

14.8a–b A Floridian idol becomes Mexican and derives from Egypt. (a) Thomas Harriot, *A briefe and true report of the new found land of Virginia*... (Frankfurt: Wechel, 1590), plate 21. Providence, John Carter Brown Library. (b) Lorenzo Pignoria, *Aggionta all'Imagini del Cartari*, p. 374.

a Jesuit priest in Goa of a certain idol with three heads, three legs, three arms, which he identifies as Ganissone, or Ganesh. Then another quick move, to Japan: "One finds similar deformities," he says, in figures that can be seen in the city of Meako (the capital, that is Kyoto), where there is a temple with a thousand images of the god Canone (corresponding to the Bodhisattva, called Guanyin in Chinese and Kannon in Japanese), "with a multiplicity of hands and arms and certain other monstrosities" (fig. 14.9).

The "certain temple" in Kyoto with one thousand identical images of Kannon might sound like a fanciful invention, but in fact it corresponds quite precisely to the monastery of Sanjusangen-do, which holds one thousand and one statues of the god.[26] The temple was described (without naming it) by a Jesuit father writing from the city in 1565, one of several Jesuit textual sources used by Pignoria. Though he did not have a visual source to work from, Pignoria's woodcutter Filippo Ferroverde offered a rendition (see fig. 14.9) that in some ways corresponds to the statues in Kyoto, even down to the two staffs held by the figures in (one of their) left and right hands.

In order to build his sequence, Pignoria had brought together information located in a variety of sources, drawing primarily but not exclusively on the Codex Ríos for his Mexican materials, and for his Asian

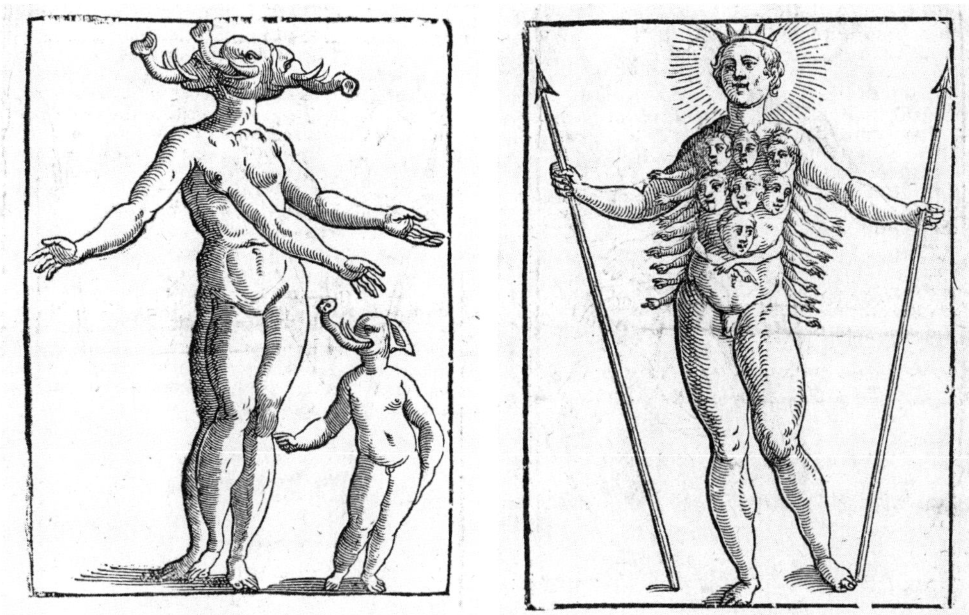

14.9 Ganesh in Goa and Kannon in Kyoto reveal their Egyptian derivation. "And the degree to which these two figures approach the thinking of the Egyptians it is not necessary to prove," says Pignoria in *Aggionta all'Imagini del Cartari*, pp. 377–78.

materials turning to Jesuit reports and Roman collections. By 1600, Rome had become a theater of the world, enabling a well-connected and ambitious antiquarian to pull these materials together and present them as an illustrated story. But what made it possible for him to imagine the story in the first place was the principle of a new world connecting Asia and America—*tutto questo che chiamano novo Mondo, tanto nell'Occidente quanto nell'Oriente*—a geographic and cultural formation that had taken shape over the preceding century. The Egyptian thesis, unevenly sustained throughout Pignoria's disquisition, was an antiquarian's way of explaining what held the Amerasian new world together.

On the whole, Pignoria is geographically tidy; Asian figures follow in sequence from the Mexican ones, even as they are all related to Egyptian culture. But once these American and Asian gods were assembled together in a highly influential publication—reduced to the same format, in black and white, unified by a single woodcutter's style, and drawn together into a vast story of cultural diffusionism by an authoritative writer—it produced a new platform for thinking about American and Asian cultures in a continuum. Given Pignoria's strong associations with Jesuit culture, it is no exaggeration to say that the Jesuit Athanasius Kircher's construction

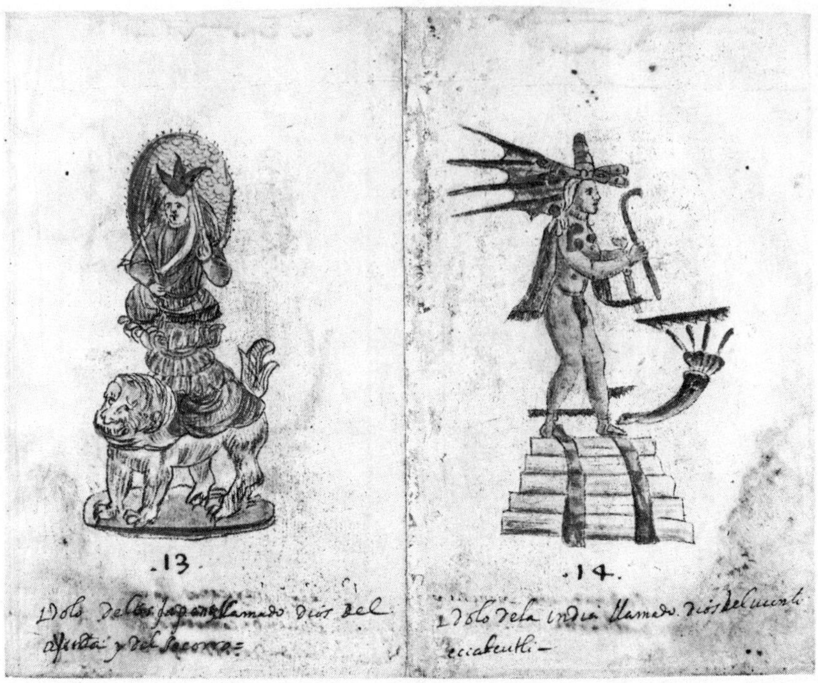

14.10 Gods of Mexico (or rather "India") and Japan, side by side. *Icones coloribus ornatæ idolorum mexicanorum, Aeguptorum, Sinensim, Japanorum, Indorum*, pen, ink and watercolor on Asian paper, each face 39.5 × 27 cm (1615–26). Rome, Biblioteca Angelica, MS 1551. (See color plates.)

of a common culture connecting Asia and America, discussed earlier, was built in good part on the basis Pignoria had established, which in turn had relied on Jesuit reports from the field and on powerful synthetic statements such as those of the Jesuit Acosta.

Pignoria's and Ferroverde's stunning suite of "Indian gods" now entered the repertoire of European iconography. A manuscript from about 1620 in the Biblioteca Angelica in Rome (from here on called the Angelica manuscript) copies each of Pignoria's figures, but now as a gallery of gods with minimal captions, without the comparisons to Egyptian gods and without Pignoria's explanatory context.[27] The figures are now out of order, allowing the various new world gods from East and West to mingle in new ways (fig. 14.10). An image of the god Quetzalcoatl, for example, that Pignoria clearly discussed as Mexican (on the right) is here called an *Idolo dela India* and is placed in sequence with an *idolo delos Japanes*.

Provenances, too, start to drift, as several Japanese figures are now called Chinese and one Japanese figure becomes a Mexican idol, and Pignoria's account of radiating Egyptian influence is reduced to summaries such

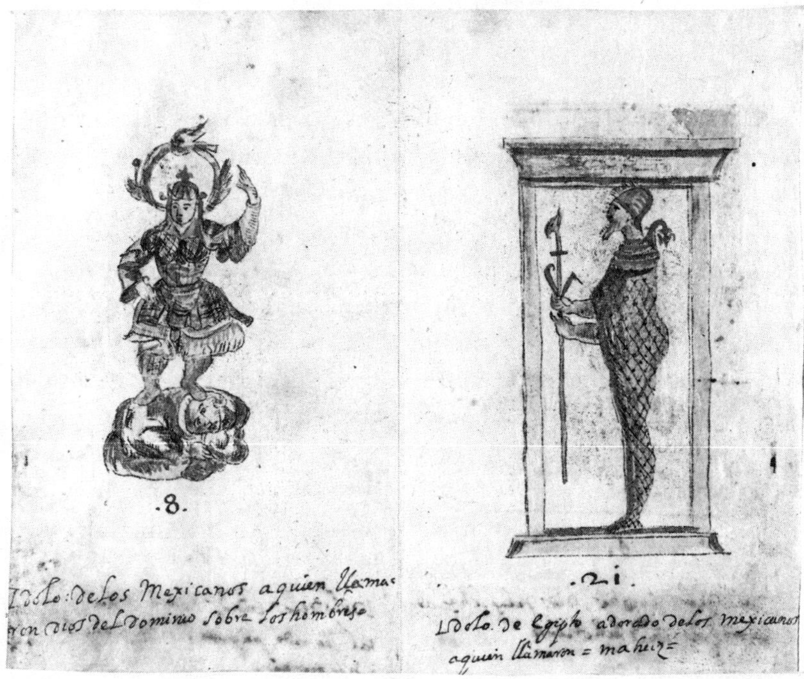

14.11 Drifting provenances. *Icones coloribus ornatæ idolorum mexicanorum, Aeguptorum, Sinensim, Japanorum, Indorum*, Rome, Biblioteca Angelica, MS 1551, pen, ink, and watercolor on Asian paper (1615–26). On the left is a figure that belongs to Pignoria's Japanese suite but here is called an *Idolo de los Mexicanos.* (See color plates.)

as "Idol of Egypt adored by the Mexicans," as if an actual Egyptian statue had arrived in America at some point (fig. 14.11).[28]

Yet the Angelica manuscript is not sloppy work; it is a carefully produced new Amerasian construction. Occasionally, the Spanish captions introduce new and correct information, such as when it identifies Quetzalcoatl in his manifestation as Eccateutli (Ehecatl), a fact not given by Pignoria (see fig. 14.11). Also, the sequence is now presented in an accordion book, each sheet showing gods on front and back, a format reminiscent not only of Mesoamerican screenfolds such as the Cospi Codex but also of *byōbu* or Japanese folding screens, such as the two that had arrived in Rome with a Japanese delegation in 1585 and had remained in the Vatican.[29] Moreover, the support used for the watercolors is a thin, dark-toned Asian paper, giving the whole object the quality of an imported artifact.

If Pignoria and Ferroverde's images are in black and white, the Angelica manuscript shows us figures in many bright colors, a color scheme close to that used in the Ríos manuscript, another book in the form of an accordion, which the world of Roman antiquarian scholarship accorded the status of a primary source from the new world. Without quite asserting it, the Angelica manuscript puts itself forward less as a copy than as a source, not merely a collection of figures copied after a recent printed book but an artifact emanating from the lifeworld that produced these gods. A nonlinear structure, the screenfold in principle allows multiple combinations to emerge, and the gods shadow through the thin paper, making for a dynamic, multidimensional object. The Asian paper and the screenfold format are new world markers, suggesting that the brightly colored Angelica manuscript is a functional totality, showcasing an extensive new world on the level of material and format as much as in its pictorial and textual content. Though produced in Rome, it was in fact an intercultural artifact, not Asian or Mexican, not even quite European, but Amerasian.

Against this background, it becomes easier to imagine how Count Zani, in 1665, could ceremoniously title his new world book a Libro della China as he gave it to his friend Cospi. It is a measure of the power of the association that even when it was renamed a Libro del Messico in 1677, everything did not snap into modern clarity. In the same 1677 catalogue of Cospi's collection, Legati also calls a turkey a *Gallo d'India* (p. 43), he speaks of elephants brought from the *Mondo Novo* (p. 11), he describes as *noci d'India* (p. 286) two mounted vases made of coconut shells from colonial New Spain (now seen with several other of Cospi's items in the Museo Civico Medievale in Bologna), he describes tobacco holders made of light-colored *terra Indiana* excavated from the lake of Mexico City, called *hicatlalli* by the locals (p. 269), because Mexican earth is in fact Indian earth. Beyond employing the generous definition of the geographical category of India, Legati also specifically assigns Indigenous productions of Mexico to Asian India, as in the case of two Mesoamerican mosaic sacrificial knife handles now in the Museo delle Civiltà Luigi Pigorini in Rome, which Legati interprets as Indian sphinxes immediately after discussing the cult of Bacchus in India.[30]

And even as Legati decides to call the Cospi Codex a Libro del Messico, China remains not far off. The manuscript is listed immediately after several Chinese implements and writings and ahead of Ethiopian and several Turkish items. The association with Asia also marked the reception of the Vienna Codex, another Mixtec manuscript discussed earlier, some of whose figures were excerpted for publication in the 1655 catalogue of the collection of the Danish scientist Ole Worm, where a sample of "hieroglyphic" writing form the Vienna codex is presented among Chinese and Japanese items as well as letters from Ethiopia, Persia, and the Malabar coast.[31] In the 1679 catalogue of the Imperial Library of Vienna, the Vienna Codex is described as a "most rare monument of the new world" and comes at the very end, concluding a list of the library's Orientalia.[32] Far from being a bizarre mistake, to name a Mixtec codex a Libro della China was to adhere to a prevailing cultural routine.

• • •

Addendum: American Idols from Java

In his 1621 treatise on the West Indies, the Benedictine monk Kaspar Klautz gives special attention to cult practices on the island of Hispaniola or Haiti, in particular the worship of *zemis*, what he calls American idols, figures made of various materials representing deities or ancestral figures of that region's Taíno people. And so that the reader "may truly see

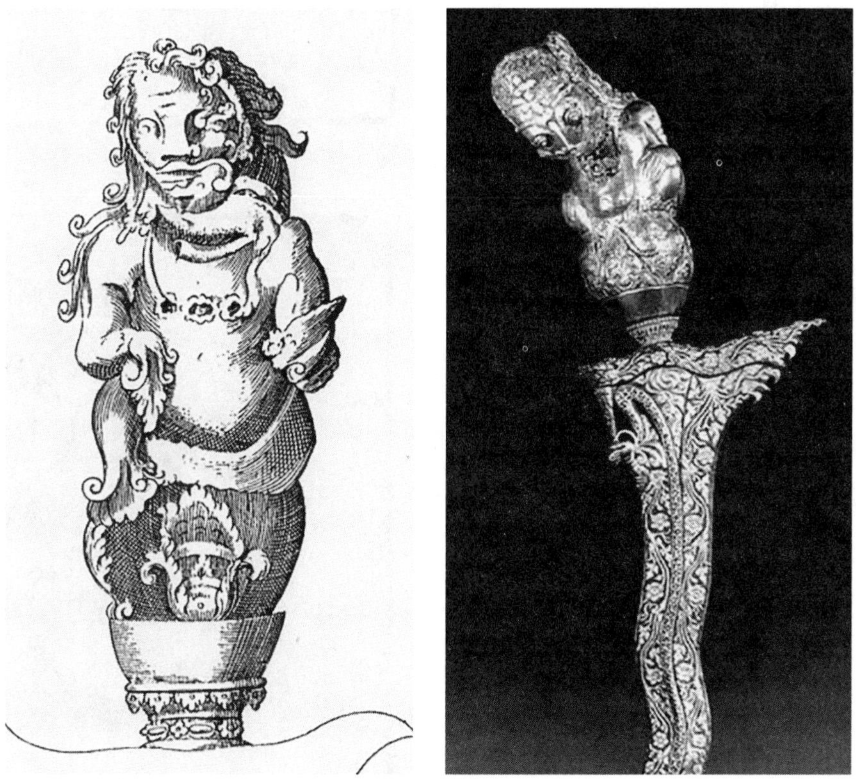

14.12a–b The diabolical American idol, a Javanese kris. (a) Wolfgang Kilian, "Zemi diabolical idol," in Honorius Philoponus (Caspar Klautz), *Nova typis transacta navigatio: Novi orbis Indiae occidentalis* (Linz, 1621), woodcut on paper. (b) Its model, a Javanese *kris* handle then in Graz, now in Vienna, Weltmuseum, made of wood, gold, and stones, 8.9 cm (16th century?). The connection between them was discovered by Christian Feest (see note 33); this illustration reproduces his figures 4 and 5.

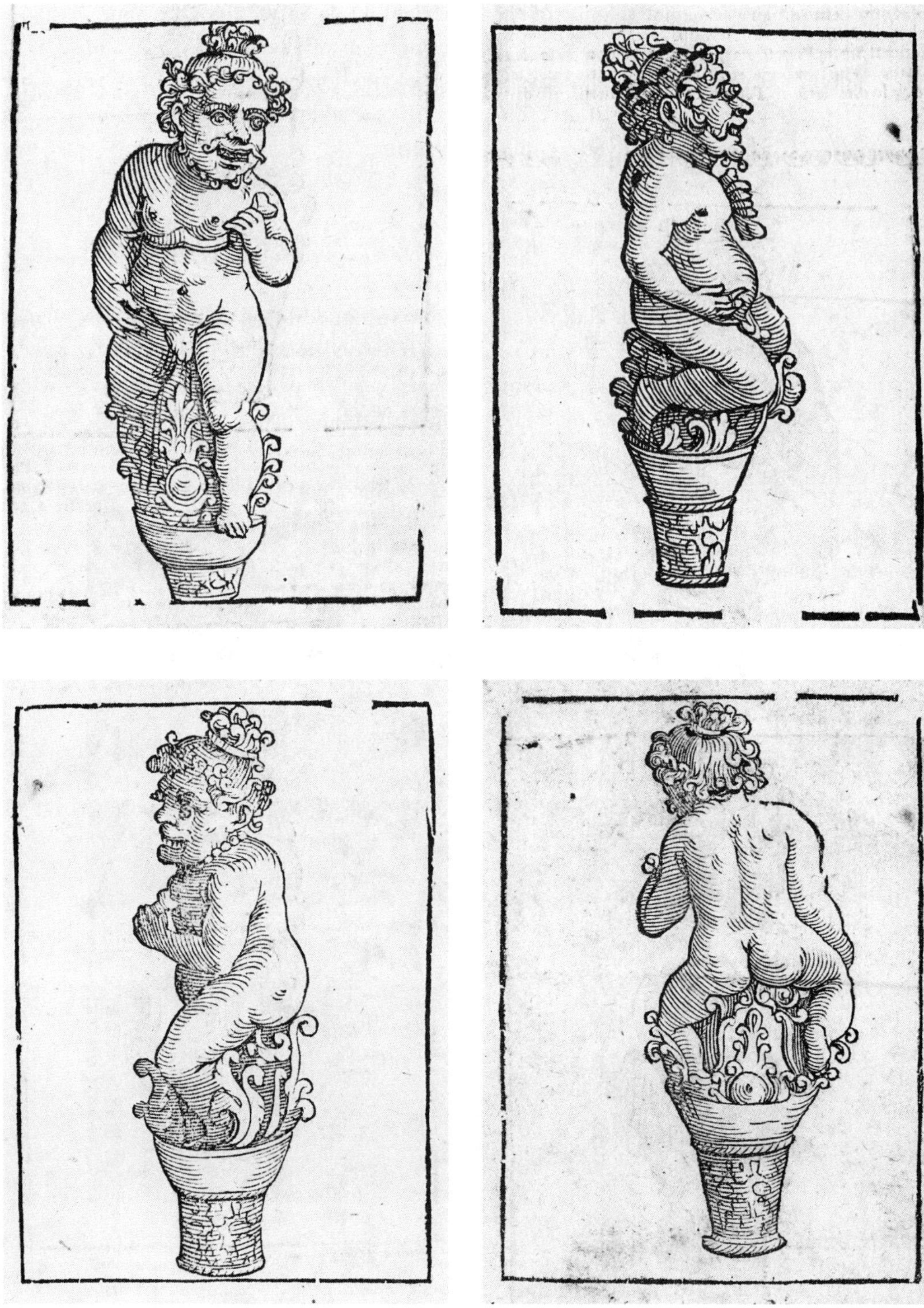

14.13 Four views of an "idoletto dell'Indie." Pignoria, *Aggionta all'Imagini del Cartari*, pp. 397–400.

and recognize the form, image and shape of their idol zemes," he offers an image of one that he saw with his own eyes in the early years of the seventeenth century in the Kunstkammer of the Archduke Ferdinand in Graz (fig. 14.12a). It was of a very hard wood, he noted, with rubies, emeralds, and gold at its base. In fact, the figure that Caspar Klautz identified as an American idol *zemi* was, as Christian Feest showed, the decorated handle of a Javanese *kris*, a type of Indonesian dagger that often carried elaborate hilts carved with the figure of a demon (fig. 14.12b).[33] For Klautz, however, this was not an exceptional item but representative of a type widespread among the Indians encountered by Columbus: "More than 170,000 statues of this kind of idols made of various kinds of materials were broken, destroyed and burned by the priests of our order of Saint Benedict in the Island of Hispaniola alone, because they are accustomed to carve or paint larger or smaller figures of these zemis on almost all of their utensils."[34] He is imagining an American island pullulating with Javanese *kris*-demons, and elsewhere in the book an engraving places a version of the Javanese figure standing on an altar in a scene of American ritual idolatry. This Amerasian assimilation happened more than once. Another Javanese *kris*, this time in the Kassel Kunstkammer, was called a "Mexican idol" as late as 1767.[35]

In the second edition (1623 and later) of his appendix on the "Gods of the Indians," discussed earlier, Pignoria introduced at the very end an additional "little idol of ivory from the Indies adorned with jewels"—yet another *kris* handle—from the collection of his friend the renowned scholar Nicolas-Claude Fabri de Peiresc (fig. 14.13).

After his sequence of gods from Mexico and Japan, we might well ask: What does he mean when he says this little idol is from the Indies? In 1623, *dell'Indie* could mean a truly dizzying array of things. It could mean that the object is from some part of Asia—sometimes India, but also China or Japan or Java—and it could also mean, as we have seen, that it is from America. But it could also refer to an object, like Klautz's *kris*/*zemi*/idol, that is actually Asian but believed to be American! Pignoria confesses he knows virtually nothing about it: "What it could mean we might perhaps be told by Time, the great manifester of all hidden things" (*Che cosa possa significare ce lo direi forse il Tempo, ottimo manifestatore di tutte le cose occulte*)."[36]

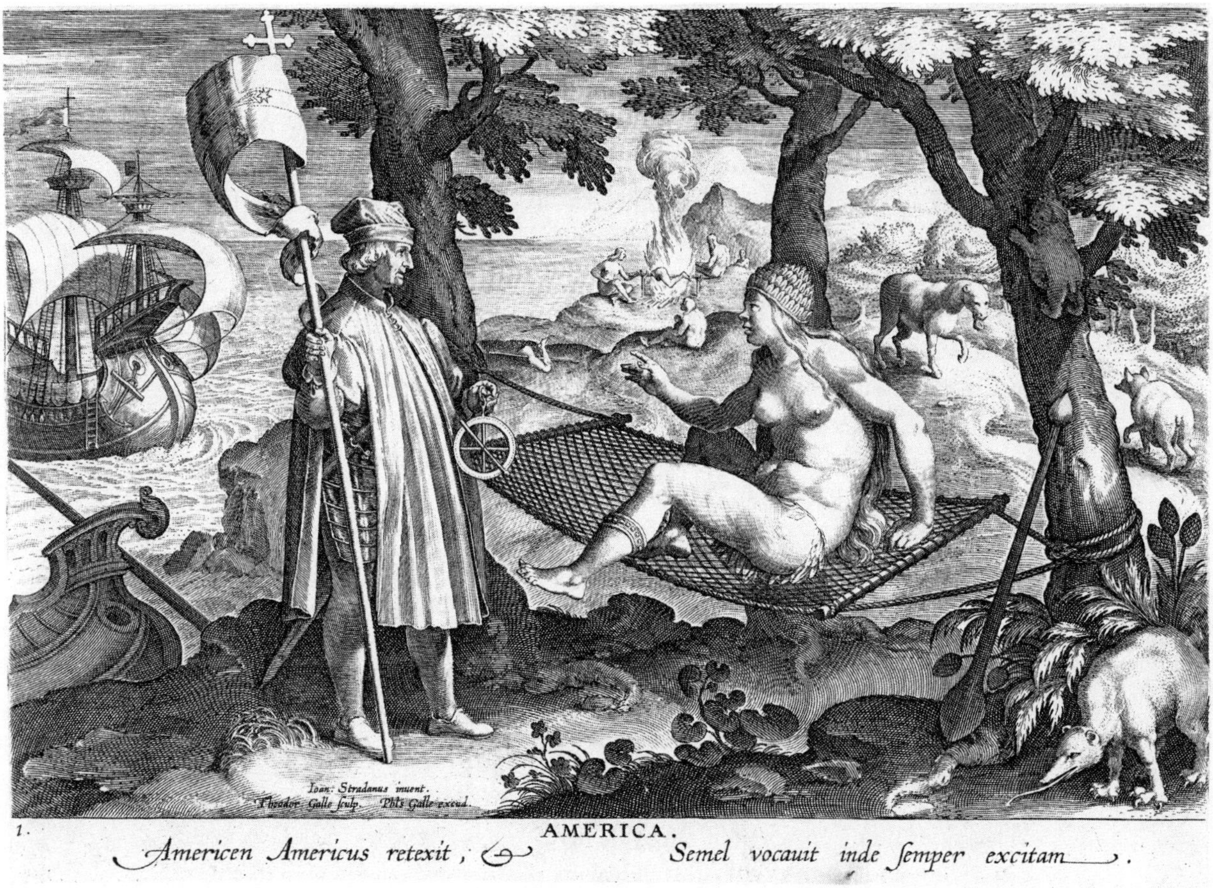

15.1 Amerigo discovers naked America, or rather reveals her as naked and names her America. Theodor Galle after a design by Jan van der Straet, called Stradanus, *America*, copper engraving on paper, 27 × 20 cm (ca. 1588), plate 1 of the print series *Nova Reperta*. New York, Metropolitan Museum.

FIFTEEN

Figuring the World I: The New World of Print

A print series published at the end of the sixteenth century under the title *Nova Reperta* (*New Discoveries or Findings*) collected and illustrated nineteen recent inventions and technologies that Europeans could be proud of.[1] Several of them, such as the compass or the production of silk or the astrolabe, had in fact already been developed in China and other parts of the world, but that did not prevent their adoption in Europe from being celebrated in the series. The first plate shows the encounter with America by the eponymous Amerigo Vespucci, or rather the awakening and simultaneous imprinting of this new land with the name of its discoverer (fig. 15.1). He is shown having disembarked from his ship on the Brazilian shore, holding a banner with the emblem of the Southern Cross, a constellation visible in the southern skies and rarely witnessed by a European, duly described in the best-selling letter on the "new world" published under Vespucci's name. The motto reads: "AMERICA. Amerigo discovers [or unveils] America; he called her but once and thenceforth she was always awake" (*AMERICA. / Americen Americus retexit, et Semel vocauit inde semper excitam*). With the ocean on the left and land on the right, we are coming upon the scene from the north, as in fact Vespucci and all Europeans approached Brazil. Light comes low from the right, as if to emphasize that there lies the west, *occidens*, where the sun sets. Holding his astrolabe, Vespucci the navigator is aware of his position. As we saw in chapter 2, he was proud to have traveled ninety degrees or a quarter of the earth's circumference southward, an achievement illustrated in the *Mundus novus* letter with a diagram of a right triangle pointed westward—the upright labeled *nos*, we the Europeans, and the horizontal axis labeled *illi*, they, the people in this southern land who stand at a right angle to us (see figs. I.1 and 2.4).

Vespucci's triangle is figured here in the quartered circle of the astrolabe he holds in one hand and is thematized in the relation between

Vespucci's standing figure and the horizontal of recumbent America, now rising into a face-to-face encounter with "us." It is easy enough to set these right-angle relations into a well-established reading of this image as an allegory of Eurocentric dominance:[2] America is being drawn up into alignment with the upright of Vespucci's zenith. On the other hand, Vespucci's account insists that he is the one who has traveled a quarter of the earth's circumference southward, with the result that this face-to-face encounter (and our looking at it) is already tilted ninety degrees "downward." Discovery upends orientation before it stabilizes into dominance.

Vespucci is well covered, wearing armor draped with a long tunic, in stark contrast to the almost naked woman in front of him, shown rising from her hammock in response to his arrival, her only weapon a nearby club. Near her we see an anteater, a sloth, and other exotic animals, and in the background are more naked figures around a fire preparing an abundant meal of human-leg brochettes. Although based in history, it is clear that this image has been composed as an emblem, with motto below, all of its elements carefully chosen to convey an idea. The animals and the cannibals—species never before seen and humans whose practices overturn the most basic rules of civilization—are there to emphasize the newness and extreme unfamiliarity of the place, announcing in the first plate the theme of new discoveries and inventions that sustains the *Nova Reperta* as a whole. But as the later engravings in the series show, some of these "inventions" were not in fact new, just new in Europe, where receptivity was in fact the mother of invention.

The Patenting of America

Even in the case of America and its uncovering, things are not so simple. The print series presents the *America* engraving as the first *novum repertum*, the paradigm of modern European discovery, yet it also attracts nagging questions about the newness of the new world. Is America really new, truly unknown to the antiquity we know? If it was known in ancient times—by the Magi (chapter 3), by the Chinese or civilizations peripheral to China (chapters 8 and 11), by Saint Thomas or tribes of Israel (chapter 13), or by the Egyptians (chapter 14)—is the real news story that she has been rediscovered after a long silence? Is that what is meant by the idea that she was asleep until Amerigo awakened her to new life, as the motto says? Or are we to understand that she was dormant because she did not in fact have a history, the life of hunting and warring and cannibalism and sleeping counting as a round that marks no time? Is the novelty, then, the act of bringing her into the order of history as European discoverers understood it? And what about her naming? *Americen Americus retexit*. The verb *tego/texit* means "to cover" and is related to words for a woven (*textilis*) covering or cloth as well as to roofing (*tectus*); *retego/retexit* means to undo or draw back the covering, to lay bare (the Latin carries that literal sense more strongly than the modern English *discover/discovery*).[3] How can it be that Amerigo uncovered/discovered America, as the motto affirms, if she was named after him? Does the newness then consist in the bestowing of a new name on a piece of land?

Not a small matter, to give a land a new name! Until Christopher Columbus and Vespucci, lands came with names given to them in the deepest past, but now, in these times, whole parts of the world were being named anew, as if the world were living through a new mythical age, an era of new foundations unfolding in real time. Or is the real newness that we are now beyond myth, beyond the parameters of received wisdom, and finally grappling with the world as what it is? And is the true novelty here, therefore, the distinctly modern awareness that the world is only available to us through the technical and conceptual tools by which we observe it? This engraving is an allegory of America and its main message is that America is nothing other than an allegory, a way of reading otherwise, a mobilizing of ways of talking about what it means to call a land new even though there are people on it, and to name it after the first one among "us" to land there and describe it.

The image behaves like an allegory, its emphatic structure inviting conceptual reading. The right-angle relationship of the two principal figures structures a series of paradigmatic contrasts—male/female, dressed/nude, upright/recumbent—even as the angle starts to close and they lock eyes. In the original drawing in the Metropolitan Museum of Art the allegorical dimension is more in evidence, as the word America is shown unscrolling (backward, in preparation for reversal in the print) on a diagonal from Vespucci's open mouth to hers (fig. 15.2). Whereas the print confines text to the explanatory caption, the motivation of text in the drawing invites us to read a fairly elaborate conceit out of it. Vespucci is speaking—speaking his own name until the last letter ends by naming her. He is framed as the active one, having arrived on his ship, having roused her and now in the moment of naming her, yet she is the one shown gesturing and speaking back at him. In the transition from drawing to print, she becomes even more active and he is no longer speaking, his upright stance now slightly taken aback.

Stradanus, a well-informed artist, used many visual models in composing his unprecedented subject, but let us focus on the standing clothed figure rousing a naked seated figure, which points us to a precursor that has not been brought forward for Stradanus's print—Lorenzo Ghiberti's

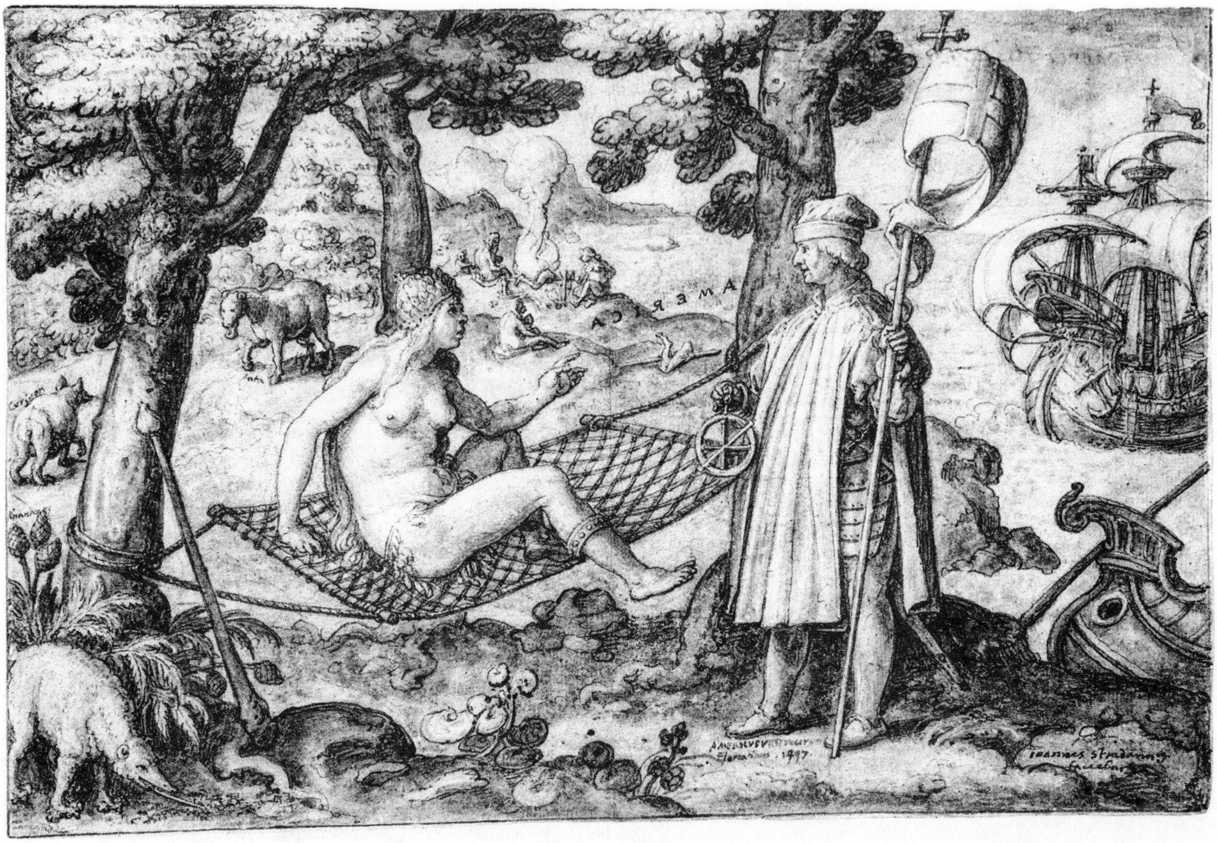

15.2 The discoverer names America after himself. Jan van der Straet, called Stradanus, *America*, pen and brown ink, brown wash, heightened with white, over black chalk on paper, 19 × 26.9 cm (ca. 1587–88). New York, Metropolitan Museum of Art. In contrast to the print, which confines all text to the legend below, here text unfolds inside the image. On the verso, Stradanus noted down excerpts from the account of Brazil in the Jesuit Giovan Pietro Maffei's widely read *History of the Indies*, published in Florence in 1588.

relief of the *Creation and Fall of Adam and Eve*, a signal work Stradanus was able to admire on the doors of the Baptistery facing Florence Cathedral (fig. 15.3). Combining motifs from both Ghiberti's *Creation of Adam* and the *Creation of Eve*, Stradanus's scene offers not only a formal parallel but a thematic one, showing Vespucci calling naked America into new life, as the motto below says. One of the main lessons of the creation story is that man and woman are made in the image of god; likewise, America is imprinted with Amerigo's name as she looks at him.

Whatever its intended meanings, the print's deep message is that the naked does not come before the clothed, but after. The Indigenous populations did not see themselves as naked; they became so under the gaze of Europeans, and in fact Europeans regularly represented them as more naked than they were. The motto is not to be read literally—we are not to understand that in fact it was Amerigo who uncovered her, that he is

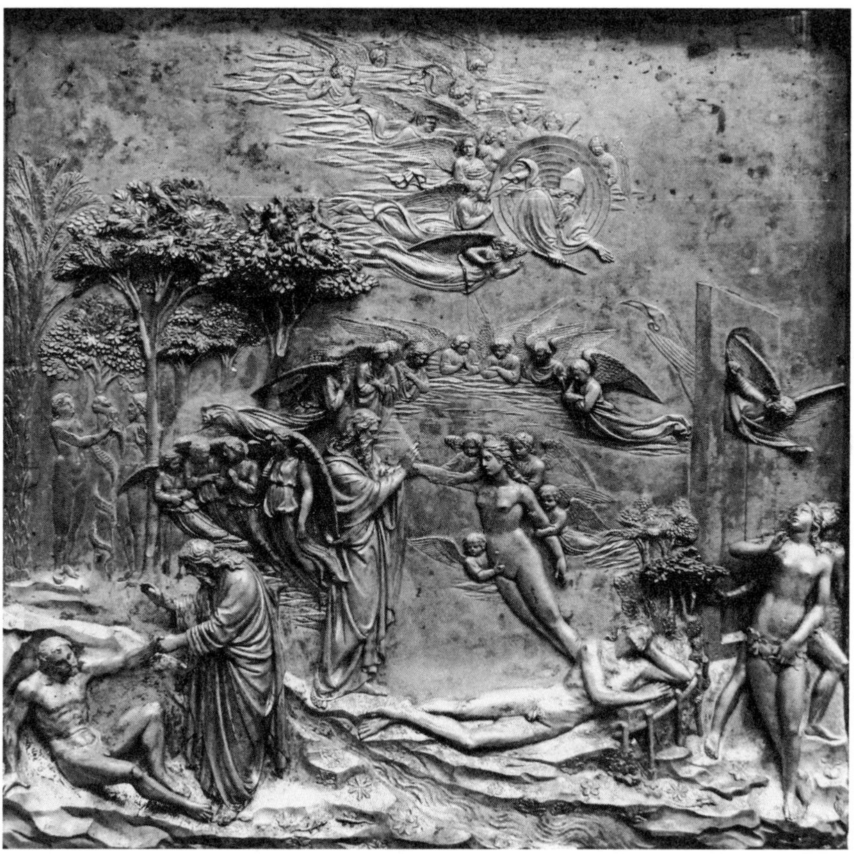

15.3 A paradigm of creation and naming. Lorenzo Ghiberti, *Creation and Fall of Adam and Eve*, gilt cast bronze, 79 × 79 cm (1425–52). Florence, Museo dell'Opera del Duomo.

the one who rendered her naked and created her thus—but there is some truth in reading it that way. Vespucci, in his authentic letters and in the famous letter on the new world attributed to him, did delineate the elements of this figure. Stradanus, representing Vespucci, did render her naked and create her thus.

The title of the image is not *The Discovery of America*, but *America*. The image of naked America was indeed a European innovation, a collaborative cultural work over many decades, well deserving of being the first in the sequence of the *Nova Reperta*. Like gunpowder or oil painting, two other inventions of the series, America as such is the invention being celebrated here; not the feat of having reached this place but America as a place and idea is the *novum repertum*. The next chapter will show that the figure of America as she came into visual form at this time was the result of decades of Amerasian sedimentation. Michael Gaudio has rightly connected this famous image to the invention of copper-plate engraving itself, the medium used to illustrate the *Nova Reperta* and also the last of the inventions illustrated by the publication, number 19, bookending the invention of America illustrated in plate 1 (fig. 15.4, and see fig. 15.1). The motto of invention number 19 reads, "By a new art the sculptor carves figures on beaten sheets and reproduces them in the press." The new medium, as Gaudio argues, is necessary to understanding how the news of new worlds took shape in this period.[4] But let us follow through on Gaudio's prompt.

If we set the *Nova Reperta*'s first and last inventions side by side, we find that the two engravings are designed as if to speak to each other. Echoing the encounter of upright Vespucci and recumbent America, the engraver's workshop is organized by mostly standing figures standing over mostly horizontal surfaces—no fewer than six working tables are shown, all of them underscored by the extended gridded floor shown in plunging perspective. The most important flat surface is the bed of the press itself, where the paper receives the impression of the engraved design, taking form as an image. But the engravings do not stay horizontal, as they are taken up and dried against the back walls, in order to be appreciated eventually face-to-face. Likewise, America is shown peeling herself from her horizontal position in order to come face-to-face with her discoverer and namer (the title page of the *Nova Reperta* labels Vespucci America's *retector et denominator*). America is shown in the process of coming into new life, her body half-rising from a hammock made of gridded lines swelling to describe a curved surface—an abstract rendering of the technique of cross-hatching used in countless engravings to create the effect of three-dimensional form emerging from shadow into light. Such lines describe

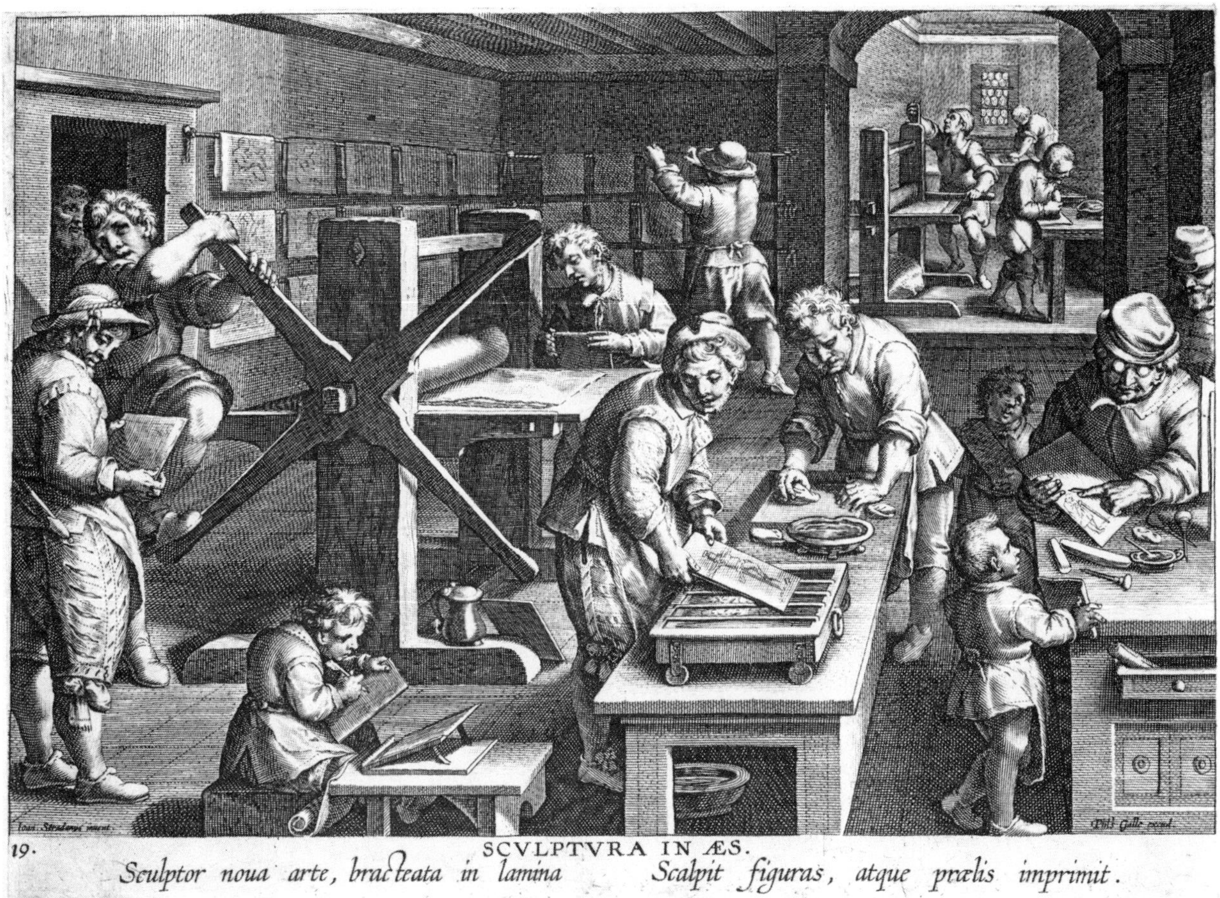

15.4 The art of engraving celebrated by engraving. Philips Galle after a design by Jan van der Straet, called Stradanus, copper engraving on paper, 27 × 20 cm (ca. 1588), plate 19 of the print series *Nova Reperta*. New York, Metropolitan Museum of Art.

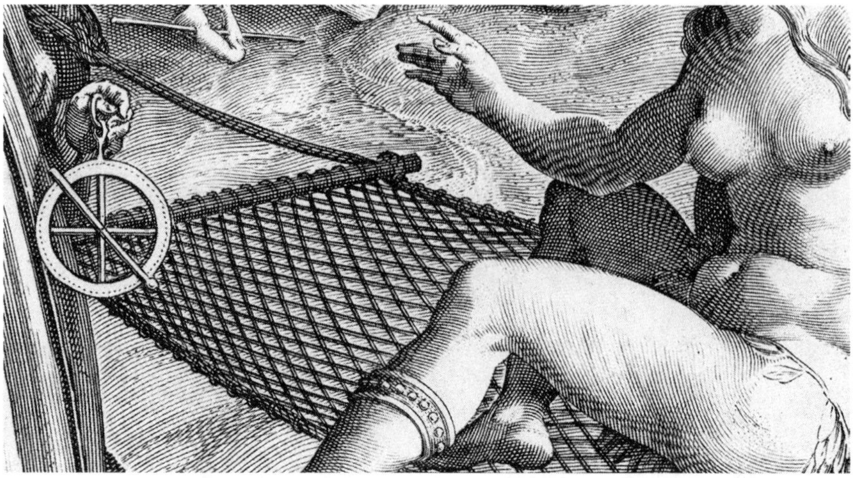

15.5 Grids that curve. Theodor Galle after a design by Jan van der Straet, called Stradanus, *America*, detail of figure 15.1.

the swell of America's powerful thighs and arms, as well as the shadier contours of the landscape (fig. 15.5). The enormous crank of the press, its massive spokes being strenuously turned by one of the shopworkers, finds its echo in Vespucci's circular astrolabe, also with four spokes, a device that works by being turned. The first and last plates of the *Nova Reperta* invite a thinking-together of the new world and the new medium. America is called into existence by Amerigo, made visible and intelligible through the art of printing black lines on white paper.

The New World as an Artifact of Print

As the success of Vespucci's *Mundus novus* letter makes clear, news of new worlds came primarily through the relatively new media of printed texts and images. Vespucci would not have come to the attention of Martin Waldseemüller, who made the decision to call the new land America after him, if not for the printed dissemination of Vespucci's reports on the new world. Together with the frontispiece of a naked man and woman used in some editions of the *Mundus novus* letter (see fig. 2.6), the text of the letter set in motion a whole imaginary of new world peoples as the polar opposites of Europeans: unashamed by nakedness, uninhibited by marriage bonds, uninterested in possessions, remarkably long-lived eaters of people. As discussed in chapters 1 and 2, Vespucci had gotten many of his ideas about these faraway people from earlier descriptions of naked and savage and long-lived cannibals on Asian islands, medieval accounts such as John Mandeville that were now, thanks to print, more widely available than ever before. In other words, Vespucci's widely read letters themselves became the media by which earlier images and accounts were processed through the new world, providing a major reference point for more images and accounts disseminated through a printing industry that was just then ramping up to unheard-of levels of production. Mandeville and Marco Polo saw a printed revival after the publication of Vespucci's letter, and because of it.

The new world occasionally arrived in samples—botanical, animal, or human specimens, as well as artifacts—but it was assembled into an imaginary above all by printed images. A very few privileged people got to handle actual items from the new world such as featherwork or masks or ivory carvings, and another few got to glimpse people from distant lands that had been transported back for display in Europe. A still rather restricted number of people had access to formal works of painting and sculpture that represented new-world or exotic subjects, though there were occasional public works, such as Pietro Tacca's *Quattro mori* at the port of Livorno or Gian Lorenzo Bernini's *Fontana dei Quattro Fiumi* fountain on the Piazza Navona in Rome, that made these themes publicly available. Yet for the vast majority of Europeans, information and images about the new world came through printed books and images, media that were beginning to reshape European civilization when Columbus embarked on his first transatlantic voyage. Just as the new medium of television became the image environment of the Space Age, shaping it as the Space Age, the new world came through the new media of print, raising the question: Were the very image and idea of the new world—and thus the image and idea of the world as a new totality—artifacts of the print medium?

In contrast to the experience of the older visual media of manuscripts, paintings, mosaics, tapestries, and sculptures, no one holding a print, or a printed book, in their hands was unaware that they were participating in a broadcast, that there were other people in other places holding the same image or the same text in their hands, and that it was the job of the thing they were holding to reach many people in different places. In other words, one of the primary messages of print media was the fact of mediality itself. Prints and printed texts foregrounded their mediality in part by being on paper, a recently developed material that had been in use before print but now was reaching an expanding public through printed books and images.[5] Optimal for easy transport and increasingly affordable, paper was part of the identity of printed images, whether or not the occasional print was pasted onto the backing of a wall or cabinet. Beyond their paper substrate, prints and printed texts were monochrome, inviting marking and coloring by readers and amateurs. With few exceptions, the traditional media of manuscript books, paintings, tapestries, mosaics, and sculptures did not invite extemporaneous markups and additions by amateur users of the sort that we have seen several times in the books and prints illustrated in this book.[6] Printed images and books reached into the lives of people, activating a new level of participation in the medium.[7]

More clearly than a work carved in stone or molded in metal, or woven in cloth, or even painted on a surface, an image made of mechanically reproduced black-ink lines on paper fairly proclaimed: "I am a reproduction; I report information from somewhere else." Bronze casting, too, was a reproductive medium, but it was an expensive and difficult process, often requiring extra chiseling and polishing work after casting, giving the results the status of rare objects. The evident fact that prints were reproductions did not diminish their credibility so much as insist on their referential function, their ability to carry information from elsewhere, whether that was another image, a figment of the imagination, a visual fact in the world, or, in the case of certain miraculous images, the "charged matrix" of the printing surface itself.[8]

Whatever their iconographic content, therefore, printed images came strongly marked as messages intended for broadcast and distribution, messages with no home but many destinations. These facts about their mediality were an essential part of the content of printed images, just as the tone of the paper was a basic part of their image structure, not hidden but recruited into their representational work. The multiple determinacy of the paper surface in drawings and prints found no equivalent in the experience of paintings, whose entire surfaces were encoded by varying applications of paint and/or gold. (Certain sixteenth-century artists and patrons did begin to develop an interest in the look of partially finished paintings, relatively rare experiments that were themselves very likely a response to the emergent appreciation of prints and drawings.) Unpainted works of relief sculpture also make the material itself participate in the image—marble goes from describing a form and then back to being marble—but the printed image results solely from the contrasting effect of the black lines printed on the paper surface, without the additional help of three-dimensional volume. In prints as well as in drawings, the paper—whether white or another tone—is underencoded; it shifts from being evident material support to becoming the surface of just about any represented thing—the water between waves, the sky, the earth, human skin. Prints make it clear that images begin with an unmarked field that is then marked to form images of all kinds. Recognized by all Europeans as a late-coming and modern invention—and memorialized as such in the

Nova Reperta—prints also paradoxically returned their viewers to a degree zero of image-making, linear marks assuming recognizable forms against a contrasting plain surface.

Paper's ability to shift in function from substrate to representational feature is basic to another related fact about printed images, what could be called their field-condition. In contrast to the traditional media of visual art, which generally relegated different categories of images to distinct formats and to prescribed spaces of various kinds, each with its own rules of decorum, prints provided a receptive and fairly unregulated field for images of all sorts. There were prints that conveyed motifs of traditional religious iconography—saint images, the Virgin and Child, the Passion of Christ—but printed sheets also hosted figures from Greco-Roman mythology, popular fables, ornamental designs, as well as current news, including visual reports on strange people from far-away lands. That range is clearly and proudly displayed in the *Nova Reperta*'s illustration for *Engraving in Copper*, where the figure on the right is shown carving a copper plate with a genre image of a blind man with a cane, while in the center we see another figure preparing a plate with an image of the crucified Christ (see fig. 15.4). Images of all kinds came out of the same printer's shop, pretty well all at the same time. Cutting through hierarchies and protocols that had governed image-making for centuries, prints hosted images of different genres on the same level playing field: black and white lines imprinted on a rectangular paper sheet. And then they turned their viewers and collectors into hosts for images of all kinds. Prints were the most demographic medium yet invented by Europeans.

No one was more aware of the universalizing promise of the print medium than the son of Christopher Columbus, Ferdinand, who became the foremost collector of prints and printed books of his era. The way he handled them throws a sharp light on the symbiosis between the imaginary of the new world and the print medium. Having accompanied his father on his fourth voyage in 1502–1504 and then having spent time on Hispaniola in 1509, when his brother Diego was governor there, Ferdinand Columbus returned to Spain and became the keeper of his father's papers and legacy. He was an avid bibliophile, coming up with the novel idea of inventorying his staggering collection of 15,000 books (including pamphlets and ephemera) from around the world, each with its own summary, in a 2,000-page *Libro de los Epítomes* now in Copenhagen.[9] His correspondingly vast collection of prints, numbering 3,204 by his death in 1539, was motivated less by an interest in prints per se—the category of "print collector" did not exist at the time—than by a desire to assemble a comprehensive image database, a universalizing aspiration made possible by the advent of printed images. The collection represented the whole range of print production—historical subjects, saints' images, mythological figures, ornamental designs, landscapes, animals, botanical items, and news broadsheets—a range of imagery that far outstripped what any earlier collection of paintings, sculptures, textiles, and gems could offer.

With a collection of this size, it became necessary to keep an inventory so as to prevent Ferdinand from buying the same print more than once on his travels—a danger peculiar to prints—allowing him to check easily and unambiguously a prospective purchase against what was already in the collection. But how does one draw up a descriptive inventory with no iconographic manual and no Bartsch numbers? Ferdinand wisely used the most digitizable criteria, categorizing his prints, first, by one of seven size designations based on known paper sizes; second, by content organized by the most basic distinctions: male and female saints, men and women (meaning non-Christian subjects with people in them), then animals, inanimate objects, decorative knots, topography, ornament, and vegetation; third, by the number of any of these in a given image; finally, by whether figures are dressed or undressed.[10]

So as to minimize ambiguity in descriptions of the image, the surface array of the prints—the way lines interacted on a sheet—is privileged in Columbus's inventory as identifying information. In the entry on Hans Burgkmair's *King of Cochin*, for example, the inventory observes that "[an Indian] with both hands holds a long stick on which is a sunshade and the king with the right index finger almost touches the stick" (fig. 15.6).[11] The "almost touching" does not occur at the level of the represented scene—the pole with the parasol is shown forward of the king's litter—but on the surface of the sheet the line describing the index finger does meet the line marking the pole. The woodblock that produced this print would have carried a continuous forked ridge at this point, like a tributary joining a river, yielding a graphic encounter that serves to identify this print unambiguously. This kind of surface description, enabled and invited by the print medium, is used throughout Columbus's inventory.

Prints informed the very concept of the new world, beginning with the basic fact that it was definitionally an emergent phenomenon, a matter of point of view; the new world was new for Europeans. As we saw in chapter 2, "new world" could mean lands never known, even to the ancients, but it could also mean lands now known firsthand and in-depth, or conquered, colonized, and converted for the first time, or simply known again in the present after a long interval. Thus it was a term that applied equally to newly encountered places in Africa and Asia as well as to the islands and lands across the Atlantic. The fact that "new

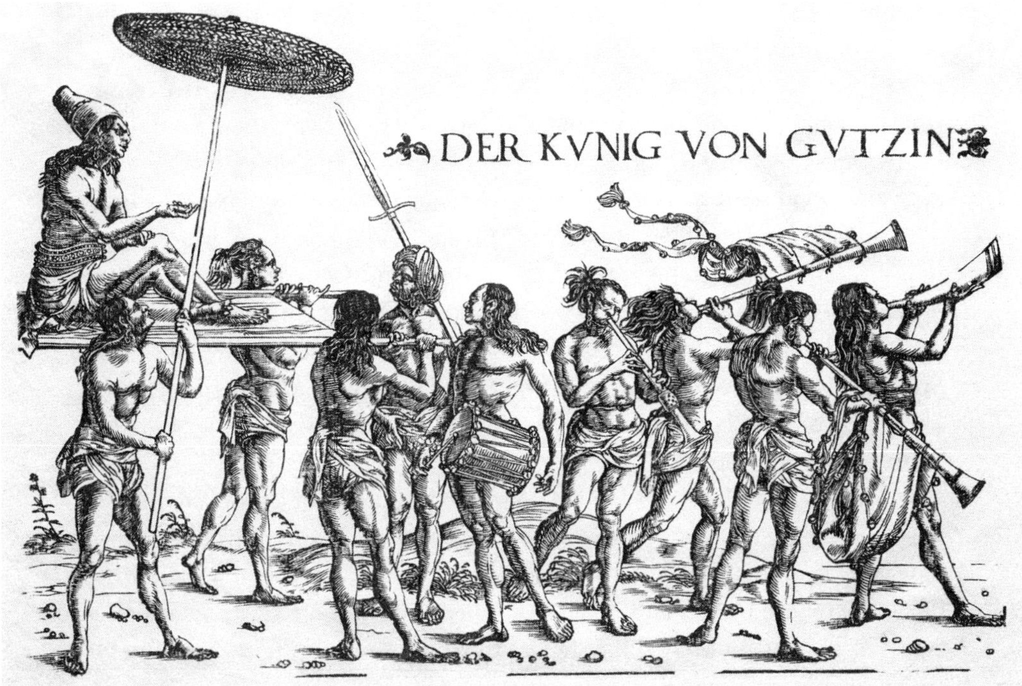

15.6 A procession of lines. Hans Burgkmair, *The King of Cochin*, woodcut on paper, 28 × 40 cm (1508). Cleveland, Cleveland Museum of Art.

world" was defined as a function of point of view was the key to its temporality, since the making visible of something as yet unknown, or known only imperfectly and indirectly in ancient times, was a process unfolding in real time, a disclosing of the earth that promised, for many interpreters, a final unveiling of the structure of time itself (chapter 7). A divinely timed revelation offered to Christians, the discovery of new worlds and the rounding of the globe were world-historical events of universal significance, offering a vision of cosmological totality that was itself proof of the truth of Christian revelation—a truth that would now be imposed on the Indigenous populations coming under European dominance.

The new world was thus a positional and time-sensitive relation, describing a reality that was far enough beyond the known world for it to be sensational news that it was being encountered now, and remote enough for it to come under a formula as general as "new world." The new world was a reality, yes, but for the vast majority of Europeans it could only be seen from afar, through mediating images—a "televisual" function, managing a relation from a distance. As we saw in chapter 7, an influential small treatise *The Position and Description of the World*, written in the late 1520s by the imperial cosmographer Franciscus Monachus who had never traveled to any of the newly discovered territories, described the process precisely as a coming into visibility, a revelation promising visual contact from a distance: "The Antarctic pole, unknown lands, seas, people beyond the Equator, the very existence of whom was not long ago a matter for continual debate—all of this has come into view [*videre contigit*, literally: come to be reached by seeing]. And so by the explorations of our Caesar a huge part of the world has opened, bared, and uncovered itself."[12] The last verb, *retexit*, is the same as the one used in the motto of Stradanus's image of Vespucci and America. The new world was defined as a function of its becoming visually accessible, and prints were the primary form of that accessibility.

A vast and complex world did of course exist outside of European images and accounts, a fact appreciated by some Europeans, yet unavoidably the new world was a mediated phenomenon and an artifact of mediation, produced by printed texts and images that insisted on their status as mediations. Again and again, prints offered European viewers fantasies of new world people, usually naked. These were real-world, present-tense Adams and Eves offered in print after print, such as we have seen throughout this volume in images of Brazilians (see fig. 2.2) and Sumatrans (see fig. 5.7) and "Indians" of various kinds (see figs. 12.2–6). On the one hand, these are the most self-evident images in the world, humans degree zero: the men fierce hunters and warriors, the women naturally strong and fertile. On the other hand, precisely because of their elementary quality, these images were graphic hieroglyphs, types representing the limits of humanity, or alternatively the earliest stages of human civilization. As Karen Ordahl Kupperman and Jill Burke have pointed out, new world peoples were described as naked even when their bodies were largely clothed, as if they had to be made to serve as the building blocks of another world, or of the whole world.[13] These images of bare life, precisely in their bareness, were always overdetermined, always ciphers waiting to be clothed in interpretation. What these naked new world figures were to the clothed figures of established iconography, prints were to the world of images. Print was the form of the new world.

For these reasons, virtually any new world representation was but a step away from the realm of allegory. The idea of representing the parts of the world in the form of female personifications—a trend, propelled by prints, that took off in the later sixteenth century—was an effect of the news of the new world, not only because discoveries of new lands had put the problem of the shape and partitioning of the world squarely on the table, but also for reasons specific to the history of image-making: the sixteenth-century practice of making figures stand for places had arisen in those repeated images, mostly printed, of nudes from the African, Asian, and American new worlds. The latent allegorical impulse inherent in new world imagery eventually led to the idea of representing all the parts of the world allegorically—though, significantly, this did not happen right away. The development of an iconography of the parts of the world came after almost a century of steady production of new world imagery that was, as we have seen in many examples throughout this study, persistently Amerasian. The cosmographer Waldseemüller in 1507 famously called America a fourth part of the world, but in succeeding maps he abandoned the designation America and folded the new world into Asia (see chapter 2), a worldview that remained dominant through the middle decades of the sixteenth century (see chapters 6, 8, 9, 10, and 11). The influential *Cosmographia* of Sebastian Münster recognized a sizable land named America yet still treated it as an appendage of Asia (see chapter 12). In hundreds of new world images produced in the sixteenth and seventeenth centuries, attributes were shared by the inhabitants of Africa, Brazil, Mexico, India, Japan, and China. This meant that when the parts of the world were distinguished and represented as allegories, attributes continued to flit, definitions continued to shift, and even the number of the parts remained unsettled. As we will see in the next chapter, the idea of naming the parts of the world, including one called America, did not overturn the Amerasian model so much as propagate it.

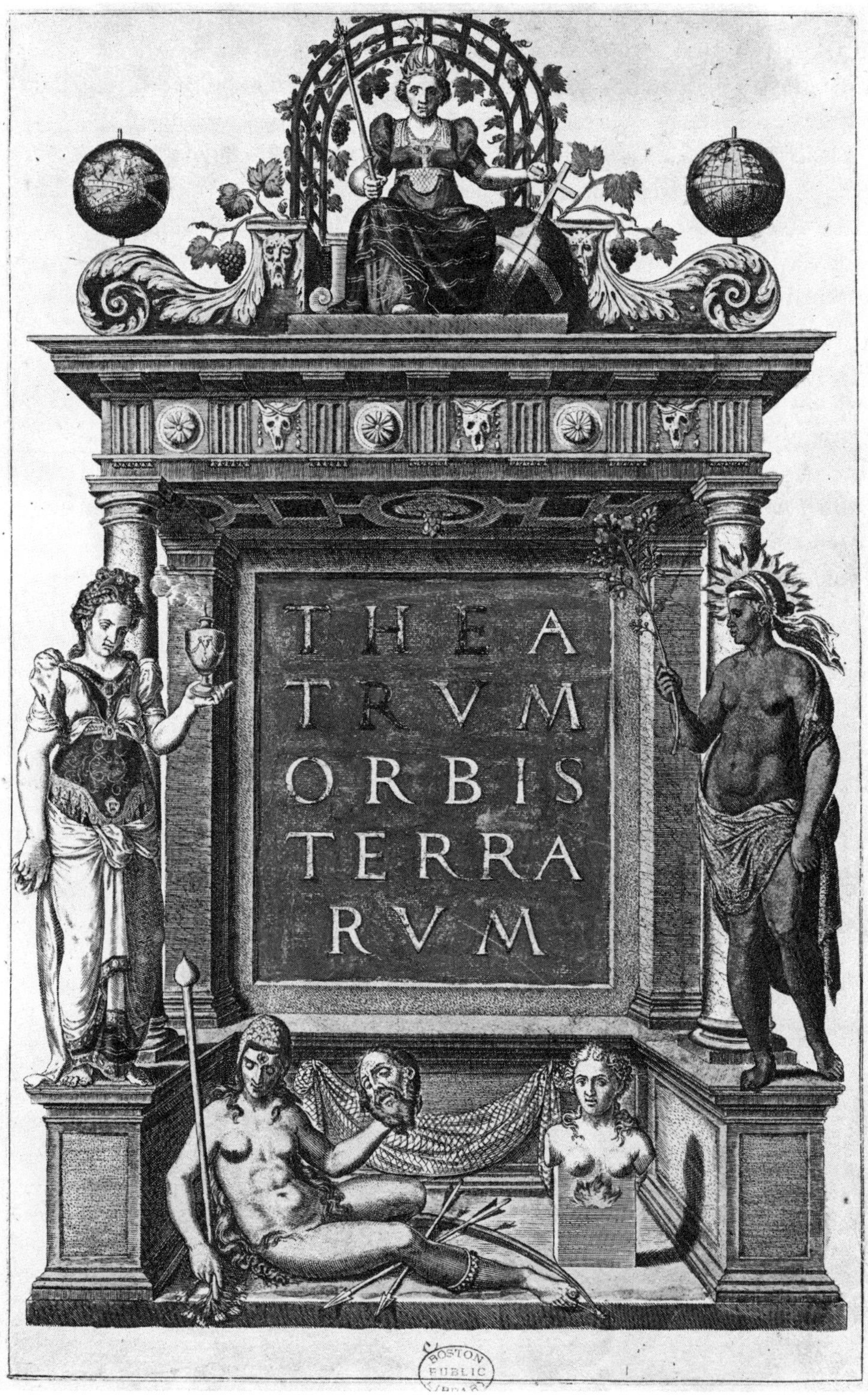

16.1 The world as theater, with several protagonists. Woodcut frontispiece to Abraham Ortelius, *Theatrum orbis terrarum* (Antwerp, 1570). Boston, Boston Public Library. Image: https://www.digitalcommonwealth.org/search/commonwealth:q524n383g.

SIXTEEN

Figuring the World II: The World in Its Parts

The traditional European scheme of the three parts of the world—Europe, Africa, and Asia—came under heavy revision as a result of the new world encounters, yet this was no simple addition of the new fourth to the traditional three. Some cosmographers maintained the schema of three, appending or folding the new territories into Asia, while others increased the number to five or six, adding America with the Antarctic regions or splitting what we call America into two parts. This chapter explores the productive variability that marks the reorganization and representation of the world in the sixteenth and seventeenth centuries, holding off where possible the imposition of modern geographical models onto the evidence. In particular, we aim to resist the tendency to conflate the early modern *parts of the world* with the idea of *continents* as it came to be defined in the eighteenth and nineteenth centuries.

The Incontinent Parts of the World

The early modern concept of *partes mundi* does not align with the post-eighteenth-century definition of continents, and the early modern use of the word *continent* most certainly does not map onto the modern use of that term. In sources of the sixteenth and seventeenth centuries, the word *continent* remains close to the present participle of the Latin *continens* ("containing"). Continent was an active principle, a holding together against the threat of a spilling over or redistribution of contents. Glossing the deranging effects of the passions, Titania in Shakespeare's *A Midsummer Night's Dream* (II. i. 92) invokes "Contagious fogs, which falling in the land have every pelting river made so proud that they have overborne their continents." The term *continent* was most often used not in a geographical context at all but as a metaphor describing dynamics of containing, but when it was used geographically, it emphasized the physical fact of land-masses larger than islands, meaning that it could describe masses smaller than what we call continents, as when the sixteenth-century geographer Thomas Cuningham defines the term *Continens* as "à portion of th'Earth, which is not parted by the Seas à sounder, but is continually in length, so that you may go from one parte vnto another without nauigation: as Saxonie, Bohemie, Sueuelande, &c."[1] Yet it could also describe much larger landmasses, as John Milton does when he collects the entirety of the world above Hell into "one Continent of easie thorough-fare" (*Paradise Lost* 10.392). If defined as continuous landmasses, as they were in the medieval and early modern periods, continents in fact overspill the modern continental boundaries, since nothing really separates Europe from Asia, as geographers from Herodotus on occasionally had to admit. Even in the eighteenth century, when the idea of America as a continent—not a part of the world but a continent—first arose, there were those who claimed that the world consisted of two continents, America on one side and Europe-Africa-Asia on the other.[2] On his epoch-making 1569 world map, discussed in chapter 11, the cartographer Gerardus Mercator proposed that there were now three continents: "the first, in the centre of which the human race was created and whence it spread, by multiplying, over all the face of the earth [essentially, Ptolemy's *oikoumene* of Europe, Africa, and Asia], the second which is called *nova India* [North and South America], and the third which lies in southern parts [his *Terra Australis*, a vast Antarctic landmass]."[3]

Mercator's most influential reader, Abraham Ortelius, embraced the three-continent idea in his *Theatrum orbis terrarum* of 1570 while proposing five parts of the world, the traditional three forming one continent and the two new parts forming a continent each (*America* and the southern continent, which he calls *Magellanica*) (fig. 16.1): "But since that discouery of America, the learned of our age haue made that a fourth part, and the huge Continent vnder the South pole, a fifth."[4] One of the first images to present the parts of the world in the form of allegorical personifications, it was also among the most influential. Five parts are shown—or four and a bit, since the mostly unknown fifth, Magellanica, is shown as an unfinished bust. The frontispiece was maintained in the many succeeding editions and translations of the famous publication, the repeated use of the plate requiring it be replaced and recut at least three times. Ortelius uses the word *continent* throughout the atlas, but always in the early modern way—not as an automatic synonym for a part of the world but descriptively to distinguish a mainland in contrast to an island, as when he reports the idea among ancient writers that England was such a large island that it might qualify as a continent.[5]

Whereas the modern term continent and the division of the world into seven of them came into consistent use in the nineteenth century, the word *continens* as Mercator and other early modern commentators used it was defined on strictly descriptive grounds as a continuous landmass; it persists in modern usage when we speak in geological rather than geographic terms of continental divides or drifts.[6] As Petrus Apianus wrote in his highly influential sixteenth-century *Cosmographia*, "A continent [*continens*] we call any solid or fixed land that is not an island, peninsula, or isthmus."[7]

In contrast to the neutral physical descriptor *continens*, macrogeographical categories such as *zona* (a climatically defined band of the earth imposed by latitude), or *orbis* (to mean region or territory, or more broadly sphere or world, as in *alterius orbis* or *orbis novus*), or *partes mundi*, or the four quarters, or the four winds, offered multiple ways of organizing the world into a system of more than one area.[8] In 1507, Martin Waldseemüller and Matthias Ringmann opined that America deserved to be classed as a fourth part of the world, adding, however, that it was an island, in contrast to the continents of Europe, Africa, and Asia.[9] Thus, it was possible to be a *pars* without being a continent, in part because the distinction between a very large island and a continent remained always unclear.[10] Therefore, to speak of sixteenth-century "personifications of the continents" or of early modern "continental schemes" or to give books titles such as *The Language of Continent Allegories in Baroque Central Europe* or *Early Modern Personifications of the Continents*, to cite two recent publications, is to pull these images and ideas proleptically into modern (nineteenth- and twentieth-century) geographical models.

One main difference between early modern parts of the world and the modern continents is that the modern continental model claims to ground its conceptual abstraction in the scientific observation of nature—these "continents" are objective physical phenomena that have now been given their appropriate geographical designation—whereas the ancient and medieval tradition of the parts of the world consistently avowed their own abstraction, the fact that they diagrammed the world into parts, that they were a way of schematizing the inhabited world's structure and history. For this reason, in contrast to the modern geographical definition of continent, the commonly used expression *partes mundi* was "in no way a technical term and neither needed a definition nor generated a discourse on the character of the *partes'* boundaries."[11] It was in the nature of the *partes mundi* to be both malleable and abstract, as in the clover-shaped Bunting map discussed in Timothy Brook's Afterword to this volume. We propose to see the parts of the world not as early forms of the modern continents but as what they were: early modern allegories.

The avowedly abstract quality of the *partes mundi* allowed the world to remain in fact quite messy while keeping its distribution into parts clearly in the realm of conceptual armature. In his *Natural History* (2.68), the Roman writer Pliny dramatized the insufficiency of our conceptual categories in the face of a restless and undefinable nature. He was certain that humans inhabited only a small part of the planet earth, a populated territory beset on all sides by water, which continually insinuates itself into bays, inland seas, and bodies of water "by which it separates Africa, Europe, and Asia." The interaction between earth and water is an active and ongoing process: islands rise out of the sea (2.87–88) or unite with mainlands (2.91), lands are engulfed by the seas (2.92–93) or they continually shake so that islands float and move (2.96). On their small parcel of earth, human efforts to organize the world according to their words and categories were at best provisional.[12] The parts were, in fact, always incontinent, and thus called for conceptual ordering. In his seventh-century *Etymologiae*, arguably the most widely read encyclopedic text of the Middle Ages, Isidore of Seville brought out geographical structure from the chaos. Basing himself in Saint Augustine, he explained that of the three parts of the world, Asia is twice as large as Europe and Africa, thus dividing the world into two halves with Asia on one side and Europe and Africa on the other.[13] A tripartite organization that resolves into a bisected structure, forming the shape of the cross, the world and its parts have a geometry and proportion that resonate with divine order.[14] The thinking of the parts of the world was always already allegorical, and that is in part why the discourse of the parts of the world found a natural home in the medium of print.

The gradual stabilization of a four-part scheme should therefore be set in relation not to the modern continents, which did not yet exist, but to the schemas of four that did exist for sixteenth-century Europeans. We encountered one in figure 7.8, a printed copy of Parmigianino's *Madonna of the Rose* that invoked Isaiah 11:10–12, where we read that the Lord "shall gather together the dispersed of Judah from the four quarters of the earth" (in the Latin Vulgate, *a quattuor plagis terrae*). This is a geometrical and encompassing idea, dividing the entire earth by a grid of four quadrants, east, west, north, and south. Then there was the formula of the four corners of the earth, as in *Revelation* 7:1: "After these things, I saw four angels standing on the four corners of the earth, holding the four winds of the earth" (Latin Vulgate: *super quattuor angulos terrae*); or *Revelation* 20:7: "And when the thousand years shall be finished, Satan shall be loosed out of his prison and shall go forth and seduce the nations which are upon the four quarters of the earth, Gog and Magog" (in the Latin Vulgate: *gentes quae sunt super quattuor angulos terrae*). Unlike the four quarters, which divide the world among them, the four corners mark out extremes, the remotest places of the earth. As quadripartite schemas, both had a role to play in the development of the new idea that the world had four parts,

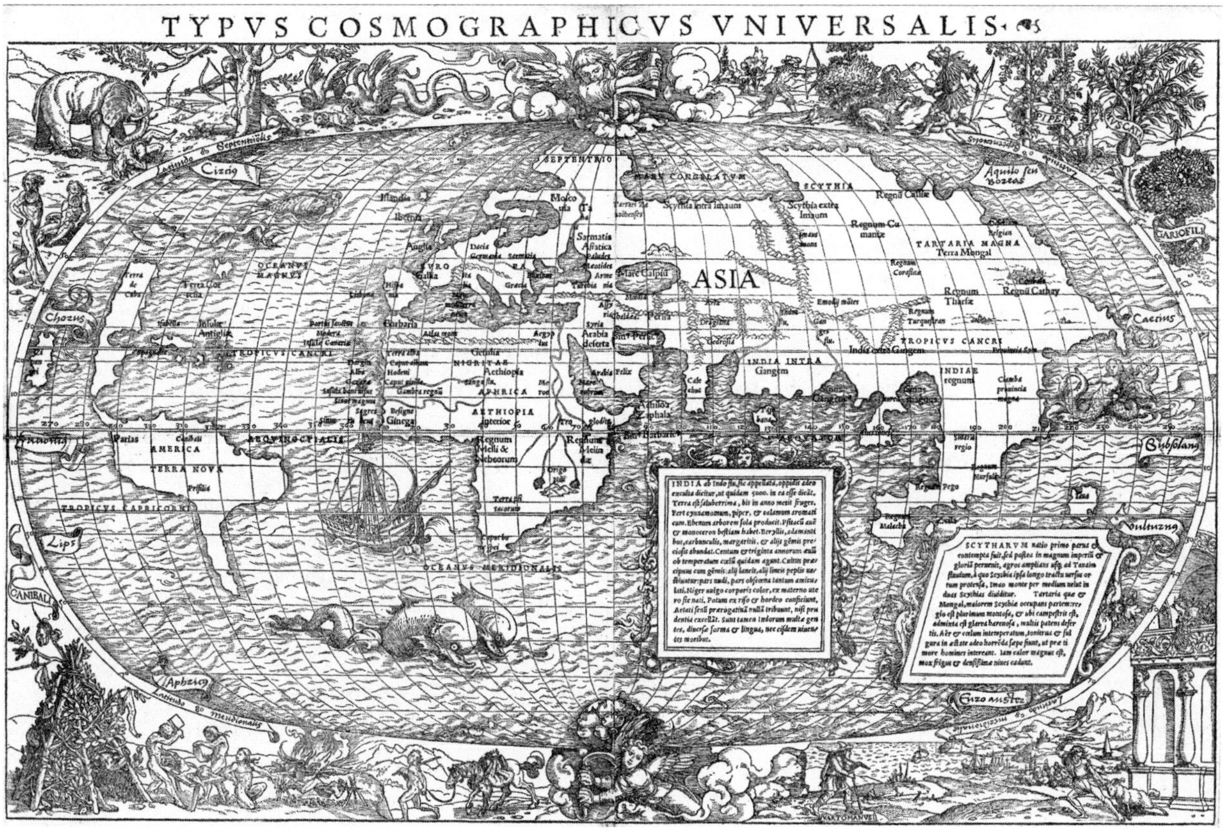

16.2 Four corner illustrations do not resolve as four parts of the world. Woodcut on paper, 36.9 × 55.4 cm. Sebastian Münster with vignettes possibly by Hans Holbein, *Typus cosmographicus universalis*, made for the publication of Johann Huttich and Simon Grynaeus, *Novus orbis regionum ac insularum veteribus incognitarum* (Basel, 1532), a widely known collection of travel literature.

especially as both quarters and corners were eminently graphic ideas, one presupposing a geometric and equal partition and the other presupposing a rectangular format with corners.[15]

A 1532 map attributed to Münster with illustrations thought to be by Hans Holbein distributes people from various corners of the earth into the four corners of the printed page (fig. 16.2), which function somewhat like the four corners of the earth of Revelation. At bottom right, under the region entitled *Kingdom of India*, we see a king leaning over a parapet while a long-haired figure below deals a blow to a large and ferocious ram of the sort described by Ludovico Varthema in Tarnassari in his East Asian travels, an account included in the book of travel reports for which this map was made (we see the wayfarer Varthema himself, labeled *Vartomanus*, approaching from the left). The other corners show, at top right,

Scythian warriors with plants growing clove, musk, and pepper, at top left Africans engaged in a deadly elephant hunt and two winged snakes, one of whom eats a goat whole, as described by Ludovico Cadamosto in another account included in the book, and at bottom left, a scene of cannibals as described by Vespucci, an account also included in the collection.[16] Strange beasts and behaviors of remote reaches of the earth are appropriately placed in the four corners or spandrels of the map, but these do not represent the four parts of the world.[17]

A little over sixty years after the Münster/Holbein collaboration, the four corners of a printed world map were filled with the parts of the world in a 1594 publication designed by Peter Plancius, though despite the use of four corners the *partes* number five rather than four (fig. 16.3). *Europa* with scepter and cornucopia sits top left, her foot on a globe topped by a cross, and *Asia* with censer on a rhinoceros presides top right, with a camel, elephants, and, incongruously, a giraffe behind her. *Africa* on a crocodile fills the lower right corner, which she shares with the figure of *Magellanica*, the Antarctic region, who is strangely shown on an elephant. Finally, in the lower left, where one might have expected America, there are instead two figures: *Mexicana* on an armadillo with a bow and arrow and *Peruana* with a feather headdress sitting on a spotted cat, and in the backgrounds of both scenes of cannibalism. More than two decades after Ortelius's 1570 frontispiece, with its four parts and a partial fifth, Magellanica, the four parts of the world were not an unavoidable scheme, even when filling four corners of a map. A similar splitting of America occurs in a 1608 map of the prominent Flemish cartographer Jodocus Hondius, where he shows the traditional medieval schema of three parts of the world populated by the three sons of Noah, which cedes place to the modern schema that includes the new world, though in depicting the parts of the world he shows five, not four, women: Europe, Africa, Asia, and then two feathered figures flanking Europe. Are the two unfamiliar and unnamed figures to be identified as *Mexicana* and *Peruana*, as in Plancius, or are they premonitions of the modern designations, North and South America?[18]

Amerasian America

Beginning in the 1570s, the imagery of the parts of the world began to be propagated primarily in printed forms, atlases, frontispieces, print series, and iconographic manuals, and also found expression in performances, ceiling and wall frescos, textiles, ceramics, and sculptures, and in seemingly endless baroque decorative schemes.[19] This new iconography was driven by the impulse to create difference, yet the materials at its disposal were predominantly Amerasian, imprinting the new iconographic

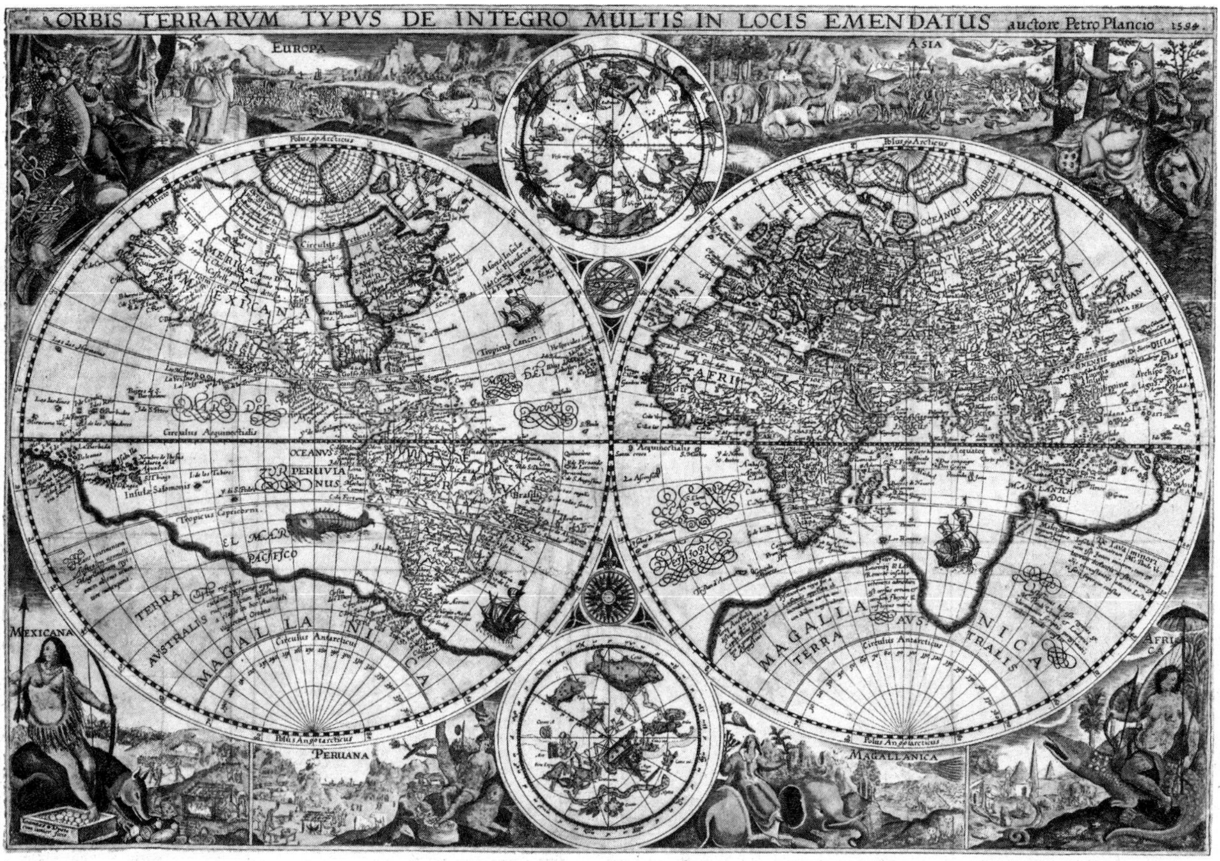

16.3 Parts of the world, or regions? Hand-colored woodcut on paper, 41 × 58 cm. Jan van Doetechum the younger, after Petrus Plancius, *Map of the World, Improved and Complete in All Its Parts* (*Orbis terrarum typus de integro multis in locis emendatus* (map of the world, improved and complete in all its parts) (Amsterdam, 1594). Like the Münster/Holbein map, Plancius's map was included in a larger publication, one of the most widely read travel accounts of the time, in this case Jan Huyghen van Linschoten's *Itinerario* of 1596.

scheme with Amerasian thinking. In fact, every one of the most characteristic features of the personification of America as it emerged at this time—nakedness, cannibalism, tropicality, feathers, and specifically the figure of the Amazon, the most persistent figure for America—had a heritage that connected it to Asia, and several identifiers of Asia and Africa were taken over from America, as we will see. The success of the new iconography thus ensured the further propagation of Amerasian themes. Like other developments we have traced, this was not a progressive history; Amerasian continuities did not simply disappear because the parts—often four but not always—were named and figured. As we will see in the next chapter, Amerasian views of the world continued to find new forms and expressions, even as the vastness of the Pacific was recognized and the iconography of the parts of the world found new expression.

Even in schemas of four parts, the iconography of America bristles with Asian and African features. A drawing attributed to Maerten de Vos in the University of Michigan Museum shows the allegorical figure of America seated in the foreground with a lion and rhinoceros in the background.[20] The rhino is based on Albrecht Dürer's famous woodcut, whose inscription clearly explains that the animal had come from India. The frontispiece of Jean Jacques Boissard's *Habitus variarum orbis gentium* (Cologne, 1581) shows the allegory of America with (African) ostrich rather than parrot feathers, and Cesare Ripa's influential *Iconologia* (1593, first illustrated 1603, here shown in a 1624 edition) shows a partially naked Amazonian America, holding a bow and arrows and standing over a human head (fig. 16.4). The crocodile that is assigned to Africa on Plancius 1594 map, discussed earlier (also used as an attribute of Africa in the frontispiece of the fifth volume of Georg Braun and Franz Hogenberg's *Civitates orbis terrarum*, also from 1594), is given to America by Ripa (who calls it a large lizard), and her headdress includes prominent feathers of peacock, native to Asia.

Even when only American features—such as feather garments and ornaments—describe America, America continues to be connected to India, as in the case of an elaborate 1599 procession and tournament at Stuttgart staging an embassy of representatives of America, including America's "Queen," where the figures were dressed in actual pieces of featherwork imported from Brazil and elsewhere, some of them carrying American artifacts, such as the Mesoamerican feather shield discussed in chapter 7 (see fig. 7.1a). These American visitors were in fact played by leading figures of the Duchy of Württemberg, with Duke Friedrich I in a gender switch playing "Queen America" herself, arrayed in feathers.[21] Although focused exclusively on America, the procession was framed as a kind of ushering onto the world stage of this new part of the world, now welcomed as a

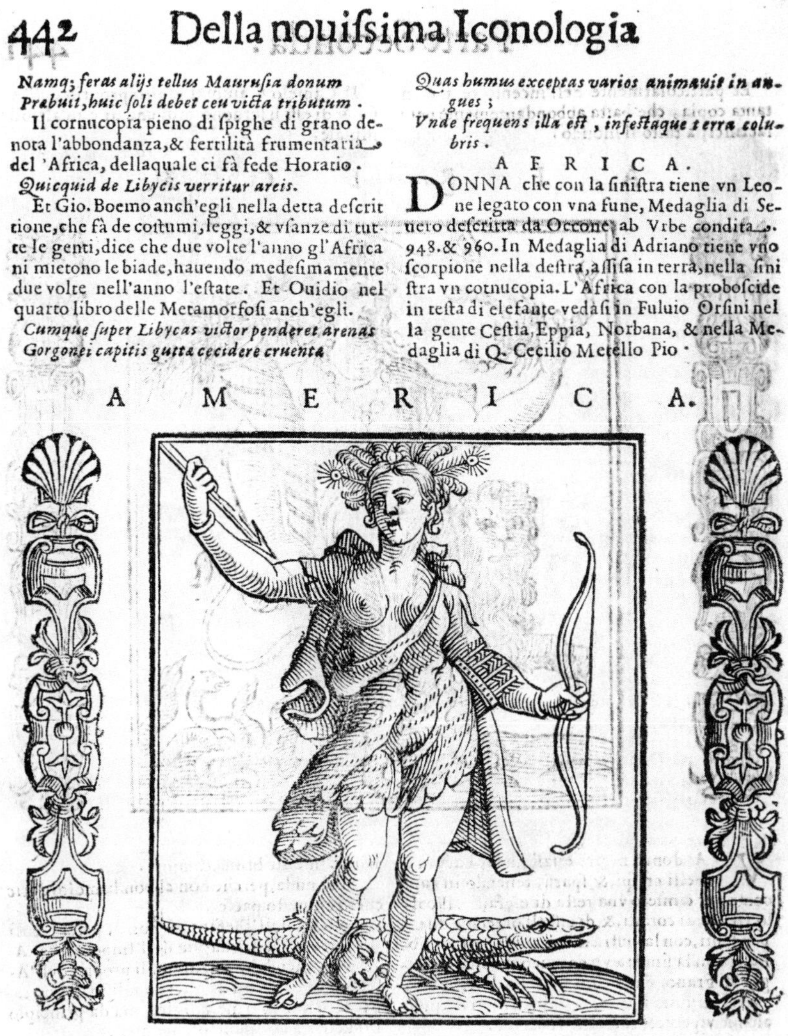

442 Della nouifsima Iconologia

Namq; feras alijs tellus Maurusia donum
Prabuit, huic soli debet ceu victa tributum.

Il cornucopia pieno di spighe di grano denota l'abbondanza, & fertilità frumentaria del 'Africa, dellaquale ci fà fede Horatio.

Quicquid de Libycis verritur areis.

Et Gio. Boemo anch'egli nella detta descrittione, che fà de costumi, leggi, & vsanze di tutte le genti, dice che due volte l'anno gl'Africani mietono le biade, hauendo medesimamente due volte nell'anno l'estate. Et Ouidio nel quarto libro delle Metamorfosi anch'egli.

Cumque super Libycas victor penderet arenas
Gorgonei capitis gutta cecidere cruenta
Quas humus exceptas varios animauit in angues;
Vnde frequens illa est, infestaque terra colubris.

A F R I C A.

DONNA che con la sinistra tiene vn Leone legato con vna fune, Medaglia di Seuero descritta da Occone ab Vrbe condita. 948. & 960. In Medaglia di Adriano tiene vno scorpione nella destra, assisa in terra, nella sinistra vn cornucopia. L'Africa con la proboscide in testa di elefante vedasi in Fuluio Orsini nella gente Cestia, Eppia, Norbana, & nella Medaglia di Q. Cecilio Metello Pio.

A M E R I C A.

16.4 America the Cannibal Amazon. Woodcut on paper. Cesare Ripa, *Iconologia* (Padua, 1624), Part 2, p. 442.

"sister" of equal standing to the traditional three of Europe, Africa, and Asia. America's identification as new suggests a clear understanding of her difference and separateness from the other parts, yet in the manuscript describing the procession she is described as "America, Grosse Königin in India"—not a great Indian Queen, but a great Queen in India. America may be distinct enough to be identified as new, but she is still a part of India.

America's ongoing connection to India comes through even in programs devoted to identifying and distinguishing the different parts of

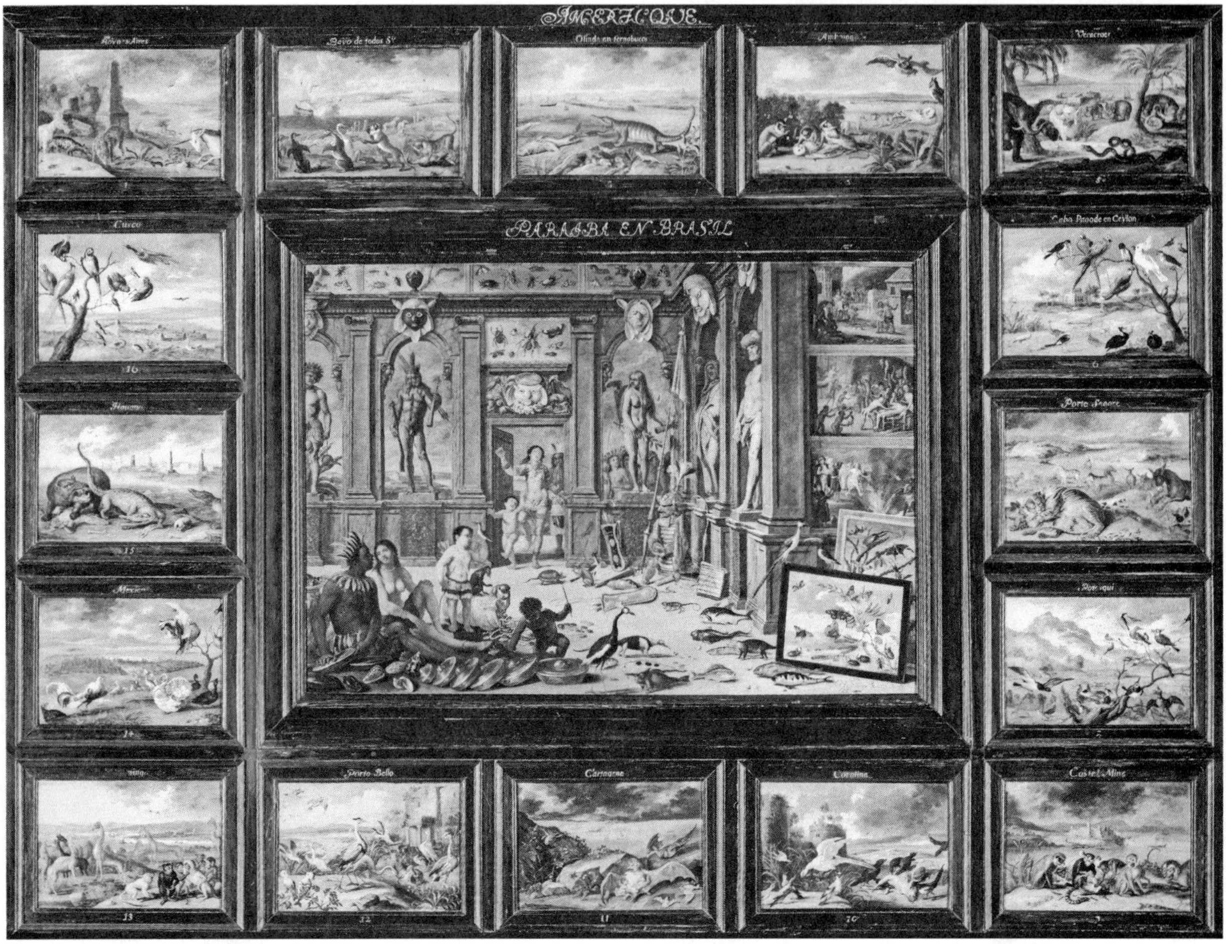

16.5 America with vignettes from India. Jan van Kessel, *America*, oil on canvas, 48.5 × 67.5 cm (1664–66). Munich, Alte Pinakothek. (See color plates.)

the word, such as in a series of paintings on copper of the *Four Parts of the World* made in 1664–66 by the Flemish artist Jan van Kessel, each representing a part of the world with a Kunstkammer-type environment of objects, sculptures, inset paintings, and people, in turn surrounded by scenes of towns and places belonging to each part.[22] The panel devoted to *America* is marked by spectacular Amerasian combinations (fig. 16.5). The eye-catching, dynamic figure of a woman with bare midriff and anklets and thighlets entering the room at center is in fact drawn from an engraved illustration in Jan Huyghen van Linschoten's *Itinerario* of 1596 showing a "singing and dancing prostitute from India" (*Inda meretrix saltando et canendo*), and the statues on the right, a turbaned figure with loincloth and a robed figure, are drawn from Linschoten's illustrations of Brahmins, "priests of the idols in India." To the right of the turbaned figure are inset paintings depicting American rites and customs, one of which shows a scene of cannibalism, and directly below, a scene of Sati (fig. 16.6), in which a widow throws herself into a fire after her husband's death, again drawn from an illustration in Linschoten.[23] The most widely illustrated meme of life in India is here used to characterize America.

In brief, Kessel's *America* works with the expanded field of India introduced in chapter 1 and studied in chapter 12, while also incorporating allusions to the Chinese-Japanese-Mexican range that came under study in chapter 13. Remarkably, in the corner of the room depicted by Kessel sits an example of Japanese samurai armor, decorated on the breastplate with Chinese characters meaning "all under heaven" (used by both the Chinese and Japanese to refer to their dominions), characters repeated on a panel next to the armor. That the Japanese armor was not simply mistakenly reassigned to America is clear from the fact that similar armor is shown in Kessel's accompanying panel representing *Asia*, where it is worn by a figure in the middle ground. The two depictions of samurai armor in fact render two existing sets of Japanese armor once in the collection of Albrecht of Habsburg and now on view at Schloss Ambras in Innsbruck (fig. 16.7); it was Kessel's decision to distribute the pair to either side of the Pacific.[24] Kassel's *Four Parts* recombine elements from the different parts, and also suggest continuities between them.

Europe as Set Designer of the World

To summarize, the structure of the parts of the world was far from a straightforward proposition in works of visual art. Artists and presumably their audiences were not always clear about which attributes went where, or even how many parts of the world there were. It is not simply that the new part, America, had to borrow some of its features from the

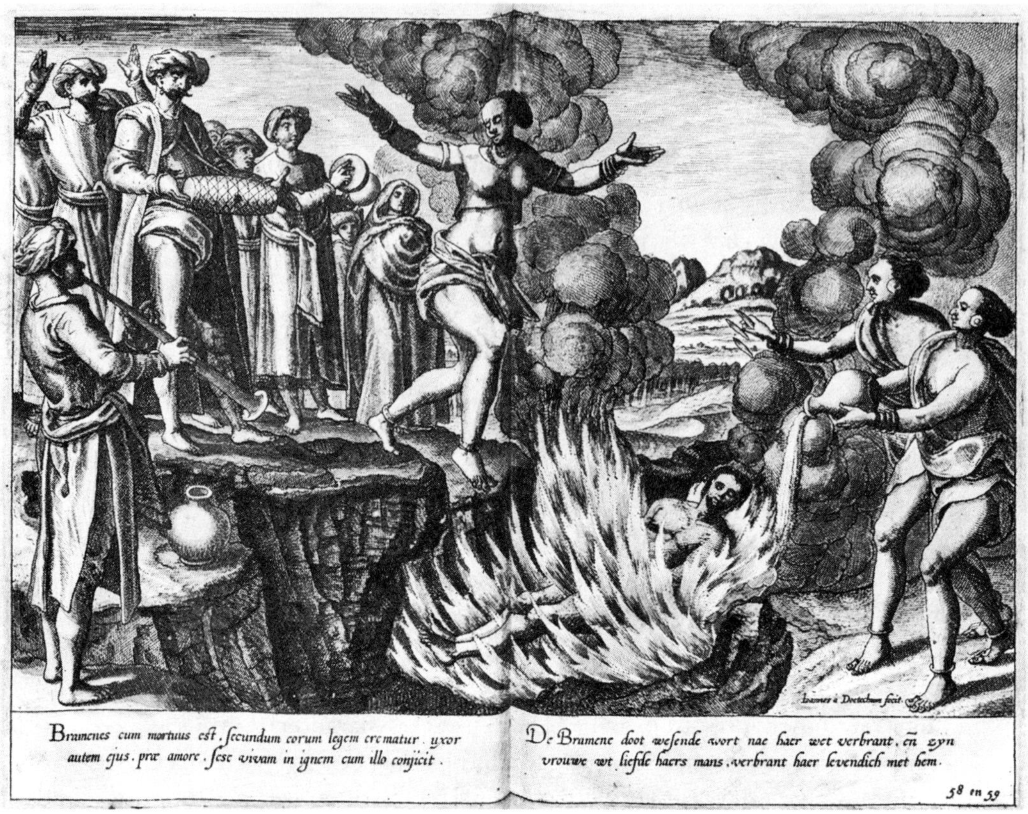

16.6 ***Sati*, the most depicted Indian ritual, in one of the most popular publications of the day.** Hand-colored woodcut on paper. Jan Huyghen van Linschoten, *Itinerario* (Amsterdam, 1596).

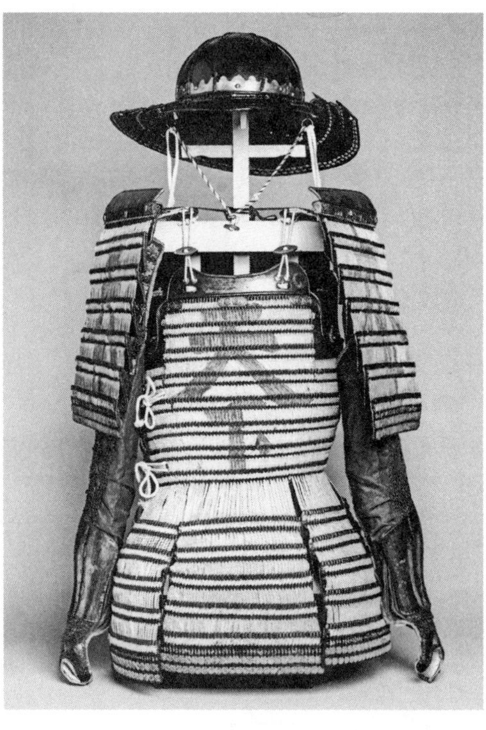

16.7 The very specimen of Japanese samurai armor shown in Jan van Kessel's *America*. Iron, brass, copper, leather, lacquer, wood. Innsbruck, Schloss Ambras, ca. 1580.

traditional three, but rather that the new iconography of the parts of the world was continually drawn into the force fields of already existing and powerful metageographical models, which intersected productively and unstably with the new quadripartite organization. One can see the zonal view of the world (see chapter 1) continuing to exert a magnetic pull well into the seventeenth century, moving tropical features such as crocodiles or palm trees or parrots around among Asia, Africa, and America. The expandable and modular conception of India (see chapters 1 and 12) also remains in play, sending gold, jewels and abundance to America and feather gear back and forth from America to Asia and Africa. The abstract geometric ordering of the four quarters of the earth also occasionally plays a role, as when the well-dressed Europe and Asia of the global north preside over the naked Africa and America of the global south. In those cases, we have a model closer to the one adopted by Jost Amman in his image of the world's clothing (see fig. 12.1), where Asia is understood as a nontropical range from Turks through Persians and Muscovites, and tropical India is absorbed into identity with America. At other times, an antipodal logic prevails, leaving Africa and Asia to either side and privileging the mutually defining face-to-face encounter between Europe and America. The overall impression one has in reviewing this image tradition—as recent books and a database allow us to do[25]—is of a constant recalibration imposed by the intersections among the different models.

The environment for these intersections and recalibrations was, initially and primarily, the medium of print (see chapter 15), which provided a unified field on which these figurations could shape and sort each other. The effort of figuration that went into the iconography of the four parts is fairly clearly visible in the allegorical figure of Europe itself, if one looks for it. Modern interpreters often endorse the readings of the figure of Europe offered in the sources themselves, seeing the crowned and sceptered figure as an expression of European dominance, as poems explicating Ortelius's frontispiece do, and as the text of Ripa insists: "The crown she wears on her head is to show that Europe has always been superior, and Queen of the world" (fig. 16.8). This claim was patently overblown at the time, as the upstart Europeans well knew; it was a reflection of European dominance in the realm of "world-making"—the representation and mapping of the world, the imaginary of the global itself.[26]

In some allegories, Europe sits on a globe, not the earth but a three-dimensional model of the earth, a signal invention of European cosmographers. In Ortelius's frontispiece (see fig. 16.1), she is flanked by terrestrial and celestial globes, a cosmographic gateway to the atlas that unfolds behind the frontispiece. In Ripa's figure of Europe for the 1624 edition, a

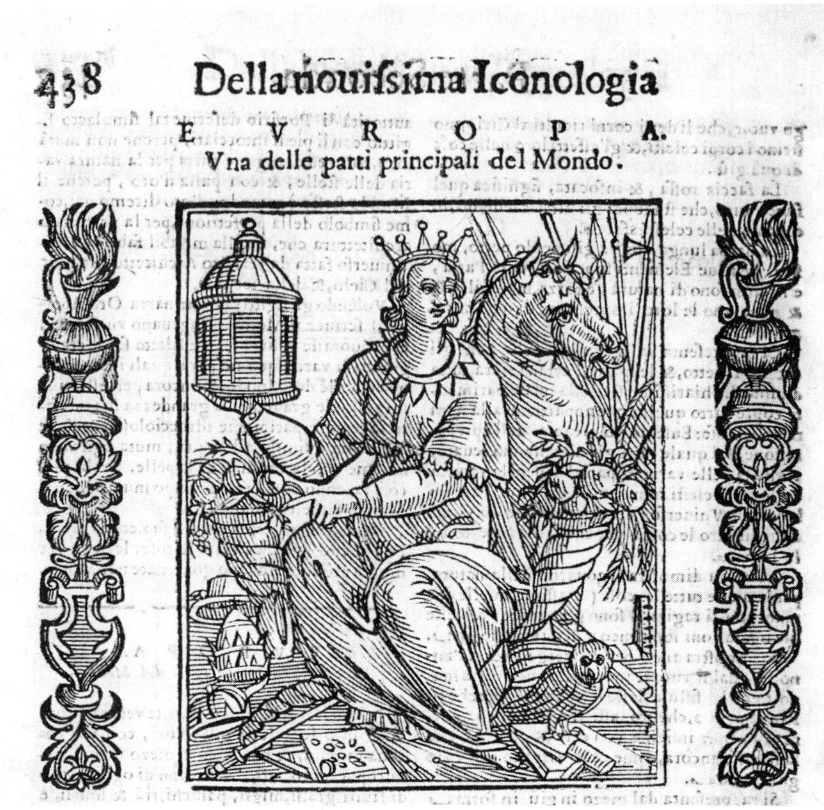

16.8 Europa as mistress of the arts. Woodcut on paper. Cesare Ripa, *Iconologia* (Padua, 1624), part 2, p. 438.

more elaborated version of the figure from the first illustrated edition of 1603, Europe's attributes are predominantly the trappings of the arts: she holds a *bellissimo tempietto*, a symbol of religion but also of perfect architecture itself, and at her feet, under the owl of Minerva, are books, musical instruments, an L-square, chisels, and paintbrushes, which "signify having had and having illustrious men and brilliant talents both among the Greeks and Latins and others excellent in painting, sculpture, and architecture." (Print-making, not shown, remains the invisible enabler.) Directly next to her right foot is a tablet with various inchoate shapes, a difficult-to-read attribute that in light of the accompanying text comes into legibility as a painter's palette, the scattered, irregular shapes on this surface representing dollops of paint, each of a different color, though in printed form they look like unnamed islands in black and white, an archipelago of forms from which some image will emerge. And to return to Ortelius's frontispiece, is it a coincidence that *America* is shown nude, below Europe's feet, for all the world like a nude study, holding a head like a studio prop, while next to her *Magellanica* is shown as an unfinished sculpture? In its own self-figuration, Europe is above all a mistress of the arts, the plastic intelligence that figures the world and the cosmos, the set designer of the *theatrum orbis terrarum*.

• • •

Epitome: Amerasian Amazonian America

How did Europe fashion the figure of what was possibly its greatest invention, America, the first of the *Nova Reperta*? Even as attributes shifted from one allegory to another, the two features that most persistently identify America—that she is a cannibal and an Amazon—were also the most clearly Asian in derivation. Like Ripa's *America*, and equally influential, Adriaen Collaert's engraving of about 1590 based on a design by Maerten de Vos shows America as a cannibalistic Amazon (fig. 16.9).

A naked female warrior sits on an armadillo, wearing an elaborate feathered military helmet and wielding a battle axe (with a curiously smooth curve, perhaps suggesting that it is made out of Mexican obsidian and not metal) and a bow with a quiver of arrows. Behind her is a battle scene, Americans without metal armor pitted against their well-equipped European invaders, and at the left margin a cannibalistic meal in progress. In chapter 1, we reviewed the Asian provenance of the new world cannibals described by Columbus and others, who drew on descriptions of Far Eastern islands in Polo, John Mandeville, and elsewhere. Cannibalism then became an identifying feature of people across the Atlantic, whether in the islands near Hispaniola or in Brazil; we see it in Ortelius's iconic frontispiece and many other images of America. And yet the cannibal identity never quite shook off its Asian provenance. Waldseemüller's 1516 *Carta marina* puts them (back) in Asia, and, in a typical example of Amerasian reflux, a *derrotero* or travel log of the 1580s, discussed in chapter 6, describes a community of cannibals called "Caribs" on the island of Cipangu or Japan.

Beyond her cannibalism, the nude female huntress that so often personifies America was based on the figure of the Amazon, a tribe whose origins were located in Scythian Asia. Herodotus had placed them on the banks of the Thermodon (Terme) River in southern Cappadocia, in what is today Turkey, and Mandeville had located "the land of Amazonia, in which there are no men, only women," somewhere between Persia and India.[27] On Caspar Vopel's mid-sixteenth-century world map, discussed in chapter 11, an inscription locates them just west of what he calls the Scythian Gulf, *Sinus Scythiacus*, somewhat to the south and west of the Scythians. As he did with

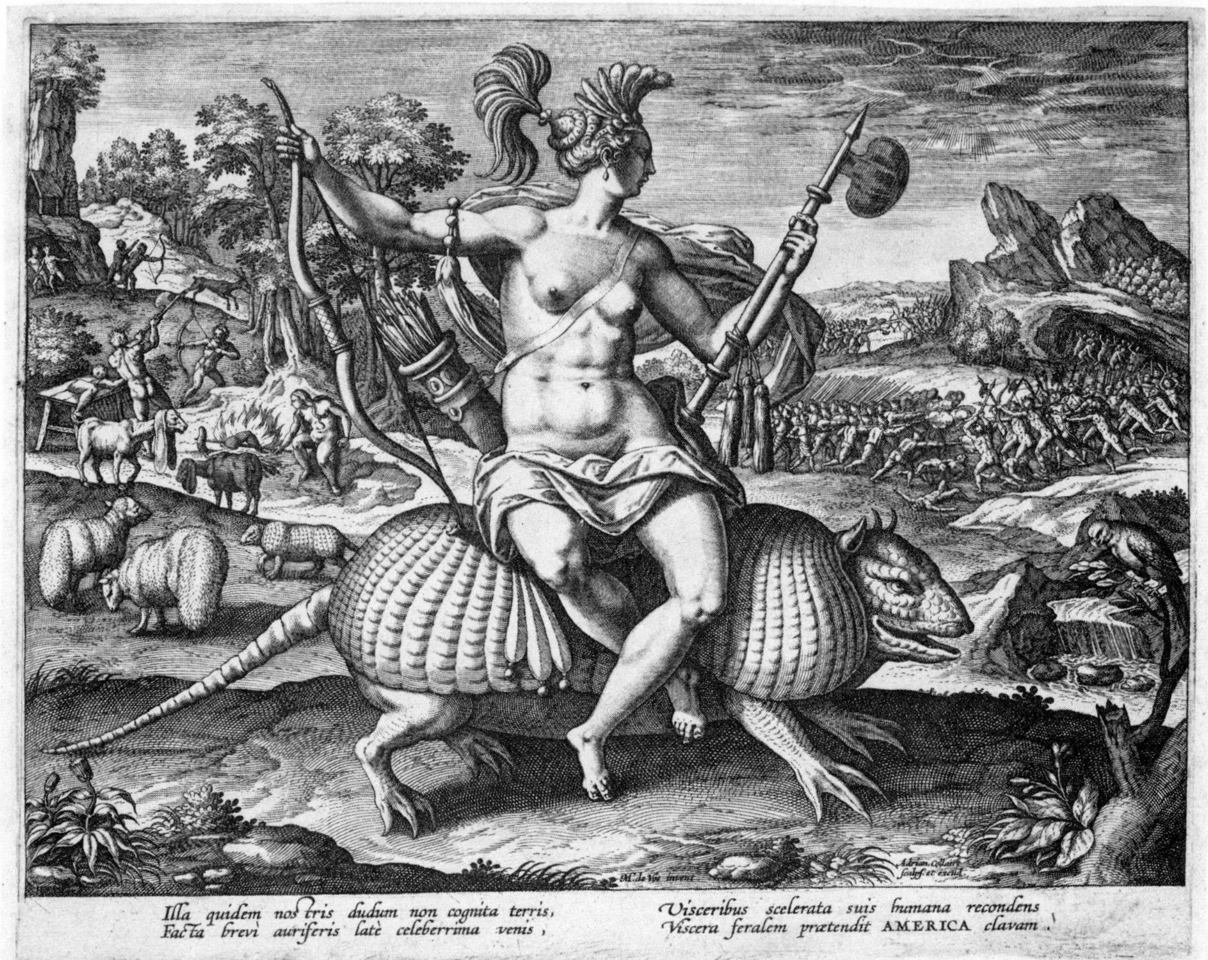

16.9 America as Cannibal Amazon. Adriaen Collaert after Maarten de Vos, *America*, engraving on paper, 21.3 × 25.6 cm (ca. 1590). New York, Metropolitan Museum of Art.

several other Asian traditions, Columbus transplanted the Amazons to the new world across the Atlantic when he reported the absence of men on the island of Matinino (Martinique), launching a decades-long series of Amazon sightings in America.[28] The Castilian writer Garci Rodríguez de Montalvo's chivalric romance *The Adventures of Esplandián* (*Las sergas de Esplandián*) of 1510 described Amazons on the "island" of California.[29] In 1517, the conquistador Juan Díaz reported having heard of Amazons inhabiting the northern shore of the Yucatán.[30] The governor of Cuba, Diego Velázquez, referred to the Amazons in his instructions to Hernán Cortés on the eve of his expedition to Mexico in 1519, and Cortés reported their presence in his fourth letter of October 15, 1524.[31] Indigenous descriptions of the matriarchal organization and culture of certain Peruvian tribes, in particular the customs of the "Inca Virgins," became identified with the Amazons.[32] The Amazon River and the surrounding jungle acquired that name during Francisco de Orellana's 1541 expedition into the area, during which reports were heard of a community called by the locals *coniu puyara* ("large women") who lived further down the valley and to whom surrounding communities offered tribute, leading the Spaniards to identify them as "Amazonas."[33] By 1535, the many reports of American Amazons had tested the patience of the naturalist Gonzalo Fernández de Oviedo, who insisted that the female warrior tribes of America are called Amazons "improperly" and "cannot be called Amazons," while allowing that they "imitate those that the ancients called Amazons."[34] The French cosmographer André Thevet tried and failed to settle the issue of Amazons in America in his *Singularitez de la France Antartique* of 1557 (see chapter 9), carefully weighing whether they were descendants of the Scythian Amazons who had migrated to America or simply a parallel phenomenon, and finally leaving the question unresolved and thus open to further speculation.[35] At the end of the sixteenth century, the English explorer Sir Walter Ralegh reported hearing of Amazons in Guiana, an empire rich in gold rumored to exist east of Peru.[36] Like the word *Indios* used to describe the populations of America and the word *cannibal* itself, the identifier *Amazonas* for the river and surrounding region is a signal Amerasian trace in modern geographical language.

The figure that most consistently represented America toward the end of the sixteenth century—the cannibal Amazon—had migrated from Asia. This is not a hidden cultural derivation that we are now bringing to light. The American Amazon's Asian provenance and her relation to her Asian sisters was a live topic of debate during the period that saw her figure propagated in books, prints, tapestry cycles, palace cabinets, civic spaces, and courtly performances. The figure of America was a conscious creation of the Amerasian imagination.

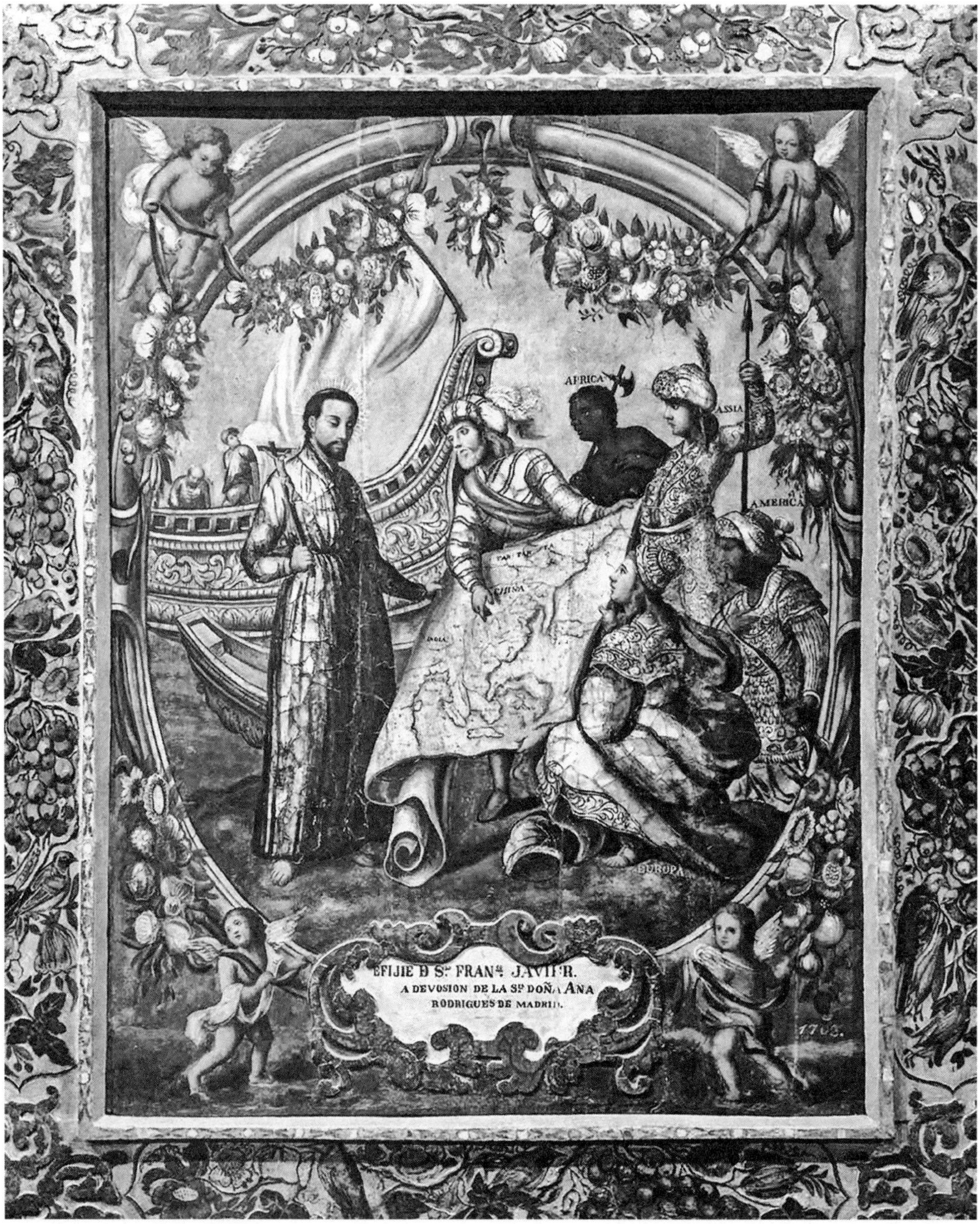

17.1 In a painting made in Mexico City, Saint Francis Xavier is presented with a map of Asia. Juan González, *Saint Francis Xavier Contemplating His Missions*, oil paint on wood inlaid with mother-of-pearl, 113 × 91.8 cm (1703). Mexico City, private collection.

SEVENTEEN

Nacreous Amerasia: The Impact of the Manila Galleon

In Mexico City in 1703, the artist Juan González produced an *enconchado* or mother-of-pearl shell painting of *Saint Francis Contemplating His Missions* for Ana Rodríguez de Madrid, the sister of the first marquis of Villamediana and the daughter of Pascual Rodríguez de Mediavilla y Rodríguez del Corral, who had come to Mexico a generation earlier (fig. 17.1).[1] Inspired by Asian shell inlay techniques found in Indo-Portuguese objects and in Japanese lacquer items that were imported into New Spain, *enconchados* were developed in Mexico by setting pieces of Native mother-of-pearl into pictures made using techniques of European oil painting.[2] Asian traditions are present in this *enconchado*, not only in the application of shell pieces but also in the entire makeup of the work, where the scene of the saint—widely celebrated in viceregal Mexico even though he never set foot in the Americas—is subordinated to a framework of ornamentation.

Aesthetics of Interactivity

What is happening on the technical level—a European-style picture embedded in and interacting with an Asian-derived ornamental framework—is reflected in the picture's subject, which shows a European saint landing in Asian territory and simultaneously gazing at a map of Asia as he plots the epochal conversion of the vastest part of the world. Both at the technical level and at the level of the depicted story, the European element is central yet exotic. Embedded in Asia yet foreign to it, the saint will need to insert himself into the ways of these cultures in order to transform and convert them from within. Or will they transform and engulf him? The official accounts of the Jesuit order tell one story, but perhaps the objects, showing the European techniques embedded into an Asian (or rather Amerasian) framework, tell another.

Native to both Asia and America, mother-of-pearl, or nacre, is a composite material produced by some mollusks as a protective inner shell layer. Both organic and inorganic, it is made up of platelets of aragonite separated by sheets of elastic polymers, a combination of staggered structure and interstitial flexibility that gives nacre its extraordinary resilience against fracture.[3] Like the colors of certain bird feathers, the characteristic iridescence of mother-of-pearl is an effect of structural coloration, which unlike pigments and dyes is not chemically inherent to the material but produced by the interaction of light with a structure of varying reflective and refractive properties. This means that its colors appear different from different viewing angles, the curving form of mollusk shells ensuring that dynamic color variation accompanies the experience of viewing as one moves the shell or moves in relation to the shell, even slightly. When an artist then breaks the shell's curved surface and embeds segments of it into a flat panel whose express purpose is to offer an image to attentive visual inspection, this variability becomes something of an aesthetic principle.

The visual play of the mother-of-pearl enters into conversation with the oil paint applied by the painter, who manipulates its saturation and color in order to describe figures and settings that will summon a scene before the eyes of the viewer. The mother-of-pearl both collaborates and interferes with the representational work of painting, giving the *enconchado* panel its characteristic quality of multifaceted shimmer. One could say that the technique of nacre inlay scatters surfaces, disrupting the naturalistic effects of the European painting technique, but one can equally well say something close to the opposite: the shell pieces introduce into the picture the stunning material and visual effects of nature itself, against which painting is revealed as what it is, a human art that imitates nature through the manipulation of pigment on panel. The overall effect is to break up the unity of the scene understood as an independent whole to be "read," and to create competing and complementary interactions at the level of material and light.

As the shell pieces send light in different directions, the viewer adapts to seeing the figures as both part of the scene and as part of an object that is itself in motion and in active relation to a world inhabited by mobile people, for almost all *enconchados* were made as mobile works. The figures belong to the scene even as they are integrated into an object made up of many materials and modes. The depicted figures inhabit a particular time (the sixteenth-century missionary saint arriving in Asia) and also other times, or no time in particular. Bringing European and Asian artistic traditions into dialogue on the unstable surfaces of a recently colonized land being refashioned as a node of global commerce, *enconchados* reflect interacting worlds and produce interacting worlds.

González's *enconchado* is based on an engraving by the Dutch artist Cornelis Bloemaert II, which was made as a frontispiece for the volume on Asia for Daniello Bartoli's multivolume history of the Jesuit order of the 1650s (fig. 17.2). The engraving shows a map of Asia unfurled before the saint, who has disembarked from an Asian junk in the background, with more Asian-style sailing ships shown on the horizon. Three male figures are turbaned, and a kneeling female figure in a jeweled headdress and silk mantle with an open sack of jewels at her feet, probably an allegory of Asia, holds open a map that shows the extent of Asia from Goa in the west to Japan in the east, Tartaria to the north to Java in the south, all clearly labeled. Behind the map is one shirtless, dark-skinned figure who represents India, though he wields a Brazilian anchor ax, a by-now familiar survival of a long tradition of entanglement in the representation of American and Asian Indians (see chapters 2 and 12).[4]

The scene undergoes further Amerasian transformations when translated into the terms of González's *enconchado*, produced across the ocean in New Spain, and not only because the technique has become mixed. The *enconchado* eliminates the figure farthest right of the engraving, who wears a tightly fitting head covering and probably was intended to represent a Chinese man.[5] What had been an array of Asian figures in the print are now globally distributed, as inscriptions are added identifying the dark-skinned man as Africa, the turbaned man next to him as Asia, and the kneeling man to the right as America (his moustache, turban, armor, and Scythian bow notwithstanding!). The female figure below with the jeweled crown and long hair, who in the print reads as an allegory of Asia, is labeled Europa in the *enconchado*. Standing as a frontispiece for the volume dedicated to the missionary activities of the Jesuits in Asia, the 1653 engraving presented Francis Xavier as the first Jesuit to mount missions in the east, emphatically locating him in Asia on three different levels—landing with bare feet on an Asian shore, greeted by Asian figures, and contemplating a cartographic representation of Asia.

Freed from the Asian context of the Jesuit history, the image as presented by the *enconchado* opens up the frame of reference, showing the saint welcomed by all the parts of the world. Furthermore, the map itself has been subtly but significantly altered in what can only be a deliberate revision. Whereas in the engraving the map shows at far right the legendary Strait of Anian separating Asia and America, the map in the *enconchado* instead shows a continuous landmass connecting Asia and America. (For the oscillation between the two geographical models well into the seventeenth century, see chapter 11.) Both at the level of technique and representation, therefore, the *enconchado* extends Saint Francis Xavier's

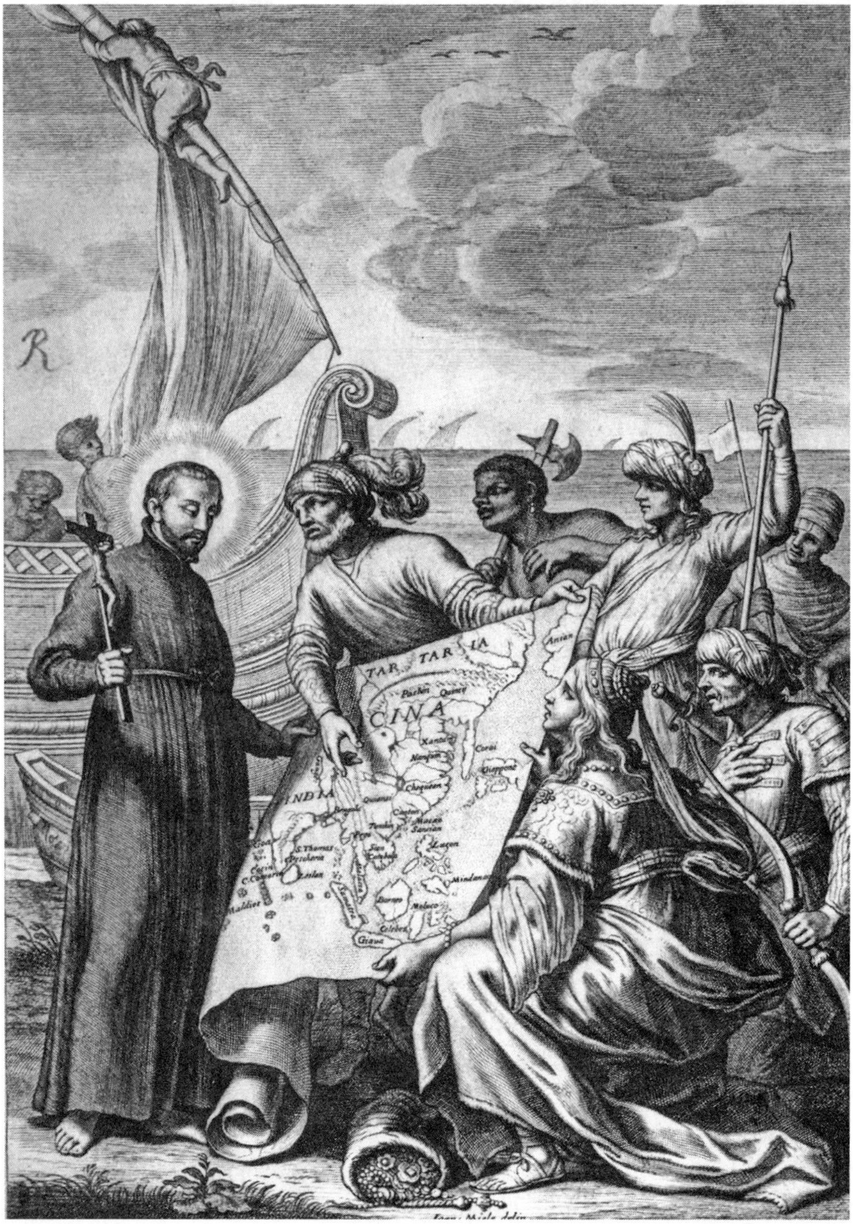

17.2 The source engraving shows a different map, with a strait separating America and Asia. Cornelis Bloemaert II, after Jan Miel, *Saint Francis Xavier Landing in Asia*, engraving on paper, frontispiece from Daniello Bartoli's *Dell'Historia della Compagnia di Giesu: l'Asia* (Rome, 1653).

already expansive worldly missions, specifically suggesting an extension from Asia far beyond the Ganges into America.

Francis Xavier's missions did open an expanded world in the minds of young Jesuits petitioning to be sent on mission to "the Indies." In the so-called *Indipetae*, letters of application to go on extra-European missions dating between the 1580s and the 1770s and preserved at the Jesuit archive in Rome, most petitioners express a general desire to go *all'Indie*, speaking of wanting to go to the *parte dell'Indie* or the *missione dell'Indie*, without naming a specific destination. A few mention *Indie orientali* and *Indie occidentali*, yet more often they speak of the Indies collectively. For example, one Camillo de Amatis says that now that the cross has been planted in *India*, *Giappone*, *Mogor* (a reference to Moghul controlled lands in India) *et Peru*, Christ is calling him and awaits him *in quelle parti*, suggesting they are all grouped together in their remoteness. Other letters make a point of their indifference to the chosen destination, as if to declare their blind obedience. An unnamed petitioner wants to go on mission to "the Indies, even though I don't know which Indies these are, nor do I care to know" (*se bene non so quali indie siano, ne mi curo ciò sabere*).[6]

Feather-Wearing Asians

It was a Jesuit pattern, part of a larger Amerasian tradition, to merge these parts of the world and in turn to mix American elements into the depiction of Asians. An engraving of 1690 by Philip Kilian illustrating a *Life of Saint Francis Xavier* shows the saint offering, in the year 1551, an image of the Virgin to the samurai Otomo Sorin, the king of Bungo in Japan's present-day Oita province (fig. 17.3).[7] The warriors in Otomo Sorin's retinue are shown wearing feather headdresses and skirts originally derived from the featherwork of Brazilian Tupi peoples and widely applied to both American and Asian figures in European imagery since the beginning of the sixteenth century. Likewise, on the altar dedicated to Saint Francis Xavier at the Jesuit mother church of the Gesù in Rome, Carlo Maratta's painting of 1682 shows the saint dying on the island of Shangchuan off the coast of southern China; a nearby local, his hands in prayer, wears a feather headdress starkly set out against the sky, a detail preserved in a 1733 engraved copy of the painting by Jacob Frey the Elder, which broadcast its composition far and wide.

Further authoritative examples of paintings for Jesuit churches confirm the pattern. Luca Giordano's 1685 altarpiece for the church of San Francesco Saverio in Naples, now in the Capodimonte Museum, shows the saint preaching to the "Indians," by which is meant Asians, among whom we see a figure with a feather skirt and another with a feather headdress. On the

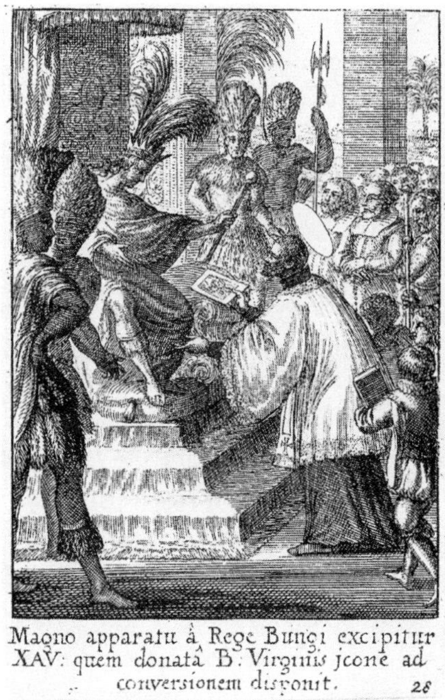

17.3 Feather-wearing samurai. Philip Kilian, Saint Francis Xavier presenting an image of the Virgin to the samurai Otomo Sorin, King of Bungo, engraving on paper, illustration in Anton Schmerling, *Vita S. Francisci Xavierii e Societate Jesu, Indiarum et Iaponiae Apostoli*… (Vienna, 1690), p. G7.

ceiling of the Jesuit church of Sant'Ignazio in Rome, painted around 1690 by Andrea Pozzo, we see allegories of the four parts of the world occupying the lower zone while saved souls rise above them toward the vault of heaven. Above the figure of Asia, who rides a camel, several saved Asian souls rise into the clouds, where they are received by the missionary of Asia, Saint Francis Xavier; more than one of them wear feather skirts of the sort often used in depictions of Americans and that by this point had become a shared Amerasian feature. Across the vault, above the figure of America, the rising figures look much like their Asian counterparts, with close-cropped hair and only slightly darker skin, suggesting a basic commonality across a range of difference. The figure of America herself wears a feather headdress, connecting her to the Asians across the vault, and she rides a striped tiger, an animal associated with India since antiquity.

Jesuit depictions showed Saint Francis Xavier converting "Indians" with feather ornaments not because anyone imagined an American episode in the life of the saint, but because feather headdresses and skirts had long since become a familiar element in the representations of Asians. This Amerasian iconography also filtered back to artists in New Spain. As the *enconchado* discussed earlier shows, works made in Mexico offered new Amerasian variations on the inherited imagery. A painting made in Mexico in 1721 shows Saint Francis Xavier baptizing an Indian ruler whose companions wear feather headdresses (fig. 17.4).[8] With the "repatriation"

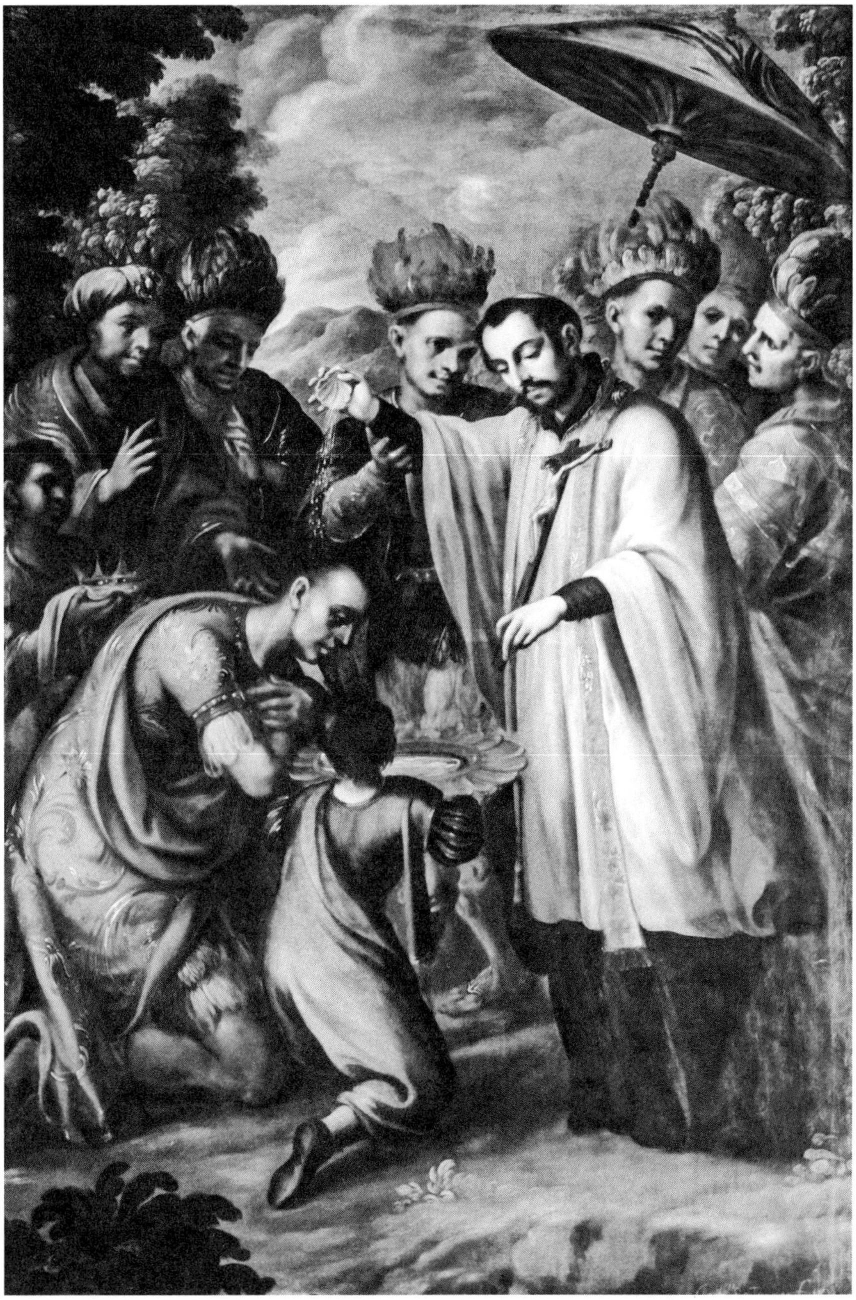

17.4 Saint Francis Xavier somewhere in Amerasia. Antonio de Torres, *Saint Francis Xavier Baptizing an Indian King*, oil on canvas, 217 × 141 cm (1721). Mexico City, Museo del Colegio de San Ignacio de Loyola.

of feather ornaments back into a painting made in America, it is reasonable to wonder: Where in the world are we?

One commentator has suggested that the painting has transplanted the saint to Mexico, where we see him "baptizing a Mexican cacique, who appears to wear a mantle of Asian silk, and figures in the background wear traditional headgear meant to recall imperial Aztec regalia."[9] A Mexican setting is, however, unlikely. It was widely known—and would have been well understood by the members of the Jesuit college for which the painting was made—that Saint Francis Xavier had never crossed the Pacific to Mexico. Many pictorial cycles produced in colonial Mexico and Peru represent the life of Saint Francis Xavier, and they are consistently well informed about the episodes of the life of the saint, respecting the near-canonical sequence of his Asian missions. Some variations in the treatment of the episodes arise, but never do the American cycles devoted to the saint invent wholesale American episodes in his biography.[10] It is more likely that this scene belongs to the well-established Amerasian Jesuit tradition of dressing at least some of Francis Xavier's Asian converts in feather gear, a feature that by this point had become thoroughly integrated into European imagery of Asia and Asians.

In fact, Torres's painting reproduces a composition found in the same 1690 *Life* of the saint discussed earlier (see fig. 17.3). A close compositional match (in reverse) for the 1721 painting can be found in one of the engraved illustrations to the *Life*, where its placement in the narrative sequence and its caption making it clear that it shows Francis Xavier baptizing converts in the subcontinent of India (fig. 17.5).[11] Like Torres's painting, the engraving shows a local ruler wearing a silk mantle, one figure in a turban, the other figures in feather headdresses, with an Asian parasol topping the scene. The Mexican painting translated a composition that is itself the result of a long-standing Amerasian mash-up, (re)introducing it into America.

The critical difference between the European engraving and the painting is the point of view, as the painting imagines the East Indian episode from Mexico, across the Pacific. From an American vantage, Torres's painting imagines a commonality between the Indians over there and those over here, as if to say: "the Indians first encountered in Asia are a lot like the ones encountered by Cortés and others here; there they wear feathers, but also silks and occasionally turbans." From the point of view of the colonial painter Antonio de Torres and his audience, there was no reason to believe that the "Indians" of Asia did not wear feathers, as so many images of them already in circulation for two centuries had shown them doing so (see chapter 12). The feather headdresses and paraphernalia

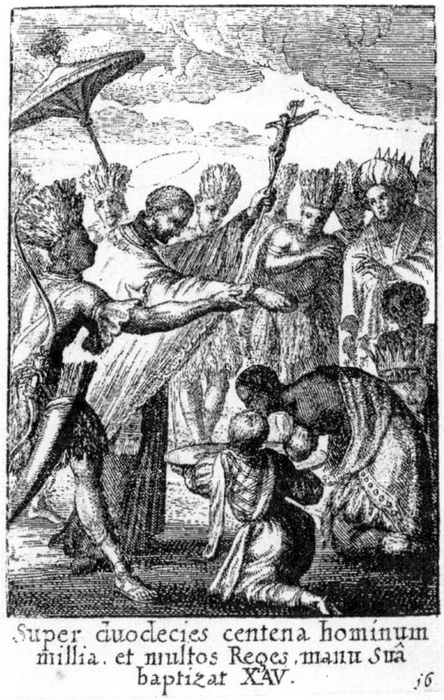

17.5 Feather-wearing Indians of Asia. Philip Kilian, Saint Francis Xavier baptizing inhabitants of India, including kings of the region, engraving on paper, illustration in Anton Schmerling, *Vita S. Francisci Xavierii e Societate Jesu, Indiarum et Iaponiae Apostoli...* (Vienna: University of Vienna, 1690), p. D7.

of both East and West "Indians" were now deeply metabolized in the European imaginary, their distant origins in Brazil buried under two centuries of image production. A Mexican audience in the 1720s, far in space and time from the Tupi of the early sixteenth century, might well *not* have identified those ornaments with Native American indigeneity. Moreover, a number of Indigenous communities from Indonesia and Taiwan and throughout Polynesia did and do wear feather headgear, a fact that could not have been lost on European visitors. It was not in fact a mistake to put such ornaments on representations of Southeast and East Asian peoples, even if the stylings were occasionally conflated with those from American sources.[12] In the Dutch writer Olfert Dapper's 1670 description of China, a depiction of Formosans (Indigenous inhabitants of present-day Taiwan) wearing feather headdresses could be another instance of Amerasian entanglement, as we have been seeing. Then again, given the well attested and continuing use of feather crowns among the Indigenous tribes of Taiwan, it could be accurate reportage (fig. 17.6a–b).

The later seventeenth century in colonial New Spain saw a vogue for images of Hermán Cortés's campaigns in Mexico, including more than one multipaneled series of *enconchados* (fig. 17.7). These depictions do not in fact show Native peoples wearing feather headdresses of the sort we see in Torres's painting. Nor are they near-naked savages. Mexica priests are shown with beards wearing crowns and impressive robes, warriors carry

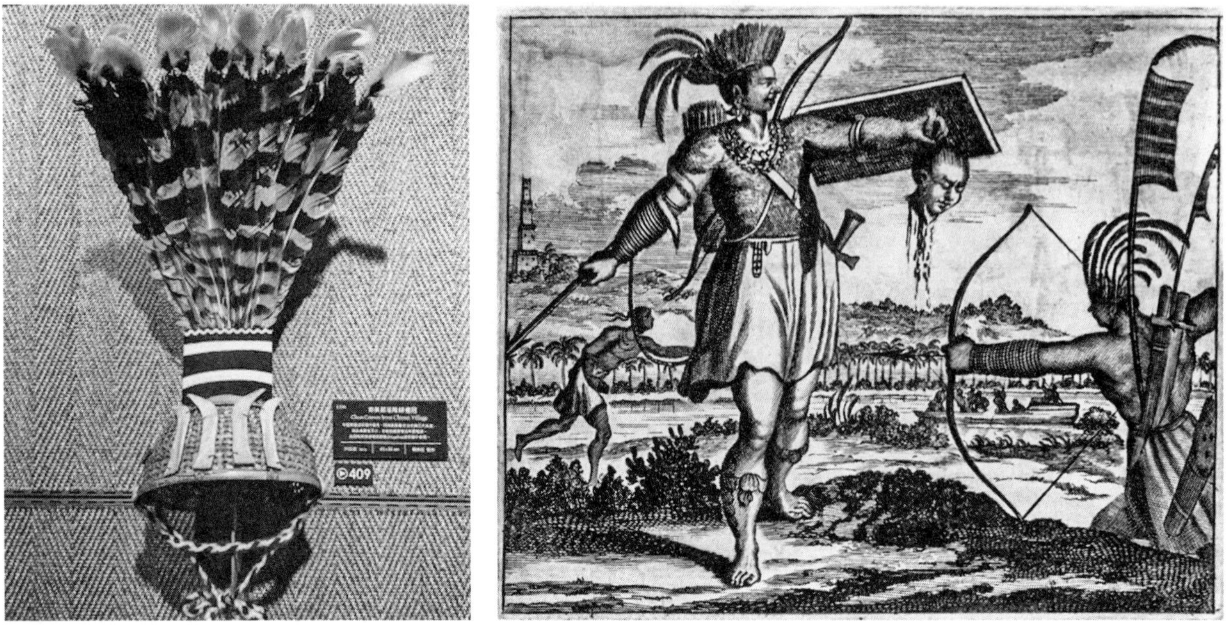

17.6a–b Feather headdresses on Formosans: Indigenous tradition accurately rendered or Amerasian entanglement? (a) Feather crown from Chimei village, Taiwan, 45 × 38 cm. Taipei, Shung Ye Museum of Formosan Aborigines. Photo by Alexander Nagel. (b) Formosan warriors, engraving on paper. Olfert Dapper, *Gedenkwaerdig bedryf der Nederlandsche Oost-Indische Maetschappye, op de kuste en in het keizerrijk van Taising of Sina* (Amsterdam, 1670), p. 22. University of California, San Diego, Library.

miter-like headgear, and the male and female Indians of high rank are shown clad in elegant dress. In fact, these American Indians look rather like depictions of Asians. To a colonial audience in New Spain around 1700, the "original" dress of the inhabitants of Cholula or Tenochtitlan was as distant and exotic as that of the Indians of Goa converted by Francis Xavier. Feathers in particular would have counted as a common inheritance, not exclusive to America but rather an expected accoutrement of "Indians" on both sides of the Pacific.

Amerasia Made Real by Transpacific Movement

Antonio de Torres's painting of Saint Francis Xavier baptizing Indians wearing silks, turbans, and feathers thus confirmed, at a basic level, a long-held assumption that the Indigenous populations of Asia must have many commonalities with the *Indios* of New Spain. By 1721, this basic assumption was then overlaid by a sedimentation of Amerasian exchanges sustained for over a century by the colonial process itself. Portuguese and Spanish colonial and missionary efforts had in fact produced a new "pan-Indian"

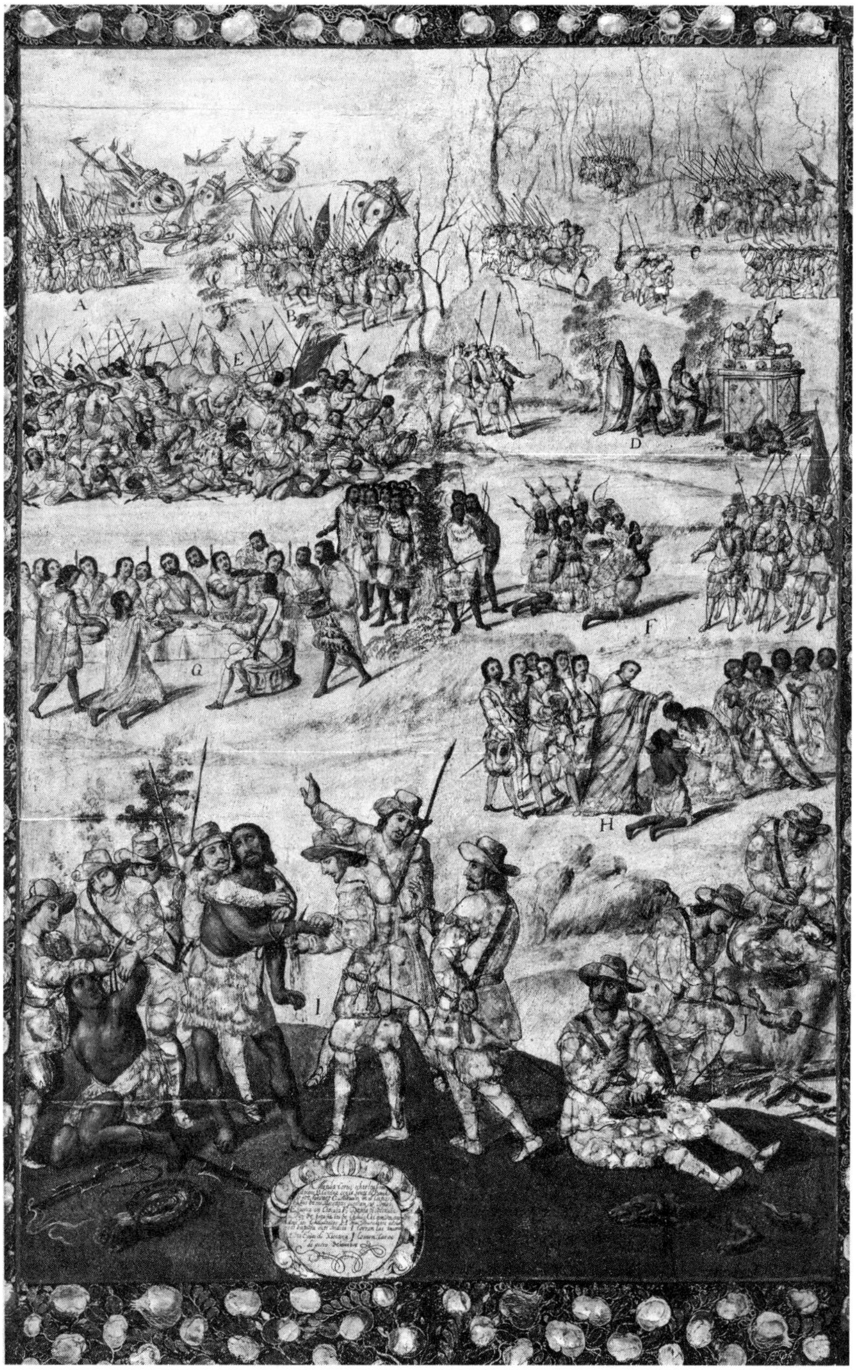

17.7 A scene from Cortés's campaign in Mexico shows an encounter with an advanced civilization. *Cortés in Cholula*, oil paint on wood inlaid with mother-of-pearl, 205 × 121 cm (ca. 1685). Madrid, Museo de América. This *enconchado* is one of six panels narrating Cortés's campaigns in Mexico. This panel shows episodes in the war of Cholula, with Cholulan priests and their gods, the surrender of their forces, and the baptism of seven Indigenous women.

identity—subjugated into a colonial class system, more or less converted to Christianity, laboring in and for a new world order—that did in fact span Asia and America. This conceptual and administrative assimilation also became a generative reality as Asians (called *Chinos* whatever their origin within Asia) used colonial trade corridors to migrate across the Pacific and then assimilate to the new environment, often intermarrying and producing offspring with the *Indios* of New Spain (see chapter 12). In early eighteenth-century Mexico there was every reason to see Amerasian affinities in a painting of Francis Xavier's Indian baptisms. Although it employs none of the material effects of mother-of-pearl, Torres's painting bears out what could be called the *enconchado* principle, reflecting and generating interacting worlds.

By the time Torres painted his 1721 canvas, the inhabitants of Mexican New Spain who gazed upon Torres's canvas were in fact quite accustomed to wearing Asian silks. An Irish Dominican friar named Thomas Gage visiting Mexico City in the 1620s noted that "both men and women are excessive in their apparel, using more silks than [woolen] stuffs and cloth."[13] To understand just how much life in New Spain was informed and invested by Asian material culture, we will need to pick up where we left off in New Spain and its northern frontier region of *Nuevo México* in the last quarter of the sixteenth century (see chapters 8 and 11). At that time, Juan González de Mendoza, writing from New Spain, produced his *History of China* (1586), the first European study devoted to the Chinese kingdom and itself made possible by the new commercial links connecting Asia and Mexico. In 1565, the Spanish launched the Manila galleon trade, a route of exchange across the Pacific that would link China and the Philippines to Mexico, and through Mexico to Europe, for two and a half centuries. Mastering in just a few years the trade winds that brought them across the northern Pacific, down the western coast of the North American continent, and then back across the ocean along more southerly latitudes, Spanish galleons began to transport large shipments of precious, fragile, and often beguiling luxury objects from Asia in exchange for Mexican silver.

In addition to silk, Spanish ships also transported huge quantities of porcelain, lacquer, pearls, and other kinds of precious objects across the Pacific. As early as 1573 two ships were reported to have brought to Acapulco "22,300 pieces of fine gilt China and other porcelain ware," mind-boggling quantities of blue and white Ming dynasty porcelain from the kilns of Jingdezhen.[14] Well into the eighteenth century, as the Neapolitan traveler Giovanni Francesco Gemelli Careri describes, the port of Acapulco was teeming with a great variety of Asian wares.[15] Merchants brought these silks, ceramics, and other items from Acapulco to Mexico

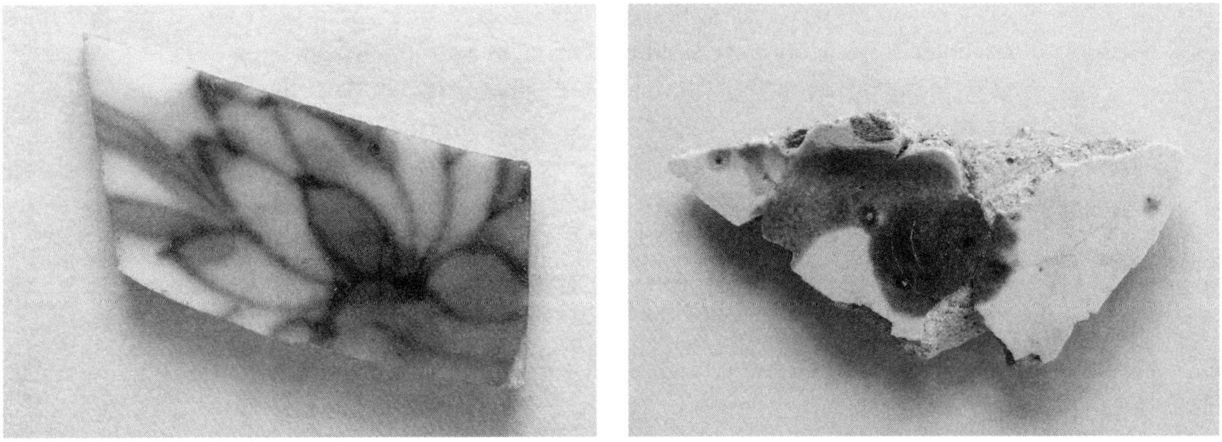

17.8a–b Chinese objects and Chinese stylings in Mexico. (a) Blue-and-white porcelain rim sherd, Ming Dynasty, 2.3 cm in length. (b) fragment of Mexican Maiolica (Puebla?), 5 cm in length, both found at San Gabriel de Yunque (1598–1610). 68.43.64 and 68.43.36, Maxwell Museum of Anthropology, University of New Mexico. (See color plates.)

City and up the Camino Real from there, or south to Peru, or to Puebla en route to Veracruz for export to Seville, though not nearly as many Asian goods ever reached Spain as Mexico.

Popular in particular for drinking hot chocolate, Chinese vessels became part of the households of wealthy settlers, even among the northernmost outposts of New Spain, leaving large quantities of Chinese porcelain sherds both in Mexico and what is now New Mexico. Already by 1600, members of the conquistador Juan de Oñate's expedition recorded owning luxury goods, including Chinese porcelain, traces of which have been found together with Mexican imitations of the technique at the first Spanish settlement in the region at San Gabriel de Yunque, founded in 1598 north of present-day Santa Fe (fig. 17.8).[16] Wills and estate inventories from the colonial New Mexican frontier also frequently list Chinese porcelain and silk, as well as other objects "from China," including furniture, ivories, and a variety of decorative arts—luxury goods that allowed settlers to signal their social status in one of the most isolated and inaccessible regions of Spain's colonies.[17]

Even as it made clear how much water separated America and Asia, the transpacific trade route brought Asian and American people and material culture into ever closer contact. The Amerasian worldview dominant during the sixteenth century still held sway, even as the Amerasian idea was substantiated by real transpacific exchanges. The idea that there was an overland passage to Asia through the northern frontier of New

Spain—Nueva México and beyond—endured as a memory even as settlers' households were being populated by Asian goods brought from overseas by the Manila galleons. As Donna Pierce provocatively describes, settlers along the northern frontier of New Spain adorned their otherwise uncomfortable and tiny frontier homes with embroidered silk cushions, curtains and canopies, lacquered chests, ivory altars, and folding screens. "The multi-storied Pueblo-style adobe compound where they lived at San Gabriel would not have been what they anticipated, and their silk canopied beds probably barely fit into the small adobe rooms with low ceilings."[18] Their luxurious rich Asian furnishings expressed the frontier hope that their fortunes would expand.

From Acapulco, where the Manila galleons landed in Mexico, Asian goods and merchandise traveled northeast along the Camino Real al Puerto de Acapulco (later, in the nineteenth century, named the China Road (*Camino de China*), an unpaved mule train that effectively connected the interior of China to the interior of New Spain.[19] The arrival of these wares spurred the production of Mexican goods that imitated and reproduced Asian forms. The potters of Puebla, for instance, soon became known for emulating Chinese work. Puebla pottery then also traveled along colonial trade routes to the frontiers of New Spain (see fig. 17.8).[20] These Mexican-made ceramics were similar in appearance to Chinese products, in particular because they also depicted traditional Asian motifs such as flowers, Buddhist emblems, encircling lines, overlapping arcades, concentric waves, scrolls, and lotus flowers.[21] To be clear, no one would have mistaken Puebla ceramics for Chinese porcelain; although Mexican ceramicists used cobalt to create blue designs on a white background as in China, they only loosely borrowed from Chinese decorative schemes.[22] Nevertheless, Asian-inspired Mexican vessels mingled with Chinese porcelain on the New Mexican table as an Asian aesthetic informed the visual culture of the elite households of New Spain.[23]

A similar conversation was inspired by Asian silk. On the one hand, locals remarked on the remarkable quantity, quality, and affordability of Asian silks; for instance, the viceroy of Peru wrote to the king of Spain in 1594 that "Chinese silk and other textiles are so cheap that Indian chieftains and even commoners are using them for clothing instead of cloth of local manufacture."[24] Everyone from Indigenous peoples to colonial urbanites, it appeared, wore garments made from Asian silks and cottons. On the other hand, however, as with porcelain, silk fabrics could be imported from Spain or made locally, from either locally produced or imported thread. The Irish chronicler Gage noted how in the 1620s, in Chiapas, "there are few Indians who have not their orchards planted with the trees wheron breed the worms which yield unto us that rich commodity [silk]. Not that the Indians themselves esteem it save that as they see the Spaniards greedy after it, [and] offering them money for it."[25]

All of this explains the development of the *china poblana* as a national symbol in Mexico: the story of the enslaved Catarina de San Juan (1606–88), a Mughal mystic (though often also believed to be an ancient princess from China) who was transported to Puebla in the seventeenth century and whose luxurious silk blouse and *rebozo* shawls set a template for what became "traditional" Mexican national dress.[26] Despite their differences, the mixing of imports and local production would have made it on occasion difficult to tell which fabrics came from Asia and which were Asian-style textiles reproduced locally. This intermingling of real Asian goods and locally crafted imitations culminated in the eighteenth century, when locals claimed that the tiles that adorned the eighteenth-century "House of Glazed Tiles" (*Casa de los Azulejos*) in Mexico City had been brought from China (they were made in Mexico), or when, in Pedro Calderón's eighteenth-century painting of the crucified Christ of Chalma, the Chinese porcelain vessels depicted below Christ, brought to Mexico through transpacific trade, were likely filled with silk flowers made in Mexico from imported Chinese silk threads (figs. 17.9 and 17.10).[27]

Asians Become Indios in America

Not only goods but also Asian people began to arrive during the late sixteenth and early seventeenth centuries as the itineraries of servants, sailors, and enslaved people tracked the movements of goods.[28] As the historian Tatiana Seijas describes, those enslaved people came from a great variety of Asian origins including the Indian subcontinent and Southeast Asia, but were grouped together and categorized as *chinos* upon arrival in Mexico despite their often dramatic social, ethnic, and linguistic differences. In New Spain, for a variety of reasons, a close identification developed between *chinos* and the Indigenous *indios*. Enslaved *chinos* were often employed as domestic servants or clerical workers in urban contexts rather than as laborers in mines or on plantations, a fact that integrated them into Mexican society socially and economically much more than enslaved Africans (by far the majority of slave labor in colonial Mexico). In addition, for the elites of New Spain, *chinos* were often indistinguishable from the Native *indios* of Mexico because of their skin color. Enslaved *chinos* often fled their owners in the hope of blending into the fabric of Native peoples, sometimes by entering into marriage with Mexican *indias*, with the ultimate goal of seeking the freedom and legal protections that came with *indio* status (see also chapter 12).[29]

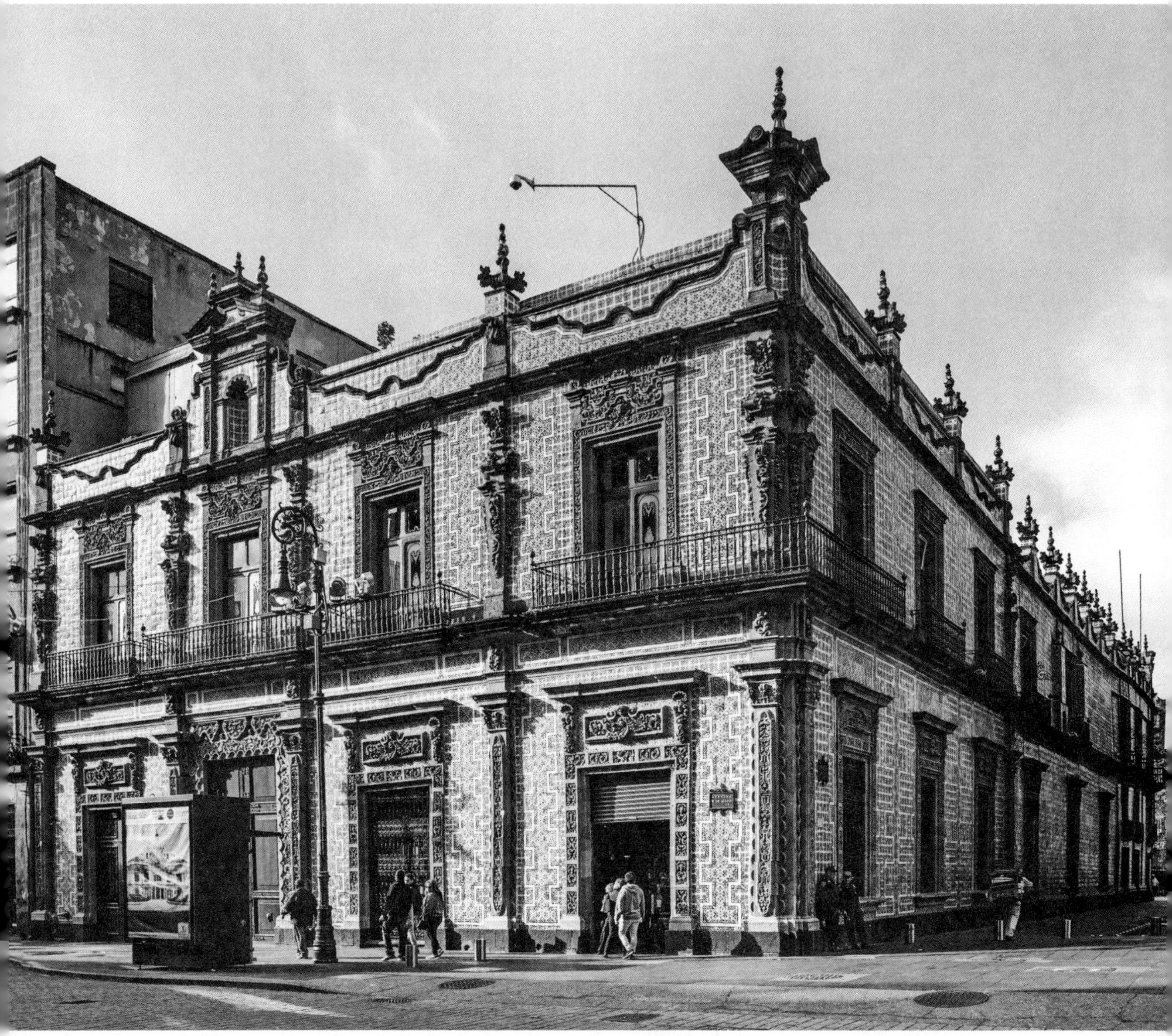

17.9 Asian-style cladding for a Mexico City palace. *House of Glazed Tiles* (*Casa de los Azulejos*), Mexico City, eighteenth century. Long believed to be of Asian origin, in fact the ceramic tiles were made by eighteenth-century artisans from Puebla.

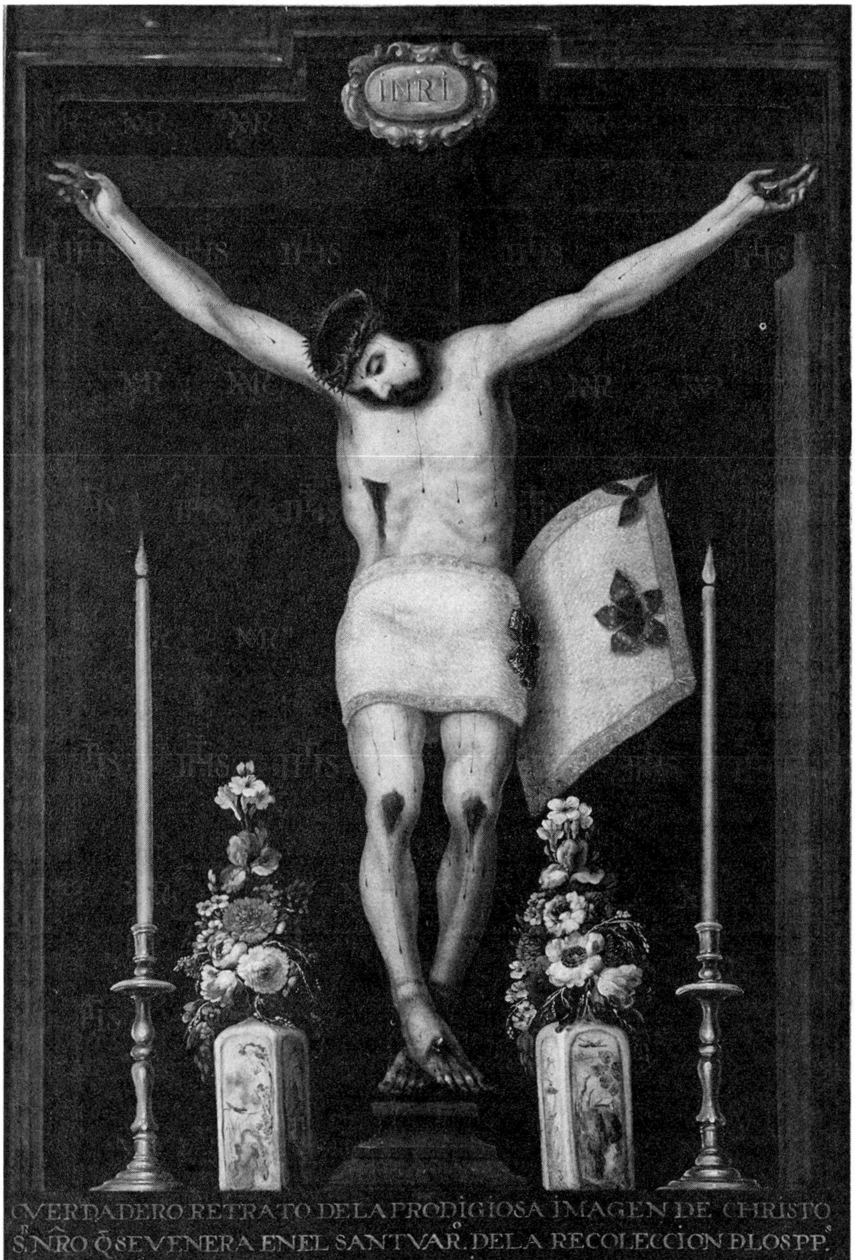

17.10 Asian and American porcelain and silk intermingle. Pedro Calderón, *Christ of Chalma*, oil on canvas, 168 × 108 cm (ca. 1750). Mexico City, Museo Nacional de Historia.

Discussions about ethnicity and the meaning of *indio* became even more complex as they moved across the Atlantic to Spain. As the historian Nancy van Deusen puts it, "It [became] difficult to identify who was an *indio* and who was not because, over the course of the sixteenth century, the use of the descriptor *indio* in Castile referred to people from the East and West Indies, China, the Moluccas, India, Brazil, Hispaniola, Mexico, and Peru."[30] In short, much like the blending of Asian and locally made ceramics and silks, in colonial Mexico Asians and Africans mixed, socially and culturally, with the free Indian population of New Spain. As Indians wore Asian clothes and Asian immigrants flowed into the New Indies and became Indians themselves, implicit and inherited Amerasian ideas became a lived condition. Given all this very real mixing, it was only logical to an early eighteenth-century painter in Mexico to imagine the (Asian) Indians baptized by Saint Francis Xavier wearing a combination of feather headdresses, turbans, and silks.

The lived visual and mental reality of New Spain insistently connected it to Asia—on the street, in the abundance of silk described by contemporary chroniclers, in the home and marketplace filled with Asian and Mexican ceramics, and in churches and missions, which also made regular use of Asian goods and textiles, and whose missionaries shuttled between Mexico and Asia. The traditional tendency to see viceregal New Spain in its relation to its Spanish overlords is being balanced by research that emphasizes a westward-facing Mexico, oriented to Asia and invested by Asian customs and stylings.[31] The lands of Mexico effectively became part of what could be called Greater Asia, as in antiquity Sicily and other Italian lands were considered part of Magna Graecia. On Vopel's great map of the world, the landmass that combines East Asia and the region of Mexico is indeed entitled Magna Asia (see chapter 11). With the advent of the Manila galleon trade, this land-based Amerasian idea was adapted to the new transpacific Amerasian reality, a Greater Asia that spanned an ocean.

Relay: Mexico City by a Transpacific Loop

The imaginary of Asia developed in Mexican depictions of Saint Francis Xavier's missions in Asia was part of a larger recursive logic whereby image techniques and formats were shaped by the transpacific exchange even as they projected transpacific imagery. Japanese folding screens or *byōbu*, for example, were adapted as *biombos* by artists in New Spain to represent both Asian and American subjects.[32] One *biombo* now in Madrid shows the Plaza Mayor of Mexico City, the viceregal palace, and some informal stalls in the city's central market (fig. 17.11). Here the heart of Mexico City is made available not directly but recursively, by a transpacific loop that

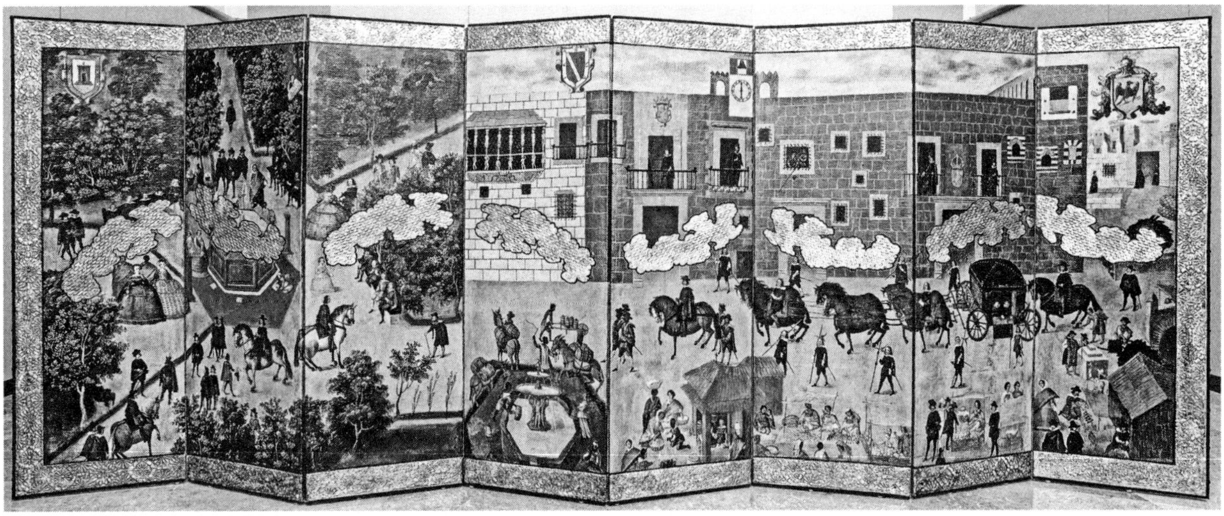

17.11 The heart of Mexico City presented to European viewers in a Japanese format using Japanese techniques. *Palace of the Viceroys and the Alameda, Mexico City, biombo*, oil on canvas with gilt decoration, 184 × 488 cm (a. 1660). Madrid, Museo de América.

made Mexico visible to itself through Asian techniques and modes of representation.

This is an image of Mexico made in Mexico but presented in an Asian format and with Asian motifs, such as gilt clouds (here made from what appear to be two cartoons that were flipped into different orientations across the screen), and from the elevated viewpoint typical of Japanese painted screens carrying views of Japanese cities.[33] The walled merchant community where Asian goods were sold in Mexico City, the Parián, was on the very same plaza represented in this *biombo*, though just out of view toward the bottom of the scene (closer to us and, as it were, beneath our feet as we look at the screen). The Parián was named after the settlement of Chinese merchants in Manila, creating "an evocative but imaginary parallel between Chinese bodies and labor over there (in Manila) and foreign things over here (in Mexico City)."[34]

In his poem *Mexico's Grandeur* (*Grandeza Mexicana*) (1604), the Spanish poet Bernardo de Balbuena describes the complexity and opulence of Mexico City, proclaiming, "In thee Spain and China meet, Italy is joined with Japan, and now, finally, a world united in order and agreement."[35] Reality had caught up with expectations—or expectations had met up with reality—when Asian goods and people arrived in what Europeans had long perceived as an extension of Asia, creating an Amerasian culture of material and genetic mixings that in turn circulated back into the world.

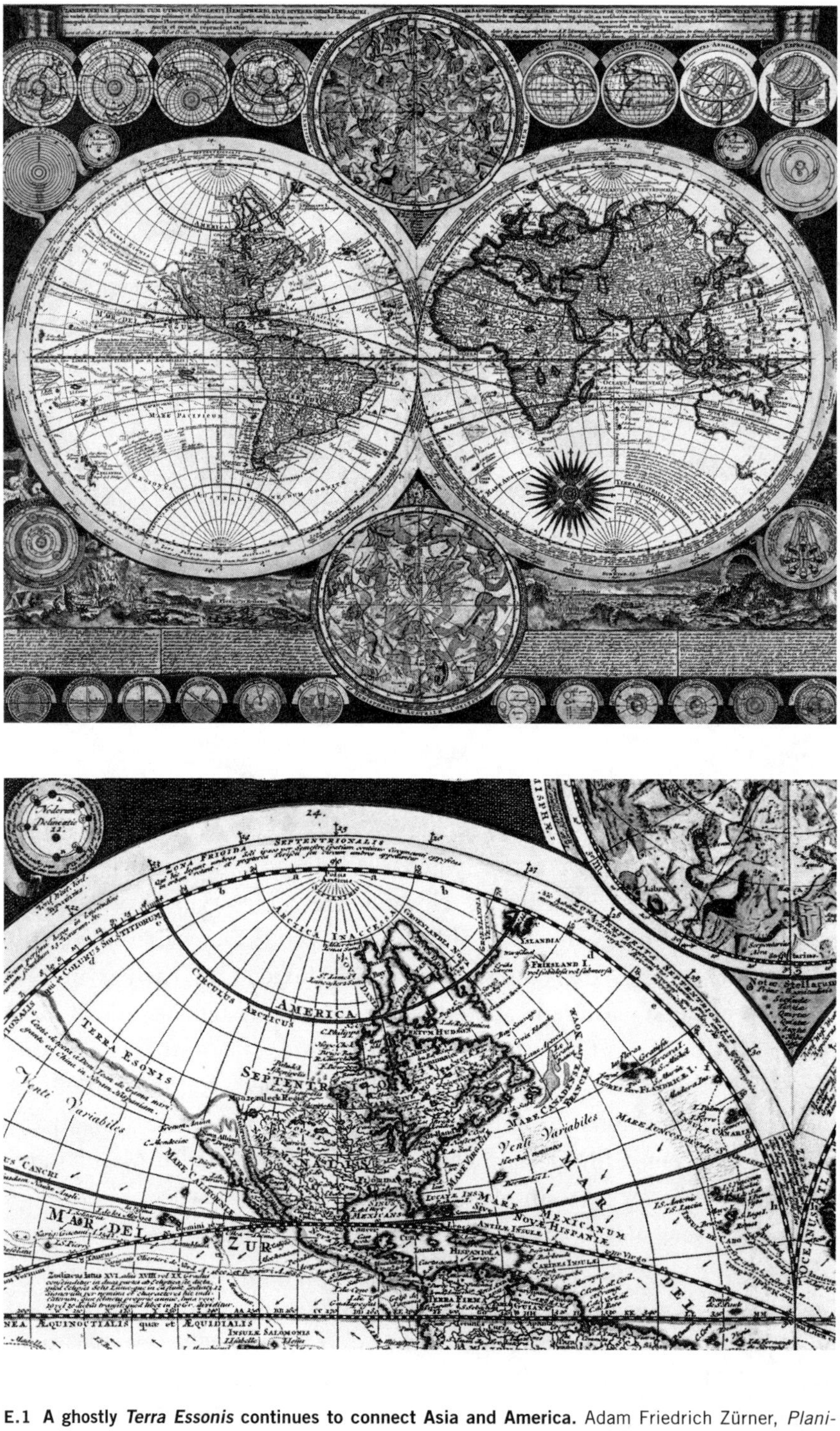

E.1 A ghostly *Terra Essonis* continues to connect Asia and America. Adam Friedrich Zürner, *Planisphaerium terrestre cum utroque coelesti hemisphaerio, sive diversa orbis terraquei . . .*, hand-colored engraving, 50.8 × 57.8 cm (Amsterdam, ca. 1700). The Barry Lawrence Ruderman Map Collection, Stanford University.

Epilogue

The story of the search for cinnamon in the new world epitomizes the history of Amerasia in all its multifaceted complexity. In his 1493 *Letter to Santángel* (see chapter 1), Christopher Columbus reports having seen cinnamon (*canela*), a plant native to India and Southeast Asia, on Hispaniola during his first voyage.[1] Bartolomé de Las Casas records that on his third voyage, Columbus brought cinnamon samples back to the monarchs Ferdinand and Isabella, though Las Casas comments that "regarding what he says about the cinnamon, aloes, ginger, incense, mirabelles, and sandalwood, I have never seen any of them on this island, or at least I did not recognize them."[2] The chronicler Peter Martyr d'Anghiera similarly notes that during their 1499 voyage, on the islands near Paria, the Pinzón brothers found cinnamon "just as efficacious for driving off fevers as the cinnamon which the apothecaries sell."[3]

These early sightings of cinnamon—one of the most prized and expensive spices in Europe, used both in food and for medicine—surely created the conditions for the later and more dramatic venture in search of it: the 1539 Andean journey of Sebastían de Benalcázar and Gonzalo Pizarro—the younger half-brother of Francisco Pizzaro—in search of the *Tierra de la Canela*.[4] The chronicler and naturalist Gonzalo Fernández de Oviedo recounts that Benalcázar thought the spice grew specifically near the Marañón River, southeast of Quito, though, ever the skeptic, Oviedo did not believe that this was the same cinnamon that was found in Asia, even if the taste and smell were similar.[5] The soldier and poet Garcilaso de la Vega, a Peruvian native who spent his youth in Gonzalo Pizarro's household, recorded that Indigenous peoples cultivated what he believed to be cinnamon in the province of Sumaco, east of Quito, where "a great many such trees grow wild and produce fruit, but it is not so good as that obtained from trees planted and tended by the Indians who trade in it with their neighbors."[6] According to the conquistador and chronicler of Peru Pedro de Cieza de León, Pizarro first heard about the presence of cinnamon from Captain Gonzalo Díaz de Pineda, who had begun to explore the mountainous regions east of Quito before fierce Indian resistance forced him to turn back. Cieza de León describes how Pizarro's expedition to the Valley of Cinnamon (*vale de la Canela*) followed Pineda's route, capturing Indians along the way and demanding to know where the trees grew. The Indians along the Napo River in the jungles of Ecuador claimed to know nothing of such spice forests, and Pizarro had them tortured or thrown to his hunting dogs in his effort to extract information.[7] By the end of Gonzalo Pizarro's expedition two and a half years later, 140 of the 220 Spaniards and 3,000 out of 4,000 Native people involved in the expedition had died. No cinnamon had been found.[8]

Yet the vision of cinnamon in America persisted. In his 1574 *Medical History of the Things Found in the West Indies* (*Historia medicinal de las cosas que se traen de nuestras Indias Occidentales*), the Spanish naturalist Nicolás Monardes affirmed that cinnamon, cloves, and pepper and other spices "only grow in the islands of the Moluccas."[9] Monardes calls the "West Indian" that Pizarro had been looking for the "Cinnamon of Our Indies" (*canela de nuestras Indias*) and describes it by noting that "the trees which bear it are of reasonable greatness, with leaves like laurel. They are all green and they never lose their leaves, which is a thing common in all the trees of the Indies."[10] Indian though it may be, the cinnamon-like plant found near Ecuador had a thicker bark that did not smell or taste of cinnamon. By contrast, it was the fruit and leaves of the Ecuadorian cinnamon that produced an aroma. Working from Amerasian premises, Monardes proposed commonality in a range of difference, allowing that the variant in "our Indies" is called cassia while the one brought from India by the Portuguese is cinnamon, yet he affirms that they "differ only in name, for all of these plants are cinnamon, thin and fine, and wherever is written cassia may be written cinnamon, and where you find cinnamon, cassia."[11]

Spices like cinnamon were synonymous with the legendary bounty of India understood as an expansive range of territory extending to the farthest islands, the Moluccas or Spice Islands. To reach and control Indian spice-producing regions and to discover new ones was to open up fabulous commercial opportunities *con mucho provecho nuestro*—to our great profit, as Monardes says. Like Marcos de Niza's story of reaching great cities of *Nuevo México* at exactly the same time (see chapter 8), the Pizarro-Pineda discovery of cinnamon was, as Monardes notes, "a thing much spoken of among the Spaniards, because one understood from the Indians that it was in great abundance."[12] Yet the question of similarity across difference persisted for centuries: were American canela and Asian cinnamon really the same? As in the case of ginseng purportedly found in America (see chapter 9), the taxonomic identity of American cinnamon was not clarified until the end of the eighteenth century, when the French naturalist Joseph Dombey determined that they were, in fact, two different species.[13]

Passages to India

The cinnamon chronicle follows a familiar pattern, revealing an Amerasian imaginary that persisted well into the eighteenth century.[14] The maps of Adam Friedrich Zürner (1679–1742) show how Amerasian cartography was reshaped as the transmission of geographical and natural-historical knowledge intensified. A German cartographer who served as the official geographer of Poland and of the Electorate of Saxony in the first third of the eighteenth century, Zürner created more than nine hundred maps in his lifetime. His *Earthly Planisphere, Both Celestial Hemisphere and Aquatic World* (*Planisphaerium terrestre cum utroque coelesti hemisphaerio, sive diversa orbis terraquei*. . .) of about 1700, for example, depicted the world through the increasingly popular double-hemisphere style map, a format that clearly separated the eastern and western hemispheres, imposing an end to Amerasian thinking, it would seem (fig. E.1). And yet Zürner depicts a large and notably blank swathe of land stretching between North America and Asia. He labels this *Terra Essonis*, a mythical land similar to *Terra incognita Australis* in the Southern Hemisphere, and outlines it with a lighter coastline than the rest of the North American continent, as if to note a lack of knowledge about this part of the world. Below *Terra Essonis* Zürner notes that its coast was described by the Portuguese explorer João da Gama (c. 1540–c. 1592), a merchant who had traveled from China to Mexico and claimed that the northeast coast of Japan extended uninterrupted far to the east. Many of Zürner's contemporaries, including the Dutch cartographer Frederik de Wit (1629–1706), the German cartographer Peter Schenk (1660–1711), and the Dutch engraver and publisher Joachim Ottens (1663–1719), all of whom worked in Amsterdam during the "golden age" of Dutch cartography, produced maps of the world that included this imagined land bridge.

Several decades later, Zürner instead calls the part of the world extending east from China the *Terra Iesso* (Jesso, Ieso), derived from the Japanese name Ezo (Yezo, Yeso), historically used to refer to the lands to the north of the Japanese island of Honshu (fig. E.2). The Venetian cartographer Vincenzo Coronelli (1650–1718) and the French mapmaker Alain Manesson Mallet (1630–1706) also regularly included this landmass in their maps, and depictions of *Terra Essonis* and *Terra Iesso* remained common for over a century.

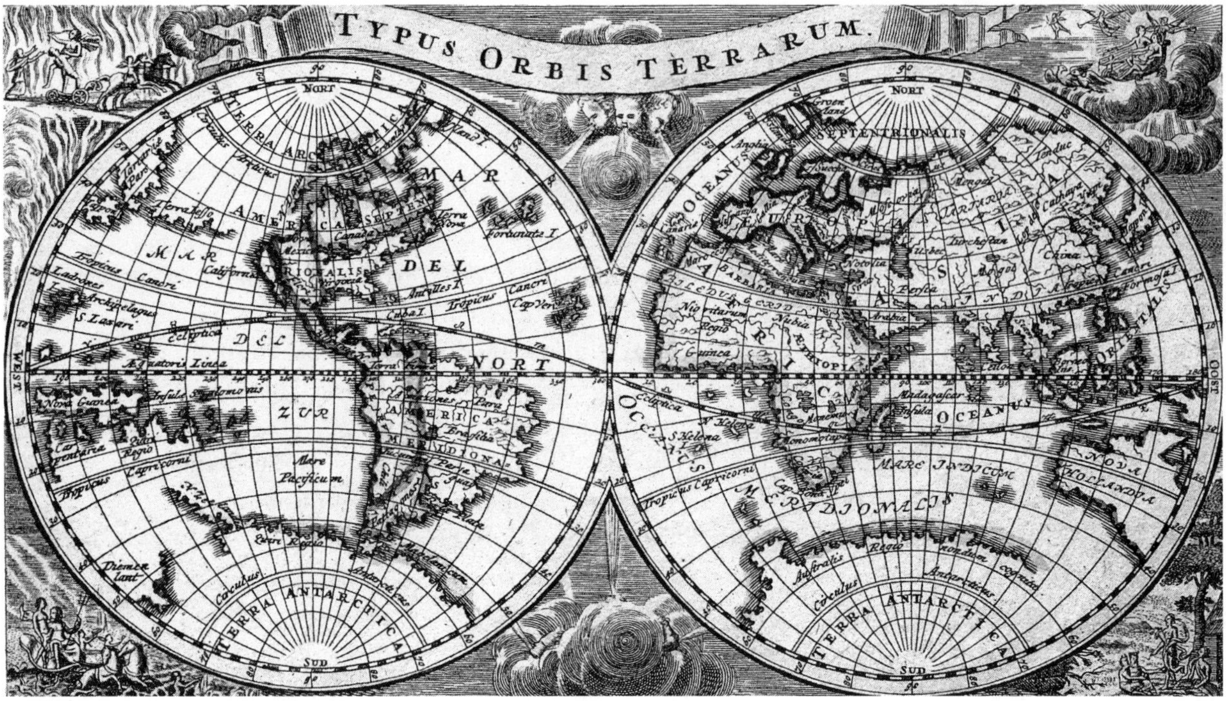

E.2 As *Essonis* changes to *Iesso*, it continues to reach across from Asia to America. Adam Friedrich Zürner, *Typus orbis terrarum*, hand-colored engraving, 19 × 14 cm (Nuremberg, 1729). The Barry Lawrence Ruderman Map Collection, Stanford University.

At other times, mapmakers showed a *Compagnies Land* or *Staten Land* in this part of the world, islands sighted by the Dutch explorer and cartographer Maarten Gerritsz de Vries (1589–1647) on his 1643 voyage to the northwestern Pacific. The de Vries voyage was one of the most thorough European explorations of the Japanese seas to date; traveling northeast of Iesso, de Vries sailed through a strait that afterward bore his name, and named islands on either side of the strait for the Dutch States General (State Land) and the Dutch East India Company (Compagnies Land). De Vries believed that Compagnies Land was perhaps not an island but part of the northwestern coast of America. In the wake of de Vries's voyage, these toponyms coexisted on the maps of generations of cartographers who preserved these features of the Pacific.[15]

At this time, it also became common to place a great variety of decorative elements, including cartouches, banderoles, and illustrations, in the cartographic space between Asia and America as a convenient way of obscuring the unclear geography of the north Pacific, as we see in Henri Abraham Chatelain's *Curious Map of the South Sea, Containing Remarkable*

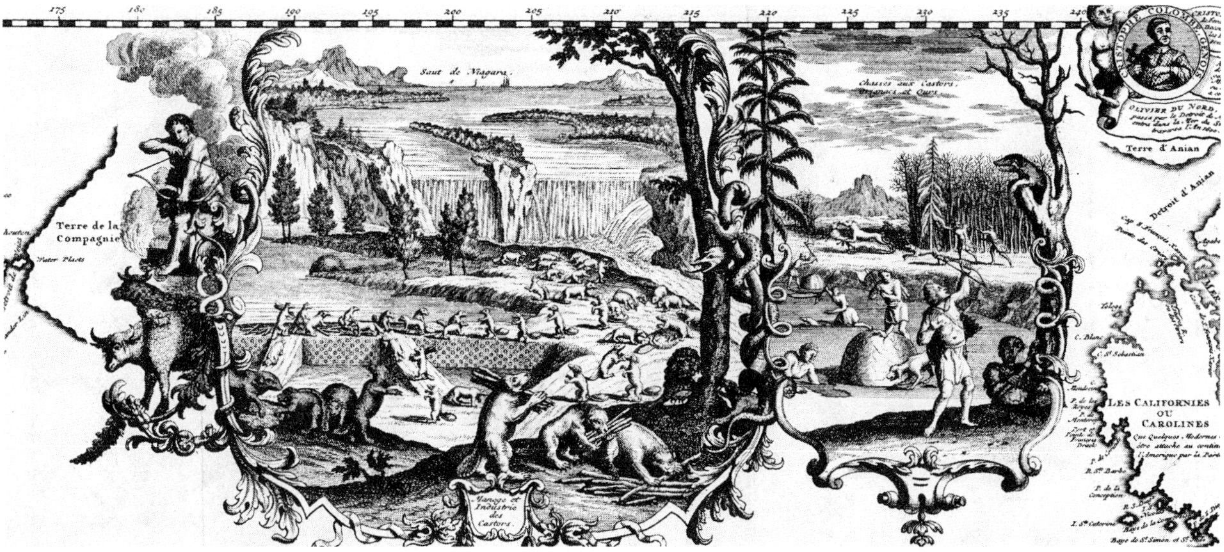

E.3 Images of industrious beavers and the men who hunted them obscure our view onto how lands connect over the Mer du Sud. Henri Abraham Chatelain, *Carte tres curieuse de la Mer du Sud, contenant des remarques nouvelles . . . mais aussy sur les principaux pays de l'Amerique*, engraving on four joined sheets, 84 × 143 cm inches overall (Paris, 1719). Collection Musée National des Beaux-Arts du Québec. Detail from University of Texas, Arlington Library.

Novelties . . . and also the Principal Lands of America (*Carte tres curieuse de la Mer du Sud, contenant des remarques nouvelles . . . mais aussy sur les principaux pays de l'Amerique*) (fig. E.3). The cartouche's vignette shows industrious beavers (an animal found both in Eurasia and North America) building dams, while fierce Indigenous peoples shown naked but for coverings around the waist wield bows and arrows and axes, a long-established and now universal code for designating Indians of East or West.[16]

With the northern Pacific now one of the remaining geographical question marks, the idea of overland migrations from Asia to the Americas, proposed by José de Acosta already in the sixteenth century (see chapter 13), became newly relevant. In his 1761 *Studies of the Navigations of the Chinese to the American Coast, and of the Peoples Located in the Extreme East of Asia* (*Recherches sur les navigations des Chinois du cote de l'Amerique, et sur quelques peuples situés à l'extrémité orientale de l'Asie*), the sinologist Joseph de Guignes argued that Amerindian peoples had arrived in a series of Chinese migrations eastward, eventually landing in a mythical land called Fusang that had been recorded by the Buddhist missionary Hui Shen in the fifth century CE, whose work de Guignes had translated. Shen had described Fusang as a land 20,000 Chinese *li* (about 7,000 to 10,000

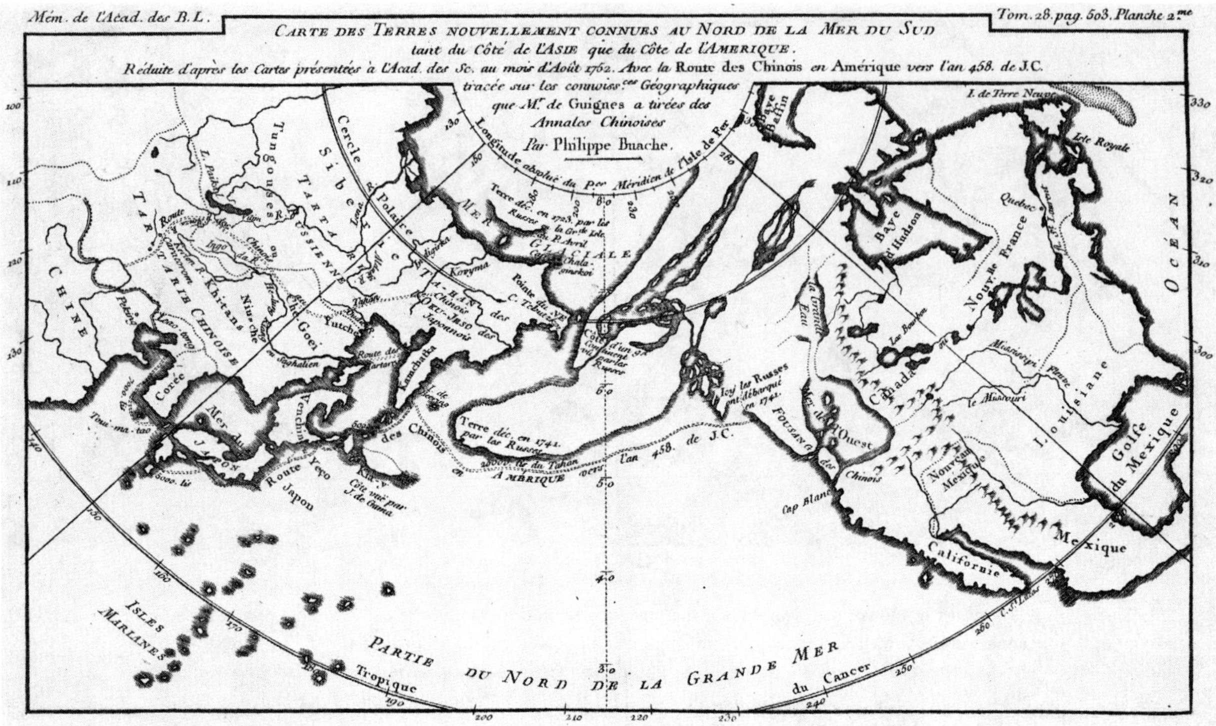

E.4 Had there once existed an ancient Chinese colony just north of the lands of California? Philippe Buache, *Carte des terres nouvellement connues au nord de la Mer du Sud,* engraving, 16.5 × 26.5 cm (Paris, 1752). The New York Public Library.

kilometers) east of China, making Fusang a Chinese colony in the Americas. Working directly from de Guignes's translation, Philippe Buache's *Map of the Recently Discovered Lands North of the South Sea* (*Carte des terres nouvellement connues au nord de la Mer du Sud*) (1752) (fig. E.4) illustrates these ideas, depicting Fusang north of Mexico and west of Canada, as well as "the Chinese route into America around the year 458" (*la Route de Chinois en Amerique vers l'an 458*). Far from breaking apart the Amerasian idea, the growth of specialized knowledge in the developing field of Sinology provided data for a more grounded theory of Amerasian exploration and cultural transplantation in the ancient world.[17]

In the 1768 entry for the word India (*L'Inde*), the French scholar Louis de Jaucourt, the most prolific contributor to Denis Diderot Jean le Rond d'Alembert's *Encyclopédie* (1751–72), explains that the ancients had named India after the Indus River. However, the ancient or Ptolemaic terminology of India for him was "useless" (*inutile*) since premodern people "had only a quite confused notion [about the Indies], and their maps, prepared exactly following Ptolemy's positions, show us this part of the world quite differently from its true nature." In exasperation, he writes, "we gave this name to foreigners who came from unknown parts; and was it not by a lack of enlightenment regarding the relationship of America to the Indies that we gave it the name of *West Indies*?"[18] Yet, as discussed in chapter 12, Jaucourt understood that the wide application of the term *Indian* could never be brought back into correct usage: "by a new abuse, which it is no longer possible to correct, in published accounts the term Indians is used to mean Americans."[19]

Jaucourt's call for enlightened clarity notwithstanding, the word Indian continued for many to name one extensive reality. In his *History of the American Indians* (1775), James Adair, an Irish trader who resided for more than forty years among the Chickasaw Indians, argued that the languages and religious customs of a variety of Indigenous American peoples, whom he calls "American Hebrews," revealed once again that they had descended from the ancient Israelites.[20] The colonial American explorer and writer Jonathan Carver's bestselling *Three Years Travels Through the Interior Parts of North America* (1778, followed by more than thirty editions), contested Adair by arguing that Indigenous American peoples had instead descended from the Tartars and the Chinese, while admitting to being unsure about the physical and geographic relationship between the continents. While some had argued that "there could not possibly be any communication by land," since "the continent of America, as far as we can judge from all the researches that have been made near the poles, appears to be entirely separated from the other quarters of the world," Carver acknowledges that others claimed that "this separation is no more than a straight, about one hundred miles over," and that "some late voyages of the Japanese give grounds to think that this straight is only a bay, above which there is passage over land."[21] He just couldn't be sure, and neither could anyone, even decades after Vitus Bering discovered the strait that bears his name. In the same year 1778, the French explorer Charles-Marie de la Condamine (1701–1774) reported seeing Amazons in South America.[22]

The full assimilation of the knowledge of the voyages of Vitus Bering and James Cook took time. Bering reached the strait that separates Alaska from Siberia and sailed through it on August 13, 1728, yet even this expedition did not definitively establish the separation of the continents, at least not immediately. Bering never saw Alaska, and even after his return, it was still not clear where the outermost limits of the landmasses lay. In 1732, when the Russian Senate reported the news of Bering's voyage to the Empress Anna and gave Bering instructions for a second voyage to the northern Pacific, some members of this audience still believed the

Asian and American terra firma could be joined.[23] According to the sociologist Eviatar Zerubavel, the physical separateness of America and Asia did not become definitive until the 1770s, when the third voyage of James Cook (1778) determined that Alaska was connected to America. That is to say, it was not until almost three hundred years after Columbus's initial landfall in the western Atlantic that the separation of the lands became settled fact.[24]

The Amerasian idea was largely supplanted in the nineteenth and twentieth centuries by the modern metageography of the seven continents. Whereas in the earlier period the word *continent* was a geological descriptor for a landmass other than an island, isthmus, or peninsula, meaning that territories both smaller and larger than the modern continents could be called such, now the number of continents was set, and the continents were identified as cultural zones, for which distinct fields of study were developed—there were now Africanists and Asianists (or more specifically Sinologists, Indianists, Japanists, etc.), and eventually Americanists.

Yet these were slow developments, and in the meantime the idea of an ancient connection between the new world and the old quietly endured. As late as 1825, in his *Voyage Towards the South Pole*, the British navigator James Weddell theorized that several of the words of the inhabitants of Tierra del Fuego resembled Hebrew. His book was owned and admired by Richard Fitzroy (captain of HMS *Beagle*, which transported a young Charles Darwin to South America in the 1830s), who in turn believed a centuries-old tradition that held that American Indians were descendants of Noah's son Ham through the line of Abraham.[25] The Irish antiquarian Lord Kingsborough's monumental *Antiquities of Mexico* (1830–48) continued to explore the similarities between Mexican and Hebrew laws and culture, in part by scrutinizing the relationship between the Hebrew language, Mexica glyphs, Egyptian hieroglyphics, and Chinese characters in a continued attempt to prove the ancient and Hebrew origin of the Mexican people, as discussed in chapters 13 and 14.[26] During the course of the nineteenth century, Americans in fact consistently orientalized the Indigenous peoples of North America and the American frontier as a means of facilitating and encouraging American territorial expansion.[27] Many nineteenth-century scholars included the builders of mounds in their surveys of American antiquity, often giving them Israelite or Asian ancestry. Josiah Priest's *American Antiquities and Discoveries in the West* (1833) for example—a best-selling classic in lay archaeology in its day—argues that America was the land where Noah's Ark had come to rest and that antediluvian Mound Builders could have been "Polynesians, Egyptians, Greeks, Romans, Israelites, Scandinavians, Welsh, Scots, and Chinese."[28]

In his *Fusang or the Discovery of America by Chinese Buddhist Priests in the Fifth Century* of 1875, the American folklorist Charles Godfrey Leland continued to argue for the existence of the ancient Chinese colony at Fusang on the West Coast of America.[29]

With or without specific claims about Asian migrations, the basic idea of an Amerasian pathway remained embedded in the American mythos, even as it was propelled by modern technology. Celebrating the construction of a railroad from coast to coast, in 1870 the bard of America Walt Whitman hailed it as a "Passage to India!" (in his eponymous poem)—nothing less than the fulfillment of Columbus's dream:

> Marking through these and after all, in duplicate slender lines,
> Bridging the three or four thousand miles of land travel,
> Tying the Eastern to the Western sea,
> The road between Europe and Asia.
>
> (Ah Genoese thy dream! thy dream!
> Centuries after thou art laid in thy grave,
> The shore thou foundest verifies thy dream.)

Amerasia Resurfaces

Today, Amerasian theories are once again in the news, as the findings of modern archeology and paleogenetics accumulate to suggest that transpacific migration and exchanges occurred long before the arrival of the Manila galleon in Acapulco.[30] Some have speculated that refugees from the fall of the Shang Dynasty in the 11th century BCE came to Mexico and helped found the Olmec civilization, theories that have mostly been dismissed.[31] More recent paleogenetic findings have shown that the Ice Age land bridge across the Bering Strait became passable only about 12,600 years, long after humans had settled in areas farther south, suggesting that the first migrations as well as later ones occurred by coastal, water-based movement down the Pacific coast.[32] Other findings show westward crossings from South America to the Polynesian Islands during the period around 1200 CE, long before Europeans undertook such expeditions.[33] Already in the 1950s, Claude Lévi-Strauss summoned a millennial history of transpacific contacts: "In contrast to the total silence of the Atlantic, a humming as of a swarm of bees sounded all around the periphery of the Pacific."[34] It may be time to revisit the meticulous investigations of the anthropologist and art historian Carl Schuster, who found extraordinarily similar ornamental patterns spanning vast expanses, even crossing the Pacific, yet refrained from proposing diffusionist theories.[35]

Erroneous as they were in many details, speculations offered in the sixteenth and seventeenth centuries about connections between the new and the old Indies may have been not entirely misguided. The twentieth-century certainty that America was disconnected from the world until the arrival of the Europeans in 1492 might itself turn out to be the historical curiosity, an episode of separatist ideology that arose in the two centuries between the early modern Amerasian imaginary and the new transpacific understanding emerging in the twenty-first century. Perhaps the modern separatist view never quite took, and a new Amerasian imaginary of sorts is resurfacing, even as demographic shifts and the dominance of China make it a reality. In the 1982 movie *Blade Runner*, set in the year 2019, the denizens of Los Angeles use a street language called Cityspeak, described by the narrator Rick Deckard (played by Harrison Ford) as "a mishmash of Japanese, Spanish, German, what have you." The lingo had in fact been invented by another actor in the film, James Edward Olmos, a Los Angeles native of Mexican origin, who also included elements of Chinese and Hungarian in his futuristic creole. This twenty-first-century Amerasian mixing at the level of street culture forms the background for the boundary crossing at the core of the story, between humans and their technical creations, human-simulating "replicants" who have varying features depending on which generation or series they belong to—some of them programmed to live only four years while others have an open-ended life; some endowed with superhuman strength and intelligence while others are troublingly equivalent to humans in their entire emotional range and neurological equipment. It is not difficult to see in this fantastical range of human alterity invented by aggressive and exploratory humans a recall of the early modern encounters with various antipodal creatures, marginally human cannibals, Patagonian giants, naked and wise gymnosophists, and fantastically long-lived new world populations. In the film, this alienation from our own fantastical creations results in a grim and violent world. In 2019 Los Angeles, wealth is concentrated in few hands and police are a military force serving the interests of the powerful. It rains all the time, a sure sign that humans have done something very bad to the world's climate. That's the film. The post-2019 reality pretty well fulfills the prediction, with the difference that the extreme rain is landing farther up the coast while Los Angeles is getting drought and fire.

A primary model for thinking about the world, Amerasia was inextricably bound up with the worst of what came to pass in new worlds East and West, including Coronado's and Oñate's murderous campaigns in search of Asian wealth or Gonzalo Pizarro's genocidal quest for cinnamon, the forced labor of the silver mines of Potosí, the oppression and routine killing of Chinese laborers in Manila, or the decimation of the North American tribes in the search for the Northwest Passage. Yet an Amerasian view also arguably produced the most sustained reflection on the "destruction of the Indies," as Las Casas named it. Las Casas laid the conceptual foundation for laws banning slavery on the grounds that these Indians were humans, part of greater India. Amerasian views of the world were also at the basis of some of the most penetrating European critiques of European institutions and biases, from Thomas More to Michel de Montaigne and beyond. A vision of distant connectivity, it was also an acknowledgment that the encounter was a form of self-encounter. Amerasia was Europe's inverted mirror, showing what was in many ways the truth of Europe, namely that Europe was also a relatively new world whose own connection to its own eastern and ancient origins—Adam and Eve in paradise, the populations to emerge from Noah's ark, the Holy Land, Greek culture, Egypt, whatever they might be—remained a persistent and unresolved cultural preoccupation from Roman times to the Renaissance. Amerasia was the product of othering, but at the same time it was a space for seeing relations of similarity across ranges of difference. A time-loop where new becomes old and old new, Amerasia challenged the already intricate temporal models of European history, theology, and art-making. It presented a world in flux, where migration continually unsettles the categories that would stabilize a worldview. Above all, its dynamism and open-endedness became a workshop for questioning the devices of worldmaking itself.

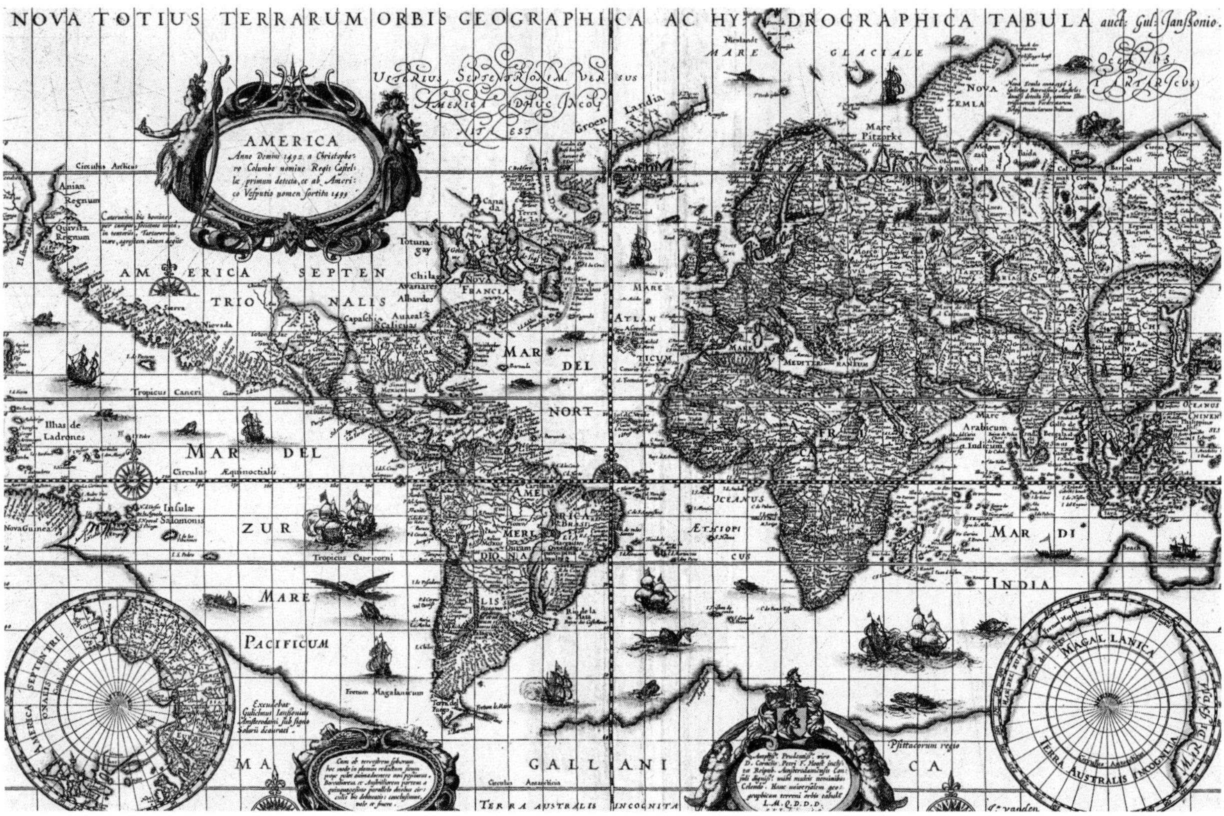

A.1 For cartographer Willem Blaeu in 1606, Europeans needed hydrography at least as much as geography to bring the world into view. Blaeu, *New Map of the Entire World Compiled from Geographical and Hydrographical Data* (Novus totius terrarum geographica ac hydrographica tabula), 1617 print of the 1606 original.

AFTERWORD

Chinese Cartographers Map the World

by Timothy Brook

The premise of this book is that Europeans encountered the world beyond Europe tentatively, experimentally, and incompletely. Their knowledge of that world was accordingly shaped as much by what they learned as by what they assumed to be the case, one effect of which was a merging of what was Asian and what was American into a zone that existed for a time as Amerasia. The gradual acquisition of geographical and ethnographical knowledge altered the ideas and categories with which Europeans managed their view of the world, yet the boundary between the imagined and the experienced resisted sharp definition even late into the seventeenth century. Some of this knowledge experimentation was due to confusion but not to indifference, as the authors stress in the introduction. Europeans simply did their best to shuffle the objects and ideas reaching them from the vastness of what lay abroad into a coherent pattern.

Their contemporaries in China, the people of the Ming, were receiving far less information about the wider world in the sixteenth and seventeenth centuries. Chinese too were not indifferent to the world when they could catch glimpses of it, but what reached them was so much less in volume and variety, arriving not as trophies wrested from conquered or compliant peoples but as debris that travel and trade, largely by others, washed to their shores. This chapter offers a glimpse of the process of organizing newly arriving knowledge of the world by looking from the other direction, not from Europe out to Asia and the Americas, but from Asia out to Europe and the Americas.

That process in China proceeded differently, as we shall see. The notion of Amerasia, for example, would have gained no traction among Asians, not because they had a clearer vision of the world—their knowledge was subject to the same sorts of elision and combination of knowledge that shaped the process in Europe—but because they had no knowledge of or relationship to America. Even less would Chinese have conceived of their place in the world as part of something called Asia, that being a European category. The process of constructing knowledge depended on where you stood and in what directions you looked, and that in turn depended on your history.

Hydrography

The world as it emerged on maps in Europe did so through the work not of geography, the study and survey of land, but of hydrography, the study and survey of watery spaces. Men on ships followed coasts, crossed oceans, navigated straits, circumnavigated islands, and peered into the distance to discern the shapes that loomed up before them. From the charts they drew, cartographers compiled maps less by massing territory into landforms than by unscrolling coastlines that wandered across the terraqueous globe, always as seen from the aqueous side. *Terra*—*terra incognita* when the shape the coast suggested did not align with existing knowledge—came later. Because movement over water was the urgent task at hand, cartographers such as Geert Kramer and Abraham Ortelius—better known to us as Mercator and Ortelius—drew continental outlines according to geometric calculations that strove not to depict how the world actually looked so much as how navigators could get from one place to another. Hydrography prevailed.

Hydrography is not a word we use today. For that matter, most map readers treat the water as nothing more than the absence of land—which may be why some map illustrators dotted watery spaces with ships under sail or monstrous creatures emerging from the deep: to remind readers that these spaces were not voids but the very zones across which mariners plotted courses and linked one port of call with the next. On his 1606 adaptation of Mercator's world map, Willem Blaeu confers on water its full share of credit by giving it the title *New Map of the Entire World Compiled from Geographical and Hydrographical Data* (*Novus totius terrarum geographica ac hydrographica tabula*) (fig. A.1). Until all coastlines were fully mapped, though, the shape of the world remained elusive. Was America part of Asia? Did Asia extend into America? The idea of Amerasia belongs to this phase of cartographic history. As long as geography could not collaborate fully with hydrography, the shape of continents would remain unresolved.

The story of China's mapping of the world has to be told differently. The geography of Inner Asia was reasonably well understood, but in the sixteenth century, when Chinese navigation was at its lowest ebb, the hydrography of the maritime world had become unknown. When the

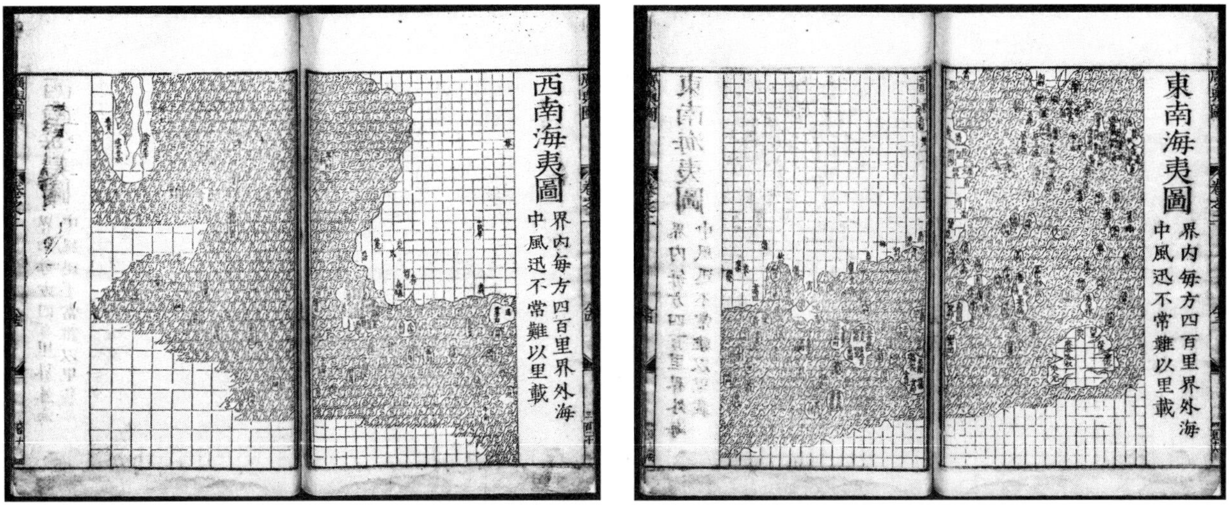

A.2 What Luo Hongxian drew when he tried to picture the maritime world southeast and southwest of China in 1555, shown here in the revised version of 1566. Luo Hongxian, *Map of the Maritime Barbarians to the Southeast and Southwest* (Dongxinan haiyi tu), as reformatted in the popular posthumous edition of *Guang yutu* of 1566. Cambridge, Harvard University Library.

founder of Ming dynasty (1368–1644) overthrew the Mongol occupation in 1368, he retrenched China within borders beyond which his subjects were not permitted to travel. Knowledge of the maritime world atrophied under this condition. When in 1525 Emperor Jiajing responded to Portuguese predation in the waters near Canton by closing the coast to ships of more than one mast, the last channels of communication with the maritime world closed. The ban was enforced, preventing Chinese mariners from learning by experience and obliging Chinese cartographers to rely on whatever fragments of earlier maritime knowledge they could scrounge until better data came along.

The Chariot and the Theatre

In 1555, thirty years after the ban was imposed, Luo Hongxian (1504–64) published China's first atlas, *Enlarged Map of the Chariot* (*Guang yutu*) (fig. A.2).[1] Fifteen years later, Abraham Ortelius (1527–98) published *Theatre of the Sphere of the Earth* (*Theatrum orbis terrarum*). Both were compilations based on the cartographic work of others; both combined image with text; and both strove to unify the materials they compiled within a consistent visual design. The point is not who got to the genre first, but why two people who experienced the world from such different vantage points produced their cultures' first atlases within the same generation.

Ortelius's story is well known. Son of an Antwerp merchant, he started life as an artisan, apprenticed as a map-colorer. In his late twenties and thirties, as he traveled widely to search for maps and meet the leading mapmakers of his generation including Mercator, Ortelius became a cartographer in his own right. Luo Hongxian came from such different family circumstances.[2] In the preface to his atlas, Luo recalls his keen interest in schematic charts as a teenager, but his training was entirely literary, preparing him to sit the civil service examinations. Passing the national exams in 1529 at the age of twenty-four catapulted him into intellectual circles in the capital where, as he phrased it, everyone discussed "the pressing affairs of the realm." Political administration was the context that inspired his interest in maps.

Luo's brilliant career ended in 1541 when he submitted a recommendation that offended the emperor. He was stripped of his rank at the age of thirty-eight and barred from the civil service for the rest of his life. Rather than lose heart, Luo launched himself into local projects serving the public interest, including surveying the land of his home county as a step toward correcting the local tax registers. In the summer of 1548, the philosopher Wang Ji (1498–1583) found Luo tramping about under the hot sun supervising field surveys: the gap between the intellectual and the artisan was closing. By this time. Luo had been working on his atlas for three years, judging from a comment in his preface that the book took him a decade to finish because "I couldn't afford to hire someone to do the work." Like the *Theatre* fifteen years later, the *Chariot* was a great success: reprinted, pirated, and plagiarized, and decisive in influencing in shaping the cartography of China that the Jesuits transferred back in Europe.[3]

Luo's atlas was mostly of China and its border regions, less so of the world beyond its borders. His main source was a fourteenth-century wall map by Zhu Siben, which he regarded highly (it has not survived) and which he spent three years searching to find. As Luo explains in his preface, his goal was twofold: to enlarge the coverage of Zhu's map, and to rework his materials into portable form. Replicating the rectangular grid for which Zhu's map was justly famous, Luo produced a sequence of forty-eight full-page maps, some of which ran in multipage sets (the Grand Canal, for example, is distributed across three maps). To impose a uniformity of scale and design, he drew every map with an aspect ratio of 1:1. The result was a square book, for which Chinese publishing offered no precedents.[4] The title, *Enlarged Map of the Chariot*, was an homage to Zhu Siben, whose wall map bore the title of *Yutu*, literally, *Map of the Chariot*, resonant with the ancient myth about the earth being a chariot on which people rode beneath the sky. Luo did not merely enlarge Zhu's map; he created something new.

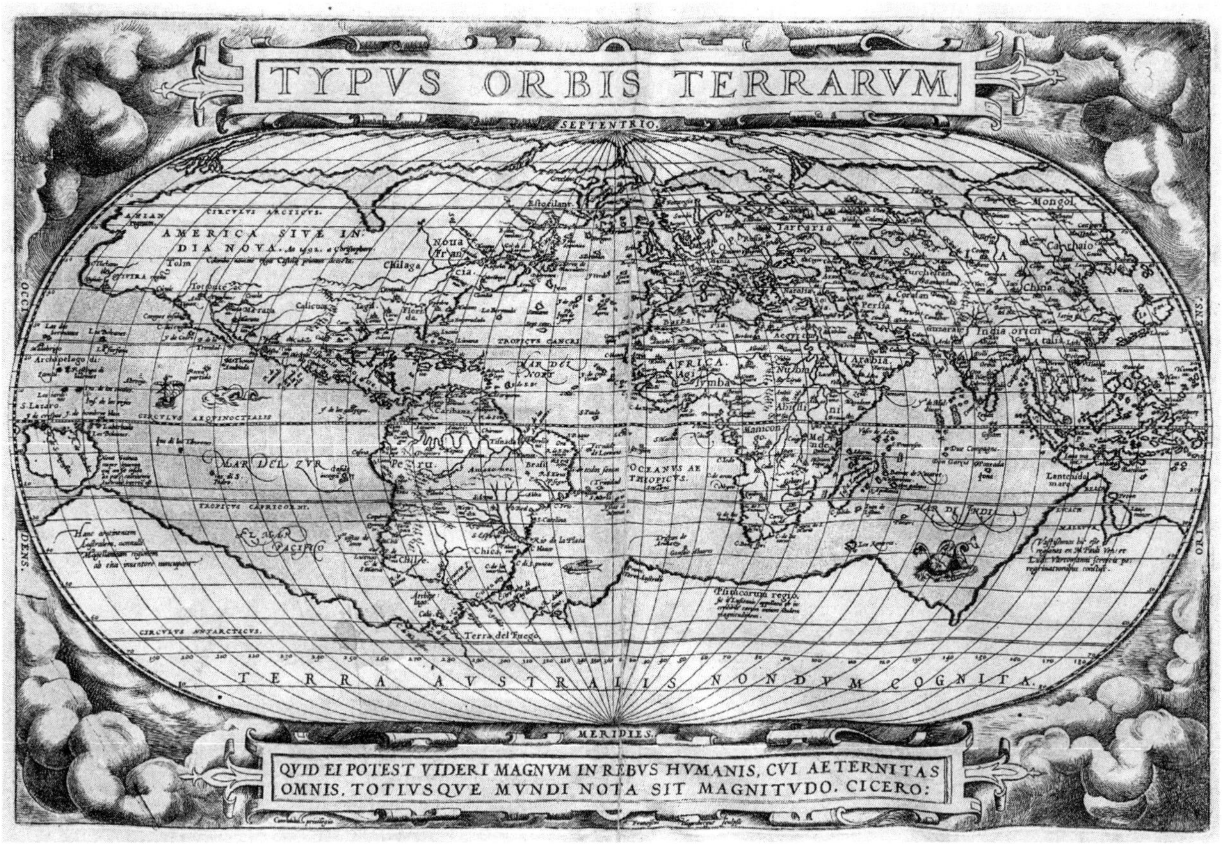

A.3 The world as visualized in the opening map of Ortelius's *Theatre of the Sphere of the Earth*, 1570. Utrecht University Library.

The *Chariot* and the *Theatre* follow different programs. The *Theatre* consists mostly of maps of Europe, though by opening with the map of the world Mercator published in 1569, followed by continental maps of Europe, Asia, Africa, and America or "the New World," it declares its ambition for global coverage (fig. A.3). The world has less of a presence in the *Chariot*. As Luo explains this program in his preface, "I started with one general map [of China] so that the viewer can see the splendor of the Ming Great State, then presented the two capital districts [Beijing and Nanjing] and the thirteen provinces, for a total of sixteen maps." The subsequent move out to the borders was for him an anxious one. "Because it is so important that we make clear the boundaries by which we Chinese defend ourselves against barbarians, I have made eleven maps of the northern border. As trouble lurks in the mountain passes out on the western border, there are five maps of these peripheral areas." Like most Ming statecraft thinkers, Luo imagined the world beyond China as a threat zone. That did not mean that knowledge of the world should be neglected. "Barbarian rulers coming to China pose a great danger, and we would be foolish if our military were unable to anticipate them. Accordingly, I have rounded out the book with a set of four maps showing Korea, Annam [Vietnam], the western regions, and the northern steppe."[5] Unannounced between Korea, his forty-second map, and Annam, his forty-fifth, appear two maps about which Luo is entirely silent. To these maps we now turn to consider what Luo understand the world beyond China.

Luo Hongxian Maps Zanzibar

The forty-third and the forty-fourth maps in the *Chariot* carry the titles *Map of the Maritime Barbarians to the Southeast* (Dongnan haiyi tu) and *Map of the Maritime Barbarians to the Southwest* (Xi'nan haiyi tu). Together they compose into a single *Map of the Maritime Barbarians to the Southeast and the Southwest* (see fig. A.2). Geography has been reduced to a silhouette, whereas hydrography fills the rest of the map with repeating waves dotted with well over a hundred islands. This is a maritime chart of the world to China's south. The blank areas along the bottom of the map where the waves stop repeating, despite the application of a grid, are simply aqua incognita.

Tracing the silhouette of the land from right to left—the direction in which Chinese viewers would read a map—we see Korea in the upper right-hand corner, then the coastline of China from the Gulf of Bohai down to Annam. The water to the east of the coast, loosely the South China Sea, is filled with islands, some of which, such as Japan, are well attested, and others of which, such as the Island of Hairy People, can be found only in mythic geographies. The continental coastline continues west onto the second panel, beginning with Laos, which is named. The coastline turns north and disappears out of the top frame, reappearing in the upper left-hand corner. South of the coast lies the Indian Ocean. Disappointingly, Luo writes nothing about this map. Perhaps he was heeding Zhu Siben's warning that "those who talk about foreign regions are unable to provide definite information, and those who volunteer information can never be trusted."

The easiest way to determine how the *Map of the Maritime Barbarians* came about is to go to the most distant point from China, where we find the place name, Sanggub. This is the Chinese rendering of the Persian *Zang-bar*, meaning Coast of the Blacks. We know it in English as Zanzibar, the tiny island off the coast of today's Tanzania. There is no evidence that as of 1555 any Chinese had ever traveled to Zanzibar. A convoy from the fourth of Zheng He's diplomatic expeditions (1406–33) did sail down the east coast of Africa in 1413, though the sole surviving Ming map of Zheng's routes marks Malindi as the voyage's southern terminus.[6] Textual records indicate that some of Zheng's ships sailed another 100 kilometers south to Mombasa, but Zanzibar lay another 240 kilometers beyond Mombasa, beyond the reach of Ming experience.[7]

The landmass on which Sangguba appears we know as Africa, a continent for which Luo had neither a name nor a concept. Its distinguishing geographical features are an outsized inland lake (Lake Victoria) and, to the east of it, a long river flowing north (the Nile). At its headwaters, Luo has inserted the placenames Zhebu Luma and Ha Nayisijin. Zhebu Luhama is the Chinese transcription of the Arabic Jibbel el Kumri or the Persian Jabāl al-Qamār, Mountains of the Moon. Ptolemy, who knew this name, regarded the Mountains of the Moon as the southern limit of the known world. Beyond it, in the terminology of one fifteenth-century attempt to reconstruct Ptolemy's lost map, was *terra Ptolemeo incognita*, "land not known to Ptolemy." Luo inattentively dropped the fourth syllable, calling it Zhebu Luma. He makes another error with Ha Nayisijin, the last syllable of which should be *hua* rather than *jin* (the characters are similar). Ha Nayisihua is the Chinese rendering of the Persian *hat al*-īstiūā, from the Arabic *khatt alaistiwa*—the equator. As the equator clips the north edge of Lake Victoria, the label is not out of place. But the equator was not a concept available to Chinese in 1555, and Luo has simply put it in as a place name.

Luo adds one more place name to Africa, an island off the east coast called Dibanu, from the Arabic, Tabarna. Ptolemy knew it as Taprobana. Sixteenth-century reconstructions of his world map located it in the southeastern corner of Indian Ocean, not where Luo has placed it by Africa. Nonetheless, Luo has duly included the island that Europeans thought was Taprobana on the other side of the Indian Ocean, putting it to his own use by dotting it with Indian place names, effectively commandeering the unnamed island to stand for India. As the authors of this volume make clear, our purpose is not to go looking for where sixteenth-century cartographers, European or Chinese, got the world right or wrong. It is to inquire into their sources, test where the boundary between what they knew and did not know lay, and consider how their decisions shaped later states of map knowledge. Unlike Ortelius, Luo drew his *Map of the Maritime Barbarians* without being at the receiving end of the new hydrographical data flooding into Europe. He had only the fragments he could find lingering in China from earlier centuries, obliging him to depict the world as others had depicted it before him.

How Ptolemy came to haunt Luo's *Map of the Maritime Barbarians* is not difficult to unravel. His prototype is a fourteenth-century world map produced under the auspices of the Yuan Great State, *Map of the Frontiers and Distances of the Amalgamated Realm and National Capital throughout the Ages* (*Hunyi jiangli lidai guodu zhi tu*). As all exemplars but one descend from a copy that Korean envoys smuggled out of China and printed in Korea in 1402, the map is usually known by its Korean short title as the *Map of Frontiers and Distances* (*Kangnido*) (fig. A.4).[8] The *Kangnido* utilizes geographical knowledge from Chinese texts going back to the Tang dynasty, which it hybridizes with hydrographical and geographical knowledge from the Mediterranean world supplied by Persian mariners who traveled to China in the fourteenth century—which is why we find traces of Ptolemy in the *Chariot*.[9]

A glimpse at the *Kangnido* reveals that Luo copied only its lower half, slicing Africa off at the Great Lakes and leaving the north shore of the Indian Ocean off the map. This foreshortening may have nothing to do with his vision of the world and everything to do with the materiality of maps. The *Kangnido* is almost three meters across and over two meters

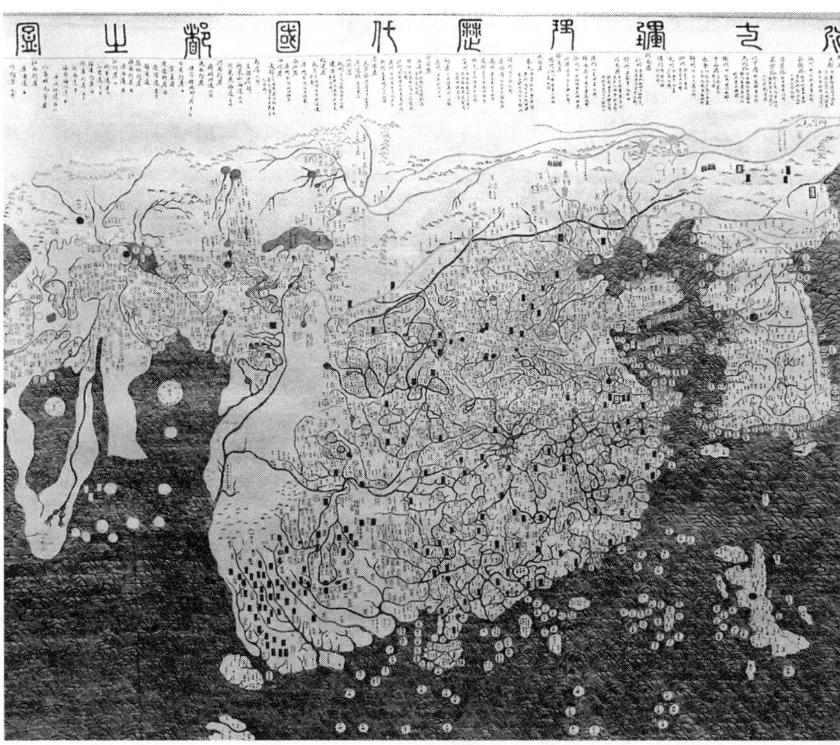

A.4 The Honkōji Kangnido was Luo's principal source for drawing the maritime world. Kyoto, Ryūkoku University.

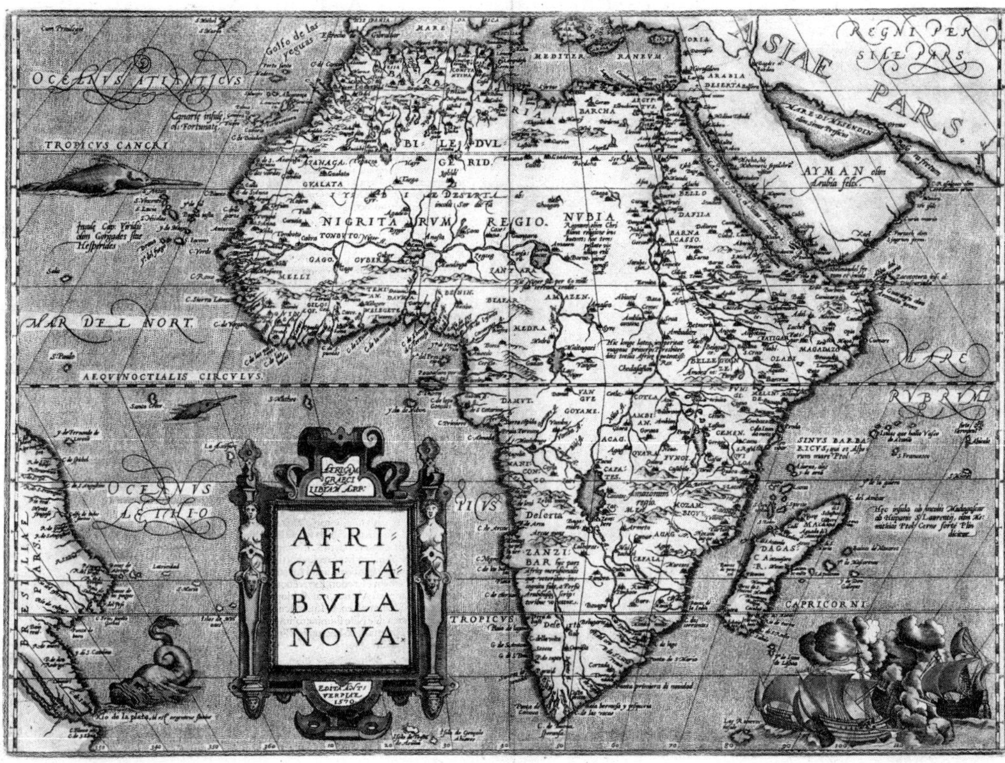

A.5 Ortelius, like Luo Hongxian, located Zanzibar on the west side of Africa. Ortelius, *New Map of Africa* (Africae Tabula Nova), 1584, reprinted from his *Theatre of the Sphere of the Earth* (Theatrum orbis terrarum), 1570.

from top to bottom, and it is the fate of large maps to get folded. Fold and unfold a map on paper for two centuries and it will start to tear along the crease. Fold the *Kangnido* horizontally across the middle, and the crease runs right through the middle of the Great Lakes. By best guess, the copy of the *Kangnido* that Luo laid eyes on was only the bottom half. What lay above the fold—the Arabian Peninsula, the Mediterranean Sea, Europe—Luo did not get to see it; indeed, he may not have even known that an upper half existed.

As it happens, no extant copy of the *Kangnido* names Zanzibar. Perhaps the copy Luo got his hands on did, but it is likelier that he picked it up from another source based on Persian hydrographical knowledge. There is, however, a contemporary who located Zanzibar exactly when Luo put Sangguba, on the Atlantic side of Africa—none other than Abraham Ortelius (fig. A.5). This uncanny coincidence simply reminds us that Africa lay at the edge of both Chinese and European knowledge in the sixteenth century, and that Zanzibar lay just beyond that edge. Luo would not have been dismayed to learn that he had mislocated Sangguba, however. He accepted the provisionality of his knowledge, quoting Zhu Siben's comment that "all who come after and view this map will recognize its errors and blunders." At the end of his own preface, Luo bids farewell with a shrug: "Correcting the errors and adding in what I have omitted I leave to my readers."[10]

The West

Filling in the missing Northern Hemisphere became possible three decades after the publication of the *Chariot*, when the first Jesuit missionaries to China brought European cartographic knowledge. Matteo Ricci (1552–1610) was eager to show Chinese what his world looked like, though he also accepted the authority of Luo Hongxian's cartography as superior to any European version of China. When he redrew the world map in the *Theatre*, he switched Ortelius's image of China for Luo's. He also moved the prime meridian from the Atlantic to the Pacific, which put Europe at the periphery and brought China closer to the center of the map (fig. A.6).

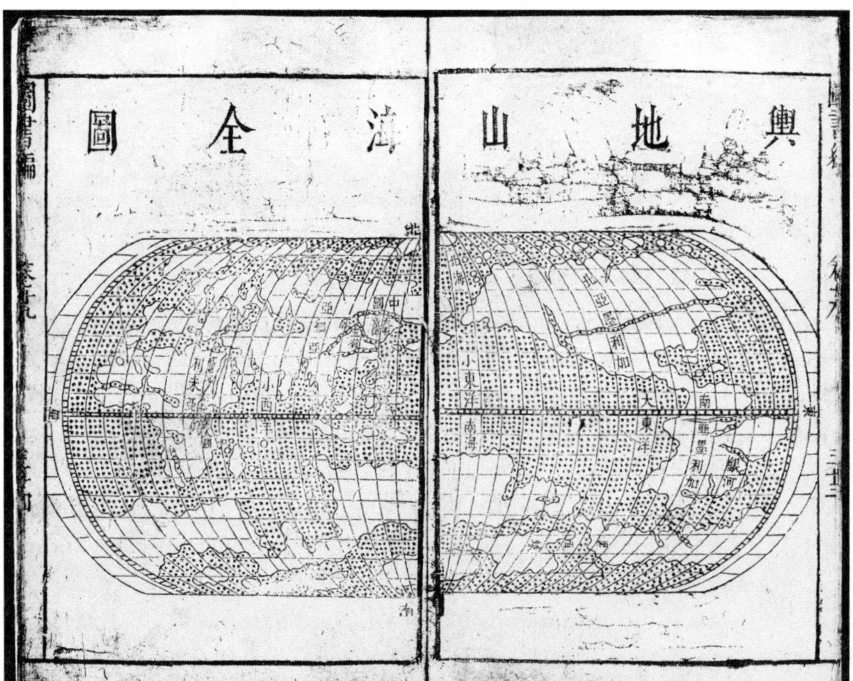

A.6 In *Complete Map of the Mountains and Oceans of the Earth* (Yudi shanhai quantu), Matteo Ricci redesigned the Ortelian map of the world for Chinese readers in 1584, shown here in the sole copy of that edition as it is preserved in a popular encyclopedia published in 1613, Zhang Huang's *The Documentarium* (Tushu bian). Cambridge, Harvard University Library.

Ricci's intention was not to curry favor with Chinese viewers expecting to find China in the middle of the map, as an earlier generation of commentary had it. Rather, it was to integrate his knowledge with theirs. In those early days, cartographic exchange between Chinese and Europeans was "open, spontaneous, and productive," in the judgment of historian Qiong Zhang.[11] Revising his vision was a means to encourage his Chinese readers find their place in his world. It also opened a path for Ricci's religious practice, which was to show Chinese that beyond China lay regions to the west, east, and south larger than they knew, and that there was more to the world than dreamt of in their philosophy.

To my eyes, Ricci's map seeks to balance the landmasses in the eastern and western hemispheres: Eurasia with North America, and Africa with South America. The effect is to reduce somewhat the size not just of China but of all of Asia. Chinese viewers must have been surprised to see that not all *terra incognita* lay to the west. That had been the long tradition of the Chinese geographical imaginary, which placed all that was foreign to the west, the direction in which lay ultimately to the Western Paradise over which the Queen Mother of the West presided. To the east lay nothing but ever more ocean.[12] This cosmography unintentionally reversed medieval Christendom's world imaginary, which placed the rest of the world in the vast continent to Europe's east, with the Garden of Eden perched at its furthest point. Hydrographical knowledge undid that certainty for Europeans in the sixteenth century. It would take longer for such knowledge to do the same for Chinese, given the lack of opportunity to explore maritime spaces.

Although Ricci displayed a world of hydrographic continents on his maps, the important direction for him was west. In his writings, he plays to China's westward orientation, setting up a scaled geography of Lesser and Greater West, such that Europe, the home of Jesus, was superior to India, the home of Buddha. Chinese knew India as Tianzhu (a transcription of "Hindu" using the character for Heaven for the first syllable). Ricci downgraded India to the Lesser West (*Xiaoxi*) and placed beyond it the Greater West (*Daxi*) of Europe. He even borrowed the authority of the West by styling himself the Scholar from the Greater West. He did the same for hydrography, redesignating what Chinese knew as the Western Ocean (*Xiyang*) as the Lesser Western Ocean (*Xiao xiyang*), beyond which—and greater than which—lay the Greater Western Ocean (*Da xiyang*), the Atlantic. This arrangement of a Lesser and Greater West, perhaps not unconsciously, reproduces the distinction in sixteenth-century European geography between *India intra Gangem*, India within the Ganges (Lesser India), and *India extra* or *super Gangem*, India beyond the Ganges (Greater India), discussed in chapter 1. In this hierarchy of zones, Greater India, as Niccolò de' Conti imagined it, excelled "in riches, politesse, and magnificence" what could be found in Lesser India. According to Peter Martyr, the easternmost boundary of this Greater India beyond the Ganges was precisely the place Christopher Columbus reached on his first voyage: the point at which East and West met. Ricci simply reverses the gaze, implying to Chinese wanting to understand the world that they should look to the Greater West for the more perfect world to be found in Europe, and more especially, to the more perfect teachings of Jesus that originated there.

West was not the only direction on Ricci's map. Ming readers would have been most surprised to see how much of the world lay to the east. Here Ricci repeats his pattern to the west by designating the ocean east of the Philippines as the Lesser Eastern Ocean and marking the open waters of the Pacific beyond that as the Greater Eastern Ocean.[13] On the far side of that ocean lay North and South America. To name the Americas in Chinese, Ricci used syllabic transcription. The unavailability of certain sounds in Chinese meant that he reworked the four syllables of A-me-ri-ca into Ya-mo-li-jia. The name appears twice on Ricci's map, once modified by *bei* (north) and once by *nan* (south).

Ricci's *mappamundi* did not explain to Chinese readers how the two extremities of the Americas and Europe related. Other evidence perplexed them; the origin of Spaniards, for instance. Were they "Franks" from Europe (using the Arab language for Europeans)? Did they not sail from the east to reach Manila rather than from the west? Or were they perhaps indigenous to the island of Luzon? Furthermore, where was the mountain of silver that kept them solvent? Ricci identifies and transliterates Potosí on the 1602 edition of his world map as Beiduxi, adding a note to say that "this mountain has many silver mines," but neither Beiduxi nor Potosí meant anything to Ming readers. The only South American place name on the 1613 print of his original map is Rio Plata, the River of Silver, though without any explanation as to how that name was coined. Despite the visible evidence of distinct continents that Ortelian geography presented, it was not clear to most Chinese where Europe ended and America began. The Atlantic Ocean appears at both sides of his map, yet in the 1602 edition, Ricci has placed the label of Great Western Ocean only to the west of Europe, not to the east of the Americas. Neither Chinese nor their Jesuit interlocutors had the term or concept of Euroamerica, not least because America was not yet a region that enjoyed the conceptual weight of Europe. But for Chinese, there may have been something of the uncertainty about what the opposite side of the globe looked like that sustained the idea of Amerasia among Europeans.

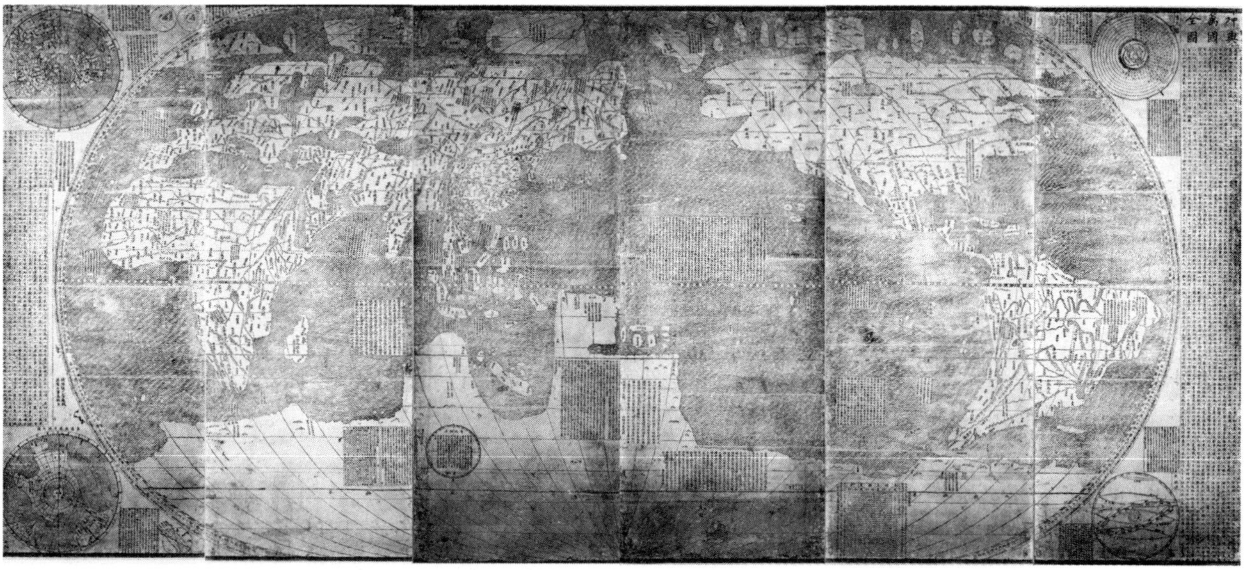

A.7 In a text of appreciation engraved mid-Pacific on Ricci's *mappamundi,* Li Zhizao declares his conviction that the principles governing East/China and West/Europe to be the same. Matteo Ricci, *Complete Map of the Ten Thousand Countries of the Earth* (Kunyu wanguo quantu), Beijing, 1602. University of Minnesota, James Ford Bell Library.

"The West"

If one locational term recurs in Jesuit texts and maps more than any other to tag what lay beyond China, it is "the West," in contrast to which China was "the East." It was a theme that Ricci and others chose to develop in order to find places for China and Europe in a global framework, and many Chinese were persuaded. We find this polarity of East and West signaled in the long appreciation that Ricci's friend (and later convert) Li Zhizao (1565–1630) wrote in praise of the 1602 edition of his *mappamundi.* Li's short essay appears as a block of text set in the empty middle of the Pacific Ocean (fig. A.7). Li is concerned to integrate Chinese and European knowledge of the world in a way that reduces the Chinese resistance to knowledge coming from elsewhere. He works his way through some of the differences, shows them to be superficial, then steps back and concludes, "Whether it is Eastern Ocean or Western Ocean, mind is the same and principles are the same, so what is not to be believed?"[14]

Despite a certain challenge to Chinese cartographic norms, Ricci's vision of the world was not rejected. Instead, map publishers in Nanjing absorbed the Ortelian image, reworking it into a new genre known as "complete maps."[15] The genre is most richly represented by Cao Junyi's

1644 map of the eastern hemisphere, *Complete Map of the Astral Correspondences, Human Vestiges, and Routes of the Nine Border Zones under Heaven* (*Tianxia jiubian fenye renji lucheng quantu*) (fig. A.8). Cao relied on Luo Hongxian's version of China to fill the center of the map. Like Luo, he also made use of the *Kangnido* to imagine the shape of Africa, though his renderings of the Mediterranean and Europe attest that he had access to the full map, not just the lower half. Otherwise, though, Cao chose to bring in many elements from Ricci's map, including oceans on all four sides of Eurasia, not just east and south. This map was so well received that it dominated world-maps publishing in China from the mid-seventeenth century through to the nineteenth.

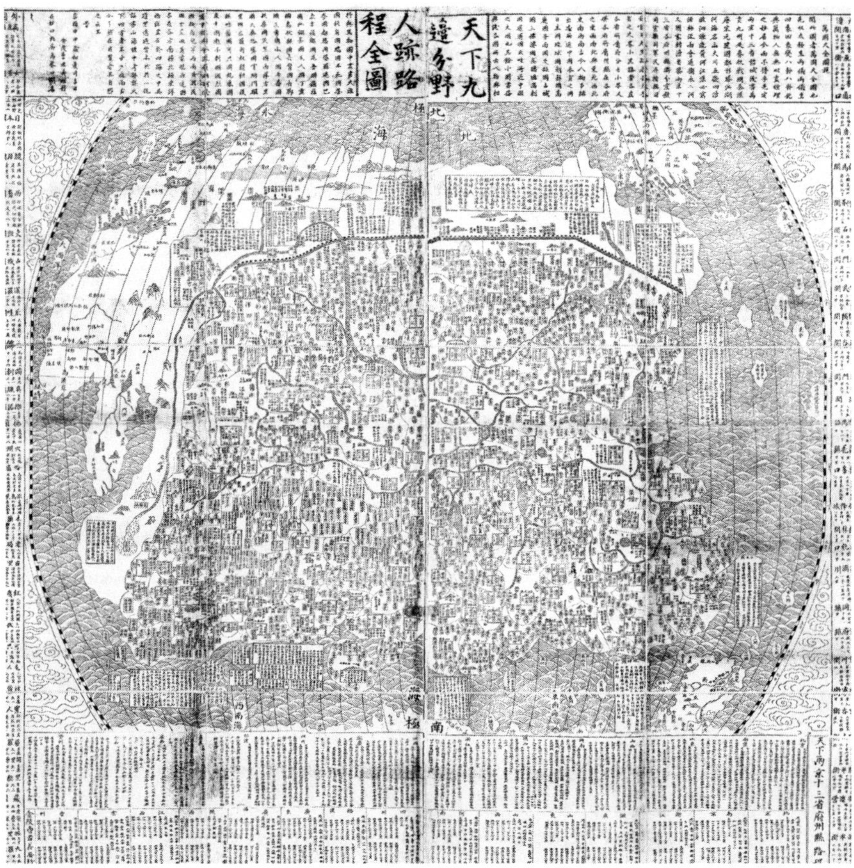

A.8 Cao Junyi, *Complete Map of the Astral Correspondences, Human Vestiges, and Routes of the Nine Border Zones under Heaven* (Tianxia jiubian fenye renji lucheng quantu), Nanjing, 1644. Cao Junyi's map, which hybridized Ortelius and Luo Hongxian, dominated world-mapping in China for the next two centuries. North America is the large island in the upper right-hand corner. London, British Library.

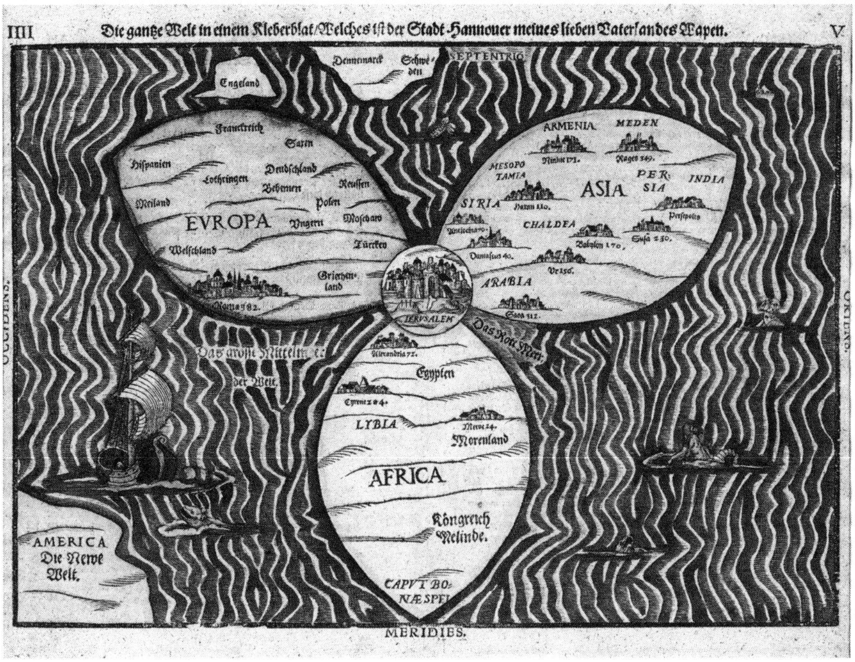

A.9 Even in the late sixteenth century, Protestant pastor Heinrich Bünting had difficulty figuring out how to fit the new continent of "America/Die Neue Welt" into his neat Christian model of the world as a three-leafed clover joined in the center at Jerusalem. Heinrich Bünting, *The Whole World in a Cloverleaf* (*Die ganze Welt in einem Kleberblat*), 1581.

The great challenge for Cao Junyi was what to do with the Americas. His solution was to squeeze an island into the upper right-hand corner—roughly where we might expect to see Alaska—and label it North America (*Bei Yamoli*), mistakenly dropping the final syllable of Yamolijia. He has decorated that island with several place names taken from Ricci's 1602 map: Arctic Circle (*Beiji jiexian*) at the top, Canada (*Jianatai guo* miscopying Ricci's Jianada, the name by which the country is known in Chinese today) in the middle, and at the bottom, Nova Hispania (*Xin Yixibaniya*) on a long peninsula that imitates Ricci's version of Baja California. If Cao's inclusion of the Americas seems curious, it is very like Heinrich Bünting's solution to the same problem in his 1581 *The Whole World in a Cloverleaf* (*Die ganze Welt in einem Kleberblat*) (fig. A.9). Grudgingly conceding that the post-Noachian biblical geography of three continents was no longer adequate, Bünting squeezed "America/the New World" into the lower left, the corner opposite to the one into which Cao fit North Yamoli.

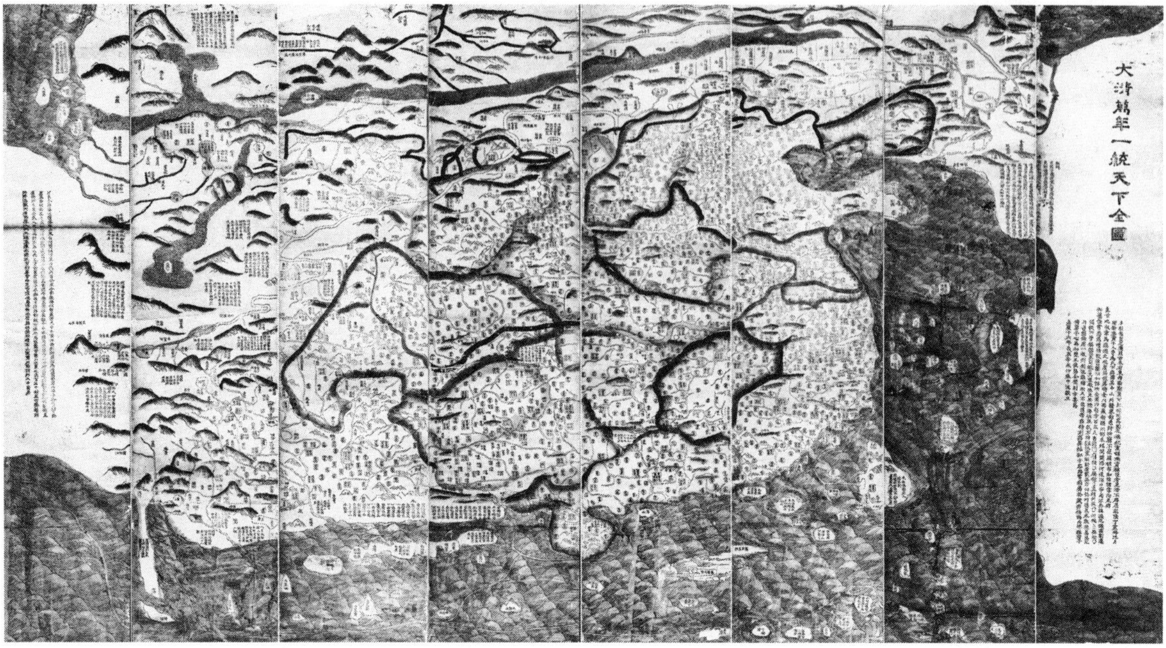

A.10 In this early nineteenth-century version of the "complete map" genre, the world beyond China has largely disappeared into an undifferentiated landmass extending off into the west and east wings of the map. *Complete Map of All under Heaven as Unified by the Qing Great State for Ten Thousand Years* (*Da Qing wannian yitong tianxia quantu*), ca. 1823. Washington, DC, Library of Congress.

Chinese knowledge of the world improved through the eighteenth century, yet "complete maps" in the style of Cao Junyi dominated the Chinese image of the world. In the opening decades of the nineteenth century, however, the genre took a turn. This shift is on vivid display in the *Complete Map of All under Heaven as Unified by the Qing Great State for Ten Thousand Years* (*Da Qing wannian yitong tianxia quantu*) (fig. A.10). Published at a time when the Qing did not yet perceive the country to be under serious threat from the West, the map evolves beyond Cao Junyi by abandoning most of the concessions he made to the Ortelian model to produce a consciously nationalistic portrait. China has been laterally stretched east and west to fill most of the map's visual field, the rest of the world downgraded to peripheral status, and the zones to the east and west of China reduced to blanks.[16] On the right-hand side, what had been the Korean peninsula on the *Kangnido* has been massively enlarged into a vast, undifferentiated chunk of *terra incognita* extending east from Korea and Japan to nowhere. On the left-hand edge of the map we can see an empty Indian Ocean beyond the Malay Peninsula and another body of water, originally descended from the North Atlantic though now confusedly dotted with islands/labels that read Hami, Luzon, Holland, Lesser Western Ocean, and Greater Western Ocean. But what dominates that side of the map is an empty landmass that mirrors the blank zone on the right-hand side. What had once been Africa has been thoroughly vacated: there's no place for Zanzibar here. In his rush to celebrate the vastness of the Qing regime, the cartographer has rendered the world beyond China not just featureless but not worth knowing. Bluntly phrased, this map marks a major retreat from the knowledge of the world that Luo Hongxian and his heirs sought to provide.

The absent world that wraps itself unseen around the far side of the globe is nameless. If someone later in the nineteenth century had wanted to give that place a name, that name would have been "the West." It is a name that has survived into the present. Reducing the rest of the world to an absent West came with consequences that are well known, as Chinese struggled through the nineteenth and twentieth centuries to negotiate a place for their nation in the new world order. Even today, some Chinese like to imagine China's position in the world in terms of a singular, oppositional relationship with an abstract West, just as some Euroamericans like to imagine their difference with China. Like Amerasia, the concept of the West exists only to the extent that anyone imagines it. Unlike Amerasia, though, it has been as much a creation of the Chinese who tried to imagine the world beyond their shores as it was an imposition of Europeans who promised the people of the Ming a West greater than the one they had once known.

Acknowledgments

Our collaboration was born in 2014, when, after a serious of casual conversations about early modern geography, we started to share and discuss the various examples of the Amerasian phenomenon we had collected. We first began to explore some of our ideas at the conference "Maps and Travel: Knowledge, Imagination, and Visual Culture, An International Workshop at Ben-Guirion University of the Negev," organized by Katrin Kogman-Appel and Nirit Ben-Aryeh Debby in June 2015. A second conference, "Making Worlds: Art, Materiality, and Early Modern Globalization" at UCLA in April 2017, allowed us to stretch further. The organizers of this conference, Bronwen Wilson and Angela Vanhaelen, in turn published a special edition of *The Journal of Early Modern History* (2019), in which our article "Amerasia: European Reflections of an Emergent World, 1492–ca. 1700," appeared. We are especially grateful to Katrin, Nirit, Bronwen, and Angela for having helped us to launch our project and hone our ideas.

Our research was awarded a generous National Endowment for the Humanities Collaborative Research Grant in 2017–19, which allowed us to complete the research and much of the writing of this book. In addition, this NEH support resulted in our digital humanities project, the companion website *Amerasia: An Inquiry into Early Modern Imaginative Geography* (http://www.ifaresearch.org/amerasia/#), in which we were able to explore our ideas in a digital and more public format. We thank Susan Halpert for facilitating access to the Vopel map at Harvard's Houghton Library, Gabrielle Roehr for her help in transcribing, translating, and editing the map's texts, and web designer Jason Varone for his harnessing the information into an elegant and usable interface.

We both did important work towards this project at the Harvard Center for Italian Renaissance Studies at Villa I Tatti, Florence. Our thanks go to Alina Payne for her help and support.

Along the way, numerous colleagues and supporters have assisted us. We thank Coco Alcalá, Sheila Barker, Robert Brennan, Shira Brisman,

David Colmenares, Jeff Dolven, Davide Domenici, Marzia Faietti, John Gagné, Blake Gopnik, Donatella Guida, Jessica Horton, Karen Kupperman, Catherine Kovesi, Lia Markey, Timothy McCall, Katharina Piechocki, Helmut Puff, Andrea Rizzi, Alessandra Russo, Suzanne Karr Schmidt, Monika Schmitter, Tatiana Seijas, Cristina Soriano, Simon Sun, Mikchiel van Groessen, Nicolás Wey Gómez, and Christopher Wood for their help, ideas, and constructive criticism.

We are especially indebted to Ricardo Padrón for his endless enthusiasm and critical feedback, to Louis Pate for his technical support, to Kenneth Hammond for his critical Sinological eye, and to Sophia Bevacqua for assisting us through our final drafts with efficiency and grace.

We feel special gratitude to our partners in life Kenneth Hammond and Amelia Saul for support as consistent as it was intangible.

Notes

INTRODUCTION: THE UNSETTLEMENT OF THE WORLD

1. As this annotation has not yet been transcribed or translated, we provide both here: "Anno post natum CHRISTUM 1521 XXX Maij Ferdinandus Cortesius prefectus Caroli V Caesaris Missus in Indiam cum classe obsedit Quinsai vel Temixtitam vel Civitatem celi celeberribum emporium Asiae orientalis. Venetijs etiam praeferendum. Et expugnavit XIII Augusti cum obsedio durasset dies 75. Sita est in medio lacis. In Circuitu habet pontes 1260 Longitudo 226 graduum M. 0 Latitudo 25 grad. Min. 15. [On the 30th of May in the year 1521 after the birth of CHRIST Hernán Cortés, commander of the emperor Charles V who was sent to India, with his army laid siege to Quinsai, also known as Temixtitam or the City of Heaven, most famous trading capital of eastern Asia, also much esteemed by the Venetians, and finally subdued on the 13th of August after the siege had gone on 75 days. It is situated in the middle of a lake. Around its circumference it has 1260 bridges. It is at longitude 226 degrees, 0 minutes, latitude 25 degrees, 15 minutes.]"

2. Christian Feest, *Vienna's Mexican Treasures: Aztec, Mixtec and Tarascan Works from 16th Century Austrian Collections* (Vienna: Museum für Volkerkunde, 1990), pp. 14–16.

3. Karl Anton Nowotny, *Mexikanische Kostbarkeiten aus Kunstkammern der Renaissance* (Vienna: Museum für Volkerkunde, 1960), p. 69.

4. Peter Lambeck, *Commentariorum De Augustissima Bibliotheca Caesarea Vindobonensi*, vol. 8 (Vienna: Cosmoverius, 1679), p. 660.

5. Christian Feest, *Vienna's Mexican Treasures*, pp. 1–8.

6. On the cartographic developments, see the wide-ranging essays in *The History of Cartography, Volume 3: Cartography in the European Renaissance*, ed. David Woodward, 2 vols. (Chicago: The University of Chicago Press, 2007). An important cultural study is Denis Cosgrove, *Apollo's Eye: A Cartographic Genealogy of the Earth in the Western Imagination* (Baltimore, MD: The Johns Hopkins University Press, 2001), esp. chap. 6, "Visionary Globes," as well as his "Mapping the World," in *Maps: Finding Our Place in the World*, eds. James R. Akerman and Robert W. Karrow Jr. (Chicago: The University of Chicago Press, 2007), pp. 65–115. On the literary implications, see Ayesha Ramachandran, *The Worldmakers: Global Imagining in Early Modern Europe* (Chicago: The University of Chicago Press, 2015), and Roland Greene, *Five Words: Critical Semantics in the Age of Cervantes and Shakespeare* (Chicago: The University of Chicago Press, 2013), esp. chap. 5, "World." On the artistic implications of a new imaginary of the world, and conversely of a new understanding of human image-making as a world-wide practice, see Alessandra Russo, "De Tlacuilolli: Renaissance Artistic Theory in the Wake of the Global Turn," in *Art History in the Wake of the Global Turn*, eds. Jill Casid and Aruna d'Souza (Williamstown, MA: Sterling and Francine Clark Art Institute, 2014), pp. 20–39, and idem, "Lights on the Antipodes: Francisco de Holanda and an Art History of the Universal," *Art Bulletin* 102 (2020), pp. 37–65. The media of printed books and maps became, in the words of Sean Roberts, forms of "connective tissue" that "bound readers and

authors across distances," both temporal and spatial. See Sean Roberts, *Printing a Mediterranean World: Florence, Constantinople, and the Renaissance of Geography* (Cambridge, MA: Harvard University Press, 2013), p. 14.

7. Peter Mason, *Infelicities: Representations of the Exotic* (Baltimore, MD: The Johns Hopkins University Press, 1998), chap. 2, "The Exotic Genre."

8. Benjamin Schmidt, *Inventing Exoticism: Geography, Globalism, and Europe's Early Modern World* (Philadelphia: University of Pennsylvania Press, 2015), takes as its subject the existence and articulation of the new category rather than the process by which it came into being, though the fact that it was the result of a historical process is clearly acknowledged, for example on pp. 325–26. Mason, *Infelicities*, p. 3, acknowledges that the word exotic was not used in the modern sense before the seventeenth century, yet affirms the birth of the "exotic genre" ca. 1500 in the wake of the first new world discoveries.

9. Martin Lewis and Kären Wigen, *The Myth of Continents: A Critique of Metageography* (Berkeley: University of California Press, 1997), p. 16.

10. On Portuguese regulatory houses, see Patrick O'Flanagan, *Port Cities of Atlantic Iberia c. 1500–1900* (Farnham: Ashgate, 2008), pp. 133–42, and Susannah Ferreira, *The Crown, the Court and the Casa da Índia: Political Centralization in Portugal, 1479–1521* (Leiden: Brill, 2015), pp. 66–68. We wish to thank Ingrid Greenfield, who is preparing a study on this subject, for clarifying these matters and providing references.

11. "Indiani dell'India maggiore mandate dal Prete Janni," Leonardo Olschki, *Storia letteraria delle scoperte geografiche: Studi e Ricerche* (Florence: Olschki, 1937), p. 206 n.75.

12. "Aithiopians, most distant of men, who live divided, some at the setting of Hyperion, some at his rising," Homer, *The Odyssey*, trans. Richmond Lattimore (New York: Harper Collins, 1991), p. 27 (1: 23–24).

13. Pierre Schneider, *L'Éthiopie et l'Inde: Interférences et confusions aux extrémités du monde antique* (Rome: École française de Rome, 2004).

14. Byron Ellsworth Hamann, *Bad Christians, New Spains: Muslims, Catholics, and Native Americans in a Mediterratlantic World* (London: Routledge, 2019).

15. For two different and sweeping accounts of this shift, see Cosgrove, *Apollo's Eye*, chap. 4, "Oceanic Globe"; and Peter Sloterdijk, *In the World Interior of the Capital: Toward a Philosophy of Globalization*, trans. Wieland Hoban (Cambridge: Polity Press, 2013), chap. 7: "Waterworld: On the Change of the Central Element in the Modern Age." See also Carla Lois, "Isla vs. continente: Un ensayo de historia conceptual," *Revista de Geografía Norte Grande* 54 (2013), pp. 85–107.

16. An important early initiative in this direction came in the essays in *Cartographic Encounters: Perspectives on Native American Mapmaking and Map Use*, ed. G. Malcolm Lewis (Chicago: The University of Chicago Press, 1998). A model study is Louise M. Burkhart's *The Slippery Earth: Nahua-Christian Moral Dialogue in Sixteenth-Century Mexico* (Tucson: University of Arizona Press, 1989). And see Pekka Hämäläinen, *Indigenous Continent: The Epic Contest for North America* (New York: Liveright, 2022).

17. Steven Feld, "Acoustemology," in *Keywords in Sound*, eds. David Novak and Matt Sakakeeny (Durham, NC: Duke University Press, 2015), pp. 12–21. More closely related to our topic and period, see the excellent essays in *Acoustemologies in Contact: Sounding Subjects and Modes of Listening in Early Modernity*, eds. Emily Wilbourne and Suzanne G. Cusick (Cambridge: Open Book Publishing, 2021).

18. An indispensable essay on this problem remains Sabine MacCormack, "Limits of Understanding: Perceptions of Greco-Roman and Amerindian Paganism in Early Modern Europe," in *America in European Consciousness, 1493–1750*, ed. Karen Ordahl Kupperman (Chapel Hill: The University of North Carolina Press, 1995), pp. 79–129.

19. A premise of several exemplary studies in the history of art: Margit Kern, *Transkulturelle Imaginationen des Opfers in der Frühen Neuzeit: Übersetzungsprozesse zwischen Mexiko und Europa* (Berlin: Deutscher Kunstverlag, 2013); Alessandra Russo, *L'image intraduisible: Une histoire métisse des arts en Nouvelle-Espagne (1500–1600)* (Paris: Presses du

Réel, 2013), in English *The Untranslatable Image: A Mestizo History of the Arts in New Spain, 1500–1600*, trans. Susan Emanuel (Austin: University of Texas Press, 2014). See also the essays in *Transforming Images: New Mexican Santos in-between Worlds*, eds. Claire Farago and Donna Pierce (University Park, PA: Penn State University Press, 2006).

20. Eduardo Viveiros de Castro, *The Relative Native: Essays on Indigenous Conceptual Worlds* (Chicago: Hau, 2015), pp. 3–37, "The Relative Native."

21. J. Jorge Klor de Alva, "The Postcolonization of the (Latin) American Experience: A Reconsideration of 'Colonialism,' 'Postcolonialism,' and 'Mestizaje'," in *After Colonialism: Imperial Histories and Postcolonial Displacements*, ed. Gyan Prakash (Princeton, NJ: Princeton University Press, 1995), pp. 241–76.

22. Hamann, *Bad Christians*, pp. 5–6.

ONE — EMERGENT AMERASIA

1. Arnold Nesselrath, "Blickwinkel/Points of View," in *Tecumseh, Keokuk, Black Hawk: Indianerbildnisse in Zeiten von Verträgen und Vertreibung / Portrayals of Native Americans in Times of Treaties and Removals*, ed. Iris Adenheiser and Strid Nielsen (Dresden: Arnoldsche Art Publishers, 2013), pp. 65–79, at p. 73; Arnold Nesselrath, "Le code secret d'Alexandre VI," *Le Figaro* (September 2014), pp. 70–77; Jessica Horton, *Art for an Undivided Earth: The American Indian Movement Generation* (Durham, NC: Duke University Press, 2017), pp. 149–51; Michael Gaudio, *Sound, Image, Silence: Art and the Aural Imagination in the Atlantic World* (Minneapolis: University of Minnesota Press, 2019), pp. 6–18; Andrés H. Rubiano, "The First Painted Image of America in Europe: A Detail from Pinturicchio's 'Resurrection' in the Sala dei Misteri," *H-ART: Revista de historia, teoría y crítica de arte* 8 (2021), pp. 286–304.

2. See Cecil H. Clough, "The New World and the Italian Renaissance," in *The European Outthrust and Encounter—The First Phase c. 1400–c. 1700: Essays in Tribute to David Beers Quinn on His 85th Birthday*, ed. Cecil H. Clough and P. E. H. Hair (Liverpool, UK: Liverpool University Press, 1994), pp. 291–328, at p. 299. On the editing of this published letter, see also Margarita Zamora, *Reading Columbus* (Berkeley: University of California Press, 1993), pp. 9–20.

3. In fact, this vessel copies a ship anchored at the port of Rhodes in a woodcut by Erhard Reuwich for Bernard von Breydenbach's *Peregrinatio in Terram Sanctam* (Mainz: Reuwich, 1486), n.p.

4. For a facsimile, transcription, and translation of the 1493 Barcelona version of the letter, see *The Spanish Letter of Columbus to Luis de Sant' Angel, Escribano de Racion of the Kingdom of Aragon, dated 15 February 1493* (London: Quaritch, 1893).

5. See Marco Polo, *The Travels*, trans. Ronald Latham (New York: Penguin, 1958), p. 295.

6. Edmundo O'Gorman, *The Invention of America: An Inquiry Into the Historical Nature of the New World and the Meaning of its History* (Bloomington: Indiana University Press, 1961), p. 78. The prediscovery documents issued by the Crown, on the other hand, including the "Capitulaciones de Santa Fe," the contract that established the terms of Columbus's enterprise, were enigmatic regarding Columbus's destination, and Asia was never explicitly stated as a goal of the voyages; see Zamora, *Reading Columbus*, p. 155.

7. In Las Casas's transmission of the diary of Columbus's first voyage, Columbus similarly reported that Cuba was Cipangu, that he had landed "off Zayton or Quinsay," and that "there were one-eyed people and others with dogs' muzzles who ate human beings," much as Odoric of Pordenone had located dog-headed men on the Nicobar Islands in the Indian Ocean and Polo had in the Andaman Islands off the south coast of Burma. See *A Synoptic Edition of the Log of Columbus's First Voyage*, eds. Francesca Lardicci and Valeria Bertolucci Pizzorusso, Repertorium Columbianum 6 (Turnhout: Brepols, 1999), pp. 58–64; and Leonardo Olschki, *Storia letteraria delle scoperte geografiche* (Florence: Olschki, 1937), p. 22.

8. See Michele da Cuneo, "Letter to Gerolamo Annari," in *Italian Reports on America, 1493–1522: Accounts by Contemporary Observers*, ed. Geoffrey Symcox, Repertorium Columbianum 12 (Turnhout: Brepols, 2002), pp. 50–63, at pp. 60 and 63.

9. See Beatriz Pastor Bodmer, *The Armature of Conquest: Spanish Accounts of the Discovery of America, 1492–1589*, trans. Lydia Longstreth Hunt (Stanford, CA: Stanford University Press, 1992), p. 27.

10. For discussions of the myriad examples of Columbus's belief that he was in Asia, see Mary B. Campbell, *The Witness and the Other World: Exotic European Travel Writing, 400–1600* (Ithaca, NY: Cornell University Press, 1988), pp. 171–76; and Dora Beale Polk, *The Island of California: A History of the Myth* (Spokane, WA: Arthur H. Clark, 1991), pp. 43–50.

11. See Helen Wallis, "What Columbus Knew," *History Today* 42 (1992), pp. 17–23, at p. 18; Valerie Flint, *The Imaginative Landscape of Christopher Columbus* (Princeton, NJ: Princeton University Press, 1992), pp. 18–19; Michael Householder, *Inventing Americans in the Age of Discovery: Narratives of Encounter* (Farnham, UK: Ashgate, 2011), pp. 21–22. For a modern edition of Columbus's annotated Polo, see *El libro de Marco Polo anotado por Cristóbal Colón, versión de Rodrigo de Santaella*, ed. Juan Gil (Madrid: Alianza Universidad, 1987). For a detailed discussion of the various ways in which Columbus imposed preexisting literary models of Asia on what he saw in the western Atlantic, see Bodmer, *The Armature of Conquest*, pp. 9–37.

12. Marianne O'Doherty, *The Indies and the Medieval West: Thought, Report, Imagination* (Turnhout: Brepols, 2013), p. 6.

13. Ibid., pp. 2–7. For the development of these traditions during the early modern period of expanded travel, see Joan-Pau Rubiés, *Travel and Ethnology in the Renaissance: South India through European Eyes, 1250–1625* (Cambridge: Cambridge University Press, 2009). On medieval European ethnographic writing, see also Shirin A. Khanmohamadi, *In Light of Another's Word: European Ethnography in the Middle Ages* (Philadelphia: University of Pennsylvania Press, 2014). On India in the early modern European imagination, see Erin Benay, *Italy by Way of India: Translating Art and Devotion in the Early Modern World* (Turnhout: Brepols/Harvey Miller, 2021).

14. See Donald F. Lach, *Asia in the Making of Europe*, vol. 1, *The Century of Discovery* (Chicago: University of Chicago Press, 1965), pp. 5–19 and 59–64; and Partha Mitter, *Much Maligned Monsters: A History of European Reactions to Indian Art* (Oxford: Clarendon Press, 1977), pp. 1–72.

15. Lach argues that by 1300, the term *India* designated much of Asia, including "the subcontinent, the East Indies, and everything in the distant East." See Lach, *Asia in the Making of Europe*, vol. 1, p. 24.

16. See *Geography of Claudius Ptolemy*, ed. and trans. Edward Luther Stevenson (New York: New York Public Library, 1932), book 7, chaps. 2–4, pp. 155–58; and John Watson McCrindle, *Ancient India as Described by Ptolemy* (London: Trübner & Co., 1885). Europeans used a variety of terms to describe India to the east of the Ganges, including Greater India, Farther India, and eventually, the East Indies; see Martin W. Lewis and Kären E. Wigen, *The Myth of Continents: A Critique of Metageography* (Cambridge, MA: Harvard University Press, 1997), p. 274. See also Bartolomé de Las Casas, *Apologética historia sumaria*, ed. Edmundo O'Gorman, 2 vols. (Mexico City: Universidad Nacional Autónoma de México, 1967), vol. 1, chap. 22, p. 109, where Las Casas neatly recaps classical understandings of India beyond the Ganges, as discussed in chapter 12.

17. John Roland Seymour Phillips, *The Medieval Expansion of Europe* (Oxford: Clarendon Press, 1998), p. 192.

18. Niccolò de' Conti, "The Travels of Niccolò Conti in the East," in *India in the Fifteenth Century: Being a Collection of Narratives of Voyages to India*, ed. Richard Henry Major (London: Hakluyt Society, 1857), pp. 3–39, at p. 21.

19. See Nicolás Wey Gómez, *The Tropics of Empire: Why Columbus Sailed South to the Indies* (Cambridge, MA: MIT Press, 2008). On the invention or "assembling" of the tropics in early modern Europe, see also Hugh Cagle, *Assembling the Tropics: Science and Medicine in Portugal's Empire, 1450–1700* (Cambridge: Cambridge University Press, 2018).

20. See Ricardo Padrón, *The Indies of the Setting Sun: How Early Modern Spain Mapped the Far East as the Transpacific West* (Chicago: University of Chicago Press, 2020), esp. pp. 107–66.

21. *Geography of Claudius Ptolemy*, book 7, chap. 2, p. 156.

22. Ibid., p. 157. On the Golden Chersonesus, see Victor

R. Savage, *Western Impressions of Nature and Landscape in Southeast Asia* (Singapore: Singapore University Press, 1984), pp. 28–33. On the "seemingly infinite" islands of India, see Jean de Mandeville, *Le livre des merveilles du monde*, ed. Christiane Deluz (Paris: CNRS Éditions, 2000), p. 312: "Ynde sont plus de V.mil isles habitables bons et grandes, sanz celles qe sont inhabitables et sanz autres petites." See also Polo, *The Travels*, p. 248.

23. *Geography of Claudius Ptolemy*, book 7, chap. 3, p. 157.

24. Conti, "The Travels of Niccolò Conti in the East," p. 21. On the European framing of *India extra Gangem* in later centuries, see Geoffrey C. Gunn, *Overcoming Ptolemy: The Revelation of an Asian World Region* (Lanham, MD: Lexington Books, 2018), pp. 181–205.

25. "L'Ammiraglio non le chiamò Indie, perchè elle fossero stato viste, ne scoperte da altri, ma perchè erano la parte orientale dell'India oltre il Gange; alla qual niun cosmografo assegnò termine o confine con altra terra o provincia per l'oriente, salvo con l'oceano: e, per esser queste terre l'orientale incognito dell' India, e perchè non hanno nome particolare, gli diede il nome del più vicino paese, chiamandole Indie occidentali" Ferdinand Columbus, *Historie del S. D. Fernando Colombo* (Venice: Francesco de'Franceschi, 1571), fol. 14r. See Wey Gómez, *The Tropics of Empire*, pp. 166–67.

26. See *Italian Reports on America, 1493–1522: Letters, Dispatches, and Papal Bulls*, ed. Geoffrey Symcox, Repertorium Columbianum 10 (Turnhout: Brepols, 2001), pp. 8–9 and 27–29.

27. See Leonardo Olschki, "I 'Cantàri dell'India' di Giuliano Dati," *La Bibliofilía* 40 (1938), pp. 289–316.

28. Along similar lines, the historian of print culture Rudolf Hirsch noted that among the earliest printed texts related to Columbus "little intrigued the general public, possibly because Columbus's search for a westward route to India was not recognized as anything beyond a mere extension of Portuguese explorations to the south and east," implying that as with audiences listening to Dati's songs, readers of this early printed material also placed Columbus's discoveries in Asia. See Rudolf Hirsch, "Printed Reports on the Early Discoveries and Their Reception," in *First Images of America: The Impact of the New World on the Old*, ed. Fredi Chiappelli, 2 vols. (Berkeley: University of California Press, 1976), vol. 2, pp. 537–60, at p. 539.

29. "Di reubarbaro ce tanta abondantia/& dicenamo daltra spetieria/loro & largento elmetallo ciavanza." *Columbus in Italy: An Italian Versification of the Letter on the Discovery of the New World. With Facsimiles of the Italian and Latin Editions of 1493*, ed. Martin Davies (London: The British Library, 1991), n.p. See also Giuliano Dati, *Il secondo cantare dell'India* (Rome: n.p., 1494).

30. "Quella terra/era di vari fructi molto ornata," "no altri stiano tucti stupiti/per labondantia che trovata habbiano/sonci gli arberi verdi & le lor foglie/chi credo che non perda mai le spoglie," *Columbus in Italy*, n.p. "È fertile el paese loro & sano/& è di frutti questo abondantissimo." Giuliano Dati, *La gran magnificenza del Prete Janni, Poemettto di Giuliano Dati*, ed. Achille Neri, Il Propugnatore 9 (1876), pp. 138–65, at p. 163.

31."la piace[v]oleza di questa gente io non sapre narrare," *Columbus in Italy*, n.p. "Et rare volta infra costor si sente alcun micidio, o ver qualche spergiuro non vi son traditori o ladra gente non aduolteri, falsi o alcun furo." Dati, *La gran magnificenza*, p. 156. Similarly, "la gienta del paese e molto affabile." Dati, *Il secondo cantare*, n.p.

32."Non sa che sia del mondo le sue isegne." *Columbus in Italy*, n.p. "Di queste magnie cose chio ti canto forse si dicho piu nol crederai." Dati, *Il secondo cantare*, n.p.

33. See Riccardo Bruscagli, "Voices from the New World: Giuliano Dati's "*La storia della invention delle nuove insule di Channaria Indiane*," *Journal of Early Modern Studies* 7 (2018), pp. 63–97, at pp. 95–96.

34. As the literary scholar Leonardo Olschki describes: "I quali, convinti che l'Ammiraglio avesse raggiunto le estreme coste orientali dell'India, ne trovarono l'immagine in questi cantari non come di un nuovo mondo, ma secondo antichissime memorie ed ancor vive tradizioni di poesia e di cultura." Olschki, "I 'Cantàri dell'India' di Giuliano Dati," p. 295.

35. In line with this way of thinking, in his *Portolano*

(Venice, 1528), a handbook of written sailing directions for maritime navigation, the Venetian geographer Pietro Coppo conflates the voyages of Columbus with those of the Portuguese, stating that "after Columbus, Spanish navigators traveled around the Cape of Good Hope, arriving in India, in Calicut, and from there traveling beyond to the most distant parts of India" ("Dapoi el colombo, li spagnoli naviganti navegando oltra el cavo bona speranza perveneno nel'india a colocut e andorno piu oltra fina nele extreme parte de India"). Pietro Coppo, *Portolano* (Venice: Augustino di Bindoni, 1528), p. 110r. Such thinking could also explain how, even decades later, a 1560 Venetian edition of Johann Boemus's *The Manners, Laws, and Customs of all Nations* (*Omnium Gentium Mores, Leges et Ritus*) makes clear that the lands on the western side of the Atlantic had been named in relationship to legends about India and Indies: the new world "was called the Indies from the India of Prester John, where the Portuguese had traded, because a Portuguese ship by luck arrived in these parts, and the pilot, seeing these new lands, called them Indies, and Columbus did the same" ("ilquale fu adimandato le Indie dall'India del prete Gianni, dove gia contratavano gli Portogesi, perche una Carauella di detti Portogesi, spinta da fortuna, arrivò in queste parti, & il Pedodota, vedendo questi nuovi paesi gli chiamò Indie, & cosi il Palombo sempre le nominò."). Giovanni Boemo, *I costumi, le leggi, et l'usanze di tutte le genti* (Venice: Francesco Lorenzini, 1560), pp. 189 r–v.

36. "Psitacci tamen inde asportati atque alia multa, vel propinquitate, vel natura, solum indicum has insulas sapere indicant." *Selections from Peter Martyr*, ed. Geoffrey Eatough, Repertorium Columbianum 5 (Turnhout: Brepols, 1998), p. 133 (Decade 1.1.11).

37. "Ex arboribus, veluti apud seres, uellera colliguntur." Ibid., p. 134 (Decade 1.1.11).

38. "Insula haec hispaniola quam ipse ophiram." Ibid., p. 146 (Decade 1.3.1).

39. "Seque non longe ab aurea chersonesso, nostri orientis ultra persidem initio." Ibid., pp. 149–50 (Decade 1.3.10).

40. "Vocauitque eius initium alpha, o, eo quod ibi finem esse nostri orientis cum in ea sol occidat, occidentis autem cum oriatur, arbitretur. Instat enim esse ab occidente principium indiae ultra gangem, ab oriente uero terminum ipsius ultimum. Neque enim absonum penitus est, cum gangetidis indiae terminos indiscretos cosmographi reliquerint, nec desint qui ab hispanis oris non longe indica littora discedere sentient." Ibid., p. 149 (Decade 1.3.8).

41. Pliny, for instance, believed that one could travel east from the Persian Gulf to the Pillars of Hercules in just a few days; Aristotle similarly claimed that only a small sea lay between the western coast of Spain and the coast of India. See Bodmer, *The Armature of Conquest*, p. 280 n.21.

42. "Ultra urbem cataii et littus indicum ultra gangem percurrerant." Eatough, *Selections from Peter Martyr*, p. 189 (Decade 1.9.9).

43. "Triginta viros, qui cipangi, alias cibaui, regionem explorarent." Ibid., p. 147 (Decade 1.3.3). On this association, see Olschki, *Storia letteraria delle scoperte geografiche*, pp. 39–40.

44. *The Discovery of the New World in the Writings of Peter Martyr of Anghiera*, ed. Ernesto Lunardi, Elisa Magioncalda, and Rosanna Mazzacane (Rome: Istituto Poligrafico e Zecca dello Stato, 1992), pp. 40–41.

45. Ibid., pp. 60–61. In a letter of August 9, 1495, to Cardinal Bernardino López de Carvajal, Peter Martyr notes Carvajal's promise to share a previously sent letter with Pomponio Leto, confirming the impression that these letters circulated among people close to Pope Alexander VI; see ibid., pp. 70–71.

46. "Lexos de allí avía hombres de un ojo, y otros con hoçicos de perros que comían los hombres, y que en tornando uno lo degollavan y le bebían la sangre, y le cortavan su natura." Lardicci and Pizzorusso, eds., *A Synoptic Edition of the Log of Columbus's First Voyage*, pp. 64 and 340.

47. "La qual dezían que era muy grande, y que avía en ella gente que tenía la frente, y otros que se llamavan caníbales, a quien mostraban tener gran miedo." Ibid., pp. 73 and 350.

48. See *The Compact Edition of the Oxford English Dictionary*, eds. E. S. C. Weiner and J. A. Simpson, 2 vols. (Oxford: Oxford University Press, 1971), vol. 1, p. 328.

49. "No podían hablar, temiendo que los avían de comer, y no les podía quitar el temor; y decían que no tenían sino un ojo y la cara de perro; y creya el Almirante que mentían, y sentía el Almirante que debían de ser del señorío del Gran Can que los captibavan." Lardicci and Pizzorusso, eds., *A Synoptic Edition of the Log of Columbus's First Voyage*, pp. 75 and 353–54.

50. "Caniba no es otra cosa sino la gente del Gran Can, que deve ser aquí muy vezino." Ibid., pp. 86 and 367.

51. Marco Polo reported the practice of humans eating other humans on the island of Andaman, where he also records that the men have heads like dogs. Columbus's own edition of Polo describes the human flesh-eaters on Andaman as having the heads of dogs. "Humanas enim carnes commedunt. Homines ibi ualde deformes sunt, nam caput (ali) qui caninum habent et oculos canibus similes." *El libro de Marco Polo anotado por Cristóbal Colón*, ed. Juan Gil (Madrid: Alizanza Universidad, 1987), p. 362. *The Book of John Mandeville* similarly notes the presence of dogs and human flesh-eating on an unnamed island near the Indian island of Gaffolos: "De celle isle vait homme vers un autre isle où il y a gentz de moult malveise nature qe norissent grants chiens et les affaitent pur estranler lors amis quant ils sont malades, qar ils ne voillent mie q'ils moerent de la mort naturele, qar ils disent qu'ils soeffrerent trop de peine. Et quant ils sont ensy estranlez, ils mangent la char en lieu de venisoun." De Mandeville, *Le livre des merveilles du monde*, p. 349. On Columbus and cannibalism, see Frank Lestringant, *Cannibals: The Discovery and Representation of the Cannibal from Columbus to Jules Verne* (Berkeley: University of California Press, 1997), pp. 1–22; Berthold Laufer, "Columbus and Cathay, and the Meaning of America to the Orientalist," *Journal of the American Oriental Society* 51 (1931), pp. 87–103, at p. 94; Michael Palencia-Roth, "The Cannibal Law of 1503," in *Early Images of the Americas: Transfer and Invention*, ed. Jerry M. Williams and Robert E. Lewis (Tucson: University of Arizona Press, 1993), pp. 21–63; Surekha Davies, *Renaissance Ethnography and the Invention of the Human: New Worlds, Maps, and Monsters* (New York: Cambridge University Press, 2016), pp. 68–72; Peter Hulme, *Colonial Encounters: Europe and the Native Caribbean, 1492–1797* (London: Methuen, 1986), pp. 13–43; John Jeffries Martin, *A Beautiful Ending: The Apocalyptic Imagination and the Making of the Modern World* (New Haven, CT: Yale University Press, 2022), chap. 10.

52. Davies, *Renaissance Ethnography*, p. 98.

53. Zamora, *Reading Columbus*, p. 7.

54. In another moment of misunderstanding—albeit not with Indigenous communities—another of Peter Martyr's reports generated Amerasian knowledge. Peter Martyr reported in a letter written to Clement VII in 1526 how Estavan Gómez, a Portuguese pilot who sailed from Spain in search of a passage to Asia (he was seeking "a new route, leading to Cathay, between the Baccalaos and Florida" for any passage "found leading to the kingdom of him whom we commonly call the Grand Khan") returned to La Coruña in Spain in 1525 and sent a message from there to the king that he had brought with him enslaved Indians, or *esclavos*. The message became garbled along the way, and "cutting off the first half of the word," the announcement reached court that Gómez had returned with *clavos*, or cloves, a product associated with the Moluccas or Spice Islands. See Peter Martyr d'Anghiera, *De Orbe Novo: The Eight Decades of Peter Martyr d'Anghiera*, trans. Francis Augustus MacNutt, 2 vols. (New York: Putnam, 1912), vol. 2, pp. 241–42 and 419–20.

TWO — WHAT DID THE TERM *NEW WORLD* MEAN?

1. See Francis M. Rogers, "Valentim Fernandes, Rodrigo de Santaella, and the Recognition of the Antilles as 'Opposite India,'" *Boletim da Sociedade de Geografia de Lisboa* 75 (1957), pp. 279–309, at p. 282.

2. "Diaz . . . digno como Josue de entrar em aquele mundo novo que bem podemos chamar a terra da promissam." Valentim Fernandes, *O Livro de Marco Paulo*, ed. Francisco Maria Esteves Pereira (Lisbon: Biblioteca Nacional, 1922 [1502]), fol. A.ij (r).

3. "As cousas novas e maravilhas das terras e gente nova e das suas cousas." Ibid., fol. A.j (v).

4. "A serviçio de Deos, e avisamento daquelles que agora vam pera as ditas Indias." Ibid., fol. 98v.

5. "Começo de oriente ate as terra do gram Cham onde ja começa de soar vosso poderoso nomem onde jazem as my nobres provicias Tencudh, Mangy, Tanguth etc. o principio das quaes segundo o meu pequeno saber achou o muy honrrado fidalguo Gaspar Corte Real." Ibid., fol. A.ij (v).

6. *El libro del famoso Marco Paulo veneciano*, trans. Rodrigo de Santaella (Seville, 1503).

7. "Item porque muchos vulgares & aun hombres de mas suerte piensan que Antilla, o estas islas nuevamente falladas por mandado de nuestros muy catolicos rey don fernando & reyna doña ysabel son elnas indias son engañados por el nobre que les pusieron de indias. E porque elna española se falla oro algunos han osado decir que es tarsis & Ophin & Cethin donde en tiempo de Salomon se traya oro a Jherusalem. E añadiendo errores a errores.... [Y] por estas islas & aun osan mas decir que fasta agora no fueron entendidos aquellos lugares dela sancta scrittura.... Yo viendo que engañan con sus vanas invenciones a muchos simples por zelo dela verdad y por cauterizer este cancer que no corrompa mas y engendre & para mayores errores." Ibid., "Cosmographia introductoria."

8. "Anteindia que quiere dezir contra india como antechristo contra christo... ansi parece que no se podra llamar India"; "Parece che asia... son en oriente y antilla la Española en Occidente en lugar y de condicion muy differente," ibid. For an overview of Santaella's understanding of the relationship between the Americas and Asia, see Serge Gruzinski, *The Eagle and the Dragon: Globalization and European Dreams of Conquest in China and America in the Sixteenth Century* (Cambridge: Polity, 2014), pp. 43–45.

9. Santaella's denial that Columbus had arrived in the Indies continued to spark debate even in the second half of the sixteenth century. In his biography of his father, published in Venice in 1571, Ferdinand Columbus continued to refute Santaella. "Here one plainly sees how wrong was a certain Master Rodrigo... and some of his followers, who join him in censuring the Admiral for naming these lands the Indies" ("Perche si vede chiaramente, quanto a torto un Maestro Rodrigo... & alcuni seguaci suoi, riprendano l'Ammiraglio, dicendo, ch'egli non doveva chiamarle Indie"). Ferdinand Columbus, *Historie del S. D. Fernando Colombo* (Venice: Francesco de'Franceschi, 1571), fols. 13v–14r (chap. 6).

10. "Columbus 1499 Letter on The Third Voyage," in Richard Henry Major, *Select Letters of Christopher Columbus with Other Original Documents Relating to His Four Voyages to the New World* (London: Hakluyt Society, 1870), p. 147. Las Casas's narrative of Columbus's third voyage similarly reports Columbus as saying, "I believe no one has ever taken this route before and the seas in [this] area are completely unknown." *Las Casas on Columbus: The Third Voyage*, ed. Geoffrey Symcox, Repertorium Columbianum 11 (Turnhout: Brepols, 2001), chap. 130.7, p. 23.

11. "Letter of the Admiral to the (quondam) nurse of Prince John." Ibid., pp. 54 and 170.

12. "Che bien dixeron los sacros theólogos y los sabios philósophos que el Parayso terrenal está en el fin de Oriente, porque es lugar temperatíssimo; así que aquestas tierra que él avía descuberto, dize él, és el fin de Oriente." *A Synoptic Edition of the Log of Columbus's First Voyage*, eds. Francesca Lardicci and Valeria Bertolucci Pizzorusso, Repertorium Columbianum 6 (Turnhout: Brepols, 1999), p. 615. According to the literary scholar Mary Watt, *Dante's Commedia* in particular had provided Columbus with guidance about the physical location of the Earthly Paradise. See Mary Alexandra Watt, *Dante, Columbus and the Prophetic Tradition: Spiritual Imperialism in the Italian Imagination* (London: Routledge, 2017), pp. 5–6.

13. *Fonti italiane per la storia della scoperta del nuovo mondo*, ed. Guglielmo Berchet, 2 vols. (Rome: Il Ministero della Pubblica Istruzione, 1892), vol. 2, p. 42.

14. See Edmundo O'Gorman, *The Invention of America: An Inquiry Into the Historical Nature of the New World and the Meaning of its History* (Bloomington: Indiana University Press, 1961), p. 83. O'Gorman claims (p. 157 n.18) that a variety of "men of learning," including the Florentine historian Tribaldo de Rossi, and the Sienese chroniclers Pietro Parenti and Allegretto Allegretti, among others, showed

"skepticism as to the identification of the lands found by Columbus with Asia." On contemporary reactions to Columbus's belief that he was in Asia, see Felipe Fernández-Armesto, *Columbus* (Oxford: Oxford University Press, 1991), pp. 95–98.

15. *Paesi novamente retrovati et novo mondo da Alberico Vesputio Florentio intitulato* (Vicenza: Henrico e Zanmaria Vicentino, 1507).

16. See Antonello Gerbi, *Nature in the New World: From Christopher Columbus to Gonzalo Fernández de Oviedo*, trans. Jeremy Moyle (Pittsburgh, PA: University of Pittsburgh Press, 1975), pp. 255–305, at pp. 258–61. As Gerbi notes, Alexandre von Humboldt compiled and annotated a scholarly list of various related expressions in ancient geographical tradition (new world, other world, land beyond the ocean, etc.) in his *Examen critique de l'histoire de la géographie du Nouveau Monde et des progrès de l'astronomie nautique aux cinquième et seizième siècles*, 5 vols. (Paris: Librairie de Gide, 1836–39), vol. 1, pp. 113–21, and vol. 5, pp. 182–84.

17. Giuseppe Marcocci, *Indios, cinesi, falsari; Le storie del mondo nel Rinascimento* (Bari: Laterza, 2016), preface, par. 6. Likewise, the historian Christine R. Johnson observes that for early modern German audiences, "it was deemed appropriate not only to combine accounts of the Portuguese voyage to India with those of the Spanish and Portuguese voyages to the New World, but also to add other material that placed the recent expeditions within a panorama of expanding European knowledge of all the parts of the world." Christine R. Johnson, *The German Discovery of the World: Renaissance Encounters with the Strange and Marvelous* (Charlottesville: University of Virginia Press, 2008), p. 25.

18. Joan-Pau Rubiés, "Travel Writing and Humanistic Culture: A Blunted Impact?" *Journal of Early Modern History* 10 (2006), pp. 131–68, at p. 137. See also Stephanie Leitch, *Mapping Ethnography in Early Modern Germany: New Worlds in Print Culture* (New York: Palgrave Macmillan, 2010), p. 12.

19. See Donald F. Lach and Edwin J. Van Kley, *Asia in the Making of Europe*, vol. 2, *A Century of Wonder*, book 3, *The Scholarly Disciplines* (Chicago: University of Chicago Press, 1965), pp. 456 and 516–17.

20. "Le Zamorin [Hindu monarch of Malabar coast] mesme, au temps que les Portugais aborderent en Calecut, fasoit sa residence à Panané . . . non fort loin de la ville. Gamma, estant encare ses navires á l'Ancre, l'avertit de son arrive: & luy feit scavoir qu'il venoit presque d'un autre nouveau Monde, avec lettres & charge du Roy de Portugal." Giovanni Pietro Maffei, *Histoires des Indes* (Lyon: Jean Pillehotte, 1604), p. 79.

21. Venice, Biblioteca Correr, Mss. Donà delle Rose, filza 447, n.11, *Leggendo diversi autori alcune cose notabili*, c. 10–14.

22. Pontus de Tyard, *Les discours philosophiques* (Paris: Chez Abel L'Angelier, 1587), pp. 273r–v.

23. Guillaume Postel, *Des merveilles du monde et principalemét [sic] des admirables choses des Indes, & du nouveau monde: Histoire extraicte des escriptz tresdignes de foy, tant de ceulx qui encores sont a present audict pays, come de ceulx qui encores vivantz peu paravat en sont retournez* (n.p., 1553), pp. 8–9. For further commentary, see Phillip John Usher, "Chopping up Columbus' Pear: World-Roaming after 1492," in *Space: New Dimensions in French Studies*, ed. Emma Gilbey and Katja Haustein (Oxford: Peter Lang, 2005), pp. 71–89.

24. "Lussisti coram te, sacro sanctoque Senatu astante, me uerba habere de ingenti beneficia quod a Deo optimo maximo grex tuus, te pastore, susceperat, quod, te praeside, Lusitanus rex fines sacratissimi imperii tui ad Indos usque produxisset, quod in nouum terrarum orbem inuentum auream attulisset aetatem." John O'Malley, "Fulfillment of the Christian Golden Age under Pope Julius II: Text of a Discourse of Giles of Viterbo, 1507," *Traditio* 25 (1969), pp. 265–338, at p. 281. The translation here differs slightly from that found in F. X. Martin, *Friar, Reformer, and Renaissance Scholar: Life and Work of Giles of Viterbo, 1469–1532* (Villanova: Augustinian Press, 1992), p. 225.

25. *Gesta proxime per portugalenses in India, Ethiopia et aliis orientalibus terris* (Rome: Besicken, 1506). This illustration is from the 1507 edition (Nuremberg: Johannes Wyssenburger, 1507).

26. A similar overlay of Brazilian imagery occurs in a 1508 broadsheet by Jan van Doesburch entitled *De novo*

mondo, where an image of Brazilian Native peoples and an accompanying paragraph lifted from Vespucci are plugged in at the top of a text describing a voyage around Africa and to India and a sequence of woodcuts by Hans Burgkmair that specifically identify those people as African and Asian. See Sandra Young, "Envisioning the Peoples of 'New' Worlds: Early Modern Woodcut Images and the Inscription of Human Difference," *English Studies in Africa* 57 (2014), pp. 33–54, at p. 42: "Under the title of 'De Novo Mondo' (that is, 'Of the New World') Van Doesborch's broadsheet sets up a kind of equivalence between the lands 'newly discovered' and those known for much longer, but sufficiently removed from parts of the world that can be identified as kin. Van Doesborch extends 'new world' discourse to regions world long known to Europe and recasts them as 'discoveries' in order to peddle a form of difference that readily becomes more explicitly racialized in a later period." We add only that Van Doesborch did not extend the "new world" discourse so much as apply the dominant form of the discourse, which commonly used the term for Asian travels and explorations as much as for transatlantic ones.

27. Amerigo Vespucci, *Letters from a New World: Amerigo Vespucci's Discovery of America*, ed. Luciano Formisano, trans. David Jacobson (New York: Marsilio Publishers, 1992), p. 45.

28. Martin Waldseemüller (with Matthias Ringmann), *Cosmographiae introdvctio: Cvm qvibvsdam geometriae ac astronomiae principiis ad eam rem necessariis Insuper quattuor Americi Vespucij nauigationes* (Saint-Dié: Lud, 1507), chap. 7, n.p.: "quarta orbis pars (quam quia Americus inuenit Amerigen quasi Americi terram siue Americam nuncupare licet)."

29. Ibid., p. 52. See Alessandro Scafi, *Mapping Paradise: A History of Heaven on Earth* (Chicago: University of Chicago Press, 2006), p. 242.

30. Alessandro Scafi, *Maps of Paradise* (Chicago: University of Chicago Press, 2013), p. 41. Christian geography placed the terrestrial paradise in the mountains of Armenia around the Euphrates. Dante placed it on the other side of the globe, the antipode to Jerusalem. The Hereford Map depicted it on an island off the coast of Cathay. *The Book of John Mandeville* (chap. 23) (c. 1360) places paradise east of the lands of Prester John in India and describes it as a fountain that divides into four rivers, on top of a mountain, high above the earth and untouchable by man. Drawing on a variety of authors, Pierre D'Ailly's *Imago Mundi* (1410) (chaps. 7 and 12) located it in the Fortunate Islands. Alvise Cadamosto placed it at the source of the Senegal River in the heart of Africa. It migrated again with Columbus to the region of the Orinoco on a high plain that he believed was the limits of the East. See Valerie I. J. Flint, *The Imaginative Landscape of Christopher Columbus* (Princeton, NJ: Princeton University Press, 1992), pp. 149–81; Dora Beale Polk, *The Island of California: A History of the Myth* (Spokane, WA: Arthur H. Clark, 1991), pp. 34–35; Marianne O'Doherty, *The Indies and the Medieval West: Thought, Report, Imagination* (Turnhout: Brepols, 2013), pp. 257–62; Watt, *Dante, Columbus, and the Prophetic Tradition*, pp. 41–50.

31. Vespucci, *Letters from a New World*, p. 4. See also Louis-André Vigneras, *The Discovery of South America and the Andalusian Voyages* (Chicago: University of Chicago Press, 1976), p. 49.

32. Ibid., pp. 51 (for the long lives of Indigenous peoples) and 61 (for their resemblance to Tartars).

33. *The Travels of Sir John Mandeville*, ed. and trans. Charles William Reuben Dutton Moseley (London: Penguin Books, 1983), chap. 20.

34. Lucian, *Macrobii*, chap. 4.

35. Ibid., chap. 5.

36. We owe this unpublished source to Kathleen Christian, who kindly shared it with us, together with her translation and the proposal of a date of c. 1515. Vatican Library, MS Vat. lat. 3410: "Cum post Reverendissimae Dignationis tuae secessum, curis aliquanto solutior, efformando filij ingenio, ac tum Latina, tum graeca litteratura instituendo incumberem: Luciani Syri Dialogos, quos ei iampridem interpretor, evolvens: In librum incidi, quo exacte quaestio illa visa est edisseri, quae pridie quam recederes post coenam apud te est habita: De illarum videlicet gentium aetate ac victu, quae in Insulis, invictissimorum Hispaniae

regum auspiciis ultra Fortunatas, paulo ante repertis, degunt. Huic Macrobios titulum, id est longaevos, facit, ubi non quidem ut solet scriptorum ille omnium festivissimus, qui lepida censura mores taxent, colloquentes inducit, sed exegematico dicendi genere curiosissimam ipse per se historiam texit."

37. Stephanie Leitch, "Vespucci's Triangle and the Shape of the World," in *Cadernos de Letras—Estudos Atlânticos: Literatura, História, Cultura*, vol. 29, ed. L. Villas Boas and A. C. de A. Cardoso (Rio de Janeiro: Faculdade de Letras—Universidade Federal do Rio de Janeiro, 2013), pp. 1–26.

38. See Jill Burke, "Nakedness and Other Peoples: Reconsidering the Renaissance Nude," *Art History* 36 (2013), pp. 714–39. On the relation of these early images of Indians to inherited European wild man imagery, see Susi Colin, "The Wild Man and the Indian in Early Sixteenth-Century Book Illustration," in *Indians and Europe: An Interdisciplinary Collection of Essays*, ed. Christian F. Feest (Lincoln: University of Nebraska Press, 1989), pp. 5–36, and Ursula Thiemer-Sachse, "Hombre bárbaro versus hombre silvestre en la Nueva España ¿Ideas exóticas de origen europeo?" *Anthropos* 104 (2009), pp. 81–92.

39. Waldseemüller, *Cosmographiae introdvctio*, n.p. [chap. 9]: "Hunc in modum terra iam quadripartita cognoscitur: & sunt tres primae partes continentes: quarta est insula."

40. Surekha Davies, *Renaissance Ethnography and the Invention of the Human: New Worlds, Maps and Monsters* (Cambridge: Cambridge University Press, 2016), pp. 99–100.

41. On the vexed question of the attribution and dating of this map, see Raleigh Ashlin Skelton, "Bibliographical Note," in Ptolemy, *Geographia, Strassburg, 1513* (Amsterdam: Theatrum Orbis Terrarum, 1966), pp. v–xx, and Alfred Hiatt, "Mutation and Supplement: The 1513 Strasbourg Ptolemy," in *Ptolemy's "Geography" in the Renaissance*, ed. Zur Shalev and Charles Burnett (London: Warburg Institute, and Turin: Nino Aragno Editore, 2011), pp. 143–61.

42. See Chet van Duzer, "Waldseemüller's World Maps of 1507 and 1516: Sources and Development of his Cartographical Thought," *The Portolan* 85 (2012), pp. 8–20, and van Duzer, *Martin Waldseemüller's "Carta marina" of 1516: Study and Transcription of the Long Legends* (New York: Springer, 2020). As studied in chapter 8, the globes of Johannes Schöner reveal a similar development, also contradicting progressivist accounts; Schöner's 1515 and 1520 globes show a separation between America and Asia, but his 1533 printed globes show America as part of Asia. In yet another case, spectral imaging undertaken by Christina Duffy of the British Library's Sloane Map (Sloane MS 117, fol. 3v–4r, c. 1535) reveals that this anonymous mapmaker also revised his depiction of the American and Asian spheres from separate to united, perhaps taking his cue from the Amerasian maps of Oronce Finé, as proposed by Chet van Duzer, "Joining the New World to Asia: Revisions to an Unstudied World Map of c. 1535," paper presented at New York University, November 20, 2020.

THREE—AMERASIAN MAGI

1. As Joseph Leo Koerner describes him, "The tassels of his breeches toss with this stride; the fluttering ribbons on his shirtsleeves [in fact extensions of the shirtcloth] rhyme with the winding road behind him." Koerner, "The Epiphany of the Black Magus circa 1500," in *The Image of the Black in Western Art*, vol. 3, *From the "Age of Discovery" to the Age of Abolition*, part 1, *Artists of the Renaissance and Baroque*, eds. David Bindman and Henry Louis Gates Jr. (Cambridge, MA: Belknap Press of Harvard University Press, 2010), pp. 7–92, at p. 7.

2. See José Teixeira's entry in *Circa 1492: Art in the Age of Exploration*, ed. Jay Levenson (Washington, DC: National Gallery of Art, 1991), pp. 152–53, with further bibliography.

3. On Cabral and Viseu, see Fernando Russell Cortez, "Pedro Álvares Cabral e Viseu," *Panorama* 4 (1968), pp. 49–55. The altarpiece had already been disassembled by the late seventeenth century. According to a reconstruction by Dalila Rodrigues, the altarpiece originally comprised eighteen panels, with two sets of panels arranged three by three to either side of a central sculpture of the Virgin.

Fifteen of these panels are extant, fourteen in the Museu Nactional Grão Vasco and one in the Seminário Maior de Coimbra. On the patronage and original location of the altarpiece, together with proposals for a reconstruction, see Dalila Rodrigues, *Grão Vasco: Pintura portuguesa del Renacimiento, c. 1500–1540* (Salamanca: Consorcio Salamanca, 2002). Rodrigues's reconstruction is debatable, however. According to Rodrigues, the sequence proceeds chronologically left to right across the divide at the center of the altarpiece, placing the Magi panel at the extreme bottom right of the structure. Another logic for the arrangement of the panels is to put on the left side the nine scenes related to the Virgin's motherhood (and Christ's childhood), ending with a now-missing scene of Christ in the temple, and on the other side the nine scenes of Christ's passion, beginning with the Last Supper. This arrangement, which respects a break in the chronology that is also a theologically justified iconographic separation between a Virgin-centered sequence and a Passion sequence, would have placed the scene of the Adoration of the Magi in a central position, in the middle row just to the left of what would most likely have been a central, sculptural image of the Virgin and Child. In this position, the Magi would be moving toward the Virgin and Child depicted in the panel and at the same time toward the Virgin and child group at the center of the altarpiece. Directly across it on the same row, on the "Passion" side, would have been a now-missing panel of the Carrying of the Cross, a piteous procession to echo, in a typical Christian irony, the triumphant left-right procession of the Magi on the other side.

4. *The Voyage of Pedro Álvares Cabral to Brazil and India, from Contemporary Documents and Narratives*, ed. and trans. William Brooks Greenlee (London: Hakluyt Society, 1938), p. 120. Giovanni Matteo il Cretico's letter was reprinted in an anthology of travel accounts of 1507 entitled *Paesi novamente retrovati*, first published in 1507, widely read, and frequently reprinted, one of several popular travel account compilations to appear in the sixteenth century (see chapters 2 and 6).

5. For the derivation from *bakkam*, see *The Voyage of Pedro Álvares Cabral*, p. 7. See also Henry Yule, *Hobson-Jobson: A Glossary of Colloquial Anglo-Indian Words and Phrases, and of Kindred Terms, Etymological, Historical, Geographical and Discursive*, ed. William Crooke (London: Murray, 1903), p. 113. For the derivation from embers, brasa, among other possibilities, see Bernardino José de Sousa et al., *O pao-brasil na história nacional* (São Paulo: Companhia Editora Nacional, 1939), pp. 97–101.

6. *The Voyage of Pedro Álvares Cabral*, p. 33.

7. "Copia der newen Zeytung ausz Presillig Landt," in *Early Brazil: A Documentary Collection to 1700*, ed. Stuart B. Schwartz (Cambridge: Cambridge University Press, 2010), pp. 9–12, at p. 10.

8. *The Voyage of Pedro Álvares Cabral*, p. 148.

9. See Maria Aparecida Ribeiro, "Penas de Índio: A representação do 'Brasileiro' na arte portuguesa," *Máthesis* 5 (1996), pp. 293–323.

10. Kathleen Christian, "Renaissance Altarpieces: The Far in the Near," in *European Art and the Wider World, 1350–1550*, ed. Kathleen Christian and Leah R. Clark (Manchester, UK: Manchester University Press, 2017), pp. 23–61, at p. 46.

11. *The Voyage of Pedro Álvares Cabral*, pp. 8–9.

12. Ibid., pp. 10–13.

13. Ibid., p. 73.

14. Richard Trexler, *The Journey of the Magi: Meanings in History of a Christian Story* (Princeton, NJ: Princeton University Press, 1997), pp. 3–4.

15. Janet L. Abu-Lughod, *Before European Hegemony: The World System A.D. 1250–1350* (Oxford: Oxford University Press, 1989).

16. See Cortez, "Pedro Álvares Cabral e Viseu." See also *Grão Vasco e a pintura europeia do Renascimento*, ed. Dalila Rodrigues (Lisbon: Comissão Nacional Para as Comemorações dos Descobrimentos Portugueses, 1992), p. 91, and José Teixeira's entry in Levenson, *Circa 1492*.

17. Hugo Kehrer, *Die heiligen drei Könige in Literatur und Kunst* (Leipzig: E. A. Seemann, 1908–1909), pp. 37 and 46. See also Paul H. D. Kaplan, *The Rise of the Black Magus in Western Art* (Ann Arbor, MI: UMI Research Press, 1985), pp. 32–34.

18. Kehrer, *Die heiligen drei Könige*, pp. 32–80.

19. Trexler, *The Journey of the Magi*, pp. 124–26.

20. In the poem by Gérard du Vivier, which was included in all French and Dutch editions of Ortelius's *Theatrum Orbis Terrarum* up to 1610: "Monstrant dedans sa main un vase de fin Or, / Remply de bon Encens, d'Amome, et Mirrhe encor." See Werner Waterschoot, "The Title-Page of Ortelius's *Theatrum Orbis Terrarum*," *Quaerendo* 9 (1979), pp. 43–68, at p. 66.

21. Kaplan, *The Rise of the Black Magus*.

22. Hugh of St. Victor (c. 1130), *De arca Noe morali*, part 6, chap. 8.

23. In Canto 26 of Dante Alighieri's *The Divine Comedy*, Ulysses recounts how he sailed west out of the Mediterranean and through the pillars of Hercules "to the west" (*a l'occidente*) (113) toward the world "beyond the sun" (*di retro al sol*), eventually arriving at the shores of what Ulysses identifies as "the new land" (*la terra nova*), on top of which is situated the earthly paradise. Dante tunnels through the earth and reaches the same spot (*Inferno* 34, *Purgatorio* 1), which is then identified as Mount Purgatory, above which is Eden, which in Dante's world had always been located in the east. For the impact of these passages during the period of Columbus, see Mary Alexandra Watt, *Dante, Columbus, and the Prophetic Tradition: Spiritual Imperialism in the Italian Imagination* (London: Routledge, 2017), chaps. 5 and 6.

24. *The Voyages of Jacques Cartier*, ed. Ramsay Cook (Toronto: University of Toronto Press, 1993), p. 37. For a discussion of this passage in a larger context of prophetic thought and new world reflections, see Karen Ordhal Kupperman, *The Jamestown Project* (Cambridge, MA: Belknap Press of Harvard University Press, 2007), p. 13.

25. "Instat enim esse ab occidente principium Indiae ultra gangem, ab oriente uero terminum ipsius ultimum." *Selections from Peter Martyr*, ed. Geoffrey Eatough, Repertorium Columbianum 5 (Turnhout: Brepols, 1998), pp. 145–50 (Decade 1.3.1–1.3.10).

26. *Epistola Albericii De novo mondo* (Rostock: Barckhusen, 1505), p. ii: "Primum igitur ad gentes. Tantam in illis regionibus gentis multitudinem inuenimus quantam nemo dinumerare poterat (ut legitur in apocalipsi) gentem dico mitem atque tractabilem."

27. "A vera cruz + chamada p(er) nome aquall achou pedraluares cabrall, fidalgo da cassa del rey de portugall. E elle a descobrio indo por capita moor de quatorze naos que o dito rey mandaua a Caliqut, y enel caminho indo topou com esta terra, accui aqual terra se cree ser terra firme em aqual a muyta gente de descriam andam nuos omes e molheres como suas mais os pario sam mais brancos que bacos e teem os cabellos muyto corredios. Foy descoberta esta dita terra em aera de quinhentos."

28. The Cantino map is named after the agent of Duke Ercole d'Este of Ferrara, Alberto Cantino, who commissioned it to smuggle back to Italy for his boss. Even up in the northern sea the southern part of Greenland is fairly accurately represented, with a banderole that reads: "This land which was discovered by order of... Dom Manoel, King of Portugal, is believed to be the extremity of Asia."

29. Trexler, *The Journey of the Magi*, p. 137.

30. *Las Casas on Columbus: The Third Voyage*, ed. Geoffrey Symcox, Repertorium Columbianum 9 (Turnhout: Brepols, 2001), pp. 31–35. All of these references to Columbus's biblical and Asian quests are discussed by Mary B. Campbell, *The Witness and the Other World: Exotic European Travel Writing, 400–1600* (Ithaca, NY: Cornell University Press, 1988), pp. 165–209. On Columbus's Arabic identifications in the lands of the western Atlantic, see Alan Mikhail, *God's Shadow: Sultan Selim, His Ottoman Empire, and the Making of the Modern World* (New York: Liveright Publishing, 2020), pp. 123–35.

31. Paul H. D. Kaplan, "Isabella d'Este and Black African Women," in *Black Africans in Renaissance Europe*, ed. T. F. Earle and Kate J. P. Lowe (Cambridge: Cambridge University Press, 2005), pp. 125–54.

32. Francesco Cappello, Venetian Ambassador in Spain, "Relazione letta in Senato, il 20 Maggio 1497," in *Italian Reports on America, 1493–1522: Accounts by Contemporary Observers*, ed. Geoffrey Symcox and Luciano Formisano, Repertorium Columbianum 12 (Turnhout: Brepols, 2002), pp. 48–49 and 109–10.

33. See the essay by Scarlett H. Strauss, "Looking Westward from Tharssis: Representing the Adoration of the Magi after 1492," on the web portal *Amerasia: An Inquiry into Early Modern Imaginative Geography*, http://www.ifaresearch.org/amerasia/#strauss-magi.

34. Andrea Mantegna's *Adoration of the Magi*, now at the Getty Museum, which has no American content, might well be a response to the most recent discoveries that were reported in the years around 1500 primarily as Asian discoveries. See Alexander Nagel, *Some Discoveries of 1492: Eastern Antiquities and Renaissance Europe* (Groningen: University of Groningen, 2013), pp. 5–43. Reviewing the known examples of the subject from this point of view brings to light elements that might have been seen in an Amerasian framework. Who in fact is the swarthy figure with the strange head covering next to the Virgin and Child in the *Adoration of the Magi* attributed to Girolamo da Santa Croce in Trieste?

35. Colin Eisler, *Dürer's Animals* (Washington, DC: Smithsonian Institution Press, 1991), p. 268, points out that Dürer owned three parrots, one of which was received from the Spanish city of Málaga, making it possible that the parrot in the *Adam and Eve* engraving was an American species. See the discussion of the problem by Claire Lipsman, "The Parrot's Tale: the Journey from Angelic Messenger to Common Commodity," on the *Amerasia: An Inquiry into Early Modern Imaginative Geography,* web portal, http://ifaresearch.org/amerasia/#_ednref23.

36. António Miguel Trigueiros, "Códices portugueses quinhentistas iluminados com moedas," *MOEDA: Revista Portuguesa de Numismática e Medalhística* 34 (2009), pp. 3–48, esp. pp. 4–16, which offers the date of 1524–26 for this miniature.

37. Trexler, *The Journey of the Magi*, p. 137.

38. Ibid., p. 140.

39. Antonio de la Calancha, *Corónica moralizada del Orden de San Agustín en el Perú* (Barcelona: Pedro Lacavalleria, 1639), p. 318.

40. Ibid., pp. 310–11. This passage is discussed by Sabine MacCormack, "Antonio de la Calancha: Un Agostino del siglo XVII en el Nuevo Mundo," *Bulletin Hispanique* 84 (1982), pp. 60–94, at p. 84. See also Sabine MacCormack, "Limits of Understanding: Perceptions of Greco-Roman and Amerindian Paganism in Early Modern Europe," in *America in European Consciousness 1493–1750*, ed. Karen Ordhal Kupperman (Chapel Hill: University of North Carolina Press, 1995), pp. 79–129, at pp. 96 and 123, where she suggests that Calancha was inspired in this view by Christian van Adrichem's (or Andricomius's) topography of the Holy Land. Indeed, on Andricomius's map of Jerusalem of 1584 we see Christ on the cross positioned outside the city and facing west. One finds this westward orientation of Christ on the cross on many other maps and images of the period.

41. As noted by Teresa Gisbert, "Los incas y los reyes magos," *Traza y Baza: Cuadernos hispanos de simbología, arte y literatura* 7 (1978), pp. 39–43, at p. 42, who compares Ale de la Puente's painting to another *Adoration of the Magi* in Ilave possibly made by an Indigenous artist, where the corresponding king is shown in elaborately and correctly described Inca clothing.

42. See Juan Carlos Estenssoro Fuchs, "Construyendo la memoria: La figura del inca y el reino del Perú, de la conquista a Túpac Amaru II," in *Los incas, reyes del Perú*, ed. Natalia Majluf with Gabriela Ramos, Elena Phelps, Juan Carlos Estenssoro, Thomas Cummins, and Luis Eduardo Wuffarden (Lima: Banco de Crédito del Perú, 2005), pp. 93–173, at pp. 160–61. Many thanks to Luisa Elena Alcalá for this reference and discussion.

FOUR — RAPHAEL'S GLOBAL PHILOSOPHY

1. We offer the date "about 1510" in view of the still unresolved debate regarding the sequence of the frescoes in the room. The evidence is helpfully reviewed by Arnold Nesselrath, "Raphael and Pope Julius II," in *Raphael: From Urbino to Rome*, eds. Hugo Chapman, Tom Henry, and Carol Plazotta (London: The National Gallery, 2004), pp. 280–93.

2. Giovanni Pietro Bellori, *Descrizzione delle imagini dipinte da Rafaelle d'Urbino: Nelle Camere del Palazzo*

Apostolico Vaticano (Rome: G. G. Komarek, 1695), p. 15: "Imagine dell'antico Ginnasio di Atene, ò vero la Filosofia."

3. For a helpful review of the identifications, some of which remain speculative, see Ingrid D. Rowland, "The Intellectual Background of the *School of Athens*: Tracking Divine Wisdom in the Rome of Julius II," in *Raphael's "School of Athens"*, ed. Marcia Hall (Cambridge: Cambridge University Press, 1997), pp. 131–70.

4. Christiane L. Joost-Gaugier, *Raphael's Stanza della Segnatura: Meaning and Invention* (Cambridge: Cambridge University Press, 2002), pp. 104–10.

5. Ibid., p. 111, Joost-Gaugier proposes instead that the figures represent Apelles and Protogenes under the guise of portraits of Raphael and a colleague. We believe these portraits are presented as Raphael and Johannes Ruysch themselves, in just the way that Ariosto and possibly other contemporary poets are introduced as themselves at the right margin of the *Poetry* (or *Parnassus*) scene on the adjoining wall of the same room.

6. James Sykes, "The Terrestrial Globe in Raphael's *The School of Athens*," *Source: Globe Studies* 55–56 (2009), pp. 53–72, at p. 68, notes these corrections and calls the globe "a synthesis of ancient knowledge and of recent discovery."

7. Dawson Kiang, "The *mappamondo* in Bramante's Heraclitus and Democritus," *Achademia Leonardi Vinci: Journal of Leonardo Studies and Bibliography of Vinciana* 5 (1992), pp. 128–35. Thanks to Chet van Duzer for sharing his observations on the shape of Africa and other aspects of the globe represented by Raphael.

8. As noted by Sykes, "The Terrestrial Globe in Raphael's *The School of Athens*," p. 68.

9. Elena Parma, *Perin del Vaga: L'anello mancante: Studi sul manierismo* (Genoa: Sagep, 1997), p. 191.

10. The bookshelves around the bottom of the room were removed by Julius II's successor, Leo X, upon his accession in 1513, when they were replaced by wood inlay decoration, which we can still see under the Parnassus fresco (see figure 4.12). The inlays on the other walls were replaced by Perino's frescoes in the early 1540s. See John Shearman, "The Vatican Stanze: Functions and Decoration," in *Art and Politics in Renaissance Italy*, ed. George Holmes (Oxford: Oxford University Press, 1993), pp. 185–240, at pp. 230–31.

11. See Plato, *Timaeus*, 43e–47c, in particular 47b–c: "God devised and bestowed upon us vision to the end that we might behold the revolutions of Reason in the Heaven and use them for the revolvings of the reasoning that is within us, these being akin to those, the perturbable to the imperturbable; and that, through learning and sharing in calculations which are correct by their nature, by imitation of the absolutely unvarying revolutions of the God we might stabilize the variable revolutions within ourselves."

12. As noted by Matthias Winner, "The Mathematical Sciences in Raphael's *School of Athens*," in *The Power of Images in Early Modern Science*, ed. Wolfgang Lefèvre, Jürgen Renn, and Urs Schoepflin (Basel: Birkhäuser, 2003), pp. 289–307, at p. 303.

13. Marcia Hall, "Introduction," in *Raphael's "School of Athens"*, p. 13, interprets these different reactions and points of view as stages in a process of initiation, from beginner to "apprentice pedagogue."

14. An approach grounded in the use of chiaroscuro in the cartoon preserved at the Ambrosiana in Milan; see Konrad Oberhuber, *Polarität und Synthese in Raffaels "Schule von Athen"* (Stuttgart: Urachhaus, 1983), p. 36. On both value and color distributions and group dynamics, see Hall, "Introduction," p. 41, and Janis Bell, "Color and Chiaroscuro," in *Raphael's "School of Athens"*, pp. 85–113.

15. Heinrich Wölfflin, *Classic Art: An Introduction to the Italian Renaissance*, trans. Peter and Linda Murray (London: Phaidon, 1961), p. 95.

16. Plato, *Republic*, 534d–e.

17. A notion recently developed by Tracy Cosgriff, "The Library of Julius II and Raphael's Art of Commentary," *I Tatti Studies in the Italian Renaissance* 22 (2019), pp. 59–91.

18. Alexander Nagel and Christopher Wood, *Anachronic Renaissance* (New York: Zone Books, 2010), p. 361.

19. Well described by Hall, "Introduction," p. 15.

20. Ralph E. Lieberman, "The Architectural Background," in *Raphael's "School of Athens"*, pp. 64–84, at p. 72,

could not decide whether the building implies a domed vault: "Nor is it clear if we are to assume a dome over the crossing or just an open drum pierced with columned windows. Judging from the light-drenched crossing we see in the fresco, a dome seems unlikely, and if there were to be no dome, windows in the drum would be unnecessary." Although our argument does not depend on the resolution of this question (both dome and drum open to sky suggest a relation to the heavenly spheres), the repetition of spherical forms throughout the fresco and below and above it would have made a hemispherical dome over the crossing the most natural form for viewers to imagine.

21. Ptolemy, *Geographia*, book 7, chap. 5.

22. Plato, *Timaeus*, 24e–25d.

23. "Neque enim absonum penitus est, cum gangetidis indiae terminos indiscretos cosmographi reliquierint, nec desint qui ab hispanis oris non longe indica littora discedere sentiant." *Selections from Peter Martyr*, ed. Geoffrey Eatough, Repertorium Columbianum 5 (Turnhout: Brepols, 1998), p. 149 (Decade 1.3.8).

24. Shearman, "Vatican Stanze," p. 198. Joost-Gaugier, *Stanza della Segnatura*, p. 61, points out that Mount Parnassus is always placed in the north, corresponding to its position on the north wall in Raphael's room (for example, by Strabo, *Geography*, 8.8.21 and 9.3.1 and 9.3.3).

25. Ibid.

26. *In hoc opere haec continentur Geographia Cl. Ptholemaei a plurimis viris utriusque linguae doctiss. emendata et cum archetypo graeco ab ipsis collata...* (Rome, 1507). A second edition was produced by the same publisher in 1508, with added pages describing the discoveries of the new world. Further citations will be to this edition, hereafter referred to as Ptolemy, *Geographia* (Rome, 1508). Ruysch's map is occasionally found in a 1507 edition, but it is not listed in the table of contents of the 1507 edition, only in the 1508, leading some scholars to believe the map dates to 1508 and was retroactively inserted in the earlier edition. See R. H. J. Peerlings, F. Laurentius, and J. van den Bovenkamp, "New Findings and Discoveries in the 1507/8 Rome Edition of Ptolemy's *Cosmography*," *Quaerendo* 48 (2018), p. 140.

27. Vatican Library, Vat. lat. 2053, fol. 3r; https://digi.vatlib.it/view/MSS_Vat.lat.2053. See Cosgriff, "The Library of Julius II," 71 and fig. 4.

28. Ruysch was evidently somewhat uncertain about this island. The current inscriptions do not include mention of Cuba, although on the east coast it lists a *C. de Fundabril*, a name given to an eastern cape of Cuba by Columbus on his second voyage. In fact, there is evidence of plate erasure in this part of the map, and still legible is an erased inscription reading "de cuba," as well as a more horizontal shape for the island. See Donald L. McGuirk, "The Mystery of Cuba on the Ruysch Map," *The Map Collector* 36 (1986), pp. 40–41, and Jim Siebold's entry on the map at https://www.myoldmaps.com/renaissance-maps-1490-1800/313-johannes-ruysch-world/313-ruysch.pdf.

29. On Ruysch's map, see Bradford Swan, "The Ruysch Map of the World (1507–1508)," *Papers of the Bibliographical Society of America* 45 (1951), pp. 219–36; Donald L. McGuirk, "Ruysch World Map: Census and Commentary," *Imago Mundi* 41 (2008), pp. 133–41; and Gregory C. McIntosh, *The Johannes Ruysch and Martin Waldseemüller World Maps: The Interplay and Merging of Early Sixteenth Century New World Cartographies* (San Juan: Plus Ultra, 2012). As Jim Siebold writes in his entry, "It is thought that he accompanied John Cabot on his expedition to North America in 1497 and 1498, or, considering the prevalence of Portuguese names on his 1507 map, a Portuguese ship leaving from Bristol."

30. Ptolemy, *Geographia* (Rome, 1508), fol. 110r: "Joannes vo. Ruschi Germanus Geographorum meo iudicio peritissimus: ac in pingendo orbe diligentissimus cuius adminiculo in hac lucubratiuncula usi sumus, dixit: se navigasse ab albionis australi parte: & tam diu quo ad subparallelum ab subaequatore ad boream subgradum 53 peruenit in eo parallelo navigasse ad ortus littora per angulum noctis atque plures insulas lustrasse, quarum inferius descriptionem assignabimus."

31. Mistranslations of Beneventanus's phrase "per angulum noctis" has caused confusion in the literature. Henry Stevens, "Historical Notes on the Earliest Discoveries in America," *American Journal of Science and Arts* 48 (1969),

pp. 299–330, at p. 316, translated it as "bearing a little northward" a reading that persists in recent literature. Henry Percival Biggar, *The Voyages of the Cabots and the Corte-Reals to North America and Greenland 1497–1503* (Paris: Protat Frères, 1903), p. 64 n.8, asserts with no supporting evidence that it "clearly means the arctic circle." Raleigh Ashlin Skelton proposed that it was an astrological term suggesting that Ruysch got beyond 90°W and reached Asia; see James A. Williamson and Raleigh Ashlin Skelton, *The Cabot Voyages and Bristol Discovery under Henry VII, with the Cartography of the Voyages* (Cambridge: Hakluyt Society, 1962), p. 305 n.4. With digital tools the term is easily found in other texts to mean the point on the horizon where the sun sets, as when the thirteenth-century theologian Albertus Magnus speaks of the sun being "in angulo noctis," that is at the point opposite to that at which it rises in the east, equating the sun being "in angulo noctis" with the sun being "ad punctum horizontis." See Albertus Magnus, *Commentarii In IV Sententiarum*, Dist XXXIII, A, Art. 20, in *Opera Omnia*, ed. August Borgnet (Paris: Vives, 1894), vol. 30, p. 312: "quando sol est in angulo noctis, scilicet in parte opposita principio sui motus: deinde alia quarta deserviet digestioni completae quousque veniat sol ad punctum horizontis." The Scottish theologian and historian John Major (ca. 1470–1550) notes in his commentary on the four Gospels that Cádiz at the Strait of Gibraltar (the so-called columns of Hercules, the westernmost point of the Ptolemaic world) is at midday when on the other side of the earth the east is plunged into night, because in that place (Cádiz) is the "angulus noctis." See *Io. Maioris Hadingtonani, theologi in quatuor Euangelia expositiones luculentae & disquisitiones & disputationes contra haereticos plurimae, praemisso serie literarum indice: & additis ad finem operis quatuor quaestionibus non impertinentibus* (Paris: Badius, 1519), fol. XCIV v.: "Gadibus ad columnas Herculis est meridies antipodibus diametraliter in oriente oppositis est nox profundis, quia illic est angulus noctis."

32. Illustrations of a gradual illuminated by Ruysch can be found in Klara Broekhuysen and Anne Korteweg, "Twee boekverluchters uit de Noordelijke Nederlanden in Duitsland," in *Annus Quadriga Mundi: Opstellen over middeleeuwse kunst opgedragen aan Prof. Dr. Anna C. Esmeijer*, ed. Jan Baptist Bedaux (Utrecht: Walburg, 1989), pp. 49–76. On Ruysch's career and on the documentary sources for his life, see Peter H. Meurer, "Der Maler und Kartograph Johann Ruysch († 1533): Zur abenteuerlichen Biographie eines Kölner Benediktiners an der Schwelle der Neuzeit," *Geschichte in Köln* 49 (2002), pp. 85–104; and Birgit Onzia, "Johannes Ruysch: Un viaggiatore tra arte e scienza," MA thesis, University of Pisa, 2014. Thanks go to Anne Korteweg for the last reference.

33. One in October 1508 is to a "Magister Johannes Ruisch clericus Traiectensis diocesis [. . .] ad bonum comptum picturarum fiendarum in cameris superioribus," and involves work by Sodoma. The second in March 1509 is to "Johanni pictori in camera bibliothece" and involves work also by Lotto. See John Shearman, *Raphael in Early Modern Sources, 1483–1602* (New Haven, CT: Yale University Press, 2003), pp. 125–26. Bram Kempers, "Een pauselijke opdracht: Het proto-museum van Julius II op de derde verdieping van het Vaticaans paleis," in *Kunstenaars en opdrachtgevers*, ed. Harald Hendrix and Jeroen Stumpel (Amsterdam: Amsterdam University Press, 1996), pp. 7–48, proposed that the first payment is to Ruysch for a room painted in the level above Raphael's Stanze, but most scholars agree it is for rooms including the Stanza della Segnatura, "superioribus" referring to the fact that these rooms are one level up from the apartments of Julius II's precursor Alexander VI, painted in the previous decade by Pinturicchio.

34. Directly above the *Urania* is a panel showing Amphitrite escaping Neptune by sailing to the island of Atlas, a scene of navigation that would have had some relevance to Ruysch. On these interstitial vault scenes, see Edgar Wind, "The Four Elements in Raphael's 'Stanza della Segnatura'," *Journal of the Warburg Institute* 2 (1937–38), pp. 75–79. On Ruysch as "the second hand [apart from Sodoma] identifiable in the vault's ornaments and monochromes," see Nesselrath, "Raphael and Pope Julius II," p. 284. Thanks to Raymond Carlson for pointing to the thematic relevance of the Amphitrite's proximity to Urania.

35. For the identification and positioning of the signs of the zodiac on this sphere, see Kristen Lippincott, "Raphael's 'Astronomia': Between Art and Science," in *Making Instruments Count: Essays on Historical Scientific Instruments presented to Gerard L'Estrange Turner*, ed. R. G. W. Anderson, J. A. Bennet, and W. F. Ryan (Aldershot: Variorum, 1993), pp. 75–87. Referring to Strabo, *Geography*, 1.1.8, 1.1.20–21, and 2.5.10, Joost-Gaugier, *Raphael's Stanza della Segnatura*, comments, at p. 108: "Strabo's struggle centers on the necessity to view the earth as a sphere. No longer is this a theoretical idea, based on the ideal shape of Aristotle's celestial sphere; instead, it is based on observation."

36. On this drawing, see Achim Gnann and Michiel Plomp, *Raphael and His School* (Zwolle: Waanders Publishers, 2012), cat. 12, with further bibliography.

37. For recent discussion of this globe, see "The Ostrich Egg and the Hunt-Lenox Globes: Commentaries and Responses," with interventions by Gregory McIntosh, Peter W. Dickson, Kurt Guckelsberger, and Stefaan Missinne, *The Portolan: Journal of the Washington Map Society* 94 (2015), pp. 47–70.

38. Bram Kempers, *Ruysch en Erasmus in Rome: Een kleine bespiegeling over multidisciplinariteit, internationalisering en kinderen* (Amsterdam: Vossiuspers, 1996), pp. 9–10, also sees a portrait of Ruysch in this part of the fresco, not however in Raphael's companion but in the bearded figure holding the celestial globe sometimes identified with Zoroaster, and that we have called Strabo, in provisional agreement with Joost-Gaugier's identification.

FIVE — UTOPIA AT THE EXTREMITIES OF THE EARTH

1. It was described as a "pulcherrima capella e musivo a Reverendissimo Bernardino hyspano tit. card. instaurata" in the 1509 guide to Rome of Francesco Albertini, providing a latest possible finishing date for the vault. Francesco Albertini, *Opusculum de mirabilibus novae urbis Romae*, ed. August Schmarsow (Heilbronn: Henninger, 1886), pp. 6–7.

2. It is likely that Tommaso Inghirami, the pope's librarian, had some role to play in the ideation of the decorative program for the Stanza della Segnatura, once the pope's library. For Christiane Joost-Gaugier, *Raphael's Stanza della Segnatura: Meaning and Invention* (Cambridge: Cambridge University Press, 2002), pp. 22–42, he was the main architect of the room's program. Inghirami's involvement provides possible context for the striking similarity to be observed between the vault of the Helena Chapel in Santa Croce and the vault design of the Stanza della Segnatura, as Inghirami was very well acquainted with the patron of the Helena Chapel mosaic, Bernardino López de Carvajal, with whom Inghirami went on a diplomatic mission to Milan, where they were welcomed by the Emperor Maximilian I from July 29 to August 31, 1496 (see Joost-Gaugier, *Raphael's Stanza della Segnatura*, pp. 26–27).

3. The basic configuration corresponds to the fourth-century mosaic of the apse of Saint Peter's, now destroyed but known from later copies, such as Giacomo Grimaldi's early seventeenth-century watercolor in the Vatican Library, though in the basilica apse the four rivers of paradise were shown issuing from a rock above the lamb, and flanking the lamb were representations of the cities of Jerusalem and Bethlehem.

4. The new world elements in the Helena Chapel were observed by Cynthia Anne Payne, "'In the Fullness of Time': The Vault Mosaic in the Cappella Sant'Elena, Santa Croce in Gerusalemme, Rome," PhD thesis, University of Georgia, 2003, pp. 134–35, who rightly interpreted them in connection with the Spanish patronage of the chapel. Edoardo Rossetti, "*Nemo crucis titulos tam convenienter habebat quam tu.* Entre profecía y devoción: símbolos y imágenes en el programa religioso y político de Bernardino López de Carvajal," in *Visiones imperiales y profecía: Roma, España, Nuevo Mundo*, eds. Stefania Pastore and Mercedes García-Arenal (Madrid: Abada, 2018), pp. 185–216, at 200–203, observed the portrait of Pope Alexander VI, who died on August 18, 1503, in the scene of the *Adoration of the Cross* directly above the *Apocalyptic Lamb*, suggesting that the mosaic was finished under his papacy and thus before that date; he also notes the depiction of another macaw (or the same one?) in the Kunstmann II map of the Bayerische

Staatsbibliothek in Munich, a map commissioned by Carvajal in the first years of the sixteenth century, where the new world bird is placed inside a depiction of paradise in the southern part of Africa, where it was located according to some traditions.

5. "Psitacci tamen inde asportati atque alia multa, vel propinquitate, vel natura, solum Indicum has insulas sapere indicant." *Selections from Peter Martyr*, ed. Geoffrey Eatough, Repertorium Columbianum 5 (Turnhout: Brepols, 1998), p. 133 (Decade I.I.II).

6. "Como soy amigo de la leción de Plinio, diré aquí lo que dice del mijo de la India, y pienso yo que es lo mismo que en estas nuestras Indias llamamos maíz. El cual auctor dice aquestas palabras: 'De diez años acá es venido mijo de la India, de color negro, de grande grano; el tallo como cañas, cresce siete pies; es dicho lobas, e es fertilísimo sobre todas las cebadas: de un grano nascen tres sextarios; siémbrase en lugares húmidos.' Por estas señas que este auctor nos da, yo lo habría por maíz, porque, si dice que es negro, por la mayor parte, el maíz de Tierra Firme es morado escuro, e colorado, e también hay blanco, e mucho dello amarillo. Podría ser que Plinio no lo vido de todas estas colores, sino de lo morado escuro que paresce negro. El tallo, que dice que es como cañas, así lo tiene el maíz, y quien no lo conosciese e lo viese en el campo cuando está alto, pensará que es un cañaveral. Los siete pies que dice que cresce, por la mayor parte, acá es el maíz algo más alto, y también mucho más, y en partes menos, segund la fertilidad o bondad del terreno en que se siembra. Cuanto a lo que dice de ser fertilísimo, ya he dicho lo que he visto, que es coger ochenta, e ciento, e ciento e cincuenta hanegas de una de sembradura. Dice que se siembra en lugares húmidos: humidísima tierra son estas Indias." Gonzalo Fernández de Oviedo, *Historia general y natural de las Indias: Islas y tierra-firme del mar océano* (Madrid: Real Academia de la Historia, 1853), book 7, chap. I.

7. See the overview of sources by John J. Finan, "Maize in the Great Herbals," *Annals of the Missouri Botanical Garden* 35 (1948), pp. 149–91, and Duccio Bonavia, *Maize: Origin, Domestication, and Its Role in the Development of Culture* (Cambridge: Cambridge University Press, 2013), pp. 14–21.

8. *The Discovery of the New World in the Writings of Peter Martyr of Anghiera*, ed. Ernesto Lunardi, Elisa Magioncalda, and Rosanna Mazzacane (Rome: Istituto Poligrafico e Zecca dello Stato, 1992), pp. 74–75.

9. See Nelson H. Minnich, "The Role of Prophecy in the Career of the Enigmatic Bernardino López de Carvajal," in *Prophetic Rome in the High Renaissance Period*, ed. Marjorie Reeves (Oxford: Oxford University Press, 1992), pp. 111–20, at pp. 115–16.

10. Fernández de Oviedo, *Historia general y natural de las Indias*, book 7, chap. 14.

11. "Throughout the Middle Ages and into the Renaissance, Christian belief in the earthly paradise rested on the duality of the place, its separateness and (through the four rivers) connectedness with the inhabited earth." Alessandro Scafi, *Mapping Paradise: A History of Heaven on Earth* (Chicago: University of Chicago Press, 2006), p. 242.

12. In a prefatory letter included in the first edition of *Utopia*, Pieter Gillis, chief secretary to the city of Antwerp and a friend of More's, attributes the uncertainty over the exact geographical position of the island of Utopia to interferences in communication at a crucial moment in the telling: "Just as Raphael was touching on the subject, a servant came up to More and whispered something in his ear. And although this made me listen with even greater attention, at the critical moment one of his colleagues started coughing rather loudly—I suppose he'd caught cold on the boat—so that the rest of Raphael's sentence was completely inaudible. However, I shan't rest until I've cleared up that point too, and can tell you exactly where the island is, latitude and all." Thomas More, *Utopia*, trans. Paul Turner (London: Penguin Books, 1965), p. 34. One person distracts More, while another, coughing, drowns the signal in noise. Signal disruptions and interferences are unavoidable, it seems, when information travels from afar, leaving the exact location of More's *Utopia* forever unclarified.

13. On the use of the term by More, see Marina Leslie, *Renaissance Utopias and the Problem of History* (Ithaca, NY: Cornell University Press, 1998), p. 64, and Jane Raisch, "Humanism and Hellenism: Lucian and the Afterlives of

Greek in More's *Utopia*," *ELH* 83 (2016), pp. 927–58, at pp. 948–49.

14. Plutarch, *Life of Alexander*, sections 64–65; Arrian of Nicomedia, *Anabasis*, book 7, sections 1.5–3.6. See also Richard Stoneman. "Naked Philosophers: The Brahmans in the Alexander Historians and the Alexander Romance," *Journal of Hellenic Studies* 115 (1995), pp. 99–114.

15. Donald F. Lach, *Asia in the Making of Europ*, 2 vols. (Chicago: University of Chicago Press, 1965), vol. 2, part 2, p. 365.

16. Martin Waldseemüller (with Matthias Ringmann), *Cosmographiae introdvctio: Cvm qvibvsdam geometriae ac astronomiae principiis*... (Saint-Dié: Lud, 1507), chap. 7, n.p.: "quam non video curquis iure vetet ab Americo inuentore sagacis ingenij viro Amerigen quasi Americi terram siue Americam dicendam, cum & Europa & Asia a mulieribus sua sortita sint nomina."

17. Toby Lester, *The Fourth Part of the World: The Race to the Ends of the Earth, and the Epic Story of the Map That Gave America Its Name* (New York: Simon & Schuster, 2009), pp. 355–57.

18. For the preceding quotations, see *Letters from a New World: Amerigo Vespucci's Discovery of America*, ed. Luciano Formisano (New York: Marsilio, 1992), letter VI, pp. 62–65.

19. More, *Utopia*, p. 127.

20. Ibid., p. 38, for Gillis's mention of Vespucci.

21. The text of the imagined procession, which Maximilian dictated to his secretary, Marx Treitzsaurwein, exists in manuscript in the Österreichisches Nationalbibliothek (Kod. 2835); for a transcription, see Franz Schestag, "Kaiser Maximilian I. Triumph," *Jahrbuch der Kunsthistorischen Sammlung des Allerhöchsten Kaiserhauses* 1 (1883), pp. 154–81. On the three woodcuts that make up the *People of Calicut*, see also Christian Feest, "The People of Calicut: Objects, Texts, and Images in the Age of Proto-Ethnography," *Boletim do Moseu Paraense Emílio Goeldi, Ciências Humanas* 9 (2014), pp. 287–303. We thank Shira Brisman for helpful discussions about the history and print sequence of this cycle.

22. Feest, "The People of Calicut," p. 299.

23. See Harry Levin, *The Myth of the Golden Age in the Renaissance* (Bloomington: Indiana University Press, 1969).

24. Cesare Cesariano, *Di Lucio Vitruvio Pollione De architectura libri dece* (Como: da Ponte, 1521), fol. XXXIv. The passage offers a typically Amerasian flipping and mingling, the Spanish said to have discovered islands in the Indian ocean, "similiter" to those discovered by the Portuguese.

25. *The Voyage of Pedro Álvares Cabral to Brazil and India, from Contemporary Documents and Narratives*, ed. and trans. William Brooks Greenlee (London: Hakluyt Society, 1938), p. 59.

26. The description of the people and dwellings can be found in *Paesi novamente retrovati & Novo Mondo da Alberico Vesputio Florentino intitulato* (Milan: Lignano, 1508), chap. 65.

27. See Line Cottegnies, "Utopia, Millenarianism, and the Baconian Programme of Margaret Cavendish's The Blazing World (1666)," in *New Worlds Reflected: Travel and Utopia in the Early Modern Period*, ed. Chloë Houston (Farnham, UK: Ashgate, 2010), pp. 71–91, at p. 82. For further examples, see Sergio Landucci, *I filosofi e i selvaggi* (Bari: Laterza, 1972), pp. 39, 46, 164, and 214.

28. Paola Malaguti, ed., *La pazzia*, http://www.nuovorinascimento.org/n-rinasc/testi/pdf/pazzia/pazzia.pdf, p. 39. See Eric Nelson, "Utopia through Italian Eyes: Thomas More and the Critics of Civic Humanism," *Renaissance Quarterly* 59 (2006), pp. 1029–57, at pp. 1047–49. We owe this reference to Grace Walsh, "Antiquity beyond the Horizon: Thomas More's *Utopia* and the New World," http://www.ifaresearch.org/amerasia/#walsh-utopia.

29. Vasco de Quiroga, *Información en derecho: Sobre algunas previsiones del Real Consejo de Indias (1535)* (Mexico City: Secretaría de Educación Pública, 1985), p. 189.

30. Quiroga, *Información en derecho*, p. 216.

31. Ibid., p. 77.

32. As the historian Silvio Zavala puts it, "Thus More's *Utopia* was to be converted into a Magna Carta of Hispano-Indian society. The task of the European should not be to transport to America *his* values, in order there to reproduce the same tortured society from which the humanist was fleeing, but to avail himself of the unformed and trac-

table mass of Indian population in order to produce from it the perfect Christian commonwealth." Silvio Zavala, *New Viewpoints on the Spanish Colonization of America* (Philadelphia: University of Pennsylvania Press, 1943), p. 113.

33. Silvio Zavala, *La "Utopia" de Tomás Moro en la Nueva España, y otros estudios* (Mexico City: Porrúa, 1937), pp. 7–15. See also Zavala, "The American Utopia of the Sixteenth Century," *Huntington Library Quarterly* 10 (1947), pp. 337–47.

34. See Ezio Bassani and William B. Fagg, *Africa and the Renaissance: Art in Ivory* (Munich: Prestel, 1988), cat. nos. 75–110.

SIX — COLUMBUS MEETS POLO, OR THE LOGIC OF ELLIPTICAL CONTINUITY

1. *Select Letters of Christopher Columbus with Other Original Documents Relating to His Four Voyages to the New World*, ed. Richard Henry Major (London: Hakluyt Society, 1870), p. 180.

2. Biblioteca Nazionale Centrale Firenze, MS Banco Rari 234 (hereafter Codex Alberico), fols. 56v–60r. Here "Mago" perhaps refers to the district of Macaca in Cuba, suggesting that at the time, Columbus believed that Cuba was part of the Asiatic mainland.

3. It is possible that this map was based on an original map made by Columbus. Hoping to obtain the pope's support and ultimately persuade the king of Spain to support the colonization of Central America, Columbus's brother Bartolomeo, who had accompanied Columbus on his fourth voyage, may have brought a copy of this letter and map to Rome in 1506 and given them to Zorzi. See Roberto Almagià, "Intorno a quattro codici fiorentini e ad uno ferrarese dell'erudito veneziano Alessandro Zorzi," *La Bibliofilia* 38 (1936), pp. 313–47. See also Sebastiano Crinò, "Schizzi cartografici inediti dei primi anni della scoperta dell'America," *Rivista Marittima* 9 (1930), pp. 5–73; George E. Nunn, "The Three Maplets Attributed to Bartholomew Columbus," *Imago Mundi* 9 (1952), pp. 12–22; Elizabeth Horodowich, *The Venetian Discovery of America: Geographic Imagination and Print Culture in the Age of Encounters* (New York: Cambridge University Press, 2018), pp. 41–58.

4. Biblioteca Comunale Ariostea Ferrara, MS cl. II. 10 (hereafter Ferrara Codex). See Laura Laurencich-Minelli, ed., *Un "giornale" del Cinquecento sulla scoperta dell'America: Il manoscritto di Ferrara* (Milan: Cisalpino-Goliardica, 1985).

5. See, for example, Ferrara Codex, fols. 9v, 10v, 11r, 20r, and Codex Alberico, vol. 2, fol. 7r and 25r.

6. "Papa Pio in l'Asia dice che Sir Nicolo di Conti tal serpenti esser optimi a magnar. Marcho Polo parla di tal serpenti in la presentia di Can Grande et sono optimi a mangiar e il fiel e medicinal. Dice haver a pie una ungia sola simile al falcon." Ferrara Codex, fol. 20v. See also Codex Alberico, vol. 2, fol. 11r. Here Zorzi is referring to the c. 1461 treatise on Asia by Pope Pius II (Aeneas Sylvius Piccolomini), which contains references to the Asian travels of Niccolò de' Conti during the 1420s and 1430s. Pius II's treatise about Asia, as well as one on Europe, was part of a universal human history, which was to include a section on Africa, never written. The Asia and Europe sections were published posthumously in 1477 as *Historia rerum ubique gestarum* in an edition owned and annotated by Columbus. On Piccolomini's treatise and its sources, see Benedikt Konrad Vollmann, "Aeneas Silvius Piccolomini as a Historiographer: Asia," in *Pius II: "El Più Expeditivo Pontifice": Selected Studies on Aeneas Silvius Piccolomini (1405–1464)*, eds. Zweder von Martels and Arjo Vanderjagt (Leiden: Brill Academic Publishers, 2003), pp. 41–54. For the passage from Marco Polo, see *I viaggi di Marco Polo*, in Giovanni Battista Ramusio, *Navigazioni e viaggi*, ed. Marica Milanesi, 6 vols. (Turin: Einaudi, 1978), vol. 3, p. 207, and Marco Polo, *The Description of the World (Divisament dou monde)*, trans. Sharon Kinoshita (Indianapolis: Hackett, 2016), pp. 104–106.

7. Ferrara Codex, " fols. 17v ("Cipangi), 18v ("Spezie"), 20v ("Marco Polo parla di tali serpenti in la provintia di Caragia, optimi a mangiar"). See also Codex Alberico, vol. 2, fols. 11r, 13v, 33v. Next to Columbus's letter from Jamaica in the Ferrara volumes—the same letter next to which Zorzi drew his Amerasian sketch map in the Florentine compendium that began this chapter, and a letter in which Columbus makes no reference to Marco Polo—Zorzi invokes Kublai Khan and the sons of Marco Polo In Cathay:

"Coblai Kan imperatore, del 1257 mandò I fioli di Marco Polo. Catajo." The main text reads, "Lo imperatore del Catajo, zà molti anni, domandò et fece gran cosa, per havere homeni intelligenti, gli insegnasino in la fede de Christo." Ferrara Codex, fol. 71r.

8. The philologist and literary scholar Leonardo Olschki pointed out that for early modern audiences, "little distinguished Marco Polo from Columbus; both opened new commercial pathways aimed at reaching the Great Khan, both revealed new peoples for potential conversion, and at the same time, new routes to discovering the location of Paradise." Leonardo Olschki, *Storia letteraria delle scoperte geografiche* (Florence: Olschki, 1937), pp. 1–2.

9. For a critical edition of and bibliography on the Ramusio edition of Polo, see *Giovanni Battista Ramusio: Dei viaggi di Messer Marco Polo*, eds. Eugenio Burgio, Marina Buzzoni, Antonella Ghersetti, *Filologie Medievali e Moderne* 5 (2015), https://edizionicafoscari.unive.it/it/edizioni/libri/978-88-6969-00-06/.

10. Ramusio, *Navigazioni e viaggi*, ed. Milanesi, vol. 3, pp. 22–23.

11. See *El libro de Marco Polo anotado por Cristóbal Colón: El libro de Marco Polo, versión de Rodrigo de Santaella*, ed. Juan Gil (Madrid: Alianza Universidad, 1988), p. lxiii.

12. "Sia vicina detta India all'Africa, e alla Spagna." Ferdinand Columbus, *Historie del S. D. Fernando Colombo* (Venice: Francesco de'Franceschi, 1571), fol. 15r.

13. See Surekha Davies, "The Wondrous East in the Renaissance Geographical Imagination: Marco Polo, Fra Mauro, and Giovanni Battista Ramusio," *History and Anthropology* 23 (2012), pp. 215–34, at pp. 226–28.

14. See Joan-Pau Rubiés, "From the 'History of Travayle' to the History of Travel Collections: The Rise of an Early Modern Genre," in *Richard Hakluyt and Travel Writing in Early Modern Europe*, ed. Daniel Carey and Claire Jowitt (Burlington, VT: Ashgate, 2012), pp. 25–41.

15. For a modern facsimile, see *Paesi novamente retrovati et Novo Mondo da Alberico Vesputio Florentino intitulato* [1508] (reprint, Princeton, NJ: Princeton University Press, 1916).

16. Massimo Donattini, "Orizzonti geografici dell'editoria italiana (1493–1560)," in *Il Nuovo Mondo nella coscienza italiana e tedesca del Cinquecento*, ed. Adriano Prosperi and Wolfgang Reinhard (Bologna: Mulino, 1992), pp. 79–154, at p. 98, and Donattini, "Giovanni Battista Ramusio e le sue *Navigationi*: Appunti per una biografia," *Critica Storica* 17 (1980), pp. 55–100, at p. 73.

17. For the following descriptions, see *The Voyage of Pedro Álvares Cabral to Brazil and India, from Contemporary Documents and Narratives*, ed. and trans. William Brooks Greenlee (London: Hakluyt Society, 1938), pp. 56–60, an edition based on the text as printed in *Paesi novamente retrovati & Novo Mondo da Alberico Vesputio Florentino intitulato* (Milan: Lignano, 1508), where these passages can be found in chaps. 64–66.

18. Biblioteca Nazionale Marciana, MS It.VI.208 (5881), fols. 118r–154v.

19. Florence, Biblioteca Riccardiana, MS 1910. See *Iddio ci dia buon viaggio e guadagno, Firenze, Biblioteca Riccardiana, ms. 1910 (Codice Vaglienti)*, ed. Luciano Formisano (Florence: Polistampa, 2006), p. 110.

20. Of Ptolemy's eight books, Europe comprised books two and three, Africa book four, and Asia books five through seven. The most comprehensive surveys of known editions of Ptolemy remain Charles E. Armstrong, "Copies of Ptolemy's *Geography* in American Libraries," *Bulletin of the New York Public Library* 66 (1962), pp. 105–13, and Henry N. Stevens, *Ptolemy's Geography: A Brief Account of All the Printed Editions down to 1730* (London: Henry Stevens, Son and Stiles, 1908).

21. Surekha Davies, "America and Amerindians in Sebastian Münster's *Cosmographiae universalis libri VI* (1550)," *Renaissance Studies* 25 (2011), pp. 351–73, at p. 352.

22. *I costumi le leggi, et l'usanze di tutte le genti* (Venice: Giovanni Bonadio, 1564), fols. 211v–213r.

23. Johann Boemus, *El libro de las costumbres de todas las gentes del mundo, y de las Indias* (Antwerp: Martin Nucio, 1556), fol. 249r.

24. Paolo Giovio, *Dell'historie del suo tempo*, 2 vols. (Florence: Torrentino, 1552), vol. 2, p. 397. The sentence mentions that it took three months, but a few sentences earlier Giovio says it took Magellan twenty-seven days

to get through the comparatively short strait at the tip of South America that was thereafter named after him, suggesting that the time of travel can indicate difficulty of passage as much as distance.

25. Huntington Library, Pasadena, MS HM 1788.

26. Along similar lines, Ricardo Padrón has demonstrated that even though Pigafetta "gave potent literary form to [his] experience of the endless, deadly, open ocean, effectively inventing the Pacific as a vast, empty watery expanse," generations of Spanish cartographers and cartographic writing in his wake embraced a "cartography of containment and [a] rhetoric of smooth sailing," thus effectively shrinking the size of the body of water to the east of Asia. Ricardo Padrón, *The Indies of the Setting Sun: How Early Modern Spain Mapped the Far East as the Transpacific West* (Chicago: University of Chicago Press, 2020), pp. 75–105, at p. 104.

27. Huntington Library, Pasadena, MS HM 1788, Derrotero del Mundo, dated 1576.

28. "Vulgaris est haec arbor in Hispaniola, reliquis que insulis, & huius India continente." Garcia de Orta, *Aromatum et simplicium aliquot medicamentorum apud Indos nascentium historia: ante biennium quidem Lusitanica linqua per dialogos conscripta*, trans. Carolus Clusius (Antwerp, 1567), pp. 224–31, at p. 227.

29. See Hugh Cagle, *Assembling the Tropics: Science and Medicine in Portugal's Empire, 1450–1700* (New York: Cambridge University Press, 2018), p. 115.

SEVEN — THE REVELATION OF THE EARTH

1. Mauricio Orozpe Enríquez, *El código oculto de la greca escalonada: Tloque Nahuaque* (Mexico City: Universidad Nacional Autónoma de México, 2010), offers a geometric and cosmological interpretation of the motif. Justyna Olko, *Insignia of Rank in the Nahua World: From the Fifteenth to the Seventeenth Century* (Boulder: University Press of Colorado, 2014) notes its appearance on various garments and accoutrements, but does not advance any interpretation of its meaning.

2. Diana Fane, "Feathers, Jade, Turquoise, and Gold," in *Images Take Flight: Feather Art in Mexico and Europe, 1400–1700*, ed. Alessandra Russo, Gerhard Wolf, and Diana Fane (Munich: Hirmer Publishers, 2016), pp. 101–31, at p. 107. On the use of ceremonial shields, see Olko, *Insignia of Rank in the Nahua World*.

3. Fane, "Feathers, Jade, Turquoise, and Gold," p. 107, describes it as "an unusual variant of the type" of the *xicalcoliuhqui chimalli* or twisted gourd shield. A concentric circle motif with fewer circles is used as the main element in another Mexica shield type, known as the golden disc shield or *teocuitlaxapo chimalli*; see Patricia Rieff Anawalt and Frances F. Berdan, *The Codex Mendoza* (Berkeley: University of California Press, 1992), vol. 3, p. 141 (f. 67r.), and for its appearance in other sources, vol. 1, "Appendix G, Shields: The Codex Mendoza and other Aztec Pictorials," pp. 242–43. Thus, the novelty of this shield might consist in combining the two shield types.

4. Alessandra Russo has emphasized the early entanglement of Mesoamerican productions with European forms and techniques. Alessandra Russo, "Cortés's Objects and the Idea of New Spain: Inventories as Spatial Narratives," *Journal of the History of Collections* 23 (2011), pp. 229–52. See also Alessandra Russo, "A Contemporary Art from New Spain," in Russo, Wolf, and Fane, eds., *Images Take Flight*, pp. 23–63.

5. *A Synoptic Edition of the Log of Columbus's First Voyage*, eds. Francesca Lardicci and Valeria Bertolucci Pizzorusso, Repertorium Columbianum 6 (Turnhout: Brepols, 1999), p. 517: "Hallaron diz que muchas estatuas en figura de mugeres y muchas cabeças muy bien labradas de palo; no supo si lo tenían por arreo y hermosura de casa o lo adoravan." The English translation on page 61 of this edition is faulty; we offer the following: "They [the Christians] found many statues in the shape of women and many heads well worked in wood. He [Columbus] did not know whether they had them for the adornment and beauty of their houses or if they worshiped them."

6. Giorgio Vasari, *Le vite de' più eccellenti pittori scultori e architettori nelle redazioni del 1550 e 1568*, ed. Rosanna

Bettarini, 6 vols. (Florence: Sansoni, 1966), vol. 4, p. 540, wrote in the 1550 edition: "E poco dopo fece un quadro di Nostra Donna in casa messer Dionigi de' Gianni, con un Cristo che tiene una palla del mappamondo"; and in the 1568 edition: "dopo fece un quadro di Nostra Donna con un Cristo che tiene una palla di mappamondo." Pietro Lamo, in his c. 1560 description of works of art in Bologna, noted the presence of the painting in the palace of Bartolomeo Zani (Dionigi's son) on Via Santo Stefano: "e fra le altre ha quel rarissimo quadro del Parmigianino, dov'è quella Madonna, che ha quel Puttino coricato in braccio col gomito sopra un Mappamondo." Pietro Lamo, *Graticola di Bologna: Ossia descrizione delle pitture, sculture e architetture di detta città, fatta l'anno 1560* (Bologna: Guidi all'Ancora, 1844), p. 12. Parmigianino certainly consulted a recent globe in rendering his sphere, yet no globe design known from the period exactly matches this one.

7. As Achim Gnann describes it, "The powerless and cautious-seeming pose [of the Virgin] is enlivened only through the dynamics of the fold-gatherings, which course through the clothing in sweeping channels that give the limbs the impression of movement." Achim Gnann, *Parmigianino: Die Zeichnungen*, vol. 1 (Petersburg: Imhof, 2007), p. 236. One early preparatory drawing in Chatsworth (Gnann, cat. 710) shows the Virgin rolling up the sleeve of the downward pointing arm (presumably in preparation for bathing the child), a motif that then lost its purpose in the succeeding drawings and in the final painting. Arthur Ewart Popham notes that "the curious and apparently motiveless action of the Virgin's right arm in the picture is explained as a survival of the mother's perfectly natural action in the drawing." Arthur Ewart Popham, *The Drawings of Parmigianino* (New York: Beechhurst Press, 1953), p. 33.

8. A detail observed by Robert Smithson, "From Ivan the Terrible to Roger Corman, or Paradoxes of Conduct in Mannerism as reflected in the Cinema," in *Robert Smithson: The Collected Writings* (Berkeley: University of California Press, 1996), p. 352.

9. Brent Dickerson, "Old Rose History and Synopsis," https://home.csulb.edu/~odinthor/oldrose.html#Damask%20Rosess. Thanks to Rosie Cullinane for sharing this reference and her thoughts on the identification of the rose. See also M. Mahboubi, "*Rosa damascena* as Holy Ancient Herb with Novel Applications," *Journal of Traditional and Complementary Medicine* 6 (2016), pp. 10–16.

10. In his brief description of the painting, Giorgio Vasari took note of the *modi straordinari* of the Virgin's clothing, with its "sleeves of yellowish veils and as it were striped with gold." Vasari, *Le vite*, vol. 4, p. 540.

11. Shannon Kelley, "The King's Coral Body: A Natural History of Coral and the Post-Tragic Ecology of *The Tempest*," *Journal for Early Modern Cultural Studies* 14 (2014), pp. 115–42, at pp. 116–18.

12. See Gaetano Giordani, *della venuta e dimora in Bologna del sommo pontefice Clemente VII per la incoronazione di Carlo V Imperatore celebrata l'anno MDXXX* (Bologna: Volpe, 1842), Appendix XLVIII, p. 75.

13. Letter of Gasparo Contarini to Doge Andrea Grimani from Valladolid, September 24, 1522. *Italian Reports on America 1493–1522: Accounts by Contemporary Observers*, ed. Luciano Formisano and Geoffrey Symcox, Repertorium Columbianum 12 (Turnhout: Brepols, 2002), pp. 136–38. On Contarini's diplomatic career in the 1520s, see Elisabeth G. Gleason, *Gasparo Contarini: Venice, Rome, Reform* (Berkeley: University of California Press, 1993), pp. 29–62.

14. Ludovico Ariosto, *Orlando Furioso* (Ferrara, 1532), canto 15, verse 27.

15. See Eric MacPhail, "Ariosto and the Prophetic Moment," *MLN* 116 (2001), pp. 30–53.

16. See Antonio Rumeu de Armas, *El tratado de Tordesillas* (Madrid: Fundación Mapfre, 1992); Jerry Brotton, *Trading Territories: Mapping the Early Modern World* (London: Reaktion Books, 1997), pp. 119–50; Alison Sandman, "Mirroring the World: Sea Charts, Navigation, and Territorial Claims in Sixteenth-Century Spain," in *Merchants and Marvels: Commerce, Science, and Art in Early Modern Europe*, ed. Pamela H. Smith and Paula Findlen (New York: Routledge, 2002), pp. 83–108. See also Seth R. Kimmel, "Interpreting Inaccuracy: The Fiction of Longitude in Early

Modern Spain," *Journal of Medieval and Early Modern Studies* 40 (2010), pp. 299–323.

17. Sydney Freedberg, *Painting in Italy 1500–1600* (Baltimore, MD: Penguin Books, 1975), p. 701 n.2, and William Eisler, "The Impact of the Emperor Charles V upon the Italian Visual Culture 1529–1533," *Arte Lombarda* 65 (1983), pp. 93–110.

18. Earl Rosenthal, "*Plus Ultra, Non plus Ultra*, and the Columnar Device of Emperor Charles V," *Journal of the Warburg and Courtauld Institutes* 34 (1971), pp. 204–28, and "The Invention of the Columnar Device of Emperor Charles V at the Court of Burgundy in Flanders in 1516," *Journal of the Warburg and Courtauld Institutes* 36 (1973), pp. 198–230.

19. See John Hewitt, "A World Map on an Oval Projection Attributed to Franciscus Monachus, ca. 1526," *The Globe* 73 (2013), pp. 17–27, and Robert J. King "Franciscus Monachus and the c. 1529 Paris Gilt Globe," *Journal of the Australian and New Zealand Map Society* 86 (2019), pp. 19–42.

20. Franciscus Monachus, *De orbis situ ac descriptione* (Antwerp, possibly 1529), n.p.

21. Ibid., "Apud Ferdinandum Culua, sive Culuacana provincia est (culuacan[i]) in qua iacet regia Imperatoris orientalis, in itinerarijs alias Cataya."

22. Ibid., "Video priores cum Ferdinandi dictis, & historia concinere."

23. Ibid., "Inde progressu viae ad fines / Mansi. Messigo modo nomen esse puto, eius meminit & Ferdinandus Cortesius, deinceps variis regionibus / perraptatis ab vrbem Themistetam profecti sunt." On Mansus, or Mangi, referring to the Southern Song dynasty, see *The Mission of Friar William de Rubruck: His Journey to the Court of the Great Khan Möngke, 1253–1255*, trans. Peter Jackson (Indianapolis, IN: Hackett Publishing, 2009), p. 203 n.2.

24. Monachus, *De orbis situ ac descriptione*: "Themistetam neotericis est, seu Tenostica ante Quinsam, ab Oderico Themisan vocata, isque propius veritatem attigit, concordi & consentiente traditione autorum, de regionis eiusdem opibus & positura. Ad septentriones a Culuacana terra. Thamachum protenditur, olim Tangut dicta, Teuis superiora saecula nuncuparunt Tebet, vel Cibet, Messigo prouincia temporibus auorum Mansi vocabulo innotuit."

25. Another publication made under the aegis of Charles V, just after the summit of 1530, was Gemma Frisius's *De principiis astronomiae et cosmographiae, deque usu globi . . . De orbis divisione, et insulis, rebusque nuper inventis* (Antwerp, 1530), with illustrations by the cartographer Johannes Schöner. The globe on the frontispiece shows us something similar to what we see in Parmigianino's summit paintings—the world from the Iberian Peninsula across to Asia, whose ultimate limits are lost to view as its vast landmass curves around the globe. However, the book's interior makes good on the title's promise, providing a description of the full extent of the world, including the newly discovered lands and America, which are presented as an extension off the coast of Asia, as in the account of Franciscus Monachus.

26. Monachus, *De orbis situ ac descriptione*: "Eximia sane atque mirabilia, quae nostro aevo designat deus, qualia nullis annalium historiarumvè monimentis prodita sunt. An unquam fando a condito mundo prius auditum, classem universum orbis ambitum circuisse? At hoc Caroli Caesaris auspiciis dedere Superi. Cardinem antarcticum, ignotas terras, maria, populos trans mundi medium limitem videre contigit, quae essent nec ne, vix satis olim constans erat opinio. At Caesaris nostri exploratoribus multo ingens orbis pars sese aperuit, nudavit, retexit."

27. See Adriano Prosperi, "America e Apocalisse: Note sulla 'conquista spirituale' del Nuovo Mondo," in *America e apocalisse e altri saggi* (Pisa: Istituti editoriali e poligrafici internazionali, 1999), pp. 15–63, and John Jeffries Martin, *A Beautiful Ending: The Apocalyptic Imagination and the Making of the Modern World* (New Haven, CT: Yale University Press, 2022), esp. chaps. 3–4.

28. "Primum igitur ad gentes. Tantam in illis regionibus gentis multitudinem inuenimus quantam nemo dinumerare poterat (ut legitur in apocalipsi) gentem dico mitem atque tractabilem." *Epistola Albericii De novo mondo* (Rostock: Barckhusen, 1502), p. ii.

29. Quoted in M. E. Reeves, "Cardinal Egidio of

Viterbo: A Prophetic Interpretation of History," in *Prophetic Rome in the High Renaissance Period: Essays*, ed. M. E. Reeves (Oxford: Clarendon, 1992), pp. 91–109, at p. 102. See also John W. O'Malley, *Giles of Viterbo on Church and Reform: A Study in Renaissance Thought* (Leiden: Brill, 1968), p. 8.

30. Egidio da Viterbo, *Scechina e Libellus de litteris hebraicis*, ed. François Secret (Rome: Centro Internazionale di Studi Umanistici, 1959), p. 161. See Reeves, "Cardinal Egidio of Viterbo," p. 104.

31. See Nelson H. Minnich, "The Role of Prophecy in the Career of the Enigmatic Bernardino López de Carvajal," in Reeves, *Prophetic Rome in the High Renaissance*, pp. 111–20, at pp. 115–16.

32. Albrecht Dürer, *Schriftlicher Nachlass*, ed. Hans Rupprich, 3 vols. (Berlin: Deutscher Verein für Kunstwissenschaft, 1956), vol. 1 pp. 152, 156, 165, 166.

33. Christian Feest, "The People of Calicut: Objects, Texts, and Images in the Age of Proto-Ethnography," *Boletim do Moseu Paraense Emílio Goeldi, Ciências Humanas* 9 (2014), pp. 287–303, at p. 294.

34. See Massimo Donattini, "Three Bolognese Franciscan Missionaries in the New World in the Early Sixteenth Century," in *The New World in Early Modern Italy, 1492–1750*, ed. Elizabeth Horodowich and Lia Markey (New York: Cambridge University Press, 2017), pp. 63–85, and Marcel Bataillon, "Novo mundo e fim do mundo," *Revista de Historia* 8 (1954), pp. 343–51.

EIGHT — COPPER BELLS

1. *La relación y comentarios del gobernador Alvar Nuñez Cabeça de Vaca, de lo acaecido en las dos jornadas que hizo a las Indias* (Valladolid: Francisco Fernández de Córdova, 1555), chap. 29, fol. xl–xlv, and *The Narrative of Cabeza de Vaca*, ed. and trans. Rolena Adorno and Patrick Charles Pautz (Lincoln: University of Nebraska Press, 2003), pp. 140–41.

2. Gonzalo Fernández de Oviedo, *Historia general y natural de las Indias: Islas, y tierra-firme del mar océano*, 8 vols. (Madrid: Real Academia de la Historia, 1853), book 35, chap. 5, p. 606.

3. See William K. Hartmann, *Searching for Golden Empires: Epic Cultural Collisions in Sixteenth-Century America* (Tucson: University of Arizona Press, 2014), pp. 134–37.

4. Richard Flint, *No Settlement, No Conquest: A History of the Coronado Entrada* (Albuquerque: University of New Mexico Press, 2008), pp. 261–69.

5. "Pues visto e muy notorio está que estas nuestras Indias en ninguna manera pueden ser parte de Europa ni de Africa, por lo que tengo dicho de sus límites; y que si han de tener participación de alguna de las tres, ha de ser con Asia. Y esto, cuando estoviese averiguado que la última tierra que en Asia estoviese al Oriente e delante del reino de la China, u otra que estoviese o haya más oriental, se juntase con la parte más occidental de la Tierra Firme destas nuestras Indias, que es lo que, está más al Poniente de la Nueva España, que acá llamamos. La cual, como no está toda descubierta aún, no se sabe si es mar ni tierra en el fin, o si está toda por allí rodeada del mar Océano, lo cual yo más creo; e mi opinión, e de otros hasta agora, más sospecha me da que no es parte de Asia, ni se junta con la que Asia llamaron los antiguos cosmógrafos." Fernández de Oviedo, *Historia general y natural de las Indias*, book 16, p. 463.

6. For the Coronado expedition alone, see the documents collected and translated by Richard Flint, *Great Cruelties Have Been Reported: The 1544 Investigation of the Coronado Expedition* (Albuquerque: University of New Mexico Press, 2013).

7. For an interactive and mobility-based alternative to approaches that immobilize "natives in their villages," see James Clifford, *Routes: Travel and Translation in the Late Twentieth Century* (Cambridge, MA: Harvard University Press, 1997), pp. 26–30. For a critique of the incarcerating implications of a discourse of the "native" trapped in their place, see Arjun Appadurai, "Putting Hierarchy in Its Place," *Cultural Anthropology* 3 (1988), pp. 36–49.

8. On these suspicions, El Turco was finally garroted by Coronado's men, though it remained unclear whether the execution happened on Coronado's orders. For the reports of various witnesses, see Flint, *Great Cruelties Have Been*

Reported, pp. 64, 73, 81, 86, 132, 139, 151, 159, 197, 205, 217, 228, 240, 249, 260ff., 269.

9. On the entanglement between Spanish explorers, multilingual interpreters, and Indigenous oral traditions in the greater Sonoran Desert, see Maureen Ahern, "The Cross and the Gourd: The Appropriation of Ritual Signs in the *Relaciones* of Alvar Núñez Cabeza de Vaca and Fray Marcos de Niza," in *Early Images of the Americas: Transfer and Invention*, ed. Jerry M. Williams and Robert E. Lewis (Tucson: University of Arizona Press, 1993), pp. 215–44.

10. Jeremiah F. Epstein, "Cabeza de Vaca and the Sixteenth-Century Copper Trade in Northern Mexico," *American Antiquity* 56 (1991), pp. 474–82, argues that the bell received by Dorantes came from the site of Paquimé (also known as Casas Grandes) in Chihuahua, a copper producing center that in fact lay to the northwest of Monclova in Coahuila, the place where most scholars agree it was given to Dorantes. Although it had stopped producing copper by this time, Paquimé was excavated and looted over time by the surrounding communities. Victoria D. Vargas, *Copper Bell Trade Patterns in the Prehispanic U.S. Southwest and Northwest Mexico* (Tucson: Arizona State Museum, 1995), argues that bells excavated throughout the present-day American Southwest came from the Mexican west coast, a view also supported by the research of Dorothy Hosler, *The Sounds and Colors of Power: The Sacred Metallurgical Technology of Ancient West Mexico* (Cambridge, MA: MIT Press, 1994). In any case, once it reached the area of Coahuila, the bell received by Dorantes could well have counted as an antiquity for the community that offered it, who according to Cabeza de Vaca "valued it greatly."

11. According to Randall H. McGuire, Southwest and Mesoamerican cultures are like "languages with many cognates, but different grammars and syntaxes." See his "Pueblo Religion and the Mesoamerican Connection," in *Religious Transformation in the Late Pre-Hispanic Pueblo World*, ed. Donna M. Glowacki and Scott Van Keuren (Tucson: University of Arizona Press, 2011), pp. 23–49, at p. 29.

12. On period European conceptions of islands and continents, as well as land and water, see Carla Lois, "Isla vs. continente: Un ensayo de historia conceptual," *Revista de Geografía Norte Grande* 54 (2013), pp. 85–107.

13. "Sabed que ala diestra mano de las Indias ouo una Isla llamada California mucho llegada ala parte del paraiso terrenal la qual sue poblada de mugeres negras sin que algun uaro entre ellas ouiesse: que casi como las amazonas." Garci Rodríguez de Montalvo, *Las sergas de Esplandián* (Burgos: Juan de Junta, 1526), p. cviii (v). The Amazons, first described by Herodotus in Scythia, often seem to hover around visions of Amerasia, as they also do in the accounts of Thevet and Ralegh (see chapters 9 and 10).

14. See Donald C. Cutter, "Sources for the Name California," *Arizona and the West* 3 (1961), pp. 233–44; Dora Beale Polk, *The Island of California: A History of the Myth* (Lincoln: University of Nebraska Press, 1991), pp. 121–32; Seymour I. Schwartz, *The Mismapping of America* (Rochester, NY: University of Rochester Press, 2003), pp. 127–71. Maps depicting California as an island were produced well into the eighteenth century. The explorer Alarcón referred directly to the island of California described in *Las sergas*; see *Descubrimientos y exploraciones en las costas de California 1532–1650* (Madrid: Rialp, 1947; 2nd ed. 1982), pp. 113–41.

15. Henry Raup Wagner, *Spanish Voyages to the Northwest Coast of America in the Sixteenth Century* (San Francisco: California Historical Society, 1929), p. 336 n.113. See also Maurice G. Holmes, *From New Spain by Sea to the Californias, 1519–1668* (Glendale, CA: Arthur H. Clark, 1963), pp. 110–11.

16. Richard Hakluyt, *The Principal Navigations, Voyages, Traffiques, and Discoveries of the English Nation*, ed. Edmund Goldsmid, 16 vols. (Edinburgh: E. and G. Goldsmid, 1885–90), vol. 14, p. 421.

17. In a 1525 bull entitled *Devotionis tuae probatae sinceritas*, Pope Clement VII referred to "an island in the sea named Yacathan of India." See Luis Weckmann, *The Medieval Heritage of Mexico*, trans. Frances M. López-Morillas (New York: Fordham University Press, 1992), p. 19.

18. Juan Díaz, "Itinerary of the Catholic King's Fleet to the Island of Yucatan in 1518," in *Italian Reports on America, 1493–1522: Accounts by Contemporary Observers*, eds. Luciano

Formisano and Geoffrey Symcox, Repertorium Columbianum 12 (Turnhout: Brepols, 2002), pp. 137–48, at p. 142.

19. Joannes Myritius Melitensis, *Opusculum geographicum rarum* (Ingolstadt: Wolfgang Ederi, 1590), p. 122. Some mapmakers thought the Yucatan was Japan; see chapter 11.

20. Luis Weckman-Muñoz, "The Alexandrine Bulls of 1493: Pseudo-Asiatic Documents," in *First Images of America: The Impact of the New World on the Old*, ed. Fredi Chiappelli, with Michael J. B. Allen and Robert L. Benson, 2 vols. (Berkeley: University of California Press, 1976), vol. 1, p. 207.

21. Alessandro Geraldini, "Itinerary to the Regions Located Below the Equator," in Formisano and Symcox, eds., *Italian Reports on America*, pp. 116–31, at p. 131.

22. See Thomas Suárez, *Shedding the Veil: Mapping the European Discovery of America and the World* (Singapore: World Scientific, 1992), pp. 81–85, and Ricardo Padrón, *The Indies of the Setting Sun: How Early Modern Spain Mapped the Far East as the Transpacific West* (Chicago: University of Chicago Press, 2020), p. 129 and fig. 24. On the islands of India in Western medieval thought, see Marianne O'Doherty, *The Indies and the Medieval West: Thought, Report, Imagination* (Turnhout: Brepols, 2013), pp. 255–57. As Thomas Suárez and Robert Padrón have noted, the island status of the Americas becomes clear when we join these two maps by Sebastian Münster that have traditionally been considered separately, the Tabula orientalis regionis and the Tabula novarum insularum.

23. Flint, *No Settlement, No Conquest*, p. 18. Weckmann-Muñoz, "The Alexandrine Bulls of 1493," p. 206, similarly notes "the American world was seen by European eyes only as a group of islands neighbouring the huge Asiatic land mass."

24. Johannes Schöner, *Luculentissima quaedam terrae totius descriptio: cum multis utilissimis cosmographiae iniciis* (Nuremberg: Johannes Stuchs, 1515), Tract 1, chap. 9.

25. Gli costumi, le leggi, et l'usanze di tutte le genti (Venice: Geronimo Giglio, 1558).

26. Hernán Cortés, *Letters from Mexico*, ed. and trans. Anthony R. Pagden (New Haven, CT: Yale University Press, 1971), p. 267.

27. See Polk, *The Island of California*, pp. 77–97 and 105–20.

28. "Instructions which Hernando Cortés gave to Alvaro de Saavedra Cerón for the voyage that he was to make with the armada to the Moluccas, May 28, 1527," in *Voyages of Alvaro de Saavedra Cerón, 1527–1529*, ed. Ione Stuessey Wright, *University of Miami Hispanic-America Studies* 11 (1951), pp. 75–88, at p. 83. See also Jorge Cañizares-Esguerra, "On Ignored Global Scientific Revolutions," *Journal of Early Modern History* 21 (2017), pp. 420–32, at p. 428. On the Morisco presence in New Spain, and the persistent analogies drawn in period sources between the conversion of the Moriscos and that of the new world peoples, see Karoline P. Cook, *Forbidden Passages: Muslims and Moriscos in Colonial Spanish America* (Philadelphia: University of Pennsylvania Press, 2016). Along similar lines, Padrón has pointed out that in the most widely read accounts reporting on Magellan's 1521–22 circumnavigation of the globe, we hear little of the horrors of crossing a vast and undifferentiated Pacific, in contrast to the extended description of the ordeal offered by Antonio Pigafetta, one of Magellan's shipmen, in his original account. Spanish cosmographers presented instead a steady hopping from island to island across a manageable body of water. See Padrón, *The Indies of the Setting Sun*, pp. 75–106.

29. "Instructions which Hernando Cortés gave to Alvaro de Saavedra Cerón for the voyage that he was to make with the armada to the Moluccas, May 28, 1527," in Wright, *Voyages of Alvaro de Saavedra Cerón , 1527–1529*, pp. 85–86.

30. Cañizares-Esguerra, "On Ignored Global Scientific Revolutions," pp. 428–29.

31. See Giuseppe Marcocci, *Indios, cinesi, falsari: Le storie del mondo nel Rinascimento* (Bari: Laterza, 2016), chap. 2, pars. 9 and 54.

32. "*Relación* of Fray Marcos de Niza, August 26, 1539," in *Documents of the Coronado Expedition, 1539–1542*, ed. and trans. Richard Flint and Shirley Cushing Flint (Albuquerque: University of New Mexico Press, 2005), pp. 59–88, at p. 75. See also *The Journey of Fray Marcos de Niza*, ed. Cleve Hallenbeck (Dallas: University Press in Dallas, 1949).

At the time, Cibola—the name for both a group of pueblos and the principal pueblo among them—was a regional center for trade in turquoise, bison hides, feathers, and shells between the pueblo cultures and the northern parts of Mesoamerica.

33. "Letters from Antonio de Mendoza and Rodrigo de Albornoz, October 1539," in Flint and Flint, eds. *Documents of the Coronado Expedition*, p. 92. See Marco Polo, *The Travels of Marco Polo*, trans. Ronald Latham (New York: Penguin Books, 1958), p. 105.

34. Joaquín García Icazbalceta, ed., *Nueva colección de documentos* (Mexico City: Editorial Salvador Chávez Hayhoe, 1941), p. 94, translated and cited in Henry Raup Wagner, "Fra Marcos de Niza," *New Mexico Historical Review* 9 (1934), pp. 184–227, at p. 223.

35. "Testimony of Witnesses in Habana Regarding Fray Marcos's Discoveries, November 1539," in Flint and Flint, eds., *Documents of the Coronado Expedition*, pp. 95–105, at p. 100.

36. Richard Flint, "When East Was West: The Oriental Aim of the Coronado Expedition," in *The Latest Word from 1540: People, Places, and Portrayals of the Coronado Expedition*, ed. Richard Flint and Shirley Cushing Flint (Albuquerque: University of New Mexico Press, 2011), pp. 105–16, at p. 109.

37. Giovanni Battista Ramusio, *Navigazioni e viaggi*, ed. Marica Milanesi, 6 vols. (Turin: Einaudi, 1978–88), vol. 3, p. 359. Ramusio's version of the *relación* was translated into English by Richard Hakluyt in 1600 (*Principal Navigations*, vol. 9); it became the authoritative English translation of this account for more than three hundred years, relaying Ramusio's depiction of Cibola far and wide.

38. In 1576, Bernal Díaz del Castillo noted that Fra Marcos de Niza's report in Mexico City described the lands of Cibola to Mendoza as neighboring the South Coast, or the coast of the South Sea (*porque le hizo relacion, que las tierras de la Cibola estavan en la comarca de la costa del Sur*). Bernal Díaz del Castillo, *Historia verdadera da la conquista de la Nueva España* (Madrid: Del Reyno, 1632), p. 235r, cited in Hartmann, *Searching for Golden Empires*, p. 213.

39. "The Relación de la Jornada de Cíbola, Pedro de Castañeda's Narrative," in Flint and Flint, eds. *Documents of the Coronado Expedition*, pp. 378–493, at p. 414.

40. Ibid., p. 421. An anonymous account of Coronado's journey also claimed that the buffalo of the plains Indians were the same kind of cows that Marco Polo had seen in China and the same humped oxen that the Venetian merchant and traveler Niccolò de' Conti had seen in Ethiopia, as described the Florentine humanist Poggio Bracciolini. See *The Journey of Coronado, 1540–1542, From the City of Mexico to the Grand Canon of the Colorado and the Buffalo Plains of Texas, Kansas, and Nebraska*, ed. George Parker Winship (New York: A. S. Barnes and Co., 1904), p. 196.

41. "The Relación de la Jornada de Cíbola," p. 422.

42. Ibid., p. 433.

43. "Aquestas Indias nuestras son cabo de la que antiguamente se llamó India," Bartolomé de Las Casas, *Apologética historia sumaria*, ed. Edmundo O'Gorman, 2 vols. (Mexico City: Universidad Nacional Autónoma de México, 1967), vol. 1, p. 109; see also vol. 1, p. 77.

44. Matthew W. Stirling, *Origin Myth of Acoma and Other Records* (Washington, DC: United States Government Printing Office, 1942), p. 1. This 1942 publication, which gave no credit to its Indigenous informants, has been updated, newly edited and with sources credited: Edward Proctor Hunt, *Origin Myth of Acoma Pueblo*, trans. Wolf Robe Hunt and Wilbert Blue Sky Eagle Hunt, ed. Peter Nabokov (New York: Penguin Classics, 2015).

45. See Francisco López de Gómara, *Historia general de las Indias* (Alicante: Biblioteca Virtual Miguel de Cervantes, 1999), chap. 212, p. 303.

46. "The Relación de la Jornada de Cíbola," p. 400.

47. "Vieron por la costa naos que traían arcatraces de oro y plata en las proas, con mercaderías, y pensaron ser del Catayo y China, porque señalaban haber navegado treinta días." Gómara, *Historia general*, p. 305 (chap. 213). See also Hubert Howe Bancroft, *History of the Northwest Coast*, 2 vols. (San Francisco: The History Company, 1886), vol. 1, pp. 45–46.

48. Hakluyt, *The Principal Navigations*, vol. 13, p. 240. See also vol. 13, pp. 190 and 243, and vol. 14, p. 134.

49. "Letter from Viceroy Mendoza to Fernández de Oviedo, October 6, 1541," in Flint and Flint, eds., *Documents of the Coronado Expedition*, pp. 309–16, at p. 312.

50. Marc Simmons, *New Mexico: An Interpretive History* (Albuquerque: University of New Mexico Press, 1988), p. 37, and George Peter Hammond and Agapito Rey, *Don Juan de Oñate, Colonizer of New Mexico, 1595–1628*, 2 vols. (Albuquerque: University of New Mexico Press, 1953), vol. 1, p. 31.

51. The explorer Rodrigo del Rio de Losa similarly argued in 1582 that the proper outfitting for the exploration of New Mexico would include material that could be used to build vessels, believing that this territory reached to straits near China. See Bancroft, *History of the Northwest Coast*, vol. 1, p. 53.

52. See Hammond and Rey, *Don Juan de Oñate*, vol. 1, p. 486. See also pp. 393–97 ("Expedition to the South Sea and the Salines"), and vol. 2, p. 699 (Fray Juan de Escalona's Letter to his Prelate, October 1, 1601).

53. See Simmons, *New Mexico*, p. 42.

54. Hammond and Rey, *Don Juan de Oñate*, vol. 2, p. 764.

55. "Con aber entonado todo aquello / Que de los más antiguos naturales / Ha podido alcanzarse y descubrirse / Acerca de la antigua decendencia / Venida y población de Mexicanos, / Que para mí yo tengo que salieron / de la gran China todos los que habitan lo que llamamos Indias." Gaspar Pérez de Villagrá, *Historia de la Nueva México* (Albuquerque: University of New Mexico Press, 1992), canto 2, p. 17, lines 292–98. On Villagrá, see Manuel M. Martín-Rodríguez, *Gaspar de Villagrá: Legista, soldado y poeta* (León: Universidad de León, 2009).

56. This sense of connectivity between Mexico and China continues to be reported in the great chronicles of the missionary orders in Mexico in the seventeenth century. The Augustinian chronicler Juan de Grijalva, for instance, describes a matrilineal structure: Mexico was the daughter of Spain, and as friars from Mexico disseminated Christianity around the world Mexico in turn became the mother to new Catholic communities in Asia: "De quien esperamos que à de ser tambien madre y cabeça, estendiendose por aquel mundo, que tiene en sus confines del Iapon, y de la gran China." Juan de Grijalva, *Crónica de la orden de N. P. S. Augustín en las prouincias de la Nueua España* (Mexico: Juan Ruyz, 1624), p. 98, col. 4. The Franciscan Juan de Torquemada's chronicle *Monarquía indiana* (Seville: Cavijo, 1615) also mingles the history of missionary work in the Americas, Japan, China, and the Philippines. For New Spanish missionaries, Mexico and Asia formed a single transpacific world.

57. Juan González de Mendoza, *Historia de las cosas mas notables, ritos y costumbres del gran Reyno de la China* (Madrid: Querino Gerardo Flamenco, 1586). See Padrón, *The Indies of the Setting Sun*, pp. 183–200; Henry Raup Wagner, *The Spanish Southwest, 1542–1794: An Annotated Bibliography*, 2 vols. (New York: Arno Press, 1967), vol. 1, pp. 116–63; Christina H. Lee, "Imagining China in a Golden Age Spanish Epic," in *Western Visions of the Far East in a Transpacific Age, 1522–1657*, ed. Christina H. Lee (New York: Routledge, 2017), pp. 43–65, at p. 43; Serge Gruzinski, *Les quatres parties du monde: Histoire d'une mondialisation* (Paris: La Martinière, 2004), p. 278 n.6.

58. All subsequent translations produced from the original Roman edition did not contain the Espejo account, resulting in two general groups of editions: those with the Espejo account and those without it. See Wagner, *The Spanish Southwest*, p. 119. In the editions of Mendoza's text that contain the Espejo account, it is located in part 2, book 3, chaps. 7–10.

59. Mendoza, *Historia del gran Reyno de la China*, part 2, book 3, chap. 8. Because this text was printed in so many editions as well as translations, our references are to books and chapters rather than page numbers.

60. Ibid., chap. 9.

61. Ibid., chap. 11.

NINE — THE SWELLING EARTH

1. Oronce Finé taught mathematics and illustration for over forty years and produced two dozen books issued in more than seventy editions. According to the historian of cartography Robert W. Karrow, where cartography was concerned, his work represented "the best being done in France." Robert W. Karrow, *Mapmakers of the Sixteenth*

Century and Their Maps (Chicago: Speculum Orbis Press for the Newberry Library, 1993), p. 190. Finé's heart-shaped map was copied and reprinted repeatedly, including in Haggi Ahmed's Turkish world map on six wood blocks (Venice, 1559), Giovanni Cimerlino's heart-shaped map entitled *Cosmographia universalis* (Venice, 1566), and in the work of the Venetian printer Giacomo Franco (Venice, 1586).

2. Tom Conley, *The Self-Made Map: Cartographic Writing in Early Modern France* (Minneapolis: University of Minnesota Press, 1996), p. 90.

3. Ibid., p. 122.

4. See Henry Harrisse, *The Discovery of North America* (London: H. Stevens, 1892, reprinted Amsterdam: N. Israel, 1961), p. 583, and Franz von Wieser, *Magalhães-Strasse und Austral-Continent: Auf den Globen Johannes Schöner: Beitrage zur Geschichte der Erdkunde im xvi Jahrhundert* (Innsbruck: Wagner Verlag, 1881, reprinted Amsterdam: Meridian, 1967), pp. 67 and 79–80.

5. "Copia di una lettera di Giovanni da Verrazzano al. Chr.mo Re Francesco re di Francia," also known as the Cèllere Codex (Vatican ms. Ottoboniano lat. 2202, fol. 171–87), reproduced, translated, and transcribed in Lawrence C. Wroth, *The Voyages of Giovanni da Verrazano 1524–1528* (New Haven, CT: Yale University Press, 1970), pp. 96–143, at p. 142.

6. Ibid., pp. 134–43.

7. See Robert J. King, "Franciscus Monachus and the c. 1529 Paris Gilt Globe," *The Globe* 86 (2019), pp. 19–42.

8. Though no copies of Jacques Cartier's royal commission for his first voyage survive, the main purpose behind this expedition was, according to Samuel Eliot Morison, "to find a passage to China." Samuel Eliot Morison, *The European Discovery of America: The Northern Voyages, A.D. 500–1600* (New York: Oxford University Press, 1971), p. 345.

9. *The Voyages of Jacques Cartier*, ed. Ramsay Cook (Toronto: University of Toronto Press, 1993), p. 14.

10. Ibid., p. 82, and see also pp. 75 and 95.

11. Ibid., p. 135.

12. Ibid., p. 143.

13. Ibid., p. 106.

14. On Jean Alfonse of Saintonge, see Carl Ortwin Sauer, *Sixteenth Century North America: The Land and the People as Seen by the Europeans* (Berkeley: University of California Press, 1971), pp. 97–102.

15. Jean Fonteneau, dit Alfonse de Saintonge, *La cosmographie avec l'espère et régime du soleil et du nord* (Paris: Ernest Leroux, 1904), p. 489. The Neapolitan geographer Giovanni Lorenzo d'Anania confirmed that Cartier had understood from new world peoples that from what we today call the Great Lakes "one could go to Cathay" (*del quale lago è congettura potersi navigare al Cataio*). Giovanni Lorenzo d'Anania, *L'universale fabbrica del mondo, ovvero cosmografia* (Venice: Il Muschio, 1582), p. 358.

16. "The lands toward Hochelaga are much better and warmer than those of Canada; and this land of Hochelaga trends toward Figuyer [or Higueras, an early Spanish name for Honduras] and Peru, in which gold and silver abound. I saw also that its natives say that in the town called Cebola, which is in thirty-five degrees of the height of the north pole, the houses are all covered with gold and silver, and they use vessels of gold and silver. These lands lie towards Tartary and I think this to be the extremity of Asia by the roundness of the world." Alfonse de Saintonge, *La cosmographie*, p. 496.

17. Ibid., p. 400.

18. Gilbert Chinard, *L'exotisme américain dans la littérature française du XVIe siècle* (Paris: Hachette, 1911), pp. 56–57, on the new geographical knowledge of the Fourth Book and for the view that Pantagruel's pilot, Jamet Brayer, was modeled on Cartier and his co-pilot Xénomanes on Jean Alfonse.

19. Pliny, *Natural History*, 8.52; Arthur Tilley, *Studies in the French Renaissance* (1922, reprint New York: Barnes & Noble, 1968), p. 52.

20. Pliny, *Natural History*, 7.2.

21. For a considerable list of early modern sources that locate long-lived peoples in the new world and East Asia, see Geoffroy Atkinson, *Les nouveaux horizons de la renaissance française* (Paris: Droz, 1935), pp. 118–19.

22. Guillaume Le Testu, *Cosmographie universelle selon les*

navigateurs tant anciens que modernes, ed. Frank Lestringant (Paris: Arthaud, 2012), fol. LVIII.

23. "Aulcuns cosmographes ont conioinet lasie avec la floride neuf espaigne terre ferme et amerique et disent icelle estre partie de lasie mais loppinion diceulx nest a ensuyuir entant quelle nappert par certaine experience ne par raison." For commentary on this passage, see Chet Van Duzer, *The World for a King: Pierre Desceliers' Map of 1550* (London: British Library, 2015), p. 165. Desceliers again placed these same toponyms in a map of 1553.

24. "Qu'elle doive estre appellée Inde, je n'y vois pas grand raison: car ceste contrée du Levant que l'on nomme Indes, a pris ce nom du fleuve notable Indus, qui est bien loing de nostre Amerique. Il suffira donc de l'appeller Amerique ou France Antarctique." André Thevet, *Les singularitez de la France Antarctique autrement nommée Amérique*, ed. Paul Gaffarel (Paris: Masonneuve, 1878), chap. 27, p. 134. For Thevet, Asia was "far from America, for the one is in the East, and the other extends from the south into the West [Estant donc ceste region si loingtaine de l'Amerique, car l'une est en Orient, l'autre comprend depuis le Midy iusques en Occident]." Ibid., chap. 66, p. 345.

25. See Frank Lestringant, *André Thevet: Cosmographe des derniers Valois* (Geneva: Droz, 1991).

26. Thevet, *Les singularitez*, chap. 63, pp. 329–36.

27. "D'autant que la partie de ce nouveau monde qui est la plus Occidentale, au pais appellé Quivira, & Anian assis souz l'Artique, & en mesme elevation que la Norvege en Europe, & la terre de Mongal en Oriente, a laquelle elle est voisine (comme dit est) n'est separé du Quinsay qu par un canal de mer, lequel n'est de guere longue estendue, qui a esté cause que ne sçachants quel tiltre plus iuste donner a ces terres Nouvelles, ils n'ont trouvé mauvais de leur attribuer le nome des Indes, non moins proprement que les anciens ont fait a toute la terre qui est pres le fleuve Indus iusqu'a l'Ocean, comme ainsi soyt que l'Inde soyt proprement celle estendue quie est dez la Gedrosie iusques au fleuve Gangé, & que le reste a esté ainsi nommé pour tenir un generalité de tiltre aux peoples, quie sembloyent convener en façons de faire. Or est il que par le rapport de ceux qui ont visité les Indes Orientales, & ont de meuré au monde nouveau, on y voit quelque similitude de moeurs entre ces deux peoples separez de peu d'espace de mer, quoy qu'a present ils ne l'entre-frequentent, pour ce que leurs voyages ne s'estendent que iusqu'aux Moluques, & Iaves, & Taprobane, mais je pense que iadis ils ont eu quelque frequentation, & que d'eux ils ont apris leur adoration du Soleil, & autres ceremonies." François de Belleforest, *La cosmographie universelle de tout le monde*, 2 vols. (Paris: Nicolas Chesneau, 1575), vol. 2, pp. 2037–38. The printed marginal notes in this section of the text read "Où l'orient & occident terrestre semblent se ioindre," "Où est proprement la terre nommee Inde," and "Indes orientaux & occidentaux participent en moeurs semblables."

28. "Depuis de venans farouches pour ne hanter personne, ils sont aussi tombez iusqu'a la brutalité de se render anthropophages, & en d'aucuns lieux si mal accostables, qu'apeine peuvent ils endure aucun estranger aborder en leur pais sans luy mal faire; comme au contrair d'autres sont si gracieux, que volontiers, ils se rendent familiers a ceux qui abordent en leur terre, comme sont ceus de la Floride, Canada, & autres terres conenues en cell pertie Occidentale, q'on nomme la nuovelle France.... Ainsi les hommes ingenieux iugeront des noms les plus aprochans de la raison, soyt d'Amerique, de nouveau monde, ou d'Indes Occidentales, car quand a moy je n'y donne sentence que tant que je voy que l'erreur commun nous semble poser loy, & leur donner le nome Indien, quoy que plus favorablement, & iustement (comme semble) on feroit, rendant l'honneur des denominations aux premiers qui en ont fait la descouverte." Ibid., p. 2038. Even though he insisted on the separation of Asia and America, Thevet himself had made a similar argument in his *Les Singularitez*, chap. 66, p. 345.

29. See Hervé-Thomas Campangne, "Framing the Early Modern French Best Seller: American Settings for François de Belleforest's *Tragic Histories*," *Renaissance Quarterly* 71 (2018), pp. 77–113, at pp. 96–97, for the relationship of Belleforest's depiction of the Taíno cacique to those found in Montaigne's "Des Cannibales."

30. "Les navigations des modernes ont des-jà presque descouvert que ce n'est point une isle, ains terre ferme et continente avec l'Inde orientale d'un costé, et avec les terres qui sont soubs les deux poles d'autre part; ou, si elle en est separée, que c'est d'un si petit destroit et intervalle qu'elle ne merite pas d'estre nommée isle pour cela." *Les essais de Michel de Montaigne*, ed. Verdun-Louis Saulnier and Pierre Villey (Paris: Presses Universitaires de France, 1965), vol. 1, p. 203.

31. "Aucuns l'appellant & la marquent dans leurs faulses cartes Mer Catayen," "Lesquels cherchans le chemin pour aller au Catai, estans advertiz par le recit fait des richesses qui se trouvoient en l'Inde plus Orientale, fierent trois navigations en la Floride toutes en vain: Attendu que ce n'estoit le chemin ne des Indes, ne du Catai aussi." André Thevet, *La cosmographie universelle* (Paris: Guillaume Chaudiere, 1575), book 213, chap. 1, p. 1001r.

32. Exchanges between Thevet and Jean de Léry expose how discussions about new worlds in the sixteenth century were often bound up in tensions between Catholics and Protestants; see Janet Whatley, "Savage Hierarchies: French Catholic Observers of the New World," *Sixteenth Century Journal* 17 (1986), pp. 319–30.

33. "Que dirons nous aussi de ce que s'escarmouchant si fort en sa Cosmographie contre ceux qui appelent ceste terre d'Amérique, Inde Occidentale, à la quelle il veut que le nom de France Antarctique... l'a toutesfois luy mesme en plusieurs endroits nõmee Inde Amerique." Jean de Léry, *Histoire d'un voyage fait en la terre du Bresil, autrement dite Amerique* (La Rochelle: Antoine Chuppin, 1578), preface, n.p.

34. Ibid., chap. 16, p. 291.

35. "Lors ceste grande terre de la Floride est fort dangereuse à ceux qui navigent du costé de Catay, Canibalu, Panuco, et Themistitan; car à voir de loin on estimeroit que ce fut une isle située en pleine mer." Thevet, *Les singularitez*, chap. 74, p. 391.

36. "Sorty que l'on est du Royaume de Xalisco... on peult aller au Royaume Oriental, de la Chine, aux Indes subiettes qu grand Cam de Tartarie: & se compte de ce promontoire iusques à celuy de la Chine, par la supputation des pilotes & bons nautonniers, quelques mille lieves, & si la terre est continente par tous, ainsi que plusieurs tiennent, on pourroit aller de ce cap cy en l'Asie & Inde." Thevet, *La cosmographie universelle*, book 22, chap. 14, p. 990r.

37. André Thevet, *Le grand insulaire et pilotage d'André Thevet* (1588), Bibliothèque Nationale de France, MS fr. 15452 and 15453, fol. 405v.

38. *Voyages of Samuel de Champlain, 1604–1618*, ed. W. L. Grant (New York: Charles Scribner's Sons, 1907), pp. 24–25.

39. *The Voyages and Explorations of Samuel de Champlain*, trans. Annie Nettleton Bourne, 2 vols. (New York: Allerton, 1922), vol. 2, p. 48.

40. "L'eau y est tres mauvaise, come celle de ceste mer," "Ce qui me faict croire que c'est la mer du Su, estant salce come ils dissent." Samuel de Champlain, *Des sauvages, ou, voyage de Samuel Champlain, de Brouage, fait en la France Nouvelle, l'an mil six cens trois* (Paris: Claude de Monstr'oeil, 1603), chap. 8, p. 25r–v.

41. An alternative etymology attributes the name of Lachine to René-Robert Cavelier, Sieur de la Salle, a seventeenth-century fur trader who explored the Great Lakes region with the hope of finding a passage to China. When he returned without success, he and his men were supposedly derisively named *les Chinois*. See Timothy Brook, *Vermeer's Hat: The Seventeenth Century and the Dawn of the Global World* (New York: Bloomsbury, 2008), p. 46 n.6.

42. "L'on croit qu'il y a passage de la au Japan." Jean Guérard, 1634 world map, *Carte universelle hydrographique*, cited in Brook, *Vermeer's Hat*, p. 48.

43. Barthélemy Vimont, *Relation de ce qui s'est passé en la Nouvelle France, en l'anneé 1642 & 1643* (Paris: Sebastien Cramoisy, 1644), pp. 9–10. See also Consul Willshire Butterfield, *History of the Discovery of the Northwest by John Nicolet in 1634* (Port Washington, NY:[1881], Kennikat Press, 1969), pp. 58–59 and 102; Gaëtan Gervais, *Champlain: The Birth of French America* (Quebec City: McGill-Queen's University Press, 2004), p. 189; Brook, *Vermeer's Hat*, pp. 49–51. While American scholars tend to affirm that he crossed Lake Michigan into Winnebago territory near present-day Green Bay, Canadian scholars tend to believe he stayed north,

reaching present-day Sault Ste-Marie and trading with the Algonquins based near Lake Nipigon.

44. Pierre Jartoux, "A Letter from Father Jartoux, Missioner of the Society of Jesus, to F. Procurator, General of the Missions of India, and China," in *The Travels of Several Learned Missioners of the Society of Jesus, into Divers Parts of the Archipelago, India, China, and America* (London: R. Gosling, 1714), pp. 215–25, originally published as "Lettre du Pierre Jartoux," in *Lettres édifiantes et curieuses* (Paris: Jean Barbou, 1713), vol. 10, pp. 160–85.

45. Jartoux, "A Letter from Father Jartoux," vol. 10, p. 215.

46. Ibid., p. 218. Jartoux's reasoning reflected contemporary thought about the flora and fauna of the Indies. Francesco Redi's *Esperienze intorno a diverse cose naturali e particolarmente quelle che ci son portate dalle Indie* (Florence: Insegna della Nave, 1671), for instance, a letter summarizing the *naturalia* of the Indies addressed to the Jesuit scholar Athanasius Kircher, also conceived of the Americas, Brazil, the Moluccas, Goa, and China all equally as "Indies." For Redi, ginseng came from China (pp. 125–26), part of this broader continuum of space that encompassed the Americas. See also Alexandra Cook, "Linnaeus and Chinese Plants: A Test of the Linguistic Imperialism Thesis," *Notes and Records of the Royal Society* 64 (2010), pp. 121–38, esp. p. 124 n.37.

47. "La plante que j'avois découverte étoit le veritable Gin-seng." Joseph-François Lafitau, *Mémoire présenté à Son Altesse Royale Monseigneur le duc d'Orléans . . . concernant la précieuse plante du gin-seng de Tartarie, découverte en Canada par le Pere Joseph-François Lafitau* (Paris: Chez Joseph Mongé, 1718), pp. 32–33.

48. Ibid., p. 19. See also pp. 17 and 41–43.

49. Ibid., pp. 50, and 54–58.

50. See Kristin Johannsen, *Ginseng Dreams: The Secret World of America's Most Valuable Plant* (Lexington: University Press of Kentucky, 2006), p. 19.

51. See David A. Taylor, *Ginseng, the Divine Root: The Curious History of the Plant That Captivated the World* (Chapel Hill, NC: Algonquin Books, 2006); Christopher M. Parsons, "The Natural History of Colonial Science: Joseph-François Lafitau's Discovery of Ginseng and Its Afterlives," *The William and Mary Quarterly* 73 (2016), pp. 37–72; Parsons, *A Not So New World: Empire and Environment in French Colonial North America* (Philadelphia: University of Pennsylvania Press, 2018); Shigehisa Kuriyama, "The Geography of Ginseng and the Strange Alchemy of Needs," in *The Botany of Empire in the Long Eighteenth Century*, eds. Yota Batsaki, Sarah Burke Cahalan, and Anatole Tchikine (Washington, DC: Dumbarton Oaks, 2016), pp. 61–72.

52. "L'Amerique ne faisait qu'un même continent avec l'Asie, à qui elle s'unit par la Tartarie au nord de la Chine." Lafitau, *Mémoire*, pp. 18 and 49. See also Cook, "Linnaeus and Chinese Plants," pp. 11–13, as well as Andreas Motsch, "Le ginseng d'Amérique: Un lien entre les deux Indes, entre curiosité et science," *Études épistémè: Revue de littérature et de civilisations XVIe–XVIIIe siècles* 26 (2014), pp. 1–39, who observes that the botanical connection laid out in the *Mémoire* of 1718 was fleshed out with a demographic theory of the Asian origin of the American populations in Lafitau's *Moeurs des sauvages amériquains comparées aux moeurs des premiers temps* of 1724, even if he avowed his uncertainty as to whether the landmasses were joined or separated by a strait.

53. It is unclear what studies he is referring to, but one possibility is the roundup article of George F. Carter, "Plants across the Pacific," *Memoirs of the Society for American Archaeology* 9 (1953), pp. 62–71; *Tristes tropiques* appeared in 1955.

54. See Claude Lévi-Strauss, *Tristes tropiques* (Paris: Plon, 1955), chap. 24, "Le monde perdu." The quotations are from p. 297.

TEN — ENGLISH REFLECTIONS OF AMERASIA

1. See Claire Jowitt, "'Monsters and Straunge Births': The Politics of Richard Eden: A Response to Andrew Hadfield," *Connotations* 6 (1996), pp. 51–64, at p. 51. The only English book to advertise itself as a publication on the new world before Eden's was the anonymous publication *Of the New Lands* (Antwerp: Jan van Doesborch, 1520). A short printed reference to the new world before Eden's text is

found in John Rastell's *The Four Elements* (1520), pp. 1r–3v. Beyond this, English references to the new world appeared primarily in fiction; see Philip Tromans, "Advertising America: The Printing, Publication, and Promotion of English New World Books 1553–1600," PhD thesis, De Montfort University, 2015, pp. 33–34.

2. Michael Householder, *Inventing Americans in the Age of Discovery: Narratives of Encounter* (Farnham, UK: Ashgate, 2011), p. 22, and Iain Macleod Higgins, *Writing East: The "Travels" of Sir John Mandeville* (Philadelphia: University of Pennsylvania Press, 1997), p. 8.

3. John Larner, *Marco Polo and the Discovery of the World* (New Haven, CT: Yale University Press, 1999), p. 160.

4. John Leland, *Commentarii de scriptoribus Britannicis* (Oxford, 1549), cited in Larner, *Marco Polo and the Discovery of the World*, p. 163.

5. See Matthew McLean, *The Cosmographia of Sebastian Münster: Describing the World in the Reformation* (Aldershot, UK: Ashgate, 2007), pp. 174–87.

6. On this process in German printed maps and globes, see Christopher Wood, *Forgery, Replica, Fiction: Temporalities of German Renaissance Art* (Chicago: University of Chicago Press, 2008), pp. 229–38.

7. In 1552, Eden became secretary to Sir William Cecil, the Earl of Northumberland, an English statesman who encouraged English global commercial enterprise, a call loudly echoed by Eden's 1553 publication. See John Parker, *Books to Build an Empire: A Bibliographical History of English Overseas Interests to 1620* (Amsterdam: N. Israel, 1965), and Parker, *Richard Eden, Advocate of Empire* (Minneapolis: Associates of the James Ford Bell Library, University of Minnesota, 1991). On translation and the growth of London as an increasingly global city, see Robert K. Batchelor, *London: The Selden Map and the Making of a Global City, 1549–1689* (Chicago: University of Chicago Press, 2014).

8. See Surekha Davies, "America and Amerindians in Sebastian Münster's *Cosmographiae universalis libri VI* (1550)," *Renaissance Studies* 25 (2011), pp. 351–73.

9. Richard Eden, *A Treatyse of the Newe India* (London: Sutton, 1553), preface, n.p.

10. Ibid.

11. Ibid. "For Solomon had a ship of Tharsis in the sea with the ships of Chiram: one ship came to the king every three years out of Tharsis, laden with gold and silver, and wrought stones, and hewn stones." See 1 Kings 10:22.

12. Richard Eden, *The Decades of the Newe World of West India* (London: William Powell, 1555), preface, n.p.

13. Eden, *The Decades of the Newe Worlde of West India*, p. 3v.

14. Ibid., preface, n.p.

15. William Cunningham, *The Cosmographical Glasse, Conteinyng the Pleasant Principles of Cosmographie, Geographie, Hydrographie, or Nauigation* (London: In officina Ioan. Daij, 1559), pp. 67 and 199. See Donald F. Lach and Edwin J. Van Kley, *Asia in the Making of Europe*, vol. 2, *A Century of Wonder*, book 2, *The Literary Arts*, 3 vols. (Chicago: University of Chicago Press, 1965), p. 370.

16. Richard Willes, *The History of Travalye in the West and East Indies, and Other Countreys Lying Eyther Way towardes the fruitfull and ryche Moluccaes* (London: Richard Jugge, 1577), p. 251v: "The extreme part of the knowen worlde unto us, is the noble Ilande *Giapan*, written otherwise *Iapon* and *Iapan*. This Iland standeth in the East Ocean, beyond all Asie, betwixte Cathayo and the West Indies."

17. Roger Hervé, *Mappemonde de Sébastien Cabot . . . 1544* (Paris: Editions Les Yeux, 1968), and Rodney W. Shirley, *The Mapping of the World: Early Printed World Maps, 1472–1700* (London: New Holland, 1993), pp. 92–93.

18. The invitation came in 1547 and Cabot returned in 1548. Heather Dalton, *Roger Barlow, Sebastian Cabot, and Networks of Atlantic Exchange 1500–1560* (Oxford: Oxford University Press, 2016), pp. 125–28.

19. Ibid., p. 127 n.68, points out that thirty years after Cabot's death Philip Jones, a former associate of Hakluyt, remembered conversations with Cabot and the mathematician Robert Recorde regarding the Northwest Passage.

20. See Roger M. McCoy, *On the Edge: Mapping North America's Coasts* (New York: Oxford University Press, 2012).

21. See Elizabeth Jane Bellamy, "Spenser's Faeryland and 'The Curious Genealogy of India'," in *Worldmaking*

Spenser: Explorations in the Early Modern Age, ed. Patrick Cheney and Lauren Silberman (Lexington: University Press of Kentucky, 2000), pp. 177–92. For Ayesha Ramachandran, *The Worldmakers: Global Imagining in Early Modern Europe* (Chicago: University of Chicago Press, 2017), pp. 135–36, Spenser's Faery myth is "more than an imperial dream of conquest, though it certainly imagines a renewed alignment between cosmos and *imperium*," representing "a nostalgic desire for order in the face of an increasingly plural world where the whole is never in sight."

22. Christopher Marlowe, *Tamburlaine the Great*, part 1, act 3, scene 3.

23. Richard Hakluyt, *The Principal Navigations, Voyages, Traffiques, and Discoveries of the English Nation*, ed. Edmund Goldsmid, 16 vols. (Edinburgh: E. and G. Goldsmid, 1885–90), vol. 1, pp. 6–7.

24. Ibid., vol. 12, pp. 36–38.

25. Ibid., pp. 41–42. On these debates, see Miguel de Asúa and Roger French, *A New World of Animals: Early Modern Europeans on the Creatures of Iberian America* (Farnham, UK: Ashgate, 2005), pp. 76–85.

26. Hakluyt, *The Principal Navigations*, vol. 12, pp. 41–42.

27. Ibid., p. 71.

28. See, for instance, ibid., vol. 14, p. 156 ("The Discourse of John Chilton"); vol. 15, pp. 319 ("A letter from Mexico, of Sebastian Biscaino"), and 421 ("The Voyage of Francis Drake").

29. Ralegh did report, however, seeing headless men or *blemi* during his voyage to Guiana in 1596; see *The Discovery of Guiana* (London: Cassell and Company, 1887), pp. 106–107. While ancient writers such as Herodotus and Pliny placed the *blemi* in Africa, later medieval geographers and cartographers such as Andrea Bianco, Guillaume le Testu, and the author of *The Travels of Sir John Mandeville* located them in Asia. In addition, while Ralegh did not believe that Ophir could be identified with Peru (he believed instead that it corresponded with the Moluccas), the discussion clearly still captured his imagination. See Walter Ralegh, *The History of the World, in Five Books* (London: Walter Burre, 1614), p. 175.

30. *The Original Writings and Correspondence of the Two Richard Hakluyts*, ed. E. G. R. Taylor, 2 vols. (London: The Hakluyt Society, 1935), vol. 2, p. 456. We thank Karen Kupperman for pointing out this passage.

31. Jack Beeching, introduction to Richard Hakluyt, *Voyages and Discoveries* (New York: Penguin Books, 1972), p. 15.

32. Hakluyt, *The Principal Navigations*, vol. 12, p. 138.

33. Ibid., p. 79, and *The Three Voyages of Martin Frobisher, In Search of a Passage to Cathay and India by the North-West, AD 1576–78*, ed. Vilhjalmur Steffansson, 2 vols. (London: Argonaut Press, 1938), vol. 2, p. 185.

34. These references, together with the relevant images, can be found in William C. Sturtevant and David Beers Quinn, "This New Prey: Eskimos in Europe in 1567, 1576, and 1577," in *Indians and Europe: An Interdisciplinary Collection of Essays*, ed. Christian F. Feest (Aachen: Rader, 1987), pp. 61–140, at pp. 71–73. See also Peter Mason, *Infelicities: Representations of the Exotic* (Baltimore, MD: Johns Hopkins University Press, 1998), p. 115.

35. Sturtevant and Quinn, "This New Prey," p. 85.

36. Samuel Purchas, *Hakluytus Posthumus, or Purchas His Pilgrimes*, 4 vols. (London: Henry Fetherson, 1625), book 1, chap. 8, vol. 1, pp. 25–30.

37. Many had attested to the presence of elephants in America, including a variety of early modern artists and printmakers; even in the twentieth century, European observers saw elephants in Mayan glyphic inscriptions and therefore linked Indo-Chinese culture to Central America. See Peter Mason, *Before Disenchantment: Images of Exotic Animals and Plants in the Early Modern World* (London: Reaktion Books, 2009), pp. 11–14.

38. See Nicholas Popper, *Walter Raleigh's "History of the World" and the Historical Culture of the Late Renaissance* (Chicago: University of Chicago Press, 2012), pp. 143–52. Along similar lines, in the introduction to his 1598 German translation of Juan González de Mendoza's history of China discussed in chapter 8, the German professor of classics Matthias Dresser argues that America was known to the kings of the Old Testament as the land of Ophir. See Lach and Van Kley, *Asia in the Making of Europe*, vol. 2, book 2, p. 348.

39. Richard C. Trexler, *The Journey of the Magi: Meanings in History of a Christian Story* (Princeton, NJ: Princeton University Press, 1997), pp. 139–40.

40. *The Jamestown Voyages Under the First Charter, 1606–1609*, ed. Philip L. Barbour, 2 vols. (Cambridge: Cambridge University Press, 1969), vol. 1, p. 51.

41. "Relation of what Francis Magnel, an Irishman, learned in the land of Virginia during the eight months he was there" (1610), in Barbour, ed., *Jamestown Voyages*, vol. 2, pp. 151–57, quotes at pp. 155–56.

42. "A Note of the Shipping Men and Provisions Sent and Provided for Virginia (London, 1622)," in *The Records of the Virginia Company of London*, ed. Susan Myra Kingsbury, 4 vols. (Washington, DC: Library of Congress, 1906–35), vol. 3, p. 642.

43. William M. Kelso, Nicholas M. Luccketti, and Beverly A. Straube, *Jamestown Rediscovery V* (Richmond, VA: Association for the Preservation of Virginia Antiquities, 1999), pp. 47–50. We thank Karen Kupperman for this and several other references cited in this discussion.

44. Thomas Morton, *New English Canaan* (Amsterdam: Jacob Frederick 1637), pp. 19–20. The Tartars continued to animate the European imagination at the turn of the seventeenth century; Cornelis de Jode's regional map of the northwest coast of America, *Quivirae regnu cum alijs versus Borea*, from the second edition of his atlas *Speculum orbis terrae* (Antwerp, 1593), had likened Indigenous peoples' tents in that region to those of the Tartars.

45. See Helen Wallis, "The First English Globe: A Recent Discovery," *The Geographical Journal* 67 (1951), pp. 275–90, and Wallis, "Globes in England up to 1660," *Geographical Magazine* 35 (1962), pp. 267–78. Further Molyneux globes were acquired by All Souls College, Oxford, by Thomas Bodley for his library, also at Oxford, and by Thomas Lawton, who donated his terrestrial globe to the Shrewsbury School in 1596. See Matthew Dimmock, *Elizabethan Globalism: England, China, and the Rainbow Portrait* (New Haven, CT: Yale University Press, 2019), p. 9. On the iconography of globes in the portraiture of Elizabeth, see also Kristen Lippincott, "Power and Politics: The Use of the Globe in Renaissance Portraiture," *Globe Studies* 49/50 (2002), pp. 121–38.

46. Adam Max Cohen, "Englishing the Globe: Molyneux's Globes and Shakespeare's Theatrical Career," *Sixteenth Century Journal* 37 (2006), pp. 963–84.

47. Introduction to William Shakespeare, *Twelfth Night*, ed. John Maule Lothian and Thomas Wallace Craik (London: Arden, 2005), pp. xxxii–xxxiii. See also Jeremy Black, *Mapping Shakespeare* (London: Bloomsbury, 2018), p. 34.

48. "Hymn to God, My God, in My Sickness," a late poem of about 1630.

49. Thomas Bundeville, *His Exercises Containing Six Treatises*... (London: Windet, 1594), fol. 243v.

50. Ibid., fol. 245v.

ELEVEN — MOCTEZUMA THE GREAT KHAN

1. Since the content of map, including its textual material and its delineations of territories, is Vopel's, we will refer to it here as the Vopel Map, even though we only know it through Giovanni Andrea Vavassore's later reprinting.

2. Marco Polo, *The Travels of Marco Polo*, trans. Ronald Latham (New York: Penguin Books, 1958), p. 237. On Quanzhou, see James C. Y. Watt, *The World of Khubilai Khan: Chinese Art in the Yuan Dynasty* (New York and New Haven, CT: The Metropolitan Museum of Art and Yale University Press, 2010), pp. 158–78.

3. For a detailed explanation of many of the toponyms on this map, as well as transcriptions and translations of many of the map's inscriptions and cartouches, see Elizabeth Horodowich and Alexander Nagel, eds., *Amerasia: An Inquiry into Early Modern Imaginative Geography*, http://www.ifaresearch.org/amerasia/#.

4. The maps of Jan van Stobnica (1512), Gaius Julius Solinus (1538), Sebastian Münster (1540), Antonio Salamanca (1550), and Michele Tramezzino (1554) also separated America and Asia. For more complete lists of maps that did and did not separate the Asian and American continents, see Eviatar Zerubavel, *Terra Cognita: The Mental Discovery of America*

(New Brunswick, NJ: Transaction Publishers, 2003), p. 41, and Edward Luther Stevenson, *Terrestrial and Celestial Globes*, vol. 1: *Their History and Construction Including a Consideration of Their Value as Aids in the Study of Geography and Astronomy* (New Haven, CT: Yale University Press, 1921), pp. 94–145.

5. Indeed, the cartouche on the Vopel map in the middle of the Atlantic, just south of the equator, states that "the peoples of China . . . belonged to the territory of the Castilians," and that "the Moluccas, filled with types of every spice, are contained within the limits of the Castilians."

6. See Ricardo Padrón, *The Indies of the Setting Sun: How Early Modern Spain Mapped the Far East as the Transpacific West* (Chicago: University of Chicago Press, 2020).

7. See Marica Milanesi, "Arsarot o Anian? Identità e separazione tra Asia e Nuovo Mondo nella cartografia del Cinquecento (1500–1570)," in *Il Nuovo Mondo nella coscienza italiana e tedesca del Cinquecento*, eds. Adriano Prosperi and Wolfgang Reinhard (Bologna: Il Mulino, 1992), pp. 19–78.

8. Lawrence C. Wroth, *The Early Cartography of the Pacific* (New York: Bibliographical Society of America, 1944), pp. 115–29. See also Wilcomb E. Washburn, "Japan on Early European Maps," *Pacific Historical Review* 21 (1952), pp. 221–36, and Padrón, *The Indies of the Setting Sun*, pp. 205–31.

9. See Wroth, *The Early Cartography of the Pacific*, pp. 116–18, and Zerubavel, *Terra Cognita*, pp. 106–107.

10. José de Acosta, *Natural and Moral History of the Indies*, ed. Jane E. Mangan (Durham: Duke University Press, 2002), pp. 304–307.

11. Theodore De Bry, *Americae*, 27 vols. (Frankfurt: Matthew Becker, 1602), vol. 9, plates 9, 10, 11. We thank Michiel van Groessen for pointing out these images.

12. "Interea dum ista agrerentur, triginta viros, qui cipangi, alias cibaui, regionem explorarent," *Selections from Peter Martyr*, ed. Geoffrey Eatough, Repertorium Columbianum 5 (Turnhout: Brepols, 1998), p. 147.

13. "[Columbus] zonse a una insula chiamata da li paesani Iamaica, ma, come lui dice, da li cosmografi Ianna maior." *Fonti italiane per la storia della scoperta del nuovo mondo*, ed. Guglielmo Berchet, 2 vols. (Rome: Il Ministero della Pubblica Istruzione, 1892), vol. 1, p. 65.

14. *A Synoptic Edition of the Log of Columbus's First Voyage*, eds. Francesca Lardicci and Valeria Bertolucci Pizzorusso, Repertorium Columbianum 6 (Turnhout: Brepols, 1999), p. 55.

15. Richard Krautheimer, postscript to "Introduction to an *Iconography of Medieval Architecture*," in *Studies in Early Christian, Medieval, and Renaissance Art* (New York: New York University Press, 1969), p. 149.

16. *Geography of Claudius Ptolemy*, ed. and trans Edward Luther Stevenson (New York: New York Public Library, 1932), p. 158. Modern scholars have argued that Cattigara either lay along the Red River Delta near Hanoi or in Southern China. It has been identified with Funan, the ancient kingdom of southern Vietnam, or placed in the Mekong River delta, which flourished around the time that Ptolemy composed his *Geography*. See Thomas Suárez, *Early Mapping of Southeast Asia: The Epic Story of Seafarers, Adventurers, and Cartographers Who First Mapped the Regions between China and India* (Hong Kong: Periplus, 1999), pp. 90–92.

17. In his 1572 history of the Incas, the Spanish explorer and historian Pedro Sarmiento de Gamboa places Cattigara in the Pacific, somewhere between Asia and the Strait of Magellan. Pedro Sarmiento de Gamboa, *Historia indica*, in *Obras completas del Inca Garcilaso de la Vega*, ed. P. Carmelo Saenz de Santa Maria, 4 vols. (Madrid: Ediciones Atlas, 1960), vol. 4, pp. 193–279, at p. 206.

18. The maps of Oronce Finé, the Paris Gilt Globe, and Münster's *Novae insulae* all show Cattigara along the coast of Peru. On Magellan's search for Cattigara, see Maximilianus Transylvanus, *De Moluccis insulis* (Cologne: In aedibus Eucharij Ceruicorni, 1523), n.p.

19. Livio Sanuto, *Geografia dell'Africa* (Amsterdam: Theatrum Orbis Terrarum, 1965), p. 15r.

20. Benedetto Bordone, *Libro di Benedetto Bordone* (Venice: Nicolo d'Aristotile detto Zoppino, 1524), p. 7r.

21. See John Hewitt, "A World Map On An Oval Projection Attributed to Franciscus Monachus, ca. 1526," *The Globe* 73 (2013), pp. 17–27. This same understanding of

global geography is expressed in the Paris Gilt Globe, which was the globe Monachus was most likely describing in his pamphlet; see Robert J. King, "Franciscus Monachus and the c.1529 Paris Gilt Globe," *Journal of the Australian and New Zealand Map Society* 86 (2019), pp. 19–42. On the career of Franciscus Monachus, see Robert Karrow, *Mapmakers of the Sixteenth Century and Their Maps: Bio-Bibliographies of the Cartographers of Abraham Ortelius, 1570* (Chicago: Newberry Library, 1993), pp. 407–409.

22. For instance, Vopel's cartouche just to the east of Florida repeats Monachus's language almost verbatim: "Peter Martyr reports that all these vast regions—Asia, Africa, Europe, and severally, India, Colhuacan, and, in the north, Sweden, Tartary, Baccalarea, and Florida—though separated by a very great distance, are connected by a continuous territory and an uninterrupted route, and, moreover, that America itself is connected to the eastern lands and to Colhuacan." (Narat Petrus Martir Asiam, Africam, Europam, & particulatim Indiam, Coluocanam, ac ad Septentrionem Suediam, Tartariam, Baccaleream, terramque Floridam omnes hasce regiones spaciosissimas, longisimoque dissitas interuallo continenti tractu & perpetuo limite cohęrere; atque ipsam pretera Americam orientalibus, & Coluocanae annexam esse). For Monachus's corresponding text, see chapter 7.

23. "*Parentque magno Cham, quem Ferdinandus Cortesius Dominus Muteezuma appellat.*" On Bargu, see Polo, *The Travels of Marco Polo*, p. 102.

24. For example, the Venetian polyglot Tommaso Garzoni's *La piazza universale di tutte le professioni del mondo* (Venice: Giovanni Battista Somascho, 1585), pp. 357–58, argued that Polo had gone to the Americas before Columbus: "We commonly attribute the discovery of the New World to the Genoese Christopher Columbus in 1492, and on the one hand to the Florentine Amerigo Vespucci, while on the other hand to Magellan, but Francesco Sansovino attributes its earliest discovery to the Venetian Marco Polo, otherwise known as Il Milione, who found new lands before Columbus, but the world did not trust his narrative as it should have." Francesco Sansovino had written about Polo's voyage to Asia in his *Venetia città nobilissima et singolare*; here Garzoni implies that Sansovino, among many others, didn't understand the full implications of Polo's travels. Offering a brief depiction of the lands that Polo and later Ludovico Varthema (see chapter 5) had visited, Garzoni describes how leaving Tartaria, "you come to the land of the Mongols and Khanbalik, and passing into the Indies along this route, you come to the land north of the Kingdom of Tangut, and the Kingdom of Mangi is in the western part, the land of Labrador, and moving south, the land of Baccalaos, Nuremberg, Terra Francesca . . . Arcadia, Florida . . . Guatemala, Nicaragua, and many other provinces that connected to new Spain." In 1588, the eminent Venetian cartographer and cosmographer Livio Sanuto began to question the association of Mexico and China, bringing into discussion the ideas of several of the cartographers discussed here. "Oronce Finé and Vopel," he noted, "believe that Mexico is Cathay." Sanuto was skeptical, noting that in the writings of Marco Polo, Haiton the Armenian, and others, the Far East and South of Asia were full of horses, yet in the account of Francisco López de Gómara we read, "In Mexico, a great fear arose in the thousands of people in that land at the sight of just one horse, which scared everyone and they fled immediately. They also together thought from the beginning that man and horse were united in one body [and], to their horror, were eaters/devourers of human flesh." Sanuto, *Geografia dell'Africa* (Venice: Damiano Zenaro, 1588), p. 17r.

25. "Ptolemy knew of the kingdom of China and makes mention of it in his Cosmography when he divides the earth, giving to Asia and to the other parts the provinces and lands which belong there and stand below his mainland. It matches with New Spain, being terrafirma up to the canal or strait that is found between the kingdom of Anian and Gran Tartaria, and China stands well near the aforementioned kingdom, as one can see in the Terrestrial Globe and the General Map of the World of the most modern [maps], particularly in that of Petrus Plancius or that of Enrico Almagren. [[And more clearly in the sphere which Fra Francisco sent to the Archbishop of Palermo with a letter, in which he deems the city of Themistetàn to be

the same as Tenuchtitlàn, or Mexico, where, he affirms, there arrived many years before Don Hernando Cortes, the famous travelers to the Orient Marco Polo Veneto, John Mandeville, and Fra Oderico of Forojulio (Pordenone), supporting this idea with various details drawn from the voyages of these men, and compared with the second Relacion of Don Hernando Cortés, believing that one could not conclude it to be any other city but that of Mexico and its empire, riches, and magnificence, that relate to the Great Khan of the Tartars, and believing him to be the same as the Khan Montezuma and his court of Themistetàn, reinforcing [this idea] by saying that Asia, by way of Culuacàn, is [part of] the lands of New Spain]]." Text in double brackets added to second edition. Gregorio García, *Origen de los indios de el Nuevo Mundo* (Madrid: Francisco Martinez, 1729), p. 8. This same edition refers directly to Monachus's *De orbis situ*, invoking the publication that two centuries earlier had argued for the connectedness of China and Mexico and revealing a continuous chain of thought about the relationship between them that continued to inform geographic thinking more than two hundred years after the Columbian voyages.

26. Michael Householder, *Inventing Americans in the Age of Discovery: Narratives of Encounter* (Farnham, UK: Ashgate, 2011), p. 22.

27. "Americus tamen Vesputius, maritima loca Indiae superioris ex Hispanijs nauigio ad occidentem perlustrans, eam partem quae superioris Indiae est, credidit esse insulam, quam à suo nomine uocari instituit. Alij uero nunc recentiores Hydrographi, eam terram ulterius ex alia parte inuenerunt esse continentem Asiae, nam sic etiam ad Moluccas insulas superioris Indiae peruenerunt. Hanc continentem Asiae superioris portionem extra Ptolemaeum, ante nostra tempora, ab Marco Polo Veneto, & alijs quamplurimis lustratam legimus." Johannes Schöner, *Opusculum geographicum ex diversorum libris ac cartis* (Nuremberg: Johann Petreius, 1533), part 2, chap. 1, n.p.

28. "Terra est, quae Mexico & Temistitan uocatur, in Superiori India, quam priores uoca uere Quinsay, id est ciuitatem coeli eorum lingua." Ibid.

29. "Post Ptolemaeum uero ultra 180 gradus uersus orieentem multae regiones repertae per quendam Marcum Polum Venetum, ac alios, sed nunc a Columbo Genuensi, & Americo Vesputio solum loca lit toralia ex hispanijs per Oceanum occidentalem illuc applicantes lustratae sunt." Ibid., part 2, chap. 20.

30. Ibid. In part 2, chapter 21, "About the islands around Asia and India and the new regions of the third part of the world" (*De Insulis Asiam ac India & novas regiones huius tertian orbis partis*), Schöner goes on to list the Yucatan, Cuba, Jamaica, and Hispaniola, together with the Moluccas, as islands in Asia.

31. Padrón, *The Indies of the Setting Sun*, p. 133.

32. See Francesca Fiorani, "Cycles of Painted Maps in the Renaissance," in *The History of Cartography*, vol. 3, *Cartography in the European Renaissance*, ed. David Woodward, 3 vols. (Chicago: University of Chicago Press, 2007), vol. 1, pp. 804–30, at p. 814 n.36.

33. On De Girava's map, see *The World Encompassed: An Exhibition of the History of Maps Held at the Baltimore Museum of Art, October 7 to November 23, 1952* (Baltimore, MD: Trustees of the Walters Art Gallery, 1952), #112. Van den Putte's map exists in one copy in the Herzog August Bibliothek in Wolfenbüttel. See Leo Bagrow, *History of Cartography* (Cambridge, MA: Harvard University Press, 1964), p. 130.

34. Iohn Huighen van Linschoten, *His Discours of Voyages Into ye Easte & West Indies Deuided Into Foure Bookes* (London: By [John Windet for] Iohn Wolfe, 1598), p. 218.

35. Antonio Galvano, *The Discoveries of the World, from their First Original unto the Year of Our Lord 1555*, trans. Richard Hakluyt (London: G. Bishop, 1601), p. 2.

36. See Giovanni Battista Ramusio, *Navigazioni e viaggi*, ed. Marica Milanesi, 6 vols. (Turin: Einaudi, 1978–88), vol. 3, p. 218.

37. Paul Pelliot, *Notes on Marco Polo*, 2 vols. (Paris: Imprimerie Nationale/Librairie Adrien-Maisonneuve, 1959), vol. 1, pp. 39–40 and 43, and vol. 2, pp. 857–58.

38. For a clear explanation of the Mercator projection,

see Mark Monmonier, *Rhumb Lines and Map Wars: A Social History of the Mercator Projection* (Chicago: University of Chicago Press, 2004), pp. 1–11.

39. See Elizabeth Horodowich, *The Venetian Discovery of America: Geographic Imagination and Print Culture in the Age of Encounters* (New York: Cambridge University Press, 2018), pp. 137–41. Books of cosmography and geography continued to list the Asian toponyms of Anian, Agama, and Pagul among the cities of Mexico through the eighteenth century. See for instance *Sistema del mondo terraqueo geograficamente descritto*, 2 vols. (Venice: Stamparia Bragadina, 1716), vol. 2, p. 171.

40. Schöner, *Opusculum geographicum*, part 2, chap. 20.

41. Richard Flint, *No Settlement, No Conquest* (Albuquerque: University of New Mexico Press, 2013), p. 18, and David Woodward, "The Renaissance Geographic and Cartographic Background to the First Century of Greater Southwest Discovery and Cartography," in *The Mapping of the Entradas into the Greater Southwest*, ed. Dennis Reinhartz and Gerald D. Saxon (Norma: University of Oklahoma Press, 1998), pp. 5–7.

42. This fact comes into view in polyfocal studies such as Serge Gruzinski, *The Eagle and the Dragon: Globalization and European Dreams of Conquest in China and America in the Sixteenth Century* (Cambridge: Polity, 2014).

TWELVE — INDIA AS A SEMANTIC FIELD

1. This hint of monarchical structure may also be carried over from André Thevet, who emphasized this aspect in his portraits of Brazilian kings in the *Cosmographie universelle* of 1575. See Frank Lestringant, "The Myth of the Indian Monarchy: An Aspect of the Controversy between Thevet and Jean de Léry (1575–1585)," in *Indians and Europe: An Interdisciplinary Collection of Essays*, ed. Christian F. Feest (Lincoln:
University of Nebraska Press, 1989), pp. 37–60.

2. Louis de Jaucourt, "Indes (Géographie Moderne)," in *Encyclopédie, ou dictionnaire raisonné des sciences, des arts et des métiers*, ed. Denis Diderot and Jean le Rond d'Alembert, 17 vols. (Paris: Chez Briasson et Le Breton, 1751–72), vol. 8, p. 662.

3. Ricardo Padrón, *The Indies of the Setting Sun: How Early Modern Spain Mapped the Far East as the Transpacific West* (Chicago: University of Chicago Press, 2020), p. 32. He continues: "the Spanish Indies . . . over the course of the sixteenth century could accommodate *either* the theory of Amerasian continuity *or* that of American insularity, or remain agnostic about the matter altogether."

4. Pierre Schneider, *L'Éthiopie et l'Inde: Interférence et confusions aux extrémités du monde antique* (Rome: Collection de l'École Française de Rome, 2004), pp. 236–37.

5. See Nicolás Wey Gómez, *The Tropics of Empire: Why Columbus Sailed South to the Indies* (Cambridge, MA: MIT Press, 2008).

6. Benjamin Schmidt, *Inventing Exoticism: Geography, Globalism, and Europe's Early Modern World* (Philadelphia: University of Pennsylvania Press, 2015), takes as its subject the existence and articulation of the new category rather than the process by which it came into being, though the fact that it was the result of a historical process is clearly acknowledged, for example on pp. 325–26.

7. Peter Mason's *Infelicities: Representations of the Exotic* (Baltimore, MD: Johns Hopkins University Press, 1998), acknowledges (p. 3) that the word *exotic* was not used in the modern sense before the seventeenth century, yet affirms the birth of the "exotic genre" c. 1500 in the wake of the first new world discoveries. Elizabeth Hill Boone, "Seeking Indianness: Christoph Weiditz, the Aztecs, and Feathered Amerindians," *Colonial Latin American Review* 26 (2017), pp. 39–61, also embraces this view.

8. Herodotus, *Histories*, trans. A. D. Godley (Cambridge, MA: Harvard University Press. 1920), book 3, chap. 98, line 3; Pliny, *Natural History*, book 6, chap. 59.

9. See Albrecht Dihle, "The Conception of India in Hellenistic and Roman Literature," *Proceedings of the Cambridge Philological Society* 10 (1964), pp. 15–23, at p. 16, and Schneider, *L'Ethiopie et l'Inde*, pp. 432–37.

10. See Marianne O'Doherty, *The Indies and the Medieval West: Thought, Report, Imagination* (Turnhout: Brepols, 2013), pp. 33–39.

11. *Selections from Peter Martyr*, ed. Geoffrey Eatough, Repertorium Columbianum 5 (Turnhout: Brepols, 1998), pp. 145–50 (Decade 1.3.1–1.3.10).

12. Florike Egmond and Peter Mason, "'These Are People Who Eat Raw Fish': Contours of the Ethnographic Imagination in the Sixteenth Century," *Viator* 31 (2000), pp. 311–60, at p. 324.

13. See Massimo Donattini, "Bolognese Franciscan Missionaries in the New World," in *The New World in Early Modern Italy, 1492–1750*, ed. Elizabeth Horodowich and Lia Markey (New York: Cambridge University Press, 2017), pp. 63–85, at pp. 69–70.

14. Andrew Laird, "Humanism and the Humanity of the Peoples of the New World: Fray Julián Garcés, *De habilitate et capacitate gentium*, Rome 1537. A Study, Transcription and Translation of the Original Imprint in the John Carter Brown Library," *Studi Umanistici Piceni* 34 (2014), pp. 183-225, at p. 211: "Videant uniuersi in Apostolico pectore nihil gratius insedere, quam huic tanto negotio vi omni, & nisu, nutu, voce, voto, te velle fideles tuos excubare, adesse vigilare, qua parte nobis verbi ostium (vt ait Apostolus) apertum est, illuc plurimos operarios destinare quo in foecundo huius Indiae cespite centeno consurgat spica fructu, quae diuitem spem alat, charitatem augeat, fidem sustentet, tanto ydolatras alacriori animo & ampliori ardore certemus ad nostrae professionis vexilla colligere in Asia, quanto Turcharum in Europa saeuitiam in nostros amplius cernimus debacchari." We thank Robert Brennan for bringing this passage to our attention.

15. All quotations in this paragraph are drawn from Bartolomé de Las Casas, *Apologética historia sumaria*, ed. Edmundo O'Gorman, 2 vols. (Mexico City: Universidad Nacional Autónoma de México, 1967), vol. 1, chap. 22, pp. 109–12. See also Anthony Pagden, *The Fall of Natural Man: The American Indian and the Origins of Comparative Ethnology* (Cambridge: Cambridge University Press, 1986), pp. 137–39.

16. Daniela Bleichmar, "The Cabinet and the World: Non-European Objects in Early Modern European Collections," *Journal of the History of Collections* 33 (2021), pp. 435–45, at p. 437.

17. This "humane" view was of course on the colonizers' terms, a means of classing the newly defined *Indios* as susceptible to conversion and integration into colonial hierarchy. Nor did the appeal to an inherently respectable Indianness mean that actual Asians from the "old" India, for all the recognized antiquity of their civilizations, were not enslaved by the Spanish; it means only that Las Casas's appeal for an acknowledgment of the humanity of the *naturales* on the grounds of their Indianness was deployed as a rhetorical tool so effectively that it acquired force of law, making it illegal to enslave *Indios* from New Spain, in contrast to Asian inhabitants of Spanish-dominated lands. During the later sixteenth and seventeenth Asians (called *Chinos* whether they came from islands close to China, the Philippines, or India) migrated to the Americas in significant numbers; ironically, a man born in Goa became an *Indio* only after successfully claiming the identity as it had been constituted in Mexico. See Tatiana Seijas, *Asian Slaves in Colonial Mexico: From Chinos to Indians* (New York: Cambridge University Press, 2014), p. 173. These judgments were made not only in New Spain but also in Spain, as colonial migrants from different parts of the empire mixed, and attempted to get themselves freed from slavery by claiming the status of *Indio*. See Nancy van Deusen, *Global Indios: The Indigenous Struggle for Justice in Sixteenth-Century Spain* (Durham, NC: Duke University Press, 2015), and Juan Gil, "Chinos in Sixteenth-Century Spain," in *Western Visions of the Far East in a Transpacific Age, 1522–1657*, ed. Christina H. Lee (London: Ashgate: 2012), pp. 139–52. The assimilation was not only discursive and then legal but also material and genetic, since intermarriage and cultural interpenetration turned the Amerasian idea into a concrete social reality during the seventeenth century, as discussed in chapter 17. This process of Amerasian assimilation shaped emergent racialized categories, for example by prompting Spanish authorities to observe and articulate similarities in the skin color of *Chinos* and *Indios*—in overall contrast to black-skinned Africans, for whom there were few obstacles to

enslavement. See Seijas, *Asian Slaves in Colonial Mexico*, p. 248. Likewise, Van Deusen, *Global Indios*, p. 191, shows that the situation prompted a refinement of racial and ethnographic analysis, where observations of skin color and awareness of Indigenous languages became "key to determining whether someone was in fact an *indio* and to which imperial domain he or she belonged."

18. Irene Silverblatt, *Modern Inquisitions: Peru and the Colonial Origins of the Civilized World* (Durham, NC: Duke University Press, 2004), p. 212: "'Indian' is not a fixed inventory of traits, a thing, making up a fixed identity. Rather, 'Indian,' like 'identity,' must be understood in its sociability, emerging in the social relations that engage human beings in time."

19. Ibid., p. 208. The "Indian" cults they promoted were in fact occasionally inflected by the Spanish presence, as when they appropriated the Spaniards' Saint James, *Santiago matamoros* (Moor-killer), who had become in America *Santiago mataindios* (Indian-killer) and now, in a reversal, became the Indigenous mountain god *Santiago apu huayna* promising to help his Indian worshippers "as long as you don't confess, don't hear mass, don't pray in church, but just dedicate yourselves to my worship." Thus, the prehistory of Christian-Muslim conflict was negatively inscribed into the new "Indian" anticolonial resistance, turning the Spanish themselves into Santiago's othered enemies.

20. Irene Silverblatt, "Haunting the Modern Andean State: Colonial Legacies of Race and Civilization," in *State Theory and Andean Politics*, ed. David Nugent and Christopher Krupa (Philadelphia: University of Pennsylvania Press, 2015), pp. 167–85, at p. 169: "They created two unequal 'republics' as the foundation for colonial rule: Native Americans and their descendants, regardless of origin or ethnicity, were classed as Indians; descendants of Iberia, regardless of origin, ethnicity, or social rank, were classed as privileged Spanish colonists."

21. Missionaries used the term *Indies* to refer to lands where evangelical work was needed, including even places in Europe; Jesuit correspondence from southern Italy in the late sixteenth and early seventeenth centuries called the lands where they proselytized in Abruzzo and Sicily the "real India" or the "Italian Indies." See Adriano Prosperi, "'Otras indias': Missionari della Controriforma tra contadini e selvaggi," in *Scienze, credenze occulte, livelli di cultura* (Florence: Olschki, 1982), pp. 205–34, at pp. 207–208. See also Luke Clossey, *Salvation and Globalization in the Early Jesuit Missions* (Cambridge: Cambridge University Press, 2008), pp. 232–33; Rachel Miller, "Converting 'the Indies' of Naples in Luca Giordano's *St. Francis Xavier Baptizing Indians* Altarpiece," *Journal of Jesuit Studies* 6 (2019), pp. 249–69, reads Giordano's altarpiece as an encouragement to see Naples and southern Italy as an alternative "Indies." More broadly, Shankar Raman has argued, India was a figure through which early modern European powers imagined and defined themselves; see Shankar Raman, *Framing "India": The Colonial Imaginary in Early Modern Culture* (Stanford, CA: Stanford University Press, 2002). Accordingly, the category of Indianness could become internalized in European geopolitical discourse, as when the Dutch claimed they were Indians in the face of Spanish domination and cruelty. See Benjamin Schmidt, *Innocence Abroad: The Dutch Imagination and the New World, 1570–1670* (New York: Cambridge University Press, 2001), pp. 87–90 and 94–95. On early modern Italian understandings of India, see Erin Benay, *Italy by Way of India: Translating Art and Devotion in the Early Modern World* (Turnhout: Brepols/Harvey Miller, 2021).

22. "Alcuni anche la chiamano atlantica & India occidentale per questa cagione, che fù nel medesimo tempo trovata, nel quale i Portoghesi caminarono l'India Orientale, ò meglio, per la similitudine de gli Habitanti con gli Indiani dell'Asia, percioche questi come quei vanno tutti nudi." *Geografia, cioè, descrittione vniversale della terra partita in due volumi, nel primo de'quali si contengono gli otto libri della geografia* (Venice: Galignani, 1598), p. 203.

23. "Gli abitanti delle Indie nuove, massime del Perù, e quelli del gran re della Cina sono senza barba con un solo pelo nel mento, vanno ignudi, così gli uomini come le donne, eccetto che le maritate portano una benda di cotone intorno alle parti pudenda; ed in lochi assai si mangiano l'un l'altro." Gian Paolo Lomazzo, *Trattato dell'arte della*

pittura, scultura et architettura (Milan: Gottardo Pontio, 1585), book 6, chap. 65, p. 452.

24. Michiel van Groesen, "Americans in Agra? Robert Coverte and the European Iconography of Mughal India," *Reading East: Irish Sources and Resources*, https://www.ucd.ie/readingeast/essay5.html. For a thorough study of the gargantuan, lavishly illustrated, twenty-three-volume work devoted to *India orientalis* and *India occidentalis* by the De Bry family of printers in Frankfurt, see Michiel van Groesen, *The Representations of the Overseas World in the De Bry Collection of Voyages (1590–1634)* (Leiden: Brill, 2008).

25. On Chinese objects in Medici collections and their coexistence with items from America and elsewhere, see Francesco Morena, *Dalle Indie orientali alla corte di Toscana: Collezioni di arte cinese e giapponese a Palazzo Pitti* (Florence: Giunti, 2005), pp. 25–71, at pp. 44–45.

26. Lia Markey refers to a 1553 inventory (Archivio di Stato, Guardaroba Medicea 30, f. 19r.) that lists "una maschera venuta d'India composta di Turchine sopra il legno" and "una maschera di legno venuta d'India composta di turchine." See Lia Markey, *Imagining the Americas in Medici Florence* (University Park: Pennsylvania State University Press, 2016), p. 171 n.24.

27. Jessica Keating and Lia Markey, "'Indian' Objects in Medici and Austrian-Habsburg Inventories: A Case-Study of the Sixteenth-Century Term," *Journal of the History of Collections* 23 (2011), pp. 283–300, at pp. 286 and 288. See also Mason, *Infelicities*, chap. 4.

28. Keating and Markey, "'Indian' Objects in Medici and Austrian-Habsburg Inventories," p. 289.

29. Filippo Sassetti, *Lettere di Filippo Sassetti: Corrette, accresciute e dichiarate con note*, ed. Eugenio Camerini (Milan: E. Sonzogno, 1874), p. 264, to Michele Saladini from Cochin, dated to 1585 without day or month.

30. Ibid., p. 314, to Cardinal Ferdinando de' Medici from Cochin, February 10, 1586.

31. Lauran Toorians, "The Earliest Inventory of Mexican Objects in Munich, 1572," *Journal of the History of Collections* 6 (1994), pp. 59–67.

32. Toorians, "Earliest Inventory of Mexican Objects in Munich," p. 66. See also Hans Thoma und Herbert Brunner, *Schatzkammer der Residenz München* (Munich: Bayerische Verwaltung der staatlichen Schlösser, Gärten und Seen, 1964), p. 364; Elke Bujok, *Neue Welten in europaischen Sammlungen: Africana und Americana in Kunstkammern bis 1670* (Berlin: Reimer, 2004); Anthony Alan Shalton, "Cabinets of Transgression: Renaissance Collections and the Incorporation of the New World," and Thomas DaCosta Kaufmann, "From Treasury to Museum: The Collections of the Austrian Habsburgs," both in *The Cultures of Collecting*, ed. John Elsner and Roger Cardinal (London: Reaktion, 1994).

33. Kate Elizabeth Holohan, "Collecting the New World at the Spanish Habsburg Court, 1519–1700," PhD thesis, New York University, 2015, especially pp. 126–35 and 171–98.

34. On the rise of area studies and Asian studies after World War II, for instance, see Bruce Cumings, "Boundary Displacement: Area Studies and International Studies during and after the Cold War," *Bulletin of Concerned Asian Scholars* 29 (1997), pp. 6–26.

35. Progress in this direction has been made in the important studies of Christian Feest, in particular "The Collecting of American Indian Artifacts in Europe, 1493–1750," in *America in European Consciousness, 1493–1750*, ed. Karen Ordahl Kupperman (Chapel Hill: University of North Carolina Press, 1995), pp. 324–60. See also Christine Göttler, "Extraordinary Things: 'Idols from India' and the Visual Discernment of Space and Time, circa 1600," in *Nomadic Objects: The Challenge of World for Early Modern Religious Art*, ed. Christine Göttler and Mia Mochizuki (Leiden: Brill, 2017), pp. 35–73, and Anna Grasskamp, *Objects in Frames: Displaying Foreign Collectibles in Early Modern China and Europe* (Berlin: Dietrich Reimer, 2019). As the historian Giuseppe Marcocci, *Indios, cinesi, falsari: Le storie del mondo nel Rinascimento* (Bari: Laterza, 2016), chap. 1, par. 28, has noted, "La tendenza a isolare . . . i testi scritti in America dagli altri, come se i primi avessero di per sé uno statuto autonomo all'interno delle rispettive letterature nazionali, non fa che aggravare la già arbitraria frammentazione di

una material che spesso non obbediva affatto ai criteri in base ai quali è generalmente suddivisa e classificata."

36. All these points and quotations are from José de Acosta, *De procuranda indorum salute*, 2 vols. (Madrid: Consejo Superior de Investigaciones Científicas, 1984–87), vol. 1, pp. 54–60 ("Proemium"). Written in 1576, laboriously edited and censored by Church authorities over twelve years, this treatise was presented to King Philip II in 1588.

37. "Avendo sempre fatto partecipe V(ostra) Ecc(ellen)tia di quelle poche medaglie che per questo buon Re mio sig(no)re ò fatte, così ora di nuovo avendo ritrattolo e fattoli uno riverso per la India, la quale ò vestito li omini et le donne colli abiti che usono in el Peru, come quella vedrá, e quello animale che pare uno cammello et una pecora così fatta e la ò ritratto da una che è qui e ve l'ò messa per essere animale raro che è buona come le nostre di lana, latte e carne, e porta soma come asino, e la ò fi(g)urata carica di fasci d'argento. La donna che porta a offerire il mezo mondo è fi(g)urata per la India provincia, come piace al s(igno)re Gonzalo Peres. Ma io l'atribuisco alla fortuna o providenzia, secondo il motto suo; e detta invenzione fu prima mia, dipoi conferitola col s(igno)re Gonzalo Per(e)s mio s(igno)re e buono amico, parendoli buona invenzione, s'è afaticato in farli l'anima e parte del corpo con il consiglio di molti litterati di questa Corte, et cosi l'ò missa in opera." Portion of a letter of Gian Paolo Poggini to King Philip II, February 28, 1562, transcribed in George Kubler, "A medal by G. P. Poggini depicting Peru and predicting Australia," *Mitteilungen des Kunsthistorischen Institutes in Florenz* 11 (1964), pp. 149–52, at p. 149. On the medal, see also the entry of Philip Attwood in *The Currency of Fame: Portrait Medals of the Renaissance*, ed. Stephen K. Scher (New York: Abrams/Frick Collection, 1994), pp. 166–67.

38. Acosta, *De procuranda indorum salute*, vol. 1, p. 196: "Neque enim de ipsa gente indorum plurimum excidit solum, verum etiam terrae ipsius effusae inarescere auri argentique proventus minus, omnia vitae subsidia lapsa referri videntur, sententia omnium una et voce conquerentium sese res indicas veluti deploratas putare a pristina felicitate delapsas."

THIRTEEN — THE BIBLICAL NEW WORLD

1. Because this passage will be referred to throughout the following discussion, here it is in full: "Entrasi di poi nel mese di marzo alli 3 di cui s'appresentò al pontefice frate Domenico spagnuolo dell' ordine dei predicatori, che venea dalle Nuove indie ovvero dal Mundo Nuovo, come se diceva, et presentogli molte cose d'indi portate. Et tra l'altra due coperte da letto fatte et tessute di pene di papagalli di diversi colori, cioè azuri, verdo, negro, giale talmente lavorate che pareano di veluto. Onde parvi di conoscere quel che habbiano nella scrittura descrivendo l' apparato del tabernacolo de Iddio ove comandava che opere plumario se dovesse ornare. Poscia vi diede stolle, manipuli et granite da camice fatte similmente et degnamente lavorate di dette penne, con altri ornamenti da sacerdoti. Anche li presentò alcuni libri molto ben dipinti che pareano figure hieroglifici, per le quali intendevansi fra loro, come noi faciamo per le lettere. Poscia li diede alcune maschere molto grosse fornite di torchine, per le quali diceva parlavano li demoni a quei popoli. Poi un cortelo di pietra giala largo due dita et lungo da due onze, col manico tutto coperto di torchini. Poi alquanti coltelli di pietra che tagliavano come rasori, per li quali si radevano. Et per tali coltelli, se conobbe di che sorte fussero quelli coltelli deli quali parla la Bibbia quando dice il signore 'Fami li coltelli di pietra da circoncidere.' Altresì presentoli un pezzo di finissimo alabastro lavorato a simiglianza di un piccolo monte sopra lo quale era posto una croce alta circa un mezzo piede di calcidonio d'un pezzo molto bella e ben lavorata, con alquanti pezzi di calcidonio in quella posti per ornamento. Molte altre cose simili vi presentò, che il pontefice n' ebbe molto piacere con li circostanti. Dela quale cose io ne hebbe alcuni libri, coltelli, co'il coltello grande co il quale uccidevano gli huomini facendone sagrificio alli suoi idoli, lo quale io diedi con un libro et con un cortelo di pietra a simiglianza di rasorio a meser Giovanni Achilino per ornamento del suo studio." Leandro Alberti, *Historie di Bologna, 1479–1543* (Bologna: Costa Editore, 2006), pp. 629–30. We have mostly followed the translation by

Davide Domenici and Laura Laurencich Minelli, "Domingo de Betanzos' Gifts to Pope Clement VII in 1532–1533: Tracking the Early History of Some Mexican Objects and Codices in Italy," *Estudios de Cultura Náhuatl* 47 (2014), pp. 169–209, at pp. 171–72. See also the discussion in Davide Domenici, "Missionary Gift Records of Mexican Objects in Early Modern Italy," in *The New World in Early Modern Italy, 1492–1750*, ed. Elizabeth Horodowich and Lia Markey (New York: Cambridge University Press, 2017), pp. 86–102, at pp. 89–90.

2. Lia Markey, *Imagining the Americas in Medici Florence* (University Park: Penn State University Press, 2016), p. 14. See also Sara Ciruzzi, "Gli antichi oggetti americani nelle collezioni del Museo Nazionale di Antropologia ed Etnologia," *Archivio per l'Antropologia e l'Etnologia* 113 (1983), pp. 151–65, and Laura Laurencich Minelli, "I due antichi *atlatl* messicani del Museo Nazionale di Antropologia ed Etnologia di Firenze," *Archivio per l'Antropologia e l'Etnologia* 123 (1993), pp. 391–404.

3. "Onde parvi di conoscere quel che habbiano nella scrittura descrivendo l'apparato del tabernacolo de Iddio over comandava che opere plumario se dovesse ornare." Alberti, *Historie di Bologna*, pp. 629–30.

4. Both the Las Casas and the Muñoz Camargo texts are cited and discussed by Alessandra Russo, "A Contemporary Art from New Spain," in *Images Take Flight: Feather Art in Mexico and Europe, 1400–1700*, eds. Alessandra Russo, Gerhard Wolf, and Diana Fane (Munich: Hirmer Publishers, 2016), pp. 37–41. Our translation of the Diego Muñoz Camargo passage is based on Russo's, with minor emendations. See Bartolomé de Las Casas, *Apologética historia sumaria*, ed. Edmundo O'Gorman (Mexico City: Universidad Nacional Autónoma de México/Instituto de Investigaciones Históricas, 1967), book 3, chap. 62, p. 325, and Diego Muñoz Camargo, *Descripción de Tlaxcala*, ed. René Acuña (San Luis Potosí: Gobierno del Estado de Tlaxcala, 2000), pp. 128–29.

5. *Descrittione dell'India occidentale* (Venice, c. 1556), cited in Domenici, "Missionary Gift Records of Mexican Objects in Early Modern Italy," p. 93.

6. Albrecht Dürer, *The Writings of Albrecht Dürer*, ed. Martin Conway (New York: Philosophical Library, 1958), p. 101.

7. "Ad orientem igitur proras uertens ophyram insulam," "Insula haec hispaniola quam ipse ophiram, de qua legitur regum tertio." *Selections from Peter Martyr*, ed. Geoffrey Eatough, Repertorium Columbianum 5 (Turnhout: Brepols, 1998), pp. 131 (Decade 1.1.5) and 146 (Decade 1.3.1).

8. Flavius Josephus, *Antiquities of the Jews*, book 8, chap. 6:4: "Moreover, the king [Solomon] built many ships in the Egyptian Bay of the Red Sea.... That they should go along with his own stewards to the land that was of old called Ophir, but now the Aurea Chersonesus, which belongs to India, to fetch him gold. And when they had gathered four hundred talents together, they returned to the king again."

9. Franciscus Monachus, *De orbis situ* (Antwerp: 1527), n.p.: "I do not wish it to be believed that Solomon sent to this island the fleet which he sent into the east in the duty of gathering gold for the jewel of the temple of Jerusalem, for I have said that this Ophira is a harbor on the shores of Ethiopia, around the torrid region and the kingdom of the Melindari, in this indeed place there is a huge abundance of gold, and it is understood that the Lusitani arrived at a port there called Opim by the Indians, which we would have called Ophira in the Greek tongue, not inelegantly. Indeed, reason convinces us that we should think Solomon sought gold from here, rather than from Hispaniola" ("Propterea tamen credi nolim Salomonem eam clas- / sem quam in orientem conuehendi auri gratia ad or- / namentu*m* phani Hierosolymitani misit, in hanc insula*m* de / stinasse, na*m* Ophira*m* illam portu*m* esse afferuerim [*sic*] in Aethio / piae ora circa zona*m* torrida*m* ac regnu*m* Melindaru*m*, eo eni*m* / loco ingens est auri copia, constatq*ue* Lusitanos portum il / lic inuenisse Opim ab indis vocatu*m*, Graeco eloquio Ophi / ram non inconcinne dixerimus, ratio enim persuadet vt / hinc potius auru*m* a Salomone petitu*m* existimemus quam / ab Hispaniola.")

10. See James Romm, "Biblical History and the Americas: The Legend of Solomon's Ophir, 1492–1591," in *The Jews*

and The Expansion of Europe to the West, 1450–1800, ed. Paolo Bernardini and Norman Fiering (New York: Oxford University Press, 2001), pp. 27–46.

11. See Giuliano Gliozzi, *Adamo e il Nuovo Mondo: La nascita dell'antropologia come ideologia coloniale: Dalle genealogie bibliche alle teorie razziali (1500–1700)* (Florence: La Nuova, 1977); Teresa Martínez Terán, *Los antipodas: El origen de los indios en la razón política del siglo XVI* (Puebla: Universidad Autónoma de Puebla, 2001); Antonello Gerbi, *Il mito del Perù*, ed. Sandro Gerbi (Milan: Franco Angeli, 1988), pp. 48–50; Giuseppe Marcocci, *Indios, cinesi, falsari: Le storie del mondo nel Rinascimento* (Bari: Laterza, 2016), chap. 2; Serge Gruzinski, *Les quatres parties du monde: Histoire d'une mondialisation* (Paris: Éditions de La Martinière, 2004), pp. 135–40. See also chapter 10 for English discussions about the origins of new world peoples.

12. The manuscript is now in the Biblioteca Provincial y Universitaria de Sevilla (Ms. 333). See Gliozzi, *Adamo e il Nuovo Mondo*, pp. 49–60.

13. See Florentino García Martínez, *Philology and Theology: Contributions to the Study of Ancient Jewish Interpretation* (Leiden: Brill, 2013), pp. 149–93.

14. Ibid., pp. 170–80.

15. Fray Diego Durán, *The History of the Indies of New Spain*, trans. Doris Heyden (Norman: University of Oklahoma Press, 1994), pp. 3–11, at p. 3.

16. Ibid., p. 10.

17. Fray Diego Durán, *Book of Gods and Rites and The Ancient Calendar*, trans. Fernando Horcasitas and Doris Heyden (Norman: University of Oklahoma Press, 1971), pp. 95–97.

18. Ibid., pp. 23–31.

19. See Erin Benay, *Italy by Way of India: Translating Art and Devotion in the Early Modern World* (Turnhout: Brepols/Harvey Miller, 2021), esp. chap. 1, pp. 29–33.

20. Durán, *Book of Gods and Rites*, pp. 57–69, at p. 59.

21. Ibid., p. 63.

22. Johannes Schöner, *Opusculum geographicum ex diversorum libris ac cartis* (Nuremberg: Johann Petreius, 1533), part 2, chap. 21, n.p. Schöner also labeled the southern tip of the South American continent as "S. Thome Terra" on his 1515 globe, even though he depicted this landmass as separate from Asia. Writing to Juan Bernal Díaz de Lugo on May 1, 1538, Fray Bernardo de Armencia offered evidence that Thomas the Apostle had been in Brazil, where he was known as Payçume, or Pay Thome. In 1549, Manuel de Nóbrega, a Jesuit missionary in Brazil, similarly claimed that Thomas the Apostle had preached in those lands. See Richard Trexler, *The Journey of the Magi: Meanings in History of a Christian Story* (Princeton, NJ: Princeton University Press, 1997), pp. 138–39, and Louis-André Vigneras, "Saint Thomas, Apostle of America," *Hispanic American Historical Review* 57 (1977), pp. 82–90. See also Grace Walsh, "Saint Thomas: Evangelist of the Indies," *Amerasia: An Inquiry into Early Modern Imaginative Geography*, http://www.ifaresearch.org/amerasia/#walsh-thomas. As we have seen in chapter 9, Jean de Léry, who traveled to Brazil in the mid-sixteenth century, believed that Saint Thomas had reached Brazil, and that the Americans were the descendants of Noah, most likely through his son Ham.

23. Durán, *The History of the Indies of New Spain*, p. 5.

24. Benitos Arias Montano expressed his views on the new world in his book *Phaleg, sive de gentium sedibus primis, orbisque terræ situ* (Antwerp: Christopher Plantin, 1572). See Jesúa Paniagua Pérez, "La vision del hombre American en Benito Arias Montano y Pedro de Valencia," in *El humanismo español, su proyección en América y Canarias en la época del humanismo*, ed. Antonio María Martín Rodríguez and Germán Santana Henríquez (Saragossa: Servicio de Publicaciones y Difusión Científica de la Universidad de Las Palmas de Gran Canaria, 2006), pp. 149–71.

25. Zur Shalev, "Sacred Geography, Antiquarianism, and Visual Erudition: Benito Arias Montano and the Maps in the Antwerp Polyglot Bible," *Imago Mundi* 55 (2010), pp. 56–80, at pp. 69–71. See also Gliozzi, *Adamo e il Nuovo Mondo*, pp. 150–53.

26. The lineage is Noah, Shem, Arphaxed, Salah, Eber, Joktan, Ophir.

27. Bernardino de Sahagún, *Conquest of New Spain*, trans. Howard F. Cline (Salt Lake City: University of Utah

Press, 1989), p. 28. See also, more broadly, Gliozzi, *Adamo e il Nuovo Mondo*, pp. 147–74.

28. Abraham Ortelius, *Synonymia geographica* (Antwerp: Plantin, 1578), p. 235; Anthony Grafton, *Joseph Scaliger: A Study in the History of Classical Scholarship*, 2 vols. (Oxford: Oxford University Press, 1983–93), vol. 2, p. 499.

29. José de Acosta, *Natural and Moral History of the Indies*, ed. Jane E. Mangan (Durham, NC: Duke University Press, 2002), for instance book 1, chap. 6, p. 27, where he clarifies these terms.

30. "The etymology of the word Ophir, and its reduction to the equivalent of Peru [remains] . . . unconvincing, for the fact is that the name Peru is not so very old, nor is it applied generally to all of this land. In the discoveries of the New World it has been a very common custom to name places and seaports according to circumstances upon arrival, and I believe that this is what happened with this realm of Peru. The belief here is that at the beginning of the discovery by the Spaniards a river, called Piru by the natives, gave rise to the name Peru for the whole land, and it argues in favor of this, that the Indians, natives of Peru, neither use nor know this name for their country," Ibid., book 1, chap. 13, p. 45.

31. Ibid., book 1, chap. 13, p. 46.

32. Ibid., book 1, chap. 23, p. 70.

33. Ibid., book 4, chap. 16, p. 200; book 4, chap. 21, p. 208; book 4, chap. 17, p. 202.

34. Ibid., book 4, chap. 23, p. 213.

35. Ibid., book 5, chap. 3, p. 256.

36. See Fra Gregorio García, *Origen de los indios de el Nuevo Mundo* (Valencia: Pedro Patricio Mey, 1607, and Madrid: Francisco Martinez Abad, 1729). On Purchas, see chapter 10.

37. See Surekha Davies, *Renaissance Ethnography and the Invention of the Human: New Worlds, Maps, and Monsters* (New York: Cambridge University Press, 2016), p. 293. For similar discussions that persisted into the eighteenth and nineteenth centuries, see our epilogue.

38. Acosta, *Natural and Moral History*, book 1, chap. 20, pp. 63–64.

39. John F. Hoffecker and Scott A. Elias, *Human Ecology of Beringia* (New York: Columbia University Press, 2007), p. 3.

40. Mikkel Pederson, Anthony Ruder, Charles Schweger, et al., "Postglacial Viability and Colonization in North America's Ice-free Corridor," *Nature* 537 (2016), pp. 45–49.

41. Bernabé Cobo, *History of the Inca Empire: An Account of the Indians' Customs and Their Origin Together with a Treatise on Inca Legends, History, and Social Institutions*, ed. and trans. Roland Hamilton (Austin: University of Texas Press, 1979), book 1, chaps. 11–12, pp. 47–66.

42. Joseph-François Lafitau, *Customs of the American Indians Compared with the Customs of Primitive Tribes*, trans. William N. Fenton and Elizabeth L. Moore, 2 vols. (Toronto: The Champlain Society, 1974), vol. 1, pp. 25–87, at pp. 49 and 80. On Lafitau's Amerasian ideas, see also chapter 9.

43. Alexander von Humboldt, *Vues des cordillères et monumens des peuples indigènes de l'Amérique* (Paris: Schoell, 1810), pp. 84–85. We quote the English translation, *Views of the Cordilleras and Monuments of the Indigenous Peoples of the Americas: A Critical Edition*, ed. Vera M. Kutzinski and Ottmar Ette (Chicago: University of Chicago Press, 2012), p. 103: "The Mexica's cosmogony—their beliefs regarding the mother of men, fallen from her original state of bliss and innocence; the idea of a great flood, in which a single family escaped on a raft; the story of a pyramidal structure raised by men's pride and destroyed by the Gods' wrath; the ablution ceremonies performed at the birth of children; the idols made of molded corn flour and distributed in lots to the people gathered within the temple walls; the penitents' confessions of their sins; the religious associations resembling our monasteries and convents; the universally held belief that white men with long beards and saintly morals had changed the peoples' religious and political system—all these circumstances had caused the monks, who accompanied the Spanish army during the conquest, to believe that Christianity had been preached in the new continent at some very remote time. Some Mexican scholars thought they detected the apostle St. Thomas in the

high priest of Tula, that mysterious character whom the Cholulans know by the name of Quetzalcoatl. There is no question that Nestorianism, blended with the dogmas of the Buddhists and the Shamans, spread through the Tartary of the Manchu into northeast Asia. One might thus assume, with some justification, that Christian ideas were communicated via the same route to the Mexica peoples, especially to the inhabitants of that northerly region from which the Toltec emerged, and which we must consider as the officina virorum [smithy of men] of the new world."

FOURTEEN — AMERASIAN HIEROGLYPHICS

1. This description draws on Ferdinand Anders et al., *Calendario de pronósticos y ofrendas: Libro explicativo del llamado Códice Cospi* (Mexico City: Fondo de Cultura Económica, 1994), pp. 123–265, as well as the summary by Davide Domenici, "The Codex Cospi," *Aztecs at Mexicolore*, https://www.mexicolore.co.uk/aztecs/writing/the-codex-cospi.

2. Published under an anagram of his name: Aurelio degli Anzi, *Il genio vagante* (Parma: Rosati, 1691–93). See Paulina Spiechowicz, "*Il genio vagante*: Valerio Zani nell'ambito dell'Accademia dei Gelati," in *Crocevia e capitale della migrazione artistica, forestieri a Bologna e bolognesi nel mondo (XVI–XVII secolo)*, ed. Sabine Frommel and Gian Mario Anselmi (Bologna: Bononia University Press, 2012), pp. 21–32.

3. "Libro venuto dalla China, con varij geroglifici." Lorenzo Legati, *Breue descrizione del museo dell'illustriss. sig. cau. commend. dell'Ordine di S. Stefano Ferdinando Cospi . . . donato dal medesimo all'illustriss. senato, & ora annesso al famoso cimeliarchio del celebre Aldrouandi* (Bologna: Ferroni, 1667), p. 38, and "Contiene questo libro non altro che geroglifici del messico." Lorenzo Legati, *Museo Cospiano annesso a quello del famoso Ulisse Aldrovandi e donato alla sua patria dall'illustrissimo signor Ferdinando Cospi* (Bologna: Giacomo Monti, 1677), p. 19.

4. "Codex iste Hieroglyphicorum Indiae Meridionalis dono missus fuit Clementi VII Pontifici ab Emanuele Lusitaniae rege cum tintinnabulis aliquot Indicis et stragula ex plumis psitacorum contexta . . . [This hieroglyphic book from Southern India was presented by Manuel King of Portugal to Pope Clement VII, together with little bells, likewise from India, and a coverlet made from parrot feathers . . .]" Lauran Toorians, "Codex Vindobonensis Mexicanus: I, its History Completed," *Codices manuscripti* 10 (1984), pp. 87–97, at p. 88.

5. "Ein buech das hinten and vornen aufgeht mit allerlei Indianischen figuren, der Hyerogliphischen schrift nit vngleich." Lauran Toorians, "Some Light in the Dark Century of Codex Vindobonensis Mexicanus I," *Codices manuscripti* 9 (1983), pp. 26–29, at p. 26.

6. "Viveno questi delle prefate insule di pan, fatto di frumento di India, et di carne; beveno una potione simile alla cervosa; non hanno carattere di lettere, ma scriveno qualche cosa più necessaria con figure di animali o ver altro, al modo che anticamente usavano Egytii, ben che questi loro caratteri non li serveno in ogni cosa." Letter of Gasparo Contarini to Doge Andrea Grimani from Valladolid, September 24, 1522. *Italian Reports on America 1493–1522: Accounts by Contemporary Observers*, ed. Luciano Formisano and Geoffrey Symcox, Repertorium Columbianum 12 (Turnhout: Brepols, 2002), pp. 136–38, at p. 137. He also reports on Magellan's just accomplished circumnavigation of the globe, strongly suggesting that Asia is now accessible by continuing to sail westward beyond these "islands" (as he repeatedly calls them) of the new world.

7. "Vidi ego his proximis annis Bononiae . . . librum ex India advectum, tygridis pelle coopertum, in quo variae hominum (et si bene memini) aliarum quoque rerum, ac animalium figurae tantum depictae erant. Et in circuitu seu limbo, ac illarum figurarum peripheria, notae quaedam, quas ego literas omnino existimavit, et si vir ille, alioque nobilis, libelli copiam ad horas non negasset, proculdubio Alphabetum exscripsissem. . . . " Teseo Ambrogio degli Albonesi, *Introductio in Chaldaicam linguam, Syriacam atque Armenicam et decem alias linguas . . .* (Cremona, 1539), c. 198r. See Laura Laurencich-Minelli, "From the New World to Bologna, 1533: A Gift for Pope Clement VII and

Bolognese Collections of the Sixteenth and Seventeenth Centuries," *Journal of the History of Collections* 24 (2012), pp. 145–58, and Massimo Donattini, "Il mondo portato a Bologna: Viaggiatori, collezionisti, missionari," in *Storia di Bologna*, vol. 3, *Bologna nell'età moderna (secoli XVI–XVIII)*, ed. Adriano Prosperi (Bologna: Bononia University Press, 2008), pp. 577–78, who proposes that the object Ambrogio examined was the Cospi Codex. Paolo Giovio, *La seconda parte dell'historie del suo tempo* (Venice: Cesano, 1552), p. 395, also refers in the context of a discussion of Cortés's conquests to "le figure hieroglíphici, con le quali solevano scrivere historie, e con diverse pitture far memoria de i Re loro. Donommi un volume di queste historie fatto di fogli tutti interi, ma piegati indietro, et coperto d'un cuoio indanaiato di tigre, il molto illustre S. Francesco Covos, segretario dell'imperatore."

8. Paolo Giovio, *Seconda parte dell'istorie* (Venice: Domenico de'Farri, 1556), p. 394; Paolo Giovio, *Historiae sui temporis* (Florence: Lorenzo Torrentino, 1551–53), part 2, p. 553. In the Codex Ríos, discussed later, folio 24r shows the sons of Patecatle and Mayaguil (Mayahuel), one described as *Aquila* and the other as *Tigre*, though he is wearing a jaguar skin: https://pueblosoriginarios.com/meso/valle/azteca/codices/rios/rios.html. The always careful new world naturalist Gonzalo Fernández de Oviedo was perplexed by the American tiger, going back and forth on the question of whether this is an adapted form of tiger or in fact a different animal. See Gonzalo Fernández de Oviedo, *Sumario de la Natural Historia de la Indias* (1526), ed. Manuel Ballesteros Gaibrois (Madrid: Historia 16, 1986), chap. 9, pp. 94–95: "Mi fin es decir que este animal podría ser tigre, y no de la ligereza de los tigres de quien Plinio y otros autores hablan." See also Antonello Gerbi, *Nature in the New World: From Christopher Columbus to Gonzalo Fernández de Oviedo* (Pittsburgh: University of Pittsburgh Press, 1985), p. 303.

9. *Vocabolario dell'Accademia della Crusca* (Venice: Alberti, 1612), s.v. "Addanaiato/Indanaiato," p. 18.

10. Leandro Alberti, *Historie di Bologna* (Bologna: Bonardo & Grosso, 1541–48), in two volumes: see the edition by A. Antonelli and M. R. Musti (Bologna: Costa, 2006), pp. 629–30: "Entrasi di poi nel mese di marzo alli di cui s'appresentò al pontefice frate Domenico spagnuolo dell'ordine dei predicatori, che venea dalle Nuove indie ovvero dal Mundo Nuovo, come se diceva, et presentogli molte cose d'indi portate. . . . Anche li presentò alcuni libri molto ben dipinti che pareano figure hieroglifici, per le quali intendevansi fra loro, come noi faciamo per le lettere." See the discussion of this and other passages by Laura Laurencich-Minelli, "From the New World to Bologna." The Dominican friar who brought the gifts to Clement, mentioned by Alberti, has been convincingly identified as Domingo de Betanzos by Davide Domenici and Laurencich-Minelli, "Domingo de Betanzos' Gifts to Pope Clement VII in 1532–1533: Tracking the Early History of Some Mexican Objects and Codices in Italy," *Estudios de Cultural Náhuatl* 47 (2014), pp. 169–209.

11. As Daniela Bleichmar notes in "Painting the Aztec Past in Early Colonial Mexico: Translation and Knowledge Production in the Codex Mendoza," *Renaissance Quarterly* 72 (2019), pp. 1362–1415, at p. 1369; the Codex Mendoza was described from the beginning as a "Mexican History."

12. See Massimo Donattini, "Bolognese Franciscan Missionaries in the New World," in *The New World in Early Modern Italy, 1492–1750*, ed. Elizabeth Horodowich and Lia Markey (New York: Cambridge University Press, 2017), pp. 63–85, at pp. 69–70.

13. See Brian Curran, "*De sacrarum litterarum aegyptiorum interpretatione:* Reticence and Hubris in Hieroglyphic Studies in the Renaissance—Pierio Valeriano and Annius of Viterbo," in *Memoirs of the American Academy in Rome* 43–44 (1998–99), pp. 139–82.

14. Don Cameron Allen, *Mysteriously Meant: The Rediscovery of Pagan Symbolism and Allegorical Interpretation in the Renaissance* (1971; Baltimore, MD: Johns Hopkins University Press, 2020), chap. 5.

15. See Margit Kern, *Transkulturelle Imaginationen des Opfers in der Frühen Neuzeit: Übersetzungsprozesse zwischen Mexiko und Europa* (Berlin: Deutscher Kunstverlag, 2013), pp. 76–99, translated as "Pictorial Theories by Missionaries in Sixteenth-century New Spain: the Capacities of

Hieroglyphs as Media in Transcultural Negotiation," *Art in Translation* 8 (2016), pp. 283–313.

16. Serge Gruzinski, *The Eagle and the Dragon: Globalization and European Dreams of Conquest in China and America in the Sixteenth Century* (Cambridge: Polity, 2014), pp. 48–59, and Byron Hamann, "How Maya Hieroglyphs Got Their Name: Egypt, Mexico, and China in Western Grammatology since the Fifteenth Century," *Proceedings of the American Philosophical Society* 152 (2008), pp. 1–68.

17. "Ninguna nación de indios que se ha descubierto en nuestros tiempos usa de letras ni de escritura sino de las otras dos maneras, que son imágenes o figuras; y entiendo esto no sólo de los indios del Perú y de los de Nueva España, sino en parte también de los japones y chinas." José de Acosta, *Historia natural y moral de las Indias*, ed. Fermín del Pino-Díaz (Madrid: Consejo Superior de Investigaciones Científicas, 2008), book 6, chap. 4, p. 206. The following six chapters of Acosta's treatise develop an extensive comparison between Asian and American written language forms. On the somewhat unusual place of Peruvian quipus in Acosta's thinking and for a helpful review of Acosta's thinking on Asian and American language systems, see Ana Carolina Hosne, "Assessing Indigenous Forms of Writing: José de Acosta's View of Andean Quipus in Contrast with Chinese 'Letters'," *Journal of Jesuit Studies* 1 (2014), pp. 177–91.

18. José de Acosta, *Natural and Moral History of the Indies*, ed. Jane E. Mangan, trans. Frances Lopez-Morillas (Durham, NC: Duke University Press, 2002), p. 284 n.1.

19. Athanasius Kircher, *Oedipus Aegyptiacus* (Rome: Vitale Mascardi, 1652–54), vol. 1, tome 3, *Theatrum Hieroglyphicum*, chap. 2, p. 10: "Et his prae reliquis Orbis terrarum gentibus, tres usas esse Nationes constat, videlicet Sinenses, Brachmanes, & Mexicanos." After this passage, on pp. 28–36, Kircher specifies that Mexican hieroglyphs are in fact far from the Egyptian, in that they represent things in the world and events in history, not an arcane knowledge—and he leveled a similar charge against the everyday use of Chinese characters. See Kern, *Transkulturelle Imaginationen des Opfers*, p. 83.

20. Athanasius Kircher, *Prodromus Coptus* (Rome: Propaganda Fide, 1636), p. 121. For this translation and further commentary, see Daniel Stolzenberg, *Egyptian Oedipus: Athanasius Kircher and the Secrets of Antiquity* (Chicago: University of Chicago Press, 2013), p. 95.

21. Acosta, *Historia Natural y Moral*, book 1, chaps. 10–14.

22. Lorenzo Pignoria, *Discorso intorno le deita dell' Indie Orientali & Occidentali con le loro figure tratte da gl' originali che si conservano nelle gallerie de' Principi & ne' musei delle persone private, Appendix to Vincenzo Cartari, Imagini delli Dei de gl'Antichi* (Padua: Tozzi, 1615). In this chapter, the 1647 edition will be cited: Lorenzo Pignoria, "Aggionta all'Imagini del Cartari," in Vincenzo Cartari, *Imagini delli Dei de gl'Antichi* (Venice: Tomasini, 1647). An important early study of Pignoria's treatise is Jean Seznec, "Un essai de mythologie comparée au début du XVIIe siècle," *Mélanges d'Archéologie et d'Histoire* 48 (1931), pp. 268–81. More recently, see Sabine MacCormack, "Limits of Understanding: Perceptions of Greco-Roman and Amerindian Paganism in Early Modern Europe," in *America in European Consciousness, 1493–1750*, ed. Karen Ordahl Kupperman (Chapel Hill: University of North Carolina Press, 1995), pp. 79–129, at pp. 87–93; Edgar Lein, "Imagini degli dei Indiani: La representación de las divinidades indianas por Vincenzo Cartari," in *Herencias indígenas, tradiciones europeas y la mirada europea*, ed. Helga von Kügelgen (Madrid: Iberoamericana Editorial Vervuert, 2002), pp. 225–58; Barbara Anderson, *Biblioteca Angelica ms. 1551 and the Origins of Ethnohistorical Illustration of Asia and the Americas around 1600 in Rome* (New York: American Philosophical Society, 2020), pp. 3–24; Sonia Maffei, "Cartari e gli dèi del mondo nuovo: Il trattatello sulle 'Imagini de gli dei indiani' di Lorenzo Pignoria," in *Cartari e le direzioni del Mito nel Cinquecento*, ed. Sonia Maffei (Rome: GBE, 2013), pp. 62–119; Maffei, *La riscoperta dell'esotismo nel Seicento: Le imagini de gli dei Indiani di Lorenzo Pignoria* (Pisa: Edizione della Normale, 2020); Sergio Botta, "Incorporating Mesoamerican Cosmology within a Global History of Religion: Some Considerations on the Work of Lorenzo Pignoria," in *Reshaping the World: Debates on Mesoamerican Colonial Cosmologies* (Boulder:

University of Colorado Press, 2020), pp. 70–99; and Paolo von Wyss-Giacosa, "Through the Eyes of Idolatry: Pignoria's 1615 Argument on the *Conformità* of Idols from the West and East Indies with Egyptian Gods," in *Through Your Eyes Religious Alterity and the Early Modern Western Imagination*, ed. Giovanni Tarantino and Paola von Wyss-Giacosa (Leiden: Brill, 2021), pp. 103–44. Thanks to Shannah Rose for the last two references.

23. On the Codex Ríos, see Ferdinand Anders, Maarten Jansen, and Luis Reyes García, *Religión, costumbres e historia de los angiquos mexicanos: Libro explicativo del llamado Códice Vaticano A, Codex Vatic. Lat. 3738 de la Biblioteca Vaticana* (Graz: Akademishe Druck-und Verlagsanstalt, and Mexico City: Fondo de Cultura Económica, 1996), and Eloise Quiñones Keber, "Collecting Cultures: A Mexican Manuscript in the Vatican Library," in *Reframing the Renaissance: Visual Culture in Europe and Latin America 1450–1650*, ed. Clare Farago (New Haven, CT: Yale University Press, 1995), pp. 229–42. Anderson, Biblioteca Angelica ms. 1551, pp. 15–17, proposes that though the images of the Codex Ríos were made in the 1560s, the text, which wraps around the images in such a way that suggests that it was not intended from the beginning, came later, and suggests that these commentaries were provided by José de Acosta and Alfonso Chacón during one of Acosta's stays in Rome, either in 1588 or in 1592–94.

24. Pignoria, "Aggionta all'Imagini del Cartari," p. 370.

25. "Et in somma per tutto questo che chiamano novo Mondo, tanto nell'Occidente quanto nell'Oriente, io ho avertito tanta la conformità frà le superstitioni Egittiane & et quelle del Paese, che ho avuto à maraviglarmi alcune volte." Ibid., p. 376.

26. Maffei independently arrived at this fact; *La riscoperta dell'esotismo nel Seicento*, p. 267.

27. Maffei, "Cartari e gli dèi del Nuovo Mondo," understood Angelica ms. 1551 to be a copy after Pignoria's treatise, a view confirmed in *La riscoperta dell'esotismo nel Seicento*, pp. 346–48. Since the manuscript includes all the figures from the 1615 edition (with the exception of three out of the four pairs of seated spouse gods, perhaps considered redundant) but does not include the figures added by Pignoria in his 1626 edition, Maffei proposed a date in the range 1615–26. Earlier, Peter Mason, *The Lives of Images* (London: Reaktion Books, 2004), p. 132, considered the Angelica manuscript to be preparatory to Pignoria's treatise. More recently, Anderson, *Biblioteca Angelica ms. 1551*, pp. 3–24, has also presented it as a manuscript made in preparation for Pignoria, proposing that the Angelica manuscript was made in the years around 1590 in Rome in the circle of the Spanish Dominican scholar Alfonso Chacón. The misunderstanding of an Egyptian figure as Mexican, discussed later in this chapter, offers the most decisive evidence in favor of Maffei's view that it copies rather than prepares the images from Pignoria's first edition of 1615.

28. This is the clearest proof that the Angelica MS 1551 is a copy after Pignoria rather than having been made in preparation for the publication. The Egyptian figure reproduced by Pignoria is from the so-called Mensa Isiaca, a Roman first-century inlaid bronze tablet in Egyptian style then in Mantua; there is no way Pignoria could have been confused about it, since he had written an extensive treatise on it in 1605: *Mensa Isiaca, qua sacrorum apud Aegyptios ratio & simulacra subjectis tabulis aeneis simul exhibentur & explicantur* (Amsterdam: Fries, 1605). An artist working for him to prepare this suite would not have made this error—mistaking the Egyptian comparandum for the American idol—since the Egyptian figure used here is in fact drawn from an illustration in Pignoria's own 1605 treatise. By contrast, there is every reason to imagine a copyist after Pignoria being fooled by the fact that in this one instance Pignoria switched the functions of the marginal figure and the main figure, putting the Egyptian figure in the main field and the "Mexican" figure in the margin. This lapse in the Angelica manuscript was also observed by Maffei, *La riscoperta dell'esotismo nel Seicento*, p. 347.

29. Donald F. Lach, *Asia in the Making of Europe* (Chicago: University of Chicago Press, 1965), vol. 1, book 2, p. 697.

30. The knives continued to be seen as Orientalia as late as the archeologist Filippo Schissi's 1814 guide to the newly

founded Museum of Antiquities at the University of Bologna; Filippo Schiassi, *Guida del Forastero al Museo delle Antichità della Regia Università di Bologna* (Bologna: Lucchesini, 1814), pp. 140–41, describes the two mosaic handles as "due sfingi di musaico di lavoro barbaro," locating them in Room VI in the third cabinet containing "cose della China, del Giappone e d'altre parti orientali," despite the fact that American items were presented in the second and fourth cabinets. A mosaic mask probably of the Mixtec god Yacatecuhtli from the Aldrovandi collection (also now in the Museo della Civiltà in Rome), is described by Schiasso as "una maschera di legno intarsiata di materie colorite di lavoro barbaro" and is also placed in the third cabinet with the *Orientalia*. See Davide Domenici, "Rediscovery of a Mesoamerican Greenstone Sculpture from the Collection of Ulisse Aldrovandi," *Journal of the History of Collections* 34 (2022).

31. Ole Worm, *Museum Wormianum* (Amsterdam: Elzevier, 1655), pp. 381–85.

32. Peter Lambeck, *Commentariorum de Augustissima Bibliotheca Caesarea Vindobonensi* (Vienna: Cosmoverius, 1679), vol. 8, p. 660.

33. Vienna, Weltmuseum, MVK 12660. The connection was established by Christian Feest, "'*Zemes idolum diabolicum*': Surprise and Success in Ethnographic Kunstkammer Research," *Archiv für Völkerkunde* 40 (1986), pp. 181–98. On *zemis*, see Serge Gruzinski, *Images at War: Mexico from Columbus to Blade Runner (1492–2019)* (Durham, NC: University of North Carolina Press, 2001), pp. 10–18; Alessandra Russo, "These [Statues] They Generally Called Çemi': A New Object at the Crossroad of Languages,'" in *The Challenge of the Object. Proceedings of the 33rd Congress of the International Committee of the History of Art (Die Herausforderung des Objekts): Akten des 33: Internationalen Kunsthistorikerkongresses*, 4 vols., eds. Ulrich Großmann and Petra Krutisch (Nuremberg: Germanisches Nationalmuseum 2013), vol. 1, pp. 77–81; and Sergio Botta, "La ausencia de los dioses taínos: Sobre el fracaso hermenéutico de la obra de Ramón Pané," *Latinoamérica: Revista de estudios Latinoamericanos* 57 (2013), pp. 161–87.

34. Honorius Philoponus (Caspar Klautz), *Nova typis transacta navigatio: Novi orbis Indiae occidentalis* (Linz: n.p., 1621), p. 49; translation from Feest, "'*Zemes idolum diabolicum*,'" p. 183.

35. Detlef Heikamp and Ferdinand Anders, "Mexikanische Altertümer aus süddeutschen Kunstkammern," *Pantheon* 28 (1970), pp. 205–20, at p. 206. And see Christian Feest, "The Collecting of American Indian Artifacts in Europe, 1493–1750," in Kupperman, *America in European Consciousness 1493–1750*, pp. 324–60, , at p. 335. See also Christine Göttler's thoughtful essay on the European reception of *kris* handles and related objects in this period: "Extraordinary Things: 'Idols from India' and the Visual Discernment of Space and Time, circa 1600," in *The Nomadic Object: The Challenge of World for Early Modern Religious Art*, ed. Christine Göttler and Mia Mochizuki (Cambridge: Cambridge University Press, 2017), pp. 37–73.

36. Pignoria, "Aggionta all'Imagini del Cartari," p. 397.

FIFTEEN — FIGURING THE WORLD I

1. See *Renaissance Invention: Stradanus's* Nova Reperta, ed. Lia Markey (Evanston, IL: Northwestern University Press, 2020), with previous bibliography.

2. From a vast literature, Michel de Certeau, *The Writing of History*, trans. Tom Conley (New York: Columbia University Press, 1992), pp. xxv–xxvii; Peter Hulme, *Colonial Encounters: Europe and the Native Caribbean, 1492–1797* (London: Methuen, 1986), pp. 1–12; José Rabasa, *Inventing America: Spanish Historiography and the Formation of Eurocentrism* (Norman: University of Oklahoma Press, 1993), pp. 23–48; Lia Markey, *Imagining the Americas in Medici Florence* (University Park, PA: Penn State University Press, 2016), pp. 133–36; Stuart Lingo, "American Bodies, Aztec Feathers, and Artistic Invention in Sixteenth-Century Europe," in *Visualizing the Past in Italian Renaissance Art: Essays in Honor of Brian A. Curran*, ed. Jennifer Cochran Anderson and Douglas N. Dow (Leiden: Brill, 2021), pp. 184–212.

3. As noted by Lingo, "American Bodies, Aztec Feathers, and Artistic Invention in Sixteenth-Century Europe" p. 190.

4. Michael Gaudio, *Engraving the Savage: The New World and Techniques of Civilization* (Minneapolis: University of Minnesota Press, 2008), esp. pp. xiv–xvii.

5. Caroline Fowler, *Art of Paper: From the Holy Land to the Americas* (New Haven, CT: Yale University Press, 2019), esp. the introduction.

6. Two major studies from a vast literature are William Sherman, *Used Books: Marking Readers in Renaissance England* (Philadelphia: University of Pennsylvania Press, 2007), and David S. Areford, *The Viewer and the Printed Image in Late Medieval Europe* (Farnham, UK: Ashgate, 2010).

7. Suzanne Karr Schmidt with Kimberly Nicholas, *Altered and Adorned: Using Renaissance Prints in Daily Life* (New Haven, CT: Yale University Press, 2011), pp. 66–69 and 93–97.

8. See Lisa Pon, *A Printed Icon in Early Renaissance Italy: Forlì's Madonna of the Fire* (Cambridge: Cambridge University Press, 2015), pp. 39–79. The impact of printing technology on protocols of credibility is a recurrent theme of Christopher Wood's *Forgery, Replica, Fiction: Temporalities of German Renaissance Art* (Chicago: University of Chicago Press, 2008), esp. pp. 155–77 and 217–44.

9. Edward Wilson-Lee, *The Catalogue of Shipwrecked Books: Christopher Columbus, His Son, and the Quest to Build the World's Greatest Library* (New York: Scribner, 2019), and José María Pérez Fernández and Edward Wilson-Lee, *Hernando Colón's New World of Books: Towards a Cartography of Knowledge* (New Haven, CT: Yale University Press, 2021).

10. See Mark P. McDonald, "The System of Print Classification and Description in the Inventory," in *The Print Collection of Ferdinand Columbus, 1488–1539*, vol. 1, *History and Commentary* (London: British Museum Press, 2004), pp. 75–98.

11. "Y uno [yndyo] con ambas manos tyene un palo largo en que esta una sonbra y el caçibe con el yndex de la dextra casy toca al palo." Ibid., cat. 2795, p. 515. See also Mark P. McDonald, "Burgkmair's Woodcut Frieze of the Natives of Africa and India," *Print Quarterly* 20 (2003), pp. 227–44.

12. Franciscus Monachus, *De orbis situ ac descriptione* (Antwerp, probably 1529), n.p.

13. Karen Ordahl Kupperman, "Presentment of Civility: English Reading of American Self-Presentation in the Early Years of Colonization," *William and Mary Quarterly* 54 (1997), pp. 193–228, at pp. 198–202; Jill Burke, "Nakedness and Other Peoples: Rethinking the Italian Renaissance Nude," *Art History* 36 (2013), pp. 714–39, at p. 726, and *The Italian Renaissance Nude* (New Haven, CT: Yale University Press, 2018), pp. 35–37.

SIXTEEN — FIGURING THE WORLD II

1. William Cuningham, *The Cosmographical Glasse, Conteinyng the Pleasant Principles of Cosmographie, Geographie, Hydrographie, or Navigation* (London: Daij, 1559), p. 113. For a sense of the range of uses of the word *continent* in the period, both geographical and not geographical, see the *Oxford English Dictionary*, s.v. "Continent," from which some of the textual examples quoted here are drawn.

2. See Martin W. Lewis and Kären E. Wigen, *The Myth of Continents: A Critique of Metageography* (Berkeley: University of California Press, 1997), chap. 1, "The Architecture of Continents." The two-part division of the world with the Indies (corresponding to America) on one side and the old world of Europe, Africa, and Asia on the other, was anticipated by the sixteenth-century naturalist Gonzalo Fernández de Oviedo; see Antonelli Gerbi, *Nature in the New World: From Christopher Columbus to Gonzalo Fernández de Oviedo* (Pittsburgh: University of Pittsburgh Press, 1985), pp. 167 and 258.

3. In the large cartouche upper left: "Dicimus autem tres esse distinctas continentes, primam e cujus medio creatum multiplicatumque genus humanum in omnem undique terram disseminatum est, secundam quae nova India dicitur, tertiam quae meridiano cardini subjacet."

4. Abraham Ortelius, *Theatrum Orbis Terrarum, or The Theatre of the Whole World* (London: Officina Plantiniana, 1606), p. 1. On the title page, see Werner Waterschoot, "The title-page of Ortelius's *Theatrum Orbis Terrarum*," *Quaerendo* 9 (1979), pp. 43–68, and Elisabeth Neumann, "Imagining European Community on the Title Page of

Ortelius' *Theatrum Orbis Terrarum*," *Word & Image* 25 (2009), pp. 427–42.

5. Ortelius, *Theatrum Orbis Terrarum*, p. ix.

6. Wilcomb E. Washburn, "The Meaning of 'Discovery' in the Fifteenth and Sixteenth Centuries," *The American Historical Review* 68 (1962), pp. 1–21, at p. 2: "Not the smallest stumbling block to our understanding has been the development of a geographical organization of the world's land masses into 'continents.' The geographers of the eighteenth, nineteenth, and twentieth centuries never fully agreed on what should be called a continent and what an island or peninsula, but they did give prominence to the word 'continent' that it never had before."

7. "Continens dicitur omnis terra solida sive fixa, quae nec Insula nec Peninsula nec Isthmus est." *Cosmographievs liber Petri Apiani mathematici, iam denuo integritati restitutus per Gemmam Phrysium* (Antwerp: Biorckman, 1533), fol. XXIX.

8. Christoph Mauntel, Klaus Oschema, Jean-Charles Ducène, and Martin Hofmann, "Mapping Continents, Inhabited Quarters and The Four Seas: Divisions of the World and the Ordering of Spaces in Latin-Christian, Arabic-Islamic and Chinese Cartography in the Twelfth to Sixteenth Centuries—A Critical Survey and Analysis," *Journal of Transcultural Medieval Studies* 5 (2018), pp. 295–367.

9. Martin Waldseemüller, *Cosmographiae introdvctio: Cvm qvibvsdam geometriae ac astronomiae principiis . . .* (Saint-Dié: Lud, 1507), chap. 9, n.p.: "Hunc in modum terra iam quadripartita cognoscitur: & sunt tres primae partes continentes: quarta est insula."

10. See the indispensable essay by Carla Lois, "Isla vs. continente: Un ensayo de historia conceptual," *Revista de Geografía Norte Grande* 54 (2013), pp. 85–107. On "the absence of a medieval definition of the concept of 'continent,'" see Mauntel et al., "Mapping Continents," p. 326.

11. Ibid.

12. Pliny, *Natural History*, trans. John Bostock (London: Taylor and Francis, 1855), 2.68, p. 101: "this speck of a world (for the earth is no more in regard to the universe), this is the object, the seat of our glory—here we bear our honours, here we exercise our power, here we covet wealth, here we mortals create our disturbances, here we continually carry on our wars, aye, civil wars, even, and unpeople the earth by mutual slaughter. And not to dwell on public feuds, entered into by nations against each other, here it is that we drive away our neighbours, and enclose the land thus seized upon within our own fence; and yet the man who has most extended his boundary, and has expelled the inhabitants for ever so great a distance, after all, what mighty portion of the earth is he master of? And even when his avarice has been the most completely satisfied, what part of it can he take with him into the grave?" Abraham Ortelius quotes this passage at the very beginning of his 1570 *Theatrum Orbis Terrarum*, and it is partly quoted, like a title, over the so-called *Fool's Cap Map of the World* engraved after 1587 (and based on Ortelius's third *Typus Orbis Terrarum* of that date).

13. Isidore of Seville, *Etymologiae*, XIV, ii.

14. David Woodward: "Medieval 'mappaemundi,'" in *The History of Cartography 1: Cartography in Prehistoric, Ancient, and Medieval Europe and the Mediterranean*, eds. John Brian Harley and David Woodward (Chicago: University of Chicago Press, 1987), pp. 286–370, at pp. 334–35, and Jonathan T. Lanman, "The Religious Symbolism of the T in T-O Maps," *Cartographica* 18 (1981), pp. 18–22.

15. A procession and tournament held in 1571 in Vienna for the wedding of Archduke Charles II of Inner Austria to Maria of Bavaria included representations of the Four Parts of the World (not Continents) together with representations of the Four Seasons, the Four Countries of Europe with their Four Rivers, the Four Winds, etc. See Robert Lindell, "The Wedding of Archduke Charles and Maria of Bavaria in 1571," *Early Music* 18 (1990), pp. 253–69.

16. See Jasper van Putten's entry in *Prints and the Pursuit of Knowledge in Early Modern Europe*, ed. Susan Dackerman (Cambridge, MA: Harvard Art Museums, 2011), p. 246 n.84, for these details and the history of the map.

17. In a 1574 fresco cycle devoted to mapping the world at the Farnese Villa at Caprarola, the artist Giovanni de' Vecchi elaborated a new use of the four corners of a world

map by occupying them with the four parts of the earth. His forms are independent of Ortelius's frontispiece of 1570 and, exceptionally, not apparently based primarily on printed sources but rather on erudite antiquarian materials, namely ancient Roman coinage with representations of the parts of the world. See Elisa Antonietta Daniele, "Portraits of the World: The Four Continents at Palazzo Farnese in Caprarola—The Figurative Code, Sources and Comparisons," in *Bodies and Maps: Early Modern Personifications of the Continents*, ed. Maryanne Cline Horowitz and Louise Arizzoli (Leiden: Brill, 2021), pp. 191–214. This left the artist somewhat at loose ends with America, who is shown as the darkest of the four figures, accompanied by none of the attributes that Ortelius was to make ubiquitous (Amazon-huntress features, cannibalized body parts, feather headdress, etc.), but instead with bejeweled face, holding a cornucopia of gold coins, and accompanied by an East Asian cockatoo.

18. Jodocus Hondius, *Nova et exacta totius orbis terrarum descriptio geographica et hydrographica* (1608). Chet van Duzer inclines towards the second option. Chet van Duzer, "The Pre-History of the Personification of Continents on Maps: Earth, Ocean, and the Sons of Noah," in Horowitz and Arizzoli, eds., *Bodies and Maps*, pp. 101–29, at p. 122: "In fact there seem to be two personifications of America, one to the left and one to the right of the personification of Europe, both wearing feathers on their heads, and one probably intended to represent North America, and the other South America. Four of the personifications are based on those engraved by Adriaen Collaert in about 1585; the fifth seems to be Hondius's addition."

19. *The Language of Continent Allegories in Baroque Central Europe*, ed. Wolfgang Schmale, Marion Romberg, and Josef Köstlblauer (Stuttgart: Franz Steiner Verlag, 2017), p. 7. See also Clare le Corbeiller, "Miss America and Her Sisters: Personifications of the Four Parts of the World," *The Metropolitan Museum of Art Journal* 19 (1961), pp. 209–23; John Higham, "Indian Princess and Roman Goddess: The First Female Symbols of America," *Proceedings of the American Antiquarian Society* 100 (1990), pp. 45–79; Sabine Poeschel, "*Studien zur Ikonographie der Erdteile in der Kunst des 16.–18. Jahrhunderts* (Munich: Scaneg, 1985), pp. 1–90; Hugh Honour, *The New Golden Land: European Images of America from the Discoveries to the Present Time* (New York: Pantheon, 1975), chap. 4.

20. See Christopher Heuer, "Difference, Repetition, and Utopia: European Print's New Worlds," in *Crossing Cultures: Proceedings of the 31st International Congress of the History of Art, Melbourne, 13–18 January 2008* (Melbourne: Melbourne University Press, 2009), pp. 244–50, at p. 248, fig. 3. A related but not identical allegory of America found on a lead plaquette of about 1580 also shows a rhino in the background. It is possible that the rhino here is standing in for the American armadillo; the point remains that the armadillo was not clearly differentiated from the rhino, a melding typical of the larger Amerasian pattern. Here our reading differs from that of Peter Mason, *The Lives of Images* (London: Reaktion Books, 2003), pp. 85–86, who reads the rhino on this plaquette and other displaced animals, such as American turkeys that show up in mythological scenes, as floating images of foreignness, no longer connected to place.

21. Eike Bujok, "Der Aufzug der 'Königin Amerika' in Stuttgart: Das 'Mannliche und Ritterliche Thurnier unnd Ringrennen' zu Fastnacht 1599," *Tribus* 52 (2003), pp. 80–110. See also Sabine Hesse, "Die neue Welt in Stuttgart: Die Kunstkammer Herzog Friedrichs I. und der Aufzug zum Ringrennen am 25. Februar 1599," in *Hofkultur um 1600: die Hofmusik Herzog Friedrichs I. von Württemberg und ihr kulturelles Umfeld. Culture de cour vers 1600: La musique à la cour du duc Frédéric Ier de Wurtemberg et son contexte culturel*, ed. Joachim Kremer, Sönke Lorenz, and Peter Rückert (Ostfildern: Thorbecke, 2010), pp. 139–167.

22. See Honour, *New Golden Land*, p. 99; Peter Mason, *Before Disenchantment: Images of Exotic Animals and Plants in the Early Modern World* (Chicago: University of Chicago Press, 2009), p. 13 n.9; Robert Bauernfeind, "Die Ordnung der Dinge durch die Malerei: Jan van Kessels Münchner Erdteile-Zyklus," PhD thesis, University of Augsburg, 2015.

23. These dependencies on Linschoten were noted by Honour, *New Golden Land*, p. 99, and Bauernfeind,

"Ordnung der Dinge," pp. 94–95, who also notes, pp. 92–93, that several motifs in Kessel's *Africa* panel were also drawn from Linschoten.

24. Bauernfeind, "Ordnung der Dinge," p. 98 and fig. 32. See also Ivo Raband, *Vergängliche Kunst und Fortwährende Macht: Die* Blijde Inkomst *für Erzherzog Ernst von Österreich in Brüssel und Antwerpen, 1594* (Merzhausen: ad picturam, 2019), pp. 224–25.

25. See Marion Romberg, "Continent Allegories in the Baroque Age: A Database," *Journal 18 5* (2018), https://www.journal18.org/issue5/continent-allegories-in-the-baroque-age-a-database/.

26. See Ayesha Raqmachandran, *The Worldmakers: Global Imagining in Early Modern Europe* (Chicago: University of Chicago Press, 2015).

27. "Amazoine, ceo est la terre de Ffemynie ceo est le roialme ou y n'y ad qe femmes." Jean de Mandeville, *Le livre des merveilles du monde*, ed. Christiane Deluz (Paris: CNRS Éditions, 2000), p. 302.

28. *The Spanish Letter of Columbus to Luis de Sant'Angel, Escribano de Racion of the Kingdom of Aragon, dated 15 February 1493* (London: Quaritch, 1893), p. 17.

29. Garci Rodríguez de Montalvo, *Las sergas de Esplandián* (Burgos: Juan de Junta,1526), page facing p. cviii: "Sabed que ala diestra mano de las Indias ouo una Isla llamada California mucho llegada ala parte del paraiso terrenal la qual sue poblada de mugeres negras sin que algun uaro entre ellas ouiesse: que casi como las amazonas."

30. Juan Díaz, *Relacíon de la expedicíon de Juan de Grijalva*, in *Crónicas de la conquista de México*, ed. Agustin Yáñez (Mexico City: Universidad Nacional Autónoma, 1939), pp. 24–27.

31. See *Instrucciones de Diego Velázquez a Hernán Cortés*, October 23, 1518, in *Colección de documentos inéditos del Archivio de Indias* (Madrid, 1864–89), ser. 1, vol. 12pp. 225–46, and Hernán Cortés, *Letters from Mexico*, ed. Anthony Pagden (New Haven, CT: Yale University Press, 2001), pp. 298–300.

32. See Beatriz Pastor Bodmer, *The Armature of Conquest: Spanish Accounts of the Discovery of America, 1492–1589*, trans. Lydia Longstreth Hunt (Stanford, CA: Stanford University Press, 1992), p. 157.

33. Gaspar de Carvajal, *Descubrimiento del Río de las Amazonas* (Bogotá: Prensas de la Biblioteca Nacional, 1942), p. 11.

34. Gerbi, *Nature in the New World*, p. 285.

35. André Thevet, *Les Singularitez de la France Antartique, autrement nommée Amérique* (Paris: Héritiers de Maurice de la Porte, 1557), chap. 63: "Some might say that these are not real Amazons, but I believe they are, seeing that they live just as the ones in Asia did."

36. Sir Walter Ralegh, *The Discovery of the Large, Rich, and Beautiful Empire of Guiana* (London: Robert Robinson, 1596), p. 23.

SEVENTEEN — NACREOUS AMERASIA

1. In virtually all the literature on this *enconchado*, the subject is identified as Saint Francis Xavier departing for Asia. See, for example, Clara Bargellini, "Saint Francis Xavier Embarking for Asia," in *Painting a New World: Mexican Art and Life, 1521–1821* (Denver: Denver Art Museum, 2004), pp. 187–89. Our reasoning for seeing this as a scene of arrival in Asia is given later in the chapter.

2. See Sonia Ocaña Ruiz, "*Enconchado* Frames: The Use of Japanese Ornamental Models in New Spanish Painting," in *Asia and Spanish America: Trans-Pacific Artistic and Cultural Exchange, 1500–1850*, ed. Donna Pierce and Ronald Otsuka (Denver: Denver Art Museum, 2009), pp. 129–49; Sonia Ocaña Ruiz, "*Enconchados*: Japanese Appropriations, Ornamentation and Light Symbolism in New Spain," *Caiana: Revista de Historia del Arte y Cultura Visual del Centro Argentino de Investigadores de Arte* 10 (2017), pp. 1–17; Donna Pierce, "By the Boatload: Receiving and Recreating the Arts of Asia," in *Made in the Americas: The New World Discovers Asia*, ed. Dennis Carr (Boston: Museum of Fine Arts, 2015), pp. 53–73; Charlene Villaseñor Black, "The Iridescent *Enconchado*," in *Iberian Empires and the Roots of Globalization*, ed. Ivonne del Valle, Anna More, and Rachel O'Toole (Nashville, TN: Vanderbilt University Press, 2019), pp. 233–69.

3. Jiseok Gim et al., "Nanoscale Deformation Mechanics Reveal Resilience in Nacre of *Pinna Nobilis* Shell," *Nature Communications* 10 (2019), pp. 1–8.

4. On the representation of anchor axes in new world imagery, see Christian Feest, "The People of Calicut: Objects, Texts, and Images in the Age of Proto-Ethnography," *Boletim do Museu Paraense Emílio Goeldi, Ciências Humanas* 9 (2014), pp. 287–303, at p. 293.

5. See Rubens's study of a man in what is sometimes described as Korean costume at the Getty, and also the central figure in his *Miracles of Saint Francis Xavier* at the Kunsthistorisches Museum, Vienna. See figures 1 and 20 and the essays gathered in *Looking East: Rubens's Encounter with Asia*, ed. Stephanie Schrader (Los Angeles: J. Paul Getty Museum, 2013). Mayu Fujikawa, "A Hint of Distant Asia in Rubens's *The Miracles of St. Francis Xavier*," *Jaarboek Koninklijk Museum voor Schone Kunsten Antwerpen 2013–14* (Antwerp: Garant, 2016), pp. 76–90, proposes that the figure would have represented for Rubens's audience not specifically Korea but possibly China or all of East Asia.

6. Archivum Romanum Societatis Jesu, Rome, Fondo Gesuitico, vol. 732, letters 24 and 49. As Camilla Russell has explained, these letters do little to demonstrate a knowledge of various places, since this was evidently not a requirement for being sent on mission; Camilla Russell, "Imagining the 'Indies': Italian Jesuit Petitions for the Overseas Missions at the Turn of the Seventeenth Century," in *L'Europa divisa e i nuovi mondi: Per Adriano Prosperi*, ed. Massimo Donattini, Giuseppe Marcocci, and Stefania Pastore, 2 vols. (Pisa: Edizioni della Normale, 2011), vol. 2, pp. 179–89; and Russell, "Vocation to the East: Italian Candidates for the Jesuit China Mission at the Turn of the Seventeenth Century," in *Renaissance Studies in Honor of Joseph Connors*, eds. Machtelt Israëls and Louis A. Waldman, 2 vols. (Milan: Officina Libreria, 2013), vol. 2, pp. 313–27. For more on the letters, see Gian Carlo Roscioni, *Il desiderio delle Indie: Storie, sogni, e fughe di giovani gesuiti italiani* (Turin: Einaudi, 2001), and Elisa Frei, "The Many Faces of Ignazio Maria Romeo SJ (1676–1724?), Petitioner for the Indies: A Jesuit Seen through his *Litterae Indipetae* and the *Epistulae Generalium*," *Archivum Historicum Societatis Iesu* 85 (2016), pp. 365–404. See also Mirela Altic, *Encounters in the New World: Jesuit Cartography of the Americas* (Chicago: University of Chicago Press, 2021). We thank Camilla Russell for her guidance in this archive and for illuminating discussions about the petitions.

7. The print, by Philip Kilian, illustrates the *Vita S. Francisci Xavieri e Societate Jesu, Indiarum et Iaponiae Apostoli*. . . (Vienna: University of Vienna, 1690), p. G7. This 1690 publication consisting only of captioned engravings was followed in 1691 by the narrated life of the saint, with newly engraved illustrations based on those of 1690. For the two related publications, see M. Gabriela Torres Olleta, *Vita thesibus et Vita iconibus: Dos certámenes sobre San Francisco Javier* (Kassel: Reichenberger, 2005), and Torres Olleta, *Redes Iconográficas: San Francisco Javier en la cultura visual del Barroco* (Frankfurt-am-Main: Vervuert Verlagsgesellschaft, 2009), pp. 129–39.

8. The painting is one of three devoted to scenes from the life of Saint Francis Xavier, which were possibly made as part of an altarpiece for the church of La Profesa in Mexico City. See the entry in *The Arts of the Missions of Northern New Spain, 1600–1821*, eds. Clara Bargellini and Michael Komanecky (Mexico City: Antiguo Colegio de San Ildefonso, 2009), p. 270.

9. Gauvin Alexander Bailey, "Religious Orders and the Arts of Asia," in Carr, ed., *Made in the Americas*, p. 102. Another view splits the difference, seeing in this scene a partial transplantation of the event to Mexico, identifying American Indians sprinkled among Asians in the scene; see the entry on the painting in *The Arts of the Missions of Northern New Spain, 1600–1821*, p. 273: "A group of Native people from the New World witness the conversion of the ruler. At the same time, emphasis is placed on the figure of Xavier, the universal missionary. The composition of Antonio de Torres establishes a connection between the saint and the American continent by placing him among peoples and in the lands where his presence had a profound impact, although he had never set foot in America."

10. See Torres Olleta, *Redes Iconográficas*, pp. 228–58.

11. Jaime Cuadriello, "Xavier indiano o los indios sin apóstol," in *San Francisco Javier en las artes: El poder de la imagen* (Pamplona: Gobierno de Navarra, 2006), pp. 200–33,

at p. 221, noted the congruence between the engraving and Torres's painting.

12. Feathers had been used to decorate clothes in China and Japan as early as the eighth century, and head ornaments made of feathers were as common in Southeast Asia as they were in the Americas. Indeed, there existed a profitable trade in kingfisher and pheasant feathers in sixteenth-century Cambodia, Borneo, and Japan. As Donald Lach noted, European artists as early as Albrecht Dürer "correctly associated colorful feathers, exotic plumages, featherworks, and feather headdresses with Asia as well as America." See Donald F. Lach and Edwin J. Van Kley, *Asia in the Making of Europe*, vol. 2, *A Century of Wonder*, book 1, *The Visual Arts* (Chicago: University of Chicago Press, 1970), p. 18.

13. Thomas Gage, *Thomas Gage's Travels in the New World*, ed. J. Eric S. Thompson (Norman: University of Oklahoma Press, 1958), p. 68.

14. William Lytle Schurz, *The Manila Galleon* (New York: E. P. Dutton, 1939), p. 27. See also Arturo Giraldez, *The Age of Trade: The Manila Galleons and the Dawn of the Global Economy* (Lanham, MD: Rowman & Littlefield, 2015), p. 147, and Linda R. Shulsky, "Chinese Porcelain in New Mexico," *Vormen uit Vuur* 53 (1994), pp. 13–18.

15. Giovanni Francesco Gemelli Careri, *Giro del mondo: Parte sesta, contenente le cose più ragguardevoli vedute nella Nuova Spagna* (Naples: Giuseppe Roselli, 1708), pp. 1–3.

16. Four sherds of high-quality Chinese porcelain from the kilns at Jingdezhen were unearthed at the site of San Gabriel de Yunque, three of which date from the reign of the Ming emperor Wan-li (1573–1619). See Donna Pierce, "Popular and Prevalent: Asian Trade Goods in Northern New Spain, 1590–1850," *Colonial Latin American Review* 25 (2016), pp. 77–97, at p. 78.

17. The inventory of belongings from a wealthy Spanish couple who immigrated to San Gabriel de Yunque from Mexico City in 1600, Doña Francisca Galindo and her husband, Captain Antonio Conde de Herrera, lists "Chinese linen," "Chinese silk," "Chinese braid," "pieces of thin Chinese fabric," and "green Chinese taffeta," thereby differentiating these fabrics from China (*de Chine*) from textiles from Holland, Rouen and Castile, as well as fabrics from Campeche, or other Mixtec fabrics. See George Peter Hammond and Agapito Rey, *Don Juan de Oñate, Colonizer of New Mexico, 1595–1628*, 2 vols. (Albuquerque: University of New Mexico Press, 1953), vol. 1, pp. 522–30. See also David V. Hill and John A. Peterson, "East Meets West on the Camino Real," in *El Camino Real de Tierra Adentro*, vol. 2, ed. Gabrielle G. Palmer, Stephen L. Fosberg, and June-el Piper (Santa Fe, NM: Bureau of Land Management, 1999), pp. 147–52, at p. 148, and Cordelia Thomas Snow, "A Headdress of Pearls: Luxury Goods Imported over the Camino Real during the Seventeenth Century," in *El Camino Real de Tierra Adentro*, vol. 1, eds. Gabrielle G. Palmer, June-el Piper, and LouAnn Jacobson (Santa Fe, NM: Bureau of Land Management, 1993), pp. 69–76.

18. Pierce, "Popular and Prevalent," p. 81.

19. While it remains unclear how or when the name *Camino de China* began to be used to refer to this royal road, this term seems not to have been applied to the route between Acapulco and Mexico City during the seventeenth and eighteenth centuries. At the time, it was consistently referred to as the "Camino Real al Puerto de Acapulco." See Ramón María Serrera, "El camino de Asia: La ruta de México a Acapulco," in *Rutas de la Nueva España*, ed. Chantal Cramaussel (Zamora: Colegio de Michoacán, 2006), pp. 211–30, and Tatiana Seijas, "Inn, Mules, and Hardtack for the Voyage: The Local Economy of the Manila Galleon in Mexico," *Colonial Latin American Review* 25 (2016), pp. 56–76. We thank Tatiana Seijas for sharing with us her research on this question.

20. Hill and Peterson, "East Meets West," p. 148.

21. See Patricia Fournier, "Ceramic Production and Trade on the Camino Real," in Palmer and Fosberg, eds., *El Camino Real*, vol. 2, pp. 153–75, at p. 155.

22. As Dana Leibsohn explains, the differences between the rougher-hewn Puebla pottery and the much finer Chinese porcelain were noticeable, and "the gap between Puebla ceramics and porcelain did, indeed, register." Dana Leibsohn, "Made in China, Made in Mexico," in *At the*

Crossroads: The Arts of Spanish America and Early Global Trade, 1492–1850, ed. Donna Pierce and Ronald Otsuka (Denver, CO: Denver Art Museum, 2012), pp. 12–40, at p. 30. According to the historian Meha Priyadarshini, Mexican ceramicists created works distinguishable from Chinese porcelains "that were meant to appeal to consumers as a local product and not as a replacement for Chinese porcelain." Meha Priyadarshini, *Chinese Porcelain in Colonial Mexico: The Material Worlds of an Early Modern Trade* (London: Palgrave Macmillan, 2018), pp. 19 and 159.

23. See Gustavo Curiel, "Al remedo de la China: El lenguaje achinado y la formación de un gusto dentro de las casas novohispanas," in *Orientes y Occidentes: El arte y la mirada del otro*, ed. Gustavo Curiel (Mexico City: Universidad Nacional Autónoma de México/Instituto de Investigaciones Estéticas, 2007), pp. 299–317. See also Curiel, "Perception of the Other and the Language of 'Chinese Mimicry' in the Decorative Arts of New Spain," in Pierce and Otsuka, eds., *Asia and Spanish America*, pp. 19–36.

24. Woodrow Borah, *Early Colonial Trade and Navigation between Mexico and Peru* (Berkeley: University of California Press, 1954), pp. 121–22, cited in Pierce, "Popular and Prevalent," p. 79. The Irish friar Thomas Gage similarly described prosperous Indian women in Mexico c. 1625 wearing *huipiles* [Native overblouses] made from "fine linen brought from China," by which he could have meant silk; see Gage, *Thomas Gage's Travels*, pp. 220–21.

25. Ibid., p. 148.

26. To be clear, the word *china* was a generic term for "servant"; since the colonial period, it also referred to a person of Asian background from the Philippines, China, Japan, or India. Terminological coincidence worked to conflate these terms. See Gauvin Alexander Bailey, "A Mughal Princess in Baroque New Spain: Catarina de San Juan (1606–1688), the *china poblana*," *Anales del Instituto de Investigaciones Estéticas* 71 (1997), pp. 37–73, and Tatiana Seijas, *Asian Slaves in Colonial Mexico: From Chinos to Indians* (New York: Cambridge University Press, 2014), pp. 8–31.

27. On the Chinese myth of the *Casa de los Azulejos*, see Priyadarshini, *Chinese Porcelain in Colonial Mexico*, p. 1. On Calderón, see Leibsohn, "Made in China, Made in Mexico," p. 32, and Pridyadarshini, *Chinese Porcelain in Colonial Mexico*, pp. 114–15.

28. See Edward R. Slack Jr., "Sinifying New Spain: Cathay's Influence on Colonial Mexico via the Nao de China," *Journal of Chinese Overseas* 5 (2009), pp. 5–27, at pp. 8–13. See also John M. Headley, "Spain's Asian Presence, 1565–1590: Structures and Aspirations," *Hispanic American Historical Review* 75 (1995), pp. 623–46.

29. Seijas, *Asian Slaves in Colonial Mexico.* See also Juan Gil, "Chinos in Sixteenth-Century Spain," in *Western Visions of the Far East in a Transpacific Age, 1522–1657*, ed. Christina H. Lee (London, UK: Ashgate: 2012), pp. 139–52. A whole new genre of depiction, known as Casta painting, emerged in the eighteenth century in an effort to visualize a taxonomy of the elaborate mixings occurring in Mexico. See Carolyn Dean and Dana Leibsohn, "Hybridity and Its Discontents: Considering Visual Culture in Colonial Spanish America," *Colonial Latin American Review* 12 (2003), pp. 5–35; Magali M. Carrera, *Imagining Identity in New Spain: Race, Lineage, and the Colonial Body in Portraiture and Casta Paintings* (Austin: University of Texas Press, 2003), Ilona Katzew, *Casta Painting: Images of Race in Eighteenth-Century Mexico* (New Haven, CT: Yale University Press, 2004); the review of the last two by Thomas Cummins, in *The Art Bulletin* 88 (2006), pp. 185–89; and Rebecca Earle, "The Pleasures of Taxonomy: Casta Paintings, Classification, and Colonialism" *The William and Mary Quarterly* 73 (2016), pp. 427–66.

30. Nancy van Deusen, *Global Indios: The Indigenous Struggle for Justice in Sixteenth-Century Spain* (Durham, NC: Duke University Press, 2015), p. 11.

31. As Seijas notes, "this history of local economic activity highlights the need to study inter-colonial exchange alongside intra-colonial trade in a way that expands our understanding of the connections between colonial Latin America and Asia beyond the flow of silver and silk. The men and women who provisioned the Galleon and supported its passengers well knew that they were part of an Empire that stretched across the seas," Seijas, "Inn, Mules, and Hardtack for the Voyage," pp. 26–27. See also Serge

Gruzinski, *Les quatre parties du monde: Histoire d'une mondialisation* (Paris: Éditions de La Martinière, 2004), p. 180.

32. See Alberto Zapatero, "Apuntes sobre la elaboración de biombos en la Nueva España," *Archivo Español de Arte* 88 (2015), pp. 173–88, and Sofia Sanabrais, "From *Byōbu* to *Biombo*: The Transformation of the Japanese Folding Screen in Colonial Mexico," *Art History* 38 (2015), pp. 778–91.

33. Peter Gordon and Juan José Morales, *The Silver Way: China, Spanish America and the Birth of Globalisation, 1565–1815* (New York: Penguin Books, 2017), p. 45; see also Sanabrais, "From *Byōbu* to *Biombo*," pp. 785–86.

34. Leibsohn, "Made in China, Made in Mexico," p. 15. See also Priyadarshini, *Chinese Porcelain in Colonial Mexico*, pp. 97–129. On the postconquest history of Mexico City, see Barbara E. Mundy, *The Death of Aztec Tenochtitlan, the Life of Mexico City* (Austin: University of Texas Press, 2015).

35. "En ti se junta España con la China / Italia con Japón, y finalmente / un mundo entero en trato y disciplina. // En ti de los tesoros del Poniente / se goza lo mejor; en ti la nata / de cuanto entre su luz cría el Oriente." Bernardo de Balbuena, *Grandeza mexicana*, chap. 3, tercets 38–39. See Gruzinski, *Les quatre parties du monde*, pp. 269–74, and 300–306, and Barbara Fuchs and Yolanda Martínez-San Miguel, "La grandeza mexicana de Balbuena y el imaginario de una 'Metrópolis Colonial,'" *Revista Iberoamericana* 75 (2009), pp. 675–95.

EPILOGUE

1. *The Spanish Letter of Columbus to Luis de Sant' Angel, Escribano de Racion of the Kingdom of Aragon, dated 15 February 1493* (London: Quaritch, 1893), pp. 6 and 17. A letter from Dr. Chanca, one of Ferdinand and Isabella's physicians who accompanied Columbus on his second voyage, similarly notes that "a kind of cinnamon has been found as well, though it is true that it is not so fine as the cinnamon we know at home. This may be because we do not know the right season to gather it, or possibly there are better trees in the land." "The Letter Written by Dr. Chanca to the City of Seville," in *The Four Voyages of Christopher Columbus*, ed. and trans. J. M. Cohen (New York: Penguin Books, 1964), pp. 129–57, at p. 155.

2. *Las Casas on Columbus: The Third Voyage*, ed. Geoffrey Symcox, Repertorium Columbianum 11 (Turnhout: Brepols, 2001), pp. 78 and 219.

3. *Selections from Peter Martyr*, ed. Geoffrey Eatough, Repertorium Columbianum 5 (Turnhout: Brepols, 1998), p. 102 (Decade 1.9.10); see also p. 58 (Decade 1.2.21) and p. 47 (Decade 1.1.11).

4. See Francisco López de Gómara, *Historia General de las Indias* (Alicante: Biblioteca Virtual Miguel de Cervantes, 1999), chap. 143.

5. "A new type of cinnamon has been found, because in truth it is not like the one we use that comes from the spice islands of Maluku and Brunei. This cinnamon is not like the one we all know except in the taste and the smell but not the form; it comes from the pods of some fruit," Gonzalo Fernández de Oviedo, *Historia general y natural de las Indias: Islas, y tierra-firme del mar océano* (Madrid: Real Academia de la Historia, 1851, book 9, chap. 31, pp. 357–58.

6. Garcilaso de la Vega, El Inca, *Royal Commentaries of the Incas and General History of Peru*, trans. Harold V. Livermore, 2 vols. (Austin: University of Texas Press, 1966), vol. 2, book 2.3.2, p. 875. Garcilaso de la Vega chronicled the Pizarro expedition sixty years after its conclusion and never personally saw any cinnamon; he could easily have added details about this plant after hearing or reading about it in contemporary sources.

7. Pedro de Cieza de León, *Obras completas*, ed. Carmelo Saenz de Sant Maria, 3 vols. (Madrid: Instituto Oviedo, 1984–85), vol. 2, chaps. 18–22, pp. 179–87.

8. Garcilaso de la Vega describes the impressive resources dedicated to this expedition, as well as Pizarro's tremendous losses. See *Royal Commentaries*, vol. 2, books 2.3.2 and 2.3.14, pp. 874 and 915.

9. "La canela, y clavo, y pimiento, y otras especias [nasce] solo en las Islas de Maluco." Monardes, *Primera, segunda, y tercera partes de la historia medicinal de las cosas que se traen de nuestras Indias Occidentales* (Seville: Alonso Escrivano, 1574), p. 2r.

10. "Son los arboles que la llevan de mediana grandeza,

llevan la hoja como de Laurel, estan todo el año verdes, que nunca pierden la hoja, que es cosa comun en todos los arboles delas Indias." Ibid., p. 98r–v.

11. "Y es todo un genero de arbol el que las produze, sino que la diversidad del lugar produze una mas fina que oltra; y assi cassia, y cinamomo es todo uno, que non differente sino en los nombres, que todo es canela delgada sina, y assi do hallaren escripto cassia pueden poner cinamomo, y do hallaren cinamomo, cassia," Ibid., p. 99r. As the food historian Andrew Dalby explains, Pineda most likely found wild trees that, observed through well-established Amerasian lenses, perhaps smelled something like cinnamon. Dalby proposes that this could have been a plant from the botanical family *Lauracea*, which included trees with aromatic wood with an aroma similar to that of cinnamon. As a result, the Spanish and Portuguese eventually gave these names that included the word cinnamon (*canela*), thereby furthering the confusion. See Andrew Dalby, "Christopher Columbus, Gonzalo Pizarro, and the Search for Cinnamon," *Gastronomica* 1 (2001), pp. 40–49, at p. 14. See also Serge Gruzinski, *Les quatre parties du monde: Histoire d'une mondialisation* (Paris: La Martinière, 2004), pp. 216–17.

12. "Era lo de la Canela cosa muy divulgada entre los Españoles, porque se entendía de los Indios que era cosa de gran riqueza." Monardes, *Historia medicinal*, p. 98r.

13. See Daniela Bleichmar, "Atlantic Competitions: Botany in the Eighteenth-Century Spanish Empire," in *Science and Empire in the Atlantic World*, eds. James Delbourgo and Nicholas Dew (New York: Routledge, 2008), pp. 225–52, at p. 231, and Bleichmar, *Visible Empire: Botanical Expeditions and Visual Culture in the Hispanic Enlightenment* (Chicago: University of Chicago Press, 2012), pp. 131–36.

14. In *Gulliver's Travels* (1726), book 2, chapter 4, Jonathan Swift describes America as reaching "about six thousand miles in length, and from three to five in breadth: whence I cannot but conclude, that our geographers of Europe are in a great error, by supposing nothing but sea between Japan and California; for it was ever my opinion, that there must be a balance of earth to counterpoise the great continent of Tartary; and therefore they ought to correct their maps and charts, by joining this vast tract of land to the north-west parts of America, wherein I shall be ready to lend them my assistance." Here the character Gulliver indicates that though the separation of the Asian and American continents was pretty much settled, he wants to reinstate the old view on the basis of new (and here fictional) evidence. By this point (for Swift writing in 1720s) it seems Amerasia was an older understanding of the world that had become ripe for revival in the space of fiction.

15. On the mythical islands and coasts of the North Pacific, see Lawrence C. Wroth, "The Early Cartography of the Pacific," *Papers of the Bibliographical Society of America* 38 (1944), pp. 87–268, at pp. 207–15.

16. Our discussion here was informed by Katherine Parker, "Northern Seas: The Mapping of the North Pacific before the Voyages of James Cook," paper presented at the Washington Map Society, November 19, 2020.

17. On Fusang, see Berthold Laufer, "Columbus and Cathay, and the Meaning of America to the Orientalist," *Journal of the American Oriental Society* 51 (1931), pp. 87–103, at p. 97. The eighteenth-century writings of Joseph de Guignes were revived and further disseminated in the nineteenth century.

18. "Qu'ils n'en avoient qu'une idée très-confuse, & que les cartes dressées exactement d'après les positions de Ptolomée, nous montrent cette partie du monde très différemment de son véritable état." "On donnoit ce nom aux étrangers venus des régions inconnues ; & même par le manque de lumieres, sur le rapport de l'Amérique avec les Indes, ne lui a-t-on pas donné le nom d'Indes occidentales?" *Encyclopédie, ou dictionnaire raisonné des sciences, des arts et des métiers*, ed. Denis Diderot and Jean le Rond d'Alembert, 17 vols. (Paris: Chez Briasson et Le Breton, 1751–72), vol. 8, p. 661.

19. "De-là vint l'usage d'appeller *Indes orientales*, ce qui est à l'orient du cap de Bonne-Espérance, & *Indes occidentales*, ce qui est à l'occident de ce cap." "On a ensuite improprement étendu ce dernier nom à toute l'Amérique; & par un nouvel abus, qu'il n'est plus possible de corriger, on se sert dans les relations du nom *d'Indiens*, pour dire *les Américquains*." Ibid., p. 662.

20. James Adair, *The History of the American Indians*, ed. Kathryn E. Holland Braund (Tuscaloosa: University of Alabama Press, 2005), p. 141.

21. Jonathan Carver, *Three Years Travels through the Interior Parts of North America* (Philadelphia: Joseph Crushank, 1789), pp. 100 and 107.

22. See Enrique de Gandía, *Historia crítica de los mitos de la conquista Americana* (Buenos Aires: Juan Roldán, 1929), p. 87.

23. Frank A. Golder, *Bering's Voyages*, 2 vols. (New York: American Geographical Society, 1922), vol. 1, p. 20, cited in Eviatar Zerubavel, *Terra Cognita: The Mental Discovery of America* (New Brunswick, NJ: Transaction Publishers, 2003), p. 61.

24. Zerubavel, *Terra Cognita*, pp. 64–66.

25. James Weddell, *A Voyage Towards the South Pole, Performed in the Years 1822–24* (London: Longman, 1825), pp. 173–74, and Robert Fitzroy, *Narrative of the Surveying Voyages of His Majesty's Ships Adventure and Beagle Between the Years 1826 and 1836, Describing Their Examination of the Southern Shores of South America, and the Beagle's Circumnavigation of the Globe. Proceedings of the Second Expedition, 1831–36, Under the Command of Captain Robert Fitz-Roy, R.N.* (London: Henry Colburn, 1839), pp. 644–46.

26. Lord Kingsborough, *Antiquities of Mexico*, 9 vols. (London: A. Aglio, 1830–48). Kingsborough draws many parallels between the Mexicans and the ancient Hebrews in his discussions of the Codex Mendoza, the Codex Telleriano-Remensis, and various monuments in New Spain. See, for instance, vol. 5, pp. 1–36, and vol. 6, pp. 481–82.

27. See Richard V. Francaviglia, *Go East Young Man: Imagining the American West as the Orient* (Logan: Utah State University Press, 2011), p. 20. We thank Jessica Horton for pointing out this study.

28. Robert Silverberg, *Mound Builders of Ancient America: The Archaeology of a Myth* (Greenwich, CT: New York Graphic Society, 1968), pp. 84–85. On the hypothesis that the Ohio mounds were originally built by the Chinese, see also Henry Clyde Shetrone, *The Mound Builders* (Tuscaloosa: University of Alabama Press, 2004), p. 44.

29. The work of a variety of European sinologists, including Emil Bretschneider, Berthold Laufer, Henri Cordier, and Joseph Needham, continued such discussions up until the First World War. See "Fusang," http://myoldmaps.com/fusang2.pdf.

30. See, for instance, David Reich, *Who We Are and How We Got Here: Ancient DNA and the New Science of the Human Past* (New York: Pantheon Books, 2018), pp. 154–85; Loren G. Davis and David B. Madsen, "The Coastal Migration Theory: Formulation and Testable Hypotheses," *Quaternary Science Reviews* 249 (2020), pp. 1–13; and Paul Wallin, "Native South Americans Were Early Inhabitants of Polynesia," *Nature* 583 (2020), pp. 524–25.

31. See Betty Jane Meggers, "The Transpacific Origin of Mesoamerican Civilization: A Preliminary Review of the Evidence and Its Theoretical Implications," *American Anthropologist* 77 (March 1975), pp. 1–27, and Mike Xu, *Origin of the Olmec Civilization* (Edmond: University of Central Oklahoma Press, 1996). Such views were already in the air decades earlier, as shown by the 1953 issue of the *Memoirs of the Society for American Archaeology* dedicated to the theme of "Asia and North America: Transpacific Contacts," in particular the essay by George F. Carter on "Plants Across the Pacific" (pp. 62–71) and that of Gordon F. Ekholm, "A Possible Focus of Asiatic Influence in the Late Classic Cultures of Mesoamerica" (pp. 72–89). See also the bracingly encompassing theories of Paul Shao, *Asiatic Influences in Pre-Columbian American Art* (Ames: Iowa State University Press, 1976).

32. Mikkel Pederson, Anthony Ruder, Charles Schweger et al., "Postglacial Viability and Colonization in North America's Ice-Free Corridor," *Nature* 537 (2016), pp. 45–49.

33. Alexander G. Ioannidis, Javier Blanco-Portillo, K. Sandoval, et al., "Native American Gene Flow into Polynesia Predating Easter Island Settlement," *Nature* 583 (2020), pp. 572–77. And recent findings have revealed an ancient Australasian genetic signature in populations of the Amazon. See Pontus Skoglund, Swapan Mallick, Maria Cátira Bortolini, et al., "Genetic Evidence for Two Founding Populations of the Americas," *Nature* 225 (2015): 104–108.

34. Claude Lévi-Strauss, *Tristes tropiques* (Paris: Plon, 1957), p. 297.

35. Carl Schuster, "Genealogical Patterns in the Old and New Worlds," *Revista do Museu Paulista* 10 (1956–58), pp. 7–123. See also Schuster, *Social Symbolism in Ancient and Tribal Art: A Record of Tradition and Continuity*, ed. Edmund Carpenter, *Genealogical Patterns: Form and Meaning*, vol. 1, pp. 37, 583, and 598.

AFTERWORD: CHINESE CARTOGRAPHERS MAP THE WORLD

1. The only study of *Guang yutu* is Walter Fuchs, *The "Mongol Atlas" of China by Chu Ssu-pen and the Kuang-yü-tu* (Peiping: Fu Jen University, 1946). Fuchs misread the rhetoric of Luo's preface, accepting Luo's disclaimer that he was merely revising Zhu Siben's work. He also crucially misinterprets a comment in Hu Song's preface to date the first edition of Luo's atlas to 1541, which is in fact an oblique reference to Luo's dismissal from court. Fuchs's many errors are widely repeated even today in the secondary literature; e.g., Theodore Foss, "Cartography," in *Handbook of Christianity in China*, ed. Nicolas Standaert (Leiden: Brill, 2001), vol. 1, p. 757. Foss's conclusion that "the European influence on Chinese cartography remained limited" (p. 763) is hobbled by the understandable impulse of earlier scholars to free Chinese history from Eurocentrism.

2. For a brief biography of Luo Hongxian, see L. Carrington Goodrich and Chaoying Fang, eds., *Dictionary of Ming Biography* (New York: Columbia University Press, 1976), pp. 980–84. The only competing claimant to being the first Chinese atlas is a Song-dynasty sequence of forty-four maps published as *Maps of Historical Geography in the Palm of Your Hand* (*Lidai dili zhizhang tu*), though that book's purpose was less to map China than to present a flipbook showing the Song to be the equal of all previous dynasties. See Hilde de Weerdt, "The Cultural Logics of Map Reading: Text, Time, and Space in Printed Maps of the Song Empire," in *Knowledge and Text Production in an Age of Print: China, 900–1440*, ed. Lucille Chia and Hilde de Weerdt (Leiden: Brill, 2011), pp. 239–70.

3. Timothy Brook, *Completing the Map of the World: Cartographic Interaction between China and Europe* (Taipei: Institute for Modern History, Academia Sinica, 2020), pp. 21–24.

4. After Luo's death in 1564, publishers of later editions abandoned the square format. In the widely reprinted 1566 edition, the page has been cut down to three-quarters of the original height and half its width, and the maps split in half across facing pages. This transformation hampers the cartography, but publishers found it easier to produce.

5. Luo Hongxian, "*Guang yutu* xu" (Preface to the *Enlarged Chariot*) (1566 edition), 3a.

6. Mao Yuanyi, *Wubei zhi* (Monograph on Military Preparedness) (c. 1621), chap. 240, p. 19b.

7. Earlier Chinese texts record Zanzibar as Cengyaoluo, not Sangguba, e.g., Zhao Rugua, *Zhufan zhi* (Description of Foreign Peoples, 1225), and Wang Dayuan, *Daoyi zhilüe* (Brief Account of Island Barbarians, c. 1339), for which see Don Wyatt, *The Blacks of Premodern China* (Philadelphia: University of Pennsylvania Press, 2010), p. 89.

8. On the history of the *Kangnido*, see Gari Ledyard "Cartography in Korea," in *Cartography in the Traditional East and Southeast Asian Societies*, ed. J. B. Harley and David Woodward (Chicago: University of Chicago Press, 1994), p. 246. Luo's debt to the *Kangnido* was first noted by Aoyama Sadao in the 1930s. Aoyama decided that Zhu Siben had copied the *Kangnido* and that Luo had simply copied Zhu, mistakenly in my view. Zhu clearly states in his preface that he regarded foreign maritime regions as "too distant to investigate" and therefore excluded them from his map. Fuchs passed this misreading to the English-speaking world in his *"Mongol Atlas" of Chu Ssu-pen*, whence it migrated to Joseph Needham, *Science and Civilisation in China* (Cambridge: Cambridge University Press) in 1959 (vol. 3, pp. 551–56) and again in 1971 (vol. 4.3, p. 500), and later to Hyunhee Park, *Mapping the Chinese and Islamic Worlds: Cross-Cultural Exchange in Pre-modern Asia* (Cambridge: Cambridge University Press, 2012), p. 165; see also Nurian Kenzheakhmet, "Central Asian Place Names in the *Kangnido*," *Journal of Asian History* 49:1–2 (2015), p. 145.

9. On the use of Tang-period place names on the *Kangnido*, see Kenzheakhmet, "The Place Names of Euro-Africa in the *Kangnido*," *The Silk Road* 14 (2016), pp. 3–4.

10. Zhu Siben, "*Yutu* jiuxu" (Original preface to the *Chariot Map*), 1b; Luo Hongxian, "*Guang yutu* xu" (Preface to the *Enlarged Chariot*), 3a. Given that Luo derived his map from the *Kangnido*, there are no grounds to argue that the shape of Africa on Luo's map indicates that Ming mariners rounded the Cape of Good Hope, contrary to Benjamin Elman's generous concession to that possibility; see Benjamin Elman, *On Their Own Terms: Science in China, 1550–1900* (Cambridge, MA: Harvard University Press, 2005), p. 125.

11. Qiong Zhang, *Making the New World Their Own: Chinese Encounters with Jesuit Science in the Age of Discovery* (Leiden: Brill, 2015), p. 196.

12. On the "undiscoverability" of the Oceanic East, see Mathieu Torck, "The Unimaginable and Immeasurable? China's Visions of the Pacific—Needham's View Re-examined," in *The Perception of Maritime Space in Traditional Chinese Sources*, ed. Angela Schottenhammer and Roderich Ptak (Wiesbaden: Harrassowitz, 2006), pp. 141–52.

13. Ricci accepted the logic of knowledge symmetry, perhaps because it appealed to his Chinese readers: if there were lesser and greater Western Oceans, there must be lesser and greater Eastern Oceans. The impulse for symmetry induced European map-colorers trained to paint the Red Sea red to apply the same color to its the Gulf of California, its approximate replica in the Americas. In the same spirit, Ricci labeled the Red Sea in Chinese as the Western Red Sea and the Gulf of California as the Eastern Red Sea. See Zhang, *Making the New World Their Own*, pp. 207, 212.

14. Li Zhizao's text is available in *Li Madou zhongwen zhuyi ji (Collection of Translations of Matteo Ricci's Writings in Chinese*), ed. Zhu Weizheng (Hong Kong: City University of Hong Kong Press, 2001), p. 225. On the powerful significance of this phrase, see Li Tiangang, *Xin tong dong xi* (Mind Is the Same East or West) (Shanghai: Huadong shifan daxue chubanshe, 2001), pp. 91–99.

15. The formation of the "complete map" genre is examined in Brook, *Completing the Map of the World*.

16. This map is examined in Timothy Brook, "China's World Map Transformed: The Complete Map of All under Heaven as Unified by the Qing Great State for Ten Thousand Years," posted online in "Depicting Glory: Rare Objects from the Late Qing to the Republic of China," Brown University Library, 2022.

Index

Locators in italic type indicate figures.

Typesetting by Meighan Gale
Layout and production by Julie Fry
Printed and bound by Sheridan Books